D0791985

# ADVANCE PRAISE FOR HOW TO LIST & SELL REAL ESTATE

*"What separates Danielle Kennedy from the normal author is the fact that she writes with her heart and mind. She is very passionate about what she writes and that passion shines through. The reality is that she's not writing from a distance—she's writing from experience. Success in real estate requires a balance of emotion and intellect, which Danielle Kennedy has and illustrates."*

Bruce Mulhearn, President, Mulhearn Gallery of Homes

*"The book is a practical, fun guide to building a sales career. It will help anyone in the business, from the rookies to sales managers!"*

David Lutton, President, The Charles Reinhardt Company, REALTORS®

*"As a devoted fan and protégé of Danielle Kennedy for more than two decades, she continues to amaze me with her ability to get basic skills across in such a smooth, practical manner. This book takes these skills to the next level and imparts methods to increase our earnings by offering even greater service to our clients . . . . I was motivated, inspired, educated, and entertained all at the same time!"*

Doris Edwards, Broker-Owner, American Dream Realty

*"Danielle Kennedy's* How to List & Sell *is a bible of practical and doable real estate techniques and practices that point you in the right direction to achieve or enhance your success. When a new agent joins our company, it is required reading. And when one of the experienced agents needs a tune up or a new slant on their business development they rely on it. All anyone has to do is put the ideas into practice and they are on their way. Every agent, as well as every office, should consider this the #1 resource in their educational library."*

Connie Hinsdale, Owner/Broker, Coldwell Banker Mountain West Real Estate, Inc.

*"From zero to $6 million in sales in just five years in a town where no one knew me—that is where Danielle has taken me. What a ride! Do yourself a favor; if you are thinking of buying a book or system that will propel you to the top, look no farther. This is it. I just purchased it for my whole team; it addresses the new technology and the tried and true. For the seasoned vet or the 'newbie' you won't need another system. Follow Danielle to success!"*

Larry Barr, 2002 Director Greater Tampa
Association of REALTORS®/2002 Florida Association
of REALTORS®/2002 Marketing Director WCR

*"I consider Danielle Kennedy's book must-read material. Danielle's unique and special teaching style conveys much insight. Danielle takes the mystery out of the real estate profession, giving readers a concise, concrete approach to real estate riches."*

Ronald G. Steele, Real Estate Investor/Licensed Real Estate
Agent, Steele & Associates Real Estate Investments

*"Danielle's open house chapter is a must-read—it works! I focused on it when I started selling real estate and jump started my business, to the tune of 47 properties sold in my first year!"*

Jerry Reynolds, Sales Associate, Northwest Montana
Association of REALTORS® Rookie of the Year

*"From the moment I opened Danielle's book, I knew this was the key to jump start my career in real estate. Having children and also wanting to resume my career, Danielle's heart of a mother came through. I've used the Breakaway Schedule and it has been invaluable to me. Thank you Danielle, I'm on my way to a successful career in real estate!'"*

Rhonda Chapleski, Broker Associate,
ReMax Horizons Group/Interlocken

# How to
# List & Sell
# Real Estate

## SOLD

## EXECUTING NEW BASICS FOR HIGHER PROFITS

## Danielle Kennedy
## Warren Jamison

THOMSON
™

SOUTH-WESTERN

Australia · Canada · Mexico · Singapore · Spain · United Kingdom · United States

**THOMSON**

**SOUTH-WESTERN**

How to List & Sell Real Estate: Executing New Basics for Higher Profits
Danielle Kennedy and Warren Jamison

**Executive Publisher:**
Dave Shaut

**Senior Acquisitions Editor:**
Scott Person

**Developmental Editor:**
Allison Abbott

**Marketing Manager:**
Mark Linton

**Production Editor:**
Chris Hudson

**Manufacturing Coordinator:**
Charlene Taylor

**Compositor:**
Cover to Cover Publishing, Inc.

**Printer:**
Phoenix Color
Hagerstown, Maryland

**Design Project Manager:**
Stacy Jenkins Shirley

**Cover and Internal Designer:**
John Robb & Associates

**Cover Images:**
Digital Stock

COPYRIGHT © 2003
by South-Western, a division of
Thomson Learning. Thomson
Learning™ is a trademark used
herein under license.

Printed in the United States
of America
4  5  05  04

For more information
contact South-Western,
5191 Natorp Boulevard,
Mason, Ohio 45040.
Or you can visit our Internet
site at:
http://www.swcollege.com

ALL RIGHTS RESERVED.
No part of this work covered by
the copyright hereon may be
reproduced or used in any form
or by any means—graphic,
electronic, or mechanical, including photocopying, recording, taping, Web distribution or
information storage and re-
trieval systems—without the
written permission of the publisher.

For permission to use material
from this text or product, contact us by
Tel (800) 730-2214
Fax (800) 730-2215
http://www.thomsonrights.com

Library of Congress Control
Number: 2002108751

ISBN: 0-324-18776-9

# CONTENTS

## Chapter 3    Build Money-Making Skills Fast with Hyperlearn and the Latest Techno Tools                   19

## Chapter 4    Confront Old Pro—And Win!                        33

## Chapter 5    The Best Fizzbo System on the Planet: Flipping Fizzbos into Your Fold                         41

## Chapter 11  Impact Listing: How Listings Are Won and Sellers Are Served by World-Class Salespeople   193

## Chapter 12  Servicing Listings Fast   240

## Chapter 13  High-Tech Promotion and the Personal Touch   264

## Chapter 14   The Subtle and Learnable Art of Capturing Customers        279

## Chapter 15   Cut-to-the-Chase Qualifying        298

## Chapter 16 Virtual Touring, In-Person Showings—And Finalizing the Sale 311

## Chapter 17 Closing Those Golden Nuggets Before They Turn into Lead 338

## Chapter 18 Negotiating for a Lifetime Customer 358

## Chapter 19   Fallout Avoidance    374

## Chapter 20   A 100 Percent Referral Business    381

**Chapter 21  Time Planning with or without Paper  396**

**Chapter 22  Self-Organization  419**

## Chapter 26  Every Day Is a Birth Day                       489

## Chapter 27  Leading Team Players to Success and Profitability                      497

# FOREWORD

As the real estate industry transitions from gatekeepers of information to translators of information, agents are looking for solutions to working with the more informed consumer. Danielle Kennedy's, *How to List & Sell Real Estate: Executing New Basics for Higher Profits* contains the field-tested and proven truths that have withstood the test of time and industry evolution. When I began my real estate career in 1981, there were very few real estate trainers. Those who were training focused on motivation rather than skill development. I was already motivated by the need for income and desire to succeed at my new chosen career. I didn't need a speaker to get me excited about what I was doing, but I did need ideas on how to find prospective clients and identify and present my marketing ideas. One of the first things I was told was to read Danielle's book, *How to List & Sell Real Estate*. I immediately identified with her because she did not rely on clichés, but rather offered readers a system of prospecting and overcoming objections.

In 1989 I moved to Las Vegas as a new franchise owner to open a Realty Executives office. I did not know anyone there and had never sold real estate in the community. I immediately became involved in the education programs for the local Board of REALTORS®. Since I was such a fan of Danielle Kennedy, I contacted her to do a program for the Las Vegas REALTORS®. At the time, the market was strong and getting REALTORS® to stop for anything was a challenge, yet more than 1000 agents came to see Danielle. I was thrilled to personally meet this trend-setter of the industry. We developed a long-term friendship based on her openness and sincerity. Her material comes from the heart and is based on truth.

Many people have said to me that Danielle is great for the basics but experienced agents need other trainers for the more advanced material. As a broker/owner of a large real estate company that only hires experienced agents, I would strongly disagree. I recently had Danielle come to Las Vegas for two days of training for our agents. The two-day event was not mandatory. Agents could decide to not return the second day if they did not feel the information being delivered was valuable. Much to my pleasure, 100 agents attended and they all returned the second day (including a few more who heard how good the program was and decided to come). Since the agents in our company average seven years in the business and average 23 transactional sides each per year, the attendance speaks for itself to the validity of Danielle's program for the experienced agent. The agents at the program bought every tape and *How to List & Sell Real Estate*. They are anxiously awaiting this new edition.

Danielle's book is the definitive guide to building a foundation for a repeatable and duplicatable business. I never tire of hearing her material. Her catch phrases are like memories of warm childhood experiences. At times I hear an objection handling technique, and I am reminded how that might have changed the outcome of an experience with a buyer or seller. One of my favorites is the *"this is a shot in the dark"* prospecting script. It works so well with the public and offers the courtesy so many consumers feel is overlooked in telephone prospecting systems. Danielle writes words and phrases that treat buyers and sellers with respect while taking control of the transaction process. Her responses are so logical, I wonder when I read them, "Why didn't I think of that?" In an age of voice mail, e-mail, and junk mail it is refreshing for someone to bring forward ideas and systems to humanize the home buying and selling process.

Danielle brings life-balancing skills to her books and training programs as well. Many agents became overwhelmed with trying to care for clients and family and produce the results of goals tacked to the walls over their desks. Danielle, with her stories of motherhood and pregnancies, lets everyone know that balance does not mean perfection. She teaches and demonstrates through her own life that choices and asking for help to accomplish goals are not weaknesses but strengths. Many of my agents, after having attended Danielle's program, came to me to say how good they felt about themselves. Danielle opens the window to the world of a top-producing agent by sharing her experiences and the material she's gained from her personal "in the trenches" real estate career. Rarely is someone with so much success willing to share so openly with others.

Real estate agents want quick, effective techniques for solving problems. The new edition of *How to List & Sell Real Estate* is formatted to be a dog-eared reference book on every desk. The concepts can be read quickly and implemented to meet the immediate situation at hand. No other trainer-author can boast the test of time for his or her material the way Danielle Kennedy can. She has presented the cornerstones of the Kennedy systems in a current, easily read book that no agent should be without. Having Danielle's materials in my office and easily at hand is like having my own consultant to assist agents resolving daily challenges. I recommend the Kennedy system to agents in a slump or to those charging forward to the next level of their careers. Either situation requires a plan and systems to handle the known steps in the march to more listings and buyer sales. Danielle removes the roadblocks and shows the way.

Danielle's new edition of *How to List & Sell Real Estate* will remind agents that the Kennedy system can be applied to today's market with astounding success. It is not a "shot in the dark" but a sure thing. This material, when faithfully followed, will produce results.

*Fafie Moore, CRS, CRP, LTG*
*Broker/Owner, Realty Executives of Nevada*

# ACKNOWLEDGMENTS

Special thanks to all my cherished students all over the world. How proud I am to be a part of your winning teams. Thanks for continuing to do your homework and raise the professionalism of this great industry.

And, with everlasting love, to my family.

*Danielle Kennedy*

# ATTENTION: BROKERS AND MANAGERS

This book is a complete, detailed, ready-to-go training program: you can simply hand it to new agents. **Call their attention to the Breakaway Schedule in the back.** The achievements called for there are keyed to, and fully explained in, the text. The Breakaway listing and selling training program will put every new agent who is determined to succeed out in the field—fast. It will quickly arm new agents with the ability to list and sell, and it will do all this without taking up your time.

**Nothing helps the new agent more than collecting a fee.** No amount of managerial encouragement approaches the power of the bankable. *How to List & Sell Real Estate* acts on the "Nothing succeeds like success" theory. It's organized so the new agent will learn before trying to practice, will acquire some expertise in a limited field, go out to operate in that limited field, and always move in a confidence-building manner from inexperience to money-making action. Although it's a tough course, this book is graduated so no single step is too formidable.

Be sure to review the book yourself. Make certain none of its techniques conflict with your local ordinances, board rules, and office polices. If an idea won't work in your situation, make a note of the items your agents are to pass over.

**There are Winning Scripts in these pages for every standard situation** your associates will encounter in residential real estate, as well as advanced techniques and insights of experienced agents. Chapters 11 and 16 have role plays for three agents plus yourself. Use all this material to inspire your present sales staff with fast-paced training sessions.

Managers, please be sure to read the new chapter on leadership, Chapter 27, "Leading Team Players to Success and Profitability."

**Danielle Kennedy** is a woman who wins at every game she plays. Her award-winning billion-dollar producing real estate career found her consistently selling 100 plus homes a year while raising eight children. Then she met the broker-owner challenge, managing three highly successful real estate offices, capturing 30 percent of the market share. With a wealth of experience to last a lifetime, Kennedy began documenting her valuable insights on how to list and sell real estate. During the last 25 years she has taught thousands of real estate agents and teams how to increase their production and avoid sales slumps no matter the real estate cycle. Entire companies, audiences, and individuals leave her training programs armed with the latest tools and fresh insights. Kennedy's client/students consistently report back to her on their documented increases in production and lasting consistency of work habits. Her best-selling books *How to List & Sell Real Estate* and *Double Your Income in Real Estate Sales* are available online or at your local bookstores and are required reading in the nation's largest real estate firms. Don't miss reading Kennedy's other popular books: *Seven Figure Selling* and *WorkingMoms.Calm: How Smart Women Balance Family & Career.*

**Danielle Kennedy**
**P.O. Box 1395, Sun Valley, ID 83353**
**Telephone: (208) 726-8375; Fax: (208) 726-9631**
**E-mail: daniellekennedy@svidaho.net**

No one knows more about building a prosperous real estate business than Danielle Kennedy. For 25 years she has smashed sales records, built lucrative businesses, authored books, produced sales training audio and video programs, and prepared as well as motivated thousands of real estate people worldwide on peak performance. Kennedy is available for half or full day seminars and special consulting work. A list of references is always available.

Danielle writes a monthly column on sales for *REALTOR*® magazine and a column on listing homes for *The Real Estate Professional* magazine. She has a Bachelor's degree in Business Communications, a Master's degree in Professional Writing from the University of Southern California, and an Honorary Doctorate in Humanities from Clarke College. Kennedy is one in only a handful of women inducted into the Sales and Marketing Executives International Hall of Fame.

**Warren Jamison** is a former real estate agent turned professional writer and speaker. A longtime member of the Authors Guild and the American Society of Journalists and Authors, he specializes in collaboration on both fiction and nonfiction. Among his co-authors are Ed McMahon, Dr. James Loehr, Jack Groppel, Ph.D., and Tom Hopkins.

**wjamison@jamisongold.com**
**Telephone: (500) 442-4151**

# CHAPTER 1

# Executing the New Basics for Bigger Profits: High Speed Breakaway

Market Share Parallels Executing the Basics ● Barriers and Fundamentals ● If You're New to Real Estate ● Should You Join a Buyers-Only Firm? ● Take Off Strong from the First Day ● Check with Your Broker ● Surface Details ● If You're Not So New ● What Do You Need to Begin Your Breakaway? ● What Do You Need to Complete Your Breakaway? ● Formula III Schedule

## Market Share Parallels Executing the Basics

Wow! It's hard to believe that a self-taught prescription of guidelines from a struggling young mother trying to find her way in the real estate business has become the "bible" of this industry. How humbled I am. I never could have imagined that the discoveries that brought me career success and financial independence could make such a long-term impact on real estate professionals all over the world! These discoveries are based on the following concepts: failing forward; self-correcting with each new prospect; fine tuning each succeeding presentation; communicating a clear, cut-to-the-chase language in order to reach more qualified prospects; and finally documenting my findings for posterity and prosperity.

It doesn't matter whether you are a new or a seasoned agent. The valuable information contained in this book is timeless. This approach to the listing and the selling of real estate has never changed. The goal is to discover the truth about the needs and desires of the buyers and the sellers that you serve. What's new is knowing how to find the prospects and then succeeding in earning their trust. This edition reveals more ways to find them and more ways to earn their trust. We are living in a skeptical world. Today more than ever we must learn how to develop long-term customer relationships.

In recent times there has been lots of discussion about how valuable the services of a real estate agent will be in the future. Will we be replaced by bankers? lawyers? technology? We are in the business of selling the most important—as well as the most intimate investment of a lifetime—the home. In the midst of this most intimate of exchanges, there is no substitute for the personal touch. The phone, the Internet, the fax, and the digital camera are merely our tools to enhance follow-up and speedy delivery of service. The threat of losing our status has little to do with technology, but everything to do with refusing to accept on-going education. When you stop perfecting the basics and only care about making your individual personal goals and agenda your main priority, you can count on becoming obsolete.

A WARNING to all seasoned agents: the biggest challenge you face is maintaining a willing attitude. Your willingness to humble yourself and go back to practicing the basics of this book will determine your future in real estate. Whenever I consult with successful companies, I always discover this unwillingness to be the biggest weakness in the company's culture. Show me a company who finds new ways to execute the basics, and I will show you a company with the biggest market share. Market share and a willingness to execute the basics go hand in hand.

This edition of the "real estate bible" is about taking the basics to a higher level of execution. This work is more valuable today than ever because we are in the age of word-of-mouth advertising. Ponder this for a moment. Remember when you first started receiving e-mails? Maybe one or two every few days? What a novelty it was to read and reply to them immediately. Today we often receive 65 to 100 e-mails a day. We are on information overload. Yes, the Internet is a wonderful source to use for research, virtual tours, and prequalifying. But people have tough time constraints. They haven't got hours to spend online researching a housing need or a question. They may do the preliminary investigation, but they rely on key individuals to make a recommendation. So technology has increased the demand for personalization. Consumers are seeking trusted friends to advise them on where to turn for housing needs. Trusted friends are often mavens of information and the community folks in-the-know; and when it comes to knowing the most professional real estate agent in the area, I hope they know who you are!

The trick is to get referrals. The heart and soul of this book is based on how to ensure repeat business. This is not a short-term prescription for capturing a prospect and closing a deal. This is an ongoing process of building and maintaining relationships and then turning them into profit centers for life. Profit centers are created when you practice multi-niche marketing. If you tap the niches we recommend in both this book and *Double Your Income in Real Estate* (Career Press, 1998), you can then create a lifetime customer who practices word-of-mouth advertising on your behalf. There is no substitute for one person's recommendation. When a respected citizen intervenes for you prior to your appearance at a listing or showing presentation, your chances of winning over the unworthy competition triples.

Executing the new basics means you merge today's most cutting edge ways to communicate with the methods introduced in this book. For example, in Chapter 5 you'll learn that flipping fizzbos* into your fold can happen faster, in some cases, by making initial contacts via e-mail. But don't underestimate the power of preparation. Study your market. Not everybody communicates in the same way. The mass mail-out still has its place in some locales. When you take the time to find out the best way to reach people, you discover the best way to get a return on your communication. This book offers communication methods that are market appropriate and time effective for your current business climate.

Take heart in knowing we have walked the talk. Yep, your coaches have seen the worst of times and the best of times in this business. None of it is scary anymore. Rising markets, falling markets—they all have their pros and cons. Maybe you have a listing on your hands for two years or perhaps 24 hours after your sign goes up, your seller receives multiple offers. Maybe the interest rates are at an all-time high or an all-time low. None of the market conditions will really matter anymore once you make this book your own. The power of these pages is in the execution of its words. The real title of this book should be: *How to List and Sell Real Estate for All Time*.

There should be no stopping you now. No more months of false starts and lost profits. Take this road map and run down this path of opportunity and prosperity. I took the risk and trekked this road ahead of you. I confronted and conquered most of the obstacles. Get moving. No more excuses. Here we go!

---

* Fizzbos are FSBOs—For-Sale-By-Owners—sellers attempting to market their property without professional real estate assistance.

# Barriers and Fundamentals

"What's the most important barrier between me and the success I want from real estate?"

You should ask yourself this question continually. The purpose of this book is to give you the skills you need to break away from whatever now prevents you from attacking your most important barrier. Once you've knocked the first one flat, you'll see another one behind it. But your second barrier won't be as difficult to knock flat as the first one was, because by then you'll know a vital fact: barriers aren't as tough as they look. They can all be knocked down or walked around. Whether you're new to real estate, not-so-new but in need of a lift, or already a high flyer, you can break away to new heights of income and professional standing. Put the systems, the insights, and the tips in the following pages to work—and soar as high as you wish.

It probably won't be easy for you to recognize your weak points. It'll be even harder to make the necessary changes in your work style to eliminate those weak points. Success doesn't come easy. It only seems easy when someone else does it—or when you look back after you've forgotten the hard work. Curiously, real estate is the best-paid easy work in the world—after you've learned the fundamentals and paid the price. If you refuse to pay the price—if you don't learn and practice the fundamentals—real estate is one of the lowest-paid hard jobs around. Even toweling off autos at the local car wash pays minimum wage. On the other hand, real estate's minimum wage is a lot less than zero because you're paying your own expenses.

That's real estate's downside now let's look at its upside. There's no ceiling. Once you get on track you can make $50,000 your first year out, double your income in the second year, and double it again in your third year.

It takes having enough expertise to work confidently with clients, solve their problems, and collect fees for doing so. Sure, you're impatient with the basics. Certainly, you want to get right at the action. But it's no good going where the action is if you can't handle it when you get there.

# If You're New to Real Estate

Is 21 days too long to wait for professional competence? If you're new to the business, quickly read through this book, and then put yourself on the Breakaway Schedule. You'll find it after Chapter 28. The 21-Day Breakaway Schedule is designed to give you a thorough knowledge of your area, its inventory, and of professional real estate skills in just three weeks. It's a 21-day cram session organized with high-speed learning methods. It's on-the-job training. It's tough—really tough. Deliberately so, because real estate *is* tough. But don't be discouraged if you can't finish it on time. Few people can. Other commitments, and often new clients discovered through Breakaway, eat into the available hours. Simply repeat the course until you've completed all of it.

Many of the most important achievements in the Breakaway Schedule don't require a real estate license. You can do it while you're waiting for, or studying for, your license. Then, when you're licensed, you'll be better prepared to work with clients. You'll have the realistic self-confidence you can only gain through hard work.

# Should You Join a Buyers-Only Firm?

Brokerage firms which only represent buyers and don't take listings are slowly changing the face of real estate practice. It's a slow change because listing income provides the greatest part of the incomes of many, if not most, established agents.

Buyers-only firms offer real estate beginners some powerful advantages.

- Quicker return. Since properties generally are on the market for weeks or months before they sell, representing buyers only means you should be able to begin closing transactions much sooner.
- You eliminate the following demands on your time, money, and expertise:
  - Working open houses. (Traditionally this is one of the most effective way to meet buyers.)
  - Working fizzbos (For-Sale-By-Owners) except when you have a committed buyer.
  - Working a farm. (This demands a considerable investment of time, energy, and money to do an effective job, but can provide a steady source of income once you have won control of your farm.)
  - Working expired listings. (This is a big money-maker for established agents, many of whom rely on this source for most of their income.)

As you can see, the advantages come with built-in disadvantages. If you become a buyers-only agent you won't be concerned with the problems of obtaining listings, but your need to know your area and its inventory of available properties is greatly intensified.

Before you decide between traditional *list-and-sell* and *buyers only*, talk to both kinds of brokers. This is a decision of overriding importance.

# Take Off Strong from the First Day

Accept three things: (1) you're ignorant of many things you'll soon know, (2) you'll frequently reveal your ignorance to others, and (3) this is part of the legitimate price everyone must pay to acquire competence in every new endeavor.

Make three basic decisions to help speed your journey to high-earning competence: (1) decide now not to be embarrassed by your freshness; (2) decide now to waste no time, not your own, nor the time of the more experienced agents around you, by apologizing for your ignorance; and (3) decide now to receive as a precious gem, any instruction offered by the top producers in your office—no matter how grudgingly, bluntly, or even sarcastically it's delivered.

Thank the top producers warmly (but briefly) for any hint of advice. Tips and encouragement are priceless, but remember: winning ways must always be learned by your own efforts, by your own study, practice, and, most importantly, by your own doing. Steer clear of the losers; they can only show you how to avoid doing what wins and then how to excuse losing.

Do what I did right, and don't do the things most agents, myself included, do wrong when starting. This book is all about doing the positives, and avoiding the negatives. Success is a series of habits and skills—and they're all learnable!

I can still see the way I worked during the first three months: the phone on a 25-foot cord under my ear while I traveled around the kitchen frying hamburgers, waving my arms like an idiot at one of my kids fighting with a brother or sister, trying to warn or caution them with a *"when I get off this phone you will be in big trouble—don't you know this is a very important customer?"* look. (Cell and cordless phones were not on the scene back then.) Slung under my arm is my brand new baby, Mary, who must have wondered what God had in mind to bestow such a nut of a mother on her. On the kitchen table is a deposit receipt with spilled milk smudging my buyer's signatures.

As soon as I can find a friend, neighbor, or babysitter to rescue me, I'm going to present the offer, smudged signatures and all. Walking into the seller's home, I'm going to look as though I don't have a care in the world. How I did those things during my early months in the business is a mystery to me now. But I did know how vital it was *not* to come in, boiling over with my own pressures and problems, and dump them on the buyers or sellers. The principals of a transaction are already cooking in a special oven reserved for people making a large and unfamiliar decision. Buyers and sellers don't need even the smallest piece of my problems; they have plenty of their own.

These were the days before any trophies for top listing and selling stood on the shelves of the pantry I used as my office; before I put up a little sign reading, "Never forget a humble beginning."

Because my beginning was indeed humble. And staggering. At the time I was six months pregnant with my fifth child, and completely unsure of myself. I looked like a tank. People couldn't believe some idiot would start a real estate career in my condition. "Why don't you just drop out and have your baby, darling." Bang. Pow. Ouch. Those early days, weeks, and months hurt. The whole experience was like a soap opera. Girl's feelings hurt daily. Girl unsure of real estate business. Girl weeps. Girls mopes. Girl hopes again.

Somehow I eked out a few good cold calls, banged on about 700 doors my first summer, and patiently courted fizzbos all over town. After about three months I had clients to work with, and I knew what I was doing. You can reach the same point by following the Breakaway Schedule for just three weeks.

When you start in real estate, you stand at the entrance of a treacherous tunnel leading to success as I did. In my case the tunnel was so dimly lit I paid for every step with bruises. While I struggled there, my survival in real estate still uncertain, I promised myself, "If I make it, I'm going to light up the way for the people who'll travel this tunnel after me." From that early resolve my speaking and writing career came.

Join me in Breakaway. Certain specific competencies enable you to nail down fees; Breakaway concentrates on them. You'll find no useless keep-busy stuff here.

Heavy work on your professionalism's foundation is included because your foundation must be solid before you can build a tower of high volume. Some of the places where this heavy work falls may surprise you. Plunge in. Make this material yours instead of time debating whether to start.

## Check with Your Broker

Many areas have rules or ordinances against some of the activities suggested in this book. For example, it may be illegal in your town to farm door-to-door as suggested in Chapter 6. Always check with your broker before trying a new real estate activity in your area.

## Surface Details

I travel worldwide conducting real estate training seminars. I'm always surprised by how much the surface details—procedures, jargon, and local rules—vary from area to area. I'm also surprised by how little the underlying truths of this people-business of ours change over time and distance. Buyers and sellers have the same basic fears in Saskatoon as they do in Schenectady, although the documents they sign may differ. If you encounter a surface detail in this book that doesn't apply in your area, skip to the next item. Better yet, figure out how to adapt the idea so you can use it.

## If You're Not So New

If you're an experienced agent, skim through the Breakaway Schedule after you've read the book. All of us have our weak points. Some of the achievements are too basic for you—skip them. Use the others to strengthen your expertise in the areas where your present level of performance doesn't satisfy you. Three weeks of systematic, concentrated effort will do wonders for your confidence and income potential.

"Wait a minute," you say, "I've been in real estate a while now—and I've been working hard—but I still don't feel competent. How're you going to change me into a pro in three short weeks?"

A fair question deserves an honest answer.

- You're the one who'll do it. I've made my start. Now it's your turn.
- Breakaway is a tough course. The days won't be short or easy.
- You can do it if you so choose. You can go all the way to top producer if you're willing to pay the price. The fee is payable only in hard effort.

Your breakthrough into top production will be painful. Accept the pain if you truly want to be a top producer. The joys of success and the knowledge of great professional growth follow close behind, making the pain of swift progress easily forgettable. There's no sit-back-and-watch to Breakaway. It's all DO, with you as the DOER, Breakaway requires three weeks of all-out effort as an investment in your future.

Can you handle it? Will you? Your answer may well determine your success in the real estate field.

Caution.

Before you skim over the Breakaway Schedule and decide, "I'm not doing this part," be aware of a highly probable fact: you're rejecting what you fear, not what you don't need. You'll be tempted to avoid precisely what will help you most—you might even make the decision so fast you're hardly aware you did.

In order to succeed, we must grow. To grow, we must endure the pain of doing what we fear until, by meeting and conquering the fear, we pass through to success. Control fear or fear controls you. It's a hard rule but a fair one, for it applies equally to us all.

# What Do You Need to Begin Your Breakaway?

Three things (on a tight budget):

- Desire to improve yourself
- Access to a cassette recorder-player
- Supply of cassettes and $3 \times 5$ inch cards

Optional tools (if you can afford them):

- Fax
- Laptop computer
- Voice mail
- Pager
- Personal digital organizer system

# What Do You Need to Complete Your Breakaway?

- Determined resolve to improve yourself
- Access to a car and the Multiple Listing Service, if your area has one
- Your real estate license and association with an active broker
- An electronic calendar, a Personal Digital Assistant (PDA), or at least an appointment book. You'll need it.

Each night of Breakaway, plan your tomorrow. Schedule how you'll accomplish your daily Breakaway commitment within twelve hours or less. Then get on with it! Avoid distractions. Waste no time on anxiety over the next step. Plunge ahead, and you'll get through in less than nine hours of thorough, effective work.

Planning tomorrow every night is just one of many important new money-making habits you'll instill in yourself through Breakaway. The program is packed with carryover ideas. These ideas will keep you on course for high income after you've completed possibly the most exciting and demanding period of your work life. But be prepared. Breakaway will crowd everything off tomorrow's action list except itself and the money-making opportunities you generate through it.

Think of it as your self-imposed **Boot Camp**—three weeks of hard work that will change you from a raw recruit into a trained soldier able to hold your own on the hard, unforgiving battlefields of real estate.

Another caution.

If you nibble around the edges of Breakaway for long, you'll lose your taste for the whole course. Don't let this opportunity to dramatically change your life slip away from you. Set the earliest date on which you can possibly begin Breakaway.

What's wrong with right now?

How about this minute?

There's no need to put off your Breakaway until a new day dawns; you can instantly blast off by deciding to, and by acting on your decision. Set tomorrow as your Breakaway's Day One. Then pick an achievement from the schedule and start making it yours now. Commit yourself to Breakaway. Stick to it. Your bank account will thank you!

One of Breakaway's greatest values lies in your commitment to an all-out investment of energy in your future. Racing the clock to meet the schedule forces extra effort and concentration. This extra output will send your abilities and performance to new heights. Completing the work on time will create an unshakable confidence in your own competence, and a faith in your own worth. These precious qualities will be of great ongoing value to you.

# Formula III Schedule

One of the earliest concepts the new real estate agent must grasp is my Formula III Schedule.

This illustration is the typical pattern of agents who never manage to balance their activity. When these agents start up, they're very enthusiastic about business development. They work the fizzbos, they hold open houses, they go farming, they work the centers of influence, and they put other prospecting tips learned in training in motion. This is good; when you're starting out you have no appointments and no business to service.

However, as soon as a sufficient number of appointments have been generated to put pressure on time, the agents who are headed for trouble cut back drastically on business development, and may even stop it altogether. Instead they start throwing themselves off balance by putting too much time into overpreparing for their appointments. These appointments *have* to work out, or these real estate agents will be in serious financial trouble because they have no new business developing.

This desperate need soon communicates itself to the public. Even unsophisticated buyers or sellers will instinctively sense the agent's desperation and back off fearfully.

Superstars also fall into this pattern by deciding they don't need to work fizzbos or farm anymore because they're getting lots of referrals. It's just another way to get badly out of balance because referrals can dry up without a moment's notice.

Never stop developing business, no matter how long you've been in real estate. Constantly picture yourself balancing three balls of equal weight and size: business development, appointments, and service. They must be kept in balance or serious problems ensue. Remember: high performance in appointments and service is essential to success, but they must be sustained by ongoing business development.

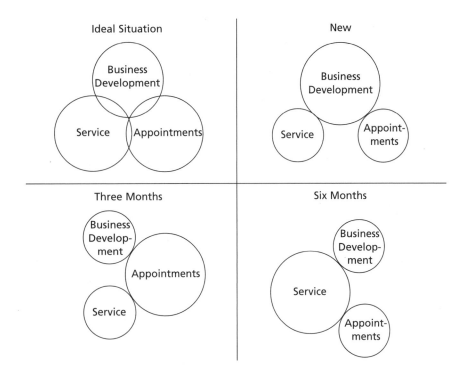

# CHAPTER 2

# High Speed Delivery for the 21st Century Consumer: The Quick-Speak Concept

The Concept ● Buyers' Phobia ● The Quick-Speak Inventory ● Money-Making Games with Your QSI ● The Jet-Powered Selling Tool

## The Concept

It doesn't matter how you get the word out. Just get it out. Use e-mail, fax, or voice mail. You need to react with speed using any of these tools when a prospect says, "I want a two-story, four-bedroom house with an off-white carpet and a big kitchen—and a family room right off the eating area. Oh, and I also want a view."

You scan a few photos and forward them. Or call the prospect back wherever you are using your cell phone. Leaving short text messages on the prospect's cell phone is a great way to react too.

"I know a home with all those things. It has two fireplaces, a wet bar, and it's air-conditioned. After we look at it I'll show you another one that's available for a lot less money. It has everything you mentioned except the carpet is bronze. But it needs replacing anyway. And we should also look at . . . ."

This is Quick-Speak. The client has the need, you have the house. There are no delays especially using digital cameras, scanning, and online virtual open houses to aid you in the process of early disqualification of property or people. No desperate search through current listing inventory while the client fumes impatiently. They ask—zap, you answer. This is competence. This is problem solving. This is doing what you're in business to do.

Of course, you'll often have to answer, "We can come close. Here's what's available. . . ." The point is, you *know*. If a house matching the specifications is available, you know about it; if not, you're certain no such house can be found in your area.

Many new agents don't understand what it takes to become successful in real estate. One essential is to know the inventory. Many experienced agents don't understand this point either. Knowing the inventory does not mean knowing how to look houses up in the Multiple Listing Book, nor does it mean spending half a day's research before showing property to every buyer. It means knowing the homes *before* you start working with a customer. It means being prepared to make money in real estate. With the advantage of the Internet, speedy delivery takes on a whole new meaning.

Of course it's harder to know the inventory. Many agents try to excuse their ignorance of the inventory by saying, "I can't remember homes unless I'm looking for a customer. Then I remember them really well. It's a lot easier that way. The inventory changes so fast."

Of course it's easier—that's why so many agents operate in this self-defeating way. It's also why an agent with a large Quick-Speak Inventory stands out from the crowd. If you've decided not to remember four-bedroom homes with pink wallpaper unless someone wants to look at four-bedroom homes with pink wallpaper, you've decided not to make much money in real estate.

The Quick-Speak concept applies to everything you need to know: not only inventory, but all the phrases needed to treat objections; all the facts, figures, and formulas; and all the winning scripts, must be on Quick-Speak if you're going to seize the instant when they can be used effectively. This knowledge on the tip of your tongue is power—big-buck earning power.

Quick-Speak means knowing all the things you need to know well enough to go far beyond merely repeating them to customers. You state them, each time, with sincerity. You present facts with close application to your customers' aspirations and abilities. Anyone can learn the phrases, but that's not enough. You need to sound spontaneous. And never bat them down by snapping off the perfect answer to every objection with mechanical precision. If you let it show how much you've practiced then you will have practiced in vain. People want to solve their problems with a sympathetic human being, not a calculator with a mouth.

Half-knowing your material makes it obvious you've memorized it; putting your material on Quick-Speak allows you to play infinite variations without losing the rhythm. Don't stop working when you have all the openers and closers down word for word. Be glad the hard work is done, and let the fun and fees begin. Be expressive with your clients; sing their song; dance to their beat and conduct them right through the closing with bright, warm, sincere interest.

# Buyers' Phobia

This is the fear of missing the best house available. If you allow even a crack of doubt to creep in on this point, your customer will suddenly develop acute buyers' phobia. They'll disappear, and seek the cure elsewhere.

The successful real estate salesperson drives this vital conviction into every buyer: he or she will show everything they will be interested in. Sometimes the salesperson has the inventory knowledge, but doesn't state it convincingly. Never groan to a buyer about how tough it is to know all the homes. Know them. And tell your people you do.

**Mrs. Buyer:** I like the colors here, but I want a larger dining room.

**You:** There's a house like this over on South Street with about these same colors. It has a very large dining room. Its yard is so small you won't have room for your garden, but would you like to see it anyway?

Here's a specific cure for Buyers' Phobia.

# The Quick-Speak Inventory

What's a Quick-Speak Inventory?

It's the total number of houses you can instantly describe without delaying the buyers by hunting around for information. Using accelerated methods, you can add five houses to your Quick-Speak Inventory (QSI) every day. By doing this, you'll soon be ready to show, without prior notice, at least three properties of interest to any buyer, and to talk knowledgeably about competitive inventory with any prospective seller.

QSI begins with a simple form to guide you to a manageable mental inventory of best-buy homes. It tells you what to look for, so your mental inventory isn't concentrated in a narrow price, location, and amenity field, but instead stretches across the entire spectrum of housing available in your chosen specialization area.

QSISS  Quick-Speak Inv

V=Vacant   O=Occupied

| *UNDER 200K* | *UNDER 150K* | | *CONDOS* | *ELM DIST* | *CLUB ESTATES* |
|---|---|---|---|---|---|
| *140 W "C" ST* | | V | *66 S NCT* | *5502 W. ACE* | |
| *1020 Bluff* | | O | *2131 4th E* | *4901 DANTE* | *65 PRESS WAY* |
| | | V | | | |
| 2 Bedrooms | 2 Bedrooms | O | 2 Bedrooms | 2 Bedrooms | 2 Bedrooms |
| | | V | | | |
| 3 Bedrooms | 3 Bedrooms | O | 3 Bedrooms | 3 Bedrooms | 3 Bedrooms |
| | | V | | | *49 S. 60TH* |
| 4 Bedrooms | 4 Bedrooms | O | 4 Bedrooms | 4 Bedrooms | 4 Bedrooms |
| | | V | | | |
| 5 Bedrooms | 5 Bedrooms | O | 5 Bedrooms | 5 Bedrooms | 5 Bedrooms |

| Fixer-Uppers | Great Terms | *VIEW* | *POOLS* | |
|---|---|---|---|---|
| | | | | |
| | | | | |
| | | | | |

© Copyright 1989 Danielle Kennedy Productions, P.O. Box 1395, Sun Valley, Idaho 83353.

I call the form a QSI slot sheet because it's short and descriptive. Call it what you like—Guidelines to Best Buys, Inventory Control Sheet—whatever. The important thing is to quickly zero in on your initial area of specialization and take a fast grip on the inventory there.

With a pencil and a plain piece of paper, make up a master form for your Quick-Speak Inventory Slot Sheet and run off a dozen copies. Use sample 1 in Chapter 24 (or download this form from the accompanying CD) as a guide. Scan the form onto your computer.

Access to homes on the Internet makes setting up your QSI even easier. First select your zone of specialization. Don't agonize over this decision. It's no problem to shift your emphasis later, and you'll profit from the special knowledge you've gained in your first specialization zone as long as you stay in your area association.

If single-bedroom units or houses with more than five bedrooms are important in your area, put them on the form. Choose the special categories most useful to you. Fixer-uppers and especially attractive terms are found everywhere; for the other three special categories select the three most important amenities in your area.

If necessary, take one of the vertical columns for additional special categories, but keep the total slots in your initial QSI to around 50. After you have about 50 homes firmly into your mental inventory, consider adding more slots. Don't limit the total number of houses in your QSI; instead, work at maintaining variety in your mental inventory of salable properties. You'll find yourself carrying 75 to 100 houses in your QSI to fill those 50 slots. The goal is to keep the most houses in your mental inventory with the least effort, because fees are earned working face-to-face and phone-to-phone with clients. The entire point of QSI is to give you the tools to earn fees with the least amount of time taken away from client work.

Building a powerful QSI in the shortest time possible, demands fast learning. It also demands keen retention.

This is easy when you know how and here's the way:

1. **Keyview houses instead of merely previewing them.** The next chapter tells you about the effective keyviewing method. Virtual touring speeds up this process.
2. **Flashdeck your QSI.** This simple method of brainclamping information fast is also detailed in the next chapter.

## Money-Making Games with Your QSI

Once you've built your QSI above 50 houses, you can increase your mental clamp on this information by challenging yourself with questions: "Name the three houses (on your QSI) with four bedrooms and the most square footage." Don't hesitate. Write down three immediately: "The tulip house on Birch. 2020 Country Club Drive. The brick-front on Aspen."

See how well you did on each question by checking your QSI Flashdeck, or your QSI slot sheet. As you do this, you'll learn even more about your Quick-Speak Inventory. The questions in this money-making game are limited only by your imagination and the keenness of your eye when keyviewing. Now you're developing your QSI into the jet-powered selling tool.

## The Jet-Powered Selling Tool

"Quick, name a three-bedroom house with a fireplace and blue carpet." By constantly drilling yourself on the 50 homes, you have an extremely useful selling tool. Follow the Breakaway Schedule given after Chapter 28 and you'll build a 50-house QSI during the next ten days. Using the speedy learning systems given in the next chapter, you can have 150 houses on QSI a month from today. Never again will you be stopped cold when customers suddenly switch specifications, as they so often do. Let's say you research homes with a view for customers, show them one or two, and then they decide to forget about a view and go for more space. The mediocre agent tells them to come back another day, and never sees 90 percent of them again. But you're prepared for this common turn of events. You drive right to some houses meeting their new requirements, knock on those doors for permission and show them right away. I've made a lot of money doing this.

Suppose a friend phones and says, "My new boss and his wife are here, and he wants to look at houses right away. Can you come over and pick him up?"

You do. Your friend's boss climbs in your car and gets right at it. "Look, I know all about this qualifying bit. I can go to $50,000 down, and I can qualify for a $200,000 loan, but I don't want to put that much money into a house. Our kids have just gone out on their own, and we might buy a smaller house than we have now. But maybe not. So show us what you've got."

If you have 50 houses on QSI, you can show him a different house every 15 minutes for *twelve and a half hours*—without stopping for meals. This will satisfy the most eager curb jumper.

"This is nonsense," you're thinking. "Nobody wants to look at houses for twelve hours, and nobody wants to see them all." Right. But if you've selected a good cross section of the available houses for your QSI, you can instantly pick out at least three houses of interest to anyone qualified to buy in your area. You come on like a champion all the way. Your customers know they'll never find anyone better able to guide them straight to their best housing buy than you.

Suppose you work in a board publishing a weekly Multiple Listing Book of a thousand or more available properties. You can't keep such a large inventory on ready recall in your mind. Fortunately, performing such a feat isn't necessary. Carrying between 50 and 250 listings in your QSI gives you a powerful machine for selling real estate.

Before you decide to amble along with only 50 houses on QSI, reflect on these two facts: (1) top producers make at least five times as much money as average producers in the same office, and (2) top producers have at least five times as many properties on QSI as average producers. High income and high QSI fly together, just as low income and low QSI grumble along together.

Top producers also don't have a superior attitude about previewing or showing listings from competing offices. If you are a true "public servant" you will not show any partiality regarding listed properties. Of course everyone wants to sell their office's listings because they make more money, but this consideration must always be secondary to the customer's need. Don't kid yourself the public knows our goals. I have heard people discuss real estate agents who won't show certain properties or who try to talk the public out of one house because it's not an "in-house" listing. In the long run, when you cooperate with all brokers and their properties your reputation within the industry and with the public will be rated as highly ethical. Take it from me, your pocketbook will also reflect your golden rule philosophy.

# CHAPTER 3

# Build Money-Making Skills Fast with Hyperlearn and the Latest Techno Tools

**Hyperlearn's Six Easy Steps** ● **Hyperlearning Techniques** ● **Specific Hyperlearn Applications**

Hyperlearn is a method of extending your perceptions and intensifying your concentration so you can more quickly grasp new knowledge and acquire new skills. It only sounds formidable; in practice it's simple. Hyperlearn is fun because the good results start at once, and you're creatively involved. Disorganized, haphazard study is inefficient and delivers disorganized, haphazard results. Hyperlearn is organized and delivers the results you want, when you want them. It's a flexible system. You adapt it to the knowledge or skill being acquired. The brief time you spend organizing your Hyperlearn course often takes you halfway or further toward mastery of the material or skill. Yes, you can put this whole system on your computer. If you carry a laptop you can practice the system anytime and anywhere.

## Hyperlearn's Six Easy Steps

The six easy Hyperlearn steps allow you to learn anything quickly.

    **1. Name it.** Define precisely what you're setting out to learn. Write down your learning goal. Be concise. Use numbers to make your goal clear and definite. Use short sentences. If you need more than a short paragraph, you're trying to include too much material in a single learning course.

Suppose your goal is, "I want to know the floor plan of every available house in my sales area; I want to know the amenities each house has; I want to be able to give buyers the prices, number of bedrooms, and—"

You stop because your goal seems too wordy and the task too big to cope with. You need to break this large learning problem down into several manageable courses. Concentrate on becoming an expert in part of the sales area fast, rather than remaining an unpaid mumbler about all of it for a long time.

Write your Chief Goal first, "To master the inventory of the entire Green Pretty Valley." Now pick a subgoal, "To master the inventory in the Elm School neighborhood."

At one stroke, you've changed a formidable goal, requiring many months to achieve, into one you can conquer within a few days—without altering your basic thrust.

2. **Concentrate it.** Gather the information you need into one place. Print the Elm School listings from last week's online new inventory. Create a file and memorize the features of each home.

3. **Understand it.** Give the information a rapid first reading to familiarize yourself with its depth and scope. Then reread it, this time carefully. Make sure you understand every detail well enough to explain it to a customer.

4. **Organize it.** Break your material down into the smallest study units possible. Express the data as single facts or in short paragraphs.

5. **Reassemble it.** Put the material into a self-created, self-teaching course. Use one or a combination of the following techniques:
   - Flashdecks
   - Solo role working
   - Blank-interval cassette tapes
   - Outlines to details
   - Mnemonic hooks
   - Feelings remember
   - Skills and senses
   - Computer files.

6. **Review it.** Go over the material twice each day, using whatever learning methods you've selected. Concentrate as you review the material, work fast, and be thorough. Do this every

morning and every night and you'll master your material with astonishing speed.

# Hyperlearning Techniques

## Create Your Own Flashdecks

All you need is a pack of 3 × 5 inch cards. Cut them in half for easier carrying and lower cost. Write one question or situation on the front of each card; write the answer or response on the back. A dozen cards make an effective flashdeck ready for instant study any time you have a few moments.

To use the flashdeck for learning, read the question, answer it, and flip the card to check the completeness and accuracy of your response. Don't hesitate. Demand test answers from yourself. If you can't answer within two seconds, read the answer on the back of the card. When you miss a question, study the answer intently. Then put the card where you'll encounter it again on review of the deck.

The time you spend organizing and writing your flashdeck cards is the most effective learning experience you can have with most types of data. From the flashdeck to complete mastery of the data through spaced repetition (twice-daily drills) is an easy downhill slide.

Shuffle the cards once or twice a week so your responses aren't keyed to a familiar card sequence. If a few questions are especially troublesome—and this is usually the case—create a constant companion deck by making a second copy of the card you're having trouble with. Carry this deck with you during the day and review it whenever you have a few free minutes. Drop cards as soon as you've learned them.

**Examples of a flashdeck card:**

|  |  |
|---|---|
| How many homes in Elm School area? | 740 |

Side 1                          Side 2

## Use Solo Role Working

First, let's distinguish between role playing and role working. Chapters 11 and 16 include role plays for office meetings. Volunteers play the parts by reading them from this book.

This is training with live ammunition. The situations agents face when they work with clients are recreated for the benefit of the role players and the rest of the staff watching. But you can't make the words yours by hearing them just once. This is where role working comes in. You can role work, solo, as often as you like. No time is wasted trying to schedule convenient times for group role playing. You get ready for solo role working by creating flashdecks and blank-interval cassettes; in themselves big steps toward memorizing the material.

## Prepare and Use Your Own Blank-Interval Cassette Tapes

To prepare a tape you need a blank cassette tape, a recorder-player, a flashdeck, and a quiet place to work for a short time. With the machine in Record mode, read the question out loud from the first flashdeck card. Then, with the machine still recording, turn the card over and *silently* read the answer. Repeat this process for each card in the deck. Simple, isn't it? But it's wonderfully effective.

Now, rewind the tape you just made and play it from the beginning. When your taped voice finishes asking a question, say the answer out loud. (Don't record your answer, of course.) Use the flashdeck to prompt yourself at first. This is a let-it-roll operation. While the blank-interval cassette plays, you're free to walk around and concentrate on what you're saying without standing over the recorder punching buttons.

Keep these four tips in mind when using this method:

1. **Speak with clarity and verve.** Work at doing this from the beginning, but don't overdo it; naturalness is the key.
2. **Visualize the situation** in your mind. Imagine the question in real life as you listen to each question. You not only need to know the answers, you also need to know the situations where they occur.
3. **Don't rush** through the silent reading when recording the blank intervals. Be sure you allow yourself a second or two to get set, plus enough time to say the full answer with conviction and unhurried phrasing.
4. **Number each card** before recording so the flashdeck will be convenient for prompting yourself and checking the accuracy of your spoken answers.

5. **Perfect your responses** by occasionally taping your replies for review. Go through the entire blank-interval cassette, then review all your answers. Make note of the responses needing further rehearsal to give them more zip and zing.

Expect to hear a host of minor mistakes; refuse to be dismayed by them. Practice perfects; ignoring a mistake usually makes it worse. Step 5 may be the first time in your adult life when you work at improving your verbal performance. You're in sales, so how well you speak bears heavily on how much you get paid. Consider how much time in the past month—or even in the past year—you have devoted to improving this vital skill.

## Turn Outlines into Details

Take your outline of the detailed material to be learned, and tape-record, write in longhand, or type the details out from memory. You can also use the answer side of a flashdeck to cue this self-testing. Check your answers for accuracy or you may thoroughly learn the wrong information.

## Create Mnemonic (nee'-mon-ik) Hooks for Nimble Numbers

Ability recalling numbers divides people into two groups. Group one has been able to remember numbers well at some time in their lives. Group two is composed of everyone else. This is all the people who keep telling themselves, "I'm no good at remembering numbers." It's easy to change this.

Every successful agent has had many instances where a snatched moment has saved a transaction otherwise lost. When a customer goes to the restroom or trots out to the car for something, you can snap off a fast phone call. Frequently a timely call held another situation for me until I could finish with the first customer and meet the second one. I've made these calls (local, of course, or charged to my office phone) while showing houses to buyers. Address books are great. Use them. Write down those phone numbers. But, if you know the number, you can be talking to the person you need to reach before you can pull out an address book and find anything in it. Your brain is eager to give you the phone number in a split-second. All you have to do is program it right and you'll remember every time. No charge.

Phone numbers are only the tip of the numeric iceberg. Interest-rate factors, square footages, prices, all the numbers you need, if they're on ready recall, will help you solidify your foundation of competence. Nimbleness with numbers contributes mightily to the relaxed, alert, I'm-on-top-of-everything attitude that does so much to reassure people when they need all the reassurance they can get to make a major decision. This positive attitude radiates from you in countless subtle ways, winning respect and building confidence. Without this attitude, you're crackling with tension and you radiate stress. Prospects pick up your stress as fear and uncertainty. Calm Confidence closes better than Hectic Hassle ever will.

None of the numbers you need to know in real estate are hard to learn. Concentrate on any number for an instant and you'll see patterns. The concentration is the first step to your goal—the ability to project the desired numbers in 10-foot high figures on the screen of your mind. Let's try instant concentration on a phone number, and suppose 547-8332 is the home phone of your client, James Fagan, who happens to be a slim guy. No matter. Choose vivid or even ridiculous images when the plain facts aren't memorable, as is usually the case.

## 547-8332

The five is alive; 47 is Fat Fagan's Waistline—8 less two 3's is 2. Visualize a very alive Fat Fagan jiggling his 47-inch waistline while yelling, "Eight minus 3 twice is 2."

Write this number a couple of times. See the figures standing high as you write them. The point is to learn this method, not the gibberish number. Practice learning the method on the numbers in your own address book. Make the dull numbers throb. If this trick eludes you right now, take a memory course at your local college, or buy a book on memory building—both are loaded with recall hooks to make memorizing numbers a snap.

## Remember That Feelings Remember

Can you remember a painful childhood accident? Most people can vividly recall such incidents and they happened many years ago and much of what happened yesterday may be a blank. Details of the long-remembered incidents were imprinted on their minds by fear and pain, without which those details would have vanished from memory long ago. You don't have to give yourself a crack on the head every time you see a house you want to remember. Pleasant emotions are effective memory clamps too.

Be alert for emotional associations you can form between events in your life and information you now wish to remember. This idea is particularly helpful in keyviewing houses. All of us can find parallels between the houses we're selling and the houses we grew up in, or have lived in since. This can apply to furnishings as well as to floor plans. A solid memory hook to hang a house on could be a grandfather clock in the hall, a clock just like your aunt's.

Another solid hook is a house where you've worked many open houses. Make a conscious effort to find these associations for a month and they'll start flowing to you, making your observation sharper and your recall keener. Make a note while you're in each house you keyview of the specifics remembered, "242 Elm, 3-bedroom, reminds me of Aunt Lou's house in Chicago."

## Use a Variety of Skills and Senses

Use every different sense and skill you can reasonably employ to perceive, express, and impress the material on your mind. Read it silently and then aloud. Copy each of the study units you've laid out for yourself word for word in longhand. Outline the basic ideas. Then, using only your outline, write the material you're learning in detail. Prepare a flashdeck and drill yourself on the facts you're acquiring. Record one of your readings of the material and then listen to your tapes. Discuss the details with someone who shares your interest.

When you're learning about houses, walk through and around them. When you're learning about an area, drive it, walk it, and fly over it if you can.

## Create Computer Files

Create a question and answer file on your computer (instead of $3 \times 5$ cards if you prefer). Quiz yourself and then check your answers with the answer key you created.

## Know and Use the Hyperlearn Process

The two essential elements of the Hyperlearn process are the following:

- Break down the material to be learned into small, easily understood parts.
- Reassemble those parts in your brain by drawing them in through as many different channels as possible. To shorten your learning time and make your recall keener and quicker, experience what you want to learn in all the different ways and with all the different senses, skills, and emotions you can bring to bear.

Remember, only full mastery of your material permits you to concentrate all your attention on the prospect. Run through your Hyperlearn exercises rapidly and intensely. Avoid distractions and slowness. Two short drills spaced several hours apart teach more effectively than one long session. Schedule twice-daily study times.

> "And while I at length debate, and beat the bush, there shall step in other men and catch the birds."
>
> —John Heywood, 1549

# Specific Hyperlearn Applications

## Learn the Named Neighborhoods Fast

Can you drive to any property in your area, from wherever you happen to be, without wrong turns or consulting maps? You're paid in proportion to the knowledge and skill you employ helping customers find houses. House hunters need guidance through the unknown to the property they can afford in the neighborhood they'll like. They, too, can study the map, research the area, and knock on strange doors, but they prefer tapping your reservoirs of knowledge. Those reservoirs had better be full or they'll go elsewhere.

There's no quicker way to lose people forever than by getting lost yourself while driving them around your own area of expertise. It's basic, but not too boring to bother with. If you have no knowledge of the territory, you'll make no money in it. If you have good knowledge, you can make good money. If you have top knowledge of the territory, you can make top money there. Learn your area's streets so well you can zip around them with blithe confidence. Make your folks glad they're working with you. It takes work. It'll take a lot less work if you apply a system to your street-learning process. The first step is to take out a piece of paper.

**Draw a map of your sales area.** Include only the main thoroughfares serving your area of primary interest. Do it fast and then compare what you've drawn to the printed map. If you're not satisfied with your accuracy or completeness, draw another from the printed map. Don't trace it. Draw it. Repeat this exercise daily, until you can quickly sketch an accurate, main thoroughfare map of your area (as you might need to do while sitting with a customer in a coffee shop). Get it straight in your head now, so you can start operating with that happy can't-get-lost feeling right away.

Many agents don't see the point of putting out further effort to learn the territory in detail. Yet, if this agent's house was going up in flames, this same agent would be enraged if the fire department wasted time figuring out how to get there. Hot buyers are aflame with impatience. Fiddle around looking for houses while they burn, and you'll send them to a better-prepared agent. You can take this lesson to heart now, or learn it after you've sent several thousand dollars to the professionally prepared agents who know exactly where to find the salable inventory.

You can lose some buyers simply by not knowing whether there's a church of their denomination in your area, and exactly where it is. Again, you can lift a fee-saving idea off this page, or wait and learn this small but sometimes crucial bit of information after you lose a sale. Experience is the best teacher, but its lessons don't come cheap.

As soon as you're familiar with the area's major streets and points of interest, you're ready for the second step: mastering the residential streets in detail. Here's how to do this efficiently.

**Define 30 neighborhoods of about 20 streets each on a printed map of your sales area. Use a pencil to draw lines around them.** These 30 neighborhoods will cover much more than your area of primary interest. The purpose is to be ready for working with buyers on short notice—a frequent event. Agents who aren't prepared to work on short notice lose lots of buyers. Don't let it happen to you. Prepare. Now.

Use main thoroughfares or natural barriers for the neighborhood boundaries. Where none are available, pick a key street to draw your line down. After you've defined these 30 neighborhoods, take a moment to put a name hook on each one so they will all stand out in your memory.

**Name each of these neighborhoods.** Choose a name from a church, school, or other landmark located there. Perhaps an intersection in the neighborhood, a park, or some other feature can furnish a distinctive name.

When the neighborhoods are all defined and named, you're ready to schedule a rapid-learning sequence. Learning two named neighborhoods a day is about right, you'll probably find. Here's how to do it:

- Study the streets and how they connect on a map.
- Set the map aside and sketch the streets from memory.
- Compare your sketch to the map and make corrections.
- Repeat the above until you can draw a complete and accurate sketch showing how the streets connect in the neighborhood you're studying.
- Make a list of the streets in the neighborhood by copying the names from the map.

- Make up a named neighborhood flashdeck (see below) and run through the cards.
- Repeat this process morning and night until you've overlearned each neighborhood. Drive the streets twice daily, remembering which named neighborhood you're in.

One of the repeating achievements of Breakaway is to thoroughly learn 2 of these 30 neighborhoods each day. Do this and you'll always know exactly where you are on 600 streets. You'll have an inexhaustible bag of tricks to save time, impress clients, and win fees. Streets rarely change. Learn them, and you'll make big money from this knowledge as long as you work the area.

## Make a Named-Neighborhoods Flashdeck

Make a 3 × 5 card for each street. On one side, write only the street name. On the other side, write the main cross streets, how you get there, and where the street begins and ends. The quickest and most effective memory tool is a sketch of the street in question.

Be sure to note the neighborhood on the description side of the card. This will permit you to mix cards into one named neighborhoods flashdeck for occasional review.

## Organize Keyviewing

When keyviewing houses, you can organize your thoughts on 3 × 5 cards so you can build up a large Quick-Speak Inventory (QSI) of properties fast. Spot a single distinguishing feature about every home you're putting in your QSI. This could be a fountain, a spectacular view, a weird decoration—anything you notice will do. Then key your memory to this feature.

On the front of each 3 × 5 card write your memory key: "Purple, hairy wall-hanging in living room." On the back of the card, jot down the following information:

> 4567 Arrowhead Drive
> CBS M/M Barnes 987-5432
> 3 bd 1 3/4 ba
> shake rf, rm 4 pool, no vu, gold cpt, clean, AM

Spelling out the abbreviations, it means: Call before showing, Mr. and Mrs. Barnes, 3 bedrooms, 1 3/4 baths, shake roof, room for a swimming pool in the back yard, no view. Gold carpet. The house is clean (but not immaculate). Priced at the market. This last comment

(AM) is your feeling, not what the listing agent said on the flyer. For your QSI flashdeck and similar purposes, it's handy to have a simple, three-term price indicator:

| | |
|---|---|
| UM | Priced under the current market: a likely-to-sell-fast bargain. |
| AM | Priced at the market. The comparables will validate this price. |
| OM | Priced over the market. This one will be around for a while. |

Have a distinguishing feature for every house on your QSI. Price. A clock like your aunt's. View. A real fixer-upper—but cheap. A cream-puff. A dull dog with lots of space. Highlight what's special by circling the item.

The most convenient way to work your QSI flashdeck, usually, is to file the cards by price. Be sure to date each *price.* Leave room on the card for price changes.

Standing around an open house, waiting for an important call, or when you're early for a meeting, pull out your QSI flashdeck and refresh your inventory knowledge. When you see "Hairy, purple wallhanging" on a card, the whole house should flash on in your head. With just a little practice, you'll be able to mentally walk around in the house and see the family room, the fireplace, the shelves in the library. You'll remember all the other pertinent details you related to the purple, hairy wallhanging.

Keen memory is merely intense concentration keyed to a detail. Everyone can have a keen memory—it takes concentration. By pulling on your hook—the key element you tied your details to—you'll be able to pull out your memory of an entire house. It's really fun to recall minor details about a house you've keyviewed several weeks before, and it can be very, very profitable.

Drill yourself with your stack of QSI cards morning and night. Polish this knowledge and it will fly you to Tahiti.

## Visual Flashdecks

Photograph houses you want to be able to identify by sight with an instant-print camera, and then write the data you want to memorize on the back of the print, Voilà: a visual flashdeck.

Use this technique to create a beautiful sales tool in no time at all for working with both buyers and sellers. Compile a visual flashdeck of:

- Distant properties
- Properties requiring long advance notice to show
- Common types of houses in your sales area for establishing price ranges

- Tract model exteriors, to speed your memorization of them, and then to show resale buyers what's available
- Best buys
- Your entire Quick-Speak Inventory

Make photos part of your keyviewing routine. An instant print of the exterior will allow you to concentrate your keyviewing effort on the interior.

## Learn Floorplans Fast

You'll be pleasantly surprised at how firm a grip you'll get on floorplans by using this routine when keyviewing:

- After walking through the house, sit down in it and make a quick sketch the floorplan. Don't look around as you do this, sketch entirely from memory.
- Jump up and check the accuracy of your sketch.
- Repeat the process until you can sketch the basic floorplan from memory.

## Conquer the Agreements

There are two ways you can become thoroughly familiar with the listing form and the purchase agreement: work with them for a few years or Hyperlearn them in a few hours. Command of this verbiage will boost your self-confidence and imbue your clients with faith in you. It will help mightily to create in your customer the essential willingness to be closed. Too many new agents delay giving these two vital forms intense study until they're sitting with buyers or sellers, and trying desperately to close. Hesitation or incompetence revealed at such an emotionally charged time will often chill the clients and kill the transaction. Don't risk it.

Here's how to acquire absolute command of the clauses in these forms easily:

- Pick up the agreements your office uses to take listings and make offers, and read them out loud. Make sure you understand every paragraph, sentence, phrase, and word well enough to explain them. Get answers to every question you have.
- Visit an escrow officer, attorney, title person—whoever is involved in closing in your state. Spend time with them and just watch their activities.
- Create a flashdeck for the paragraphs of each vital form: on one side write the number, on the other write the exact, complete text of the paragraph.

- Drill yourself with the flashdeck until you know exactly what's in each agreement form, and precisely where everything in it is.

This won't seem like wasted effort after you've had a distraught seller say, "I can't find where it tells what happens to the earnest money if the buyers back out." You can scurry over and frantically scan the form to answer the question while she thinks, "Don't you even know your own form? Am I dealing with an amateur?"

How much better if, without glancing at the form, you immediately say from where you're sitting, "Paragraph 12* covers it, Mrs. Nagle." This action quietly shouts, "I am a competent agent. Your interests are safe in my hands." Large fees are won on a series of just such small wins!

## Write Offers with Hyperlearned Phrases

Being able to write clear offers is a vital skill. Loosely phrased offers frighten sellers. How would you phrase an offer if your buyers want

- To sell their house first?
- To assume the existing low-interest loan?
- To be assured the landscaping will be properly cared for until they take possession?
- To do, or be protected against, any of the other things that frequently come up during purchase negotiations in your area?
- To lock in the desired interest rate in a buyer's agreement?
- To close concurrent with the closing of the buyer's present home, sold but not recorded?
- To rent back prior to the closing (not a very smart thing to do but sometimes necessary)?
- An all-cash offer?
- A geological report within a certain time frame (or any other valid inspection that could affect the ultimate value of a home)?

## Take a Quick Fix on These Phrases

- Examine your office's files of closed transactions, note the most common situations arising on offers, and study the wording used for those situations. Pass over complex, unusual circumstances.

---

* The form used in your area probably covers this information under a different paragraph number.

Concentrate on learning the solutions to the most frequently encountered questions first.

- From this study, create a list of effective offer-to-purchase phrases in flashdeck form. On one side of a 3 × 5 card, write the deposit receipt problem. On the reverse side of the card, copy the most effective phrase you've found dealing with that particular circumstance. Avoid rambling sentences. Choose the shortest and most precise clauses.

- Practice working fast and accurately under pressure by writing up offers with intense concentration for 30 minutes a day until you are supremely confident in this area of real estate expertise.

## Buy Software

Lots of people still like to do things the old fashioned way. Perhaps 3 × 5 cards or making maps to help you learn is precisely your cup of tea. But if you are a true techie why not save oodles of time and purchase software with maps of whole neighborhoods? Specific directions to anywhere you want to go are included. Stay on top of the latest software by browsing trade shows at the National Association of REALTORS® or any of our state conventions. And take yourself shopping outside of real estate. Your local computer store is always adding new products that are real estate friendly for the Hyperlearn system. Browse online too.

# CHAPTER 4

# Confront Old Pro—And Win!

**How to Win Fizzbo Listings from Old Pro ● Eight Tips on Winning Any Listing from Old Pro ● When Old Pro Has an Offer on Your Listing ● What Old Pro Hates ● When You Have an Offer on Old Pro's Listing ● When Both You and Old Pro Have Offers on a Third Agent's Listing ● Hearing Simultaneous Offers on Your Listing**

It used to be an advantage to be an Old Pro. By today's standards, however, Old Pro may infer stubborn and stuck. I am amazed to see so many seasoned agents unwilling to put in the down time to get trained on the latest technology. Some Old Pros wonder why they keep losing the listing or never get the buyers that the new and the willing agents do. It has much to do with becoming ripe and rotten versus staying green and growing.

In this chapter I assume that Old Pro is really on top of all the best ways to deliver service. Much to my dismay, I see many new agents when they find themselves competing against an old-timer of considerable reputation, assume they're beaten, merely go through the motions of trying, and let Old Pro collect the fee by default.

New agents should seek and welcome encounters with established agents who have an impressive track record. Win or lose, these encounters are instructive. Dwell on the positive benefits of such a learning experience, and refuse to worry whether your inexperience shows. Seize each of these exciting learning opportunities, wring all the knowledge you can from them, and you won't be inexperienced for long. Let's consider the basic situations where you'll find these priceless learning opportunities.

# How to Win Fizzbo
# Listings from Old Pro

Since the new agent has more time, he or she holds an important advantage over Old Pro in working this aspect of real estate practice. Fizzbos (FSBO—For-Sale-By-Owner) are heavy time-eaters. Old Pro will swoop in and gobble up a fizzbo now and then where he or she is referred, has a buyer for the property, or just feels like it. But the top producers (with rare exceptions) can't work constantly in the For-Sale-By-Owner field. Referral business brings in most of their production; if they try to work fizzbos heavily, they'll have to neglect their referrals.

If you're a new agent battling for a fizzbo over a period of time with Old Pro, take heart. Time is with you. The longer the fizzbo holds off making a decision, the better your chances are of eventually winning. You have the staying power and the determination; you are rapidly plugging the gaps in your knowledge and skills; you are closing in fast on Old Pro's lead in expertise. It'll take time for you to match Old Pro's inventory knowledge of the entire sales area. You can't match her whole bag of skills overnight. But you can, within days, learn enough about the seller's neighborhood to convince him you are the upcoming expert on his location. Do this by concentrating on his block and neighborhood. Old Pro can't concentrate to this extent; he or she must cover a wider area. And, when people think about who is keeping current on their turf, your knowledge of what happened there last week will be much more important to them than Old Pro's knowledge of what happened there last year. Knock on doors. Talk to the people. Find out who is thinking of selling, who is getting promoted, and what people think of the neighborhood today. You're in a far better position than Old Pro is to discover what's happening now on the block because you have the time to do it.

# Eight Tips on Winning
# Any Listing from Old Pro

- Concentrate on one situation. Overprepare for it.
- Keep your cool, your humor, and your integrity.
- Be professional and courteously assertive.
- Emphasize your strong point: you have more time for thorough promotion (especially open houses) and for servicing the listing.
- Defuse Old Pro's advantages by quickly conceding his or her fine reputation. Then describe your office's enormous fund of knowledge and skill and say it's available, if needed.

- Don't fight on unfavorable ground. If you're competing for a listing in the farm an Old Pro is actively working, don't try to prove you know more about their chosen neighborhood than Old Pro does (though you might be able to show more knowledge about *one house* in it). In this situation, you're in the running only if the sellers are disenchanted with Old Pro for personal or business reasons, and they very well might be.
- Believe in and act on this maxim: "I win by demonstrating my own competence; I lose by casting doubt on my competitor's competence." You can't have clean hands if you throw mud.

Try to have the appointment after Old Pro. If this isn't possible, say to the seller, "Could I have just one more chance to talk to you before you make your final decision? I know Old Pro is an excellent agent, but please don't list with someone based on pricing. Any of us can agree to a price."

It's critical, when you're up against Old Pro, to use a listing presentation manual to make sure you fire all your ammunition.

Role play your presentation to your spouse, or another beginner in your office. Rehearse presenting the seller's net sheet and the guidelines to market value. Find out if you and the prospective seller have a mutual friend. If so, call the friend to enlist help. Say to your friend, "In real estate, I get by with a little help from my friends, so could I ask you a favor?" (Don't pause.) "Mary and Bud Johnson have asked both me and a competitor to give them a market evaluation on their home. Sometimes if a mutual friend not in real estate puts in a good word, I have a better chance of getting the opportunity to serve them. Would you call Mary and Bud and possibly put in a good word for me?"

# When Old Pro Has an Offer on Your Listing

(Practices vary from state to state. Check with your broker on how this is handled in your area.)

You set up the appointment to meet Old Pro at your seller's home. Naturally, you don't want to look inept. Avoid it by taking the time to thoroughly research your listing long before any offer can come in. Have a complete guidelines to market value already prepared. Visit all the houses on the list so you know how comparable those houses are. Know them well and be able to talk knowledgeably about them.

Never forget that Old Pro is human too. He or she is not a machine, or some super tough-skin. Every Old Pro has been humbled, frustrated, and defeated many times in this business. Old Pro may be supremely confident or suspicious, alert, and unconfident. He or she may be desperately pressed for time and wholly unprepared. However, Old Pro will probably come to the meeting very well prepared because of the long-time accumulation of knowledge and constant updating.

As a new salesperson, you'll always be confronting the Old Pros in the business. When I was new, I looked up to the big producers in the board because they were where I wanted to be. I realized how much more they knew than I did, and I never tried to be something I hadn't earned the right to be yet. But I wanted Old Pro to respect and like me, and to think I was taking my job seriously.

My first summer was strange. In those days, there were only 100 members in our board. We all met for coffee and rolls every Thursday morning at a savings and loan office. Then we'd follow each other's cars and preview all the new property listed during the previous week. The first few times I walked into the S & L's coffee room, people from each office were banded together in tight little groups, and I was alone—and pregnant. Everyone seemed to stare at me. I'd try to hide in a corner but my tummy stuck out like Mammoth Mountain. Sometimes they'd look at me and giggle, or whisper. I felt angry and isolated—but I had conviction. "These people think I'm pregnant, fat, and dumb. I'll show them I'm pregnant, rich, and smart." First a listing of mine came out on caravan. It was a mile too high but there I was, parading around my own listing with all these other brokers.

"It's beautifully done but overpriced," they said as they stepped through, and "Whose listing is this?"

"Mine, thank you."

"It's too much money."

"The seller and I are reasonable people," I'd say quietly. "Bring us a prospect and we'll work with you."

"Bong," they'd think, "Who is this little pipsqueak?"

Then I got another listing. And then an offer. My first offer involved a high-flying lister and farmer from another office. I practiced, drilled, and rehearsed before I presented. Old Pro was happy. I was happy. I told him after the offer was accepted, "It's such a privilege to sell your listing. You are a legend in your own time." Always stroke Old Pro's ego. He loves it. I sure did later. Then I sent him a thank-you note, "Thanks for the opportunity to work with you. I appreciate your patience. I'm sure you remember what it was like to be the new kid in town when you first moved into real estate. Keep me posted on our transaction and I'll do the same. Danny."

He told everybody in his office how I was a hard-working lady. If Old Pro is impressed, he'll tell his buddies about you. Then you've got one office on your side and you go for the others little by little. How do you think so many of my listings sold during the first year? Lots of Old Pros worked with me because I dug in and did my part.

# What Old Pro Hates

Here are three examples of what often occurs when New Agent has an offer on Old Pro's listing.

**1.** New Agent tells Old Pro and her seller the photo in the Multiple Listing Book isn't very attractive, and if she were Old Pro, she'd have it retaken for the seller. Old Pro thinks, "Another smart aleck."

**2.** Old Pro, during the presentation offer, explains to his seller what this offer means to him in dollars and cents by breaking down the seller's net sheet. New Agent interrupts Old Pro when he gets to miscellaneous charges and says, "You've only plugged $100 in there. I always use $200, because I want to cushion my people extra high, and avoid any last minute shocks. I really think we ought to use $200 here." Old Pro knows New Agent heard another agent say this, and sees through the big dealer act.

**3.** New Agent tries to become fast friends with Old Pro's sellers. Always address Old Pro (who is acting as listing agent) in a respectful manner, "For you and your sellers we are offering . . ."

In all of these examples, the New Agents made an enemy of Old Pro, gained nothing now, and set themselves up to lose much in the future. This is a people business, and Old Pros are people too.

# When You Have an Offer on Old Pro's Listing*

Use this dialogue to secure Old Pro's cooperation now, and start building solid rapport to bring you many benefits in the future.

"Hi, John. I'm Danny Kennedy of Sell Fast Realty. I haven't had the opportunity to work with you yet, but I hear you're one of the pros. Anyway, I have an offer on your listing and I'm excited and eager to present it as soon as possible."

Be sure to say this. Sometimes Old Pro gets lazy, would rather keep his dinner plans, and present your offer the next day.

---

* Check with your broker and make sure these suggestions conform to the customs of your area.

"Please call me back immediately. I'm anxious to meet you and present this offer. I've spent a lot of time making sure it will meet your requirements."

The key is friendly persuasion—humility with firm confidence. You may be new, but you're definitely one of the up-and-coming pro agents. Your attitude displays this to Old Pro.

Old Pro says, "Tell me your offer before we go over there."

**Caution.** Protect yourself. Don't tell *anyone* what the offer is until you're with the seller.

"Old Pro, I'd rather wait and discuss it when we're both in the presence of your seller. This way your seller won't think you and I and my customer are in cahoots."

When you present the offer, tell Old Pro in the sellers' hearing, "John, I know how much these folks respect you."

Expand on this a bit, and then say, "First, I'd like to give all of you a little background on my buyers. Then I'd appreciate it if you'd present the terms and price, John—unless you'd prefer to listen along with Mr. and Mrs. Sellers, and shoot questions at me after the presentation. Which would you prefer?" Tie downs work with Old Pro, too.

Give Old Pro the opportunity to make the choice. If Old Pro is the buyer's agent, and you are the lister, then reverse the words: "Old Pro, would you prefer to have me sit back and listen with the sellers while you present the entire offer—and then ask questions afterwards?"

# When Both You and Old Pro Have Offers on a Third Agent's Listing

Introduce yourself to Old Pro.

"I certainly wish we were meeting under better circumstances, but I guess our customers have the same taste. We must both be doing something right."

Insist on presenting your offer alone with the seller and her agent, and not in the presence of the competing agent. If you're alone with Old Pro before the offers are presented, keep the talk light. Chit chat, trade tips on other properties, but don't discuss your offer or your clients. Not a word.

# Hearing Simultaneous Offers on Your Listing

As a first-year salesperson climbing rapidly to the top, I caught my share of icy stares from Old Pros. Some of them want to see you get good, especially if they've given you a few tips, but they aren't comfortable if you get too good too fast. So don't push them unless you have a reason to.

One evening an early listing of mine drew six offers. At least three of them involved strong-willed Old Pros. The "Woman in the Shoe" (my nickname around town because of all my kids) lined up those six agents at the property and said, "My sellers and I are honored to have six offers. I wish we could accept all of them. So here's the procedure: We'll listen to all six in the order you arrived here tonight. Then we'll do one of two things: accept the best offer, or make a counteroffer."

Of course I wanted my sellers to get some reassurance regarding the financial strength of the individual buyers as well. How frustrating to walk away from strong prospects only to find out the offer accepted (though it looked appealing on the surface) was from a risky buyer. It's always great to get some loan interviews set up prior to the offer. Then the seller can get some input from a loan representative or lending institution during the time of the offer for further reassurance. In the case of multiple offers, keep the hotline phone number of your state association's on-call attorney handy; you must be very sure you're giving correct advice in what can easily become a complex situation. Never put your sellers in jeopardy. Giving incorrect advice could make them liable to pay more than one real estate fee if two parties of buyers perform as agreed.

Everyone had a better way to handle the situation of six offers at the same time. Some Old Pros had their buyers outside in cars waiting to consider counteroffers. It was a touchy situation. I had called the Board of REALTORS® in the afternoon for advice on the proper procedure. I told my sellers I'd done this, and asked for their confidence. I kept my cool, although when you have to deal with a couple of cocky buyers' agents, it can make you seethe under your smile. It was a difficult time for those six agents too, and afterwards I sent them all thank-you notes. At the time, I knew I had to extend myself to avoid making anyone mad.

Sooner or later you will run into the simultaneous-offer situation on one of your listings. When you do, plan ahead to avoid upsetting anyone and to keep control. Maintain good eye contact with each agent as you take them into a separate room with the sellers. Say to them, "We certainly appreciate having more than one offer. Please understand I have a fiduciary relationship with my sellers. I must guide them to the best decision for them, without bias."

Keep in mind that someday you will be a seasoned campaigner. The secret now is to ask Old Pro to remember when he or she was the new kid on the block, "Frustrating and confusing, wasn't it?"

New agents: you haven't quite earned the right to throw your weight around. Have a little respect for your elders; you are not yet one of the walking wounded. The key word here is *compassion*.

Why should feisty youngsters have respect for entrenched old-timers? Because the Old Pros are the people who know where it's at and how to get it. They're the ones who did most of the business in the past, and they'll keep on doing most of the business in the future. They aren't afraid of the capable, hardworking newcomer—it's the incompetent, careless clowns who worry them.

The Old Pros will be around tomorrow, and ten years from now, still doing good business. They'll sell a few of your listings whether they like you or not, but if they like you, and respect your professional ability, they'll sell lots more of your listings.

Sure, confront Old Pro when you must. Play hard, but fair. Win his respect and the fee if you can. If you can't, it's a big win just to gain Old Pro's acquaintance, confidence, and respect.

# CHAPTER 5

# The Best Fizzbo System on the Planet: Flipping Fizzbos into Your Fold

**Bring in 100 Listings with One Winning Move ● Make Money with Five Fizzbo Tactics ● Give Fizzbos the Full Treatment ● Put Your Winning Move to Work ● The Four-Kinds-of-Buyers Listing Close ● Avoid Futile Double-Calling with the Fizzbo X-File ● Call Fizzbos from an Open House ● Fizzbo Details ● Start with Fizzbos**

Fizzbos are the wonderful people who put out signs reading, "For-Sale-By-Owner." Happily for new and old agents alike, there are always plenty of them around. Whenever I've needed to rejuvenate my business fast, I've done it by hitting the FSBOs (fizzbos).

Experienced agents often need to rejuvenate their activity when their production has fallen off and they want to get back on track. They do it quickest with the for-sale-by-owner people. The same applies to new agents—fizzbos are a quick way to get on the fast track to higher earnings for the first time, too. What a great place to start a real estate career!

The need for your services as a real estate professional will continue to grow because financing and the other aspects of real estate knowledge will continue to become more complex. Every year owners attempting to sell by themselves will encounter greater difficulties. To solve the difficulties, owners will turn more often to highly trained full-time real estate professionals.

The best choice among a bewildering array of available loan packages is just one of the complex areas buyers want to be reassured about before they commit to buying a home. As a result of this multiplying loan, legal, and liability complexity, the public mistrusts the average homeowner who is trying to sell his own house. For-sale-by-owners are part-time, unlicensed people trying to market their most valuable asset—their home. Without an agent to act as a buffer and conduit between buyer and seller, fizzbos often fail to hold together any sales they succeed in making for the 30 days or longer it takes to reach closing time.

When do most real estate agents do most of their work—after the sold sign is posted on the front lawn. Buyer's remorse, changes in loan amounts and rates, possession problems, geology reports, plumbing, and so on, all crop up before the close. The average homeowner is ill-suited to represent himself on such touchy topics. This is why you should never give up on any fizzbo you have good rapport with. Even after the homeowner tells you the property is sold, changes often occur. Fizzbo sales have high fall-out rates. You should be waiting to help or to immediately list the property. After a false sale self-destructs, the homeowners have probably had it with playing real estate agent.

You need one effective tactic, one winning move, one system you know produces. Once you have your single fizzbo system perfected and are consistently bringing in salable listings with it, your success in real estate is assured. The fizzbo situation lends itself to the use of a single system because you have complete control over who you approach, when and how you approach them, and whether or not you'll call back. So throw yourself into perfecting your winning move.

# Bring in 100 Listings with One Winning Move

Most agents devote little or no quality time and effort to developing their methods to a high level. They always *act* in terms of getting the *one* listing or sale in their minds at the moment. They may believe they're taking a longer view, but when it comes to action, they do little beyond improvise their next phone call, door-knock, or face-to-face meeting. They function entirely outside the concept of perfecting systems for gaining listings and closing sales. They operate on the play-it-by-ear plan. They continue on this basis throughout their real estate careers, however long or short. Leaning this way and now that way, they never put together an act good enough to make enough money to raise them safely above the mediocre stage.

Don't drift in this aimless manner. Acquire a system able to manufacture salable listings from the fizzbo raw material at a steady rate. Think in terms of developing a system capable of winning 100 listings at prices realistic enough to allow 80 of them to sell.  Calculate how much money 80 listings sold at your area's average price times your listing brokerage split would bring you.

$$\frac{\$ \underline{\quad \text{(average price)} \quad} \times 80 = \$ \underline{\quad \text{(a)} \quad}}{\$ \underline{\quad \text{(a)} \quad} \times \underline{\quad \text{(split)} \quad} = \$ \underline{\quad \text{(in your pocket)} \quad}}$$

The sum you're going to earn by learning how to grab fizzbos adds up to important money, doesn't it? Thinking positively about adding this substantial amount to your assets gives you a different viewpoint. It's an effectiveness-expanding exercise; do it often.

To earn this sum, you'll need discipline, determination, and desire. Earning it will involve study and practice. Earning it will involve working to a schedule and managing your time well. Earning it will involve going in rejection's way. But now your corrected viewpoint will put rejection into its proper perspective. The rejection you'll brush aside earning this sum of money will leave no more impression on your mind than the contrails of yesterday's jet flight overhead.

You'll be working with people in all their human caprices, confusions, and contrary convictions. To do this successfully, you must be flexible. Every phizbow is different. Some fizbeaux are impatient, get-it-on types; other fizzboughs are slow and suspicious and poor listeners. Know your system so well you concentrate on the person, not on what you're supposed to say next. You'll often need to compress your plan into fewer words, omit parts of it, or repeat some of it over and over in different words. You'll need to psych up for the crucial periods, and tune all your antennas for signal catching.  You'll need to know when to move right into the close, and when to make an emergency landing to wait out a storm.

Your single system to consistently produce salable listings from fizzbos will be the one you create yourself to exploit your strong points, and to meet the needs and conditions in your area. The two most important steps toward developing a well-paid fizzbo business are to:

**1.** Design a clear-cut system and work your system hard. Some of your systems first parts won't work for you; replace them with other ideas. Constantly think in terms of perfecting your performance.  Build a list of repetitive phrases that are able to lead you to a steady flow of salable listings from fizzbo contact.

**2.** Select and adhere to a schedule for working with fizzbos at the most effective times where you operate.

First, select the basic tactic for you to win victories on the fizzbo playing field. Five choices are given under Decision A. Select one, perfect it, and start the fees rolling your way before you consider spending time on a second fizzbo tactic. You'll probably never need the second fizzbo tactic. Concentrating on one will leave you more time for other aspects of successful real estate practice.

Details for each of the five tactics follow Decision D.

# Make Money with Five Fizzbo Tactics

All of the following methods can be implemented using e-mail, short text-messaging on beepers and cell phones, voice-mail messaging, or regular mail delivery. Face-to-face contact is your main goal. So fire away and use whatever speed tools you can to accomplish that goal.

## Decision A: Select a Money-Making Fizzbo Tactic

1. **Send a letter a day.** Preprinted letters combined with phone calls pave the way for a successful listing meeting. Over 60 percent of American households are two-career families. This means both folks may be at work when you try to call on their fizzbo ad. It sounds dumb, but they advertise and then disappear. A lot of two-career fizzbo couples are what I call "forced fizzbos." They had their house on the market with a broker. Communication was at a low level ("Every time I call those owners, they aren't home."). No offers ever came in. The listing expired. Six weeks went by and the sign was never picked up. Finally the husband threw it in the side yard. The owners' opinion of real estate agents is bleak. Frustrated and desperate, they decide to sell it themselves. If a sharp agent can get a foot in the door, I know this two-career couple would love to get the business of selling their home off their backs.

2. **Provide a free service package.** Once you've done the preparatory work, you can use this phone tactic on every fizzbo popping up in your sales area, and put off researching individual houses until their owners send you clear come-and-list-me signals.

3. **Knock on the door,** after researching market values in the area.

4. **Phone for an appointment.**

5. **Send an e-mail.** E-mail is very user friendly for both letter-a-day and the free service package. You can send the contents of the package (various forms) as an attachment.

## Decision B: Decide How You'll Find the Fizzbos

1. **Drive the streets.** Of course, you must be careful to drive below the speed limit for residential areas. With practice, and by routing yourself on a map, you can cover a large area in one early morning hour when there's little traffic. Late in the evening is also a good time. My first sale was a fizzbo I found in the middle of the night. They gave me a one-party show (a written agreement to pay brokerage if I sold the property to my customers, who were named in the document). I had already shown my buyers everything in the area and I thought they'd buy from me if I could find a house they'd get excited about. I knew what they wanted, and where they wanted it, but there simply wasn't such a house available at 6 P.M. when we stopped looking. Worry about losing my buyers to another area kept me from sleeping, so I got up and drove their favorite neighborhood once more. On a street I'd just covered a few hours before, I found a brand new FSBO sign. The sellers had just decided to move, and after dinner the man tacked up his sign. Before they sat down to dinner the next night, they had accepted my customer's offer. When you have the buyer, cruise those streets no matter what the hour.

2. **Read the newspaper ads like all the other agents do.** Many agents have never seriously considered automobile search for fizzbo as a regular part of their routine. They may occasionally list a fizzbo they stumble onto, and do it rather easily, but they continue to rely on serendipity and newsprint for their supply of fizzbo prospects. They never consider that there may be a fundamental difference between fizzbos who advertise and those who only put up signs on their property.

   "But they are the same people," you may say.

   Many are. But many aren't. Therein lies the opportunity. Some sellers believe the easiest way to find a strong agent is to stick a For Sale sign in front of their house. Some fizzbos are too broke to advertise and some are too stingy. A few can't make the necessary decisions. Some never placed an ad in their lives and have no idea how to do it. Others know how to advertise but just can't get around to it. And some know a fizzbo-negative fact: more agents than buyers read and call on fizzbo ads. There are hundreds of reasons why fizzbos fail to advertise beyond tacking up a sign on their property.

To be sure, some fizzbos will place ads but won't put a sign on their property. Searching by car isn't necessarily the surest method of finding every fizzbo. But it does have these advantages:

- You'll find many fizzbos before the pack does.
- You'll find many fizzbos before they spend money advertising, which heavily commits many people to the sell-yourself idea.
- You see the property before you speak to the owners, so you can talk knowledgeably about their property, their neighborhood, and how to solve their house-selling problems.
- Some fizzbos will be the easy-to-list *Wow-do-we-need-help!* types.
- Some fizzbos will be those couples who both work. No one is there to show the house or answer the phone, so how do they expect to sell it themselves? Most of the both-work fizzbo couples haven't figured out a simple fact: by effectively keeping their house off the market during the week, they cut themselves off from the main buying stream. Real buyers need a home so badly it's their number one priority; they're house-hunting all week long. But on the weekend, when the both-work fizzbo couple can be home, the lookie-lews and the bargain-dreamers are out in full force. Often, the agent who lists the both-work fizzbo couple is the first person with the persistence to track them down.

If you work the ads, pay special attention to the offbeat or throwaway publications with the smallest circulations and therefore the lowest ad rates. Advertisers in such papers are the least determined to stick with the fizzbo thing.

Car-search is not necessarily the best of the two methods; working the ads is not necessarily the least time consuming. Try both methods. Let results, not laziness, decide which is best for you.

**3. Go on-line and search.**

## Decision C: Selecting the Fizzbo Opportunities You'll Work

Whether you work the ads or hunt in the field, you've limited the area in which you seek fizzbo opportunities. Now consider what system you'll use to select the fizzbos you'll work on within your chosen area.

**1.** Work all of them as you find them.
**2.** Select the houses with the most appeal to you.

3. Select the price range or type of housing you believe is most in demand.

4. Select the best buys.

**1 and 2:** Working every fizzbo you find means you work with lots of poor prospects. Selecting only houses with great appeal to you, without regard to demand or value, will load you up with unsalable listings, devouring your time, energy, and enthusiasm.

**3 and 4:** Your selection process is simply time management. You choose to manage your time well, or poorly, by your actions—or failure to act. What is good fizzbo time management? Every day, do everything you can to list the properties most in demand and priced to sell before you give any time to the poorer prospects. Be careful not to immobilize yourself worrying about which opportunities are the best. The point isn't to spend time debating which of two prospects is the better one to work on, the point is to be continually on the lookout for salable opportunities, and to work on them first.

## Decision D: Select an Effective Schedule

Timing is vital. Late Sunday afternoon is a great time for closing fizzbos who are discouraged by a poor turnout and no action over the weekend. Of course you can't do it all during four Sunday hours. And other aspects of real estate compete for your time. You'll need to block out times during the week to follow up with all the fizzbos you're working with now, and to initiate your program with new fizzbos. You'll need to set goals for how many new fizzbos you'll take on each week, for how many old fizzbos you'll continue to work with week after week, and for how many fizzbo listings you want to take.

Here are the details and the phrases to pump success into each of the five basic money-making fizzbo tactics:

1. **Send a letter a day.** You can run this system on all fizzbos in your sales area, without any research beyond learning each fizzbo's name, address, and phone number. Enclose one of your business cards with every mailing. If you use this method via e-mail be sure to reference your Web site.
   - *First day:* In a large brown envelope, send a blank copy of your purchase agreement. Hand write on one of your memo sheets (with your photo and phone number):

     "Sorry you're leaving us! Here's a copy of the form you'll need to sell your house. If you'd like an explanation of any of its terms, please give me a call. No obligation. Sincerely, _____" Sign your first name, and enclose your card. You can write those words once, and then print a handful of copies.

- *Second day:* In a regular #10 correspondence envelope, send them a blank sellers' net sheet and this note, also handwritten on your memo sheet:

     "Here's the form we use to figure your net walkaway dollars. Please feel free to give me a call if you don't have the formulas to figure these items. Again, no obligation, Sincerely, _____" Be sure you don't say "if you don't know how to figure these items," which implies you think they're stupid if they can't.

- *Third day:* In a Christmas-card-sized envelope, send a blank Guidelines to Market Value form and this handwritten message:

     "We use this form to summarize the market price setting facts. If you'd like me to develop this data for your home, please give me a call. No obligations, of course. We're here to serve you. Sincerely, _____."

- *Fourth day:* Wait until they've received the day's mail. Then, knock on the door, or phone, and say: "Hi, I'm Al Vaughn with Belmont Realty. Are you getting the forms I've been mailing to help you market your home?"

     You've already given them service, and demonstrated a nonabrasive persistence. They'll usually feel obligated to give you some information about the house. From their response to this contact, decide whether to (1) try for an immediate listing appointment; (2) put them on the Full Treatment (spelled out later in the chapter); (3) put them on Letter-Every-Saturday; or (4) drop them as an unpromising situation.

2. **Send a letter every Saturday.** This plan calls for you to send them something about selling their home once a week. Mail it on Saturday so they'll have it on Monday, right after their house didn't sell over another weekend. Each week, send them a handwritten update on the market, plus one of your newsletters, a reprint spelling out why it's so tough to sell your own home, a flyer telling them something about selling their house (such as setting the stage), or some similar item. Mail on Saturday, and then call them every Wednesday or Thursday evening. Each time you call, consider whether you should intensify your

campaign to list them. E-mail and text messaging works great here too.

**3. Provide a free service package.** Work up a package of written material to help the fizzbos market their house, and then offer this package to them free during an evening phone call. The package should provide information they can use, and it should also introduce them to the complexity of real estate transactions.

Once your free service package is ready, you need only compile the list of fizzbos you want to call, and you're all set for your evening phoning session. Because no time is spent in research, this system does not require a high success ratio. You can call large numbers of fizzbos, and deliver the package only to those who give you encouragement. This gives you a select group to concentrate your follow-up efforts on.

Avoid calling during the day with this tactic; call in the evening when both husband and wife are more likely to be home. Avoid delivering the package the same night you call. This is too sudden for most people and frightening to some. Making an appointment for a later night has a reassuring, professional ring to it.

The package consists of flyers and blank forms. The flyers should be neatly typed on the company letterhead and have your photo and name printed on them. If you don't have personalized letterhead, type your flyer on a regular company letterhead, rubber-cement your photo to it, and have a quick-printer run off some copies.

Put one copy of each form in each service package. Be sure all these papers are fresh and clean, not creased and dog-eared. As you make up a batch of these packages, protect them in large envelopes.

Here's the list of items for your free service package (download all the following forms to your computer from the CD accompanying this text).

## Forms

- Real Estate Purchase Contract and Receipt for Deposit (or whatever agreement form is used in your state for making offers). Get this form from your office or broker.
- Buyer's Net Sheet
- Seller's Net Sheet
- Power of Attorney (in case only one of two buyers will be able to be present when the contract is finalized). Get this form from your office or broker.
- Guidelines to Market Value

# Flyers

- Advertising Rates and Numbers to Call to Place Ads in Local Newspapers
- How to Get Your Home Ready for Sale
- How to Set the Stage for Your Open House
- Federal and State Financing Plans Possibly Available to Finance the Purchase of Your Home (This will necessarily be complex.)
- A Brief Discussion of Conventional Home Financing
- Fixed-rate Mortgages
- Adjustable-rate Mortgages
- Your latest (or best) newsletter
- Items You'll Need to Complete Your Sale (List such things as termite inspections, roof inspections, appraisals, assessor's parcel numbers, legal descriptions, building permits for any improvements, title insurance, and so on.)

# Other

- "Want to Sell Your House in a Hurry?" This compact article has good houseselling information for homeowners, and it makes a powerful case for using an agent. Write to Reprint Editor, *Reader's Digest*, Pleasantville, NY 10570.
- Title Insurance Rate Card
- Reprint of the most complicated magazine or newspaper article you've come across recently about housing prices, interest rates, and the availability of mortgage funds.
- Guest Log Sheets. Make these up on blank paper. Type across the top on the long way of $8\,^{1}/_{2} \times 11$ paper:

## GUEST LOG

| Name | Address | Phone | Remarks |
|------|---------|-------|---------|
|      |         |       |         |

Run horizontal and vertical grid lines to the bottom of the sheet. Don't put anything like "Courtesy of Harry Hotseller, Go-Get-Um Reality," on the Guest Log Sheets, or the lookers coming to the fizzbo's open house won't sign them. Give every fizzbo three or four copies. Win a fizzbo's confidence and you'll get a chance to work with the list of house hunters gathered on these log sheets. When they have collected a few names, offer to run back to the office and make a copy of the sheets.

- Preliminary Title Report. (Select an intricate report from your office's files of completed home resale transactions so the fizzbo will gain some insight into the complications arising here. Your copies should have identifying names and numbers blacked out.)
- Sample Escrow Instructions, if this is applicable in your state or province.

There's the package. Winning scripts in this chapter give you the phone and face-to-face conversation, and cut-off points to make this system a time-effective producer.

**4. Knock on their door.** Here are two winning scripts you can use when driving around your area to get something going. Many successful agents simply can't drive past a fizzbo sign in their area without stopping to knock on the door because they've already made so much money doing this. Set aside at least half a day a week to look for fizzbos with the intention of charging right up and talking with every one you find. Between 3 and 6 P.M. on Friday is an excellent time because more people are home and they seem to be in a better mood—maybe it's payday and the start of two days off.

## First Knock-on-the-Door Winning Script

"Hi. I'm Danny Kennedy of Sell Fast Realty, and I noticed your sign out front. (Don't pause here.) As you know, the real estate market changes constantly and for this reason you should have a knowledgeable local professional to call to answer a quick question even if you are marketing your own home. So here's my card, and if you need a fast answer about how your home stacks up against the competition or are wondering about some other aspect of marketing your home, give me a call and I'll be happy to discuss the situation with you."

After their response, you may want to give them some pertinent information, "The interest rate on Treasury Bills dropped half a point this morning. This can affect the sale of your house because mortgage interest rates tend to follow Treasury Bill rates."

## Second Knock-on-the-Door Winning Script

"Hi, I'm Danny Kennedy with Sell Fast Realty, and I was wondering if you're cooperating with real estate agents in the marketing of your property on a one-party basis."

They'll usually ask what you mean.

"Well, for instance, in today's market the buyers being transferred in are even more conservative than before. These are people who have cash and can buy in this market. However, most of them want to be represented by an agent because of the time and distance involved in their move.

"So, when a buyer of mine especially loves an area, I often ask a for-sale-by-owner if I could show his property on a one-party agreement. This agreement applies to just the one person or couple I represent, and makes it possible for me to expose your property to the one buyer. If I *am* able to sell them on your property, I'd bring you a written offer to buy.

"The offer would be backed by a substantial good-faith cash deposit. If you decide to accept my buyer's offer and sell your home to him, I would then be entitled to receive a fee when the sale is completed. The agreement is made in writing, of course, because it's a common business arrangement.

"Here is the advantage of the one-party agreement: You can continue to market your home to everyone else in the world, and still have the opportunity to sell to my buyer if you choose to do so. So it's a winning situation for you both ways."

Always use the low-key approach with the for-sale-by-owner. Never get pushy; never act as though you must have the listing. Learn to think and act decisively without putting must-haves in your life. Must-haves always create more barriers between you and your goals.

Many fizzbos are suspicious. They want to believe your buyer will cruise the area and find them anyway. This means the harder you push, the more you'll convince them they should wait for your buyer to knock on their door. To avoid this, approach every fizzbo in your area of interest as soon as possible with the one-party agreement idea. Then return every week to remind them of the opportunities to sell they may have missed by not agreeing in advance to cooperate with you when you do have a buyer.

Act with purity of intention with everyone—and especially with the for-sale-by-owner. Truly want the same good things for everyone you'd want for yourself in the same situation.

Be patient and don't give up. Some fizzbos have to be worked a little at a time for months before they list. I've heard many agents say, "Those people will never go with a real estate agent." I always cringe at this comment because I've seen the same thing happen over and over: A few days or weeks later, the ex-fizzbo pops up on the schedule of new listings, listed by persistent Pauline who hung in there.

## Another Winning Script

"Hi, I'm Danny Kennedy with Sell Fast Realty—I know you're marketing your own property and don't want to be bothered with agents—but you should have my free service package."

Pause here to get a response. They may agree to getting anything free, ask what your service package is, or tell you they don't need it. Practice responses for each comment to bridge into your main speech:

Fizzbo: If it's free, okay.

Your response: There's no obligation at all. My free—

Fizzbo: What is it?

Your response: I'll be happy to tell you about it. My free—

Fizzbo: I don't need it.

Your response: It'll only take a moment for me to tell you about it—why not listen and then decide? (Don't pause here.) My free—

Your response is, "My free service package is prepared especially for you. It gives you the information you need to market your home and there's no obligation. In fact, you'll find it'll save you time because you can use it to speed things up when other agents call. I promise I'll just drop it by and not bug you to death. In these days of ever-increasing competition in the marketplace, you should have someone you can call on locally during the marketing of your home, someone who won't just be after the listing."

Give the owner time to respond at this point. Of course, whenever they agree to let you drop off the package, switch into making an appointment to do so.

Many owners say something like, "What's in it for you?"

Your response is, "Maybe nothing but good rumors—after you see my package and perhaps get a few answers from me, either now or at some time in the coming weeks. You may at least be able to tell some of your friends you know a real estate agent who is really interested in giving service. Many people don't want to market their own homes for a variety of reasons; perhaps someone you know will want professional help with selling their home in the future.

"Perhaps you'd be willing to pass my name along for them to consider if you're impressed with my service. Word-of-mouth advertising is the best kind there is, and it's what I'm always trying to deserve. So, can I drop my free service package off at six this evening, or would around eight be a better time?"

5. **Phone for an appointment.** For both knocking and phoning, it's vital to check for recent sales on their street and the streets on either side of fizzbos. Before you knock on the door,

or phone them, you should have the sales information from your comparable file memorized for those streets, or on a Guidelines to Market Value form in front of you. If the fizzbo knows more about their home's value than you do, how are you going to convince them they need your expertise?

Your first contact, whether by phone or door, is merely the take-off. You have the flight ahead of you. Success with fizzbos demands persistence—but it also requires recognizing unpromising situations. Decide on how many fizzbos you can work in a week giving them the Full Treatment outlined next. Contact new fizzbos, but do it less frequently now, and be more choosy about which of them to take on for persistent follow-through.

Whenever you draft a new fizzbo for Full Treatment, drop the one you're already working on with the least promise of giving you a salable listing. This way, you'll constantly upgrade the quality of your fizzbos. Quality here means the likelihood of obtaining a lucrative listing.

If you're using Tactic 4, and you've driven past their house, be sure to flash your knowledge fast when you call. Even if the newspaper with their ad just hit the streets, the chances are several other agents have already called them. If so, you can be sure the fizzbo is tired of talking to agents who know nothing about their house except what's in the ad. They put their castle on the market and the world yawned. As far as they know, no one has even bothered to look at it—until you called.

Here's how you open the conversation. Say it all in one breath:

"Hello, I'm Danny Kennedy with Sell Fast Realty. You're the party with the lovely two-story home on Elm Street with the white picket fence?"

Of course, all of the above strategies can be translated to e-mail communication.

# Give Fizzbos the Full Treatment

Give them forms.

Lend them flags, arrows, and signs.

Go see them late every Sunday afternoon, and call, or drop in, once during the week. Be quick. Get in and out fast. Always tell them something they don't know about new sales or listings, or other developments affecting the salability of their property. Never tell them all you know. Aim at leaving these impressions: (1) you're busy, but interested in serving them, and (2) you have more vital information than you have time to pass on to non-clients.

As soon as they're talking pleasantly to you, say, "If things change and you decide to list, do you have an agent in mind?" What you're looking for is a *no* to this question (unless they say, "Yes, you."*) and a *yes* to the next key question, "If you do decide to take advantage of professional real estate service, will you consider appointing me as your full-time representative?"

As soon as you have established some rapport with the fizzbo (but not before, or you'll shoot yourself in the foot every time) you must ask the key questions above.

If they answer, "Well, I guess so. My husband's cousin, Bob, just got his license and Jim wants to let him try. But I don't want us to suffer through his learning curve." Note the winning list scripts in Chapter 11. "If I list, I'll list with my friend," is an excellent script suggestion to use with people who have relatives or friends in the business. If this option doesn't work the first time, wait until Cousin Bob drops the ball, and his listing expires. When they're mad at him, even more anxious to sell, and ready to think realistically about price, they may recall your earlier conversation—especially if you've kept in touch.

## Put Your Winning Move to Work

Outline your fizzbo plan and your fizzbo goals in writing. Do this fast because you'll make changes and improvements as you work your plan and achieve your initial goals. Constantly think in terms of developing a *system* instead of bouncing around doing whatever seems like a good idea at the moment.

Never let your systematic plan show. People resent being processed like fish in a cannery. Personalize your scripts with references to the interests and situation of the individuals you're talking to.

Always be alert for opportunities to skip any steps of your system when they're not required with a particular prospect. Know when to close. If you fail to recognize when you've gotten the listing, and relentlessly plow through your entire routine, you'll often talk yourself right back out of the listing.

Also be alert for steps of your presentation it would be wise to repeat. Don't keep talking about point Q to someone whose eyes are glazed over in puzzlement about point L. Keep checking with the prospect in a friendly way. Be very careful here. On the one hand, make sure you're getting through. On the other hand, don't seem to

---

* Rehearse how you're going to respond when they say this. You're close to getting the listing; be careful you don't talk yourself out of it.

suspect they may be slow-thinkers. Many people are quick to take offense at any such hint.

Your schedule must be flexible enough to allow you to work with hot buyers until they buy, rigid enough to keep you in contact with old prospects, and open enough to bring you into contact with many new prospects each week.

Ask your fizzbos to consider who their potential buyers are. Ask them why those buyers go to the trouble of scouting around by themselves, unless they're determined to save the fee themselves. Now let's consider the listing close.

# The Four-Kinds-of-Buyers Listing Close

This is a great winning script if you use it right. Don't waste its impact by hitting fizzbos with it when they're fresh on the market and bursting with false confidence. Wait until you've built some credibility and rapport with them through several visits, during which time marketplace has introduced a glimmer of reality into their thinking.

How soon this can happen depends on their personalities and pressures. I've seen it happen within a week. More often, the process of facing reality takes several weeks, and it can stretch out six months or longer. When you feel the time is ripe, stop by on a Sunday afternoon and say something like the following.

"Hello, Mr. Botkins. I thought I'd just stop by on my way home from the open house I held on Elm Street and compare notes. Did you have pretty good traffic today?"

"Well," Mr. Botkins says, "I always get a lot of traffic every time I put out my open house sign, much more than when I had it listed with an agent last year, but for some reason I don't have a check in my hand yet."

"I can understand how frustrated you must feel, Mr. Botkins." Since it's true, I add the following statement because it helps people see me beyond my real estate role. "Before I got into real estate professionally, I was a for-sale-by-owner myself, so I know what you're going through.

"Can I give you some information I acquired about the buying public after I got into real estate professionally? This information could help you market your home, and it won't take long."

Notice how I tell them I acquired this knowledge after entering the business, which piques their interest and causes them to think I'm going to give them the answers they need. If possible, proceed to the kitchen table with both Mr. and Mrs. Fizzbo and begin the following winning script.

"You see, Mr. and Mrs. Botkins, there are **four distinct kinds of buyers** out there. The first kind are people making their **first purchase of a home**. Most **first-time buyers** are afraid of people selling their own homes because they feel those sellers have far more experience than they do. To the first-timer, purchasing a home is a frightening experience. Their Aunt Mabel says the bottom is going to fall out of real estate prices before Christmas; Uncle Ned tells them to keep their money in the bank in case times get tough.

"Without the help of a third party to guide them through all the unfamiliar decisions involved in buying a property, they simply won't make the purchase. They're afraid of a For-Sale-By-Owner because they know an owner has only one property to sell them. First-time buyers don't buy until they find a real estate expert they trust and enjoy working with.

"Buyers of the second kind are the nearby **house changers**. These are local people who can take their time looking for their next home. They're only interested in the bargain of the century. They know the for-sale-by-owner isn't paying a brokerage fee, so they automatically deduct the fee off the top when they look at the price you've put on your house. Their aim is to find a seller in trouble or someone who has underpriced their home through ignorance of its true market value. They work the for-sale-by-owners hard, and there's no way they'll let the seller save a dime. If they weren't set on saving the brokerage fee for themselves, these buyers would work through an agent.

"The third type of buyer is the **investor**. If you think the house changer is tough on price, you haven't met an investor yet. Investors are especially difficult to work with if the sellers are under pressure to move fast or have any trace of a financial problem making them more vulnerable. Investors want bargains, but they also need counseling—most of them don't understand all the ramifications of the tax laws or have the thorough knowledge of an area's values such as a real estate professional possesses. So most investors work through agents to save time and assure themselves of access to more properties.

"**Out-of-the-area buyers** are the fourth kind. Most of them need a house right now. Whether they're being transferred in or are moving here on their own, their house hunting time is limited. And they're suffering from the culture shock of moving to a new area. They don't know the values here; they don't know the communities they can choose among; and they're almost always unfamiliar with our entire region.

"Usually they fly in. Often, instead of renting a car, they'll depend on the real estate agent they've been referred to for transportation. These people are under heavy pressure to make a quick decision, and they need all kinds of questions answered fast—about schools, business services, travel conditions, and so on.

"They want to have their own local representative, someone they can trust to look after their interests. When they go back to wind up their affairs wherever they're coming from, they want to know they have a reliable representative here who'll keep them informed and carry out their decisions by phone.

"When I'm working with out-of-area buyers, they'll often see a for-sale-by-owner sign and say, 'I'd never walk in cold turkey and try to deal directly with an owner. I'm a babe in the woods around here.'

"What's the bottom line in all this? The only buyers you have much chance of getting an offer from are the local house changers and the investors—the toughest kinds of buyers out there. These people won't pay top dollar—they won't even pay market price—they'll only go for a giveaway.

"I can get you the fair market price for your home at this time. How can I do this when you can't? Simple, I am a full-time real estate professional. Listing your property with me means I will expose it to the people who can and will pay fair market price—first-time buyers and out-of-area buyers. Would you consider listing your home with a part-time agent?"

They'll probably say, "No way. Absolutely not!"

"After 'testing' your property for the past (add length of time), I'm sure you'll agree it requires a full-time marketing commitment. In short, you are a part-time, unlicensed individual trying to market your most important asset—your home.

"If you decide to take the commitment to *sell*, not *test*, seriously, please consider me—a full-time, committed, licensed real estate expert."

Then show the Listing Presentation Manual with its testimonial letters, and so forth, as discussed in Chapter 11.

The previous script has kept me in for-sale-by-owner conversations for years. It works because it's solidly based on truth. Modify my words to fit your style and reflect your situation honestly, and this script will work as well for you as it has for me.

Its purpose is to make the owners face facts and think "We're not getting the proper kind of exposure trying to sell it ourselves. Dealing with local bargain hunters is tough—I can't do better than I could by going through a professional. It's hard to be patient with most of the people who come in here wasting my time, and the ones I think want to buy don't trust me. I don't know enough about real estate. There are lots of things about financing I just don't understand."

After you deliver the Four-Kinds-of-Buyers script, pull out a Sellers' Net Sheet and work out numbers for them. Figure the brokerage fee and go over each item with them. When you get to the brokerage fee, point out the truth: they really don't have it to play with—bargain hunters deduct it anyway.

# Avoid Futile Double-Calling with the Fizzbo X-File

You need a fast-working file to tell you whether you have already called a given fizzbo. Calling them repeatedly is great—if you know that's what you're doing. Not knowing means you blunder; knowing means you can build rapport by taking a different line on subsequent calls. Just as important, you also save the time, and avoid frustration talking to especially hostile fizzbos a second time. Here's how to set up your file so it saves time.

Tape each fizzbo ad to a 3 × 5 card and write the phone number in large figures in the upper right-hand corner. Abbreviate the name of the publication and show the date of the ad. File the cards by phone number, lowest number first. Then, the next time you work a batch of fizzbo ads, it's quick work to check the phone number in the new ads against your existing cards.

On the card shown on the following page, "MB9/7" means you saw this fizzbo's ad in the September 7 issue of the *Morning Bugle*, a local newspaper. Tape the ad to the back of cards to keep all the details handy. The notations and circles in the first call box show you reached a man at the number at 11 A.M. on September 7, a Friday. The day of the week is worth noting (write "F") because it alerts you to the possibility the man works nights, from home, or is unemployed.

Another local publication you check regularly for fizzbo news is a bargain-ad paper, the *Dollarclutcher*. The next week, checking the *Dollarclutcher*'s ads against your fizzbo cross file, you pull this card. After entering "DC9/14" in the second ad box, you dial the number again. The man answers.

"Hello. This is Alex Campbell with Fastrunner Realty. I talked to you last week. Are you getting as many calls from your ad in the *Dollarclutcher* as you did off your *Morning Bugle* ad?"

Fizzbo X-File Cards save time and organize the information, but ordinary 3 × 5 cards will work. Chapter 24 has more details about fizzbo X-Files, and tells you where to get them.

FSBO X-File

| MB<br>9/7 | DC<br>9/14 | | | 123-9876 |
|---|---|---|---|---|

| WHERE/WHEN ADS WERE RUN BY THIS FSBO | PHONE NUMBER |
|---|---|

| | MAN'S Jerry | **M** |
|---|---|---|
| Stone | WOMAN'S Rita | **W** |

| LAST NAME | FIRST NAMES |
|---|---|

4126 Barmie Dr          Westport

ADDRESS

CALL RECORD

| DATE: | TIME: | DATE: | TIME: | DATE: | TIME: | DATE: | TIME: |
|---|---|---|---|---|---|---|---|
| 9/7 | 11  AM | 9/14 | 8  AM | 9/16 | 9  AM | | AM |
| PERSON REACHED  M | | PERSON REACHED  M | | PERSON REACHED  M | | | M |
| Call 9/14 | | Call 9/16 | | Appt for 9/17! | | | |

Danielle Kennedy Productions, P.O. Box 1395, Sun Valley, Idaho, 83353

# Call Fizzbos from an Open House

Should you admit you're on an open house, when calling other *sellers*? Certainly. It's one reason why you call fizzbos late in the afternoon; so you can tell them, "I've called all my buyers—all the ones I haven't already shown this house to and I've called all the neighbors around here, and a lot of them came over."

Tell the fizzbo, "Call your neighbors, and invite them to your open house." Why give fizzbos a great idea like this one? *Because they won't act on it.* If they start to, the first grumbler they hit will stop them cold, and the experience is certain to inject new respect for the real estate professional into their blood.

Will the first grumbler stop *you* cold? He shouldn't. You're the professional, the trained telephoner, the get-it-done type. You're aware of a saving grace, every hard *no* you hear gets you closer to a soft *yes* able to put money in your pocket.

Without a reverse directory, the fizzbo will be limited to calling the neighbors whose names he knows—people who already know about his open house.

Chapter 9 has additional tips on working fizzbos from an open house.

# Fizzbo Details

Talk to the stay-at-home fizzbo ladies in the morning. Try to make an afternoon appointment to visit. If you can look at the property before an evening appointment, you'll be able to prepare a better Guidelines to Market Value form. Have the cold, hard facts for the evening appointment because they are often essential to closing fizzbos on listing with you.

All agents need to immediately identify themselves and not allow the homeowner to think for an instant she may be talking with a possible buyer of her property. This is a real must. You can't build trust on a foundation of deceit.

Identifying yourself will get you a quick shutoff now and then. Expect this—but don't let it tarnish your honor. One of the pillars of your integrity and professionalism should be your unfailing respect for the rights of others. By choosing to always respect the rights of others, your rights get respected more often than not. Even a quick shutoff has its benefits—you know immediately you're not going to make any headway with this person *this morning*. You can try again later. For now, congratulate yourself on not wasting time. Thank them for being frank with you. If they've been instantly nasty, your courteous response will make a valuable good impression for future contact.

Always be alert for fizzbos who are ready to stop fooling around and get their house listed and sold now. With some people, the mood strikes suddenly—and doesn't last long. Always be ready to cut the preliminaries and write up the listing. Always be equally ready to back off when you're pressing too hard.

Top producers don't work for-sale-by-owners because fizzbos take up too much of their time. So, to be a top producer, you should avoid fizzbos, right? Wrong. The top producers have less time for each fizzbo than you do, of course. With the kind of fizzbos who have to be nurtured toward listing through a series of visits (preferably spaced close together) the top producer is at a disadvantage—but you can give prospects six hits to a top producer's one.

## Start with Fizzbos

They're where I started. The new agent is the only one who has the time to work the fizzbo field widely, heavily, and with the consistency and persistence it takes to close them.

Many fizzbos compile a list of people who come through to look at their house. These people are often bona-fide prospective buyers, although some will be bird dogs for other agents, lookie-lews, and people interested only in distress situations. Volunteer to help the fizzbos and they'll usually give you their visitor list.

If some of your clients or friends go fizzbo, don't snarl at them. Smile warmly and sincerely—be careful not to let your friendly smile turn into a *you'll-soon-see-what-a-dummy-you-are* smirk—and say, "If you sell it on your own, I'll be happy to answer any questions or guide you."

"Well, uh, thanks. But I don't want to take up your time if you're not getting anything for it. I think we can manage okay."

"Fine. But if taking up my time is your only reservation, there's a way you could pay me back for helping you without costing you a dime. Are you keeping a list of the people who come through your open houses, or of those who call?"

"Well, we haven't bothered. Actually, I hate to ask."

"Let me tell you how to set it up to help you and the buyer. Suppose you go along for a while, it doesn't sell, and you decide to drop the price. Calling everybody who expressed interest could find a buyer in a hurry at your new low price."

"I don't want to tell them I might drop my price later. It's the same as saying our price is too high."

"I agree. Say, 'Look, if it doesn't sell by June 1, I'm going to list with Danny Kennedy of Sell Fast Realty, but I'll reserve the right to sell to you without brokerage if you'll give me your name and address.' Then hand them the Guest Log Sheet."

"Might be a good idea."

"If I help you with the processing, perhaps you'll consider giving me a copy of the list. I'll call them and see if I can help them find another house."

"Naw, it sounds kind of sneaky to me."

If they say something along this line, you pushed too soon, before you built confidence in your integrity in their minds.

## Work the Buddy System

Work the buddy system in your office, not the stab-in-the-back system. What you send up comes down—on your own head. Let me tell you a true story about a good listing I got from an office where backstabbing was the guiding rule. Only the names have been changed to protect the guilty.

Mr. Bell was trying to sell his own property and, of course, he wasn't having any luck. I was working on him, knowing he was close to a decision.

"If I don't have a sale in the works by July 15, I'm going to list with Jack Toeline of Selzip Realty," Mr. Bell finally said. Jack was the agent Mr. Bell had brought the property from three years earlier.

Mr. Bell liked Jack, and Jack had kept in touch with him. I was keeping in touch too—I hadn't given up. One afternoon Milton Cutter, another agent from Selzip Realty, saw the fizzbo sign in front of Mr. Bell's house and stopped in. As it happened, Jack Toeline had been in to see Mr. Bell the same morning.

When Mr. Bell told Milton Cutter he'd just talked to Jack, Milton said: "I'm amazed. Jack is so busy he barely has time to return his messages. He's already got all the business he can handle."

Did this backstab allow Milton Cutter to steal business away from his co-worker, Jack Toeline? No way, Mr. Bell was turned off on the whole Selzip organization. Even though he liked Jack, he wasn't about to list with a company whose agents were fighting among themselves. He wanted to list with a company whose agents got along together, helped each other, and all tried to sell each other's listings. Since I was Mr. Bell's number two choice, I wrote up the listing.

When it sold and I collected my fee, I started thinking beyond just not knocking the guy who works at the desk next to you. Why be neutral? Why not help each other instead of simply not knocking each other? Why not use the buddy system? Here's how it works.

Two strong, experienced agents, let's call them Wendy and Eloise, decide to buddy their fizzbo calls. They divide up the fizzbo opportunities in their service area, and decide on Wendy taking the west side of town and Eloise working the east side of town. In other words, they come up with a simple way to avoid conflict. Then they put the plan in operation. The first day Wendy works the west side and Eloise works the east side, calling all the fizzbos.

The second day they trade lists of fizzbos phoned, and Wendy calls the people on the east side of town, the fizzbos Eloise talked to the day before. Meanwhile, Eloise is calling on the people Wendy talked to the day before.

Let's run through one of those calls. Eloise calls up a fizzbo she knows Wendy talked to yesterday and identifies herself and her company.

"Somebody called me from your company yesterday."

"Oh, was it Wendy Fullbright? She's very active in your area."

"Yeah, I think so."

Eloise says with much enthusiasm, "Well, I'm not going to try to compete with Wendy Fullbright. She's one of the best agents in town. She sells a lot of property."

The buddy system works best when both agents knock on the doors and meet all the people in person.

"Somebody from your office has already been here."

"Oh, really? Who?"

"Well, I think she said her name was Wendy, or something. I've got the card right here. Yeah, Wendy Fullbright."

"You're lucky to have Wendy Fullbright interested in your property because she sells a lot of houses around here. Well, I better be going—no need for me to stay here and take up your time since you've already talked to the best in our company."

The owners love it; people like to work with organizations whose members pull together.

## Bring the Whole Gang Over to Meet Mr. Fizz

You've been stopping in on Sundays, you've given them the four-kinds-of-buyers script, you've worked the buddy system, but they still aren't quite ready to approve the agreement. Try another tactic.

"Mr. Fizz, Tuesday is our sales meeting at Sell Fast Realty. I'd love to bring my team of experts out to see your property. They're all working with customers right now and—you never can tell—one of them may know a buyer who'd fall in love with your place. When this happens we could work a one-party agreement on a showing. And I really want you to meet all these people—they're the best in the business."

Say it enthusiastically. Sellers can't resist enthusiasm when it comes to marketing their homes.

## How to Scare People and Lose Friends

A fizzbo opened his front door one Sunday afternoon and there sits a beautiful potted plant with an envelope on top. "How thoughtful," he says, and opens the envelope. Inside is a newspaper clipping about another for-sale-by-owner in town who was abducted and robbed at gunpoint by someone posing as a buyer. There's also a note from an agent saying, "Be sure this doesn't happen to you."

This is a true story. The agent's tactic to intimidate people didn't work, and he wasn't the type to give service and deserve people's trust. He soon left the business.

## Build Future Business with Today's Fizzbo

My first fizzbo experience wasn't too thrilling because, in a strong seller's market, the Millers *were* able to sell it themselves. But I had promised to help, so I shopped the loan for their buyer, did some footwork for everyone, and the Millers moved to their new home a couple of miles away. Eighteen months later I got a come-list-me card from someone I'd never heard of. When I went there and wrote the listing, I stopped next door to thank the Millers—who had told their neighbors about me.

Don't look only for the quick dollar—you're in this business for the long haul. Working the fizzbos is like any other form of prospecting—it's a great way to get the word out about who and where you are.

## Fizzbo Follow-Up Via Internet

E-mail is a quick, noninvasive way to stay in touch with your fizzbo prospects. Also, you can use short text-messaging on mobile phones or beepers. But don't rely on it as your only means of communication. If you fax or e-mail you may want to leave a message on the prospect's voice mail that you have faxed or e-mailed. It may seem to be overly cautious but it has always paid off for me. So many times people fax and never follow-up, only to find out it never went through as planned. Never take anything for granted in this business.

## Fizzbo Chat Rooms

As you begin to build trust with the fizzbo you may want to invite him to take advantage of your chat room visits. Why not set up a fizzbo chat room? You may want to limit the time you take questions each week. Inform your fizzbos by e-mail, voice mail, or an electronic newsletter the days and times when you are available to solve problems or answer questions. This is a great way to stay in touch and build the relationship.

Work those fizzbos until it hurts.

# CHAPTER 6

# Epidemic Selling: Sow That Farm and Reap, and Reap, and Reap

Infect Your Neighborhood ● Learning My First Farming Secret ● The Different Farms ● Four Sizzling Starter Letters ● Selecting Your Farm ● Annual Turnover Rate ● Organizing Your Farm ● Working Your Farm File ● Coping with E-agent ● The Evergreen Listing Farm ● More Farming Secrets ● Farming Tool Decision Day ● Professionalism ● Your Attitude on the Farm ● Avoid Careless Slips ● Every Door Is Different ● Speed Counts ● Humility Helps ● Success Breeds Success ● Notice the Best-Looking Homes ● Handling Exceptional Properties

## Infect Your Neighborhood

The world's greatest real estate salespeople know that building a reputation in a specific territory (farm) is the number one secret to their success—not overnight success—long-term success. And it all begins with working the territory. Think of it as picking your spot to infect and then slowly but surely starting an epidemic of business. This word-of-mouth method of creating a lifetime worth of referrals is your only guarantee for security in this business. What you will learn in this chapter will create an invisible army of supporters that will consistently make sure that your name and your company is the first choice in the minds of all those people this army influences. And in this electronic age, it can all happen even faster than when I started by foot to get the word out. (Everything in this chapter can be applied using technology.) Here's how it all began for me.

# Learning My First Farming Secret

"Kennedy, I know it's tough not getting in on the great floor time here," my manager told me a few weeks after I started in real estate, "but you can turn it to your advantage." Nell Shukes was trying to cheer me up. With nothing to show for many hard hours except a couple of unpromising Fizzbo situations, I needed cheering up.

"Tell me how, Nell."

"Do what that kid out in Simi Valley is doing."

"What kid?"

"Tommy Hopkins."

That was the first time I'd ever heard his name. "So what's he doing?"

"Breaking records," Nell said. "I've been trying to break his record all year. I came close, but—" Nell leafed through her messages and then looked at me.

"For Halloween, he rents a truck and loads it up with pumpkins. Then he puts on a ghost costume and drives around his neighborhood giving away pumpkins. For Christmas, he throws parties for all the neighborhood kids."

"But how can that pay off? All that expense—"

"There are four or five hundred houses in his neighborhood, Danny. It's active—about 20 percent turnover—and he's getting it all."

"Then he's averaging two listings a week!"

"Right, and he sells most of them himself."

"Four transactions a week!"

She nodded. "Plus the referral business he's doing outside his farm. It does add up."

"His *farm*?" If I'd heard the term before it hadn't sunk in. Pumpkins, Christmas parties, farms? This is the real estate business? My mind was reeling. "Nell, I can't afford a truckload of pumpkins. So far, it's all been outgo: babysitters, gas—"

"You don't need to spend a dime now. The storeroom is already jammed with rain hats and other giveaways. You can reimburse the company later out of your earnings."

When you're seven months pregnant, hiking to several hundred houses handing out plastic coasters is sorely lacking in appeal. "I can see how the pumpkin truck and the parties would make an impact, but these little giveaways—who cares? If I could start big, like this Tommy did—"

"Danny, let me tell you how big Tommy Hopkins was when he started. He couldn't afford a suit, so he wore his high school band uniform to the office and out farming."

"You're kidding me!"

"Danny, he did the best he could instead of stalling. He knocked on the doors, handed out the scratch pads, and told the people about himself and his company. It worked. He started getting listings, and when he collected a fee, he put a chunk of it back into better farming tools—"

I'm not sure I heard the rest of what Nell Shukes told me about Tommy Hopkins just then because I was thinking, "If that nut can knock on doors in a band uniform, I can knock on doors in a maternity dress." The idea of actually doing it took hold, and I left Nell's office with fire in my eye and hope in my heart.

I've never forgotten our conversation. Four years and eons of experience later, listing and selling awards put me on the same speaking platform with Tommy Hopkins in Palo Alto. Once again he inspired me, this time to become a national real estate trainer. Now let's talk about how *you* can set a sizzling pace on *your* farm.

# The Different Farms

## The Best Farms

Some of the best farms can't be delineated on a map. One of the most effective real estate farmers I've ever heard of, David Garris in Laguna Beach, CA, played tennis at 7:00 A.M. every morning for years with doctors and executives at his country club.

He didn't hang around the tennis courts all day. He was too busy with his real estate business. But he always found time to line up some early-morning tennis partners. He made a point of inviting new members to join him for tennis. Invariably they were pleased to be noticed and, whether they played tennis with him or not, he became acquainted with them.

It took him time to build that farm. There were thin periods in the beginning, times of doubt, but he persevered. Now he gets come-list-me calls from friends of club members who are golfers, not tennis players. The good word gets around, especially when you keep spreading it yourself, in the right way for you and for the working environment you've chosen.

Ask yourself: What's my comfort zone? How many homes can I farm? Would I be better off working a club, civic organization, or sports group than an ordinary farm?

Three to four hundred homes make a good farm. Over that number, you lose control. Don't take on more than you can handle. You should visit with everyone in your farm at least three times a year—preferably four times. You should have something useful with your name on it in their houses all the time. You should send them a note, or a newsletter, or leave a giveaway on their doorknob every month. As soon as you can afford it, stage at least three super promotions a year. The next chapter gives you details and promotions for every month.

## People Farms and House Farms

The tennis player's farm is a specific group of people: the members of the country club. Their real estate holdings are scattered over a large area and the tennis player reaches those properties only when personal contact at the club has set the stage for a further step. His is a people farm.

The house farm is a specific group of dwellings outlined on a map and concentrated in one or a few areas. The agent reaches the owners through their properties.

In a house farm, people come and go; the houses remain. The reverse is true in a people farm; members of a club often change homes, or invest in rental property, without leaving the club.

Whether you have a house farm or not, you always have a people farm. Call it the Everybody-I-Know Farm, and include everyone who isn't loyal to another real estate agent. Don't leave people out just because they live far away. They, or one of their friends, may decide to move nearby at any moment.

Think about your Everybody-I-Know Farm. It exists. Out there somewhere are more people who know you than live in your house farm. Are you cultivating them? Do they know you're in real estate?

An Everybody-I-Know Farm, properly worked, returns invaluable referral business from small efforts. The next section tells you how it's done. First consider whether some of your interests or hobbies are served by clubs. Clubs are able to give you valuable new contacts while you enjoy some much needed recreation. If so, get active in those clubs or groups. Have fun. Avoid obligating yourself to a heavy schedule of club duties. Explain how your real estate business requires you to work unpredictable hours, especially evenings and weekends. Then take part in your group's fund raisers, tournaments, and social activities with gusto whenever you can squeeze them in.

Let all the club members know you're in real estate when you get the chance. Don't push it. Let the subject come up naturally. It will—frequently. You'll soon find that you'll get a good shot at other members' real estate business merely by demonstrating courtesy, friendliness, and a willingness to participate energetically in your group's social activities.

## Your Everybody-I-Know Farm

It all begins with the list, and your first resource for names is you. While studying for my license, I used spare moments to organize my mailing list. In a green cardboard box, filed A to Z, I put a card for everyone I could remember since I was ten years old. As soon as my license was hanging on a wall, I sent my letter of introduction to everyone who wasn't so close that a handwritten note, also shown in the next section, was required.

Make up the list first. If you're already busy in real estate and looking for more business, you won't be able to spend much time pulling this vital list together. Try adding three names to your list every morning, starting today. Do that and, one year from today, you'll have 1,095 names on your list—the equivalent of three regular house farms! How long can it take each morning to put three names and addresses on cards?

I use 4 × 6 inch cards because they have room for lots of information, and several changes of address. Start by copying current addresses out of your Christmas card list and whatever little address books you have squirreled away. At the same time, address an envelope. In the envelope place your latest newsletter, a copy of your Profile of a Champion, your printed letter announcing your entry into real estate, or a form letter especially written to tell friends you're well qualified to handle referral business.

Don't do a junk mailing. Send only one of these items at a time. On the front write, "Hi, Jeannie. See over." Then on the back jot some friendlies and ask, "Whatever happened to Deanna Droptfrumsyte? What's her current address?" In this way, work through all your old rosters from church, school, a tour of service, previous employment, and clubs.

Add the people you're buying from now, and those you've bought from in the past. List former neighbors and distant relatives. What about customers and suppliers in your former occupation? As you work with these old rosters and memories, names long forgotten will pop up. Jot them down, one to a card. You'll remember some faces but the names will elude you. Can you think of someone who would know their address if you could remember the name? If so, jot down in the middle of the card whatever you can remember: "Tall, skinny kid in the mailroom. Was studying advertising in night school. Liked to do imitations."

You can't force your memory, but you can encourage it. Go over the cards once in a while just before going to sleep. Visualize the person you're trying to remember and the scene you knew them in. Sooner or later, the name will jump out at you.

Get on the Internet and find phone book reference sites. Spend an hour once a month checking your "names only" cards against directories of the cities you think your old friends might be living in. Some of the people you find listed will give you the addresses of other old friends. You'll be surprised at how rapidly your list will grow with only brief but systematic regular effort.

Mail to your Everybody-I-Know Farm at least twice a year, but no more than four times a year. Send one of your newsletters, or a specially written form letter. Each time, ask them to tell anyone they hear is moving in your direction about you. Say you are a capable, hard-working real estate expert who takes great care of clients and customers. It works. People feel important saying, "I know a sharp real estate agent out there." Your friend's friend would rather work with someone recommended by a friend than with a stranger in a strange place.

Don't neglect the contacts you've spent a lifetime gaining. Tell them where you are, what you're doing, say you're good at it—and make sure you really are.

When you address these letters, don't write, "Mr. and Mrs. Prospect." Write, "The Prospect Family." You don't know what's happened at their house during the last few weeks or months. Sensitivity in writing and in one-on-one negotiations with people is so important. The divorce rate is high. People pass away. If you mail a letter addressed to "Mr. and Mrs. Prospect" and their family has suffered a cruel shock the week before, it's going to hurt.

For your introductory letters, break your Everyone-I-Know list into two parts: close friends and relatives in the first part; everyone else in the second. Your close friends should be informed first by a handwritten note. Use your personal stationery or blank paper rather than your company's letterhead (with or without your imprinted name and photo). You are sending a handwritten note to reaffirm that you have a personal relationship which does not preclude your also having a business relationship with them. Using your company's letterhead will say to some people: "We used to be friends, but now I'm changing our friendship to a business relationship." Writing on plain or personal stationery says, "We're friends and I'm in business now." Take the time to tailor your handwritten message to fit each of your close friends and relatives. You'll find it is time well spent.

Although it's important to inform your friends first that you've gone into real estate, these people are the last ones who will come through for you. Their support will come—when you've earned the right to service their real estate needs. Don't be hurt. Because they know you so well, or think they do, they'll discount your abilities until you've won your wings working with other people.

The other day a note came from a friend telling me she'd just entered the business. I was pleased to get the information directly from her. Some people might think it's pointless to write someone who's in real estate saying they've gone into it too. I took her joining my industry and thinking enough of me to tell me so as a compliment. Send a letter to real estate people? Certainly. Send it to everybody. We all need each other's help. If you have friends in real estate, be sure to tell them you're coming in because they'll need your help later on and you'll need theirs.

# Four Sizzling Starter Letters

Create files on your computer for all of the following documents.

1.  **Introductory letter to people you know very well.**
    Keep it short because it's vital to write these letters by hand.

    *Good Morning _____,*

    *Guess who's gone into real estate? I'm proud to say, "I have." For a long time I've had a deep concern and interest in our community. I've lived here for _____ years, and during those years I've (describe your community service, clubs joined, and so on).*

    *I know the properties here and have a deep pride of ownership in our home. Now I want to take these qualities into the active market. I want to ask you for your trust and confidence in important real estate matters.*

    *Do you feel I'm worth the risk?*

    *I hope so, because I've dedicated myself to marketing our wonderful community to people like yourself who have my love and respect.*

    *Sincerely,*

2.  **Professionally printed (or computer-generated) introductory letter.** Mail it first class (hand addressing is best) to everyone you haven't sent a handwritten note announcing your entry into real estate.

    *Hi Friend,*

    *Yes, I want to call you friend, and I hope you'll consider me one. Everyone needs a friend in real estate—someone you can trust with such important matters as your security and your investments.*

*Would you place this kind of trust and confidence in me?*

*You may ask, "Why should I?"*

*Here are a few reasons:*

1.  *I am honest. I don't shade the truth. My word is good.*
2.  *I am reliable. If I tell a client I'll do something, wild horses won't stop me from doing it.*
3.  *I have time for you. Most people today are "too busy." I'm never too busy for you!*
4.  *I'm a licensed real estate agent. This means I passed a state licensing examination that required much dedicated study.*
5.  *I am constantly taking courses on all facets of real estate: appraisal, negotiation, financing, and so on. I'm taking these courses for you—to serve you better.*
6.  *I live here and have pride in and concern for our community.*
7.  *I have dedicated myself to serving our community by active participation in (name the service organizations you belong to and are active in).*
8.  *I am proud to be associated with Sell Fast Realty, which many people, myself included, believe is the finest real estate organization in Green Pretty Valley.*
9.  *If you give me the chance, I promise I'll prove I care, and that I'm highly capable of serving your best interests.*

*Thank you for taking the time to read this.*

*Sincerely,*

When you send out several hundred letters saying "I'm reliable," you're making quite a statement about yourself. Think it through. Get yourself organized fast, because you'll have response from a large mailing—you'll have things to do and people to see. At first some of these people will only be testing you. If you've been disorganized, kept irregular work hours, and done only what you had to do, set up a realistic work schedule. Keep to it. Prove your reliability to yourself first—if there's any doubt in your mind— as you put together this mailing list and letter mailing. Get your briefcase, desk, auto, and—most important of all—your mind, organized to handle real estate business. Go over every item on your office's checklists for processing new listings, reporting sales, opening and following through on transactions, working up-time, writing ads, holding open houses. Make sure you understand everything. The Breakaway Schedule at the back of this book has a program to make you an expert fast.

There's a lot to do. At the beginning, before the business makes you busy, get as much of this initial organizing out of the way as you can.

## 3. Introductory letter to your farm.

*Consider me a new friend!*

*How do you do?*

*I'm Danny Kennedy. My home is just around the bend from you on Gridiron Drive, and I'm also a real estate counselor. Since our neighborhood is my favorite, I'm delighted to be its specialist for Sell Fast Realty.*

*This means I know all the developments on real estate listings, sales, and new neighbors here. I'm well posted on our entire area's cultural activities, tax proposals, and school bond issues. I also keep current on specialty shopping open now or due to open soon, and on other community services and events—from attorneys through handymen and physicians to zoo admission hours. Please call me if you have a question you want answered.*

*You might even get a good recipe or two from me now and then. I'll be distributing memo pads soon for your convenience. Please consider me a friend and a community professional who is deeply committed to keeping our neighborhood one to be proud of.*

*Sincerely,*

## 4. Follow-up letter to be sent 60 days after letter 3 goes to your farm.

*Hi Neighbor—*

*Can we be friends?*

*A good real estate agent who believes in the town he or she lives in and serves its residents should be considered a friend. So please think of me that way.*

*I am your home-town representative for the area served by the Birch Street Elementary School, and I keep current on all properties marketed in the entire Green Pretty Valley. I know the streets, schools, shops, and churches. If you need home-town advice, you may lose out if you don't talk to me. Keeping current with our local scene is my work and what I love. Just ask my broker. I spend many hours studying and working to be a better me—for you.*

*Cordially,*

*P.S. Watch for my handy notepads!*

Here is a year-end letter to be mailed the last week of December to the old and prospective clients in your updated Everybody-I-Know list.

(This letter must always reflect confidence and optimism. If you don't have both, don't send it.)

*Hi!*

*Am I lucky. Because this year I had the opportunity to serve _____ clients in our home town. As 2009 winds down, we know it has been a good year for owners of real estate. The average days on the market for property in our area was just ____ days. The financing picture was flexible. Interest rates were a bit high as the year ended, but that figure must be compared to the rapid appreciation rate of __ percent. As so many astute buyers demonstrated during the year, a person would be unsound to let the interest rate stand in the way of a smart real estate purchase.*

*The general economic trend was stable according to an article in* The Wall Street Journal *dated _____.*

*Here are some predictions for the coming year:*

*(Quote from* Kiplinger, Board Room Talk, Wall Street Journal, Forbes, New York Times, *or any large out-of-state newspaper—distant prophets carry more weight.)*

*"Building starts will be slow during the first half of the year," according to _____. A slowdown of new construction, of course, throws additional buyers into the resale market.*

*"Car sales will hit _____," states the _____. "Retail sales are expected to reach _____, and personal incomes will set new highs at $ _____," says the _____. This means more people will have more money to invest in better homes for their families.*

*The outlook is bright. People will be spending money, and real estate will continue to be a first priority in millions of households.*

*All in all, we have strong reasons for confidence. I hope to see you during the coming year. Please consider me a friend. Realtors are the best kind—we care about your security!*

*Cordially,*

Your wrist should hurt the first year. Grab any reason for writing a note. (Personal notes have more meaning now than ever.) If someone in the grocery store says, "I heard you're in real estate," go home and write that person a note, "Thanks for mentioning you know I'm in real estate because I need people to know it. I've got to spread the word now about myself being in the business." People will do it for you if you ask them to nicely.

Be alert for the people who'll be your heralds, and make sure you keep feeding them stuff to talk about: your first listing, your tenth, your sales, copies of your ads.

Sustain the momentum your mail campaign starts, but don't sit back and wait to be overwhelmed by its results. Prospect. Work with fizzbos. Call on expired listings. Hold open houses. And farm, farm, farm—get out there and knock on those doors. Behind them is where the money is.

## Selecting Your Farm

Define the available areas on a map, and take a quick count of the houses involved. You should be looking for about a 300-house (or housing unit) farm. As soon as you're familiar with what's available, start to rate your choices on these three factors: diversity, affinity, and promise.

**Diversity.** Variety in floor plans, exteriors, amenities, and values is desirable in a farm for an important reason beyond the obvious one of attracting a variety of buyers. The market often moves in parts rather than as a whole. Three-bedroom moderns may be hot sellers when four-bedroom rustics are cold; demand may be brisk in the top price ranges when it's dormant in the low ranges; and a few weeks later all these conditions may reverse. Trapping yourself in a narrow price, style, and amenity range can make your ride to success a rough and jolting one. Avoid it.

To get a location and price spread able to furnish a steadier income, consider the advantages of farming 100 houses in three different areas. Such noncontiguous farms aren't harder to work. You can diversify in this way without paying any significant time penalty.

**Affinity.** You'll feel more at home in some areas than in others. This feeling may strike you with great force just driving through, or you may have to spend hours there with your senses open. Walk the streets. Talk to the residents. Take time to develop your feelings before you commit yourself to a farm. It's vital to feel enthusiastic about the area and in tune with the people there. Get into all the neighborhoods you're considering in the evenings and weekends, and talk to everyone you can. Open yourself up. Be receptive. Taste the flavors and sniff the breezes until you're certain which area you want to throw your efforts into.

**Promise.** Use the past turnover rate as a guide in making your decision, but this too can change. An area with a high turnover rate may be coming to an era of long-term stability; an area with a low turnover may be about to move. Don't go on blind faith—discover why it should move or you'll be stuck with a low turnover rate.

Why would a stable neighborhood suddenly start to break up? The reasons may be complex and unknowable, or simple and obvious to the attentive eye. Sometimes an area around an elementary school consists mostly of first-time homeowners who, as newly married couples in their twenties, moved in at about the same time. Real estate turned over slowly while their incomes gained on the mortgages and the babies. The now thirty-something couples glimpse new vistas as larger families and growing incomes shrink the satisfactions of yesterday's dream cottages. Promotions open new horizons. Then an influential couple moves out and up; two years later their entire group of friends has scattered. Now the neighborhood's property will turn over rapidly for quite some time because change is in the air. You can conduct that entire movement if you know the score—and get to the performance on time.

# Annual Turnover Rate

The annual turnover rate for a given farm is easily determined. Your Multiple Listing Service will have the records of sales by street. Count the number of sales made last year on all streets of interest, and then count the houses on those streets. Divide the total number of sales by the total number of houses: The result is last year's turnover rate.

In the 309-house farm you're considering, 63 houses were sold last year, giving a turnover rate of 20 percent, which is very good. The calculation is: $63 \div 309 = .20388$, roughly 20 percent.

You may love an area, but does the property there turn over? The time to think these things through is before you choose your farm. Once you make your choice, charge ahead for total control. The first step is to organize your farm.

# Organizing Your Farm

Organizing your farm means "organizing *yourself* to become the world's outstanding expert on your farm." Here are four time-effective methods of quickly grasping the in-depth knowledge of your farm required to gain firm control of it. A burgeoning real estate practice and a rapidly rising income will sprout from gaining control of your farm.

Convert all of the following to documents on your laptop, if you own one.

1. **Farm file.** Contains information about the homeowners.
2. **Deed details folder.** Holds the dry, rarely changing stuff of records: legal descriptions, assessor's parcel numbers, exact lot sizes.
3. **Farm flashdeck.** Provides a simple technique for speedily learning the names of everyone on your farm.

**4. Property catalog.** Collects information about the houses, their improvements and amenities, and the grounds they stand on.

Part of your farm file is obsolete every time a family moves out. If you have collected information there about the house, you must re-copy it, or crowd in data about the new owners. Confusion results. Avoid these problems by keeping your property catalog separate. Once compiled, your deed details folder will never need updating. The farm flashdeck reduces what most agents believe is an impossible task—learning everyone's name in the farm—to a readily accomplished goal you'll quickly achieve.

The methods are detailed in the following four sections.

## Set Up the Farm File

The farm file must be a convenient system for recording new details about the people in your farm; the system must be equally convenient for reviewing those details quickly in the field.

Some agents like to use file cards for their farm file. I preferred a three-ring binder with a divider for each street. On the back of each divider I staple a list, typed in easily-read capitals, of the people on that street. At first, to refresh my memory, I always pull over to the curb and run my eye down a street's occupant list before turning the corner.

MARK & LINDA BROWN (Billy, Wanda)
RICKY & LILA HARTFORD (No Kids)
JUNE & HARRY LARSON (Chad, Baby Nancy)

Behind each divider is a special page for each family. On this sheet I gather the friendly things I learned talking to people—good for starting the next conversation with them. The address, names of the owners, and their phone number head the paper. Below that I enter facts about their children and pets. I use the top quarter-page for this information, and give a brief description of the property as seen from the street, leaving space for adding more details later.

The next quarter-page I reserve for what they told me about their leisure time interests, associations, and hobbies. On the bottom quarter-page I record what they volunteered about their jobs and career interests.

By always entering certain kinds of information in about the same place, I can more quickly review my farm file, more readily see what I don't know about each family, and more surely avoid showing ignorance of something they've already told me.

Write a small, legible, permanent record as you go, not a huge scrawl that'll soon fill the page. Transfer a street's pages to a clipboard if it's more convenient. Discipline yourself to write concisely and readably as soon as you're alone.

At the top of each page's back, note the dates you visit each family and their reaction to you. Gather this information as you go or you'll get confused: going around your farm twice probably adds up to six hundred visits.

When I was farming, I used ordinary ruled notebook paper. It's handier, to keep the items used on every contact on the front side of the page. Farm File, in Chapter 24 ("Money-Making Forms and Checklists") and also on the accompanying CD, allows you to do just that.

A glance at your notations of visit dates, homeowner reactions, and at the other facts about each family you've recorded, enables you to begin each new visit where you left off your previous one. You'll find people paying friendly attention to you because you're paying friendly attention to them by remembering details about their lives and interests.

Know who is on your team, and who their friends are, but remain the professional at all times. Nothing will turn your farm's crops to weeds quicker than becoming known as the neighborhood gossip.

Where do you get the homeowners' names, addresses, and phone numbers to begin with? A fast and convenient source, if one is available in your area, is the reverse (crisscross) directory. This useful directory lists telephone subscribers by street and number. Use this valuable tool for all its worth, but recognize it has limitations: people were moving while it was being printed; it won't tell you who owns rental property; and it won't have people with no phones, unlisted phones, or new phones.

Start the rapport-building stage of farming as soon as possible. The sooner you're through the initial stages of this period (rapport-building should continue as long as you work your farm) the sooner you'll be able to gain effective control of your farm. So get out there today and make your first visits. Keep them brief. Keep moving. As you go, gather and record information. All you need to start is determination and a few sheets of notebook paper.

Divide your farm into 30 groups of about 10 houses each that you can conveniently visit by parking your car once. You shouldn't always work your farm the same way, but for the first three to six visits, the 10-house group will work fine.

Visit one group of 10 houses each day, and make prospecting calls to verify the names and addresses given in your reverse directory for two groups of 10 houses. You'll soon be calling at houses where you feel confident in calling the people by name.

As you walk the areas, record the addresses not given in the reverse directory. Bypass those houses unless someone's out front and you get into an easy conversation with them. After exchanging pleasantries, they'll usually introduce themselves.

Information on properties not appearing in the reverse directory will be in your deed details folder. The next section tells how to create one.

## Create Your Deed Details Folder

In some areas, title companies will furnish you with owners' names, legal descriptions, and similar data on a courtesy, no-charge basis. Call your title company representative and ask for a farm package. In regions where this isn't done, your best source may be the assessor's office, which is often found in the county courthouse.

Legal descriptions, assessor's parcel numbers, and lot sizes usually stay the same for many years. Since you rarely need this information except when writing up a listing, there's no need to carry it along when door knocking.

Avoid copying deed details by hand except onto a listing form you can double-check for accuracy. Errors in this information are time consuming, embarrassing, and troublesome at best; at worst, they'll cost you a lot of money. Avoid errors by working from photocopies of official or title company records.

Once you have your own photocopies, a few minutes with a pair of scissors and a copy machine will give you the data in the format you prefer: legal or letter size. Make two sets, one for your office and the other for the farming kit you carry in your car. This assures you of having these vital details handy and accurate whenever they're needed. Once it's made, your deed details folder probably will never need updating as long as you work a given farm.

## Flashdeck Your People

The flashdeck's goal is to clamp the names of everyone in your farm into your memory as quickly as possible. Then associate those people with a house you can visualize: their home. Only facts you will memorize should appear on the farm flashdeck cards.

On side 1, write the family surname only. On side 2 of each card, enter the first names you find in the reverse directory. Add the names of spouses and children as you discover them.

As you work your farm, compose a brief description of each house. Add details about the interiors later. Start with the outside and

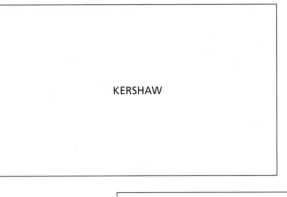

| | | | |
|---|---|---|---|
| | | | Lulu 5 |
| HUSBAND | Joe Kershaw | CHILDREN | Steve (about 8) |
| WIFE | Mary | | |
| HOUSE | This is the Tiptoe through the tulips house Outside reminds me of a cozy cottage by the sea—window boxes w tulips, freshly painted white picket fence | | |

Farm Flashdeck

describe what distinguishes each house from neighboring structures in the most accurate, emotional, and *favorable* phrases you can think of. Use this opportunity to develop your sensitivity to the sales features of your farm's properties. Emphasize the positive elements of the real estate you've appointed yourself the world's expert on. Truly, one of your highest-priority goals must be to become the world's foremost expert on your farm in the shortest possible time.

Review your farm flashdeck twice daily until you've over-learned the facts in it. If you have an assistant, have them input all the homeowners in your farm into the computer. If you do not have an assistant, hire someone a few times a month or even quarterly to update your computer files. (The flashdeck learning system was described in Chapter 3.)

## Use the Property Catalog

The people come and go, but the houses stay. Farm expertise is knowing about both. Pay keen and systematic attention to the houses as you learn about the people and you'll acquire this complete, double-barreled farm knowledge faster, and retain it longer.

Compiling a property catalog for your farm spurs your observation. Writing down the facts you observe is a learning process; reviewing the facts you've entered in the catalog cuts your memory grooves deeper. If you're been telling yourself you have a poor memory, you'll be delighted at how easy it is to install 300 instant-recall images in your brain, one for each house in your farm, when you do it systematically. Piggybacked on each of those images will be others—the owners' faces, names, and details about their interests, children, and prospects. When you've acquired only a part of this knowledge, you'll find it building on itself. It might happen like this.

Al Pike, a new agent who is working smarter, not harder at a social gathering finds himself talking to a man he's never met before. Al introduces himself, but doesn't mention his business yet because he feels it would be too pushy too soon.

"I'm Dick Taylor," the other man responds.

"Someone named Taylor lives on Maple Street. Are you the one?"

"Sure am. Have we met, Al?"

"We haven't, but its a pleasure to greet you now, Dick. You live in the beautiful white colonial with the huge oak tree in front, don't you?"

"You're right." Dick gives Al a quizzical look. "How do you know all this?"

"I'm with Shakey Shacks Realty, and I specialize in the area you live in, Dick."

"I guess you do. Very impressive how you tied my name up with my house. I'm surprised I haven't heard of you before this."

"I decided to specialize in your area just three weeks ago, so I've still got a lot to learn about it."

"Well, you're moving fast, I can see that. Say, you should talk to Lindsay Long. Do you know him?"

"Only that he lives on Maple Street, too."

"Right. Well, he's been offered a job on the coast. I think he's going to take it. You ought to talk to Lindsay right away."

"Thanks for the tip, Dick. Would it be asking too much for you to give him a call and put in an ice-breaking word for me?"

"Glad to, Al. Anyone working as hard as you are deserves a break."

Many sales have been made by a sharp agent who knocked on a door and said, "I have a buyer who wants a home exactly like yours. Are you thinking of selling in the near future?" The answer quite often comes back as, "We *are* thinking of selling. Do you really have a buyer, or is this just a gimmick?" The industry's image and this great ploy should never be tarnished by using it as a foot-in-the-door scheme.

Used with integrity, it can readily result in a listing or even a double-fee transaction. These opportunities flow from knowing every property in your farm, not just those currently for sale.

Your small loose-leaf notebook makes an ideal property catalog. Many people want, and will pay extra money for, certain amenities. Record in your property catalog which properties have them. Make note of the colors, number of bedrooms, and unusual features. Compiling this catalog gives you a thousand conversation openers with the residents of your farm. Make the most of this opportunity to learn about the houses and their owners—but don't be nosy. Judicious questions don't arouse hostility. Avoid asking a homeowner for information you can gather by looking at the house or at the public records.

Avoid asking questions you don't know the homeowner can answer. People usually know how many bedrooms they have, but not the total square footage of the house. Remember what the rancher told his son, "Never ask a man where he's from because he might not be from Texas, and then he'll be mad at you for making him own up to it."

Ask, "What do you like best about this house?" It's not nosing around for details the homeowner may think are none of your business, it's asking for an opinion. People like to be consulted. If your *like-best* question goes well, follow it up with, "Would you be offended if I asked you what you like least about this house?"

Before asking any questions at all, of course, identify yourself and state your purpose. "Good morning. I'm Tillie Newcomer with Sell Fast Realty—and I'm the specialist in this area. I'm just going to take half a minute to say hello and leave a memo pad, and ask just one question for the property catalog I'm compiling on this neighborhood. This is a three-bedroom house, isn't it?" (Of course, you'd only ask this question in a custom home area, where the answer isn't obvious, as it would be in a mass-built tract.)

"No, we have four bedrooms."

If they're closing the door on you, give them a bright, "Thank you," and head for the next house. If they seem willing to talk for a moment, use the what-do-you-like-best opener.

Notice how Tillie handled the bedrooms question. She was fairly sure it was a four-bedroom house, but she said, "It's three, isn't it?" and handed the homeowner a win. Suppose Tillie had said, "You have four bedrooms here, don't you?" to the owner of a three-bedroom house. The homeowner then has to say, "No, we only have three." It's not a win, and the owner's standing there thinking, "Why am I talking to this klutz who's taking up my time and making me feel bad?"

Suppose you guess that a house has four bedrooms, say three to be safe, and the homeowner answers, "We only have two bedrooms."

| | |
|---|---|
| Noted _____<br>when<br>walking<br>by | 19345 Maple                          3 bedroom, 2 ba.<br><br>2 story Colonial—white eagle over front door. Huge oak tree in front yard. Sweeping brick wall. Tucked against hill. No view, but quiet.<br><br>RV acc. poss. (There's room for recreation vehicle access and storage.) |
| Learned _____<br>when<br>Dick<br>invited you in | Elegant dining room with smoked mirrors. Gold carpet. Yellow check lino in B & K.<br><br>Owners                                        Dick/Rachel Taylor |
| Space _____<br>for<br>changes | |

You can save the win by quickly saying, "I'm amazed. It's such a big house—you must have some very impressive-sized rooms here."

Avoid assumptions such as, "And, of course you have a swimming pool like everyone else on the block does," Agent Footmouth says to a pool-less lady.

"We're the only underprivileged family on the block," she snaps, and slams the door in Footmouth's face.

# Working Your Farm File

At the end of the farming day input all the interesting facts in a journal notebook. I would sit in my car and do my journal entries. Because I own a laptop now, I type into my laptop all the information I need about my clients. Whether you use a hard bound or an electronic notebook, include helpful details.

One day you sell a house in your farm on West Street. It's the work of a moment to compare the ages of your buyers' children to those on West Street they'll be living near. You journal it right away before you forget. On your next sweep through your farm, you knock on a door and say, "Hi, Mrs. Hall. I just sold the house across the street. And guess what? They have a daughter Kelly's age." Or you share the newcomers both like to bowl, since you know the Halls do, too. People want to know who's coming into the neighborhood. You're not disclosing anything personal.

## Coping with E-agent

Did you select a farm where an agent from another office is powerful—though not in total control? It's pointless to challenge an agent who has total control of a farm. You can take total control of some other farm with less effort than it'll require to make a bare living fighting someone else's total control. Talk to the homeowners. If half of them tell you that Millie or Jack has the whole neighborhood tied up in a sack, go elsewhere. But, in any desirable farm, you're likely to find one strong agent already operating there. He or she has been taking a steady flow of listings out of the farm for some time, but hasn't taken total control. Let's call this entrenched agent, *E-agent.*

Here's how to cope with E-agent. It your gender is the same as E-agent, take heart, he or she has no advantage there. If you're of the opposite sex, also take heart. Some people prefer working with a man; others prefer working with a woman.

Never have anything but praise for the entrenched agent, or keep silent. You never know when you're talking to one of E-agent's bird dogs (spies), or someone who'd like to make mischief between the two of you. Be sure the grapevine is passing good things back to E-agent; there's no sense in goading him or her into strenuous competition to get even for a careless remark you've made.

E-agent has strong points and weak points. He or she has been tough about taking listings at market price, or has taken overpriced listings and had them hang around forever without selling. Maybe E-agent knocks on doors but doesn't hand out giveaways; maybe he doesn't put out a newsletter. If he uses a newsletter, it has a certain slant. You take a different slant, Chapter 7 tells you about giveaways and super-promotions and Chapter 13 about newsletters.

Notice what times and days E-agent farms. Then go farming at a different time. Find out—by casual conversation with someone who seems friendly on the farm—if E-agent specializes in sending out written material. If he's so busy he relies on mail, then you rely on face-to-face contact—it's usually the most cost-and time-effective method.

E-agent has loyal fans. Stay away from them. Get your own.

Hang in there. E-agent most likely won't. He's been getting a nice business from your mutual farm for a long time—with less and less effort expended. Persevere, because perseverance is the hardest game in real estate, and it pays off best.

Compete hard, but don't let it show—don't make E-agent come out and fight. You can't bank brag. Do him little favors. The only important thing is listings sold. Do your best to sell E-agent's listings because then the new owners are *your* clients.

Never forget to work on achieving your personal goals, not beating E-agent's record. Paddle your own canoe and let E-agent paddle his; the river is wide enough for both of you.

# The Evergreen Listing Farm

There are three common methods of farming. Let's discuss them in order of popularity.

**"I hate it, but I hit it when I have to."** This is a labor-saving system of farming. Not much needs to be done because not much is expected. Devotees of this method tolerate other office's signs in their farm quite well; what really upsets them is another agent from their office working expireds or fizzbos in their farm.

**"I really worked it—once."** Nothing happened, so why continue? Door knock on a dull afternoon, send a kid around hanging newsletters—and the ungrateful public refuses to respond. Okay, so I tried farming and it doesn't work—forget it—farming is a waste of time.

**The evergreen attitude.** "My goal is effective control of my farm. Steady income requires steady effort. To reap regularly, I must fertilize frequently."

Effective control of a farm begins when you're taking one-third of the listings produced there—and selling them. Except in special circumstances, such as when your office has a commanding location, writing two-thirds of the listings from a given farm is about the best you can reasonably expect to achieve over an extended time span. Sellers loyal to the agent they originally bought from, and those with friends or relatives in the real estate business, impose such a limit. There'll also be an occasional maverick with whom you can't click.

A very active farm has an annual turnover of 25 percent, but let's assume 20 percent. In a farm of controllable size (about 300 houses), this means 60 listings per year. Writing 40 of those listings, selling 10 of them yourself, and promoting other brokers to sell the other 30 earns one fee per week. This is effective control of your farm and of your bank account.

Set your goal at one transaction per week from your farm. It's achievable if you're willing to make the effort. Keep that goal constantly in mind whenever excuses for not pounding the pavement or hitting the phone tempt you. Give farming a high priority. Schedule heavy time and effort for it—and then do it. As you get busier and busier, get more and more efficient. Your farm made you busy and prosperous; maintain your powerful thrust there.

Too many agents think of farming as a distasteful chore—and it shows. You've got to feel good about the homeowners before you can expect them to feel good about you. Psych yourself up until you know you're the best agent who'll offer real estate services to them. You're not necessarily the most experienced agent, but you can be the most determined to deliver thorough service in your farm. Even the newest agent can make this commitment.

## The Three Stages

Gaining effective control of an evergreen farm (a farm that continues to produce yield) has three stages:

- Getting to know me
- Getting to like me
- Getting to love me

Each stage takes about six months. If you've selected a good, active farm and work it properly, you'll get at *least* two listings during the first stage, four during the second stage, and eight during the third stage. After 18 months you'll approach effective control—where your presence is so strong it discourages competition. At this crucial point many salespeople become too busy and slack off working their farms. When the confusion clears, they often find an aggressive competitor is gaining rapidly on them. Your farm needs frequent attention. Your attention can't be constant, needn't be regular, but it must be frequent.

Let's consider those three stages to effective control of an evergreen farm in detail:

1. **The getting-to-know-me stage.** Before you start, realize you need patience. Most of the people who quit farming didn't have the necessary patience. They did one-tenth, or perhaps nine-tenths, of the work necessary to make it pay. Then they got discouraged—and allowed all their effort to evaporate. During this first stage, giveaways are essential to get you in the door. Memo pads with your picture on them are great. Have a note printed, or inserted with a spot of glue (your pad printer can do this) near the end of the pad: "Time to call Danny Kennedy for another memo pad." You'll get calls and sometimes a lead to a listing in the neighborhood at the same time.

Rain hats, litter bags, and an endless list of goodies are available. Make your choices, and then get out there and hand out those giveaways.

Your words at this stage are very important, "Hi, I'm Danny Kennedy with Sell Fast Realty. I hope I haven't interrupted. I'm a real estate expert who specializes in your home town. I'll only keep you for a minute, but I want you to know I keep tabs on what's going on in this community." (Mention something topical like: tax relief, a new fire station or public pool, or school bonds.) "And I also keep current on homes sales and listings in your neighborhood."

Don't be afraid to use the word "expert." *Webster's* defines *expert* as, "One who has acquired special skill or knowledge in a particular subject." Based on *Webster's* definition, you are a real estate expert, aren't you?

Keep it simple and basic. At the end of this sales dialogue use these dynamite words, "Thanks for talking to me." Many of the people behind the doors on your farm are afraid of strangers. They are afraid of a small woman too. A fearful attitude isn't only a problem men have. The fear isn't necessarily of physical danger—it's an instinctive fear of the unknown. So a large part of our work is to alleviate the fear of the unknown by making ourselves known in a pleasant way.

2. **The getting-to-like-me stage.** Think for a minute about the representatives of mortgage and title companies who drop into real estate offices soliciting business. One day you see Martin Smith's card and memo pad on your desk. You've never heard of Martin Smith, and don't think you need him, so you throw away his card. A couple more times you see his card on your desk, and you keep throwing it away. Then one day Martin Smith comes in and he introduces himself and you small talk for a moment. A week later you're calling a client whose number you've jotted on a memo pad—and you notice Martin Smith's photo and name printed on that pad. But it still wouldn't occur to you to call Martin Smith, a title company representative, when you need title insurance. Then one day a problem comes up.

You're preparing a listing appointment packet for presentation tomorrow. You have no time to spare. A call comes in. A document that was missed when the client came in for settlement must be signed immediately by your buyer in order for the transaction to close the following morning. Martin Smith, who until now has been a face only vaguely connected with a name, happens to be there. He says, "I'll be glad to help you out. I'll drive the 60 miles to get it signed." Aha—the moment of truth arrived. You not only know him—you like him! He can be useful as well as informative. Martin Smith is now in a position to obtain—not only some of your title business—but also some business from the other agents in your office. Because you're going to tell them about how good old Marty saved you from a tight time squeeze. As long as his title work is competitive in price and quality, he's now part of the team. He's no longer one of the problem people you smile at and get rid of as quickly as possible.

The same forces work in the farm. When you finally arrive at the right place at the right time, you enter the getting-to-like-me stage, not only at that one house, but at all the neighbors who talk to those people. For example, it's mid-May and you're out farming as you walk up to Alice and Phil Cooke's door. Alice and Phil have the itch for a swimming pool. He's sitting at the dining room table filling out an application for a home improvement loan. When he comes to the application's question about the present value of their home, Phil yells, "Hey, Alice, what do think this place is worth?"

"How should I know?" Alice calls from the back yard. "Is that our doorbell?"

Phil opens the door and stares as you say, "Hi, Mr. Cooke—I'm Danny Kennedy, the real estate expert from Sell Fast Realty. Is there any information you need about real estate these days? I'm right on top of things."

"Hey, you are just the gal I need—the face on the memo pad, right? Listen I'm filling out a loan application, and they want to know the value of my house."

"No problem, Mr. Cooke. Let me run to my car and get my current listings and comparable records. I'll give you an up-to-date market evaluation in five minutes." The getting-to-like-me stage is accomplished. You are useful and informative and not after anything but his confidence. Obviously, he's not moving. But you helped. He tells the neighbors to the left, right, and down the street, "Kennedy is okay. She's not just after the buck. She'll give you service whether you're moving or not."

In this stage be careful not to become a pest. Don't let them say, "Who is this clown hanging around the neighborhood all the time?" Act busy in your farm. Move. You're being watched. If you're in the neighborhood too much, they'll say, "When does he sell houses?"

Watch your timing, and step out briskly in your farm. Drive through, wave, and act busy. Even though you don't visit someone, even though they don't have that person-to-person contact with you every time, once you're in this getting-to-like-me stage, driving around the neighborhood and acting busy there, keeps you in their minds.

Recommend nice homes for a home tour, or something special like "The Most Beautiful Homes on the Block" award Tom Hopkins talks about in his seminars. If your local newspaper occasionally does a photo story on some of the area's outstanding houses, find out how they're selected and try to get homes in your farm included. If a charitable group in your area conducts an outstanding home tour as a fund-raising event, be on the lookout for homes in your farm you can recommend for the tour.

If your area has no tour, develop a plan for one and call the program chairpersons of various charitable organizations. Ask to appear on their program at their next meeting to propose a fund-raising tour for their organization's benefit. This is a powerful way to make yourself known in the community, and talking with homeowners about whether they'd like their home singled out as a showplace is a powerful way of creating a significant presence in your farm.

Make spot checks on your buddies in the farm. From day one, cultivate the group of homeowners in your farm who are naturally friendly and helpful. Some people are more open and you'll know them when you see them. They open the door and say "Good morning. Beautiful day, isn't it?" Lean on your newly acquired buddies in the getting-to-know-me stage. On each block, visit two or three buddies and say, "I'm on my way to the office to show property. I just wanted to see if I can do anything for you in the area of real estate—How's the memo pad supply?—Talk to you later—Bye now." Boom, on to the next spot check. Soon you'll pop onto a juicy tidbit on one of your spot checks—"Hi, Dan—say, the Walter kids are telling my kids their new home will be near Disney World in Florida. Something's up—check it out." Three cheers for spot checks in the getting-to-like-me stage!

**3. The getting-to-love-me stage.** When they're putting the bread on your table, you've reached this happy state. You should use a more personal approach now. Send birth announcements when a baby is born in your farm. Drop the parents a note saying, "Congratulations on the new addition. I hope Father's nerves are calming down, and Mother is getting some rest. If you think you'll need more space later, remember me."

Now your sign is the one seen all over the farm. People are watching to see if you make any mistakes. A friend calls and says, "Is your agent doing a good job for you? Is she keeping the promises she made? Is she keeping you informed?"

"No, she isn't. She's gotten too big for her britches."

The caller asking these questions is thinking of moving, or has a friend who is. How much better if your client says, "Yes, she's done a marvelous job. She's really a fine agent."

During this getting-to-love-me stage, remember, bad rumors spread rapidly. You can lose your farm as quickly as you built it up.

"She returned messages fast when we wanted to list. She followed up while it was on the market real good. But, now that the property's sold, we can't even find out whether the buyer is getting a loan okayed. Am I burned up. But what can I do?"

One irate lady can do plenty. She can ride over your farm like Attila the Hun with phone calls telling everyone who'll listen what a rotter you are. No real estate farm will ever be so lush its crops won't fail if left untended. Allow yourself to become too busy with other things, too disorganized, or too tired, and the labor and money you expended building up your farm will be wasted.

# More Farming Secrets

## It's a Numbers Game

By striking out 1,306 times, Babe Ruth set one of the longest-held records in baseball. However, we remember his 714 home-run record. Even the legendary Babe had to take two slaps for every kiss. Thomas Edison's ratio was far lower. He had hundreds, perhaps thousands, of fruitless experiments patiently carried out to achieve each successful invention.

Count the harvests you reap, not the never-sprouting seeds you planted. Sow widely, and sow often. Talk to as many people as you can. Follow up every opportunity you sniff, never look back and grumble. Look forward through your victories to more successes. Real estate is a numbers game.

## Find the Best Time to Farm

Find out the best time to visit when you first begin farming. Hit two or three houses at different times of each day for two weeks and discover when most people are home. Friday afternoons, between 3 P.M. and 6 P.M., and Saturday mornings between 10 A.M. and noon, were my most effective times. After I covered my farm twice, those were the only times I went farming because by then I was too busy to door-knock during the less-effective times of the week.

## Always Have a Reason

Always have a reason for follow-up notes and phone calls. For example, you're in your farm talking to a lady. She really doesn't want to talk about real estate, but has a question about the school bond issue, or she's heard something about the school system she wants verified. As you're chit-chatting, she says, "I'd really like to know what the scoop is on this." She doesn't specifically say to you, "Find out."

Don't tell her you will, which becomes a promise you might not be able to keep. Instead of promising, do it. Go back to the office after farming and find out what she wants to know. Then drop her a note, or call her up and say, "Remember when we were talking about the school bond issue? Well, this is the story—"

Have a good reason. This is always an effective rule to keep in mind. When you have a reason for contacting them, it's not, "Why is this pesky agent bugging me again?" You're giving out information; you're a professional doing the job right.

## Beat Square? Try Wacky

One day another agent and I were talking about the people on our farms we hadn't clicked with, and how we might get some of those people on our team. We decided to go out right then and see what we could learn from each other by knocking on problem doors together. The plan was for her to take the lead in my farm, and for me to take the lead in hers. I won the coin toss and we went out to hit three houses on my farm first.

We knocked on two doors, found no one home, and were walking past another house when my friend pointed at it and said, "You're doing good here?"

I shook my head. "There's a 'No solicitors' sign, a big one, right on the door. No way you can say you didn't see it."

"Danny, let's see what'll happen if we blow her a kiss." My friend headed for the door. I followed, reluctantly, and kept well back when she knocked.

A grim-faced woman opened the door and, after giving my friend a wilting stare, said, "Don't tell me you didn't see my sign."

My friend fluttered her hands, shook her head, and protested in a bewildered tone, "But I don't smoke!"

The lady opened her mouth, couldn't find words, and finally chuckled. Then she said, "Oh, all right, come on in." We had a nice chat, and the lady invited us back any time we were in the neighborhood. After a few months, a relative she referred bought a house from me, and two years later I listed her house.

It was a shot in the dark and we were in a wacky enough mood to try it that day. Our light-hearted approach ultimately made our pockets heavier.

Why not? Why be grim when you can be cheerful? People pay to see comedians, but the only attention cold stone faces get is from pigeons.

## Keep a Record

Keep a record of all sales and listings in your farm. Recording this information in the order it happens makes it easier to summarize and helps you spot important new trends. Within 60 days of starting to work a farm, using the information you've gathered and analyzed from the Multiple Listing Service, you should be able to tell prospective sellers and buyers something like the following:

"Three years ago 49 houses sold in this immediate neighborhood at an average price of $150,000. Two years ago 57 went for $158,000, and last year 66 homes brought an average price of $160,000. So far this year the lowest any house has sold for is $151,000, and the highest price paid is $185,000. At the rate it's going I expect 75 houses to sell this year at an average price of $167,500."

Your listeners will be impressed.

People will ask you to repeat the information, so be sure you've got it right, and can back it up with records. It takes effort to pull together the information necessary to make this short speech, but it pays big dividends in reassurance. Your buyers not only know they've got a knowledgeable agent on their team, they know they're buying a good investment. Your prospective sellers are reassured to learn you know the area better than they do, and they'll be more inclined to accept your pricing advice. Check out every reported sale as you work your farm and find out what each sold property is comparable to. If 1234 Elm Street sold for $200,000 a month ago and you know nothing else about the house, the price information won't help you a bit to advise a buyer or seller about a property at 4321 West Avenue. But if you know they are both two-story, four-bedroom homes of about 3,000 square feet with similar amenities, Elm Street's sale makes a significant statement about West Avenue's market value. This statement will carry weight with mortgage company appraisers and loan committee members; it should give guidance to the seller, and it will be considered by an intelligent buyer.

## Publish a Monthly Newsletter

Sounds overwhelming? It isn't when you set it up right. Create a simple format, set a schedule, gather market information, type it, have a quick-print shop run off copies, and get them out. Detailed tips for doing all this quickly, reliably, and cheaply are given in Chapter 13, *High Tech Promotion and the Personal Touch*.

Why bother? Because the monthly newsletter gives you a constant presence in your farm. People will notice if you consistently deliver professional market facts about their neighborhood. If they suddenly find themselves sellers, they'll want the agent who can do them the most good. Tell them you are their best choice twelve times a year—it's a powerful convincer.

## Get Out There!

The hardest part of farming is leaving the office. Details by the dozen conspire to delay you. Excuses multiply. "I'll just do these two things, make one more call, and then I'll go farming. Oh, but I've got to—"

This can—and usually does—go on all day. Schedule your farm time like an appointment with a buyer. When that time comes, go do it. That's all—just go do it when the time comes. At the end of the year you'll be thousands of dollars richer for following this simple resolve.

## Farming Tool Decision Day

Pick one day each month to make your decisions about farming tools. Mark the date in your appointment book for the rest of the year or, if you use the tickler 1/31 system discussed in Chapter 22, staple a reminder in the appropriate day's folder. The 10th of each month is a good date to make your final decision on the item you'll hand out during the fourth following month. This allows your supplier 110 days to imprint the items and get them to you well in advance of need. If you order early, you won't be tracing shipments when you should be handing out the giveaways in your farm. Ordering early also allows you to shop for price, and to refuse or return poor quality merchandise.

# Professionalism

Professionalism furnishes the real estate agent with both armor and weapons. The armor is your attitude of concern to help qualified buyers while safeguarding sellers' legitimate interests.

Be friendly, relaxed, and natural—while making clear by action and speech that your professional responsibilities come ahead of your personal whims. Never indulge in idle chatter about your pet peeves, problems, and pleasures. Stick to business. Talk about your clients' interests, concerns, and opportunities instead of your own. Maintain, under your friendly and relaxed manner, a reserved position of dignity.

Professionalism's weapons are knowledge well learned and skills carefully practiced. Know your job. Let people become aware, by deeds instead of words, of your time's considerable value. Treat your time with respect and you'll find others respecting it too.

Among the burdens of success at farming are the chatty types who give you a lot of referrals and get a bit possessive of you. They're inclined to call up at any time and want you to run right over. Although you're grateful to them, you can't let them control your time. Let's take a professional approach to handling a possessive person's phone call.

"Danny, can you come here right now? My girlfriend from Oak Park and her husband just dropped in and they really think Hilton Head is neat. They're interested in taking a quick peek at a few houses. Who knows? Maybe she'll be able to get him down here. I sure hope so, because we're such great friends, and—"

When two women, or two couples, get together on a visit, they often catch "house hunting fever." The hosts are proud of their hometown or second vacation home, and the visitors are more interested in looking at homes than at the high school gym. Sometimes they just want to be entertained at your expense. Even if you don't pick up the lunch check, your time, especially your weekend time, is a heavy expense. Ask to talk to the visitor.

**Agent:**  I'm so happy you love our area. But are you really serious about investing in our area?

> **Visitor:** I don't know. It depends on what you have in my price range.
>
> **Agent:** How long will you be here today?
>
> **Visitor:** Just this afternoon.
>
> **Agent:** My schedule is pretty full this afternoon, but I have lots of information on this area. I can put together a presentation of some representative properties available right now in your price range. (The flyer packet discussed in Chapter 9 is ideal for this.) I can drop it off in about 20 minutes on my way to an appointment. Will this fit in with your plans?

# Your Attitude on the Farm

Treat people with the best of good manners. Use an approach of alert cordiality, so they'll feel a pleasant compulsion to reciprocate your friendly attitude. Be sensitive. Never press when they're troubled or busy. Above all, avoid even the suspicion of trickery or underhanded tactics. You farm to build confidence and trust, not to breed fear and suspicion.

# Avoid Careless Slips

Careless slips of the tongue can get back to people in your farm. You're there to list and sell real estate professionally, not to pass judgment on people. Be careful what you say, and be careful what you write in your farm file. Someone can look over your shoulder, or the book can be mislaid.

# Every Door Is Different

Plan your presentation, practice a dozen openers, but remember that you're dealing with human beings. Look at the person who opens the door. You've got a memo pad in your hand and a split second to react and adapt your planned presentation to the circumstances. If they only open the door a crack so a wolfhound can bark at you, don't stand there saying, "I'm Danny Kennedy of Sell Fast Realty, and let me tell you, the real estate market is fantastic." Sneak your memo pad through the doorway crack and say, "I'm sorry for the interruption. I'll come back another time." Then beat it out of there.

Every door is different. Mrs. Verbose answers the next door. She's a little old lady who hasn't seen anyone breathe for weeks. "Oh,

Danny, you're the one with the memo pads. Come on in." She pours you tea, gives you cookies, and tells you about her long-lost relatives. You could be there all day. There's a time when you'll have to say, "Goodbye, Mrs. Verbose. I've got to go. But I'll be back and talk to you."

This is a people business first, and a property business second. Gear your outwardly visible emotional level to each person.

Before you start doing anything not already common real estate practice in your area, check with your broker. Local ordinances, or your professional association's rules, may prohibit some tactics. For example, some areas have rules against cold calling for listings. Other places won't permit agents to go door-to-door. Before you order give-aways, make sure you'll be allowed to hand them out. Before using any new method, make sure it's acceptable. Before you dive in, make sure there's water in the pool!

# Speed Counts

When you have the chance to put out *Just Listed* or *Just Sold* door-hangers, speed counts. If these transactions are of special interest to the fizzbos or other prospective sellers you're working with, phone or visit them with the news. These are professional, nonintrusive reasons to contact them, and nothing enhances your image more than listing or selling a property comparable to theirs.

However, you can't know everyone who might be thinking of selling in your farm. Some people are secretive, others are struck by sudden changes. Get those new door-hangers out fast (with the seller's permission, of course), while they're still news and before another agent does.

# Humility Helps

Humility helps you pass around many a pitfall dug by pride. Real estate agents walk a narrow line between enthusiastic confidence on the one hand, and unfeeling pride on the other. Some of us stray from the narrow line and offend people—to our serious financial cost.

After you really have control of your farm, drop notes to people, or go see them and thank them.

"I never could've won my sales award without your confidence."

"I really appreciate your support—I couldn't have done it without you."

Memorize those phrases and use them often. And, on a day you think you're Mr. King Pin, put a sign on your desk saying, "Never forget a humble beginning."

# Success Breeds Success

Work your farms hard, get some priced-right listings, put the *For Sale* signs up, slap the *Sold* riders on promptly, and you'll start getting calls like these.

From a young woman you don't remember (farm file shows you caught her home only once, and she didn't seem too impressed), "Jerry just called. He got the promotion and transfer we've been hoping for. I told him you're the hot agent around here, and he wants you to come out tonight and put our house on the market."

From someone on your farm you've spoken to several times, "Hey, call up Nancy Dowd. I've been telling her about you. Yeah, and her listing expired at midnight last night . . . the other office didn't take care of her right. Yeah, call her up and I think you've got the listing."

Now your name riders are all over the farm. You have a good month, another, and then three. Lots of people are calling in, lots of good things are happening, and your name goes in the paper: top lister, first in sales, and so on. Tape a newspaper clipping of the ad or article and send it, with a thank-you note, to the people who've been giving you leads. Tell them, "I really appreciate your help. I couldn't have done it without you."

Encourage people to feel they have an emotional stake in your success with notes and attention. Don't be stingy with praise and thanks for help. People like to play a part in a winner's success. Your recognition of your team players does more than anything else to build the local referral team you must have before you can list and sell in high volume.

# Notice the Best-Looking Homes

Well-kept homes usually have the best-informed owners. The pride and commitment they've lavished on their home often extends to concern for their entire neighborhood. They'll say, "Those people down the street haven't cut their lawn in six months, there's big trouble behind their door."

Don't carry gossip, but do keep your ears open for clues to the future and how you should deal with people. Knowing an unfriendly woman has marital and financial problems makes it easier to cope with and overlook her initial surliness. Persevere. A series of short, friendly contacts can gain her trust. You'll then be in position to help and advise if difficulties require the sale of her house.

Be especially attentive to the people who keep the best homes in the neighborhood, even though they seem to be the least likely to move. You have a common interest—the well-being of their neighborhood. Be kind to your best-kept homeowners: thank them for their help, and reward them with appropriate invitations and small gifts.

## Handling Exceptional Properties

Some properties won't conform to the usual pattern in your farm. Pay special attention to them. If most of your farm consists of well-kept residences, investigate any poorly maintained house. If the tax bills are being sent elsewhere (the assessor's office can tell you), an absentee owner probably has rented the house. Because the owner is some distance away, the renter may feel he can let the property run down.

Take a photo that shows the property's condition, and send it with a nice letter to the owner. Say nothing about the property's condition; simply say you specialize in the area and are well qualified to help with real estate matters. Don't write, "I can solve your *problem*," and perhaps stir one up for yourself. The occupants might be pet relatives or in-laws.

If the property qualifies for this treatment, you'll be able to make some photos from the sidewalk to make your point, effectively but subtly. This can bring you a client and get a blight in your farm cleaned up.

If there are vacant lots in your farm, become an expert on their offering price, terms, and the requirements for building a house on them.

Any vacant lot not offered for sale in a built-up area might have formidable title problems, or it might just be lying there waiting for an aggressive agent to work at getting it listed and sold. It's to your advantage to breathe new life into the neighborhood by getting those lots built. To qualify as an expert on your farm, you must know the current status of every property on it.

If there are a few retail business properties within your farm, or on the fringes of it, get to know the managers. If you can use their services, consider trading with them. Hairstylists and barbers make great bird dogs.

# Winning Scripts

- "May I ask your permission to give you a complementary memo pad?"
- Former client: "Are you busy right now?"
- Active agent: "Things are hopping, Jeannie, but I'm certainly never too busy to talk with you. What's up?"
- Spreading the word in your farm about your new listing: "Your neighbors chose me to sell their home. Wouldn't you like to choose your new neighbors? Do you know of anyone who's looking in this area for a home?"
- Never linger when farming. "I'd love to stay, but I have another appointment."
- "I know that I could market your home for you. Is there a chance you'd consider me?"

**Getting-to-know-me stage, long form.** Use this approach when they seem friendly. Have a giveaway in your hand.

"Good morning, I'm Danny Kennedy with Sell Fast Realty, and I'd like to take this opportunity to tell you I know your street, your neighborhood, and your town on a professional real estate level. In other words, I'm an expert on the property here. I'm not bragging, but I have earned the right to say this by hard work. So I hope you'll call on me for all your real estate and community information needs. May I have your permission to leave this memo pad with you?

"Thank you so much for your time."

During this crucial *getting-to-know-me stage*, it's important to take a matter-of-fact attitude about your right to be at their door. After all, you are the specialist in the area, so you *must* keep up with the happenings and trends there.

One way is to take a survey on your second or later visit. Create a form listing your survey questions and make copies for each property in your entire farm. Your questions could cover such things as the following:

- How many bedrooms do you have?
- How many members are there in your family?
- How long have you lived here?
- Is this the original building, or have you added some rooms?

If you ask these questions after you've developed rapport, and after you've explained how you're updating your records for the area you specialize in, most people will be happy to talk to you.

**More getting-to-know-me scripts.** "Hi, I'm Danny Kennedy with Sell Fast Realty. The lady down the street said someone in the area might be relocating. Do you happen to know who she meant?" (Isn't there always a lady down the street who's telling you something?)

If they say they don't know, smile and ask, "Would you folks be thinking of relocating in the next three months?"

You're looking for the few who'll say *yes* or *maybe* to that question, of course, so be prepared for this answer. Inquire pleasantly for more details about their plans. Work gradually into the real estate decisions they'll need to make. Volunteer to get them some specific bit of information your discussion reveals they don't have about their possible move. Schedule yourself to keep in touch with them.

If they say *no* to your question about moving in the next 90 days, tell them, "As you know, real estate needs can come up unexpectedly. Here's my card. If you have any questions in the future, please give me a call."

Let them say something and, if it goes well, add, "I'll be stopping by from time to time to see how you're doing and give you up-to-the-minute market information. Would that be all right?"

Break off courteously with the few people who answer this question negatively, and make a note of them. You're not done with your farming day until you send a handwritten note to all the people who said they didn't want market updates. Here's a sample.

> *I hope I didn't offend you by stopping in today. I am a full-time real estate professional who specializes in your area, so many of your neighbors like me to keep them updated monthly on real estate developments affecting your neighborhood. From now on I'll be contacting you by mail only, but feel free to call me anytime—no obligation, of course. Thanks for talking to me.*
>
> *Cordially,*

Here's another opener to use when you're out door-knocking.

> *"Hi. I'm Danny Kennedy of Sell Fast Realty. Here's my newsletter with up-to-the-minute information affecting property owners in this area—which is my area of specialization."*

**Getting-to-know-me stage, short form.** "I hope I haven't interrupted you. I'm Danny Kennedy, the real estate representative from Sell Fast Realty for this area. Please accept this memo pad with no obligation. And please remember—I'm an expert on the property here. Call me if you have any questions about this area. Thanks for listening."

**Getting-to-like-me stage, long form.** "Hello. It's nice to see you again. How's the memo pad supply? My shipment of litter bags just came in, so I thought I'd drop one off for you. Have you heard about _____ Industries? They're moving into town, so lots of their people will need homes here. We're really excited about this at Sell Fast Realty because this development is going to have a beautiful impact on your property's value. I'm looking for homeowners who may want to sell soon. I hope you'll keep your ears open for me, and pass on anything you might hear about people who are leaving this area. Have a good weekend, and thanks for talking to me."

Since you didn't directly ask for the listing, they won't feel threatened. But you did drop the hint. It depends on the tempo of the person behind the door whether you use the long or short form. Use the short form if they fidget.

**Getting-to-like-me stage, short form.** "Hi, Mr. Oasis, I'm Danny Kennedy with Sell Fast Realty, and I'll just take a minute. My office is excited about the new company moving into town. If you hear about anyone who might be moving out, please let me know because we've got buyers who want to move in. I hope you'll remember me, I'm Danny with Sell Fast Realty. If it's okay I'll leave this memo pad with you."

**Getting-to-love-me stage, long form.** "Hi, Jack. Things are really popping. Did you notice my sold sign across the street? Well, we marketed it in just 48 days. And guess what? The buyers are collectors too. I think you'll enjoy them. Say, Jack, I'm really running out of homes. This is such a darn nice area I can never find enough houses around here for sale. I need help. Do you know of anyone who might get transferred or want to sell soon? Thanks for everything."

**Getting-to-love-me stage, short form.** "Hi, Sue. I don't know if you've noticed, but I've been busy around here listing and selling property. Do you happen to know anyone who may want to relocate? Can I tell them you mentioned their name to me? Thanks for everything."

# Client Contact Management Systems

Farming has never been easier. The electronic age allows us to farm without invading. You can e-mail at midnight and by morning be ready for another form of prospecting because you did your farming for the week last night.

The important issue is keeping the territory organized. That is how you keep the business epidemic growing and going. Start with the right client contact management software system. Once you decide on a system that you like (National Association of REALTORS® in Chicago can help with options) buy it. Then be sure it gets out of the box and off of the floor of your garage. Hire a techie from the local junior college to show you how it works and to input names. Don't be frugal about this. It will pay off.

Your property catalog, farm file, deeds detail folders, and more can all be put in your computer. Once the system is up and running you will be able to easily manage follow-up. Follow-up is often a weakness. In a paperless world where everything has a document and a saved place on your computer, the chances of you losing little pieces of paper that contain important information go way down. Don't become obsolete by drowning in your own paperwork.

# CHAPTER 7

# Online or Offline: Danny Kennedy's 12-Month Farming Almanac

## Online or Offline

The information in this chapter is timeless. The methods work in all business climates. What you need to decide is how you want to send the message. You have more choices now than when I began building my business epidemic. I could knock on a door, place a phone call, or send out a mass mailing. But today you can do all of that plus more. Your newsletters can be sent electronically. You can leave a monthly farming message on short text-messaging systems, voice mail, E-mail, fax. But the important thing is that you communicate.

## Blitz Your Farm

Start with inexpensive giveaways and a consistent newsletter. Then, as the fees come in, invest part of them in your drive for control of your farm. The ideas are here; move as fast as you wish. What income would you have earned if you had listed half the houses sold in your farm last year? Figure out this key number, and decide if you can afford not to dominate your farm by investing at least 15 percent of your farm income in promotion.

# Farm by Plan

Set up a 12-month almanac for your farm. Do it on your laptop to really save time. Have a giveaway planned for every month. Do it on your own; you don't need your company to do it for you. If they're providing farming tools, fine. Use their materials. If not, take the initiative and do these necessary things for yourself. It's your farm and your career. Take charge of them both.

*People who don't remember you won't call you.* They don't even know you're there. A long step in the right direction is to have your memo pads sitting beside their phones, with your photo, name, and phone number staring up at them. However, not much will happen until they connect a warm body with a cold photo. When an occasional glance at the memo pad recalls a person they've talked with face-to-face, that *essential-to-success* feeling of familiarity begins to develop.

# "I've Seen You Around"

Put the common reactions to work for you. We all tend to trust the familiar and distrust the unfamiliar. People often say, "I've seen you around," as though having seen someone before automatically makes them more honest, capable, and likable.

"I've seen you around, so you must live and work near here. We probably know some of the same people. You're not a fly-by-night. We have to cope with the same weather, traffic, and school problems. Maybe our kids know each other. You're going to be around tomorrow. We've at least got this much in common: we've both chosen the same part of the earth to live on. I know where I can get back to you."

Of course, no one consciously goes through these thoughts each time they recognize someone at their door, but the feeling of familiarity goes through them. "You're part of the community. To some degree I can trust you. I'll treat you with a touch more courtesy and respect than I would a total stranger." You can build trust and confidence on this foundation.

The essence of farming is to impress your image on their minds so when they think of selling, they'll also think of you. *People who don't remember you won't call you.*

It takes more: People who don't remember you as **the real estate expert in *their* area** won't call you when they decide to move. This is why the verbal techniques on the following pages call for you to constantly repeat, "I am the local real estate expert who is ready to help with any real estate question at any time."

# Operating in a Vacuum

Giveaways you personally hand to homeowners have enormously greater impact than those hung on doorknobs. For example, one day I noticed an unprofessionally dressed man distributing frisbees for a competitor on my farm. They were beautiful frisbees. They were imprinted with my competitor's picture, name, phone number, office, slogan—the works. In two colors yet! And Mr. Unprofessional was doing a good, fast job of setting them on doorsteps. He had been properly instructed to bypass houses with For Sale for signs on them for other agents—no problem there.

While I stood at a front door, waiting for someone to answer my knock, I watched the man hustle back and forth across the street, hitting house after house for my competitor. Her system was so easy. All she had to do was pick an item out of a catalog, place an order for shipment to a delivery service, and write a couple of checks. No pounding the hot pavement, no risking rejection, no getting all rumpled and tired. Just order the work done, let the phone ring, pick it up, and make those listing appointments.

Trudging to the next house, I debated whether to quit for the day rather than confuse people by being at their door when they spotted the frisbee. Then Mr. Unprofessional hurried around a corner, and a pack of grade-school-age boys appeared. They were racing each other to see who could gather the biggest stack. I kept on farming and never saw another of those frisbees. The boys had swept my farm clean of them.

Don't operate in a vacuum. The real world is quirky, full of surprises, and it hands out very few free lunches.

Let's call the agent who put her faith in frisbees, Edna Goeasy. She never figured out the real reason why her frisbee promotion sank without a bubble because a family emergency called her away the week they were distributed. Edna just knew the delivery service dumped her expensive giveaways in the trash instead of handing them out as instructed—but she wasn't there to make sure. The supervisor swore he had spot-checked the job, and Edna had to pay his bill. She paid for a lesson but didn't learn it.

An effective farm program builds your image as the area expert and also keeps you in close touch so you'll often know who's thinking about moving early enough to zero in on them before they make a decision. If your farming program bumps along, and gets done only when you're in the mood, the chances are you're not building toward control of your farm.

# Plan and Review

Plan your farm program a year in advance. It's not necessary to order everything, or to develop every detail right now, but the general outline should be tentatively set *now*. Find out **now** what lead time is required for the giveaways you'll need later. Schedule the dates **now** when you must place your orders to be sure of timely delivery. Working well ahead of need is simply a habit. Playing constant catch-up is also a habit, an expensive and time-consuming one.

Planning a year's farming activity is easy. Start with an annual event in your community, or an annual promotion in your company, or a holiday. Work forward to the current month, and back through the full year. Open a computer file or label a folder, "Farming—Next 12 Months," and collect in it all your ideas, schedules, and brochures on giveaways and promotions.

In your electronic planner or appointment book, write a reminder for the same day of each month to review your next 12 months' farming plans, to order what needs ordering, and to evaluate how your current promotion is going. Should it be repeated next year? Tentatively decide *now*.

Considering the entire year's farm program only once a year is bad practice because you'll be influenced too much by two ephemeral factors: the market's state at that one moment, and how well or poorly your last promotion went.

Your initial plan should be simple. List the next 12 months on the left side of a page. Then jot down next to them possible farming activities for each month. This chapter will give you many ideas. If your company runs cooperative promotions occasionally, consider what the most appropriate tie-in would be for the month before and after. Tell your people of the coming event in your monthly newsletter, and then remind them of it afterwards.

This plan-a-full-year-and-review-it-monthly approach will bring many things into sharp focus, including some unrealistic expectations and misleading ideas. **Only relentless repetition achieves results**.

Don't expect too much too soon. Farming requires preparation, planting, and nurturing before a big harvest can be reaped.

"Dare to be different," people say. It's really easy—at least in theory. Just follow a sound plan long enough for it to work for you; do this and you'll stand above the crowd. Almost everyone else quits after one or two quick passes through a farm.

# Two Vital Points

When selecting items and activities, keep these two essential considerations firmly in mind.

**1.** Farming activity must reflect *favorably* on you.
**2.** Farming activity must reflect favorably on *you*.

Let's examine these two different ideas separately.

**1.** Farming activity must reflect *favorably* on you. There's nothing worse than getting a hate letter written in crayon. I guarantee it'll ruin your whole day. If you sponsor a free show or have a drawing for the kids, be very careful to think everything through. Talk to others about your ideas. Imagine the scene you'll stage so you can organize it to keep everything going smoothly. Talk to a few of the kids. Get their ideas. *And make sure you don't carelessly leave one or more children out.*

If the kids in the farm don't like you, you've had it with the parents. You want the kids to scream happily and the dogs to bark joyfully when you come around. "Oh, she's here again. I like her. When Dad gets transferred and we have to sell our house, Mom, she's going to sell it for us, isn't she?"

The whole family should like you. Pay attention to all of them, and work carefully to avoid getting any of them mad at you. Hollywood says there's no such thing as bad publicity, but being true at the box office doesn't make it true where the listings are signed.

What's worse than getting a hate letter written in crayon? Realizing you spent money to make the kid write it. You can be just as upset—and financially hurt—after spending money giving out a gimmick you think is funny or different if part of your homeowners think the item is offensive. Many imaginative ideas stand between the dull and the dangerous. Build your reputation as a strong real estate agent without risking backlash. Make your selections thoughtfully.

**2.** Farming activity must reflect favorably on *you*. It's absolutely no good at all to put on a whizbang promotion unless people identify you with it. The husband comes home and says, "Where'd we get this neat little gadget?" The wife answers, "Oh, somebody hung it on the door. You know, it's one of those giveaway things." Cost? Considerable. Results? Zilch.

Once you have control of your farm, you'll be so strong your name may come up whether you or a competitor supplied the item. Reaching this pinnacle requires frequent contact, and notable promotions *strongly identified with you* spread throughout the year. When you have control, you can stand in the back of a truck, handing out pumpkins to kids you're calling by name. The first year, you'd better figure out a way to attach your name, photo, and phone number on the pumpkin, and you'd better hike up to the door and hand it to each homeowner. But it's all lost if you only come through your farm three or four times between each October's pumpkin-hand-out time.

# Rating Scale

A rating scale will help you choose among the various promotion possibilities. Never use any giveaway scoring less than 50 points out of a possible 100.

| | |
|---|---|
| Acceptable cost | 25 points |
| Uniqueness | 20 points |
| Identification as detailed below | 55 points |

Allow identification points for each item you can have imprinted on the giveaway itself. However, if your identification imprinting is only on discardable packaging, cut the points in half.

| | |
|---|---|
| Your photo | 20 points |
| Your name and phone number | 20 points |
| Your company's name and location | 10 points |
| Your slogan | 5 points |

This scoring system is heavily weighted against mass giveaway items on which your advertising message can't be imprinted. It favors imprinted memo pads and newsletters, the two most cost-effective promotions I know. I made a lot of money because I established and maintained identity. Nothing does this as cheaply and reliably as imprinted memo pads and newsletters backing up an active door-knocking program. However, I believe it would be a mistake in most farms to limit giveaways to those two items. Think of them as the foundation of your farm program.

Now let's look at ideas to fill out your 12-month farming program. Additional tips on these promotions are given in Chapter 13.

## Farm Chats Online

I recommended in Chapter 5 on fizzbos that you set up online chats. Create a chat room that you publicize with times and dates when you are available for a chat. This works especially well in the farm. About half way into the getting-to-know-you stage of farming you may want to introduce weekly farm chats. During these chats you can talk about recent sales that you are allowed to discuss. You can give gardening hints. Post community events. Keep everyone in your neighborhood updated on cultural, business, and market activity in your farm. After all, you are trying to establish yourself as the expert. What better way to do it than staging farm chats online? You can cover a lot of territory that way. Notice that in the 12-month almanac the newsletter lead story is the same topic as the online monthly chats. Other topic ideas include, how to stage your home, moving up in the community, local interest rates, and whether it's a buyer's or seller's climate.

## January Through December: Giveaways, Super-Promotions, and Winning Scripts

### January

- *Giveaways.* (one each month)
  - A calendar of local sports and cultural events you've compiled
  - Imprinted memo pads
  - Cookie cutter of house, snowman, dog
- *Winning scripts.* "Hi, Mrs _____. I'm Rosa Guerra with Gallegos and Pak Realty. Here's a little something to start the new year off. I hope you'll— (tell about the unique set of cookie cutters you're going to give them through the year, if this is your plan) —enjoy it. And I hope you'll remember me if you have any questions or needs in real estate."
- *Memo pad message.* "Every month (every other month, every third month) this year I'm planning to run by with a different cookie cutter. Just my way of saying thanks for thinking of me when you think of real estate—Liz."
- *Newsletter lead story or online farm chat topic.* "All Last Year's Sales Prices in This Neighborhood."

Give the average prices broken down for the number of bedrooms frequently found in your farm.

| | | |
|---|---|---|
| 2-bedroom homes | $_____ | average |
| 3-bedroom homes | $_____ | average |
| 4-bedroom homes | $_____ | average |

Also give the high/low range.

- *Newsletter bottom lines.*

  "Knowledge is of two kinds. We know a subject ourselves, or we know where we can find information upon it."

  —Samuel Johnson

  "If real estate is the subject, you know where to find information: Call me."

- *SUPER-promotion.* Stage an Ice-Skating Night. Provide the firewood and hot refreshments, if outdoors, the admission fee, if indoors.

**Farming Technique.** A common mistake is to regard newsletters as being interchangeable with giveaways. "This month I'll just hand them a newsletter," has stalled many a promising farming program. Newsletters are powerful when used to support a strong face-to-face door-knocking and giveaway program. Used alone they will fall flat. Chapter 13 tells how to create a newsletter able to contribute mightily to your rapid takeover of your farm, and shows how you do it with little trouble and at low cost. Just don't expect the printed page to door-knock for you, open the doors, and make the impressions giveaways will. But the newsletter is a broad canvas; paint the picture of your professionalism on it. Giveaways are the free program and newsletters are the commercials; so don't leave the commercials out of the program.

# February

- *Giveaways.*
  - Tax preparation booklet
  - Heart-shaped potholder
  - Cookie cutter of heart, diamond or square, half-moon
- *Winning scripts.* "Hello there, I'm Betty Jones with Sell Fast Realty. Happy Valentine's Day. Here's a little remembrance. I keep current with our local resale housing market, so call me if you have any questions."

- *Memo pad message.* "Hope your Valentine's Day will be a sweet one in every way—your local real estate expert—Betty."
- *Newsletter lead story or online farm chat topic.* "What We Can Expect the Local Resale Housing Market to Do This Year."
- *Newsletter bottom lines.*

"A house is made of walls and beams; a home is built with love and dreams."

—William Arthur Ward

"What is more agreeable than one's home?"

—Cicero

- *SUPER-promotion.* Throw a dance party for your farm. Rent a local disco or a hall.

**Farming Technique.** Only a few hours each week are really effective times for farming. You'll want to make the most of those vital hours. You'll want to concentrate on people, not fumble with farming materials. Several days before you're planning to farm, take a moment to practice how you'll handle your handouts from door to door. Remember, as you go, you'll want to make notes about the people you talk to. If your materials will be awkward to handle loose, drop them in light plastic bags. Fold the end of the bags around rubber bands, and staple them closed. Then all you have to do is carry a few of the filled plastic bags and hand one to each homeowner as you plant your verbal seeds with them. No fuss. You're free to talk, listen, learn, and make notes.

The rubber band allows you to hang the bag on the doorknobs of no-answers. The memo pad messages are for the no-answers.

- *Good idea.* Hand-copy the current memo pad message on 50 or more pads ahead of time, and use them only on no-answers.
- *Better idea.* Write the message on two sheets of your pad, paste them down side by side, and make 150 copies. When you cut these sheets in half, you'll have 300 messages—enough for your whole farm. (I recommend memo pads half the size of a regular 8 ½ × 11-inch typewriter sheet.) Chuck one of these messages in every one of your plastic bags, along with your giveaway, imprinted memo pad, and newsletter. Then give the same thing to homeowners who answer as you hang on the knobs of no-answers. Keep it simple.

## March

- *Giveaways.*
  - Kites for the kids

- - Fuzzy green shamrock for lapel
  - Imprinted shoe horn
  - Cookie cutter of shamrock, egg, cat
- *Winning scripts.* "I'm Sue Chalmers of Selzip Realty, your local real estate expert. I hope the kiddies, and even Mom and Dad, enjoy flying our special family kite. Have a good month and thanks for your time."
- *Memo pad message.* "Hope you have the luck of the Irish this month. Please keep this pad handy for writing reminders, and please remember your local real estate expert—Sue."
- *Newsletter lead story or online farm chat topic.* "What Every Homeowner Should Know Before Selling a Home." Give tips on setting the stage.
- *Newsletter bottom lines.*

  "A verbal contract isn't worth the paper it's written on."

  —Sam Goldwyn

  "What this world needs most today is happy homes. Not rich homes. Not frustrated homes. Not empty homes."

  —Elsie Landon Buck

- *SUPER-promotion.* Rent a local bowling alley for a few hours and invite the farm to a night of bowling on you. Give out trophies for high score, low score, and most balls in the alley.

**Farming Technique.** The purpose of super-promotions is to make a heavy personal impact on your farm, so the more personal you make the super-promotions, the greater the success you'll have with them. Never leave your invitation on the door knob. Tell the people about it face-to-face. Few people will be interested in all your events. It's why you do something different every time.

# April

- *Giveaways.*
  - Rain hats (these were super successful for me)
  - Car litter bag with spring motif
  - Forget-me-not flower seeds (or any seeds) for Mom
  - Cookie cutter of umbrella, boat or banana, arrow
- *Winning scripts.* "Good morning. I'm Kathy Dibrell of Green Pretty Valley Real Estate. I wanted to stop by with this rain hat—maybe it'll come in handy to keep you dry. Have a great month, and I enjoyed talking with you. Don't forget—I'm here to serve all your real estate needs."

- *Memo pad message.* "Isn't spring great? Hope you get to enjoy the fresh outdoors when the sun is out. Real estate sales are soaring this spring. Remember me, your local area expert—Kathy."
- *Newsletter lead story or online farm chat topic.* "Thinking of Selling? There's No Better Time of Year Than Summer."
- *Newsletter bottom lines.*

"April prepares her green traffic light and the world thinks Go."

—Christopher Morley

- *SUPER-promotion.* Stage an Easter Egg hunt at the local park or country club.

**Farming Technique.** Complete your property catalog (see previous chapter) this month by asking questions as you work your way through the farm. Explain how you're compiling the catalog to better serve the community.

## May

- *Giveaways.*
  - Mother's Day marigold plants
  - Pencils imprinted with your name, phone, and slogan
  - Cookie cutter of Mom (figure with skirt), hand, triangle
- *Winning scripts.* "Hi. I'm Helen Early of Selzip Reality. Here's a little remembrance for the holiday. Thanks for your time, and if you have any questions about real estate, I'm your local expert."
- *Memo pad message.* "Happy Mother's Day—and think of me if you need any real estate service—Helen."
- *Newsletter lead story or online farm chat topic.* Write a profile of a good neighbor—a feature story about someone who lives in your farm and has contributed outstanding service to the community.
- *Newsletter bottom lines.*

"A smile increases your face value."

—Old Mohican adage

"May, with alle they floures and thy grene,
Welcome be thou, faire, fresshe May."

—Chaucer

- *SUPER-promotion.* Treat your farm to a night of baseball. Rent a bus and take over a section of the ballpark.

**Farming Technique.** Hand out plants or seeds the Friday or Saturday before Mother's Day. I advise against farming on that day.

# June

- *Giveaways.*
  - Barbecue apron for Dad
  - Father's Day soft drink or beer can holders
  - Cookie cutter of Dad figure, auto, hexagon
- *Winning scripts.* "Hi there, Mrs. _____. I'm Jim Andrews with Partners Realty. Here's a special holder for Dad for Father's Day. Enjoy it, and have a Happy Father's Day, and I hope you'll remember me any time you're thinking about real estate."
- *Memo pad message.* "Here's a special holder for Dad for Father's Day. If you need more room this summer, give me a ring and let's talk about it. Your old real estate buddy, Jim."
- *Newsletter lead story or online farm chat topic.* "Our Local Athletes." (Be sure to mention every student in your farm who goes out for sports.)
- *Newsletter bottom lines.*

  "However small it is on the surface, it's four thousand miles deep, and that is a very handsome property."

  —C. D. Warner

- *SUPER-promotion.* Get the kids started off right on summer vacation by sending an ice-cream truck around handing out free goodies. Be sure you're standing on the running board.

**Farming Technique.** Hand out can holders or something the Friday and Saturday before Father's Day. I advise against farming on Father's Day.

# July

- *Giveaways.*
  - Safety tips booklet
  - Car game for kids
  - Imprinted back scratcher
  - Cookie cutter of flag, sunburst, star
- *Winning scripts.* "Hi. Mrs. _____. I'm Karen Shepherd with Green Pretty Valley Real Estate. I specialize in this area, so if there's any real estate information you'd like, I hope you'll think of me. Here's a _____ and thanks for chatting with me."

- *Memo pad message.* "Important enclosure—a safety tips booklet to hang in the kitchen. Enjoy the summer and call me for help on real estate problems—Karen."
- *Newsletter lead story or online farm chat topic.* "Homes Are Selling Faster (Slower) This Year Than Last. Why?" Then tell them why.
- "I'm an expert on real estate throughout Green Pretty Valley, but I specialize in the Summit neighborhood's fine homes. In Summit, 21 homes were sold during the first half of this year, up from only 17 in the same period last year. This is almost a 24 percent increase. Why did it happen, and where will this selling surge take us?"
- *Newsletter bottom lines.*

  "The house of everyone is to him as his castle and fortress, as well for his defense as for his repose."

  —Sir Edward Coke, 1619

- *SUPER-promotion.* Watermelon feast for the kids. Stage it at a local park. (Get permission well in advance.) Give invitations out one week before the event and specify when the watermelon truck will get there. Be sure to emphasize it's a "First-come, first-served event. Come late and you may miss out." Line up lots of mothers to help control the kids. Have plenty of plastic trash bags, napkins, plastic forks, etc. Think through the cleanup and disposal problem. Some trash disposal companies will deliver a small bin to a site and remove it the next day for a nominal charge. Events like this can be terrific if thoroughly planned and carefully executed. Arrange for someone in your office to cover for you during the event as though you were on vacation. You can't work with a last-minute buyer then, no matter what. Schedule this for mid-morning, not afternoon. Kids get impatient. And have a little something extra to give each of them when it's over, so you can send them home happy. Balloons with your imprint on them are great for this.

**Farming Technique.** Wear your name, not your nametag. A T-shirt with your first name or nickname blazoned on it is a terrific farming tool. People will call you by name as you hand them a giveaway—and they'll be far more likely to remember you.

# August

- *Giveaways.*
  - Coloring books for kids

- • Car games for kids
- • Cookie cutter of girl child, boy child, circle
- *Winning scripts.* "Hi. I'm Jeanne Cushing of Red Carpet Realty. If you'd like more information about any aspect of real estate, please call me."
- *Memo pad message.* "Here's something to keep the youngsters busy in the car. Have a nice summer—Jeanne"
- *Newsletter lead story or online farm chat topic.* "Ideas for Inexpensive Travel." Go to a local travel agency and offer them free publicity in return for some tips. You might acquire a good bird dog or two this way.
- *SUPER-promotion.* Get together with some other agents, rent a local cinema for a morning, and put on a free movie for the children in all your farms. You'll be surprised how small the shared cost will be. Arrangements should be started at least six months in advance. Print invitations. Use them as a farm handout.

**Farming Technique.** This is another good month to emphasize kids. Many mothers find summers especially difficult. You can win their gratitude by providing some diversion for the "There's nothing to do around here" element at their house.

## September

- *Giveaways.*
  - • Fall events calendar
  - • Fall car litter bag
  - • Cookie cutter of apple, mushroom, horse
- *Winning scripts.* "Hi, Mrs. _____. I'm Janis Van Dorn with Sell High Realty. Were Stevie and Susan glad to get back in school?" (Add a real estate reminder.) "Enjoy the fall season, and thanks for being so nice when I drop by."
- *Memo pad message.* "With all the things to remember in September, I thought an extra pad would be handy. Your local real estate expert, Janis."
- *Newsletter lead story or online farm chat topic.* "Back to School Tips for Our Neighborhood."

  Call or visit your local store managers and list their specials and back-to-school sales. Include what's selling best this year. Then write your second story around the local housing market's performance over the summer just ended, and conclude with a prediction about what will happen to housing during the balance of the year.

- *Newsletter bottom lines.*

"Eden is that old-fashioned House we dwell in every day without suspecting our abode until we drive away."

—Emily Dickinson

- *SUPER-promotion.* Stage a moonlight hayride for the romantics in your farm. Your local riding stable may be able to handle this for you, or you may need to bus your people out into the country.

**Farming Technique.** Avoid farming the last few days before school starts. You'll find the mothers will be much more relaxed and talkative the day after school begins.

## October

- *Giveaways.*
  - Trick-or-treat bags
  - Stick-on spook decal to be ironed onto a T-shirt
  - Halloween candy
  - Cookie cutter of pumpkin, teepee, face (profile)
- *Winning scripts.* (Wearing a costume). "Hi, don't be scared—it's really me, Meredith Osborn with Selzip Realty. I hope this _____ will make Halloween a bit more fun. I never did crazy things like this before I became a real estate expert . . . but it's a lot of fun."
- *Memo pad message.* "Happy goblins! Call me if you have any questions for your local real estate expert—Meredith."
- *Newsletter lead story or online farm chat topic.* "Turkey Drawing Next Month at the Gordon's House."
- *Newsletter bottom lines.*

"I wouldn't join any club that would have me for a member."

—Groucho Marx

- *SUPER-promotion.* Hire a truck and pass out pumpkins a few days before Halloween.

**Farming Technique.** Wear a funny nose, witch's hat, or half-mask as you pass out the trick-or-treat bags or pumpkins.

## November

- *Giveaways.*
  - Local and neighborhood directory

Compile it yourself. Include all the babysitters and yard-chore boys you can find in your farm, plus any other neighborhood services. Include emergency phone numbers, a list of nearby doctors and dentists, shoe and TV repairmen, and so on. (Keep your imprint small, but readable.)
- Imprinted ball point pens
- Cookie cutter of turkey, cornucopia, cow
- *Winning scripts.* Talk about your lumineria promotion next month. Introduce yourself and remind them you're the local real estate expert.
- *Memo pad message.* "Happy Thanksgiving to you and yours. When I count my blessings I think of the people I represent in this neighborhood"—Linda Malloy with Tarbell Realtors.
- *Newsletter lead story or online farm chat topic.* "Join with Your Neighbors to Create a Special Wonder This Year at Christmas. It's Free and It's Fun!"

   "A local real estate agent (me, of course—I'm the local real estate expert who really cares about this neighborhood) is donating the materials for lumineria. Every homeowner who wants to join in producing this charming effect during Christmas week will be provided with three of these simple lamps. In Mexico, villages glow at Christmas with a special soft loveliness only lumineria can bring. Let's do it here! It's free, it's lots of fun, and it takes less than five minutes each night to set them out. I'd love to tell you about it. Just give me a call any time, or I'll see you next month.

   "I hope you'll be heralding Christmas week this year in this gentle, heartwarming way."
- *Newsletter bottom lines.*

"My house, my house, though thou art small, thou art to me the Escorial."

—George Herbert, 1651

- *SUPER-promotion.* Give away a free Thanksgiving turkey.

**Farming Technique.** Hold your drawing at someone's house in the farm. This requires developing a farm friend who'll stage this event for you. Women agents can have their friend put on a 10 A.M. coffee klatch with prizes for the best cookies made with your cutters. (Appoint a committee to do the judging—don't make the decision yourself.) Also have several door prizes building up to the turkey drawing. Stick around for the clean-up, and give your hostess a nice gift. Men agents can have their wives handle this, and simply be present at the drawing, or schedule the event for the weekend when their hostess's husband is home.

## December

- *Giveaways.*
  - Holly trees
  - A unique Christmas tree decoration ordered in quantity, perhaps in January for the following Christmas at overstock prices.
  - Cookie cutter of tree, Santa, bell
- *Winning scripts.* "Hi, Mr. and Mrs. _____ with Sell Fast. Plant this holly tree and as it grows let it remind you of the way your property is growing in value, and of me, your local real estate expert. Have a wonderful season. And thanks for your time."
- *Memo pad message.* "You're probably out Christmas shopping but I wanted to stop by and leave my holiday greetings. I'm hoping you'll enjoy using this cookie cutter. Thanks for all your courtesy toward me this year—Danny."
- *Newsletter lead story or online farm chat topic.* You may prefer to send a hand-addressed "Am I lucky" letter like the one in Chapter 6 instead of your usual newsletter. Or you can summarize the year's events in finance and real estate as your lead story.
- *Newsletter bottom lines.*

  "And I am praying God on high,
  And I am praying
  Him night and day.
  For a little house—a house of my own—
  Out of the wind's and the rain's way."

  —Padraic Colum

- *Christmas cards.* Yours will get lost in the deluge of cards descending on every home every year, except where you know the people quite well. Omit sending them to most of your farm. You can save this money and time, and no one will notice.
- *SUPER-promotion.* Light up your entire farm with lumineria.

  For about the cost of nice Christmas cards, you can create a very striking effect in your farm during the week prior to Christmas. Expect to spend some extra time encouraging the project along. The plus is, you'll be working with your farm people to enhance the quality of their lives, and you'll find the lumineria project reflects wonderfully well on you and your career. Be sure to call your local paper and tell them about it when your streets are glowing softly.

The materials are simple: small candles, sand, and small white paper bags. The homeowners put the bags on their curb in the evening with the sand inside to hold both the bag and the lighted candle upright. Get sand by the sack at your local building supply, arrange to buy bags and candles wholesale, and save lots of money. You'll find suppliers in the phone book.

**Farming Technique.** Talk this project up in the daytime, and get people's permission to bring the lumineria at dusk so they can be lighted and put out on curbs immediately. Once you get this project started, it will grow on its own. Acquire the materials well in advance, and start actively promoting the idea early in December. Placing rows of lumineria at a few key locations, where people driving in and out can see them, will give the idea a big boost.

Obviously this should not be done in high fire-risk areas, or where rain or high winds are likely. Consult your local fire department first.

# CHAPTER 8

# Global Prospecting

The World Is Your Oyster ● Dealing with the Fears ● Using Non-pushy Expressions ● Piddle the Prime at Your Peril ● Know Your Turf ● Prospecting by Foot ● Prospecting by Phone ● Phone Technique ● Winning Scripts ● Prospecting from Open House ● Cold Canvassing by Foot or Phone

## The World Is Your Oyster

Isn't it great that the electronic age allows us to prospect across the globe in seconds? With the click of the Send icon on a computer or a quick call on a cell phone, we can speak directly to clients from the United States to London without any third-party interruption. You know their cell phone numbers and they know your cell phone number. There is no excuse for poor follow-up in this high-speed age of communication. Most obstacles don't center around outside forces.

## Dealing with the Fears

My finger pushes the door chimes button. It's like pushing a fire alarm when you're ten years old and there's no fire and you're scared you can't run away fast enough. Only now I can't run. So I just stand there with my adrenaline-charged-blood pounding.

What can I say?

"I'm Sally Tompkins, and if you wanna move quick, I'll be glad to help you?" What a terrible thing to say. She'll step on my corns.

What makes me different from the two dozen other agents who've rung this doorbell before? Oh rats, I woke up her baby. Now I can hear her coming. She even walks like she's mad. I never realized footsteps could sound mad.

"What do *you* want?"

"Can I use your phone? I'm so scared I need to call my shrink."

Wouldn't it throw her? Somehow I have to throw her off the defensive. Somehow I have to break through what separates her *she* from my *me*. Somehow I have to get her shoes off so I can put them on.

I know about the fears of prospecting. I remember them well. In 1972, when I started in the business, the entire Board of REALTORS® met in one spot for the weekly caravan. We'd follow each other around and visit maybe 15 houses.

I was pregnant again—very much so when I went on my first caravan. As I got in the car with two veterans of the business, these ladies gave me the evil eye. One said, "Just go home and have your baby." She laughed at me.

"You don't have that much to lose in the next three months. Do you really think you have to do this?"

I felt terrible. I did go home. I cried and said, "I quit." Then, somehow, I pulled myself together and got back in there. No matter what the evil-eyed lady said, or anyone else thought, I knew I had plenty to lose by giving up three months: all the contacts I could make, all the knowledge and experience I could acquire, and all the much-needed fees I hoped to earn. I didn't need her disapproval. I already had four beautiful reasons not to start work, and another on the way. But every today gives us reasons to put off paying the price of success, and every tomorrow brings more reasons for waiting—if we're looking for them. There are lots of rationalizations for not prospecting:

"It's already been overdone."

"It doesn't have to be done."

"It isn't worth doing."

"It just isn't done anymore."

Instead of looking at those reasons, let's look for reasons why we *can* start, and start *now*, to pay the price of success. All these reasons are not true.

Many of the most successful agents are constant door knockers. Prospecting is a proven method. It works. The only things stopping us are our fears. Yes, I've been stopped. I've gone home, beaten in heart and soul. I've tossed and turned through the night, and healed my wounds with tears. Then, after the healing, I went back to knocking on strange doors and phoning people I'd never met. I used every crutch I could find to boost my spirits—as long as those crutches didn't take up too much time, or stop me from working. The first 18 months of my real estate career, all my business came from prospecting and for-sale-by-owners. It's how it all started.

Prospecting is part of the dues in this business, part of the price you pay for success. Do it right, do it heavy, do it fast, and there'll come a time when you won't have time for it anymore. Long before it happens, you will have banked lots of success in its most tangible form.

Looking back, I know I was lucky; circumstances forced me to go out and find business. At the time, I didn't feel so lucky. I had no floor time because of my pregnancy. I had to be my own one-woman advertising agency. The most logical place for me to start was door-to-door canvassing. The very first time I went door-knocking, it rained. My first thought was, "I've got brains enough to come in out of the rain. Forget about door-knocking, put a log in the fireplace at home, and read a good book about selling real estate."

Fortunately, I had some freebie rain hats, and I realized there couldn't be a better time to give them out. So off I went to canvass in the rain, a raincoat wrapped around my big stomach.

I told the wives who answered my knock, "If you want to go out today, you might want to use this rain hat I brought you. Compliments of Danny Kennedy." It made an impression. There I was, dripping, a look of total honesty on my face, all eagerness to begin my new career. Several of the women asked me in for a cup of hot tea. Then they'd show me their new wallpaper and, pretty soon, they'd be saying, "Let me think. Do I know anyone around here who wants to sell? My neighbor next door may get a transfer." I would ask for the neighbor's name, and if I could mention to the neighbor how I found out they might move. It always seemed to help if I could say, "Marge sent me." I think people subconsciously approved of me because so-and-so approved of me. So much business came out of those rainy days I was sorry to see our dry summer come. By the end of the first summer, I'd covered about 700 homes.

I really got to know the people. I wrote letters to them every month. In these letters I would give little tips about their property. If invited out to give an evaluation, I always put a handwritten thank-you note in the mail the next day. I felt more comfortable with personal stationery than company letterhead. The personal touch worked well for me.

I was trying to get across how much I *cared,* and if they listed with me, they'd get something different. I didn't want to be the ordinary real estate agent. I wanted to be the person they could depend on, the person who cared. I've always felt the difference in this world involves just one thing—*caring.* Either you do or you don't. And I cared.

There's always a reason not to go canvassing. It's raining, it's too hot, too cold, too windy, too early, too late. I've heard all the little voices busily talking inside every head thinking about going prospecting.

"I hate it. And I slept lousy last night. I wouldn't be any good out there today anyway."

"People are getting sick of me."

"All I'll get out of this today is sore feet."

"I think I'm catching a cold. I better take it easy."

With a new baby at home, plus four more little ones, if I couldn't think of an excuse, they'd provide me with one. I was always struggling and fighting inside to make myself get out there. Some people think I was immune to all these canvass diseases. But the truth is, I suffered with all of them more than most agents do because, every Friday afternoon and Saturday morning for more than three years, I pounded the pavement and knocked on doors. That works out to be about a full year of canvassing.

Slowly it gets easier. The fears fade away. There comes a time when you've ducked every punch too many times to be taken by surprise. You can handle it. But you don't love it. Never, ever, did I spring out of bed on a Saturday morning, quivering with joy because I could go canvassing. It's hard work, but it pays extraordinarily well when done right. And there are moments of great satisfaction in it too.

# Using Nonpushy Expressions

"Would you be offended if I _____?" Many heavy prospectors use this expression a lot. Put it in your quiver and it'll shoot down a lot of birds for you too.

When you ask permission to give people something, to meet them, or just to talk to them, it softens the blow. You have no hold on people in the prospecting situation, and you won't be able to work with any but the most submissive types unless you come on easy. You're calling them at their home to say that they may need you. But their phone works both ways—if they'd felt the need to talk to an agent right then, they'd have called one. So show lots of deference when you disturb private people by dialing their number or knocking on their door. Convey this message to them by your manner, "Mr. or Mrs. Homeowner, you're in control here, I'm not pushing you." Better to exaggerate your deference than to come on too strong in cold calling or door-to-door canvassing.

- "Thanks for talking to me."
- "I hope I haven't interrupted you."
- "I hope I haven't offended you."

Their defenses start tumbling down when they realize those defenses aren't necessary because you're not a pushy person. Then they're open to the idea you're someone who has something to offer, someone who won't press them at an inconvenient time. Combine assertiveness with softness in such a way as to assert yourself without making people feel pushed. This means you're always ready to back off and always ready to try them again at another time. There are more numbers in the phone book than you'll ever call. If rejection makes your gorge rise, if you take it as a challenge you must beat down, canvassing will give you a rough ride to nowhere.

- "Would you mind if—"
- "Could I have the pleasure of—"

Phrases like these enable us to softly and assertively sell our product.

## Piddle the Prime at Your Peril

There are only a few optimal prospecting hours each week, and they go quickly. Don't piddle them away. Keep in touch with old clients at other times. Use your prime time for drumming up new clients. Organize beforehand to get the maximum performance from those golden hours. Chapter 24 has two handy items for prospecting: a checklist of items to have at your elbow when you're calling, and the Fast Fact Grabber form (available on the accompanying CD).

Whether you use an electronic entry pad, the Fast Fact Grabber form, or a plain notepad, start jotting down facts right away. Don't wait until you strike pay dirt—you'll lose many important details able to cement your relationship with prospects who are slow to reveal an active interest in buying or selling soon. Action-imminent people are cagey. They're afraid they'll be knee deep in fee-hungry agents if they let one of them know they're about to move. So don't pounce if you sniff action. Accumulate facts, build rapport, and work on the prospect slowly.

Gather and record facts on every call and you'll soon be doing it automatically and effortlessly. Unless you acquire this habit quickly, you'll find yourself having the following expensive frustration. After talking intently with homeowners for a long time, you finally flip their switch to *on*. Then—because you've forgotten things they've already told you—you have to ask them to repeat some key details. This flips their switch to *off*, and your listing is lost.

Immediately after completing each call, if the situation is worth pursuing, schedule a specific time to call the person back. The Fast Fact Grabber has space on the back for this purpose. Do it as soon as you hang up the phone.

You never know when you'll find the right key to their door. After a rocky conversation, I've often said, "Thanks for talking to me." As I start to hang up, the prospect says, "Wait a minute." And then he or she spills it. They're sweating out an unwanted transfer, and so on. Remember, some people warm up slowly. Accept this as being okay. Every fee has a different price tag connected to it.

Skim over the notes you keep, and write out plainly any scribbles you won't be able to decipher when your notes get cold. Complete all your notes and plans for each call right then, so you won't confuse one call with another, and then quickly get on with your next call.

# Know Your Turf

News on your local scene gives you ammunition to fire when prospecting. Be constantly on the lookout for such news. You need reasons to call people repeatedly, and new information about the community provides you with something both useful and cost-free to give to the homeowner. Observe everything you can. Be active and visible. Go to your local college's library and see what services they offer the adult nonstudent. Make appearances at public events of all kinds. Your local papers are an excellent source for community events, especially the local throwaway newspapers.

Be a fountain of information about your area. Talk to everyone you can (always being alert for opportunities to tell them you're a knowledgeable agent, and to give them your card, memo pad, or flyer packet).

Know what's going on in your area 24 hours a day. Whether or not you're interested, some of your clients will want to know about the night life. So stay informed, or you will limit your clientele.

# Prospecting by Foot

## Look Before You Knock

Train yourself to be alert as you walk up to every door. Search for a sign reading, "Don't ring bell, baby sleeping," or "Daysleeper, don't disturb before 1 P.M." Notice the things such as toys left about, new landscaping improvements, and the property's condition. Don't eavesdrop, but allow sounds to reach your ears of an argument going on inside, a child being disciplined, or any other indication that another time would be better for a farming contact. Avoid blundering into emotional situations. Try to get out of there quickly whenever your timing isn't good.

To avoid letting this become an excuse not to make calls, set a quota for actual contacts, and keep at it until you've actually talked to your quota of active occupants. Push your antennae out when you first head for a particular house, and start getting yourself in tune with those people. Have a dozen different opening lines so overlearned you don't have to give a thought to yourself. Put all your attention on the house you're going to.

Perhaps there's a fountain there, abundant flowers, or something the homeowners have done to make the front of their house special. When they open the door, comment on it, "I really like your waterfall."

"My husband put it in. It took him a month."

It's simple, but it's a rapport builder.

## Knock, Don't Ring

Strangers and bill collectors ring doorbells, friends knock. Be a friend. Knock, step back, and turn your body and face to the side. If you don't look like you're going to leap on them the instant they open the door, you're more likely to pass the peephole inspection.

Chapters 6 and 7 have many tips and expressions for door-to-door canvassing. Most of the telephone phrases and winning scripts in this chapter work beautifully on door-to-door situations.

## Prospecting by Phone

Tony Dulvoyse sits down to prospect. We don't hear anything for half an hour except paper rattling and a chair creaking. Then Tony dials. The conversation is a bummer; it lasts only 27 seconds. Tony gets a cup of coffee and talks for 19 minutes with another agent. They both agree the market is lousy. Tony returns to his desk and calls another name in the reverse directory. No answer. Encouraged, Tony immediately dials the next name. He reaches an ex-sailor who immediately switches the conversation to the Second World War, and relates his adventures on the *Yorktown* during the Battle of Midway. Half an hour later, with the battle still in doubt, the ex-sailor suddenly breaks off the conversation to answer the doorbell. Tony spends the next 15 minutes reconsidering the whole idea of phone prospecting. He finally decides to give it another try—next week sometime.

Avoid this failure with your phone technique, by setting quotas, and using technology to be more efficient.

## Cell Phonology

All the techniques that pertain to normal phones pertain to cell phones. But the beauty of the cell phone is you can make your prospecting calls from places other than your desk. Make calls right after your run, while resting in the park, waiting at the doctor's office, or in an airplane before the door closes. There is no end to the list of places to call from— a remote island during vacation. And nobody has to know where you are. You now find more time in a given day to make your calls because you are not stuck to a desk.

If someone gives you his or her cell number, be sure you do not abuse it. As much as e-mail and voice mail are noninvasive, cell phones are extremely invasive. It's okay to call someone from your cell phone, but be careful about calling another cell phone without permission. Make sure the reasons are solid and then you will not lose the respect of the prospect. The prospect knows that if you call him on his cell it must be important. That's a good thing.

Watch out! Cell phone bills can be horrendous. Get yourself a good deal, with lots of free minutes. And don't always use the cell phone. The phone methods in this chapter are timeless, so don't just rely on new technology to prospect. Use the older, cheaper ways too. It all works. Just do it!!!

## Short Text Messaging

It was popular in Europe first. Mobile phones containing short text messaging. In Britain, for example, Short Message Service has been used to promote everything from Cadbury chocolates to the latest films. The marketing technique involves sweepstakes or electronic coupons as an enticement to get folks to the movies or a store.

A message can pop up on someone's phone without interrupting them. The recipient reads the message and decides to delete it or respond. You could send, "This is a shot in the dark, but if you are interested in moving, there is an extremely well priced property in the Hancock Park area. A rare find."

Beware of wireless spam with any of these methods. It is important to target the right people for these messages. Use the same policy as you would follow in cold calling.

Short text messaging can be extremely valuable in the area of follow up. So many times you do not want a long conversation with a prospect or client. You just want to pass along information and then let the person digest it. So go ahead and use the latest and greatest electronic marketing tools. But follow the principles set out in this chapter with any tool you use.

## Psych Up, Not Down

Organize to prospect by equipping your desk with headphones and a jack so both hands are free while you make calls. Gather the items you'll need into a kit before you sit down to prospect. Have several opening lines in your mind. Write down a goal for the number of calls you want to complete. Schedule a definite starting and stopping time. The purpose in all this is psyching *up*. Throwing yourself into an activity you *know* you're unprepared for is psyching *down,* which means a little voice in the back of your head is crying, "You'll be sorry. You don't know what you're doing; this will be terrible." Shut the pesky little voice up the only way you can—*by preparing*. Don't set a staggering goal for your first session—it sets you up to lose.

Set yourself up to win. Schedule ten calls. During each call, key the facts you gather into your computer or scribble them on a piece of paper. Then review them right after the call and put them in good order. Or eliminate the rewrite by using the Fast Fact Grabber form while you're on the phone. Be sure to write down any effective phrase you used. Take the time to rejoice over any small victory you win, and further psych yourself up.

When you bungle a call (we all do now and then), look on it as a small win too. "I learned something I'll never say again." Complete ten calls and take a short break. Be alone. Walk around the block. Psych yourself up again. You've finished ten prospecting calls in one session, that's more than most people with real estate licenses will make during their entire real estate careers. Congratulate yourself! Already you're a winner—and you're on the road to great success.

Now think about scheduling another phone session. What about making another ten calls, and then taking another short break? How about making this your regular prospecting program? Ten calls. Then get out of the office and stretch your legs. Let your mind go blank for a few moments. After your refresher, you're ready to take a strain again.

## Bang 'em Out (1)

I've watched successful prospectors work the phones, and I've seen dismal failures work the phones. Here's the main difference: Successful prospectors talk longer and they make more calls per hour. How can they do it? Simple. **They piddle away far less time between calls.**

## Bang 'em Out (2)

Prospecting is a numbers game. You can't be successful at it unless you make a large number of calls. Think in terms of hearing *no* a hundred times to get one good, solid *yes.* (Keep a tally; you'll do better.) You can't make a lot of calls unless you use your time wisely. This means organizing all the little details, staying at it, and minimizing the time between calls.

## Bang 'em Out (3)

One hundred completed prospecting calls will always get you one immediate appointment to show property or a visit to a house going on the market soon. By averaging one call every 72 seconds—*no* answers don't take long—you can line up a firm appointment in two hours. Take an extra hour or two while making those calls so you can pursue all the leads you have unearthed, and after three or four hours you'll have five or ten possible clients to follow up with in the future.

To organize your phone prospecting farm, file a 3 × 5 card on each person under the date you're to call them again. All you need is one set of 1 to 31 date-file guides for the current month, and one set of January–December monthly file guides. If you don't use a 3 × 5 card system or a computer to keep track of details, log each call on a Fast Fact Grabber and file them alphabetically in a three-ring binder. Remember, voice mail, e-mail, and text messaging all count as bona fide calls.

# Phone Technique

## The Fee Winner

The fee winner consistently exhibits the following skills:

- Breaks off negative conversations quickly, courteously, and firmly
- Builds rapport on small wins with promising prospects
- Takes one step at a time

- Progresses steadily toward obtaining an appointment
- Loses little time between calls
- Makes notes to keep facts straight during each call, and to make future call-backs more effective
- Speaks clearly
- Uses common words and standard English to communicate with, and inform, prospects
- Talks like a friend
- Is relaxed and unhurried during prospecting calls
- Wants results now, but also realizes many situations can't be developed into active business now. Next month will arrive right on schedule, and business will be needed then—today's prospect is tomorrow's hot buyer or seller.
- Works efficiently on future business without jeopardizing present business
- Calls prospects back at the precise time they suggest
- Is well organized for prospecting

## The Fee Loser

The fee loser falls into the following bad habits:

- Gets entangled in negative conversations. When finally off the phone, insists on telling the entire office what an idiot the other person was.
- Doesn't know how to build rapport. Makes one great leap for the appointment, finds the chasm too wide—yeeeeoooow! Splat.
- Is very busy doing nothing around the office between calls
- Depends on memory. Forgets vital details. Doesn't use a Fast Fact Grabber.
- Mumbles
- Uses real estate jargon, slang, and obscure references to impress prospects, but succeeds only in confusing and annoying them
- Pushes like a salesperson
- Hassles prospects with an impatient manner
- Wants results *now*. Has no interest in, or capability of dealing with, future call-backs able to produce business later.
- Has never bothered to get organized for efficient prospecting and follow-up

## Vocal Variety, Clarity, and Speed

Can a discouraged-sounding voice encourage anyone to become your client? Think about it. What your voice says to people goes far beyond the meaning contained in the words you speak. A second line of communication, more powerful than the words spoken, is set up by your voice. This second line is the variety and color of your tones, the clarity with which you pronounce your language's sounds, and the speed at which you talk.

Variety, clarity, and speed always reach the emotions of your listeners; your words sometimes reach only their ears. If you tell a prospect how knowledgeable, enthusiastic, and capable you are in a flat, monotonous, discouraged tone, with words carelessly slurred together and spoken with tiresome slowness, your listener hears two conflicting witnesses. The first witness is your words, and your listener knows you direct them to further your own purposes. The second witness is the variety, clarity, and speed of your words. If these qualities testify against your words, your listener senses they've escaped your control, and for this reason must be believed. Your words are found guilty of perjury, and you are sentenced to oblivion as far as this person is concerned.

Within the words, and the other sounds you make, are other witnesses who can also swear against you. Too many "uh's," too many interminable sentences, too much slang and jargon (or too little, if you're talking to a trendy type), irritating repetition, too many vague terms—all these can testify. All these unprejudiced messages are more readily believed than your words.

Pull your act together. Convert all the witnesses in your voice to your cause. Set your portable cassette tape recorder by your phone when you prospect. For faster auditing of your phone mannerisms, record only your end of the conversation. Record when you talk, press the Pause button when the prospect talks.

Listen to the cassette and you'll discover improvements you can make in your prospecting techniques. Practice your improvements. Record your calls and play them back. Get together with another enthusiastic and upwardly mobile agent to critique each other's taped performances on actual prospecting calls.

## The Best Times to Prospect

The best times to prospect depend on local laws and customs, climate, and season. The following prime and no-no times are valid in many areas. Determine which hours are best and which are to be avoided in your area by inquiry, and by checking the results of your effort in the field.

**Prime Time.** Here are my best phone prospecting times, from least effective to most effective. If your available time is not close to the best times here, no problem. Making calls in the electronic age with e-mail, voice messages, text messaging, and cell phones, makes any time a good time to call. But even with the technology tools, I still like the following schedule:

- 10 A.M. to noon, weekdays
- 3 P.M. to 4:30 P.M. weekdays
- 7 P.M. to 8:30 P.M. weekdays
- Noon to 5 P.M. Saturdays
- 3 P.M. to 6 P.M. Sundays
- 3 P.M. to 6 P.M. Fridays (Everyone's in a good mood.)

The two best phone prospecting times are also the best times for open houses. Why not do both? See *20/20/20, Go Like 60 Goal Plan* in the next chapter.

**E-mail Time.** Anytime is e-mail time. The most noninvasive way (along with text messaging) to connect is on the Internet. This is the advantage of computer communication. Use photos whenever appropriate because it can drastically improve your capture ratios with the right prospect.

**No-No Times.** Never prospect, either by foot or phone at the following times:

- Before 9 A.M. on weekdays
- Before noon on weekends, unless you see unmistakable signs of wide-awake adult activity as you walk by
- Between 5 P.M. and 7 P.M. any evening, because people are usually eating dinner then, and interruptions irritate them
- After 8:30 P.M. For many people, this is getting late to hear from strangers, and there are lots of early-to-bed, early-to-rise folks around
- Whenever there's a major sports event on TV
- And, of course, never prospect on religious and national or local holidays

## Use the Crisscross Directory

If your office has a crisscross (by-street) directory, you have access to an invaluable prospecting tool. When I used to prospect, I called any names I recognized first. This builds confidence. Calling people I know slightly, or who are friends of someone I know, usually gives me something to work into later conversations with the people I don't know at all. By doing this, I'm going to hit a friendly conversation or two. Those wins will boost my morale, and they'll encourage me to call the strangers on the page.

For example, in the crisscross, I see the name *Dabney* on the street I'm calling. I don't know the Dabneys personally, but I do know Mary Jackson plays tennis with Mrs. Dabney.

So, when she answers my call, I say, "Hi, Mrs. Dabney. I hope I'm not catching you at a bad time." Leave just a short pause here, but don't give her too much time to think up reasons for not talking to you. "I'm Danny Kennedy with Sell Fast Realty, and I think we have a mutual friend."

"Who are you talking about?"

"I understand you play tennis with Mary Jackson."

"Yes, quite often."

"Mary and I have known each other for a couple of years through our church group. I just thought I'd call to mention I'm with Sell Fast Realty, and I keep quite actively involved in real estate sales and listings in your neighborhood—and also with general community affairs. Do you know of anyone who may be interested in making a move in the near future?"

"Off hand, I can't think of anybody."

"Thank you for trying. If someone does come to mind, or even if you folks are considering a move, I hope you'll think about using me to assist you."

"Okay."

Pause. Give her just a brief moment to volunteer something. If she doesn't, say, "Thank you for talking to me, Mrs. Dabney. Goodbye."

You're looking for immediate results when you cold canvass—but never overlook an opportunity to build the pool of people who know of, and respect, your abilities in your chosen field. So I'll send Mrs. Dabney a thank-you note the same day, "Thanks for talking to me on the phone today." I'll slip a reminder of our mutual friend into the note, too, "Please say hello to Mary for me when you see her."

The impression made by a brief phone call is very slight, and Mrs. Dabney wouldn't remember me by it alone. But the phone call followed by a thank-you note (it must be mailed the same day) has a good chance of causing Mrs. Dabney to mention me to Mary. If Mary responds with some favorable comment about me—and I'd never use Mary's name unless I was sure she would—I've made three strong impressions on Mrs. Dabney. By entering her address into my send-newsletter-quarterly file, I'll be able to keep building my reputation in Mrs. Dabney's mind four times a year (with tiny effort on my part because I'm working with flexible and efficient systems).

You can use this discourse when you *don't* have a mutual friend, by beginning your call with, "I keep quite actively involved in—." Now you're making the true cold canvass call. Without encouragement, linger not. Find an appropriate software package with crisscross directory information.

## Stage a Telethon

One of the greatest ways to get shy agents rolling on the telephone—and have a lot of fun at the same time—is to stage a Tuesday Night (or any night) Telethon. Ask your broker for permission to organize one with other agents or, if you're a broker, organize one for your associates.

Pick the hours between 6:30 P.M. and 8:30 P.M. All the salespeople can chip in and buy nutritious snacks. (No eating while phoning, please!) Notify the staff at your regular office meeting, "A week from Tuesday we're having a Telethon." Pass around a sign-up sheet to see how many promise to participate. Then divide up the calling areas by page number in the standard phone book, by street in the crisscross directory, or by farm areas. Award a prize to whomever makes the most appointments (perhaps a facial at the local salon, or a free haircut and style at the barbershop).

Here's what each person needs for the telethon:

- A mirror set by the phone. (Use it to monitor your expression. If your face frowns, your voice will too.)
- A small cassette recorder if you want to tape yourself, or others
- A Fast Fact Grabber form to write down facts about the people called
- Your appointments book or time planner to record appointments
- Your own inventory book and the Multiple Listing Book in case the conversation turns into property inquiries
- Your comparable file. (Be careful not to give them too much information over the phone. Do this in person with a Guidelines to Market Value form. This form is available on the accompanying CD.)

Here are some scripts with powerful phraseology you can use at the telethon.

"Good evening. This is Danny Kennedy with Sell Fast Realty. Are you Mr. Walter Frankel?" Pause. (Be very businesslike and confident. Ask this because crisscross directories are often wrong.)

"Yeah, why?"

"Well, Mr. Frankel, my company is conducting a special telethon tonight to update our records of people living in the community. We wanted to be sure you still live there. Our job is to know things like this, in order to be sure the right people know where to contact a good real estate agent if they need one."

"I don't need one."

"Well, I'm glad to hear you're happy where you are. But, may I ask, have you noticed our signs and activity in your area?"

"Yeah, so what?"

"What do you think? Does it look like we are doing the job? We're part of this community like you are, and we want to do the right things. Have you heard any negatives?"

"No, but you're bothering me now."

"Well, I'm glad you haven't heard anything bad. Thank you. I'm sorry for the interruption, but I know something now I didn't know before I talked to you." Pause.

"What's that?"

"Walter Frankel doesn't think Sell Fast Realty is all bad. And I thank you. Goodnight, and the best of everything."

"Good luck, kid."

On calls into any street where your firm has recently sold a house, use this approach.

"Good evening, Mr. Jones. Danny Kennedy with Sell Fast Realty here. I'm just making a quick call to tell you about your new neighbors. Have you met them?"

"What are you talking about?"

"The Schaefers, who lived right down the street from you, have just moved to Denver. We marketed their home for them in 20 days to a lovely family with school-age children. Do you have any youngsters in elementary school?"

"No. So you're the guys who sold the Schaefers' house, huh? How much did they get?" (Usually this question is driven by plain nosiness, although it may indicate they're considering selling.)

"Since the transaction has closed, I can give you the information." (If it hasn't closed say, "I'm not at liberty to say because the transaction hasn't closed yet, but if you're really interested in neighborhood values, let me prepare a Guidelines to Market Value for you in your home.")

Additional effective scripts for telethons and regular prospecting are given later in this chapter. Your best scripts, probably, will be those you create yourself. The key is to always have a reason for calling and to use it as a catchy, *take 'em off guard* opener.

Here are some winning cues for your scripts:

- Our signs and activity in the area
- Recent sales
- Voting night. The night before elections, have a telethon and kill two birds with one stone. Remind people to vote (the volunteers

at the polls, who are also homeowners in your farm area, will love you) and remind them about the tax proposition, or any such issue that affects them as homeowners. Caution: Don't try to impose your own political views on the people you call.

- Cultural events: "Hi. I'm Danny Kennedy with Sell Fast Realty. Just making a call to remind you of the spring home tour tomorrow sponsored by our company. Have you ever thought about selling your beautiful home?"

There are as many openers as there are people. When you put a group of enthusiastic agents into one room for a telethon, creativity flies. Learn from each other and have fun.

## Offer an Online Chat Night

Instead of telethoning, you can offer a seminar online for your targeted calling list. Topics could include: current market conditions, values in the neighborhood, a home buyers seminar. Video conferencing online is another option if you have the proper equipment.

# Winning Scripts

## Twelve Opening Lines

These scripts are just starters. Take five minutes now and write another dozen to fit your climate, your region's special idiom, and your personality. Always identify yourself first.

1. "I hope I haven't interrupted, but—"
2. "Good morning. I hope this rain hasn't got you down. Here's a rain bonnet—"
3. "Hello there! Can I take a minute of your time?" (Point to your watch.) "Just time me. I'm _____ of _____ Realty."
4. "Hi. I'm _____ with _____. May I leave this memo pad with you as a token of my appreciation for your smiling at me this morning?"
5. (After noticing a freshly cut lawn) "Good morning! Your lawn looks beautiful; you've done a great job with the landscaping."
6. "Hi, Mother . . . Well, how does it feel to have the kiddies back in school? Here's a memo pad for September to remind you of things to get done after summer vacation."
7. "I'm _____ of _____ stopping by to say hello, and to distribute another set of cookie cutters, compliments of our company."

8. "Hi. there, Mrs. _____. I'm Nellie Collins of Reliable Realty. Are you as happy here as you look? . . . Great. Well, if you know of anyone who can't stick around and enjoy this lovely block, could I ask a favor? Mention my name. They may not know a top-flight real estate agent."

9. "I've got something to tell you." (Relate some news item about a store opening, a house sold and a new family moving in—anything except juicy neighborhood gossip.)

10. "Guess who's back with a smile, a newsletter, and a _____." (Name whatever you've got in your hand to give away.)

11. "It's me—your friendly old agent from around the corner who helps move folks around."

12. "I'm just stopping by to say hello, and to give you _____."

# Prospecting from Open House

## Winning Scripts for Calling Everyone from an Open House

"Hello. I'm Matt Butler with Seven Pines Realty—calling you from just down the street—where I'm holding an open house for one of your neighbors right now."

Pause now, and they will often ask you which house. If they do, chat about the house, and invite them over to see it. Tell them the time you'll be there, and then say, "My sellers here are very sorry to be leaving this beautiful neighborhood, and I certainly understand why. Do you share their enthusiasm for this area?"

Answers to this question will fall into three groups.

1. *"We like it here."* Respond with, "I was sure you'd say that. Do you happen to have any friends or relatives who'd like to move here and share this wonderful neighborhood with you?"

   "No."

   "Perhaps someone at work?"

2. *"We don't like it here."* This may indicate a desire, or need, to move. Don't pounce. Let the conversation develop naturally.

   "I'm sorry to hear it. Would you be offended if I ask you why? I'd be very interested to know." Be very careful to ask this question sympathetically. You don't want them on the defensive, and you don't want to pant with eagerness to move them out.

3. *"It's okay. I guess we're neutral about it."* With some low-key people, this is equivalent to "I hate it," or "I love it." Here are eight tacks you can take to develop how they really feel.

- "Do you think we're too close to the city?" (too far from the beach? the mountains? the city?)
- "Is this area convenient to your work?"
- "Do you enjoy living in this state?"
- "Does the aroma of the glue factory bother you?" Every area has at least one minor negative you can exaggerate and use here—substitute smog, congestion, summer heat, winter cold, or both. Maybe it's hurricanes, frequent brush fires, morning fog, too much rain, or too much sun. Anywhere in California you can always ask, "Are you concerned about earthquakes?" and get a response. The purpose is to get them talking.
- "How long have you lived here?"
- "What do you think of our schools?"
- "Do you think the shopping is good around here?"
- "What do you think about the restaurants (cultural opportunities, sporting events) in this area?"

When you pick up a hint that they may be moving, or if you've simply had a friendly conversation, conclude with, "I've enjoyed talking with you. I hope I haven't taken too much of your time. Would you be offended if I dropped off one of my handy memo pads for you after my open house?" Don't pause. "I can't stay more than a minute because I have a commitment" (you can truthfully say this even if your commitment is to walk your dog) "but I'd like to meet you while I'm right here in your neighborhood. Would it be all right? About five?"

Then add this prospect to your People-I-Know farm so you can routinely keep in touch and efficiently build your credibility as a real estate expert with this new person over a period of time.

## Calling Expired Listings from Open House

Many listings will be passed around from office to office until finally, after a year or more, the sellers agree to the price and terms the first agent probably advised them to offer. Work expired listings. Call them from open houses. Be especially alert for present fizzbos who were listed by another office in the past.

Success goes to the agents who use their time effectively to work with more people. Here's a general opening line for expireds.

"Hi. This is Danny Kennedy with Sell Fast Realty. I'm just updating my listing book and I was wondering if your property is still available."

Notice I did *not* say, "Is it still for sale?" or "Has your house sold yet?" Those questions remind them of their failure; mine reminds them of their opportunity. And it gives them a chance to say *yes* instead of *no*. If they have already renewed or listed with another broker, asking if their property is available doesn't create problems with your competition.

When they do say *yes*, which is most of the time, you've created an opening for, and put them more in the mood for, making an appointment with you to hear your listing presentation. Lead into it by asking them another question, "Can I show it?"

# Cold Canvassing by Foot or Phone

"Hi, I'm Alex Hawthorn with Helena Homes, and I'm calling to ask your help. We just sold a lovely home in your area, and we need another home to sell because we're working with a lot of buyers in this office. Do you know of anyone who's thinking of selling?"

"I specialize in selling homes in your neighborhood. No one in this world knows more about the real estate between Elm and Birch than I do."

After a good phone call, drop by their house an hour or two later, hand them your memo pad, and say, "I just had to meet you after our great talk on the phone this afternoon. I've got to run to an appointment now but I just wanted to say thanks so much for your courtesy."

Always finish by repeating your name and affiliation, "I'm Alex Hawthorn with Helena Homes. I specialize in your area."

E-mailing and text messaging will work with this method if you feel stopping by would not be appropriate with this prospect. Use common sense and sensitivity. Use different methods of communication to work with each individual case.

# CHAPTER 9

# Open House Bonanzas

Open Houses Are a Hot Option ● The Odds ● Hold the Right Houses Open for the Right Reasons ● Twig or Berry? ● Productive Open Houses Are Planned in Advance ● Multiple Open Houses ● Partner Open Houses ● Weekday Open Houses ● Virtual Open Houses ● Invite Success ● Hand Out Flyer Packets ● Before an Open House ● Use Low-Cost Automatic Selling Devices ● More Money-Making Open House Ideas ● During Open House ● Winning Scripts ● Capturable Customers and Clients ● Lock Up and Turn Off Lights ● Bring Your Own Banana

## Open Houses Are a Hot Option

Be careful. There are so-called old pros in the business who are going to tell you that holding open houses are a waste of time. The worst advice you could take! The quickest way for a new agent or a seasoned slumping agent to get a grip and get back into the black in her account, is the hot option—the open house. You will discover in this chapter just what a good open house entails. You'll also get some of my newest open houses marketing methods. It's all good. So get cooking!!!

## The Odds

Where the agent has failed to prepare for an open house with a high degree of professional effort, the odds are at least 250 to 1 against someone walking in and buying it. Yet agents who understand this promotional method make big money. These agents do a good job of showing the house they're holding open because doing so is an essential element in their success. They take good care of their sellers' interests *and* effectively work the other six reasons for holding houses open.

If you have difficulty believing those 250 to 1 odds, you're probably equating *visitors* to open houses with present-time buyers. Looking at houses is a hobby with millions of people. Most of those millions will buy somewhere, sometime. But *somewhere* may be a thousand miles away, and *sometime* may be nine years from now.

Many agents throw themselves into trying to capture every walk-through as a client or customer, and suffer great frustration at their inevitable failure. Others react to the public with dull indifference. Successful agents meet all visitors with relaxed alertness and a pleasant, helpful attitude. You should make some preparations for every open house.

- Work smart at building traffic to it—before and during the event.
- Check out the financing in advance. Know for certain whether there's a prepayment penalty. Have at least one loan source tentatively lined up.
- Have a list of any special conditions, no-go items, things the seller has agreed to correct, amenities outside the home a prospective buyer might overlook (a nearby walkthrough to the elementary school, for example).
- Have your Guidelines to Market Value and Buyer's Closing Costs (these forms are available on the accompanying CD) on the listing filled out and handy, along with forms for writing up offers and a calculator. Be ready to do business. Opportunity has a light knock and a short attention span, so be ready to seize the moment.

# Hold the Right Houses Open for the Right Reasons

The **right houses** are

1. located where arrows can bring good traffic,
2. priced at the market,
3. suited to the weather, and
4. attractive from the curb.

The **right reasons** are

1. to capture a present-time buyer for the house held open,
2. to capture present-time buyers for your other listings,
3. to capture present-time buyers for any property,
4. to make contacts with present-time sellers (can lead to listings),
5. to contact future buyers,

**6.** to contact future sellers, and

**7.** to maintain good relations with your sellers.

# Twig or Berry?

The people who come into any open house can be divided into twigs and berries. **The twigs are:**

- spies for your seller—often just busybodies who weren't asked,
- no-dough dreamers,
- sellers, already listed with another agent, checking their property's competition,
- owners of similar houses looking for decorating and landscaping ideas,
- recent buyers of the same type of home worrying whether they got a good deal, and
- simply curious time-killers of all kinds and descriptions.

**The four varieties of berries are:**

- sellers or buyers moving up, sideways, or down within your sales area,
- buyers moving in,
- sellers moving out, and
- investors.

Berries come through your open house in different stages of maturity:

**Ripe:** These are need-to-move-now people who are pushed by outside forces or internal emotion

**Semi-ripe:** Interested and qualified folks who aren't pushed.

**Green:** Individuals facing a possible change of circumstance, and people who want to move now, but believe they can't yet because of real or imaginary obstacles.

Many twigs will be candid. "I just listed my house with Dick Ewell of Port Republic Realty. He said I ought to look at this one."

"Sure," you respond, "I know Dick. He's a nice guy and a fine agent. You're in good hands." Then show Mr. Honest-feller through with the utmost courtesy. Maybe it'll get back to Dick and he'll do the same for you. In any event, you behaved professionally. You've had a chance to practice your sales speech, and that's all you can take out of this situation.

Some twigs never admit the real reason they came in. Don't fall into the trap of thinking you've failed miserably every time visitors won't give you their names. Don't beat yourself trying desperately to say the magic word and turn a twig into a client. It can't be done. I'm not advocating hanging back, watching suspiciously, until the new-comers declare themselves. Between suspicious hang-back and hard-sell pounce, there's plenty of room for a variety of relaxed and friendly approaches. Keep your house presentation low-key and nondominating.

Put gentle pressure on them to talk and reveal themselves by generous pauses; avoid beating them down with torrents of words. When your mouth is on, your ears are off. What *they* say is more important to you than what *you* say. Ask cordial questions in a relaxed and non-threatening way. If you watch and listen carefully, they'll soon tell you, by words or action, whether they're twigs or berries.

Once you discover they're twigs, of course remain cordial. Practice your presentation on them if you feel like it, or save your energy. It's no defeat to miss a twig—there's just no juice there. Stay friendly, enjoy the conversation, and never forget your botany: berries grow on twigs. The no-dough dreamer you're nice to this afternoon may tell their close friends, Mr. and Mrs. GottaMoveNow about you tomorrow.

Above all, protect your enthusiasm. Keep it bright and sharp for when you get the chance to pluck berries. If your enthusiasm is fragile, avoid shattering it by chopping too hard at twigs. Your most effective afternoon-long approach will depend on your personality and energy level. Bubble over with all the twigs if it's your nature—but don't dive into the pit of despair when people leave without responding. You were simply chewing on a dry twig, not a juicy berry. No harm done—unless frustrations with twigs make you pounce on the next genuine, ripe berries you see, and drive them off.

Hang loose. Think of funny things. Stay up. Mr. and Mrs. Gotta-MoveNow are coming through the door any minute. Be relaxed and ready to charm them.

## Productive Open Houses Are Planned in Advance

The secret of the top producer is this validation (see Chapter 27): "I do the most productive thing possible at every given moment."

You're on open house. "Okay, I'm eating cookies, I'm drinking pop, I'm sitting here with my feet up, the music's playing, and I'm waiting. Somebody? Anybody! Come in here and buy this house from me!"

If there's a dog in the garage, you're hoping it'll bark when someone drives up, so you can jump up, brush the cookie crumbs away, and look busy before the people get in there. This is doing the most productive thing every available moment?

Say to yourself, "What can I do right *now* to generate business?" That's better, but not good enough. Say to yourself the *Monday before* an open house, "How can I generate business while I'm holding the open house this coming weekend?" Then you can prepare. You can have the neighbors' phone numbers and names from the crisscross directory, your list of expireds, your copy of the local papers with the fizzbo ads. Even if you don't have your farm file completed yet, you can work up enough of it to keep busy calling this next weekend.

## Location Is the Number One Ingredient of Successful Open Houses

Hard-to-find houses are sold by escorting buyers to them, not by holding zero-traffic open houses there. Avoid inconveniencing your sellers without purpose, and avoid wasting your time. Hold only easily-found houses open. Not more than four arrows should be required to guide house hunters to your open house by the most direct route from a main thoroughfare. If five or more arrows are necessary, reconsider your other choices—another one will probably generate more traffic.

## Choose a Well-Priced Listing

It's counterproductive to hold open houses on clearly overpriced properties. Stoppers get the wrong idea about your area. Neighbors come in and think, "If the professionals expect to sell this place for *that* much— wow! My creampuff's worth at least $10,000 more than this dump."

You're in a bad position. You can't knock the price because it's your listing (not that you ever should) and you're talking to a neighbor who may report what you say to your seller. The price is too high, you know it all too well, but you're forced into defending it. This can lead to an expanding set of priced-out-of-the-market, and therefore unsalable, listings. Such listings are worse than useless; they'll cost you money and maim your enthusiasm.

Unless your ambition is to work hard and earn little, give properties with at-the-market prices first call on your open house time.

## Choose Between Price and Location

This weekend you can hold open Greedy Street or Hidden Hollow. Greedy Street, at a well traveled and easily-flagged location, is joltingly overpriced. Hidden Hollow, so hard to find people swear it isn't there, is priced snap-up. Which should you hold open?

**Do the Bounce-off.** Team with another agent for a Greedy to Hidden play. Take the walk-ins alternately. Keep your cars nearby, all warmed up for a fast run to Hidden Hollow with your new prospects. How do you avoid knocking Greedy's price?

A prospect says, "How much are they asking?"

You tell him. He staggers, then gasps, "Are they serious? I mean, how much bargaining pad is packed into their price?"

"The only way to know is to make an offer. I'll be happy to assist you in finding out."

"No, I was just asking. I had no idea property was so high here."

"A premium location like this isn't what everyone is looking for, of course. We have another fine home on Hidden Hollow listed for—" You name the price. "Unless you see it, you won't know the fine values available here in Green Pretty Valley. It's a lovely home but hard to find. I can take you and Mrs. Bysmartz to view it in a jiffy. We can be back here in less than fifteen minutes. Would you like to see it now, or after—"

Both agents should work Greedy Street together, rather than having one waiting at Hidden Hollow. There are four reasons to work together.

**1.** One agent always stays at Greedy Street, to keep that house open and well-looked-after, while the second agent takes prospects to the other property. Never close down an open house during the hours you've asked the owners to be away. This is a direct injury to their interests, for which they will be properly resentful. You can't capture more customers there if it's closed up.

**2.** The rapport that one agent builds with prospects is largely lost if they're sent to another agent.

**3.** Many of the prospects will never reach Hidden Hollow on their own.

**4.** Working bounce-off together causes less fee-sharing dissatisfaction than working at separate houses.

## Weatherwise Is Saleswise

It's July. It's ninety degrees in the shade. Your open house doesn't have air conditioning and people are driving up in air-conditioned cars to look at it. They walk into your oven—and right out again. Even if they stayed, would they think about the floor plan? Would they want to buy it? Hardly. While you're standing there, hot and sticky, how good are your chances of capturing them as customers to look at other, cooler properties?

Not too good.

When it's hot, hold air-conditioned homes open. When it's cold, pick one with a nice hearth, a big family room, and lots of homey appeal. Get the owner's permission to build a fire in the fireplace, turn on cheerful music, and fill the air with the good old smells of baking.

## Multiple Open Houses

Avoid boredom.  Avoid starvation. Why hang around a homeowner's refrigerator all day while sitting at a deadbeat open house?  Do what they have done in Australia for years.  Hold multiple open houses in one day.  Pick 4 to 8 hot locations. (Decide how ambitious and motivated you are.) Then in two-hour increments, open each house.  Run the ads for these open houses online from your web site, in the local newspapers, and send flyers and invitations.  All the ideas in this chapter apply.  Just increase the number of open houses.  You will be amazed at how resourceful these multiple additions will be for you.

## Partner Open Houses

Hold open houses in pairs or teams. It is safer and definitely more effective. If you are a top producer and always carrying a large inventory, you need help. Talk to the brightest and most enthusiastic of the new agents. Ask them to sit at some of your hottest locations. They can do it in pairs. But wouldn't it be great if you teamed up with a couple of newbies and showed them how it is done? When those prospects walk through the door, strut your stuff. Let me see how a real pro holds an open house. Train the new talent on the spot. Then let them have a turn. You will get more inventory sold and they will start building a bank account. Don't you wish someone had given you such an opportunity?

## Weekday Open Houses

Entrepreneurs, professional people, and relocation prospects prefer house hunting in the middle of the week. So why are you just holding weekend open houses? Relocation prospects and affluent buyers who have moved multiple times, consider house hunting hard work. It's a job. And they would rather put in the work time on the weekdays so they can enjoy golf or the family on the weekends. So open those houses in the middle of the week between 11 A.M. and 4 P.M. You will be amazed at the number of qualified prospects who will come through your door.

# Virtual Open Houses

If you want to stay in bed late every now and then, why not bring your laptop under the covers and hold a few virtual open houses? Just do a spam e-mail to all of your hottest prospects and direct them to your web site or your current online open houses so that they can browse in the privacy of their own homes. And guess what? You can literally offer this service every day of the year. Just be sure you keep up with the changes in the tour. There is nothing worse than leaving sold properties displayed online. So if it takes a smart assistant to keep your web site or open house tour current, don't be cheap. Hire the help!!!

Here comes a bunch of ways to make any type of open house option you choose exciting. It all applies, even electronically.

# Invite Success

Call the seller on Tuesday.

"Mrs. Johnson, would an open house this Saturday be convenient for you?"

"Sure."

Mail the invitations on Wednesday.

"Would it be okay if I send out some invitations?" This comment is effective with sellers who have difficulty sticking with plans to be gone.

"I have quite a program of mailing invitations to my own list of buyers. The advantage is that we greatly increase our chances of finding a buyer fast. The disadvantage is that we can't postpone the open house after the invitations go out."

Many agents prefer working with a computerized mailing list. However, if you're going to address them by hand (certainly the warmest, friendliest way) the good old 3 × 5 card file makes the fastest-working, easiest-to-update, mailing list. Build up your list to include all present and past clients, all drop-ins from your guest log of previous open houses, and the personnel or human resources directors of all companies within commuting distance.

Local hotels and motels, where people thinking about moving into the area might be staying, are also excellent places to send your invitations. Ask them to display it at the registration desk, or by the coffee shop cash register. The hotel clerk may let you drop a flyer in each guest's mail slot.

And don't overlook the neighbors, any of whom may have friends or relatives interested in the area. A crisscross telephone directory makes it easy to locate everyone living near your listing.

## Use Your Client's Phone

You may want to reserve your cell phone for incoming calls. If so, ask permission to use the home's phone for local calls only. This item should be on your checklist for making open house appointments.

"I'll be the person representing you at the property while you're gone Sunday. When no one else is in your home will it be okay if I make some phone calls? Of course they'll all be local calls. I'll be very careful to charge any toll calls to our office phone."

The owners may call in to tell you something or to see if there are any messages for them (but certainly *not* to check up on whether you're actually there!). A busy signal may upset them if they're not forewarned. If you don't get a chance to clear the phone situation with them beforehand, on the note you always leave after an open house write something like,

> *"Dear Jim and Betty: Seven couples came through today. Their general response was. . . . Thanks so much for setting the stage so nicely. I hope you don't mind, I used the phone to return some pertinent messages today, and to drum up more visitors to see your house. They were all local, nontoll calls. I appreciate the opportunity to work at your home from 1 to 5 this afternoon.*
>
> *Sincerely,"*

## Remind Sellers to Set the Stage

During your listing presentation, you educated the sellers on setting the stage properly (see "Danny's Dozen that Brings Your Sellers More Money" in Chapter 12). When you hold the house open Saturday, be sure to remind them about stage-setting in your note so they'll take care of it right for your Sunday open house. "You've done a beautiful job of keeping your home sharp and bright. This effort will pay off for you."

## Get the Sellers Gone, Gracefully

When you come to open the house, either you or the sellers must leave. While you're making the appointment on Tuesday, if they aren't enthusiastic about clearing out, explain how people reach the decision to buy. Buyers must first become emotionally involved in the house. Buyers must imagine themselves doing their own thing, surrounded by their own furniture.

"If you're present, Mr. and Mrs. McComb, or if you leave Granny and the kids, they're overpowered by the feeling they're intruding into someone else's space instead of standing in their own future home. Let buyers dream a little. They've got to. It's the only way houses are sold. Let's put this powerful process to work for us.

"People coming through open houses often ask me right off: 'Is this your home, or are you an agent?' They're always relieved when I say I'm an agent because then they know they can relax, react as buyers, and say what they think without offending anyone."

If your sellers persist in wanting to stay home, ask why. Press for answers in a courteous manner.

"It's vital for us to understand each other because you have a lot at stake here. Are you concerned about something valuable getting damaged or taken?" Suggest putting the precious items in storage.

"Are you uncertain whether I know all the features of your home well enough to show it to its best advantage?" If they hesitate here, ask them to go over every detail with you again. With people of this sort, you should already have notes. Check them again. Add copious details if necessary. Exhaust your sellers.

If all else fails, tell them they aren't emotionally ready for an open house yet. In negative moves resulting from illness, divorce, death, unwanted transfer, or money problems, this must be handled with great sympathy and tact. Even when the move is generally a positive one, and they are happy about where they're going, often there's regret about friends and activities being left behind. The last thing you want is despondent or anxious sellers hanging around, charging the air with tension.

"It's not worth the emotional stress you'll go through, Mr. and Mrs. McComb. We'll wait a couple of weeks and let you both get used to the idea. Then we'll talk about an open house again."

"But we can't afford to wait two weeks. We want our house sold now."

"The purpose of open houses is to find buyers. People rarely buy the first house they walk into. So, actually, all our open houses help sell yours."

"So you've said. I still want *our* house held open."

With strong conviction in your voice say, "Thanks for your co-operation. I really appreciate it. I know it's not easy at a time like this. Now, which afternoon will be most convenient for you to be away?"

"Well—Saturday, I guess."

## Operating Theories Regarding Open Houses

"I can't expect someone to walk in and buy the house I'm sitting on more than once a year. This means I have to hold 100 open houses to get 1 sale—unless I *make more happen.* I won't accept 1 sale for 100 days' work. I'm going to earn a lot more, so I'll prepare effectively. I'll hold the right houses open. While I'm there, I'll work efficiently to make good things happen. It's up to me, not luck."

When and if you make the above decisions, you've taken the second most important step to making open houses pay off big for you.

What's *first* in importance?

Action.

Great ideas are inspiring, but completed action is bankable.

## Fish Where the Fish Are

You catch more this way. Open houses don't placate sellers, sales placate sellers. The best way to get agents to notice your listings is to sell one of theirs. Hold houses open to *capture new customers*. Select them and act with this objective in mind.

## Organize Backup Before Needed

Mr. and Mrs. Hotbuyer walk in. You relate well to them. They want to see houses now, because they're catching a plane back to Homeville at 8 P.M. They're tired of tooling around; they want to buy now.

It'll never happen? Don't you believe it. I've had buyers like this walk in several times. The fee is there, just waiting to be grabbed—if you're ready.

If you have a good grip on the inventory. If you've done your homework on qualifying, financing, and closing. All you need now is someone to take over your open house or floor time. Lining up an agent to do this for you is a lot easier to arrange if you work it out beforehand. Here's where close cooperation within your office pays. Be part of this close cooperation; the only way to get it is to give it.

## Write Ads for the Open House Yourself

As the listing agent, you should show the ads to the seller for approval on Wednesday, or call them and read it over the phone.

"How's this sound? Does this sound good?" Read it out loud and then laugh, "Ain't it great!" Have fun. Sizzle with life. Keep them enthusiastic. Keep their spirits up. Every time you do something to sell their house, try to involve them in it. If you can't involve them, at least keep them informed.

When you write the ad for the open house, always write an ad aimed at a certain kind of buyer. A two-bedroom house appeals to retired or newly married couples. Make this the ad's theme, "Open house this weekend, all newlyweds, all retired people." To zero in to what the market appeal is for a given house, think of broad groups of buyers. Check with your manager first; one person may be in charge of coordinating ads.

## Screen Walk-ins Carefully

I used to give flyers on the house to everybody who came through an open house. I'd say, "Feel free to go through and I'll be happy to answer any questions you may have." Then I realized I was as important to the buyer as he or she was to me. They need to pick your brain. Don't put everything on a silver platter for them so they can say, "Thank you, goodbye."

So now I follow the winning scripts in this chapter. When they ask if a flyer is available at the door, I'm likely to say, "We can probably dig one up while you're previewing the property." Then I proceed with the script and demonstrate the features of the home to them.

It's often better not to have a flyer on the property you're holding open. You can say, "Let me do a personalized worksheet for you with all the pertinent financial information." Having flyers on the open house often makes it too easy for an excellent prospect to get through the door too fast for you to make any connection. Work a little harder—and make a lot more money—by having all the details on that house memorized, not printed.

# Hand Out Flyer Packets

The packet should contain:

- two business cards, one stapled unless you can insert it in a die-cut slot, the other loose
- flyers for all your other listings. Put in at least six house flyers, preferably with a price spread indicating the range available in your sales area. If you have less than six listings of your own, exchange flyers with other agents in your office.
- a flyer on the latest electronic technology you and your office are using to help them find their best buy fast
- other brochures promoting your firm
- a "Profile of a Champion." It promotes you. Chapter 13 tells you how to write the profile. Make this the last page of the packet.
- a company wrapper to cover your packet with an air of competence. If your office doesn't furnish one, find report covers at office supply stores.

Fizzbos, dissatisfied sellers whose listing with another office is about to expire, and homeowners just reaching the decision to sell will be impressed by this graphic display of your advanced marketing methods. Buyers interested in a future move to your area are more likely to keep your packet, and call you later, than any one of the dozen business cards they've picked up on their fast swing through your area. You've demonstrated competence, professionalism, and local knowledge very effectively to the need-now buyers we're all looking for.

Do not include material promoting your area in the flyer packet. It adds bulk, diffuses your purpose, and renders fuzzy what otherwise would be the sharp image of an exceptionally competent agent. Make area promotion a separate handout and give it only to the deserving.

## Promote Your Area with a Giveaway Package

Chambers of Commerce, land developers, banks, city and county governments, and special districts will often give you a supply of brochures extolling your area. You'll probably acquire a variety of folders and documents from these sources that would be awkward in stapled-packet form. If so, pull them together with a highlights flyer and give yourself another plug. Put it all in a glassine envelope, with your highlights flyer on top so it'll be visible from the outside. Here's a sample of the flyers you should create or find for your Area Highlights Giveaway Package.

- Highlights flyer
- Green Pretty Valley is growing. New jobs, new businesses are coming
- Lake Lotsafishnfun brochure
- Green Pretty's schools score high statewide
- List of local churches
- List of cultural activities
- List of leisure time activities in Green Pretty Valley
- List of professional and amateur sports available
- Chamber of Commerce roundup of facts and figures
- Newspaper article on Zap Corporation to build research center in Green Pretty Valley and employ 500 engineers

**Gathered for Your Convenience**
**by John Magruder**
**Quaker Road Realty**
Since _____ serving all of Green Pretty Valley
with friendly professionalism.
Let's talk about the good living here.
No obligation, of course.
Office 555-987-6543 Home 555-123-4567

# Before an Open House

Visit the property. List the house's features and extras. Find out the transportation methods to all levels of school from the house, and where the schools are located. Drive the neighborhood and familiarize yourself with what's nearby—parks, churches, shops. Know the good points and bad points. Know all the houses for sale in the immediate area, including the fizzbos—where they are, their condition, price, and features.

# Use Low-Cost Automatic Selling Devices

Low-cost automatic selling devices can hold a buyer for you if you happen to be momentarily busy with someone else. On a slow open house it can impress a prospect with your professionalism enough to swing another listing or sale your way. Here are three possibilities: (Use all three in occupied homes of cooperative sellers.)

**1.** Program your laptop to run your electronic listing presentation continuously.

**2.** With the seller's permission, run a video extolling your area's attractions on their TV.

**3.** Buy four inexpensive, lightweight wood easels from an artists' materials store. Have the store cut illustration boards (the double-weight kind won't warp quickly) to desired size for your easels. When you paste your items on the board, use white paper cement, not rubber cement that soon stains through. Use a T-square and ruler to position your items neatly.

### Easel 1

Good: Your "Profile of a PRO" flyer.

Better: Typed sales story detailed below

Best: Sales story typeset by a commercial art shop on reproduction paper to look like printing or printed on your color printer.

Use this model to compile your own powerful sales story.

"Orange County's Saddleback Valley has six distinct communities, each with its own unique advantages:

- El Toro
- Laguna Hills
- Laguna Niguel
- Lake Forest
- Mission Viejo
- San Juan Capistrano

"Between 2000 and 3000 houses and condominiums are usually for sale here in the valley. Finding your best home in this vast inventory is no easy task. Knowledgeable professional service will save you time, effort, and money—perhaps a substantial amount of money. Our business is knowing where the values are.

"I've qualified myself to give you that professional service by (summarize your professional awards and accomplishments) intensive training, and constant study of our local housing market.

"Let's talk about your needs. I'm a full-service Multiple Listing agent, ready to ably represent you in the purchase of any real estate in the Saddleback Valley. There's no cost or obligation, of course. I'm here to serve you."

Add a small (about 4" × 5" maximum size) *recent* portrait of yourself to the illustration board. Why, if you're in the house? If several people are milling around, a good prospect might not know who you are, feel uncomfortable asking, and do the easiest thing—walk out.

### Easel 2

Mount in large, neat letters: "For you." Arrange on that board in peg-board pockets or on shelves some flyer packets, business cards, buyer-catcher maps.

### Easel 3

Place this legend: "Welcome. Thank you for coming in. I'm proud to present this outstanding property.

"On the kitchen table you'll find more information about Saddleback Valley and real estate values here. Please give me an opportunity to answer all your questions." Sign your first name.

Before your sellers object to you offering other properties at their open house, explain how no one buys without believing they are getting good value for their money. "The sooner I can educate your buyer, Mr. McComb, the quicker your sale is made."

### Easel 4

Illustrate an informal story lesson about your area. Add boards one at a time, as you develop or find interesting material to paste on them. Leave this easel empty, with a stack of story boards lying against one of its legs. People will ask, "What are they? Can we see them?" That's your signal to launch into your talk. A pointer is handy to direct attention to details. Start with orientation maps highlighting the main traffic routes, relate the various communities to each other, and locate points of interest. Keep each board simple. Put your name (no slogans or phone numbers) on each board in clear, easily read letters. After the maps, add other boards that show aerial, panoramic, or sunset views of your area; schools; recreational facilities; shopping centers; parks; prevailing wind patterns; outstanding homes; historical photos; charts of seasonal temperatures, construction trends; or average prices. The possibilities this method provides to subtly establish yourself as *the agent with the expertise* are endless. Stay alert to prospect reactions and you'll soon find yourself developing some boards that will always get a laugh, and take you light-years closer to winning your listeners as customers.

Sometimes (glory be!) an open house really jumps. Several parties show up at once, and the heavy traffic keeps on coming. It starts suddenly, for no apparent reason, and just as suddenly it stops. While it lasts, you're on your own. Only what's already in your head, and what's sitting around the house, can help you.

Prepare for heavy action. It pays. If you want to go electronic, do all of the above on a laptop!

# More Money-Making Open House Ideas

## Safety First: Hold Vacant Properties Open *with a Partner!!!*

Vacant dwellings in good condition and well located for traffic flow make terrific open houses. Why? Because you can capture customers there and take off—to show other property more in line with their needs—with no worries about owner backlash. Your sellers aren't inconvenienced by having to stay away or spiff up the place. However, be sure to work these open houses with a partner: it is safer and if things get hectic you can handle more traffic with two people.

Here are some things to do before holding an open house at a vacant dwelling:

- Several days before holding a vacant house open, check it out.
- Flush every toilet. If there's an overflow problem, get it fixed before a homelooker's kid comes squishing out on a Sunday afternoon.
- Make sure the utilities are on. Your rule should be, "No lights, no water—no open house." If the weather requires heat or cooling, insist on having them functioning too.
- Bring your cell phone. Unless you can bang out calls, the house must be exceptionally well located to justify losing touch with the world during the most important hours of your week.
- Leave a card table and three chairs at the vacant house so you can work effectively while you're alone, and also offer seats to a house-seeking couple. How long will people stick around if they have to stand? Many won't stay for very long.

## Open on Professionals' Day

Many doctors and dentists take Wednesday or Thursday off, as do other professionals and businesspeople. In many areas those two days will outdraw Monday, Tuesday, and Friday.

Don't expect many stops during a midweek open house, but what traffic you do get (other than curious locals) will often be the best kind—*ready-and-able-to-buy-now* prospects. Because people moving into the area from distant points usually look for a home without regard to the day, you stand a better chance of picking up these hot buyers midweek than on weekends when there's more competition.

A well-located, easily flagged vacant house makes the best mid-week open house because your schedule remains flexible. At the last minute you can skip the open house and show property to the buyer who just phoned in. Guard your flexibility. Don't advertise the mid-week open house, and don't definitely commit to it with your seller.

## Use Giveaways

Have a supply of memo pads with your name on them to use as cof-fee coasters. When you give a memo pad to walk-throughs, say, "Take notes on any interesting houses you see this afternoon." They'll be doing it on your memo pad, with your phone number and picture on it.

## Bake Cookies?

Why not? Your supermarket has prepared dough. All you do is slice, lay on a cookie sheet, pop in the oven, and the house is filled with the fresh fragrance of home cooking. (Get your sellers' permission, of course.)

If you're contemplating your first venture with an oven, have a trial bake at home. During the open house, keep your sellers' kitchen shipshape, and leave it spotless.

For the most fragrance with the least fuss, put a few drops of vanilla on a tin plate and bake in the oven.

## Make Up *Sold* Door-Hangers During Open House

This is important. Will you have time right after selling this house to print its address on labels and stick them on 300 hundred *Sold* door-hangers? Activity tends to come in bunches. You may be swamped by then. If you have those *Sold* cards already made up and ready to hang, you'll find time to hustle around your farm with them—and take a few bows from the people you meet while you're hanging them.

But, if you don't have the door-hangers made up, this tedious chore *and* the effort of hanging them is staring you in the face. It's easy to put it off until tomorrow, then next week, and then another week slips by. Finally you realize three things: your sale isn't news anymore, you're not going to put those door-hangers out, and you've lost a powerful boost to your momentum. Don't lose that powerful boost. Until you can afford to hire an assistant to do things like this for you, do this job on your first open house.

- It increases your commitment to selling the house.
- Having the house numbers of all your houses memorized makes you look professional. You'll remember it too—after writing the number 393 times, or sticking all those labels on.
- Most important—those door-hangers will get hung promptly— when they're news—when they'll do you the most good.

Do you leave them out as you work? Certainly. What if someone comes through and sees this stack of *Sold* door-hangers?

"Yes," you say, "I *am* confident this house will sell soon. It's a very sound value, and—" It's a great lead-in for your sales speech. People like enthusiasm and confidence. And among the neighbors you've invited to the open house and the other walk-throughs are some people thinking about selling, not buying. Impressing them with your energy and spirit won't hurt your chances of listing their property.

There's another reason for making these *Sold* signs up in advance. If you don't get them hung fast, someone else may beat you to it. What prevents the agent at Sellzip Realty from telling the people in your farm about the sale you just made via one of his *Just Sold* door-hangers? It's the truth: The house has been sold, and he isn't saying he sold it.

Then you come along later with a similar door-hanger announcing the sale of your listing. Guess who looks like they're trying to ride someone else's accomplishment? The number two person does, and if you're slow off the mark, it'll be you.

The residents of many areas don't recognize street names only a block or two away from them. The impact of *Sold* door-hangers is greatest on the people who live on the same street, less on people who travel the street on which the sale occurred. It has almost no impact on people who don't know whether the house is located on the other side of town.

Get those door-hangers out fast, especially along the same street. I suggest hanging them the morning after the sale, when you go back to put your *Sold* rider on the property's *For Sale* sign.

That afternoon, run a flyer with a sketched map of several nearby streets. By stapling that flyer to more *Just Sold* door-hangers, you can greatly expand the area in which the news of your sale will have strong impact.

Keep your sketch simple so people will instantly see that the just sold property is nearby.

## Put a Hook on Your Maps

Maps can be prospect-catchers too. Write something like this across your sales area maps (do it legibly—people won't take time to decipher messy writing):

"For knowledgeable help in locating your dream home, and for skilled assistance negotiating the best possible terms for purchasing it, call (your name) at (draw an arrow to your office's phone number printed on the map). Home Phone 555-123-4567. Don't hesitate to call if you're just looking. No obligation, of course."

The last two sentences are important. They take the pressure off the prospect. Otherwise it comes across as, "Don't bother me unless your furniture is already in the moving van."

Also staple one of your business cards to the map. Sure, it's likely to get torn off—that's why you write your message on the map but sometimes a prospect will take your card off and file it.

## Take Your Fizzbo File

Take your laptop and access your fizzbo file and take the local papers where fizzbos advertise. Saturday and Sunday afternoons are great times to call for-sale-by-owners—the ones you don't have time to see later. They're home. They're thinking, "Buyer, where are you?" They'd probably like to talk to someone—anyone.

Give them your cell phone number. Offer to consult over the phone should they have any uncertainty about handling something with a possible buyer.

Keep your call brief, unless they hold onto you. Identity yourself first, then ask if you're interrupting someone who's there looking at the house.

See Chapter 5 for the full discussion on working with fizzbos.

## Take Your Farm File

With no other preparation than the minute it takes to put your farm file in your car, you're ready for an effective day, even if traffic is light on your open house. Take your farm file to every open house.

With your farm file you can make dozens of brief, image-building calls into your farm, inviting people to your open house. To people you don't know yet, make cold canvass calls, looking for people interested in buying the house you're sitting on, buying any house, or listing any house.

## Call Expired Listings

Open house afternoons are great for calling expireds. You'll occasionally hit an expired who is unhappy with their former agents because they didn't hold open house often enough.

What an opening! Tell them you're calling from an open house with the client's permission. Invite the expired over to see how professionally you work open houses. Tell him about your flyer packet, your giveaways, and all your neat action.

"I get *buyers* from open houses. It's a great tool. I use it all the time."

You don't have to say one word against his former agent. Don't be drawn into discussing anyone's failures. Not only might the other agent be the expired's friend or relative, it's dangerous ground ethically. You can't strike at another agent without harming the industry's image, and your own image is interlaced with the industry's.

Since they probably won't come, try for an appointment to see them later. If you get a *no*, mail your flyers with a note. Then a few days later, call them again. And again. And again.

## Call Neighbors

During any season, there's probably no better time to prospect, to make cold canvass calls, than Saturday and Sunday afternoons. This also happens to be the prime open house time in many areas. So why not do both? Don't just sit there. Take the crisscross directory and work the immediate neighborhood by streets.

## Target Cold Calls
## from Your Open House

Upgraders are an important source of real estate transactions. These rising families have received the promotions, built up the equities, or otherwise acquired the funds enabling them to move up.

Whenever you get a listing, consider where, within economical phoning distance, trade-ups for the house might come from. Then take your crisscross directory to the open house and bang out 100 calls seeking a trade-up. This technique is most effective when you call into the area you serve—you might acquire listings as well as buyers.

"Hello, Mrs. Smith?"

"Yeah."

"I'm Kathy McComb with Cedar Run Realty. I'm calling you from an open house we're holding today in a beautiful river-view home. Do you happen to know anyone who'd be interested in a large three-bedroom home with a nice-sized family room and a lovely covered patio?"

"No."

"I'd like to invite you to visit our open house. It's on Via San Pedro, just follow the signs off Marguerite."

"We're not interested."

"I won't keep you, Mrs. Smith. Thanks for talking to me." Be sure to pause at this point, or you'll always miss out on the goodies.

"Uh, you're in real estate?"

"I sure am—Kathy McComb with Cedar Run Realty."

"Do you ever do anything in El Toro, Kathy?"

"I'm over there nearly every day."

"Well, we're thinking of selling. Jack wants to go south."

Something like that will happen at least once every 100 calls. Once every 20, more likely. The above conversation took about 40 seconds. Making 100 cold canvass calls takes time and it's hard work. But it gets easier; the first 100 calls are the hardest.

# During Open House

## The 20/20/20 Go Like 60 Goal Plan

When warm bodies walk in the front door, obviously your cold call plans slip out the back. Your primary aim at any open house is to capture all *capturable* clients and customers who stop there. On light-traffic open houses, be careful not to get so involved in secondary activities that you're not thoroughly prepared to do a superlative job showing the property and picking up customers when people do walk in.

But don't be nervous about being on the phone when someone walks in. It's easily handled. If you're talking, simply say, "Someone just walked in—I'll call you right back, thanks, goodbye." Gentle click. Get off the phone fast. Don't give them a chance to tell you not to call back.

Saturday and Sunday afternoons are the week's most valuable hours. Don't default on them by doing nothing but keep-busy paperwork. Fizzbos are home. Just-transferreds are home. Movers-up are home. The people who know who's doing what are home too.

Call them. Prospect. Drum up traffic for your open house. Fertilize your farm with phone calls. Develop your own plan for getting the most out of those golden hours. Use your plan on every open house. Refine the details as you go. Here, for starters, is a schedule for an open house advertised for 1 P.M. to 5 P.M.

*I would only follow this schedule and stay (with a partner) at an open house this long on one condition:* THE PROPERTY MUST GET AMAZING FOOT TRAFFIC DUE TO EXCELLENT LOCATION!

Otherwise create a two-hour schedule. This will eliminate baking cookies and will drop your calling or e-mailing (don't forget to bring your laptop) to half the number of people suggested on the 1 P.M. to 5 P.M. schedule.

| | |
|---|---|
| 11:45 | Have a quiet, high-energy lunch, able to carry you through a busy afternoon and into early evening. |
| 12:30 | Set up arrows and flags. |
| 12:40 | Say goodbye to owners. Open up the house. Set the stage. Turn the lights on. Open the drapes. Put your prospect-catchers on the kitchen table. Set up your automatic selling easels. |
| 1:00 | Tour the property. Review out loud all the neat stuff you're planning to say to prospects. |
| 1:10 | Slide a sheet of cookies into the oven and brew some coffee. |
| 1:20 | Call 20 neighbors from the crisscross directory. Invite them to drop by and munch a cookie, sip some coffee, and see the house. |
| 2:20 | Call 20 people in your farm. (If you work eight open houses a month and do this every time, you can cover a 320-house farm *six times a year* this way, without putting in any more time than you now are.) Note: you have to reach 20 active people in your farm; indigent relatives, kids, maids, and no-answers count zero toward 20. |
| 3:20 | Eat one cookie. Relax 5 minutes. Start your note to your sellers. Then call fizzbos until you have an appointment after the open house, or until you've reached 20 of them. |
| 4:20 | Take these last 40 minutes to complete any calling you couldn't do before. |
| 5:30 | You're still here. In summer, 5 to 5:30—or even 6—is often the best time of the day for stops. But don't schedule your open houses that late. Preserve flexibility. If your owners return, leave. If you have a fizzbo appointment at 5:30, close promptly at 5:00 so you can recover your flags and take time to lock up properly, and to psych yourself up properly. |

Close up methodically. Give close attention to this task. The fine impression you've made on your sellers by how you handled the open house can be spoiled now by a moment's inattention, by forgetting to lock up or turn something off.

Complete your note to your sellers. Keep it upbeat, friendly, and honest. "Thanks for allowing me the pleasure of playing hostess here today. And many, many thanks for your wonderful cooperation in setting the stage so beautifully. We had 3 stops . . . I appreciate the opportunity to serve you."

Sixish:  Recover all your flags and signs. Be careful not to leave them sagging out there, irritating the neighborhood.

Finally:  Head for the appointment(s) you lined up with your 20/20/20 calls.

When making the fizzbo appointment, be sure to cover yourself— in case someone stops by and delays you right at closing. Tell your fizzbo it could happen, and of course they'd want you to work with those people, who might turn out to be buyers for the fizzbo's house.

This schedule, followed faithfully, with calls made in a bright, friendly, and confident manner, will give your career and income a tremendous boost. Resolve now to put those golden hours of quiet, open house time to work.

## Place Arrows with Care

Always ask permission before you put a directional sign on someone's property. Not only is it common courtesy; not only does it build rapport for you, your firm, and the industry; not only might you make, or renew a contact that could lead to a listing; but you avoid an irritated homeowner who turns your sign around or lays it down.

Remember—you're intruding into someone's territory. Kids sometimes feel this more strongly than their parents.

Never have the sign in your hand when you ask permission to put it up. I did this until I was turned down a couple of times. Some people can't handle this kind of presumption except by saying *no*. Be modest and pleasant.

Say, "May I have your permission. . . ." Then, after getting their okay, go to your car and get the sign. This may seem like a small thing—until you're refused by someone who controls a vital corner for directing traffic to your open house. And don't use too many arrows and flags because it shouts, "Beware—this is a hard-sell guy."

## Here We Sit

Here we sit alone on a Sunday afternoon, in this strange but familiar house. The sellers think our open house sign has the magic to bring the perfect buyers and their precious pocketbooks floating down into our arms and make them buy. We know better. While we wait for the perfect buyer to float, we phone. And phone. And phone. And e-mail, e-mail, e-mail.

It's amazing how working the territory hard makes the time fly on even the slowest open house. And it digs up business too. But better yet, hold more than one house open and you will never be twiddling your thumbs again.

## An Open Door Says, "Come In"

Whenever weather and insects permit, leave the front door open during your open house, especially if it can be seen from the street. An open door says, "Come on in. You can walk right out again if you don't like the situation inside."

A closed door means they have to ring the doorbell and stand there like dummies until someone opens it. Or should they walk right into a strange house, and risk making a social mistake? Decisions, decisions.

You may say, "If a little thing like that stops them, they can't be serious buyers."

Not necessarily. Many people head straight for a real estate agent to save themselves the stress of blundering up to strange doors, unexpected and unescorted. Shy people need homes too, and they often make your most loyal customers once the ice is broken.

If it's too hot, cold, or windy to leave the front door open, stake out a sign on the grass reading:

**WELCOME**

**WE'RE EXPECTING YOU TO**

**WALK RIGHT IN—PLEASE DO**

On the back of that sign, where your house hunters will read it as they leave, drop your name on them one more time under the words:

**THANK YOU FOR STOPPING**

## Role-Play First

What's the first thing to do after the signs are up and the stage is set? Role-play. Talk to an imaginary prospect. You're alone—you can do it without embarrassment. There's nothing like practice to put customer-capturing phrases, and house-selling tie-downs, on the tip of your tongue.

"Is this your first visit to Grand Junction?"

"Isn't this a pleasant patio?"

"You can almost sniff the aroma of steaks cooking on the barbecue, can't you?"

"Wouldn't this be a cozy room to spend a rainy night in?"

Make notes of all your good stuff. Review it two or three times during the afternoon. Keep those notes so you can quickly get them fresh in your mind the next time you work the same open house.

## Use Your Guest Log Right

Guest logs hurt more new agents than they help. One sure way to turn them into a small disaster is to make a big deal out of trying to get everyone who comes through the door to sign it. Relax. A guest log is an occasionally useful minor tool—and that's all it is.

Leave it out in a conspicuous place, preferably on an eating bar, where it's easy to write in. Jot down a couple of names at the top of the page because no one likes to be first to write on a blank page.

And never ask anyone to *sign* it. Sign is an alarm-ringing word—people have to *sign* mortgages, installment contracts, and marriage licenses. Use these phrases instead:

"Would you mind leaving your name in our guest log?"

"Could we have your name here to remember you by?"

"Would you be offended if I asked you to enter your name in our guest book?"

"We'd be proud to have you registered with us."

"If you'll leave your name in the guest book, I'll *mail* (emphasize that you'll *mail* to them, not *call*) flyers to you now and then on outstanding properties in this area."

Use every other line of the log for remarks. After the first name you fill in, write something like, "Might move here next fall. Wants my newsletters. Add to mailing list." Under the next name write, "May be interested in three-bedroom with lake view. Send info re: the Brown house. Not in a hurry."

It reads in a nonthreatening way. Things are going to be *mailed.* No heavy phone calls. Leave your guest log out where it can be seen. It's one more way to convey the idea, "I'm a busy professional who's too busy to hound anyone. But I can be of real service if you need my expertise."

Remember to build rapport first, then go for their name. If you can't build rapport, don't shove the log at them; doing so marks you as a fumbler.

Have a list of items you can mail to prospects: a brochure on the country club, a new map, your newsletter with prices and local events. As you talk with people, stay alert for something you can mail them tonight. Enclose a short note, "Here's the brochure on the lake we were talking about this afternoon. . . ."

This gives you a perfect excuse to call them in three days to make sure they received your flyer on your area's schools, or whatever you sent them. You're not bugging them. Just a friendly call. Your friendly follow-up call will often be an essential step toward earning a fee.

## Handle Office Walk-ins and Open House Walk-throughs

Floor-time walk-ins and open house walk-throughs are different animals—keep this difference in mind. Office walk-ins say, in louder-than-words action, "We want to work with an agent. Solve our housing problem without making us mad and you've earned a fee."

Open house walk-throughs (newcomers seeking a home) make the opposite statement, "We drove past 20 realty offices getting here. If we wanted to work with an agent, we'd be with one now. We're just looking. We're on our own. We want to size up this area, see if we want to live here, maybe find out what the for-sale-by-owners are doing. Perhaps we can't afford this neighborhood; maybe we can afford a better one; possibly we can't qualify for anything right now. It's our business, not yours. At this time, we're just sniffing around—"

There's often an exciting final kicker to this unspoken speech, ". . . unless some really sharp agent handles us just right."

With the office walk-in, you move directly into the qualifying phase. Your company's image and location dropped a golden nugget in your lap. Not so with the open house walk-through: there you've been given just one swing at the ball—and the pitcher is tough on the unprepared.

## Be Security Conscious

When they walk in the door, they're strangers. Strike a happy medium here. You want to know where they're going, from room to room, to make sure they're not picking up anything belonging to the owners, but you also want them to feel comfortable. What I like to do at an open house is to take the hostess approach by standing at the door and saying something like, "Welcome to our open house. If you have any questions, feel free to ask. I'll stay about ten steps behind you so you can look at your own pace."

If the people look hesitant as they come in, suggest, "If you'll step this way, I'll be happy to show you through the property."

A lot of them will just follow because they're not sure of how the house flows. If they have questions, they'll ask. Keep your eye on what they're doing—in a relaxed, casual manner—because they're people you don't know, and you're guarding the house. You don't want to smother people when they walk into an open house. Let them know you're there, but don't overwhelm them.

## Never Leave an Occupied Open House

If someone comes in and says, "I want to see property right now," and you've qualified them and know they're a hot prospect, call the office and get someone to take over for you, or make another appointment. This is hard to do, but you have an obligation to the owners of the house you're holding open. If the owners come home an hour early and the place is locked up, or the neighborhood spy sees you go, it's very embarrassing, and it might prove to be disastrous.

## Beware of Sellers and Neighbors Disguised as Buyers

It happens all the time. You're being watched. It will be subtle and un-obtrusive in most cases. How you handle the open house is important for future listings in your farm area. If you're not in your farm, how you conduct yourself will have a lot of bearing on your company's image. How you answer key questions about the homeowner's property will be remembered and repeated to your seller.

Tune in on a conversation between a neighbor and your seller a few hours after an open house:

"You should've seen it—she was doing a bad job—cookie crumbs all over the place—she wasn't keeping it nice and cleaned up and she was telling people more about the house three blocks down than she was about yours. And get this, the first thing she said when we walked in was, 'They're soft on the price.'"

# Winning Scripts

The Buyer's Analysis for Better Service questions in Chapter 15 and the Winning Scripts in Chapter 8 all have a series of questions that are powerful in open houses.

Your tone and manner must be friendly, relaxed, and interested. Before you get into what a walk-through couple can afford, be sure to cover what they like and want. Establish rapport first, then ease into qualification. If you press too soon, without first taking time to develop rapport, your chances of gaining them as a customer are poor.

Most people looking at open houses want to be left alone. They want you to answer questions when they ask them, not before.

The best way to handle people coming through is to *not* fight their desire to be left alone. Here's an introductory script that'll meet that and allow you to work with them.

"Hi folks. Feel free to go through by yourselves."

"Aha," they think, "just what we wanted—to be left alone."

Then you say, "But before you do, I would like to point out just one thing." And then demonstrate the house.

I can hear you saying, "Hold on—I thought you told me to let them go through alone."

No—it's what you tell them. But if you let them do it alone, you won't reach your goals. How can you build rapport when you don't talk to them?

For this plan to work, you have to learn how to demonstrate the house. Get there early. Find out everything special about that house so you can point out things they're unlikely to notice. It's worse than worthless to trail them around saying obvious things like, "This is the kitchen."

An example of telling them a feature may come when showing the back yard. "It looks like this property ends at the fence, but it really goes down this gentle slope and includes those flowering peach trees."

If they have any interest in the property, they'll ask about the trees. "How many are there?"

"Fourteen—and the owner tells me they all bear fruit."

Anything like this will perk them up and get the conversation flowing. Continue demonstrating and weighing their responses. Remember not to get so wrapped up in your demonstration that you fail to interact with them. Your whole purpose in making the demo is to interact with them. It's a two-step process: demonstrate, pause; demonstrate, pause.

At an open house when the buyers look like they want a much cheaper home than the one you're working, preface the price by saying, "We have many lovely neighborhoods in this area where prices start at (name the lowest-priced property on the market) and go all the way up to (name the highest priced). This one is only (name the house's price).

Always ask, "Are you presently working with another broker?" If the prospects are working with someone else, and they feel loyalty to the other agent, I want to honor their loyalty whether it's to someone in my company or not. I also want to save my time for prospects who show me a better chance of earning a fee. When they say, "Yes, we're working with another agent," respond pleasantly with, "Fine. I'll be glad to give your agent all the information about this property that I can."

Three situations often come up here:

1. They're interested in the property you're holding open and it's your listing.
2. They don't like the open house, so it doesn't matter whether it's your listing or not.
3. They like the house and you're working another agent's listing.

Here's how to cope with these three different circumstances

1. Cooperate with their agent. Offer to call him or her, to deliver information. Don't try for both ends of the fee when they've told you they're working with another agent and it's your listing. You can't do this without seeming greedy—and maybe losing out entirely.
2. If they're not interested in the present house, tell them about your other listings. If you strike no spark, switch your emphasis to selling your community. The more people who move into your area, the better it is for you.

   Avoid pressuring them. Flow with their indicated interests and establish yourself in their minds as an area expert, not only on its houses, but also on its amenities and opportunities. Suppose their loyalty is to an out-of-area agent, and they're looking in your area without the salesperson along. If they decide to buy here, some agent in your area will probably capture them as customers. It might as well be you.

   Build rapport before you ask whether their broker specializes in another area. If they're trying to get out the door without being rude, let them go. But if they're hanging around, go for an appointment to show property.

   In this situation a feeling of solid rapport is essential. Establish that they'll work through you if you find what they want. Be friendly and candid. Explain how your time is your stock in trade. Don't set yourself up to spend a week showing property and then have someone's cousin or fraternity brother come in to present the offer and collect the fee.
3. Most people, even those who've bought several houses, don't have a clear idea of how the real estate business works. Because you're holding the house open, they assume you must be the listing agent or will somehow get a portion of the fee. More

than likely, the thought that it's not your listing will never cross their minds. They just want an agent they feel confidence in to represent them—and them only—in the transaction. When they walk into an open house, they intend to bring in another agent for the purchase negotiations if the house interests them. Loyalty isn't involved.

When you see buying signs and it's not your listing, make sure the prospect knows it isn't yours. Explain carefully how you'll look out for their interests with dedication and skill. Emphasize that in-house transactions, where the sellers' and buyers' agents both work out of the same office, account for about half of your company's business. Convince them that the in-house transaction's feeling of mutual confidence, and the speed with which paperwork can be handled, puts them and you in a stronger position, rather than a weaker one, to negotiate the best possible terms for them.

"Do you know anyone who lives or works near here? Maybe we have a mutual friend."

Drill yourself on all your area's activities, especially those involving children, so you can zing in things like, "Your children look very athletic. Did you know that we have a very strong (name the sport) program here? Last year our boys' (girls') team was in the play-offs, and. . . ."

"Have you seen Lake Mission Viejo yet? It's big—124 acres, and has great fishing, boating, and swimming. Are any of you excited about these sports?"

Know the craft stores, the playgrounds, and everything, else that offers opportunities for leisure-time activities in your area. Be ready to talk about the activities with mass appeal *and also the more specialized interests.* Know about the photography, chess, curling, skating, and square-dancing associations; know the drag-racing, skateboarding, and ice-fishing places. Any time you show even a little knowledge about an activity a buyer is especially interested in, you're a long pass closer to a touchdown.

# Capturable Customers and Clients

## Seven Statements You Should Make

You should make these seven statements to every serious prospect who comes through your open house door—provided they're true.

**1.** "**I'm a full-service Multiple Listing agent.**" Many people, particularly first-time buyers, don't realize that agents will research their needs and take them around to see a lot of houses—all without charge. When they see Green Gulch Realty's sign on a property, some of them think they have to call Green Gulch to see it. It's a mistake to operate as though all of the buying public understands how the Multiple works. To make statement 1, you must belong to an organization authorized to use the Multiple Listing MLS trademark.

2. **"I'm a hard worker. I understand how important a real estate decision is to you, and I will do everything possible to make sure you get the finest service."**

3. **"I want to prove myself to you. You deserve the best in professional representation. Real estate is a person's most sound lifetime investment."**

4. **"I'll make every moment count. I know your time is precious."**

5. **"I'm a pioneer here."** (Say this if it applies, as it often does in the newer neighborhoods and communities. Newcomers like to associate with pioneers because pioneers are believers in the area and know it well. In mature communities, say "I've been here a long time." Be sure to declare it if you have. Your prospects will be impressed and pleased.)

6. **"Let me give you the royal tour of our community."** Never forget they have to buy the community before they'll buy a home in it.

7. **"I feel a responsibility to do right by you. I hope you'll consider me a prime resource for the solid information and hard work it takes to find exactly what you want."**

## Take One Step at a Time: Leaps Scare Off Capturable Prospects

Suggest to the lookers, "Let me make up a list of houses that might meet your needs."

"Okay. Then we'll drive by and see if we like any of them."

This is a counterstroke. They're not ready to commit to an appointment yet. You don't need to press for an appointment—what you need is a way back to them.

"Terrific. Should I phone the list to you, or mail it?"

"I'll call you—I've got your card."

"Sounds great."

Let him off the hook. They aren't ready for action yet. You want to hang in with them, yet lose the least amount of time. Talk a little.

Then say, "I know of three houses you might want to drive by."
(Here's where your Quick-Speak Inventory pays one of its many
dividends.)

"Just let me give you the addresses so you can run by them on
your way home."

Pull out one of your Show List forms (this form is available on the
accompanying CD) and jot down the addresses and a few other details.
Two of the houses aren't your listings. Tell them you can represent them
to obtain the best possible price—and go on to say you're a full-service
Multiple Listing Agent. Try again for their names, "So I can put it together in case you see something you like and want to call me back."

## Phone Phrases for
## Upping Attendance

Identify yourself as soon as they answer, and then say,

- "I hope I haven't interrupted your Sunday, but if you're in the
  mood for looking at houses, please stop by and see me. I'm
  holding a home open two blocks north of your house, just over
  on Magnolia."
- "I represent your neighbors, Martin and Christel Zweig. Do you
  happen to know them?"

When you've made courteous reply to their answer, go on with,
"I'm the special agent (*special* rather than *listing* agent) servicing their
property. They're leaving us, unfortunately. Do you enjoy this neighborhood as much as the Zweigs have?" Listen to their reply.

"Well, good. Do you know of anyone who might want to invest
in this fine area? The reason I ask is because I am holding the Zweig
property open today and I'd be glad to contact anyone you think might
be interested in living here in our wonderful community."

## Build Your Clientele
## with Note-Taking Habits

Immediately after each looker leaves your open house, record everything you can remember on your laptop, or on cards. Try dictating
everything you recall into your cassette recorder. Using a tape recorder
will encourage you to recall more things about the people, to visualize
them more clearly, and this process will intensify your memory of them.

Prospects want you to remember what they like and don't like.
They're insulted and diminished when you forget, flattered and made
to feel important when you remember. Retaining many of the little de-

tails they drop about themselves helps you to understand what they'll like in a house, and what will turn them off. It delivers a far more powerful, "You are important to me," message than anything else you might say.

## Find Your Way Back to the Hesitant Prospect

Here's where your questioning techniques and note-taking habits really pay off. A couple comes into your open house and, in your relaxed manner, you draw information out of them. The man is elusive; he doesn't want to be pinned down. Not until late in the conversation do you discover that he's being transferred into your county. At this point, their baby starts crying and they quickly leave.

You immediately jot down all you know about them:

"M/M Field. Chuck and Marcie. One child, new baby, Laura. He's slender, thinning blond hair, glasses, nice big toothy smile. Doesn't say much, voice soft. Marcie, short, red hair and freckles. She does the talking."

As you write, you're visualizing this couple and impressing their distinguishing characteristics on your mind. You add, "Chuck is an electrical engineer, being transferred in by Sparks Corp. She's a nurse, not working now."

You add a number of other details, what colors she likes and so on. They came in at 4 P.M. on Sunday, took one of your flyers, and you doubt you'll ever hear from them again unless you do something about it. You don't know where they're staying, or where they're coming from except it's out of state.

Monday morning you call Sparks Corporation. The receptionist says she's never heard of Charles Field. You ask for Human Resources and identify yourself.

"Yes, Mr. Field is scheduled to start work here on the 15th."

"He's interested in a house I was holding open yesterday. Could I send you some information about the house so you could forward it to him?"

You don't ask for his address directly because this gives Human Resources the perfect opening to get rid of you fast with a, "We're-not-allowed-to-give-out-that-information-sorry-I-can't-help-you-goodbye." Zap. You're dead.

Instead, she's thinking, "I don't want to be bothered with this." So she says, "Mail it to him directly so he'll get it sooner. His address is—"

Write the Fields, ". . . enjoyed talking with you last Sunday very much . . ." Of course you don't relate how you got their home address. There's no need; you identified yourself to his company and stated your legitimate business. By the time the Fields get your letter on Wednesday, they'll think one of them gave you their address. Chances are, you're the only agent who got back to them. You've scored points with the Fields by making them feel important. Follow up your letter with long-distance phone calls. You have a clear course now. Fly it, and the next time they come to town you'll have an appointment to meet them at the airport and show them property.

## Handle Two Separate Parties

When two separate parties walk in your "Quick Overview of Green Pretty Valley" notebook, your "Popular Floor Plans and Price Ranges" notebook, your flyer packets, and your storyboards and self advertisements on the four easels (described earlier in this chapter) will keep the overflow people busy while you talk with the first ones to come in. Say to your first couple, "This is a four-bedroom home with a bonus room and a view, priced at $210,000. Is this in line with your needs?"

They answer:

- "No, we don't need this much room."
- "Well, I don't know, we're just looking."
- "Maybe."

You say, "Fine, I've developed this compact presentation of the most popular floor plans here in Green Pretty Valley. Price information is in there too. Would you like to look at this for a moment while I greet these other people?"

They answer, "We didn't want to go over $150,000."

You say, "Terrific. We have several lovely properties in that range. Take a look at my compact presentation while I greet these other fine people for a moment."

They answer, "This is beautiful."

You say, "Wonderful. Make yourselves at home. Feel free to look around. I'll check with you in a moment after I've greeted these other fine people."

You do. Then make your decision, based on your immediate perception of what's best for you, of who to stick with, or whether you should keep moving back and forth between the two groups. Don't allow the decision to be made for you by whoever happens to be the gabbiest or the pushiest. Simply break in, smiling, and say, "Excuse me. I'll get back to you in a moment," if your attention is being monopolized by a chatterbox.

## Hide Your Multiple Listing Book

You impress prospects by what you know, not by what you dig out of the MLS while they stand there, drumming their fingers, wondering why they're wasting time with an agent who doesn't care enough, or know enough, to be properly prepared for prospects.

# Lock Up and Turn Off Lights

This is another basic, obvious detail. But if you, as an owner, were to come home after being away for the day because of an open house and find closing-up details neglected, you'd be on the phone fast too. Be careful about closing up. Don't rush. And don't have your mind on getting home, or on working with a buyer, until you've finished your open house properly. Closing down your seller's home is important; it deserves a few minutes of your undivided attention.

# Bring Your Own Banana

The first open house I worked started off poorly and got worse. At the last minute I thought about signs. By the time I'd rushed around borrowing them, I was late.

The owners gave me dirty looks and drove off. I walked inside. The tension didn't go away. Finally I realized why—hunger. I'd passed up breakfast for lunch, and then missed lunch. Not only was I hungry, I had nothing to do. I'd brought only a pad of deposit receipts.

All through that long, dispirited, weak afternoon, I sat there. Only two couples, neither very interested in the house or my services, came through.

It was a small house. There was nothing to read. There was nothing to eat either, except four big beautiful bananas on the kitchen table.

I didn't dare look squarely at those bananas. My will wouldn't handle it. I kept telling myself, "Eating a client's food is stealing."

Playing it safe, I stayed in the living room—but I couldn't stop thinking about those luscious bananas. Four bananas. But the owners had two kids of banana-eating age. A banana would be missed for sure. At 4:00 I was shaky blue with boredom and hunger, but I knew there was no way I'd let myself touch those bananas.

I kept my resolve until about 4:15, when suddenly it melted. I crept up on the kitchen table like a Comanche, seized one of the bananas, ripped off its end—and stared at wax!

Since then, I've always brought my own banana. This idea soon expanded to include bringing everything I'd need to effectively work an open house. Then I took it a big step further. Before every kind of appointment, I began taking a moment to visualize the coming situation. I thought about preparing mentally, about psyching up when it was called for, and about gathering the necessary gear to be productive when I got there.

Sometimes it takes a lot of forethought. But it's always worth it. Spend the necessary moments visualizing where you'll be, what you'll be doing, and what attitude and items you'll need. Spend those moments early, while there's still time to prepare. Hold multiple open houses. Partner. Hold weekday open houses. Keep moving and working. Bring the laptop and don't forget to . . . bring your own banana . . . and prosper.

# CHAPTER 10

# Any Time Is Up-Time

## You're Up

I never had the added bonus of up-time. In the beginning of my career I was considered a part-timer due to my pregnancy. (Part time is a state of mind. There are plenty of people who look full time but are part time and vice versa.) With electronic messaging, the Internet, e-communication, cell phones, and so on, you can create up-time even when you are not on the floor schedule. Just make your personal up-time prospect time your priority for at least one hour every day.

Most active agents have at least one cellular phone. By putting their voice mail or personal phone numbers on ads and signs, they receive most of their calls directly. While this reduces the message-taking chores of the up person, it also makes it even more vital that the agent perform effectively when handling incoming calls from potential customers.

The phone rings. You answer pleasantly, and *briefly*. Some people answer the phone with a speech: "Good morning. Thank you for calling Eagercluck Realty in beautiful Green Pretty Valley. This is Rosemarie Eagercluck speaking. How can I be of service to you on this glorious spring day?"

"By shutting up, and letting me tell you what I want," your caller thinks to herself.

Other agents think they sound busy and important if they answer the phone with a grunt, or a growled hello. Already the caller is sorry he called. Grunts and growls on a business phone are often taken to mean, "I'm in no shape to handle new business."

Note: The following information is directed to both the agent-on-call or the call receiver. Call receiver programs are popular at some companies.

# The Best Opener

"Sell Fast Realty, this is Mary."

This simple statement of your company's name, followed by your name, is the best opening line you can use. Saying those few words pleasantly conveys a great deal. You're brisk, business-like, and friendly; your caller has reached the office he wanted to reach; he's talking to a person important enough to be known by name. And your straight-to-it manner has subtly said, "It's okay to get directly into the reason for your call. In fact, I'd rather you would."

Avoid saying, "How may I direct your call?" or any other phrases used by salaried receptionists. Salaried receptionists are fine people but you're not one—you're an agent who works on commission.

An up-call is any call from a prospect the up-people can legitimately try to bring in as their own customer. When people call in asking for another agent, it's larceny to try and take the caller over. These things become known, and they cause trouble. Play square. Make supporters instead of enemies in your office; foster cooperation instead of score settling.

When you take an up-call your purpose is to make an appointment, not to help the person eliminate the property he's called about. Bear in mind it's often not possible, so make your try with determination and a light heart. Your caller may be checking to see how his own listing is being handled, or killing time waiting for the agent he's already decided to work with.

Converting calls to appointments is where the money is, and the only place it is, on up-time. Those calls will come in sandwiched between all kinds of routine calls. When they do, it's your duty—to yourself and your company—to concentrate on getting the appointment to the exclusion of all else.

Your back-up person should be quick to pick up the phone when you wave your hand in a prearranged signal to show you're occupied.

It takes concentration to convert a prospecting call into an appointment. Here is how it's done.

# Winning Scripts for Ad and Sign Calls

1. **Avoid giving the buyer immediate control by stating the property's price.** The following introduction is a winning script to use on all ad calls:

    "Stones River Realty, this is Liz McCleary."

    "I'm calling about the 'Rainbow's end' house in your ad. Can you give me the price?"

    "Certainly. I'll put you on hold for just a moment while I get the information." Come back on the line in no more than 15 seconds and say, "Another agent is using the 'Rainbow's end' file right now. Will you be where you are now for another five minutes?"

    Usually they'll respond with something like, "I can be."

    "Fine. If you'll give me the privilege of knowing your name and number, I'll call you right back."

    Some of them won't tell you their name and number, which is a practical way to separate calls worth your time from the worthless ones.

    When you call back those who do tell you, you're in a far stronger position. You know their name and number, and they've asked you to call them—so the first threads of a relationship are in place. Now you have a good chance of arranging a meeting with them. Had you simply given them the price when they asked for it, the odds are about 80 to 1 against ever hearing from them again.

2. **If your ads tell everything, you won't get many calls.** Whatever basic fact (price, address, terms) the ad doesn't give will be the thing most callers want to get out of you. They'll want to do it fast so they can get off the phone with you and go about their business. Here are three ways of coping with this problem. These responses work whether callers are trying to get the price, the address, or any other bit of information.

    • "Thank you, Mrs. Summers. I'd *love* to give you the facts on the property. In fact, I'll be happy to drop off a copy of the property fact sheet. Would you be there at two this afternoon, or would you rather come over here now and pick it up?"

    • "Thank you, Mr. Turner. I'd *love* to give you the facts on the house you're interested in. May I ask, have you ever looked for property and been frustrated because everything you looked at wasn't to your liking? Or perhaps when selling your own home, you've been frustrated because most of the people coming through weren't right for it? Well, we do things differently here. You and our homeowners are too important. We promised them we'd interview everyone prior to showing their property because time is important both to you and to them. So, could you stop by our office in the next hour, or would you rather I'd meet you somewhere else early this afternoon?"

- When they won't let you off the hook, say the price and in one breath add, "it's-in the-range-you-had-in-mind?"

"My price range is a lot less," and the caller gives the figure, sounding wounded.

"Terrific," you say, with enthusiasm. "We've got several beautiful properties in your price range."

If you allow the faintest hint of disappointment or condescension to creep into your voice, you've lost the caller. You can trade a bit of free enthusiasm for a fee here.

**3. You've held your prospect past the price problem.**
Continue with, "I know I have just the right property for you, but I'm going to ask you a few questions—you don't mind, do you?"

With the caller's permission, ask, "How many are there in your family?"

Use this roundabout way instead of asking directly how many children they have. Through tragedy or disappointment, *how many children* may be a very sore point. If they give you any number over two, after telling you they're married, fill in your knowledge of their basic housing needs. Suppose your caller says there are five people in his family.

"Are the other three all children, or do you and your wife have some adults living with you?"

"Our three children live with us."

"So I'll understand your needs correctly, what are your children's ages?"

Usually they'll volunteer the sex of their children along with their ages. If they don't, ask.

"Is your six-year-old a boy or a girl?"

Keep notes of what your caller tells you. If you've forgotten the answers you're trying his patience to get now, you'll lose more credibility than you can afford to sacrifice when you meet him. Use a Fast Fact Grabber form (available on the accompanying CD and shown in Chapter 24) to organize this information, or design your own form.

As soon as you have the answers to your questions about the caller's family, you have to make a quick decision. This is the earliest you can take the next step without sounding insincere, but it would be better if you knew more about their likes and dislikes as to house style, interior colors, and amenities. But if your caller is getting impatient, another round of questions now may get you the "I gotta go, goodbye" shutoff. There's no defense against it. Unless it's an easy flowing conversation, and you're hitting it off well with the caller, go with what you have now.

4. **Tell your caller about possible property.** "I saw a terrific property yesterday; it might be exactly what you're looking for. I believe it's just come on the market, so it's not on the Multiple Listing yet." (Don't you always know of such a property?) "Let me check out the particulars and call you back. Will you be where you are now for the next 30 minutes?"

"I can be."

"Great. What's the number there?"

5. **Getting the phone number on an up-call is a mid-size win.** Once you have the number, he'll readily give you his name. Call him back in ten minutes. You know his price range, the number of bedrooms he needs, and something of his preference from the house he called about originally. From your Quick-Speak Inventory, you'll be able to jot down at least three houses on your show list of likely interest to your prospect. But, before you ring off, you have two more things to do. Your caller has told you his name is Tom Jordan.

"Mr. Jordan, I know you've circled other ads in the paper (or looked at other properties in the area if he called from a sign) and I'd love to help you with them. Which ones interest you?"

If he gives you this information, you'll be able to learn more than he can about those houses by calling the listing offices and telling them you have a customer who is interested in one of their offerings.

The second thing you must now do is make sure Tom Jordan gave you his real phone number. The method of spotting phony numbers is given later in this chapter.

6. **You struck out on questions 3 and 4.** But your caller hasn't hung up on you, so keep whacking away with the following

string of questions. Any one of them may open up a line of discussion able to take you in to an appointment close.

"What feature in the ad interested you most?"

"What's causing you to think of moving this way?"

"Do you own your home now, or do you rent?"

"Will you keep your present home as an investment, or will you sell?" *or*

"Most people need to sell their present home before they buy another one. Is this what you plan to do?"

"Are you calling from your home, or are you already out looking?"

"Have you seen any houses in this area yet?"

"How long have you been looking?"

"Have you seen anything you like?"

"What area do your friends live in?"

7. **If you're flying high with the prospect, really hitting it off well, don't go on too long before you press for a name and phone number.** Be frank about it. There's no better technique than reality. Use it whenever you can.

"We've been talking for a few minutes now." (Even if it's been half an hour, never say it's been a *long* time.) "I feel confident of being able to serve all your real estate needs. In case our conversation gets cut off unexpectedly, let's stop right now and arrange an appointment. Which hours do you prefer—daytime or evening?"

Now be quiet. If your caller isn't playing games, he'll make the appointment with you. If he or she is playing games and weaving away from the appointment, thank them kindly for calling, and ask them to call again if they'd like to work with you.

8. **You've made the appointment.** They're coming in. If it's happening fast—before you're off floor duty, have your backup take over. While you wait for your new customers, work as close to the door as you can. They said they'd be there at 1:00. At 1:00 the door opens. A couple you've never seen before comes in, so you take the initiative.

"You must be Mr. and Mrs. O'Brien. I'm delighted to have the chance to meet you. I introduced myself on the phone. I'm _____. (Repeat your name now because they may have forgotten it and, as you do so, hand them one of your cards.) It's a privilege to have the opportunity to serve you."

Now follow the coffee and qualifying routine given in Chapter 15 in Winning Scripts.

## Spotting Phony Numbers

"By the way, I want to make sure I have the right number." Repeat the number they gave you, but transpose two digits: they said 123-7654, you repeat back 123-7645. If they correct *you,* it's a good call. If they don't correct you, they've probably given you a phony number. But you're not certain yet. So play along with them to the end of the call. Then think of a reason to call them back: a question you forgot to ask, or you just got a message postponing your afternoon appointment, so you could meet with them right away after all. Have a plausible reason for phoning back because they might answer. They might've given you their right number, and simply have been too preoccupied to notice your intentional transposition when you repeated it back. But, if they didn't correct you, the odds are they gave you a wrong number. Checking it out will save you the trouble of getting ready for a pair of no-shows.

## Putting Someone on Hold

"Thank you for waiting. I really appreciate your patience." Get back to the caller often if she's holding for another agent in the office. Make sure all callers realize they've reached a superior office where the people really care about giving service.

## Spirited Teams Make More Money

Playing square with your comrades in the office builds a team spirit clients and customers feel, appreciate, and value. Every time you're tempted by a gray area, put yourself behind the other agent's eyes, and imagine how you'd like it if you were on the other end of the same situation. It takes the whole team to build team spirit. You can start a rebirth of the team spirit in your office. You don't have to be "Goodie Goodie Shined Shoes" to do it; simply set a good example of fairness, of leaning to the other agent when the case isn't clear cut, and tell the other agents you're acting with enlightened self-interest—which is exactly what you're doing. Working in an office where strong team spirit has built mutual trust and respect among the associates is not only more satisfying, it's also financially more rewarding.

Some agents need more time than others to learn they can't expect their co-workers to take good messages for them if they don't take good messages for their co-workers. Unrecorded or wrongly recorded messages can lose big money, or cause big trouble. Take messages with care.

Never tell a caller, "He's not in." Those are mean little words when used by themselves. Many agents say those words with a *Go-away-I'm-busy* note in their voice as though they want to discourage the caller from bothering them with a message.

Saying, "Not in," often makes the caller ask, "Do you know where I can reach him?"

Some thoughtless salespeople create problems by volunteering information in this situation. They create problems for the other agent and for themselves too; callers often report such incidents with great glee when they finally get through to the person they're calling. Here's a sampling of trouble-making phrases:

- "I haven't heard from him all day. He's just part time here, you know."
- "I think he took off for the beach."
- "He's out of town somewhere—maybe on vacation. I don't know when we're going to hear from him again." (Translation: "If you're in a hurry, get yourself another agent.")

People who want to work in an office with an uplifting spirit and money-making ways say something like:

"Dranesville Realty, this is Karen."

"John Forney, please."

"John's out in the field, but I'll hear from him soon. May I have your name and number? I'll make sure he gets your message as soon as possible."

## Create a Trust-Enhancing Environment

Create an environment able to inspire confidence in your integrity, stability, and competence. It's enormously easier to deal with people who trust you. And people will trust you if you don't jangle their alarm bells. Many people who buy houses equate cleanliness and order with honesty and competence. Maintenance of the building is management's responsibility, but the night-time cleaning crew can't pick up during the day after trash-unconscious associates. Dispose of plastic cups and fast-food clutter swiftly. Don't let newspapers accumulate. Do your part. Your office's image is inseparable from your own.

Not only the surroundings you work in, but the way you dress and your personal grooming, your eye contact and body language, your manner and tone of voice, your entire posture and attitude, are part of the environment in which your customers' confidence will bloom or wither.

You never get a second chance to make a first impression. If you have a desk so messy even finding a pen on it would be difficult, they'll wonder how you'll ever find them a house. Your desk should be clean and orderly. Place on it items that show you mean business, like an amortization book, a legal-size pad, and net sheets. Display your real estate trophies and certificates around your desk. People like to know they're dealing with a winner.

Have a family photo on your desk, to show you're something besides an agent, you're a human being too. "Oh, he's got a family. Maybe he isn't such a bad guy after all," they'll think. They'll absorb the fact and feel more comfortable with you. Have you ever gone into a doctor's inner office and noticed, with a twinge of surprise, the family photos on his desk? Reassuring, wasn't it, to realize he doesn't appear out of no where in a white coat each morning to do whatever he does to people? Your doctor has a family, and his concerns are similar to yours.

Let your personality and interests show. But just let the tip of the iceberg be seen (or talked about) because your customers are far more interested in themselves than in you.

## What Walk-ins Fear

Peoples defenses are raised when they walk into a real estate office to announce their desire to buy or sell. They're thinking, *"Here I am—ready to be ripped off."* Never let walk-ins think they're doing something odd. Never allow walk-ins to feel they don't belong, or aren't welcome. And never, never let them wonder if coming into your office was a mistake. All too often, after being ignored for two endless minutes by people who continue to talk on the phone without showing a flicker of interest in him, a walk-in is thinking along those lines. He doesn't know the system. He doesn't know the up-gal went out for doughnuts, and the backup-guy went to the bathroom without telling anyone to take over the floor. He doesn't know everybody else takes him for the man Mac called to fix something. Another walk-in, another walk-out.

Other offices do the scramble. Inside the front door is the usual row of desks. A prosperous-looking couple walks in. Instantly, thickets of eyes stare at them, and panic grips the air.

"Yikes—who's up?"

"I think Jack is."

"But the dang fool just went downtown."

"Gimme the schedule. There it is, Wednesday morning. You're up, Jean."

"I was up yesterday. This must be Thursday."

"Oh, my! *I'm* up."

There should be an up-desk or a secretary's desk at the front of the office, if the room is large enough. When someone walks in, the up-person or the secretary immediately gives them a pleasant, "Good morning. May I help you?"

If no secretary is on duty, the up-person should be seated close to the entry area. Everything needed for the qualifying interview should be handy, along with sales and listing kits.

# Tea Cart, Be-Back Book, and Sign-Out Sheet

Floor time can be efficiently organized on a tea cart. On its top and a shelf or two, there'll be plenty of space for the following items:

- Office's master inventory file of listings
- Notebook or file containing copies of all current ads
- 3 × 5 file box, with dividers for each salesperson, so it's easy to check for their messages
- Call record book in duplicate. After a message is recorded, the original is torn out and filed behind the divider of the salesperson called, and the duplicate remains in the book to insure no messages are lost.
- Sign-out sheet. A page for each day provides a place for every agent in the office to leave instructions to the up-person as to how their messages are to be handled at particular times, and when they'll call in or return to the office.
- Be-back book, or a page in the listing and ad notebook, provides a place for the up-person to record the name of any prospect, walk-in or call-in, who might return later. Whenever this happens the current up-person tells the agent who recorded the prospect's name that a customer or client has come back to work with her or him.

When a buyer walks in, the up-person greets him, and then signals for the backup person to take over the floor. As unobtrusively as possible, the backup person comes forward and takes over the up-desk, or wheels the cart back to his or her own desk. This allows the up-person to concentrate on converting the walk-in to a client or customer.

A warm welcome kicks those conversion attempts straight at the goal. But if your walk-in had to face 12 eyes in a staring contest, and then had to ask for help before being recognized, the game's nearly lost. Why start from behind? This is not the time when silence is golden. This is not the time to make your walk-in feel isolated. Ideally, windows will allow one of the staff to see people coming before they reach the door. The secretary, or whoever sees them, should say in a calm voice, "Someone's coming in."

The up-person, if seated in the back, should immediately come forward and act as the host or hostess. The prospects walk in the door and there's no time lag. Someone immediately gives them a friendly, "Welcome to Quarles Realty. May I help you?"

"I need a map."

"Fine. I'll get you a map." He hands it to the walk-in—who then walks out. The prospect is never seen again. The up-person didn't say one word able to catch the golden nugget and start it rolling toward his bank account.

Let's try it again.

## Electronic Tea Cart

All of the above can be put on a laptop. (Scan sign out sheets or be-back book forms and people can call in the instruction for you to complete.) Then you have a paperless organized space while doing your up-time. Anytime!!!!

# Five Winning Scripts for Walk-ins

Cultivate a bright and cheery manner, and an enthusiastic but business-like tone whether you're face-to-face or on the phone.

1. **Your office has a sign out offering free maps.** A man comes in and says, "I need a map."

    "You've come to the right place, sir. Are you new in this area?"

    "No, I'm looking for a friend's barbecue party, and I'm having trouble finding their home."

    "Hey, have a good time at the barbecue. Here's your map—and a memo pad and my card. If you ever need any real estate services, or more maps—or even if you're just in the neighborhood drop in and say hello. Bye—nice talking to you."

    Make the person feel glad he went into your office. He might get transferred tomorrow. Or find out at the party about a friend who has just decided to sell and tell him about you. You've got an instant to make an impression. Be sure he goes away feeling your office's reason for being open is to serve *him*. It's a feeling many people will remember a long time.

2. **A confident-looking couple on an area-scouting expedition come in.** "You've come to the right place for a map, folks. I'll be glad to get you one. Is this your first trip to the valley?"

"Yes, we're looking here for the first time today. But, quite frankly, we haven't decided to work with an agent yet. We want to take a map, drive the area, stop at some open houses—and see the new model homes. We just don't want any pressure right now."

"Fine. If you don't find what you're looking for at the model homes, we have several resales of the same quality. Many of our sellers here in Green Pretty Valley have taken great pride in home ownership, and buying one of their homes is like buying a model. Sometimes it's a lot better, because everything's done. And our availability might be greater than what they have in new home sales. So, please, before you make your final decision on a new home, come back and see me if you have the chance. You might be very pleased you did."

Then hand them a prospect-catcher map you have ready.

"And, just to give you an idea of what's available on the resale market, here's some information on several outstanding properties we represent in this office." Here's another place to use the flyer packets from Chapter 9.

3. **If they're not running for the door, try for their name.** "By the way, I'm Jim Carleton of Mesilla Realty—?" This and a friendly smile will usually draw their name from them.

"I'm Harry Lookwell."

If they come back, it will probably be after you're off floor duty. Your office should have a "Be-Back Book" (A page in the up-book will do it.) "M/M Harry Lookwell—Jim Carleton." If the Lookwells come back, whoever's on the floor should then call Jim Carleton and say, "The gentleman you talked to while you were on the floor—the one you put in the Be-Back Book— he's here now. He'd like to give you the opportunity to work with him a little bit."

So, it's important, when you hand them the map, to say, "Here's my card. I'm with Kelly Realty, and I'm here to serve you. May I ask your name?"

"John Pelham, but I'm going to the models."

"Fine. Mr. Pelham. If you want to, feel free to stop back later today. Maybe we can help you get more familiarized with resale homes. It's a big-dollar decision, and lots of people want to make sure they've seen everything of interest before making it. Have a nice day."

4. **A man and woman walk in.** They look unsure of themselves. *Up-Person*: "Welcome to Quaker Road Realty. May I help you? (No pause here.) My name is Emily Matthews?" (Remind them to tell you their names by saying yours as a question.)

"We're Bob and Lana Reynolds. We want to look at houses."

"You've certainly come to the right place, Mr. and Mrs. Reynolds. We're one of the fastest-moving real estate offices in this area, and we're here to serve you. May I ask how you heard about us?"

(They answer.)

"Thank you so much for choosing our firm. It's a privilege to meet both of you, and hopefully we'll have the opportunity to work together until your housing needs are filled. The first thing I'd like to do is invite you to be seated at my desk," or, "—to join me in our conference room. Perhaps both of you would enjoy a cup of coffee."

(Walk them back to your desk or to the conference room and pull out the chairs.) "Make yourselves at home. Please excuse me while I prepare a bit of coffee for you both." (Bring two of your imprinted memo pads back to the conference table.) "Here you go. You might want to use these memo pads for a coaster, and then make notes on them while we're out touring property."

5. **A couple walks in after seeing a sign.** House hunters sometimes find it more convenient to walk in than to phone after seeing one of your company's signs on a property, or reading one of your ads.

Again, the up-person should be in the front third of the office and on the alert. "Welcome. I'm Terri Wing with Kraskova Realty. Can I help you?"

"We saw your sign over on Vista del Lago and we'd like to see the inside."

"Wonderful. Would you like a cup of coffee while I call for an appointment to show the home?" Take them back to the conference room, sit them down with their coffee and, after building rapport for a few moments, get into the qualifying interview. Use the buyer's analysis for better service form (available on the accompanying CD). Chapter 15 covers this crucial step in detail. Qualify them. Work in the light, not in the dark.

## Up-Time Is Opportunity Time

Up-time is rightly called opportunity time—but don't rely on it for your income. Consider any business you acquire through working the floor as a bonus, and organize yourself to constructively use the quiet moments while you're up. The business is out in the field, not in the office.

# CHAPTER 11

# Impact Listing: How Listings Are Won and Sellers Are Served by World-Class Salespeople

The principles of listing in this chapter are timeless. We may not be cutting out pictures or gluing together listing presentation manuals anymore. We may not even have marketing or ad firms create brochures or manuals for us because we have it all now on computers/laptops. But the contents of what is important in this presentation format are still valuable. So adjust everything you read to make these principles computer friendly. Unless, of course, you still prefer hardcopy graphics.

Before you can be a strong lister, you must have a strong listing philosophy. Much more than a craving to make a lot of money is required. You must believe in yourself, in your ability and determination to promote and negotiate the large issues, and in your willingness to follow through on the smallest details. You must be fully aware of this truth: Although the money is there, it isn't there merely for the taking; it has to be earned with timely and effective work.

Three factors determine salability: price, condition, and location. If condition and location are favorable, price then becomes the key factor.

# Strong Listers Have
# the Best Protection

Each day, all of the available real estate in the nation calls for bids in a vast, silent, slow-paced auction. In the process, Montana's cattle ranches compete for mortgage funds with Florida's condos. Most buyers are limited by their roots or work, and consider only the properties available within a small area. However, each year, more buyers widen their horizons and compare Maui to Miami before buying in either place.

With few exceptions, effective demand comes down to two things: the will to own now, and the ability to deliver the necessary cash, whether borrowed or owned. Every real estate transaction involves impermanent people in semipermanent decisions. Circumstances are changing for the buyers while they wait for their transactions to close. Will-to-own-now is the sum of many emotions held together by anything from a thread to a chain of logic. In a stable market, individual decisions to sell roughly match individual decisions to buy. When either supply or demand exceeds the other, conditions are ripe for the herd instinct to aggregate the emotions of millions, and create price pressures too great to be long maintained. The reaction, the counter movement, must come. It always does and we know this. So why should a sudden shift in effective demand ever take us by surprise?

During my sales career the money market was constantly changing, just like it does now. I especially remember one 12-month period when the mortgage market fell in to a sorry state. People couldn't buy a resale home in California with new conventional financing unless they could make an initial investment of 40 percent. My volume for the year was four million dollars, which mostly came from the 92 listings I took during those 12 months. Many of them had assumable loans, and many of my sellers were willing to take back second mortgages for part of their equity. While I was working frantically to keep up with my opportunities, I heard on every side how pointless it was to take listings because who could find buyers with enough money to plunk down 40 percent?

I couldn't find many 40-percenters either, but I certainly located, and closed, lots of assumers. Strong listers have the best protection against the market's whims if they adapt to its changing conditions. Listings taken and listings sold are the heart of real estate. The more listings you take during periods of high demand, the more you'll be able to take when demand drops off. By concentrating on obtaining and marketing listings able to interest buyers in the tightened situation, strong listers insulate themselves from the worst of a cold market's chill.

The only way you can protect yourself is to think ahead and prepare for the next change. **Wherever your market is now on the cycle—rising, falling, or stable—it's preparing to change.** It will probably change sooner than you expect. We tend to live in last week and today. Successful listing agents look beyond today, beyond next week, and pass their foresight on to their sellers.

Your listing goals and methods should be very different in the rapidly rising market, the falling market, and the stable market. Bear in mind that some parts of your marketing area, or some types of houses within it, can be falling while other parts or types are rising.

# Before the Listing Presentation Appointment

Careful preparation makes or breaks the listing presentation. Before you go on a listing presentation, be sure to do the following:

- Drive the area
- Compile a Guidelines to Market Value (GMV)
- Note overimprovements

## Drive the Area

Look for properties not in the record: fizzbos (for-sale-by-owners), exclusive listings, new listings, recent sales. Research all the activity you find. Knock on the fizzbo doors, call the listing agents, and get any information not in the record.

There's a good chance that two things just happened: (1) another house nearby just sold and, (2) your prospective listees know it. You come in for a listing appointment with the Smiths and the first thing Mr. Smith says is, "How much did the Halls get?"

The best way to handle this is to name the price the Halls sold their home for (if the sale has been recorded), and then firmly steer the conversation away from pricing. You don't want to talk money until you reach your game plan's time for working on this crucial and touchy matter.

But you can't go this way if you don't know what the Halls sold for. In fact, you don't know what house Mr. Smith is talking about, or even whether a family named Hall lives in your farm. If you knew all the family names in your farm, you could now say with assurance, "No family named Hall lives in my area of specialization, so the sale was elsewhere. What street. . . ."

This confident statement also conveys, "I know this locality extremely well; I really am *the* expert on the property here."

But you have to answer Mr. Smith's question. As you realize it's been two weeks since you've driven your entire farm, your palms get sweaty. You know a lot could've happened during those two weeks.

Now all you can do is throw a rock at the bear, "You must be talking about the four-bedroom house on West at Elm. It sold for X$*. I'm not sure the name was Hall though. By the way, I love your living room paneling. Did you put it in yourself?"

Smith won't let you off the hook. "Dick and Nancy Anderson sold the place on West at Elm. Haven't you seen the Hall's house?"

When in trouble, speak confidently, give pertinent information if possible, and ask a subject-changing question. You could minimize the damage if you could now say, "Sure. It's the two-story stone-front. Nice house. Must've just sold. I'll call right now and find out what it went for."

You could bail yourself out this way if you knew the house. But if you don't know fact one about it, all you can say is, "I'll find out what Hall sold for and get back to you."

"Well, I hope so," Mrs. Smith says. "The Hall's place is just like ours, and it sold fast. I'm surprised you don't know about it. Anderson's was on the market for ages. Gus, is there any point in talking with this *person* until we know how much the Halls sold for?" As you slink out, Mr. Smith mutters, just loud enough for you to hear, "Some expert."

Picture it happening to you. Imagine it vividly. Then you'll never forget to drive the area before a listing presentation. It doesn't matter whether your appointment is in your farm. Sellers usually don't know or care about the farming concept. Are you an expert on the real estate around here, or aren't you? It's that simple to them. So drive the first few streets around a listing appointment. Allow yourself time for checking when your search turns up activity you didn't know about.

## Virtual Tour Comparable Listings

Be sure you go online and check any new listing additions in the market area you are surveying. Yes, driving the area is important. But virtual touring and surfing the net for new listings pays off too. Another office might have just put something on that you are unaware of that is pertinent to your upcoming presentation.

---

* X$ stands for a dollar amount relevant in your area now.

## Compile a Guidelines to Market Value (GMV)

Select and enter on this form (Chapter 24 has a sample and it is also available on the accompanying CD) the sales, expired listings, and current listings most like the property you hope to list.

Where do I get this information? By visiting the properties involved. If you can't get inside, drive past. Then—in order of convenience—gather more data from the following sources:

- Your personal comparables file, your office's comp file, your Multiple Listing Service's records
- The Internet, or other computerized or microfilm services
- Title insurance companies, in some states or provinces
- The county assessor's office

Have the information fresh in your mind, and concisely written on a Guidelines to Market Value form, when you keep your listing appointment. What if there are no comparables? Particularly in areas with older homes constructed by many builders, this can be a problem. There are two ways to deal with a lack of comparables:

**1.** Widen the area you can draw comparables from by establishing price differentials between your locality and other localities. Do this by comparing average prices *paid* (ignore asking prices, of course) per square foot. Call a friendly real estate agent in the other locality for the information you need. With just this one bit of research, you can determine that houses in Westport, where you operate, sell for 8 percent more per square foot than similar houses in Eastport, a town just outside your board's jurisdiction. Armed with this price differential, you can use comparable sales in Eastport to establish value in Westport with conviction by the simple process of adding 8 percent to the prices paid.

**2.** Contact a loan representative and discuss the property you need to establish value on—its location, lot size, age, condition, and so on—and get his opinion on the loan the property would carry for a qualified buyer. Then take it one step further with the lender. Prepare a buyer's profile net sheet prior to the appointment.

Don't just consult with the loan representative, ask him to prepare a buyer's net sheet proposal using a double income requirement. Use a middle-of-the-road figure of closed sales from the area. This allows the seller to get a perspective on what it will take a buyer to qualify for her home. We need to get the attention off of the seller. If we don't start prepping the seller about what a buyer profile is for her home, negotiations will be a big problem later in the process. Remember you can do this without paper. Just get the buyer profile net sheet on your laptop. Your loan rep can send it to you as an attachment to e-mail.

## Note Overimprovements

Many owners put a great deal of money or personal labor into improving their homes. Unless they're knowledgeable in these matters, or have been well advised, these improvements, installed to their own taste and for their own pleasure, won't add what they cost to the value of the property. I've had clients who felt they should get $3 back for every $1 they spent on improvements—when in fact their expensive decorating experiments actually *lowered* the value of their property.

When you walk in for a listing appointment and see room additions, costly wallpaper, exotic details, and many expensive extras, make careful notes—and get in a good frame of mind to fight for validity when it comes to pricing. Sellers don't understand how hard-eyed appraisers from lending institutions view expensive frippery—they don't think it's worth much. It's important to the sellers and their pride, but we still have to look to the market and contend with its realities. We can go only so far in recovering the cost of overimprovements if the house is going to sell. Generally, this won't be as far as the sellers are counting on going.

Carefully evaluate how emotionally involved the sellers are in their overimprovements as you tour their property. Acknowledge the sellers' comments with interest. Be sincere with your compliments.

"It's a pleasure to tour a home as lovely as yours." As you work with them and the Guidelines to Market Value form, be very sensitive. The seller's pocketbook is sensitive, and their hands with their blisters are sensitive! You'll find effective phrases for this situation in this chapter's Winning Scripts section.

Always carry a Listing Presentation Manual (LPM) when you keep listing appointments. The following section explains why you should have one, and how to create an effective one.

# The Listing Presentation Manual (LPM)

## Objectives of the Listing Presentation Manual

The good of the Listing Presentation Manual is to do the following:

- To build the sellers' confidence in the salesperson and the salesperson's company

- To build the salesperson's self-confidence
- To break barriers with client prospects
- To improve presentation quality
- **To win more listings**

You can go interactive and put your entire listing presentation on a CD-Rom business card. Just slide it into your computer and up comes everything that must be a part of your listing presentation. With a slick laptop presentation you can even include video clips of satisfied sellers and buyers. The initial cost of this high-tech video production may be too hefty for your budget. But if it is not, once you have it in place, the CD-Rom business cards are under $5 to reproduce. But remember you do not have to go interactive. Either way, a listing presentation should be as professional and as confidence-building as possible.

Some agents are tense during the listing presentation, which transfers their uncertainty and tension to the prospects. Having an LPM organizes your thoughts and keeps the interview moving. Your LPM will repay many times the concentrated effort necessary to create a good one—and to practice using it effectively.

Creating an LPM focuses your mind on developing a superlative presentation. Before you're there in reality, it projects you into the listing situation in your imagination so you can practice your lines, perfect your manual, and then go out and close more listings.

## How to Create a
## Listing Presentation Manual

Go interactive if possible. As you read this next section, figure out how you can cover all the objectives on your laptop. I love paperless presentations. Communication is 80 percent eyes and only 20 percent ears. Think about this as you plan your LPM.

Before you start putting your LPM together, ask yourself these questions:

- Why do sellers need an agent? What can a broker do for them that they can't do for themselves?
- What makes my company better than other companies?
- Why should the sellers select me?

You begin by selling the industry, go on to selling your company, and end up concentrating on your own value to them. They don't need you if they don't need an agent; they don't need you if they don't need your company's services; so sell them on those two concepts before narrowing it down. Fill the stage with scenery before you bring on the star—yourself.

There are two points of special impact in any presentation—the beginning and the end. The end is the more effective of the two because it's closer to decision time. For this reason, end on yourself.

There's another reason for orchestrating your presentation this way: If your accomplishments and general greatness are the opening number, people may think you're taking an ego trip on their time, and they'll be offended. Save yourself, not for the finale, but until the mood's set and your audience is warmed up. However, with your competent manner and control, sell yourself all the time. The reality is—it'll be you and the sellers all the way for 90 days. You're the one they're thinking about working with on a day-by-day basis. You're the one who'll represent them as the hammer strikes the anvil when an offer comes in. They must have faith in your professional abilities or they won't list with you. Make sure your presentation doesn't simply sell the industry and your company. Sell yourself. Do it with finesse, subtlety, and conviction.

Put together the best LPM you can today. Then build on this nucleus. The items needed for your Listing Presentation Manual are given in effective working sequence in Chapter 24. Presenting phrases for use with the manual appear in this chapter's Winning Scripts.

# LPM Preparation

## Keep Your LPM Speech Spontaneous

Memorizing a listing presentation speech from beginning to end is disastrous. It means you'll give the same speech to the just-fired and the just-promoted; the angry divorcee and the devastated widower; the sophisticated and the naive. It's like saying, "You're all the same to me, all you people I give this pitch to." Prospects catch this put-down and remain prospects until an agent comes along who recognizes their uniqueness and special sensitivities. The beauty of having your presentation outlined on your laptop is that you can be spontaneous. Spontaneous does not mean "shooting from the hip." You have all your ducks in a row (in this case on your laptop via photos, forms, videos, and so on) and then you tell the story around the visual.

If you're irritated by interruptions and have to get back on track before you can continue, your presentation is to canned, and it's going to hurt you. Change the sequence. Practice the parts, not the whole. The Listing Presentation Manual is only a guide. Always personalize your speech to your prospects' situation. Be sure to skip the parts without close application to the case at hand. Be ready to move ahead quickly if your listeners show boredom with unnecessary detail.

Encourage sellers to ask questions. Give full answers, and linger a little in the areas of special interest to the sellers. Talk with them, not at them. Keep these people involved. Get lots of feedback by relating the items in your LPM directly to their lives, the house they want to sell, and where they're going.

Photos in your LPM of you holding a *Sold* sign, and shaking hands with other sellers, provide many opportunities for happy and effective talk.

"There's Fanny and Jack Gordon. They needed a bigger house just like you folks do. I was able to find them a beauty. By the way, they're skiers too—maybe you'd like to meet them someday."

## Determine the Sellers' Motivation

Without pressing too hard, try to find out why they're selling before you have your meeting with the husband and wife. Unless you know why, you can't give them the best possible service. Unfortunately, many sellers believe otherwise. They think, "If we let the agents know we've got to sell in 60 days, they're going to gang up on us and beat down our price. By keeping them in the dark, we can get several thousand more dollars for our house." Many a wife or husband receives strict orders from a fearful spouse to withhold the truth.

This usually results in disaster for the sellers. The agent goes along with unrealistic pricing, thus allowing the sellers to think they've won an important battle. Time passes and there is no action. Then the sellers panic. Who gets trampled in the panic? The seller *and* the unwary listing agent. The listing expires or is canceled and the house sells through another office in a week at thousands under market. Ignorance of how the real estate market works, and the first agent's failure to gain the sellers' trust, led to these fiascoes.

Variations on this theme are played out constantly in real estate. The best defense against price games-playing is a genuine concern for your clients' welfare, sensitive alertness, and a frank attitude toward and thorough knowledge of pricing.

Sometimes sellers are reluctant to discuss their true motivations for understandable personal reasons. Where a family is breaking up, serious illness threatens, or careers and financial security are jeopardized, revealing true motivations may be too painful an experience for your sellers. Be empathetic. Credit them with more than unreasoning greed.

Financial or personal problems may make them feel desperate, or such a large decision as a house sale may have sharply distorted their ordinary personalities.

We deal with people, not with bricks and stucco—sometimes it's easy to forget this, especially if we've been in real estate for a long time. Everyone is different. They come from different backgrounds; they're bound for different destinations; and they'll travel different routes to get there.

A seller calls me and says, "Come over and list the house." Not until I get there does it come out about the divorce. They've been married 5—maybe 25—years. When I come in for their listing, I'm the one who's going to put the *For Sale* sign on their house. I'm chopping at their roots; I'm the symbol of what's happening to them. Where's the empathy if I hustle in there bubbling with enthusiasm, success, and good cheer?

"Wow, the market's really going great! I'm having a terrific year, folks! Yeah. Now let's take a look at the rest of this sweet little home of yours. Gee, it's neat. I like what you did with the wallpaper, and I *love* this carpet."

Don't chirp on and on at deeply wounded people. Don't bubble at all when you take a listing where a death, divorce, or other grievous event has just struck. Try to understand what they're going through. Do the job as quickly and professionally as you can, and then get out.

Why is it so important to know why they're selling as soon as possible? Because it'll tell you how to act during your meetings with them—it'll even tell you how fast to walk while you're touring the property, and whether to be relaxed and jolly, or crisp and business-like, during the listing interview.

## The Prospects Are Talking to Other Brokers, But You Haven't Presented Yet

If they're considering three agents, the ideal position is to make your presentation third. I usually win when I'm last, if only because they're tired by then. But if you're first, and then they're going to talk to Tom Green, and afterwards to Sara Rice, it's often "Who was the first agent? Oh well, let's go with Sara—she's here."

So, if you think you can pick your position on their schedule, try to find out who the competition will be.

"Hmm, I already have an appointment early this evening—who else is coming over tonight?"

Their answer, and your judgment on the two *how heavy* questions below, provide the basis for your decision on what course to fly now. This decision has an important bearing on your success ratio and it must be made instantly, so think through every aspect of it in advance.

- How heavy is the competition I'm facing for this particular listing? Can any of them close powerfully?
- How heavy an impression have I made so far on these prospects?

When you're competing against a strong closer (and it only takes one to do you in) but you haven't already made a strong impression on the prospects, your best chance is to present before the strong closer does. When the sellers are ready to make a decision (scheduling appointments with three agents indicates that they are) the first one up can always get the listing. Then you'll get a call from the successful agent canceling your appointment with the prospects who are now his clients.

When you're competing against agents whose closing abilities you doubt, and you believe you've already made a strong impression with the prospects, shoot for the last spot. Be sure to say, "Now, you won't list with one of those other agents before I get there, will you? I'd be so disappointed if you didn't give me a chance to serve you."

Tips on closing listings are given under *Five Excuses From Sellers* in this chapter's Winning Scripts.

## Aim for the Kitchen Table Before You Head for the House

Coming in the house loaded down with gear for your presentation intimidates people. Right away the sellers are worried about the hard sell. Travel light. Have what you'll definitely need in your hand, and leave the rest in the car.

*How will I carry all my listing materials into the house?*

Will I stagger in with ungainly packages under both arms and in each hand? What do I need to have with me? NOW YOU CAN HAVE IT ALL DOWNLOADED ON YOUR LAPTOP.

**1.** Laptop/listing folder (See the role play in this chapter.)
**2.** Calculator
**3.** Clipboard
**4.** Multiple Listing book
**5.** Listing Presentation Manual
**6.** Listing form downloaded in your computer, already filled out as far as possible. Be sure you can access the form and complete it once you get to the home. Use it on Microsoft Word.

If you'll be more comfortable walking in with everything neatly in place in an attache case, then select an LPM format able to fit inside one. Think about the front door situation. You want to feel cool, relaxed, and friendly. You also want to look, and be, efficient. Organize so you'll have all those qualities going for you.

It's important to get in sync with the seller—if they're meticulous, you be the same. Be sensitive to their needs and ways of doing things.

The rehearsal and research phases are over when you walk in their door. You're on stage. Now you perform. Will you walk out to a standing ovation—the signed listing? Whether or not you do depends on preparation more than performance.

If you muff a line, smile, and try again. Without damaging your chances, you can say, "I didn't put that well. What I mean is—." You can correct minor flaws in your performance as you go along if you have to, but you *can't* remedy a lack of preparation after the meeting starts.

# The Listing Presentation

## You Can't Get a Second Chance

You can't get a second chance to make a first impression. The first 15 seconds are critical. Be relaxed, alert, and friendly. Above all, be on time—which shows by action how important you think the meeting is.

Never light up a cigarette or carry one in a house. Use their names a lot so they know you know who they are, and because it makes them feel important.

## Rapport

Build rapport from the moment they open their front door. Keep on building rapport while you're still standing in the entry meeting everyone. Build rapport not only for yourself, but also for the company you represent. The reason you're there—because of what you've done or who you know, or because you took a come-list-me call on floor time—doesn't alter your need to build rapport for both yourself and your company. They're not considering employing just you; they're also considering employing your company's name, know-how, connections, prestige, advertising, office location, and entire staff. So build rapport for yourself and your company, especially during the early moments of the contact.

## Tour the Property
## Through the Buyers' Eye

Say to the seller when you begin the tour, "Let's pretend, as we go from room to room, that you are the *buyers*, not the sellers. See your home through a prospective buyer's eyes." Those few words which can change the perspective of the seller will help price the home more realistically. So many sellers I knew always did a double take when I told them to look at the house from a buyer's viewpoint. Suddenly they noticed that the carpet would be replaced if they were not moving, or the need for new drapes or appliances.

Once you have them seeing their home more from a buyer's perspective, then you can shift the discussion back to why they are moving. If you haven't already determined their true motivation to sell, keep alert for openings to talk about it, or for clues to the reason popping up during the property tour.

Adjust your tour manner and pace to their mood and reason for leaving. When it's a move brought on by divorce, someone's passing, or another tragedy, don't linger and exclaim over their plaques, trophies, and family mementos. Walk through with your clipboard, make quick notes, and move on. Be reserved, professional, and respectful.

Your attitude should be completely different in the happy situations. Don't try to hurry when Daddy laid every brick in the walks, planted every shrub in the yard, and stuck up every roll of wallpaper in the house. Daddy is going to tell you about all the hours he spent doing it; about every brick laid, every hole dug, and the time the glue bucket spilled; and how little Stevie helped him every step of the way. Share his enthusiasm—unless you want him to find someone else who will. The property tour is short or long, as determined by the sellers' motivation, not your mood or schedule.

Organize the items you walk in with for easy carrying. Then, as you go through the kitchen on the property tour, say something like, "Mind if I leave some of these things here for a bit?" and set everything except your clipboard on the kitchen table. This table, of course, is where you want to be sitting when the tour is over and you get down to business. Kitchens are friendly places where families gather; living rooms are formal chambers where tense people sit back and stare at strangers who want something from them.

## Now You're at the Kitchen Table

What sellers want boils down to just three requirements:

- More money

- Less trouble
- Fast action

"Sure, we want all the money we can get. But I don't want to fix the cracked sink in the garage. And I want our sale to go fast, too." Be aware of something else your sellers want: peace of mind. They want to feel safe with you. So conduct yourself with integrity and win their trust.

As soon as you're all sitting at the kitchen table, give them the listing presentation by going through the LPM. During the presentation, tell them about yourself, tell them about your great company, compliment them on their house, and then get down to the key item—money.

Roll out the Guidelines to Market Value now. If you have a laptop all these forms should be in your computer. This form is often called "Competitive Market Analysis," a term many proud homeowners find insulting.

## Score When You Explain Financing

Say, "In keeping with seeing your home through the buyer's viewpoint, let's pretend you are buying your home back and the buyer's profile sheet I am about to show you is what it will take to qualify for your home."

Explaining this complex subject gives you another opportunity to score points—or to anger people. Using confusing jargon and acronyms to rattle off a quick rundown of the available financing methods is showing off. They'll know you're trying to look indispensable by making them feel stupid. Demonstrating disrespect for their feelings is no way to build trust.

It's not necessary to make a dazzling display of financing knowledge; it will come out naturally as you make your simplified explanations. The clients' questions will give you ample opportunities to display your professional expertise. As you do so, keep this thought upper-most in your mind: **Never make a client feel stupid.**

Start with the existing loan on the property. Review how they bought, and then explain how a similar loan would be written today; what interest rate, term, and downpayment would be involved; and how much income a buyer would need. Discuss whether their loan could be assumed by a buyer, or if the property could be sold subject to the existing loan. Then pass on the other financing methods appropriate and available for the price range of their offering.

Don't lecture. Keep it a three-way conversation between you, the wife, and the husband. Drop in good words like, "I know it seems complicated, but that's just because you don't work with it every day like I do."

## Preoccupation Is Everyone's Pet Peeve

Maintaining eye contact when people talk to you is vital. A glassy stare focused above their heads is not eye contact. Look them in the eyes most of the time.

Not being preoccupied with other matters is also vital. If you've got things on your mind when someone is telling you something important about their property, they'll see your mind and eyes drift away. The prospect will then drift away from you. Don't fall into the trap of thinking you can think your faraway thoughts, nodding wisely while they prattle, without offending them.

We brokers and managers are often guilty of this with our sales associates. They come to us, all excited and happy, and we're so bogged down with urgent but petty details, our hearts and minds aren't really there with them. They see this, it kills their enthusiasm, and they leave us alone. Having messed up the important part of our managerial function, we're now free to get back to squashing grasshoppers.

Be very careful on a listing presentation to be 100 percent with your clients. Leave your problems at home or in the office. Before you head for the appointment, start psyching yourself up for it. The first step is to put everything else out of your mind.

## Specific Listing Form Tips

**All Facts Must Be Accurate.** The buyers' agent will rely on the information in the listing and pass it on to the buyers, who can then claim they based their purchase decision on this information.

**Don't state the house's square footage, the lot size, or any other quantity unless** you've verified the information and are prepared to rest your case on its accuracy. Buyers who think they've bought 1800 square feet, and then measure only 1672 square feet after moving in, might get very upset. If you gave 1800 square feet as the house's square footage in the listing, and the price the buyers paid works out to $120 a foot, they're going to feel cheated by $15,360— and a court may agree.

*NT.* Some agents write square footage as "3250 *NT*," meaning "3250 square feet, Not Taped." What they're really saying with *NT* is something like this, "Somebody told me the house is about 3250 square feet, but I didn't measure it myself. I'd like you to think you're getting 3250 square feet, because it sounds like a lot, but if the house is actually smaller, don't blame me." They will blame you, and you'll find out what *NT* really means—*Nasty Trouble*.

**Describe Pools Carefully.** Pools are another source of post-sale problems. Pool builders sometimes round the inches to the next higher foot—and they often measure to the outside of the coping. Homeowners will say, and believe, their pool is 20-feet wide when the water width is only 16 feet, 6 inches. Measure it, or simply state there's a swimming pool. Call it stunning, shimmering, fun-filled, exotic, custom, free-form, delightful, or large—but don't get specific unless you know your facts.

**Keep the Fluff Out of the Facts, and the Facts Out of the Fluff.** A sharp line exists between the opinions you express in the remarks section and the specific facts called for in the listing form's spaces and boxes. If you add facts in the remarks section, keep them concise and accurate; when you express opinions there, keep them generalized and descriptive.

"Large ranch home with pleasant, well-lit rooms," announces itself as opinion; "1800-square-foot ranch home with imported Italian ceramic tile entry and top-of-the-line Great-Stuff® carpet," states facts. If the carpet falls apart and the buyers call in a floor man, who tells them the carpet is the cheapest made and the tile is local nonceramic, they're going to send you the replacement bill. Will you lose a sale because your description reads, "Large ranch home with gorgeous tile entry and carpet"?

**Don't bind your sellers to a specific move-out date** on the listing by stating, "Possession on August 30, 20___." Tie the possession date to the day the transaction closes (settles). This makes possession move with the time the property is on the market.

## Working with the Guidelines to Market Value Form

How you use this market analysis technique often determines whether or not you get the listing. When you're sitting at the kitchen table in the prospects' home, don't look over the form and say, "Well, now, this house on Pine Street is a little nicer than yours." You can use a market analysis so beautifully—if you guard well what you say. See *Guidelines to Market Value* in the Winning Scripts section.

**Use a Range.** Let's consider a four-bedroom house with five comparables listed on the Guidelines to Market Value (GMV) form.

The comparables list the same house, same square footage, roughly the same kind of property; some have pools, some have views. I see a range from X$ to X$. Write across the top of the GMV: "Range—X$ to X$." and say to the sellers, "This is what the market will bear on this particular kind of property right now, based on whether or not it's got a pool or a view."

Make the origin perfectly clear: You didn't put the range on these properties; the public did. While you're explaining this, your sellers are sitting there thinking, "Okay, somewhere in this range is where we sit. X$? Well, this one had a pool and a view. Ours doesn't. But the X$ one doesn't have a view either. Hmm."

Already, you've got them framed in. That's what you want to do, frame them into a reasonable market value price.

**Don't Compare Their Home to Someone Else's.** Don't do it at all, even if the sellers bring it up.

"Well, you know, we saw the Clarks' house down the street and quite frankly, ours is a lot sharper."

"Yes, I've seen it. Some things there appeal to certain buyers, but some things about your house definitely appeal to certain other buyers."

Take a negative and turn it into a positive, but don't compare. Comparing gets you in trouble.

**Seller's Net Sheet.** Wait to do a seller's net sheet (this form is available on the accompanying CD) until after you've discussed the GMV with your prospects. After you've looked at all the prices and have seen what's sold and for how much; after you've discussed what's expired, what's listed, and how many days these various properties have been on the market; then you're ready to face setting the price. Now they know one sold for X$ with no pool, and one sold for X$ with a pool. Another house with no pool has been on the market at X$ for 190 days. Say something like this to the seller, "Looks like this one is too high; the market just won't pull its price."

Study the GMV at the kitchen table. Analyze it. Watch your body language. You're concentrating on the Guidelines to Market Value form. You may have every figure on the form memorized, but when you're sitting there with your sellers, you're studying it as deeply as they are, as though it was the first time you'd seen the information.

## What the Salesperson Must Keep in Mind to Price It Right

Once you have the range established, you can start to zero in on the right price, the magic figure able to encourage offers without being a giveaway. At this point, the sellers are going to say, "Okay, what do you think our home is worth?"

It's an emotionally charged question. Say something like, "Let's think about these things before we make the final decision."

**Location.** Does this house back up to a busy highway? What's the market activity in the immediate three or four blocks? Are there a dozen or more properties already for sale here? only two or three? none? Does this location carry a prestige premium?—or a lack-of-prestige discount?

**Condition.** Be thinking, "What do I have to tell this couple to help them get their offering into proper market condition? How can I say what has to be said diplomatically?"

**Price.** Will the seller stay within the range? You should know by now, based on his reaction to the Guidelines to Market Value. You've gone over the guidelines and he said, "Well, the house on Maple Street had a pool and it sold for X$. We don't have a pool, but I can tell you something—our fabulous view makes up for their pool!"

How can a view make up for the lack of a pool? You can't swim in air. This problem is not peculiar to areas with pools. Sellers everywhere say, "'A' makes up for 'B'." They'll try to equalize any condition.

"Sure, our street is dangerous, but we've got the biggest backyard in this end of town. It makes up for our problems out front."

Comments like this from the sellers, as you grind on the GMV together, tell you that you'll have to fight the price. You'll fight more effectively by taking side cuts. If the missing amenity is a pool, don't talk about pools. Make your point without hitting too hard. Tell a story about something none of the houses on the Guidelines has. See *Horse Lots* in Winning Scripts.

**Terms.** What financing is available now? Tell them about this in as much detail as they'll accept. What ratio of loan to appraised value is available 60 percent, 70 percent, 80 percent, 90 percent, 95 percent—even 100 percent? What points will a buyer have to pay as a loan origination fee?

Professional people don't necessarily know much about financing a home. Doctors have no special reason to know about real estate. Many lawyers are too busy with their specialized practices to keep current on real estate financing. Get down to basics with all your people and explain everything.

**The Sellers' Motivation.** The sellers' reason for moving, their needs, and their emotional make-up are going to determine how their house gets priced.

If the new house they've bought won't be ready for six months, and they think the market's going up X$ in the meantime, they'll set their price higher than anyone else. "We're in no rush," they'll think, even though they're unaware of the yearly buying pattern in your area.

People who have been transferred act very differently. Many companies pay the brokerage on the sale of their transferee's present home, and take care of moving costs. People who change homes frequently to take new assignments often have a realistic view of house pricing.

Are the sellers gamblers or worriers? Some sellers need to carry a house vacant for several months before they can get realistic. Others feel overextended and want to get out from under fast.

You need to know their motivation. Pick them up during the afternoon preview and the evening presentation. You've got to, or you'll never get them to okay the magic figure that gives you a *salable* listing.

## "I Like the Number"

"I like the number," my seller said, explaining why he wanted to set his price $20,000 too high. Other sellers add their airfare from across the country, their monthly mortgage payments, or what they paid their gardener. The oddball "cost" items popping up in a house's price aren't limited by reason.

This entire approach to price setting is very *un—un*businesslike, *un*realistic, and *un*necessary. The sellers are entitled to all they can net out of their house. No justification is required. What their costs were is irrelevant to the issue of what the market will now pay for their property.

But some sellers actually believe their costs set the price their property will sell for. We are, of course, talking about a normal market, not one in which buyers are driving up prices by frantic bidding.

Many people flip their switch from *buy mode* to *sell mode* with no carryover insight into how a buyer of their property will feel, even though they've just bought a house and felt absolutely no interest in the problems and goals of the persons who sold it to them. Not only do many people compartmentalize their buyer-seller feelings in the same day or week, some do it in the same breath. With their seller's hat on, they have an amazing ability to totally block out the simple facts governing buyers:

- Buyers won't knowingly pay too much.
- Buyers want to get a good deal.
- Buyers aren't interested in paying for sellers' mistakes.

- Buyers don't care how much money the sellers need for an initial investment on their next house, to start their new business, or whatever else the sellers have in mind.
- Buyers actually check to see what other properties are available, and they compare values.

The sellers who block out these universal buyer attitudes aren't too dense to see the truth; they simply don't want to. You'll generally have little difficulty explaining, and getting agreement to, the first four facts. The fifth one will probably give you the most trouble because most sellers—even those offering a common, drab house in need of care—think theirs is a unique and highly desirable prize far superior to similar properties. Tread softly here. Such sellers sail a dreamboat on a pond of delusion. It works something like this, "If buyers are shrewd, my dreamboat won't float. Therefore, buyers are stupid. Anyway, I only need one buyer—just one guy smart enough to have the money to buy this house, and too dumb to know it's overpriced."

## Overpriced Listing Tactics

This discussion applies only to when there are comparable houses available at the lower value set by market action. Don't use these ideas unless the market has clearly established values, and the overpricing is extreme.

What is extreme overpricing? Where there are many comparable properties with few differences, the salable price range will be narrow; where there are few comparables and many differences, the salable price range will be broad. No simple rule of thumb will fit all cases.

I've carried listings as long as 13 months before finally selling them. This involved constant consultation with, and step-by-step education of, sellers too headstrong to listen. I hate to let go, but sometimes it's the best thing. When the sellers know you disagree with the pricing, they're tempted to search for an agent who does agree. Then, 9 months later, the house sells at the price you said it would 270 days earlier. You've lost the one fee, but how many more did you make during the period with the time you saved?

"What is the most profitable way to operate?" You need to keep asking yourself this vital question. Measure the opportunity in hand against those you could acquire with the time and emotional energy you will spend servicing your overpriced listing preempts. If you can hang in there with small loss of time, it's the most profitable way to go. But if you are a high-volume salesperson, the overpriced listing may be costing you too much in time and enthusiasm. Perhaps a less-active agent will have the patience to work through the pain and educational process that difficult, overpriced sellers require.

As a new salesperson, I tended to hold on until my sellers saw things the market's way, no matter how long it took. Then, as my volume increased, working with seriously overpriced people began to take too much time away from servicing reasonably priced clients who would listen to me.

Many agents start strong by writing a number of overpriced listings and for a few weeks think they're taking over their farms. Then the listings start to expire; the word goes out that they never sell anything; and, before long, their signs have all disappeared. Suddenly they discover their newsletters, door-knocking, clever giveaways, and close personal contact avail nothing. They decide that farming is passe, mid-Twentieth Century stuff. Working with buyers is the key to quick success.

Except for one small detail, they did everything right on their farms. Unfortunately, most of the real estate profession's problems are packed into that one small detail. When the small detail explodes into a clutch of angry, haven't-sold sellers and expired listings, it becomes painfully obvious how large of a detail, price is in the scheme of things.

Many agents feel they have no choice. They must take overpriced listings. If they don't, someone else will. But will the other agent gain an advantage by letting his sign sag for 90 days on Tewhi Terrace?

What's your game plan? Do you take every listing you can, regardless of price, and hope for the best? *Or do you take an overpriced listing only when there's an understanding to reconsider the price unless it's validated by offers within an agreed-upon time?*

The problem may arise from confusion on the sellers' part. They may believe an agent's function is to sell property for more than it's worth. They may think it's easy to get market price. They may feel they'd be "giving my home away" if they sell at the market price. These false conceptions may be too deeply rooted for words to wash them away. Try, but don't be crushed if you can't talk their price down. If you fail at first, back off and allow time's pressure to push them into reality. When their overpriced listing with Eagercluck Realty expires, go back in for it with redoubled confidence. You'll probably be able to add it to your readily salable inventory. Just don't say, "I told you so."

Sellers need to sell, and they won't unless they price realistically. If you never push sellers hard to make their price realistic, you're failing to protect their interests. It's a serious failing—serious enough to destroy you as a listing agent.

Aim for the second or third listing as where the money is. With very obstinate sellers, payoff might be delayed until the fourth or fifth time the house is listed. It may seem too risky to decline the listing in hopes of catching it at a more realistic price after it expires, but you're certain to save energy, time, and money for more promising opportunities by not promoting the unsalable.

When considering whether to accept an overpriced listing, don't think about the fee you'd earn if a one-in-a-million buyer comes along who has no regard for value but does have all cash. Don't think about the huge initial investment it'll take to get the appraisal past a loan committee. Instead, think about defending the too high price to buyers, as you'll be obliged to do. Think about the cost of flyers, the pressure to hold the house open, the phone calls about why it didn't sell—all the listing service time.

If the property is in your farm, consider how it'll look to have your sign fade and sag there for months. Worse yet, when the seller is furious with you and finally ready to accept market price, your sign comes down, another office's goes up, and the property sells within days. It's not the right scenario for your fast takeover of your farm.

Imagine a better situation as the nonsolds drive past the signs of your activity—especially your *Sold* riders—as they come and go. Some gray morning it'll hit them, "If only we'd listened to the agent who's selling all the houses around here, we'd be long gone by now." Then you get a come-list-me call.

Of course, if sellers agree to reduce to a realistic figure after a limited market-testing period, it's always best to take the overpriced listing. Decide in advance what your tactics will be when faced with an overpriced listing. There is no perfect solution able to score in every instance, and you may be successful with methods other agents can't make work.

Your decision is also complicated by the season. Allow for the seasonal buying pattern in your discussion with the client. Lay the groundwork for your return by asking them to consider what will happen if your forecast is correct and they list with another firm for 90 days at what you believe is 15 percent over market. After 90 days, you think they might reduce their price by 5 percent and list with a second office, again for 90 days, and still at 10 percent over market. After six months, where will they be in relation to your area's usual peak selling season? After six months—will they remember you? They should, if they live in your farm and you're in effective control there.

Don't always take overpriced listings. Don't always walk away from them either.

## Market Forecast

After you've toured the property, and worked through your Listing Presentation Manual, tell sellers what the market is like.

Say (if it's true), "You know, the marketing time lately has been running 90 to 180 days. It used to be you could sell your house in 20 days around here; no more." Tell them what the market's like *now*.

Collect articles from the business and realty sections of magazines and newspapers backing up what you're saying. Put these articles in your Listing Presentation Manual. Homeowners usually don't have this information; they rely on you for it.

## Overpromises

Be careful what you promise sellers; people think you mean it. If you tell someone, "I'll get you the moon for this property," they'll expect the moon.

"This so-called agent of mine, Betty Bignews, convinced us she was going to sell our house for X$. So we signed a 90-day listing. Now she wants us to extend her listing even though she's never brought us a single offer. The Panama Canal will freeze over before we'll renew with her."

Agents don't control what their listings sell for—unless they buy them. You're an agent, not a buyer; talk like an agent.

## Take Command of Listing Remarks

If you run off your sparkling sales blurb without regard to the space limitations of your Multiple Listing book, you'll force someone else to edit the description and make decisions only you and the seller should make. Save time and trouble, and look professional, by doing the job right the first time.

The following "remarks" were taken from a recent entry in the Multiple Listing book issued by my board:

> $500 BNUS TO S/O W/FULL PRC OFR. OVER 2100 SF LXRS LK LVG W/FNTSTIC LK/MTN VU, PRSTGS LOC, QIET CDS NOTE UPGDS: CERM NTRY, NWX FLRS, PLSH CPT, WTBR, CERM CTRS, TRSH COMP, INDR LNDRY, & MW.SM LNDR SV PPP

How many busy real estate agents have time to decode this cryptogram? I called the listing agent for a translation. Here's what he meant:

> $500 BONUS TO SELLING OFFICE WITH FULL PRICE OFFER. OVER 2100 SQUARE FEET OF LUXURIOUS LAKE LIVING

WITH FANTASTIC LAKE AND MOUNTAIN VIEW. PRESTI-
GIOUS LOCATION ON A QUIET CUL DE SAC. NOTE UP-
GRADES: CERAMIC TILE ENTRY, NO-WAX KITCHEN AND
BATHROOM FLOORING, PLUSH CARPET ELSEWHERE, WET
BAR, CERAMIC COUNTERTOPS, TRASH COMPACTOR, IN-
DOOR LAUNDRY, AND MIRRORED WARDROBES IN MASTER
BEDROOM. PLEASE STAY WITH SAME LENDER TO SAVE PRE-
PAYMENT PENALTY. DON'T LET THE SMALL DOGS OUT.

The board typist, who did a superb job of compressing nine lines
into four, had to give up on the last sentence. Unfortunately, it was the
most important one to the sellers. The agent told me they were furious
because their precious poodles got out. You can try to blame this on the
board, but your sellers will hold you responsible—as they should in
this case.

Such problems are easily avoided. First, find out exactly how
much space you have by counting the number of spaces your Multiple
Listing book allows per line of remarks. Then write your remarks to fit,
and print off a few copies of this note:

> Board Secretary: Please type the remarks exactly as shown. They will
> fit.
>
> Thanks, _____

Clip one of these notes to each one of your listings when you
submit them to the board.

**Writing Effective Remarks Fast.** Before you write your
throbbing description, list everything it is essential to say. As the sellers reel off four times as many details as you have space for, list them
in two columns: *must go* and *if possible.* The if-possibles will never
make it, but you don't have to tell the sellers this.

Once you've written all the must-gos in the shortest form busy
agents will understand, count the spaces used, deduct that from the
total available, and the remainder is your *selling remarks* limit. Don't
waste time writing and polishing 100 words when you only have room
for 35.

# The Delicate Art of Pricing

"How much for our home?" they ask, their faces pokering the soft distress only their eyes betray.

But who can put a price on love, warmth, and security? Sure, it's
windows and walls and rugs and grass. I've seen thousands, sold hun-

dreds. But the numbers game is gone when you're sitting across from two people and their hopes, dreams, joys, and sorrows. He paneled the den; she papered the kitchen. Here they argued, and there they made up. The cause of the quarrel is long forgotten, only the sweetness of its settlement is remembered. The master bedroom—a private place to hold one another, make love, laugh, and cry. Each room evokes special memories—and marks many paths they can't trod again.

Into this home I come, the stranger, to tell them the worth of this prized place of their caring, to set a value on this nest of their yesterdays. I'm to say what the highest bidder will pay for the priceless—for this dwelling hallowed by a joyous time now ending for them. "We've been happy here," they say.

Yes, but the thing must be done. They tell me so. Then let me do it—with intuition—with understanding of their next move—with empathy for their new dream—with a sharing of their bright dawning hope. Let me be firm. Let me be strong. But, oh, please, let me be *delicate*.

# Listing the Caseys: A Role Play in One Act

Cast:    Your manager
Danny, the agent
Harry Casey
Martha Casey

Designed to be read by four people at an office meeting, this role play trains the agents who participate and the other agents present at the meeting who form the audience. The person playing Danny, the agent, should read the play beforehand and prepare for the ad-libs. No other rehearsal is required if all four members of the cast have their own copy of this book.

The manager or broker conducting the meeting reads the manager's part (all of which is directed to the audience). Volunteers play the other three parts. The agent may be a man or woman associate.

Props required: three chairs, three coffee cups, a table (a desk will do). Danny carries a clipboard and a Listing Presentation Manual.

(Lines to be spoken to the audience are given in parentheses like these.)

[Stage directions are enclosed in brackets like these.]

***Manager:*** (Our play is *Listing the Caseys*, _____ and _____ have consented to play Mr. and Mrs. Casey. Our agent, Danny, will be played by _____. The time is a Saturday afternoon in football season. The scene is the Caseys' front door in our town. We're about to observe our agent arrive for a listing presentation. He/she has done this dozens of times, and his/her success score on listings is terrific. As you'll see there are reasons for his/her great batting average. Besides what you observe, Danny also has an impressive inventory of houses on Quick-Speak, keeps excellent records, and drives the area thoroughly prior to an appointment. Our agent comes in knowing all his/her lines. We all know the key to any successful performance is preparation.)

*Danny:* Good afternoon, Mrs. Casey. I'm Danny _____ and we have a 2:00 appointment. Am I right on time? I sure tried to be. (Of course, I wouldn't say this if I wasn't on time.)

*Martha:* Yes, you are. Do come in, Danny. We were expecting you. Let me go get Harry. He's in the back watching football. [She walks away.]

*Danny:* (Aha! Football. Nothing makes a man madder than someone intruding on his Saturday football. I better do something quick.) [Harry enters.]

*Danny:* Harry, I'm really sorry. I make it a policy never to interfere with clients watching football games. Can I return at a more convenient time? [Looks at audience.] (I'm dead serious about this. It's inconvenient to come back, but not as inconvenient as losing the listing.)

*Harry:* Gosh, you're the first agent who's appreciated how much I like football. But Danny, we've got to get this show on the road, and I have two more agents coming in later. We better get on with it. If you notice me running to the TV from time to time, don't be offended.

*Danny:* Heck, no. I'm a real fan myself. Harry and Martha, do you think we could do two things now? Number one, give me a cook's tour of your home and, number two, can I set my things down on the kitchen table for our meeting after the tour?

*Martha:* Be my guest.

[Danny sets the Listing Presentation Manual/laptop on the table, and retains the clipboard.]

*Manager:* (Notice how Danny takes control here after finding out Harry's attention can be taken away from football. But, had Harry been unwilling to hear the presentation, Danny would make another appointment to come back later.)

*Danny:* Harry, do you mind if Martha gives me the tour? Then you can watch the game until we get back here to the kitchen. Unless, of course, there's something you want to show off.

*Harry:* Great idea. I'll just watch the old tube and let you two do your thing. Martha, I like Danny. He (she) isn't trying to cut me out of seeing the game.

*Martha:* Well, Harry, are you going to play me or trade me?

*Harry:* Very funny.

*Danny:* Okay, Martha, let's see this lovely home of yours. And let's pretend as you show it to me, that you are considering buying your house, not selling it. Try to see it through a prospective buyer's eyes.

*Manager:* (Martha and Danny take the tour. Harry bursts in every now and then to point out the brick fence he built himself, and the mirrored wardrobe in the bedroom.)

[As the manager talks, Danny and Martha go in one direction, Harry in another. Martha points, and Danny looks, scribbling furiously on the clipboard.]

*Danny:* You certainly have a lovely home, Martha. Let's go back to the kitchen now. Perhaps you and Harry and I can talk about how your property fits into the local real estate market.

[Martha waves Danny to a seat at the table, pulls out three coffee cups, and pours as Harry comes in. They all sit down.]

*Danny:* How's your team doing, Harry?

*Harry:* Lousy.

*Danny:* Then let's get on a better topic. You and Martha have a lovely home. You have certainly done a lot to enhance this neighborhood. How do you feel about leaving?

*Manager:* (This is an important question. If the reason for leaving is good, Danny knows marketing and pricing of the property will be easier. Generally, distraught sellers—those who move for reasons beyond their control—are tougher to work with. Examples of distraught sellers include a split-up where one party doesn't want the divorce, a lateral move by a company to another part of the country, a pair of empty-nesters moving to a smaller house because their children are grown up. All these people have unhappy thoughts about leaving their cherished homes.)

*Harry:* Well, I've just been promoted to Sioux City, and we're pretty excited about the job and pay raise. But there *is* one problem. I just got back from Sioux City, and I find I can't get as much house there as we have here in River City.

*Danny:* All we can do is try for the top dollar here, and not compare this market with Sioux City. But I can understand how it's a big disappointment to you.

*Harry:* Yeah, but the promotion is good. So what's this area like right now?

*Manager:* (Danny must maintain good eye contact now with both of them.)

*Danny:* Interest rates are running about ____ percent.

[Danny locks eyes with one of the Caseys for a few seconds, then turns head to eye-lock with the other while speaking.]

The average number of days a house is on the local market here, before being sold, is 72 at this time. Considering the season, our market action is brisk, and weekly sales this year are running about 5 percent ahead of last year. Generally, the market is bright at this moment.

But we have to remember the season. We're coming up on the holidays, which usually start slowing the market down about now.

*Manager:* (Danny adapts the market evaluation to the current situation each time he/she gives it. The market evaluation is a powerful display of expertise, and belongs in every listing presentation.)

*Harry:* After the holidays, what do you think the market will do? Take off?

*Danny:* I don't expect it to take off, but I do think it'll continue to be brisk, and keep on running about 5 percent ahead of the year-ago figures.

*Martha:* Wow, then things look good.

*Danny:* In general, yes they do, Martha. May I ask, how did you hear about me?

*Harry:* The owner of the corner gas station says you come in there all the time, and really seem to be a busy one. Plus your picture is always in the paper.

*Danny:* I work hard at being a true professional. But I always ask that question because it is nice going in knowing if the homeowners have confidence in me right up-front.

*Harry:* But I have two other hotshots coming over later.

*Danny:* Great. Now, let's get back to the business at hand. I'd like to tell you a little bit about my company, our philosophy, and myself. May I demonstrate my Listing Presentation Manual to you?

*Harry:* Okay, but will you wait one second? I gotta check the score.

[Harry runs out, then trots back and sits down again. Danny flows with this naturally, smiling and leaning back in the chair.]

*Danny:* [When Harry is back.] First off, let me tell you a little bit about our company—

[Ad-libs a sales speech about your company: how long it's been operating; how many people are on the staff; if you're in the top six; where your office ranks on the board in volume; what the relocation connection is; what the advertising program is; how impressive the office decor or location is. Harry and Martha may interrupt several times to ask questions or comment.]

*Harry:* Okay, Danny, let's get down to bare facts. What can we get for this place?

*Danny:* Well, you mentioned you have other agents coming in. Do me one favor. Please don't choose a broker based on pricing. We all have the same facts of record and, quite frankly, I hope you'll make your choice based on ability, integrity, and track record. Will you do this for me?

*Harry:* Sure. But what will I get for this place?

*Danny:* First, Harry and Martha, let me take out my Guidelines to Market Value form. Heaven knows, I don't want to compare your home to others because it's so special.

*Manager:* (Danny's pauses and sincere manner make an important contribution to rapport at this point.)

*Danny:* You both have really done an outstanding job here. But the appraisers from the lending institution we'll be working with after the sale always come back to me and want the facts of record.

*Martha:* Who are they?

*Danny:* Well, when the property sells, the buyer needs to qualify for a new loan, and so does the property. Qualifying the property means we have to get an appraisal on the property high enough to carry the new loan. Of course, the appraisal has to reflect the values in the neighborhood. Shall we look at the Guidelines to Market Value?

*Manager:* (Before they look at it, Danny always talks about the Guidelines to Market Value form so the sellers understand its purpose.)

*Harry:* Okay, shoot.

*Manager:* (Note the agent's concentration on both sellers to pick up their body language, and any defensiveness they might show.)

*Danny:* [Points with pencil.] Notice this property about two blocks from here. It sold 10 days ago for X$. It's very similar to yours. I believe the carpet was installed just prior to marketing the property.

*Harry:* Yeah, but did they have a brick wall? My carpet is only six years old—and it looks good.

*Danny:* [Calmly.] I definitely am not trying to compare your property. I'm just trying to establish value. No, they had a wood fence, but I just want you to know what's out there, and what sold.

*Harry:* I know this one, Martha. Your stupid friend, Rosie, lived there. She cleans house like Jack the Ripper. Every two years she lights the top of her stove to burn off the grease. Can you believe she got X$ for her dump?

*Martha:* Honey, you're right, she's a messy housekeeper.

*Danny:* It sold for a higher price because its owners were willing to sell "subject to" their existing loan.

*Harry:* What?

*Danny:* Well, the seller didn't need a lot of cash, and the buyer didn't have much. So the sellers carried back a lot of the paper, instead of getting paid off in cash. The buyers took the property over subject to the seller's present loan. Do you want to consider doing the same thing?

*Martha:* Heck, no. We need all our cash for Sioux City. And we want this loan paid off, right, Harry?

*Harry:* Right.

*Danny:* Well, just keep in mind how those special financing arrangements made Rosie's house marketable at a higher figure to a certain type of buyer. Special terms have value too, even though she wasn't the housekeeper you are, Martha.

*Harry:* There certainly are a lot of special circumstances in this real estate business, aren't there?

*Danny:* For sure, Harry.

*Manager:* (We'll skip over their review of four more properties.)

*Danny:* Since we've looked over the Guidelines to Market Value, I'm going to write the range right here. In the sold houses, it's X$ to X$. On the listings, X$ to X$. Harry and Martha, do you see yourself in these ranges?

*Manager:* (Danny isn't afraid of silence. Right now is one of those times when the ability to keep quiet is of vital importance.)

[Harry, Martha, and Danny sit looking at each other, without speaking, for several seconds. Danny doesn't move, Harry and Martha fidget.]

*Harry:* You tell me, Danny. My contact at the gas pump tells me you're the one who has the real estate brains.

*Danny:* Thanks, Harry, I appreciate it. But please keep in mind one solid fact: When we list a house, we have only heard from its owners. Sellers can set the price wherever they like. But for the property to sell, we also have to hear from a buyer. And—unless it's sold for cash—the property has to have sufficient value *an appraiser can document* to qualify for a new loan to complete the sale. It boils down to a willing seller and a willing buyer getting together on a good price for both of them. So the market values are set by folks like yourselves, together with qualified buyers who are interested, emotionally and physically, in your home. I'm just the mediator. But here's what I'd like to do—
[Pauses, staring at the guidelines form.]

—How about if I prepare a seller's net sheet for you at this point? I'll pull a figure out of my hat off your Guidelines to Market Value form here. This will give you an idea of what you'd net—in dollars and cents to you at the closing—if you sell at a number in the general vicinity of what I'm going to put down.

*Harry:* Okay.

[Danny pulls out a seller's net sheet form and works quickly at entering amounts on it.]

*Manager:* (Danny will figure the price at X$, knowing full well it's on the low end of the range, based on the comparables. Our agent wants to get Harry and Martha used to the scale of value they're in, and frame them in on a salable price. It takes guts to pull a figure out and put it on the net sheet with a critical seller, but it has to start someplace, and the logical time comes right after the Guidelines to Market Value form is studied.)

*Danny:* Let me explain each of the charges on this net sheet, Harry and Martha.

*Manager:* (Everything down the line is explained, including prepayment privileges. The sellers should be impressed with the agent's thorough knowledge of the net sheet.)

*Danny:* Harry and Martha, please add up these figures to be sure I didn't make a mistake on this net sheet. I don't want to give you any false information.

[Harry and Martha study the net sheet intently.]

*Manager:* (Danny knows the figures are right. The point is to involve them.)

*Harry:* So this means we come out with about $132,000 after our loan is paid off?

*Danny:* Yes, approximately, barring any miscalculation you may have given me on your loan balance, or anything of the sort.

*Martha:* Harry, we were hoping for more like $165,000.

*Harry:* Yeah, especially when I think of Sioux City's prices.

*Manager:* (Danny doesn't say a word while they're talking to each other.)

*Martha:* Yeah, but remember, Danny said we can't figure Sioux City prices into the decision, honey.

*Harry:* What do you mean? If it's money, it counts.

*Danny:* Oh, I agree, Harry. No one wants to see you get more for your property than I do. But, the thing is, if I'm not honest with you, you won't appreciate my stroking after it takes too long to market your home. Then a new, and more honest, agent might come along, list it at market value, and sell it quick.

*Martha:* You're honest, Danny. But do you think we could get, or maybe even list at X$?

*Manager:* (Danny originally gave the low-end target price of X$ in order to have room to come up to a higher asking price.)

*Danny:* I suggest a maximum asking price of $359,900. The hundred dollars under $360,000 makes a big difference in the buyer's head. I figure this number allows $900 to $1,900 for a negotiating pad. Am I in line?

*Harry:* Danny, I do want to get some other opinions.

*Danny:* Certainly. But may I tell you about some of the deadlines we REALTORS® are up against? In order to get your home on next week's caravan, your listing has to be in the board office by _____. Also, if you give me the opportunity to work for you, I'll personally greet everyone at your open house by serving a progressive Mexican lunch. The finest agents in our town are my friends, so I'll send out special invitations to all of them. Plus I'll send a sharp photographer out to shoot both the interior and exterior, and then I'll personally make up a special brochure of your home.

*Martha:* Harry, let's do it. Remember, you and I wanted to go up to the city tomorrow to see Mary and Dick, and I hate having to interview more agents.

*Harry:* Well, I don't know.

*Danny:* I could work an open house for you tomorrow, and get the ball rolling, if you aren't going to be here. I love writing ad copy, so I could shoot an ad into today's late edition if there's time.

*Harry:* Yeah, but what about your cousin's friend—the agent guy.

*Martha:* Oh, yeah, maybe we better talk to him.

*Danny:* Who is your cousin's friend?

*Harry:* Howard Jensen.

*Danny:* Oh, yes. He's with Vibration Realty. Nice guy. He's a Multiple Listing agent like we are. He could still sell it, you know.

*Martha:* He could?

*Danny:* Sure, I would be exclusively representing you as your listing agent on all offers, but I cooperate with all other agents who bring in a buyer besides myself.

*Harry:* Well, aren't you going to sell it?

*Danny:* I certainly am going to try, but the neat thing about a Multiple Listing agent is that you have a team of _____ [ad-libs the total number of agents on your board] on your side. I get along very well with Howard and most agents in the board.

*Martha:* Well, Harry, I think Danny's pretty thorough. Let's just cancel the other appointments.

*Harry:* Well, okay, but now I'm going to tell you why, Danny. You didn't insist on taking me away from my football game.

# Winning Scripts

The front door opens where you have an appointment to give a listing presentation. If the owners are both standing at the door, make eye contact with each of them in turn. If not, zero in on the second person as soon as you see him or her.

"Hi, Mr. Shepley. I'm _____ with _____ and I really appreciate your letting me stop by." Pause at the entry hall and look in all four corners of the living room ahead of you. If you're properly psyched up, your alertness and intensity will create a presence, a feeling of subdued excitement, an expectant mood, a feeling that something good and important is going to happen now that the expert is here. Your presence commands respect, and allows you to exert control.

If this is a referral appointment, say, "I'm very happy the Prestons recommended me when you told them you needed a market evaluation on your home."

"Aha," thinks Mr. Shepley, who wasn't listening when his wife reminded him, "This is the fireball real estate agent Jack was telling us about." Having identified you, several of Mr. Shepley's defense barriers fall flat. Always mention your referral connection in front of both of them when you have their full attention because one of the couple may never have been told you were recommended. (And remind them early, so you benefit throughout the interview from the greatly expanded credibility a recommendation gives you.)

"I represent Palfrey Realty, now one of the top four brokers in the area. I'm really proud to be a part of our team. I wonder if I might ask you a favor? (Don't wait for an answer.) Can both of you give me the grand tour of your home now? I need to walk through so I can appreciate what you've done before I can counsel you."

## Five Excuses from Sellers

Many situations require you to choose a course and stick to it, win or lose. So you can't always convince prospects to list. But you don't have to win them all (which is lucky, because that's impossible). Go with your hunches. You can't develop intuition unless you listen to its first whisperings. If you don't get a hunch, play the odds. If you don't know the odds, act with confidence. Always move and act with confidence. Expect to fail more often than you succeed. Accept the reality, be comfortable with it, because it's how the numbers work out, especially at first. Following are five excuses sellers frequently give for not employing you, and five ways to convince them to do so.

**1. "I'll sell it myself and save the fee."** This is the for-sale-by-owner's whole game. Chapter 5 tells you how to tame this tiger.

**2. "I'll think it over."** When they say this after my listing presentation, I always ask, "Have you definitely decided to make a move now?"

If they answer, "Oh, yeah, we're moving. In fact, we're already talking to some other brokers."

I say, "Is there something I've missed? Are there questions in your mind? Something I haven't told you or covered? Is there a barrier between us I can overcome and break through?"

Be frank and honest with people. They're just human beings. Encourage them to be frank and honest with you. Find out why you don't have a signed listing in front of you.

If they say, "We want to sleep on it, or we want to talk to someone else," and come up with a bona fide reason such as, "This is the first time we've ever sold a home. We'd really prefer to get two or three other opinions," then honor their feelings. Pressure only goes so far.

If they have an appointment at 2:00 the next day with another broker, tell them, "Before you make a final decision, give me one more chance to see if there's something I can do for you—maybe something someone else has told you they can do. Just give me one more chance." Always end on this note. Then try to make another appointment with them after they've talked to the other brokers.

**3. "We want to buy a new house before we list."** I don't feel bad about this if their new house (from a builder or developer) won't be ready for several months. But if they're talking about purchasing a resale home before they list, say, "If you plan to make an offer on another house before yours is on the market, does this mean you have the necessary funds to close on the new house before selling your present home?"

"Oh, yeah. We've got the money in a savings account."

If they have the money, fine. If not, tell them now about the problems they can have trying to buy their next home *contingent* on their present home selling.

If they're leaving your sales area, you have a worthwhile chance at a referral fee by lining up a broker for them in the region where they're moving. If they're staying in your sales area, they're probably not committed to another agent regarding the house they'll buy, or they wouldn't be talking to you about listing the one they'll sell—unless they're building, or planning to buy a new house from a developer.

Be alert for these opportunities. Many people won't volunteer this information; they'll let the more alert and effective agents pry it out of them. In many cases, they aren't sure precisely how to proceed. It's a big decision; in this case two big decisions—with lots of things to worry about in the wee hours of the morning. So people often take the long way around when meeting their wants or needs, especially when the decisions are easily postponed.

Just don't let the dollar signs flash in your eyes when you discover they're in the local market for a house. Be relaxed, cordial, and interested. Let them be comfortable with you. Try for a small commitment first, a relaxed, "Let's see what's available" trip for an hour or two. Then thoroughly prepare and give these people the highest priority on your time. The odds are you're working for two fees here, or none.

If their answer to your question about the necessary funds to close on the new house before selling the present home is negative, you'll learn a lot from the exact way they phrase it.

- "Well, isn't there some way we could be sure of where we're going before we let go of this place?" These people need help. Talk basics.
- "Oh, no. We'll make our offer contingent on this house selling." This couple is more sophisticated about real estate. Use a little jargon on them.
- "I don't want to wind up owning two houses and making two payments. But we've got to have a place to live. I can't see spending a fortune storing my furniture and living in a motel in my hometown, and I darn sure don't want double payments."

This man thinks timing his sale to fit his purchase is a difficult problem fraught with unknown perils able to break out unexpectedly. (He's right.) The important thing is what he's just revealed to you, probably unintentionally. He'd welcome a strong agent taking charge of coordinating both the sale of his present home and the purchase of his new one. The only way to work with him is to earn two fees. Spend a little time telling him you're an expert and you can handle it. Then go out and find him the house he wants while you're lining up a buyer for his place. He's told you where his shoes are. Put them on. He wants to be sure of owning one house, no more and no less, all the time. Assure this man you'll protect him from a double move. He'll probably flex a little on price, on either end, and he'll probably bend a little on what he wants his new home to be like too, just so he can be sure of a roof over his head without risking owning two homes at once.

Most people don't worry much about all this until the last few hours. They just assume it'll all work out okay, as it usually does—by the sweat of an agent's brow.

If you haven't had experience with contingent offers, Chapter 23 tells how to develop a sales dialogue explaining this subject to your clients.

**4. "If I list, I'll list with my friend."** "Consider me your friend." Smile and continue on. "You know, close friends can't be detached about each other. Isn't friendship sort of an agreement to filter out someone's imperfections so the good things shine brighter? It's a great concept for friendship, but it's a poor one for business.

"Being realistic is the best policy when you're selling real estate, and it's hard for anyone to be both close to, and impartial about, the same person. This puts too heavy a burden on friendship. You have a great friend in the business, which I respect, but keep in mind your need for professional service and opinion. Even though your friend says, 'I'll be realistic with you,' it's almost impossible because of the rose-colored glasses a friend wears."

**5. "Another broker said our house is worth X thousands more."** "Mr. and Mrs. Sellers, don't choose a broker based on price."

Nearly every time I would go out on a listing presentation, the owner would say, "Well, after we're through talking to you, we're going to call in two or three other brokers." After you've toured the property, gained empathy, moved in with their mood, worked the sellers' net and the Guidelines to Market Value; after you've run the full 26 miles giving the whole listing presentation, make a strong move. Look at them and say, "Please do me—and, more importantly, yourselves—a great big flavor by not selecting a broker based on who comes in here with the highest price. Please remember we're all talking about your asking price, and talk is cheap. An agent with a price higher than the market will pull isn't offering to buy at that price. All of us have the same records; we're all Multiple Listing brokers. If you decide not to follow the market and price your house higher, I can do it too. And I'll back you 100 percent. I may not want to do it because I want to solve your problem. You have a need to sell here, so I may fight you a little bit on price. But please don't choose me based on pricing. Choose your broker for professionalism, for integrity, and for willingness to work."

A real estate friend of mine recently said, "When I give a seller a price lower than another broker's, the other broker always gets the listing because he put more money on it." Talking further with her, I found she wasn't facing the issue squarely. She was treating it as an unmentionable. It is hard, but you've still got to talk about it with your sellers.

"Choose me for my know-how and my honesty—and the pricing we can work out."

## Guidelines to Market Value Form

**Appraisers.** "The reason I brought this Guidelines to Market Value form with me today wasn't to compare your home to others, because we know we can't compare anybody's house with anyone else's. We can't compare anyone's kids with anyone else's. We're all unique; we're all originals every single one of us—." We've got to get this point across to the seller.

"—but the reason I brought it is those darn appraisers. You know, we can set a price, and sell it for that price, but then the appraiser comes out from the bank, and says, 'How did you arrive at this price? Can you substantiate it?' Then we've got to go back to the records and prove the value is here."

You must explain all this to the sellers, because most of them don't know about the part appraisers play in home sales.

**Horse Lots.** Are you familiar with this term? In some suburbs and developments in rural areas, riding horses can be stabled on certain properties called *horse lots*.

A family walks into a real estate office in such an area. "We want a house on a horse lot. We're all riders. We love horses. Let's go look at the horse lots you've got."

The agent says, "I know a place you'll love. You can't have horses there, but it's got a terrific tennis court. So you swat tennis balls instead of horse flies. Same difference."

The horse-loving family immediately walks out on this thick-headed agent. In the next office they find an accommodating agent who sells them what they want.

Any time your property omits something of special importance to certain buyers, you eliminate them. You don't replace them with others unless the omitted amenity is reflected in the property's price.

**Defining Price.** Have you ever asked a prospect, "Well, Mr. and Mrs. Jenkins, what do you want to get for your house? Do you have a figure in mind?"

They're going to look at you and say, "You tell us. You're the expert, the pro, the champ. You're the best. Now you tell us."

Reply with, "Thanks for the compliment. But you and the mystery buyer will become the experts. *Market price* is created by willing buyers and willing sellers, not by real estate agents. It's why you shouldn't choose a real estate agent based on price. We all have the same facts of record. These facts are used by appraisers when your house is sold and a new loan is placed on it."

You've got to get this across to the sellers. They think you're pricing their house like an appraiser. You're not an appraiser; you're the third party who creates a channel to new owners for the property they no longer need. You're the mediator, the negotiator; not the czar of price. Don't let sellers get upset with you for following what the market, the law, and the whole environment has brought about. Don't let them confuse you with the problem you're there to help them solve; don't let them blame you for prices you're not responsible for.

**Bailing Out.** I've found it helpful to discuss pricing along these lines. "You're entitled to every penny you can get for your house. When an investment increases in value, the owners make money when they sell. When an investment decreases in value, the owners lose money when they sell. You don't need to make excuses for taking a profit because nobody would cover your loss if you were to have one.

"A lot of forces are at work determining what the selling value is including the supply-demand ratio and timing—two important forces. The market makes prices. Sellers acting alone don't set the price, because they're all competing against each other for the buyers in the marketplace *at that time.* Buyers acting alone don't set the price, because they too are competing—against the other buyers in the marketplace *at that time*—for the most desirable, best priced properties, the properties offering the most value for the least money.

"In setting your price, please don't fall into the very common error of approaching it from the standpoint of your costs. If you want to sell *now,* determine what price range the market will *pay now*.

"I have never talked to a buyer who had the slightest interest in bailing out a seller, or in paying more than market price. Buyers want to buy right. Of course they sometimes get emotional; they sometimes pay a little more for a house if it really turns them on, but they do it to satisfy their own whims, not the seller's need.

"Now, let's talk about what the market says is a fair price for your house today."

**Put Them Eyeball to Eyeball with the Truth.** "Let's figure out how much it would cost you to buy your own home at the price you're thinking of asking, X\$_____. The most common arrangement is X percent down, and the current interest rate is X percent, so the buyers' monthly investment would be X\$, plus property tax and homeowners' insurance. So, at your price, we're looking at the buyers' housing cost being X\$ a month. If you decide to go that high with your asking price, I'm with you 100 percent, but I'm going to have you take responsibility for the price. Maybe we can re-evaluate it after we get some buyer response.

"Now let's talk about the appraiser. The lender tells him, 'We're looking at a risk of X\$, so this property darn well better be worth it now—and after the economy's taken a hard bump too. We're loaning our depositors' money, so we've got to be careful.' The appraiser will take the lot size and your house's square footage into consideration as he compares it to other properties sold recently in this same neighborhood. But he'll simply lump the upgrades into one category: excellent, good, or poor. It's rough on you and me, but it's the way appraisers do this, and we have to be aware of the realities.

"When we come into the Multiple Listing book and appear on the caravan sheet with your four-bedroom home, the other agents—the sharp ones who do all the business—will know quite a bit about your house just from its location. If they feel it's overpriced, they won't show it. They won't even preview it because they're always pressed for time. And they don't want to irritate their buyers by showing them overpriced properties, so why should they take the time to see a house they believe is too overpriced to sell?"

I constantly ask questions like, "How do you feel about this?" Questions give the sellers a chance to confide in me.

"Do you agree?"

"Does this sound reasonable?"

"Are you satisfied on this point?"

"Do you see what I'm saying here?"

You have to get your points across, and the only way you can know you're doing that is to get them to talk, to voice their objections, to air their gripes about the system, and to speak of their true feelings. You need to say the right phrases, but you need to listen to the sellers even more.

One of the winningest scripts is the gold-grabbing silence of the superb listener. Such listening takes every bit as much energy and attention as does delivering an effective sales talk.

Make the sellers aware that they are not to come back at you if there's no activity, and a price re-evaluation will be in order in a couple of weeks. However, if they get their price no one will be happier for them than you will be.

**Take Overpriced Listings Very Carefully.** Take overpriced listings cautiously. Don't let yourself be pulled into carrying overpriced listings in a buyer's market by wishful thinking about getting the prices down later, especially if the sellers aren't strongly motivated to sell.

**Deadlines Are Closes.** But deadlines can close you *out*, if your timing is bad, instead of closing you *in* on a listing. Here's how it works. You've made a strong listing presentation and feel you're almost there—but the sellers want to wait. You're the last of three agents they've heard. They can't quite make up their minds and want to think it over. Your office caravan is Tuesday; the Thursday Board of REALTORS® caravan deadline is 5 P.M. Tuesday; the following week's Multiple Listing book deadline is Friday at 5 P.M. Here's what you say:

"I know how you feel. You're thinking. 'We can wait a few days; we're not quite ready emotionally to take the final step.' It *is* a big decision. But, actually, you've already made the big decision (to take your new job a thousand miles away, to buy your new house, whatever applies) and now you're doing a very understandable thing: catching your breath for a few hours."

Smile understandingly. "A few hours delay can't make much difference, can it?" Pause briefly. Whether they say anything or not, continue with, "Well, let's talk about it. Waiting those few hours can cost you a bundle—let's make sure it doesn't happen. First of all, our office caravan is every Tuesday morning. Tomorrow. We have a hard-driving team, and all of them are working with buyers. So, a few hours delay wipes out showing your home to our office for a whole week. Then comes the next deadline. Five P.M. tomorrow is the cutoff for getting on Thursday's Association of REALTORS® caravan. So we miss it for a week. Well, you may say, 'What's a week?'"

Your next lines will depend on what the market's doing, and what the season is. (Any facts you give now must, of course, be true at the time.) "Sales have dropped every week for the past four weeks. It's not much of a change—but every week the activity is a little less than it was the week before. When we have a condition like this, buyers realize the market is going down and wait for better prices. This action cuts sales further and increases the downward pressure. It's why we have these up and down cycles in real estate and, frankly, I think two months ago would've been a better time to have your house on the market. We can't roll back the calendar, but we can make sure no more time gets away from us.

"Next week, probably 30 couples will buy here. This is what we're all telling each other. But the market often moves with suddenness, and turns yesterday's sound assumptions into tomorrow's wishful thinking. You want to sell. Considering the season, we can forget about the market taking off during the next few months. But we can't forget about it getting worse. You're going to give someone the assignment to sell your property soon. Why make it tougher on yourselves by waiting? It's not a question of it being tougher on me to sell your house next week, because I'm going to be selling houses next year, and the year after that. I'm thinking about your situation.

"You should have your house listed in the next issue of the Multiple Listing book. It should be on Thursday's caravan. Our office should come through here tomorrow morning, and start comparing it to their buyers' needs. All I need to get this aggressive sales program moving is your approval right here." Slide the listing form over to them. "Shall we proceed?"

**Rising Market.** What do you say if the market is rising? You're sitting in their home in February, at the beginning of your heavy selling season.

"Mr. Seller, the four top-selling months here are March, April, May, and June. Sales peak in June, hold constant or slide off slowly through August, and then drop sharply to the off-season lows. Those folks who are fortunate enough to market their homes now, at the beginning of our heavy selling season, can expect top dollar and minimum selling time—*if* their conditions and location are right. In this situation, we can project a bit of appreciation into our listing price. But remember, a price too much over the market will discourage showings and offers.

"Let's see, X$ is the top market figure right now for a comparable sale of this size home in your neighborhood. The sale occurred just 10 days ago. Prior to that, the figures were X$ and X$. I'd suggest a spring maximum list price of X$. This gives us a projected cushion, and it's still believable in the marketplace. The spring forecast is good, and sales are beginning right on schedule to make their slow climb to the peak, so I feel comfortable with X$ at this time."

**Nonrising Market.** If you don't expect the market to rise this spring, adapt this dialogue to the current situation.

"Mr. Seller, March through June is our most active selling period, but last year's rapid appreciation, coupled with the stock market going South, drained off all chance of further increasing prices this spring. So I'm convinced our sales prices will remain constant for another 6 to 12 months. Until demand catches up with supply, and rising income brings the buyers' ability to qualify up to higher levels, I don't see an economic base able to support higher prices. Last year's rapid appreciation has hurt us, and brought on the correction period we're in now. Please bear this in mind when we agree on price."

Such speeches are highly effective when they flow smoothly out of your mouth. You'll find the material for them in your ongoing study of published economic figures and forecasts. Your public library will have copies of the most prestigious financial publications.

Make your own forecast of future sales activity and price levels in your sales area. Write down your predictions, and refer to them after the facts are in. Figure out why you were right or wrong. The more careful and thorough your predictions are, the smoother and more convincing your sales speeches will be.

**Overimprovements.** The sellers have a 2200 square foot, four-bedroom home.

"I've compiled the data on all the four-bedroom homes within a six-block radius on the market now, and I've also compiled a list of similar four-bedroom homes sold within the past two months. I've also shown the expired listings—the unsold properties."

Break the list down and tell them why each expired didn't sell. "This listing was higher than the market could bear." (You're not blaming the agent or the seller—you're blaming the market.)

Get a range for selling. "Is this somewhere in your frame of reference, Mr. Seller?" Usually, the sellers will now give you the sales price they've been thinking of.

If the seller says, "Those properties don't have the improvements we have," pause, look at your Guidelines to Market Value form with great concentration, and name a price, "X$." I talk to myself a lot in front of an overimproved seller.

Give the seller a track record of the market. An agent must read newspapers, go to seminars, and be in the thick of the market in order to speak with authority in this situation.

"Your home is really beautiful. This is my area, and I've sold many homes here, so I know yours is one of the nicest. I hate to do what I have to do next, but you know I'm a licensed real estate agent, and to get licensed I had to go through certain training. In order to practice real estate, there are certain codes of ethics and procedures I have to follow.

"So, at this point, I need to do something out of obligation to you. I'm not comparing your home to any others because it's special, but my problem is this: you're so close to this house. There are so many good memories for you here—and everything you've done is the best—it all means it's very hard for you to be as objective as I am.

"I deal with people every day and I know how the people who will be coming in here think. I know they'll appreciate your home, but no matter how well beauty and art and loving care are appreciated, they still have to be backed up with facts.

"Quite frankly, if we don't discuss this, later on you'll be upset with me. You've put a lot into this house, and it shows a strong sense of responsibility to be such a good homeowner. Now, if I get the opportunity to be your representative, I feel we should go over these facts."

## Agree on Pricing

If you're not honest with a homeowner, later on another agent will be. If sellers complain about the information I've presented, I say, "If I don't give you the real facts and figures, someone else will, and I'll have failed to act responsibly toward you. The asking price is your decision, but a selling price takes three parties: you, a buyer, and a lending committee."

If the sellers still want to go with a high price, say, "Okay, I'll go along with this price, and from here on out, I'm behind you 100 percent. But do two things for me. First, give me the chance to come back in two weeks to re-evaluate the price, based on public reaction. Second, be aware that I'm not taking responsibility for your price. You set the price on this house, not me."

If you don't make this clear up front, they'll say later, "Well, you told us we could get X$ for our house." But you never said that. During the listing interview, ward off this evil by writing on the seller's net sheet how the price was arrived at. Jot down something like, "Mr. and Mrs. Shepley feel their house is worth X$, but my analysis indicates, and I recommended to them, a price of X$ to sell in this market." Make a copy for your file, initial the note, and give it to the sellers.

Then, if your sellers later try to blame the nonsale of their home on you, tactfully remind them of the recommendation you made when taking their listing. Never do this angrily. Mention your recommendation and sympathize with their need and desire to take all the money they can out of their house. But stand clear—keep yourself separated from the market.

"It's the market. The market simply won't put your number on this house today. It's the old law of supply and demand."

## Acquaint Sellers with Your Marketing Program

"I'm going to advertise your property once a month in my own personal ad in the _____."

"Our company's advertising program will feature your house on _____."

"I'm going to bring our office staff through on our special office caravan next Tuesday. As I said before, our team is strong. Year in and year out, we sell ____ percent of our own listings."

"I'm going to bring the Board of REALTORS® caravan through here next Thursday. The entire board will be invited to see your home. I'd like to serve refreshments on Board of REALTORS® caravan day, so let's discuss this now."

"The Multiple Listing Service will have this property in the next book. It'll come out a week from Wednesday."

"I'm going to make up a temporary flyer to have for next Thursday's caravan."

"I'll make up a brochure with three pictures and a printed description. I'll leave a stack of them here for people coming through, and distribute them to the other offices. I've got my own list of out-of-area buyers and brokers I'll send your flyer to, and, of course, it'll go in the flyer packet I give all the agents and prospects I contact wherever I go."

## Explain How Advertising Works

One of the mistakes agents make with sellers is to assume sellers understand how the process works. They don't. It's no wonder sellers get so upset when they don't see their house advertised—no one has corrected their erroneous ideas. Sellers think a newspaper ad—with its photo of the home and a few printed words—will make a buyer call the real estate company and say, "I've found my dream house—I could tell from the ad—I just know it's the one I'm going to buy." Sight unseen, sellers assume a buyer will go wild over an ad.

We have more modest goals when we advertise, don't we? We don't expect to sell a house with a classified ad; we just try to make the phone ring. All the ad can do is give an up-person a chance to make an appointment. We know there's a long, hard road to travel between the phone call and a completed sale. However, many successful trips down this road begin with the ad-generated phone call.

So I like to say, "Mr. Sellers, all properties advertised with our company can sell your home. It doesn't matter whether your house is advertised or not. You see, a buyer may call us on a three-bedroom home priced at X$, but they don't know the price yet because we're going to give price information to them on the phone—and we find out they need four bedrooms for not more than X$. Then we're going to tell them about your house—after I qualify them in the office, of course. But first I have to get them in. What I'm going to say when they call in on the ad is, 'Yes, this particular property is X$. It's a three-bedroom home, and it's lovely. Does it sound in line with what you're looking for?' They'll say something like, 'Oh, no, not at all.'

"Then, Mr. Sellers, I come back with, 'We have some terrific properties in several price ranges,' and I'm off and running to convert them to your property. Just because you don't see your house advertised in the *Bugle* every morning doesn't mean we're not working on it. Our phones are ringing every single day!"

Explain this to your sellers. Otherwise, you'll be hearing, "I want my house advertised every day. I want my house held open every day for two weeks. *Every* day. We want action with a capital A."

Sellers don't understand how this business works. You have to explain it to them. If ads aren't the main source of buyers in your company, explain why they aren't. Perhaps classified ads don't bring in enough business to justify their cost in your area.

"This area's unique advantages brought you here, Mr. and Mrs. Sellers, and they are the very reasons why classified advertising doesn't make the phone ring here. It's because we're so close to the city—the people just drive out. It's because we're so far from the city, people come out for the weekend; because of the lake or the college or because we're so much like a resort." Give them the reasons applying in your locality.

Then tell your sellers, "The sign we'll put in front of your house is a 24-hour billboard. It's what really makes the phone ring in this area. You see, people aren't afraid to call an agent and ask about a property. They don't hesitate to tell us, 'it's too high,' or 'I need more bedrooms than it has,' or even, 'I'm looking for a steal.' They know they won't be talking to the owner, and maybe get put down hard. The 24-hour front signs are what make the phone ring around here—and our sign is a particularly effective one."

"Nationwide, this has been proven. Effective broker house-signs make the phone ring more than all other kinds of advertising combined."

Then tell them about the other things your firm does, and you do, to gain the business coming from ads in other areas. If your firm belongs to a national relocation referral network, tell them how it makes the phone ring and brings in customers.

## The One Percent-Edge Approach to Holding or Raising Your Fee

This is an effective method with all motivated sellers, but especially with expired listings and property that's been on the market for a long time. Here's what you say.

"You have many options as a homeowner to get your property marketed. A very important part of selling your home is motivating the (state the number) agents in our Board of REALTORS® to see your home and then interest their buyers in it.

"In a market such as this, the homeowner suffers and so do agents. As an extra incentive, let's offer this property at a fee 1 percent higher to the selling agent than is customary."

People who are transferred or are otherwise motivated for a fast sale often see the value of taking this approach. When you're working with someone you think will try to grind you down, the 1-percent-edge approach often allows you to at least take the listing at the customary fee. To make this work, you usually have to talk about the fee before they do.

Here's another version.

"Mr. and Mrs. Brillson, you've said you're interested in a fast sale, but you also need to sell your home at the top of the market in order to have the funds necessary to buy your next home."

Wait for them to answer—they'll always agree.

"Mr. Brillson, if you said to me, 'I want you to handle the total sale of my home; I don't want it on the Multiple Listing Service; I want all offers to come through you.' If you wanted the sale handled this way, I'd be hard-pressed to help you. What I'm saying is, I work very closely with other agents, not only in my office but also in other offices. I've worked hard to develop a reputation as an honest person who is easy for other agents to work with.

"What we need to do is excite those other agents because it will tremendously increase the number of buyers who will be exposed to your home. I suggest that instead of placing your home on the market at X$, let's increase the price by 1 percent and at the same time, increase the brokerage fee to the selling agent by 1 percent.

"Now this doesn't guarantee a sale, but it does guarantee your property will be shown to far more of the qualified buyers coming into this area than would otherwise be the case. Your property will be a favorite listing in all the offices here—and the icing on the cake is, it doesn't cost you anything to get all the agents here on our side."

## Fight the Fee-Cutters

In many cases, a demand for a lower than customary fee will come up before you've had the opportunity to establish sufficient rapport to bring it up yourself. Here's an effective response in these cases.

"Mr. Cassidy, a lot of people believe I can approve this. But my broker is against playing favorites. If we do, we cheat the rest of our clients. You see, we have many homeowners committed, in writing, to us at our standard fee. Our company considers it highly unethical to have a special arrangement with only a few homeowners unless it's disclosed to all our clients.

"This attitude on our part is extremely important to you. If we would conceal a special arrangement with you from our other clients, what guarantee do you have we wouldn't do the same thing *to* you? When we talk about the price of your home we're talking big dollars—and it's vital to you to associate yourself with people you can trust."

On higher-priced homes, you can often dispose of this question by saying, "When marketing your home, Mr. and Mrs. Collingsworth, we want to appeal not only to the new and inexperienced agents—we also want to reach the top producers. I'm referring to the highly successful agents who earn more than X$ a year. These people sell most of the properties; they're always working with buyers—and they just won't show property carrying a reduced fee. In other words, going with a reduced fee means you've reduced your chances of selling drastically. Do you really want to do this in *today's* market?"

# CHAPTER 12

# Servicing Listings Fast

**Start Servicing Fast ● Advanced Caravan Technique ● Communicate with the Sellers ● Never Wing It ● Getting the Price Down Less Painfully ● Coping with the Messies ● Danny's Dozen to Bring My Sellers More Money ● The Thorough Stage-Setting Program ● Beware of Overnight Panic ● Avoid Possession Hassles ● Winning Scripts**

The secret to building a relationship that will warrant a lifetime customer is the servicing aspect of the real estate business. Many salespeople are very enthusiastic when it comes to capturing clients and closing or listing them. But once the chase is over, the challenge ends. There are agents who are very short-term thinkers; they do not deliver what they promise. When you are working with an agent who does not value service, perhaps it is your listing and his buyer, the transaction can close with a lot of hard feelings on the customers' part. If this is the case, then forget about winning that customer for life.

The secret to building a strong relationship is to exude the same enthusiasm throughout the entire process. Buyers and sellers remember how a transaction closes, not opens. Never forget the goal is to create a lifetime fan. That means you deliver knowledge with speed and in the midst of the process you get closer to the customer. They trust you. With these thoughts in mind, let's take a look at the best way to service customers.

The problems related to servicing listings fall into two distinct areas. The first is where the buyers come from—the world outside the listing. Various aspects of buyers are discussed in the next six chapters.

In this chapter we concentrate on the second problem area—the sellers, your relations with them, the property itself, and its price. Remember, **correctly priced listings require no servicing because they sell fast. Real estate agents should remember this great and profound truth**, but they must also remember that most listings cannot be brought in at quick-sale prices. Therefore, to be a successful listing agent, you must study the skills of servicing listings, and learn how to motivate sellers to do what must be done to get their property sold—within their time limits.

## Start Servicing Fast

Sometimes we work so hard at getting a listing, we feel it's all over when the sellers finally sign. However, this is only the beginning. You've been hired—now you get to do the job—sell the house! Don't let any time go by while you rest up from your labors; do all the servicing you can when you write the listing. Before you leave them do the following:

- *Prepare the sellers* for the reality of the marketing process. Forewarn them, so they'll know what to expect. Inform them about how the process works, so they'll be cordial, resigned, and cooperative; not startled, angry, and on the phone to you complaining about people you have no power to control.
- *Convince them to leave when the property is shown.*
- *Convince them how vital it is to set the stage for a showing.*
- *Convince them to banish the negatives.*

The Winning Scripts at the end of this chapter will help you accomplish these goals.

The seller is the most important person in our real estate world. Remember open houses don't sell property. Price and terms sell property. So first consider the financing available for the property. If the only houses currently being sold are owner-carrybacks at extremely favorable terms because mortgage money is tight, you can't justify investing your time in any listing requiring a new conventional loan.

Second, look at similar houses in the neighborhood and at the prices those properties sold for. You have to, because the buyers will. The new lender—if there is to be one—will, too. Unless the sales price conforms to the lender's value formulas, there is no sale. But the sellers hated it when I compared their house to others. In their minds, nothing compares.

I didn't want the sellers to think I was indifferent to their home, and would "give it away" if they'd let me. Usually sellers don't know about market cycles, or understand that they can set asking prices, but only a buyer—by buying—can set a selling price. Many sellers are unrealistic. I didn't want to alienate them and lose the listing, nor did I want to take the price so high we'd never (within the longest listing period possible) get within negotiating range of what the market would pay. I wanted to compromise on a reasonable figure.

Servicing priced-right listings demands skill, knowledge, and close attention, but these are the happy situations. There's lots of action. Your sellers stay excited. A low offer comes in and you can prove the asking price is right. Before long you've brought buyer and seller together and the property is sold. Now you're off working on other opportunities instead of burning time and energy trying to explain to unrealistic sellers what they find unexplainable: why their property hasn't sold.

Remember, if the price isn't realistic, you can do everything else right—you can work very hard, you can spend lots of money promoting the property—and earn nothing. In the last chapter, we talked about overpriced listings and what to do with them. This concern is still with us in this chapter—your number one service item is to adjust the price to a realistic level relative to the value offered and the sellers' timing.

## Advanced Caravan Technique

Your office should have its own caravan each week before the regular Board of RELATORS® caravan for all offices. The office caravan takes place immediately after the weekly office meeting. It's an important tool for listing agents; often the sight of the sellers' kitchen table carpeted with our staff's business cards is the final push to nail down the listing. Yes, we caravan houses before the listing is nailed down, when requested.

Empathize with your sellers. The sellers go through a lot of trouble to glitter up the house. Then the salespeople go whish-woosh, in and out, and they're gone. The poor owner will think, "All my work—and they weren't here ten minutes." Tell her beforehand she's working with professionals who know what to look for, and that they see a lot fast.

Another idea I've found makes a terrific impression, and we've never had a complaint about our caravaning speed since we started doing it. Leave a rose. Your florist will put the roses in vases for you, and deliver them to your office during the meeting. Also, leave a short note (see example below) if the sellers aren't there. Write your note before the caravan so you can give all your time to showing the house to your staff while they're on the scene.

> *Dear Diane and Mark,*
>
> *Thanks for doing such a beautiful job setting the stage. I hope this is the start of a very happy transaction between you and Sell Fast Realty.*
>
> *Helen*

Now we'll assume you're working with a realistically priced property, not a throwaway, but a fair, at-the-market priced home. Much effort, skill, and knowledge are still required to create a sale. An important part of this effort involves securing the sellers' wholehearted participation in what must be a cooperative venture if the best price is to be obtained quickly.

# Communicate with the Sellers

## Give Them What They Want

One of the most important parts of servicing the listing is to keep in touch with your sellers. It is easier now than ever. E-mail is an excellent way to stay in touch. BUT BE SURE THEY READ THEIR E-MAIL DAILY! Otherwise you have to use other methods. Update sellers constantly with every significant development like sales, new listings, changes in financing, and the general market condition—everything bearing on the salability of their house. Do this and they'll never blame you if the property doesn't sell; they'll blame the marketplace.

My longest listing was 13 months, but I told the seller what was going on every single Monday morning. The house had bad problems. My seller hung in there with me, and I was able to hang in there with him, only because I kept talking to him. I didn't keep him in the dark. It's all they want—to be loved—like everyone else in this whole wide world.

And, they want a sale.

## Call Every Monday Morning

Failing to keep in touch has cost more listings than any other single cause. You can't let an unrealistic seller stew in overpriced isolation, and at the same time build the credibility to get a reduction to salable levels. Their house isn't getting shown. If they aren't hearing from you, they'll think you aren't working on getting their house sold. And they may be right.

When you call a seller and he says, "I haven't heard from you in a couple of weeks."

You can reply, "Well, I've tried to get you, but your line is always busy," or "—but no one ever answered." Those are great lines if they're true. If not, can you blame your sellers for getting upset when their largest asset languishes on the market without a flicker of interest from the public, or even from their agent?

*At the very least,* call all your sellers every Monday morning. If you're too crowded by clients in the morning, do it Monday afternoon, Monday night, or Tuesday. Without fail, the first of every week, call every listing you have. Tell your sellers what's happened to similar properties in the marketplace, and report on any activity on their listing.

## Protect Yourself Against the Always-Busy Phone

What about sellers whose phones really are always tied up? On the *back* of one of your letterheads, jot down every time you call:

7/19

| 9:00 A.M. | Busy | 9:35 A.M. | Busy |
| 9:15 A.M. | Busy | 11:05 A.M. | Busy |

At this point, flip over the page and write them a pleasant note. Mention your calls noted on the reverse side. Some people don't realize how much they (or their children) keep their phone busy. Don't let a minor item such as this damage your relationship. The burden of proof is on you. Drop by and hang the note on their door if they aren't there.

## Make Promises You Can Keep

If you tell your sellers you're going to call every Monday morning, then call them every Monday morning. If you say, "I spend Wednesdays with my family, but I'm on duty most weekends," then be active on the weekends and make sure they know it. Tell them, "I can't be reached on Wednesdays, but I'll call you every Friday between 4 and 6." Then do as you said you would, and you'll save yourself a lot of trouble. Make promises you can keep and then keep them.

One of my sellers asked me to join his family in prayer about the listing before he would sign it. His house was a wreck. Two weeks later he gave me a hard time because his house hadn't sold, and he urged me to cooperate with God. I told him he should do likewise because God means for us to make some effort too—so would he please clean up his house and give us both a better chance? This didn't go over too well, so I suggested he reflect on how God looks on the welfare of buyers, and this devout man finally saw the point. The next time I visited them, cleanliness was next to Godliness, and their house sold soon afterwards.

# Never Wing It

You've proclaimed yourself the local area expert, and a competent professional in the general practice of residential real estate. This doesn't mean you must have the answer to every conceivable question. Never put yourself in the position of talking with clients about subjects you aren't qualified to discuss. Don't hesitate to say, "It's outside my area of specialization." When the conversation strays from your area of expertise, an occasional "I don't know" dispels any suspicion that you are a tiresome know-it-all.

# Getting the Price Down Less Painfully

On a Sunday night, after several weekends of open houses, might be a good time to get a price reduction, if it's indicated. Your sellers are feeling down and out. They may not have been willing to listen to you before, but now they have the public's response. You may be able to sit down with them and say, "We've had four weekends of open houses. Based on the Guidelines to Market Value I brought out a month ago, it looks like the public is telling us the same thing. Let's think about the price a little bit. . . ."

They're going to be more receptive to realistic pricing after the public has validated your opinion. **Caution:** Don't wait too long. Stay in tune with your sellers. If you're slow in seeking a price cut, they may blame you for their house not selling.

# Coping with the Messies

## Wait Them Out

With messies who are moving away on a certain date whether their house sells or not, bring in a cleaning crew when the house is vacant.

Clean-up labor goes further when there's no furniture in the way, and it lasts longer in unoccupied houses.

Think ahead. Consider the seasonal buying patterns, the length of your listing, how well you relate to the sellers, and how realistic their price is. Can you hold the listing long enough to make this work?

## Build Curb Appeal

A few hours of labor and very little money will often increase curb appeal enormously. I'm always amazed when people put a house on the market for big dollars and then let their kids dig holes in the front yard.

Part of your job is to put some pressure on them, so they'll think, "If my agent sees this, he will be right on our necks about it." So the sellers yell at little Hector and keep him in line. You've got to keep the pressure on with some people—being sensitive so it doesn't blow back in your face. Always come on with a firm but considerate manner.

"I'm sorry to mention this, but I'm afraid of the front yard now. Let's say an agent drives up with some buyers, and they've already seen ten houses. They're a little tired. Your house might be just what they're looking for. But when they drive up and see those big holes in your front slope, one of them says, 'I don't even want to see the inside. Go on to the next one.' The buyers drive off. This kind of thing happens all the time. Please understand me; I'm not trying to interfere. If it weren't my job to get your house sold, I wouldn't say anything because I know you've got a lot on your mind right now, but the front slope needs a little attention."

## Remember That
## Buyers Have Noses Too

One of my sellers had a houseful of pets. You went through the entry sideways because of the rabbit hutch. The living room was a zoo—literally. Every little creature had contributed to the unusual aroma in the house. I suggested they take one of two actions: reduce the price substantially or move the zoo. They moved the zoo. But the house still smelled like a zoo—to everyone except the owners. They wouldn't accept the truth about the sense of smell being our most easily fatigued sense. We simply can't smell an odor we are exposed to for several hours every day as keenly as someone who isn't accustomed to it can smell it. They didn't believe my delicate comments about Essence de Barnum driving off buyers. So I waited. When their new home was completed they moved into it. In this house the zoo had its own open-air shed. I closed their old home up tight, let it steam for a week in July, and then took them back for a sniff. They got the point.

"What should we do?" they asked. The walls were painted early bullfighter, and the carpet was different in every room to match a toreador's every mood.

I told them, "Get a crew in here and rip out the carpet and pad. Rent some large fans and let them blow air through the place for a few days. Then repaint the whole interior off-white. Finally, put down honey-colored carpet—one color throughout. Come over every day and bake vanilla in the oven. Do all this and you'll be able to recover your fix-up cost in the price—and it'll sell promptly too."

They did, and it did.

## Remove Destructive Decor

Sometimes the decor makes a house unsalable even when it's priced under the market. A friend of mine took a listing from a collector of medieval weaponry. Swords, sabers, and scimitars covered every wall; a nasty-looking collection of maces, and other ancient head crushers hung from every ceiling light. Buyers laughed at first and then felt oppressed. No offers were received until the house was de-militarized because the owners moved away with their obsolete arsenal. Then it sold promptly.

## If You're Slightly Unsure of Yourself

If you're a slightly unsure, new salesperson and really can't give the "paint the inside, cut the grass, de-junk the place" lecture to your sellers, make up a flyer like, "Danny's Dozen to Bring My Sellers More Money." Hand a copy of this flyer to each of your sellers. (Put one in your Listing Presentation Manual too.) It's a crutch, but don't hesitate to use crutches until your legs are strong enough to run on. I never hesitated to, or failed to grow out of any of them. You won't either. Think of a catchy name for your flyer such as:

- Arnie's Assortment of Able Ideas to Bring My Sellers More Money . . .
- Betty's Bundle of . . .
- Bernie's Bag of . . .
- Carl's Collection of . . .
- Clara's Carton of Clues to . . .
- Ellen's Emeralds for Selling Your Home for More . . .
- Frank's Famous Ideas for . . .

- Gerta's Group of . . .
- Hank's Hard-Hitting Tips to . . .
- Xavier's Zingers . . .
- Yolanda's Yummy Tips for Upping the Yield
- Zack's Stack of Zippy Tips for . . .

You get the idea. A touch of light-hearted alliteration can relieve the tension when you ask your sellers to put their shoulders to the wheel and grunt to get their house sold.

# Danny's Dozen to Bring My Sellers More Money

1. **Cultivate curb charisma.** Some of the best buyers are the most impatient because they need to make a decision fast. If the view of your house from the street turns them off, they might not even stop. Shape up your front yard.

2. **Take a critical look at your house's front.** If it's weathered looking, if anything needs repair, or if anything needs to be hauled to the dump—eliminate these problems. Don't turn your buyers off outside before the inside can turn them on.

3. **Never stay in your house with house hunters.** Let the agent handle it, and remove yourself if you possibly can. Remember, the agent has worked for many hours with these potential buyers, knows what they're looking for, and how to work with them. Let him or her do the job without interference.

   You may think an agent isn't showing the important features of your house, but the agent knows buyers aren't sold by details until they've become emotionally involved with the big picture of your house. The presence of any member of the sellers' family can't help, always unnerves possible buyers, and often prevents a sale. Don't put this obstacle in your path. Leave when buyers are coming.

4. **Give your dogs and cats a vacation.** They need it and so does your pocketbook. Having pets around (especially aggressive dogs) when you're selling your home can be incredibly expensive. Many people are acutely uncomfortable around some animals, and simply can't think *buy* when their minds are on *bye*.

5. **A few cans of paint and putty to brighten up your home's interior** are the best investment your can make when you're selling a house.

6. **Drips do more than run up your water bill.** They focus the attention of possible buyers on your house's entire plumbing system, and cause them to worry. Fix these little problems before they cost you a sale.

7. **Squeaking doors and creaking floors,** torn or missing screens, cracked glass, and anything in need of repair dampens the house hunter's enthusiasm. Many buyers believe there will always be ten problems they haven't noticed for every one they see.

8. **Hide (or neatly arrange) everything connected with work:** lawnmowers, garden hoses, vacuum cleaners, and all the gear you used to fix up the house. Accent everything connected with play and relaxation: sound systems, skis, toys in the kids' rooms.

9. **De-clutter.** Repack compactly, dispose of unneeded items, or rent storage space and move out as much material as you can. Your home's storage space can't look adequate to a buyer if you've got it jam-packed.

10. **Turn up the shelter.** If it's hot, cool it; if it's cold, light a crackling fire.

11. **Harmonize the elements.** Turn the music on softly and the TV off. Turn on all lights, day or night. Open the drapes in the daytime.

12. **You can sell pride of ownership faster and for more money.** It's called cleanliness, and fresh cleanliness has more buyers than used dirt. Put sparkle in your bathrooms and kitchen, and you'll take lots more silver out.

After you've discussed debunking, cleaning up, and fixing up with your new clients, you should explain setting the stage.

# The Thorough Stage-Setting Program

Sellers should run through the stage-setting items any day when buyers may appear. Compile a checklist suited to your area, and go over it with each of your sellers as soon as possible after securing their listing. Here are some points to discuss with them.

## Watering

Little water drops all over the plants and lawn give a delightful, fresh feeling in summer, and all year long in dry, warm climates. Suggest that sellers time their sprinkling so the dewy effect remains when the buyers are likely to appear. Hosing down the walks also adds sparkle. However, leaving hoses strewn around, and gardening tools lying about, not only looks tacky, it spoils the dream by reminding house-hunters of chores instead of the good life.

## Lawns and Grounds

Explain to your sellers how important it is for the yard to look appealing and well cared for. When the work is done, it looks easy; when it's undone, it seems formidable.

Lawns should be mowed and edged, hedges cut, trees trimmed, and weeds eliminated. If possible, bare ground should be covered by gravel or bark; at the very least it should be raked and kept moist.

Lawns with patches of dead grass can be greatly improved with a few square feet of sod from the local nursery. It's surprisingly cheap, and anyone can successfully install it. All it takes is to notch out the old dead grass with a spade or trowel, cut the new sod to fit, and stomp it into place. What a difference it makes!

## Drapes and Window Coverings

Consider each window and room separately. Is the view pleasant, or do you see the neighbor's trash cans? Are the window frames attractive when exposed? Are the drapes themselves more striking when opened or closed? Does the room show better by sunlight or lamplight? When you are not certain, opt for sunlight. Buyers want to see, and light encourages them.

What you're doing here is showing your product to its best advantage, not concealing its defects. The buyers can open the drapes and see the trash cans, but they're still reassured because there are drapes to hide this from their own guests. You are working here on effect more than substance and on emotion more than fact. Keep this in mind as you direct sellers in setting the stage for the first time.

## Lighting

Tell your sellers to switch on every single lamp and light in the entire house every time they prepare it for a showing or go out.

## Music

What's the mood of the house? Select music that enhances it, rather than whatever happens to be your, or your sellers', favorite. Loud country music playing in a stately home furnished with antiques is as out of place as a Bach fugue playing in a family room paneled with knotty pine. Soft and romantic music is the choice for the place just made for two. When in doubt, go with something current, snappy, and not too loud.

You're selling lifestyle along with walls and floors, so harmonize all the elements. Have your sellers play recorded music suitable to the house each day they leave. For a specific showing, the right selection can be a powerful mood-setting influence. Tell your sellers to make mood music part of their stage-setting drill.

## Get Ready! Get Set! Set the Stage!

Lights on. Drapes open. Music playing softly. Fireplace blazing on a cold day, air conditioning going on a hot day.

**The sellers are gone.**

Beds made. Kitchen sparkling. Everything in its place. Pets at grandmother's. Windows cleaned to invisibility. Lawns mowed. Hedges trimmed. Tools in the garage.

**The sellers are gone.**

The buyers come. They linger. "I don't know what it is about this one, but I feel good here. You know—it's like home," the wife says.

"Looks like an easy place to take care of," replies the husband. "There isn't anything we'd have to do. The company will move us in, and I can hit the job the next day."

**Ring. Ring. Ring.** It's the buyers' agent calling you. "I've got an offer for you. Say, you know, your listing sure showed well."

## When Is the Stage to Be Set?

**Set the Selling Stage Every Day.** Selling a house is a continuous, ongoing, daily performance. Use the analogy of a stage play to dramatize your enthusiasm; sellers like it. Specifically, the stage should be set:

- For your office caravan
- For your Board of REALTORS® caravan
- Whenever the house is shown
- Whenever open house is held there
- Whenever your sellers leave the house during the day, and especially on weekends

Sellers should keep their house showably clean at all times, and be ready every day of the week to go through the whole stage-setting

process, and *then leave.* Not all sellers will give you this kind of cooperation. If they're overpriced, the market is slow, and you don't expect
many showings, you may be well advised to conserve their patience
and energy during the *Let's-test-the-market-with-a-high-price* phase
buyers may insist on going through. Then, when they've become realistic and more in the mood to cooperate, come on strong about constant
stage setting.

## The House Is Home

On a raw, overcast day with a cutting wind, an agent ushers two shiv-
ering people into a cold, dark, silent, and empty house. The buyers
walk quickly through, and then hurry back to the warm car. They drive
on to the next listing. This house is also empty, but the lights are on,
and it's warm inside. Soft music shuts out the sound of the wind. In the
fireplace a cheery fire is crackling behind a screen. This time the buyers don't hurry back to the agent's warm car. They take their time, look
the place over carefully, and mentally move in. This house feels like
home. It's already sheltered them once, and the idea of making the
arrangement permanent is entrancing. They sit down at the kitchen
table with their agent and write up an offer.

This offer, which your sellers accept, came about because you
persuaded the sellers to light a fire and then leave, as part of a thorough
setting-the-stage program. Their property has sold quickly because
you've promoted it well, and because they've done their part by setting
the stage whenever a phone call told them their house would be shown.

## Furnished or Vacant, Which Sells Better?

There's no hard-and-fast rule to the Furnished or Vacant question, but
it's good to have an answer in case you're asked. In most cases the sellers don't have much choice, they either have to stay until it sells, or
they're under considerable pressure to move before it sells. If you're
dealing with a situation where they have no choice, make them feel
good about whatever they have to do.

Some buyers love to look at vacant houses; others are uncomfortable in them. Some buyers can't stand anyone else's taste in furnishings, and get so wrought up reacting to the decoration that they
don't notice the floor plan. Most buyers, however, will be somewhat
more comfortable looking at neat and clean furnished houses if the furnishings don't crowd the rooms and make them look tiny.

Some sellers living in a small house have it jammed with furniture and gear while they're preparing to move to a larger one. Tell them, "Put some of these lovely pieces of furniture in storage. The fees you'll pay will come back to you many times over in selling this house sooner and for more money."

Being vacant and unfurnished is not a serious sales problem in smaller homes, for example, those under 1700 feet. As the size increases, it becomes more and more important for the houses to be at least partially furnished. Large empty houses, especially those over 4000 feet, seem like acres of empty space if left totally unfurnished.

# Beware of Overnight Panic

Sellers can swing from hanging tough to panicky overnight. Never forget this. Keep in close touch with your sellers. Keep yourself aware of their mood, never let them feel abandoned. Keep them posted on what the market is doing. If it's tightening, stay ahead of it and them.

## Hanging in There with Hang-Tough Sellers

Be quick to tell the most obstinate hang-toughs to make a serious price cut now, before the market drops even further under their price. Note in your file when you tell them to cut, and how much. Collect facts to help you defend your competence in a firm, confident, and convincing manner. With a hang-tough seller, you'll often have to defend your actions. They'd much rather blame their high price on your advice, and change agents when they lower the price to where you told them it should be in the beginning. Since they're the judge, prosecutor, and jury on this question, you've got to have your facts straight and solid or you'll lose the case.

## Less Now, or More Later—Maybe

(What follows applies primarily to the stable or falling market. It has little application to a sellers' market.)

Many times a seller considering an offer gets skewered on this hope, "Maybe I can get more." The same hope skewers many agents too. Offers rejected by the seller have a way of looking better and better as time passes—especially if no other offers are forthcoming. Sellers are natural history-revisionists. After a few weeks they often turn your quiet urgings of acceptance into damnation of the offer by faint praise.

If you believe an offer on your listing is realistic, come on strong with the sellers. Tell them, "In my professional opinion, this offer should be accepted, although I will loyally support any decision you make."

Dwell on this. Make sure they won't ever claim you didn't urge them strongly enough to accept the offer. Have them initial a note stating you urged them to accept the offer.

Suppose a higher offer comes in a day or two later. If you've done a thorough job with your Guidelines to Market Value, it's highly unlikely another offer from a different buyer will immediately come in for more than two or three percent above the price you've already urged them to accept. Not a large possibility, but it does happen, and it's happened to me.

Your sellers then tell you, "Lucky we didn't listen to you. If we had, we would've lost X tax-sheltered dollars."

You reply, "I'm really happy it worked out the way it did. Sure, there's egg on my face, but better sweet egg than rotten egg. Since an emotional buyer happened to come along—a best buyer, we call them—ready and willing to pay your price—I'm really happy for you. And what great timing! I wanted to play the odds—and they're about 99 to 1 you wouldn't have seen an offer like this before the one you turned down started to look real good—but you took the risk, and won! Terrific! Just don't check out the details of how those folks happened to show up right when they did. It'll scare you how chancy it was. Not inevitable at all. But, the important thing is. . . ."

However, you pocket the listing fee. In return, accept the egg on your face in good grace.

In the far more common situation, where the offer is rejected and there's no second offer, you remain the unpaid listing agent of an unsold property—for the remainder of your listing contract. If you came on strong for accepting the one offer, you're in an immeasurably stronger position to fend off the seller's natural tendency to gripe at you because the house hasn't sold. Be careful, of course, not to say "I told you so." It's much better to make sympathetic noises whenever the subject comes up.

"I understand—it was a difficult decision. Next time, we'll be forewarned." Not, "Next time we'll know better."

Suppose there's another party who's interested in the house but won't make an offer. All the closing techniques fail, yet the prospects continue to make buying sounds while your seller is considering an offer he really doesn't want to take.

What you have is a garbage-can banger, not a buyer. Tell your sellers this person is not ready to buy. What someone *might* do tomorrow, next month, or two years from now lies in the uncertain future. There's only one kind of buyer—the for real, now kind. All others are future-maybes, whose eventual buy is dependent on fate's favor, changeable plans, tastes, and prospects.

A prospective buyer who makes a realistic offer, signs a purchase contract, and puts deposit money behind it, pays your seller a substantial compliment. Much professional effort and marketing expense were required to secure the offer. You should not allow your sellers to brush it aside lightly—*they'll* hold it against you if you do.

# Avoid Possession Hassles

Binding your sellers to a specific move-out date on the listing (for example, "possession on August 30, ____") exposes them to possible legal problems. Instead of a specific date, tie the date the buyers will take possession to the settlement day ("possession 2 days after settlement").

When the offer comes in, again make sure possession is based on the day title changes hands—and isn't named as a specific date. Unless you do this, a last-minute paperwork problem may delay the closing and put your sellers in the position of having agreed to give the buyers possession before settlement.

You can then be caught between the buyers' insistence on moving in on the *agreed-upon* possession date, and your sellers' refusal to move out before they have their money. This can be time consuming for you, and expensive (also for you) if the buyers are living in a hotel and their furniture arrives by van on the stated day.

The time to negotiate possession date is when the offer comes in. During the weeks or months elapsing between the day the sellers list and the day they consider an offer, the circumstances governing the exact timing of their move can change drastically. There's no better time to get the possession date established than when the sellers are considering the offer. They can't realistically do it when they list; they don't know when they'll get an offer, or how much more time must pass after they accept an offer before settlement will occur. But when the offer is being considered, this timing is an important part of the offer. Urge your sellers to make their move-out decision before they accept the offer.

Can they be out on settlement day? Do they want one, two, or three more days? Will the buyers agree to allow them to stay after settlement (close of escrow)? Make this part of the accepted purchase offer. If necessary, use a counteroffer just for possession. And make sure your sellers understand exactly what they're agreeing to on this point. It doesn't seem too important when everyone is thinking about selling price and money, and moving day is a month or more away. Then moving day suddenly arrives and your sellers turn balky because they haven't made the arrangements.

Avoid this sticky mess by showing a friendly interest in their moving preparations as the transaction progresses from accepted offer to settlement. "Well, I guess you're all set to move. You didn't have any trouble lining up a mover, did you? Somebody told me the movers are busy right now."

# Winning Scripts

## Prepare the Sellers for the Market Process

Tell sellers what will happen and how quickly they may need to set the stage. Doing a thorough job of preparation can fend off complaint calls about things you can't prevent. Tell them, "Other brokers will call at 1:30 and say they want to show the house at 2. You rush around and set the stage beautifully. It's not convenient, but you leave anyway. You're gone two hours, come home, and a moment later the doorbell rings. It's the agent, and he has his buyers with him. You'll probably let them in, but maybe you'll think, 'Why couldn't this person be more considerate?'

"Please remember the way real estate works. Agents can't make their buyers arrive on time—or arrive at all. Buyers make appointments and expect to go right out that day to see property. If the agent waits until the buyers actually arrive to call you, then he'll have even less warning to give you. Buyers who are late for appointments buy houses too, so we want to work with them. And maybe the buyers were unavoidably delayed.

"You might get a call ten minutes before the agent wants to bring people through. Sometimes agents come to the door with buyers in the car. They shouldn't—but some prospects won't conform to a schedule. Many spur-of-the-moment buyers are this way because they've got to make a decision fast."

Explain all this to your sellers. "These situations can be aggravating, but they can pay off with a quick sale for you, too."

## The Sign Is Out Front

Tell your sellers, "A stranger may come to the door and say, 'Can I see your home? I noticed the *For Sale* sign out front and I might be interested.'"

Forewarn your sellers by telling them, "Don't let anyone in without an agent. Here are three of my business cards. Keep them by your front door. Unless lookers have a real estate professional with them, tell anybody who wants to see your home, 'This is the agent who's handling my property. You can call her office for an appointment, or if you want to see the house right now, I'll call the office and get an agent to bring you through.'

"The person at the door will be a stranger. Let us find out who he is. It's our job, not yours."

## Convince Them to Leave When the Property Is Shown

Tell your sellers, "I want you to leave in order to protect you emotionally, too. I know you love this house, and I know every brick went into it with love. When some guy comes in here and says something like, 'this brick job sure is bad,' or 'the drapes aren't right with the window,' your feelings are going to be hurt. House-lookers say careless things when something doesn't suit their particular taste. It doesn't mean their taste is any better than yours—it's just different. Sometimes they say something like this to drive a better bargain by pretending they don't like your house.

"Or they might say, 'Oh, I love this place. It's my dream house! We're going to run back to the office right now and make an offer!' What you don't know is, they say this about every house they see. I want to save you from the emotional ups and downs. I don't want to see you go through it all. So, just leave, and I'll tell you what the response was."

## Turn Them into Firm Believers in Setting the Stage

"You know, selling a house creates an abnormal situation. It's not normal to have strangers walking in and out of your house. You want to get this process behind you as soon as possible, and the way to do that is to think of your home as a theater. From now on, you're putting on a performance. It's like staging a play.

"Buyers won't get into the buying spirit unless the scenery's right. They need to dream a little to imagine the exciting new lifestyle they can live here. Let's set the stage right and make it easy for them to get into the buying mood."

If your sellers both work outside their home, tell them to turn on all the lights to show off their house every morning when they leave for work.

"I know your electric bill's going to be a little high for about a month, but it'll be worth it to you many times over. Imagine an agent coming into your house with a buyer when it's dark inside. The agent may have seen your house on the caravan, but he was concentrating on the floor plan and the amenities, not on where the light switches were. So all of them come in and stumble around.

"Finally the agent finds a light switch, and then runs over to open the drapes. He can't find the pull cords right away. While he's hunting for the cards the buyers get impatient. 'Oh, forget it,' they say, and walk out. Everything about your house might have been marvelous for them. If they'd taken the time to see the whole floor plan, they might've bought it. But the stage wasn't set, and they didn't have the patience to set it for themselves. Most buyers won't. We've got to do this for them."

There are two steps to setting the stage: fix-up and turn-on. It isn't hard to get people to switch the lights on and open the drapes, but the fix-up can be as tough as it is essential. If the house needs work, it may strain your diplomacy to get them to do it. If the house is dirty, it can overstrain your diplomacy. Telling people their home is unclean, or needs work, risks making enemies. Not talking them into doing the cleanup and fix-up makes enemies because you can't sell their unsalable property. The first is a risk and the second is a certainty; so take the risk and avoid certain disaster.

## Convince Them to Fix the Problems

Fixer-uppers can be sold—at fix-em-up-and-make-a-bundle prices. It's workable, if the sellers can accept putting their home in this category. Sellers usually prefer to think it doesn't belong there. When you list a house in bad condition, use this approach:

"I want to see you get the best, the absolute best, market price for your home. I want people to come in here and be excited. So you've got to help me. I can't do it without you, and gosh, I know—hey, I've got finger marks on my walls too. Those darn little kids! You know, you gotta keep repainting every year. But, I think we better paint the walls."

In the kitchen, the dishwasher is worn out. Open it a crack and it falls apart. Take the problem back on your shoulders. "Oh, I know, I've used my dishwasher so much. . . ."

Be nice but get this point across: Buyers will be turned off if the house is shown in its present condition. Replace the dishwasher, repaint the walls, trim the hedge.

"This home needs work—but I understand. Okay? I really understand."

Cover every item you can think of. "I hate to tell you this, Mrs. Atkins, but we've got to clean the oven. Some women today want to see what the oven looks like because they're very meticulous, and they think, 'If the oven is dirty, maybe none of the appliances will work as well as they should.'"

If the seller says, "I don't know if our water heater will make it to the close of escrow (settlement date), but I'm not about to spend the money to replace it. I'll never get that money back out of the house."

Tell them, "Let's think about this. I know how you feel. It's not a new house, and it didn't have a new water heater when you bought it. But the water heater was working, wasn't it?"

"Yeah, sure."

Put your seller back in his buyer shoes, "When you moved in, you assumed you could take a hot shower after you finished putting things away, right? You would have been pretty upset if there wasn't any hot water. So right away you'd be on the phone asking, 'What are my rights?' Well, the buyer has the right to presume appliances are in working order. (State laws vary. Check yours.) I don't want you to have a legal problem or see a last minute hang-up delay the settlement. You'll save money by avoiding the hassle. If I were you, I'd replace your water heater right away."

Making this point often helps, "Most of the value of a home, of course, is in the land, the location, and the structure. Call those things the iceberg. But what affects buyers just as much is the tip of the iceberg: cosmetics like fresh paint, and elbow-grease items like trimmed hedges and shiny bathroom fixtures. Nothing adds more value for less money than clean-up, shine-up, and paint-over. I know how busy you are. I understand what you're going through right now (add something here about their new baby, his long commute, whatever fits) but your house will sell faster and for more money if you'll—" (tell them what needs to be fixed up).

## More Dirty-House Dialogues

Make an appointment to show them the "competition." You may have to use a little pressure, because they may suspect—many times without even admitting it to themselves—what you're up to. Show them just one or two perfectly kept homes for sale in roughly their price range. Pick houses not noticeably new, or the lesson will be lost.

Talk money to them. Everybody understands money. "I don't know how this woman finds time to keep her kitchen so spotless. Look at this—" Point to a gleaming faucet. "My housekeeping certainly doesn't match hers except when I put my house on the market. She probably didn't keep this place this sharp month in and month out either—but she'll get an extra X thousand $ for it. Oh, yes, squeaky-clean houses sell for at least X thousand $ more in this market. And they sell faster, too. Much faster."

If your seller doesn't get the point, repeat your "see the shine" tour with her once a week or twice a month until she does. Of course, the person responsible for the dirty house may be a *he*, not a *she*. Gender doesn't matter on this question; what matters is whipping the place into shape so it'll sell.

By this time you should have a clear idea whether the sellers are unconscious, lazy, or both. The person who is aware of the problem will make excuses, "I know this place is a bit dirty, but I just can't seem to get it together. . . ."

"I know how it is. Don't I ever! I really understand. Why don't you let me swing a cleaning crew in here for you? I've seen clients get a dollar back for every two cents they spent on a cleaning crew."

"Really? You think it can make that much difference?"

"Absolutely."

"My husband would have a fit if I even mentioned it. He'd tell me to do it myself."

"But you can't do it and work too, can you? Ask him if he knows how to get a dollar back for every two cents he spends. The clean-up needs to be done, and we're talking about a lot of extra money you both can make here. And not only money is at stake; the house could sell much sooner if we brighten it up. Cleaning crew or you, it needs to be done, and the sooner the better. I'll call you tomorrow and see what you think then."

## The Intruder Theory

If a listing is too jammed with items or junked up to show well, say to your sellers, "You know, when prospective buyers go into someone else's home with the idea of buying it and living there, they have serious problems seeing themselves in the new house. Some people tell me they'd rather look at vacant houses, because then they can visualize how their furniture will fit into the rooms. I don't think they want to mention it—but the fact is, a lot of people feel uncomfortable in the role of buyers. It's like they're pushing the sellers out of their home—or they're intruding. A lot of people really have a thing about not intruding. This is part of the reason why it's so important for the owners to be away during a showing, so the prospective buyers can feel as relaxed as possible. But, if there's so much physical presence of the family, if the place is crowded with furniture, the walls are covered with family photos and awards and hung with the family's hobbies and interests, a lot of buyers are overwhelmed by this feeling of not belonging.

"I think that's what we have here. You've made great use of this house; you've really lived here and made it your own. This is as it should be—until you decide to sell. Now, however, the way things are in your home, it's tough for buyers to put themselves in here mentally. And they have to move in mentally before they'll make the commitment and sign the papers to do it physically. The quickest way for you to take your money out of this house and get on with your lives is to make your ownership less powerfully felt. If you'll put a lot of these precious photos and other items into storage, it's really going to make money for you, speed things up, and cut down on the number of times you'll have to get your house ready to show.

"Here's a card from Save-Most Storage on Fabricante. You can rent space by the month there. Believe me, you'll make more money if you store—(specify what)—until you move."

## Trash and Clutter

Tell your sellers, "Rent a big bin from the local dump and clean out your garage, side yard, attics, closets, drawers, and nooks and crannies. Half the things we save we'll never use again".

"Keep trash cans stored in the side yard or in the garage. On trash pick-up day, be sure to put those cans out of sight immediately after they're emptied.

"It's a real shock to house hunters if they step out of an agent's car and see empty trash cans rolling around on the lawn. It might happen all the time at their home, but when they're buyers, people are finicky.

"All bikes, trikes, big wheels, papers, candy wrappers, and whatnot should be *out of sight* at all times when you're living in the house-showing fish bowl. One eight-year-old boy had a thing about wadding up paper and throwing it around. His mother was otherwise an immaculate housekeeper, but she'd given up on the boy's paper obsession. We couldn't sell her house until the kid went off to camp—those wads of paper lying around made the whole place look junky."

## Talking Sense to Mr. Sellhigh

Most sellers want to base their price on what they need for a new house, or on how much they've spent on their present one. Sellers are prone to think buyers are emotional folk who don't much care what they pay as long as they get what they want. Sellers don't care much about the interest rate the buyers will have to pay, or how large the buyers' monthly payments will be. They'd like to sell their house at next year's prices.

Buyers, on the other hand, feel the strong position money takes when it talks. Sellers tend to think buyers compare prices and values carefully, and will compromise on their wants to drive a hard bargain. Buyers have no interest at all in paying over market prices. In fact, they feel entitled to buy at bargain prices.

You have to explain this to many sellers. The conflicting buyer-seller viewpoints provide many of the reasons why agents are needed: to bring the principals together at today's prices. Prepare to do so. Memorize the following speech. Then compose two or three more ways of saying much the same thing in different words. You'll find such speeches profitable and time saving.

"The market is made by willing buyers and willing sellers (call them by name here). I know your needs are important. I empathize with your needs—but we have to be realistic if we're going to make anything happen for you. We can't put a price on this house to validate your next move. Your price also has to validate the market, or no buyer will buy. If you wait for the buyer who won't look at any property except yours, you'll wait a long time. Not one buyer in a thousand will do this. People shop carefully for houses, and even if they didn't, appraisers appraise carefully. If the loan isn't approved, we can't close the transaction and cash you out.

"You want a sale, and you want it soon. So let's not lose sight of the basic element in making or breaking our chances of a sale—correct pricing. Buyers want to buy right. They can't conceive of paying more than market value, and in the market we have today, with (insert the number of listings available on your Multiple Listing) properties available for them to choose from, they know they're in a strong position. Today's buyers have a wide range of choice—and they know it.

"I am legally bound to present all offers, but I can't control the marketplace. I am behind you 100 percent as far as not gossiping about the price of your property behind your back, but I must tell you now, I am giving you full responsibility for rejecting this offer because it's right at the prevailing market price.

"If we allow this offer to die, and then, sometime in the future, wish we had accepted it, I want it understood now—and remembered then—how strongly I recommended accepting it. I understand your problems, and I feel for your needs, but we must always be realistic."

Then make a note on the communication log in the file: "Agent highly recommended acceptance of _____'s offer on _____(date) _____."

## Winning a Listing Extension

Here's my agency's letter to persuade sellers to extend their listing with us. The first time it was used, it won an extension long enough to allow one of my associates to sell a realistically priced house. This agent had kept in close touch with the sellers throughout the listing period, but the final extra touch to bring in the extension was this letter.

*Dear Max and Corinne,*

*We know you are upset because your house has not sold—we are too! We work very hard for our clients and you are top priority on our list. Let us tell you what we are planning on doing to successfully market your house in the future:*

- *Award a $500 bonus out of our pocket to the selling agent.*
- *Handwritten notes to the top producers of all the real estate companies in the area.*
- *Recaravan the property with refreshments for the area agents.*
- *New flyers to remind agents again about the price and of your willingness to participate in financing the sale.*

*All we are asking for is time. Granted we have had it for six months but, as you know, we are going through a low swing in the real estate cycle. Now that the "good" season is approaching, let us have a chance to prove to you that no other agent can do more for you or will work harder than I will.*

*Please give me this opportunity to continue to serve you. It means a great deal to me.*

*Sincerely,*

**Caution:** Never take an extension for granted. If you have not communicated with a seller for weeks, do not e-mail or fax or leave a voice mail regarding extending the listing or reducing the price. That's rude. Extension requests take time and only work when a good relationship is already in place. People do not like to be used. Anyone who has not earned an extension or a price reduction—through constant servicing—should exit the scene fast!!!

# CHAPTER 13

# High-Tech Promotion and the Personal Touch

**Five Promotion Concepts** ● **Real Estate Writing Tips** ● **Style** ● **What Makes an Ideal Web Site?** ● **High-Tech Marketing** ● **Getting Newsletters Out Fast** ● **Writing Your Profile of a Pro** ● **Listing Remarks** ● **Your Name Is Your Trademark** ● **Your Product** ● **Imprinted Memo Pads: Your Most Effective, Year-Round Farming Tool** ● **Buying Giveaways**

Consumers fall into many categories. There are consumers who use the Internet and those that do not. There are consumers who let a third-party resource do all the checking for them before they choose a product or service. Then the resource reports to the consumer on the most qualified business. In the age of word-of-mouth endorsements people just do not have hours to surf the Internet to find out who is offering the best discount on computers, books, or cars. So they rely on information people give them to get the scoop on what's hot. This also applies to real estate. I hope you have an army of supporters spreading good rumors about you behind your back because that type of blessing is worth more than all the promotion secrets this chapter has to offer.

When it comes to promotion, you must approach the consumer from every angle. Use referrals from Internet sites, mail outs, print ads, and so on. You need it all. It just has to be effective. This chapter gives promotional ideas for being effective both in a paper and a paperless world. But never forget, especially in this paperless electronic communication age, the handwritten thank you note with a postage stamp gets more immediate attention today than ever.

The most effective promotion in a situation may be a few timely words spoken quietly to the right person, or it may be 20-foot high words towed across the sky by an airplane. Successful promotion communicates. It reaches people. It causes them to do something they would not otherwise do. It causes them to phone you, to go see your listings, or to remember you at the right time.

*Somebody who can act gets the message.* This is successful promotion. That's all it is. The message in real estate is simple; it can be said in fifteen words: "I am the agent you should work with. This is the property you should buy." Everything else is just icing on the cake.

However we must ice the cake! Some very successful agents deny that they ever use promotion. "None of the old Hollywood stuff for me. All I do is talk to people." There are agents who have built a thriving business this way—the tennis player in Chapter 6 is one of them. Yet the tennis player *is* promoting himself effectively every time he calls a new member with an invitation to play an early morning game. He's promoting his message by introducing the new member over the tennis net to one of his satisfied clients. Sometimes the most effective promotion is the most low-key.

Take a look at the farming almanac in Chapter 7. You'll find ideas for farm promotions you can create yourself, find locally, or buy through the mail. The most successful agents match their promotion methods to their sales goals, not to their own personal preferences.

An agent successful in promotion realizes her own taste is not an infallible guide to what's effective in promotion *in her farm.* She constantly seeks feedback from the public about which messages are getting through and which ones are being ignored. The common fabric of her promotions are verve, persistence, and innovation.

Avoid stereotyping yourself as only an orange picker, or business will be slow for you when all the oranges are crated and only apples are ripe on the trees. Learn to pick apples too. More important, let the world know you pick apples. The agent with a flair for the flamboyant can work effectively on soft sell merely by picking up the phone. The faceless soft seller, who is unknown to anyone beyond his or her circle, can divert an entirely new flow of opportunities with a single spectacular promotion.

If you suspect your image is a bit stodgy in spite of considerable success, hire an elephant and a trainer to give your customers and their kids a ride. Send them up in a hot-air balloon, or drive them around town in a double-decker London-style bus. People who never could remember your name will start saying they've known you a long time. Everyone will think you're just a little bit crazy—in an exciting, entertaining way—and they'll give you the large helping of extra respect such agents command. Being ignored is the most expensive state there is in real estate. You can't afford it!

Promoting yourself, promoting listings, and promoting buyers are the three legs of the tripod of promotional success. All three factors are related to each other. Newspapers charge the same whether your ad pulls 50 phones calls or 0. Printers charge the same whether your flyer is a winner or a dud. Which is cheaper: a $26 ad which produces nothing, or a $52 ad that puts you in contact with a buyer who drops a juicy fee in your pocket? Doubling the size of your ads isn't necessarily the solution; doubling the thought behind your advertising is.

"Effective promotion produces income. I do as much of it as I can afford." If you agree completely with this statement, you're ready to make big money through promotion. But if you consider promotion to be an expense of limited value, to be avoided whenever possible, you will gain nothing from it. Money is only one-fourth of the price you must pay for a successful promotion. The other three-fourths are enthusiasm, effort, and insight. Unless you are enthusiastic about your promotion, unless you complete the work required to carry it off on time, and unless you direct the entire operation thoughtfully, your money will be wasted.

# Five Promotion Concepts

1. **If you aren't enthusiastic about your promotion, how can anyone else be?** Stop whinning about the costs of advertising and start banking on the earnings from advertising and promotion.

   "Sounds great," you say, "until I have to file for bankruptcy."

   You're thinking about costs again! It's ok to consider costs. You'll need to budget carefully so you can complete any plan you start. And there is a limit to how fast you can afford to increase your income. Promotion can be effective only when it's balanced against the other demands on your time, energy, and money. And remember, effective promotion can only make money for you if you're capable of handling more business when it's rapping on your door.

2. **Give promotion first call on your most creative time.** You may easily afford the expense of failed promotions,

but are you willing to give up all the income a well-managed promotion would bring you? No work in real estate is more demanding of your most creative thought and follow-through than promotion. No work in real estate returns greater rewards for effective effort than promotion.

3. **Work well ahead of deadlines.** Last-minute-rushitis is the most common plague to inflict promotional activities with failure.

4. **In every promotion, tell people who you are, where you are, and what you do.** Even on the one-shot, get-business-now ads and promotions, never miss a chance to build your image. If you miss the one-shot ad, you'll still benefit from the long-term image-building effect.

5. **Be careful of your money until you discover what's effective.** Think of ways to gauge the response you're really getting from your promotions. This is more difficult than it sounds, but it's vital to promotional success.

# Real Estate Writing Tips

Gather the specific details you want in your ad on a fact sheet, and decide what to include. You can't write an ad until you know all the facts you're going to give and how much ad space you can afford. Since real estate moves so fast, don't waste time or space on details you don't have the complete facts on. Before you get the last detail down, the house may be sold.

When writing flyers, use the home's strongest point as a hook in your lead-off sentence. Put your third most important point somewhere in the middle to sustain interest. The second-strongest point comes last, so your send-off will sing. The bottom line is when buyers decide to act on your flyer or forget it. Put the power there.

Between the lead and the end, write all your other points in a natural, smooth order. The direction will be dictated by your opening sentence. If you start with the gorgeous carpet, don't jump to the outside for point two and write about the well tended hedge in front. Having begun inside, run through the home's interior features before you mention location, landscaping, or exterior style.

If your flyer says the kitchen is huge, the backyard is huge, and the fireplace is huge, your readers will be bored by all this hugeness. People don't want to look at boring houses. One of these *huges* could be *bonus-sized* and another *extra-large*, if *big* and *large* aren't powerful enough for you. Or they could be *enormous, gigantic, mammoth, immense, king-sized, vast, ample, colossal, extensive, generous, giant-sized, imposing, large-scale, lavish, massive, capacious,* or even *deep* and *wide.* Check your word processor's thesaurus for synonyms of *huge.* Give your expressions of size a pleasant variety. In print, *Roget's International Thesaurus* classifies synonyms but is slower to use. Develop your own list of synonyms in an "important information" notebook.

## Style

Avoid using abbreviations on printed business forms, flyers, and brochures. It looks tacky and commercial. Unless your company is known by its initials or abbreviated form, spell out the name in full. And give the full, nonshortened address in small type, including the Zip code. Giving all this information on your memo pads allows people to tear off a sheet and send it to a friend with a note saying, "This is the sharp agent I was telling you about." And it's all there: name, address, phone number, the business you're in, and your photo.

Show your phone numbers in a concise, clean, and clear way such as:

Office 000/123-4567
Home 500/987-6543

Avoid abbreviations before phone numbers such as:

Off: Off with what?
Res: Is it a bug killer? Why sound pretentious by calling your home a residence?
Bus: Do you drive a bus, or call this number for a bus, or is it code for "Don't call me unless you mean business?"

## What Makes an Ideal Web Site?

Besides bringing you customers, the ideal agent web site will answer many of the questions buyers and sellers frequently ask, and save you time.

A great promotional site will accomplish the following:

**1. Load fast.** Web surfers (potential buyers or sellers) are impatient. Many of them have slow computers and Internet hookups, and graphics take lots of time to download. Resist the urge to pack your site with huge photos of glorious sunsets, green hills, and happy children.

2. **Give contact information.** Include your phone and fax number, e-mail address, office mail address, and a map for out-of-towners to find your office.

3. **Show your photo in color.** But it doesn't have to appear on every e-mail. If you are working with out-of-state buyers and they're e-mailing you from a hotel, it can get very expensive. If they're waiting for your message on a counteroffer, they'll be annoyed watching your photo come through again—for the fiftieth time!

4. **Present a thumbnail-sized photo of each of your listings.** Clicking the small photo enlarges the photo and brings up a page giving all the basic details except address. Take it a step further and offer video clips/virtual tours from room to room. If you can't afford to make it really top-notch, just use the still shots.

5. **List your qualifications as a professional real estate agent.** Include your awards and your number of years in this business (if this is your first year, forget this one).

6. **Provide for easy site navigation.** Use a clickable list of pages where additional information can be found. This page list, usually placed in a column on the home page's left side, might include the following features:

   - **Home page.** Gives contact information and a bulleted list of your qualifications.
   - **Client testimonials.** You cannot have too many testimonials. How do you get them? First, deserve them. Give the customer first-rate, first-class service. Second, ask for them. (You can do this by phone, fax, e-mail, or voice mail, but do it!)

     Say "I have an urgent request. Can you put your comments about my service in writing in the next 24-hours?"

This is what I call high-stakes language. It is ok because your clients love you and you have earned the right to ask. But remember, when you use high-stakes language be very *clear* and *logical* explaining why you need the letter so fast.

Say, "I go out on job interviews every day. Would you ever go out on a job interview without a reference letter? My future truly does rest in your hands."

- **View my listings**
- **Virtual tours** Internet users love these tours! They use them before the contact. Recent surveys cited in *Real Estate Professional*

magazine show that 88 percent of web users said that they searched the Internet prior to looking for specific homes. These same consumers are finding their agent on the Internet too. Make sure you have an impactful presence!

- **Area homes for sale**
- **Online chats (this is optional)** On this page post when your homebuyers or homeowners online informative chats will occur. Have Frequently Asked Questions (FAQs) prepared in case participants don't respond right away when the session starts. Don't post this on your web page unless the chats have become weekly or monthly. These online information sessions can provide you with good contact names. Be sure you have a place for prospective clients to type their e-mail addresses. Also include a box to check to let you know if prospects are interested in an online chat. Some may want to wait for the regular weekly session. Other prospects may want to ask you questions privately. It's like calling Fizzbos and offering them a "free service package" This lets you to get your foot in the door.
- **Frequently Asked Questions (FAQs)** If you are not interested in holding regular online chats on your web site, then list some frequently asked questions by buyers and sellers. Arrange the questions so that to every few questions, you can give something like this as your answer, "It depends on the circumstances. Please contact me for an answer tailored to your specific needs." Caution: Don't make that the answer to every question. Provide some solid and informative answers to FAQs too.
- **Community churches**
- **Community cultural facilities** Have a direct link with the Chamber of Commerce or a list of events. Consider a link with your local theatre company. Out-of-area prospects love being directed to great entertainment in between house hunting.
- **Mortgage information** Include a sample lender qualifying form. DON'T HAVE IT FILLED OUT! Just display it and say, "e-mail or call me to find out the particulars of qualifying."
- **Mortgage calculator**
- **Rent vs. mortgage after-tax calculator**
- **Investment opportunities**
- **Real estate information**
- **Current newsletter**
- **Sign up for my free e-mail newsletter or online chat**
- **National homes for sale**
- **National investment opportunities**

# High-Tech Marketing

You can produce more results at a lower cost in time and money than ever before with the immense power of today's high-tech marketing. You can use high-tech methods to vault over the competition—or you can ignore high tech and be left behind. Today's consumer uses the Internet to shop and is a partner with the online service provider. So if a prospect needs real estate, he will go online to discover information. But the information is only as good as the real estate agent who is providing it. You are still a key element in the process. The method of communication has changed—Internet, e-mail, fax—but an agent is still needed to bring buyers and sellers together.

## Start Building a Team from Day One

So what a computer-challenged new agent can do to harness the force of high tech? If your first option, learning to be a high techie yourself, isn't realistic, go to Plan B. Find a computer whiz kid at your local junior or senior high school who is willing to get your High Tech Programs (HTP) up and running in return for small money now and more when your first high-tech transaction closes. However, avoid making long-term commitments that are too generous as you build your team.

Are you intimidated by the prospect of writing a newsletter? Maybe grammar and spelling aren't your strengths. The same place you found your computer whiz kid has English teachers willing to bang out your newsletter. Building a team like this can be done with little or no money to start. It's all a matter of finding the right people (individuals you like and trust, who like and trust you) for your team.

## E-mail List

Your first high-tech marketing job is creating an e-mail list for your farm. Then you can send your newsletter at virtually no cost to everyone on your list. More than one-third of all American homes send and receive e-mail, and these numbers are increasing rapidly. However, be aware that at least half of e-mail users are strongly opposed to "spam," (unasked for and unwanted commercial messages). If you spam your farm, you will probably do yourself far more harm than good—so don't do it. Spamming often instigates viruses, so it's a turn off all the way around for the receivers.

What's the answer? Developing your newsletter's subscriber list the hard way—one name at a time.

## First Flyer

Even before you list your first property, print a flyer announcing your-self and your e-mail newsletter and ask readers to subscribe (at no cost, of course). Promote your first flyer and newsletter every way you can think of: at garage sales, to for sale by owners, in stores and restau-rants, and at community meetings. Promoting your newsletter pro-motes you as a real estate pro and you'll get some listing calls this way.

## Newsletter

What should your newsletter contain? Include only news about your farm: all sales and listings of properties, upcoming garage sales, clam-bakes, and whatever else is going on in your farm. It's like publishing a local no-cost newspaper. Ever notice the signs people put up about lost pets? Call those people and ask if they'd like you to describe their missing dog or cat in the newsletter. Put out a special edition for them. You'll make a friend—and a potential client—for life.

Each newsletter should contain a few ideas about preparing a home for sale, mortgage rate trends, flood insurance, or anything else of interest to homeowners in your farm. Make sure you cover devel-opments that will affect the value of property in your farm, such as business openings and closings. Keep your newsletter crisp and tightly focused on your farm.

Several national services produce and sell newsletters. However, these newsletters are aimed at a national or regional audience. You can find better uses for your money until you have a thriving practice going.

Begin publishing your monthly newsletter as soon as possible, before you have even one person on your e-mail subscriber list. Print it at a local copy shop and hand it out wherever you can. If activity war-rants, publish on the first and fifteenth of each month, or even weekly as soon as you have a steady flow of your own new listings to an-nounce. Since it's so easy to do, send both the e-mail and print versions of your newsletter.

Direct mail, (post office mail) isn't high tech, but there are high-tech ways of utilizing it. Effective direct mail depends on the quality of your mailing list. Check with your title company to see if you can get a computerized list of all the owners of properties in your farm. The title company list will have snail-mail addresses (but rarely an e-mail address). With this list, begin a direct mail campaign. Always include a letter and the print version of your latest newsletter, and ask them to subscribe to the e-mail version. Assure them your subscriber list will remain confidential and will never be sold.

# Your Business Web Site

As soon as you can, set up your own web site. (See *What Makes an Ideal Web Site?*). First select and register a domain name. You can do this for as little as $19 per year. Use a search engine and search for "domain registration," then your computer whiz-kid can guide you. Keep it simple so it will load quickly. Once you have a site, promote it on your business cards, letterheads, and—most importantly—on your listing signs. Archive all your newsletters on your site so prospects can see past issues.

# Digital Cameras

Why pay a photographer to shoot your listings when digital cameras are so inexpensive and easy to use? Share the cost with other new agents if necessary. You'll need to produce the following:

- Thumbnail photos of your listings for your web site
- Virtual tours of your listings for your e-mail newsletter and web site
- Shoot your own virtual tours and put them on your web site. Your computer whiz can figure out how to include the virtual tours with your e-mail newsletter. Imagine—in your Print version you tell people about the virtual tours available to subscribers of your free e-mail newsletter. When you make a listing presentation, tell prospects—or better yet, show them on your laptop—how you'll present the virtual tour of their home to potential buyers.

# Search the Internet for Referral Alliances

Your computer whiz can do your searching for you. First, study where the buyers in your farm are coming from, and their characteristics. Then romance real estate people in those areas and establish referral relationships.

# Use Your Own Genius and Energy

As you develop your real estate practice, stay alert for new ways to utilize all the latest tools. Become an early adopter of new technologies; lead the pack instead of playing catch-up. But always remember that real estate is a *people* business. Developing people skills so that buyers and sellers will have faith in you will always be the most important factor in building a successful real estate practice. That's the heart of this book, my friends. High tech can create opportunities to serve more people, but that's all it can do. With each new opportunity, you still have to develop trust in clients' hearts. That only comes when your desire to serve their interests is genuine.

# Getting Newsletters Out Fast

The secret to newsletters is to set up a format and stick to it. Electronic newsletters save lots of time. The newsletter format is built right into your word processing software. Then you know exactly what you need. Whether you go paperless, hard copy, or both, your big job is automatically broken down into several smaller ones.

Choose a lead story of interest to your farm. (Chapter 7 gives ideas for every month). In your lead story, don't try to compete with the major publications. Do what they can't do: Tell readers what's going on inside your farm. Print the news about the good things: the babies born, the promotions, the vacations, and who won the local bridge club's tournament. Drop in a joke or a quote.

There's the program. Now comes the commercial—a brief item of real estate news. Give a few facts. Where do you get facts? From experts. Give them real estate facts in every issue, and your newsletters will work harder for you. Tell readers the average number of days homes were on the market before selling, the average price of houses sold, or compare activity last month to the same month last year.

Keep it simple. Print it on your letterhead—the one with your photo printed on it. Include a few graphics from your letterhead. Then drop it off at the local quick printer.

And always get in this message, "I am the real estate expert for your neighborhood. If you want more information about real estate, please call me." Say it in different words each month, but say it.

# Writing Your Profile of a Pro

A profile of a pro is simple. Just substitute information about yourself for the details given here about Kate Bancroft. Print it on your picture letterhead. Make copies and staple them as the final sheet on the packets of listing flyers you give to open house walk-ins.

> ### Kate Bancroft
>
> Born in Small Pond, Arkansas. Graduated from Pathfinder High School, Denver. Attended UCLA, Westwood, California. Her husband, John Bancroft, is a mechanical engineer.
>
> The Bancrofts have a ten-year-old son, Sean, who is active in soccer. Family activities include backpacking, tennis, and camping.
>
> Kate specializes in the Meadowlark area, but keeps fully informed on all real estate offerings in the entire Green Pretty Valley.
>
> For knowledgeable, understanding care of your real estate needs, call a professional: Kate Bancroft.
>
> Office phone 123-4567; home phone 765-4321.

You can write something like this about yourself the first day you're in real estate. You're a professional the moment you decide you'll do what separates the pros from the piddlers and losers. You're not obliged to beat the details of your newness into the heads of every prospect you contact.

## Listing Remarks

Don't burden your listing remarks with scrubby details like the new dishwasher unless your Multiple Listing book gives you lots of space. If you only have a line or two left after putting in what has to be said, write something bright to make agents want to see the house. Here are some ideas:

- Your buyers will give you rave notices for showing this lovely. . . .
- She'll love you forever, sir, if you purchase this. . . .
- Mom will love cooking in this gourmet kitchen while the whole clan lives it up in the adjoining family room complete with. . . .
- This colonial castle features a special. . . .
- Zowie—your own private spa. Think of the possibilities.

## Your Name Is Your Trademark

You can use all the bells and whistles technology has to offer, but people won't call you if they don't remember your name. Make it easy for them. Difficult names aren't necessarily a disadvantage, but blurred ones are.

*Harold L. "Hal" Sturgis* isn't a real estater's trademark, it's confusion. *Hal Sturgis* is crisp and memorable, and it's the way Hal should print it on his letterheads and business cards for maximum impact.

*Zoltanovich P. Buttersnichel* doesn't need the *P.* as much as *John R. Hall* needs the *R.* It's surprising how often the Halls of the world drop their middle initials, and the Buttersnichels slap theirs on everything.

Consider how good a trademark your complete legal name makes. When it's longer than people will use in ordinary conversation, it's too long for an effective, money-making trademark. Consider using the shorter version of your name—the one you actually go by—on business cards, flyers, and letterheads. Sign your full name only on legal documents. If you don't like your given name, or find your last name too long, shorten one or both of them. Zoltanovich P. Buttersnichel becomes Zolly Butter when he tells everyone it's his label, and uses it exclusively whenever he orders something with his name printed on it.

Before you start your next promotional campaign, consider whether a more colorful and shorter name will be remembered better. If yours is long and difficult, an easier, more vivid version will swing some extra fees your way. A name able to stick in people's minds is money in the bank.

# Your Product

In the area of promotion, real estate agents are a lot like a product manager in charge of marketing a brand of soap, cigarettes, or sailboats for a large corporation. Successful product managers win public recognition for their products by endlessly repeating the same trademarks, slogans, themes, and colors. Over long periods of time they maintain a family resemblance as one advertising campaign succeeds another. When necessary, they update their advertising to remain fresh and current. They change—yet keep the same elements. These managers build on, instead of wasting, their past efforts. They carefully select their new pattern from what is consistent with their old pattern. Instead of scattering their efforts, astute product managers concentrate their efforts on consistency—and achieve impact even with a small budget.

How does all this apply to a sales associate making the rounds of a farm? Very closely. The photo on your imprinted memo pads should be a recent one. It should show you as you usually look when working real estate, not as you dress for Mardi Gras. Use the same photo, the same slogan, and the same style of type on your business cards, letterheads and newsletters. Maintain the same complete visual package as closely as possible on all your giveaways. Follow the pattern as much as you can on display advertising too.

If you dress flashy when first bouncing through your farm in December, then dress sloppy when dragging back through in January, and finally achieve a conservative well-dressed appearance when prospecting briskly in February, can you expect people to remember they've seen you before? They won't remember Flashy or Sloppy either; they'll just think three agents have been calling on them.

Select a suitable style of business clothing and stick with it. Change gradually with the styles, don't switch wildly from day to day. Don't wear the same dress or suit every time you farm either, Think about presenting a consistent image of dependable professionalism when selecting your wardrobe. Think about the same things when selecting and developing all your farming and working tools, whether the item in question is an automobile, or a flyer.

Consistency counts. A bright, brisk, business-like manner counts. Confidence counts—if it doesn't come off as arrogance. All these things weigh heavily when your identity score is suddenly totaled up—as it is every time someone on your farm decides to sell.

You have a product to manage: yourself and your marketable services. Manage your product's advertising with care. Concentrate on consistent repetition—and achieve impact even with a small budget.

## Imprinted Memo Pads: Your Most Effective, Year-Round Farming Tool

Here's what goes on your memo pads:

- Your company's name, address, and phone number
- Your name, photo, and home phone number
- Your slogan if it's brief (about half a dozen words at the most)
- Plenty of space for your clients and customers to write on
- Emergency phone numbers (fire, police, and so on)

Two cost-effective sizes are

- $5\frac{1}{2}" \times 8\frac{1}{2}"$
- $3\frac{5}{8}" \times 8\frac{1}{2}"$

Print the emergency numbers in light gray so they can be written over. It costs a little extra, but it's worth it to have special final pages printed with, "This is the last page! Time to call Danny for another memo pad."

# Buying Giveaways

The giveaways you need for farming and other promotional use can be bought from companies listed under *Advertising Specialties* in the Yellow Pages. If you live in a small town, computerized Internet purchasing may be your best source. Your local telephone company office or public library will have a directory of 800 numbers and the Yellow Pages from the nearest large city.

**All giveaways must be imprinted.** If it's impossible to imprint the item itself, imprint the packaging. Keep the imprint as simple as possible, and avoid crowding in several slogans. For your name, use upper- and lower-case letters rather than all capitals because it's easier to read. Choose a serif typeface (with small hooks on the end of the letters, like this) instead of sans serif (with all straight lines, like this) for the same reason.

Unless you can generate your own computerized graphics, have a commercial artist paste up your imprint with set type, and tell him or her to make a dozen "repro proofs" to send to your various giveaway suppliers. The repros are also handy when you run display advertising. Have the artist select bold type (if it fits the style of your letterhead and business card) so the imprint can be reduced in size and still be easily read. If your company name doesn't clearly specify it's in real estate, add, "Serving Your Real Estate Needs" below your name. If you omit this line, many people will associate you with insurance, automobiles, or tulip sales.

# CHAPTER 14

# The Subtle and Learnable Art of Capturing Customers

Customer Profiling ● Revving Up for Relo Action ● New People ● The Essence of Client-Capture ● Buyers' Tango ● The Proof-of-Competence Phase ● Capture Both Partners ● Tune in Emotionally ● Shoot Your Best Shot and Don't Worry About Competition ● Recognize Lonely Charlie ● Smile Mysteriously ● Lunching with Buyers ● Expanded Folk Wisdom ● Another Window of Understanding ● Don't Tell Them You're New ● Use Your Buyers' File Constantly ● The Hungry Breath ● Winning Scripts ● Lender Qualifier Form

## Customer Profiling

As you hunt for qualified prospects, remember the privacy factor. Today more than ever privacy is an issue. When a buyer is referred to you, there is a built-in trust factor. Usually in the higher-end market, a referral buyer seems to be more willing to give you the confidential information you need to assist in the house hunt. But when there is no referral, when you are working to find prospects from a targeted list, it is important to think about the best way to market to them *before* you begin your prospecting. Are they renters, move-ups, empty nesters? You need to customer-profile before you even make the contact. Because knowing who you are trying to generate business with, makes an enormous difference in the success of the pursuit. It is so important to use the customer profiling information the right and honest way. If you do, you will overcome the first hurdle of customer resistance. Sales companies spend lots of money today on targeted lists that give accurate customer profiles.

# Revving Up for Relo Action

How would you customer-profile the relocation buyer? In many areas, national relocation firms have become an important factor in real estate sales because they know the customer profiles before they call us. This information is very valuable to the real estate agent. Large corporations frequently transfer employees from one part of the country to another. When the transferred family sells their home, these large employers often pay the brokerage fee and recommend a real estate office in the area the employee is moving to on the advice of a relocation firm.

In other words, national relocation firms provide a flow of *profiled* buyers coming in and sellers going out—qualified, right-now buyers, and sellers with no time or interest in going fizzbo. Since relocation firms provide some of the finest clients and customers around, they must get the finest possible service—or they'll take their considerable business elsewhere.

Making sure the finest service is given to the relocation client begins with an organized system for working with referrals from the first phone call. The key person who handles referrals in your office must be prepared to do two things any time he or she picks up the phone: (1) provide accurate information about the area; and (2) ask the right questions about a family being referred.

The well-prepared relo specialist in your office would say something like this to whoever calls from a relocation firm.

"Thank you so much for giving us the opportunity to serve your client. Here at Sell Fast Realty we pride ourselves on the thorough and professional way we counsel the people you send us. In order to do this in the most beneficial way, I need some details about the client.

- "How many are in the family?"
- "Where are they relocating from?"
- "How long have they lived there?"
- "What size home do they have now, and what is its value?"
- "How much equity do they have in it?"
- "Do they have to sell their present home before they can buy here?"
- "Is the company purchasing their present home?"
- "How many times has this family been transferred in the last ten years?" (If they've moved frequently, plan on using a great deal of empathy with the wife.)
- "Do both the husband and the wife work outside the home?"
- "Are they happy about the move?"

- "Do they have any special requirements, such as being near their church?"
- "What is the new position of the person being transferred?"
- "Is this transfer a step up or sideways for them?" (Is it a promotion or a lateral move?)
- "Will they come out to look together, or will one of them come alone?" (If one will come first, find out which one, the wife or the husband.)
- Ask all the obvious questions—their name, phone number, address, ages of the children

Follow up the relocation lead by immediately calling the transferring family.

"Hi. I'm Danny Kennedy with Sell Fast Realty in Green Pretty Valley. (Mention your connection with the relocation company.) I'm looking forward to doing everything possible to make your move here pleasant."

Give them an opportunity to respond. Then continue with, "Do you have any questions about Green Pretty Valley you'd like to ask?"

After you've offered to answer their questions, they'll be more receptive to answering yours.

"I was given some information about you and your family to help me serve your needs better, but I'd like to check some of those facts."

Then go through the list of questions you asked the relo firm and verify the facts they gave you. The information you already have will allow you to phrase your questions tactfully and avoid sensitive areas. As you talk with them, get more details about their likes and dislikes, and note what they tell you in the file you're building on them. Ask as many questions as you can about their present lifestyle without seeming nosy.

Discover, if possible, what they're hoping to find in your area. With many people, you learn most by letting them talk. Use questions such as, "Is your son interested in sports?" Few mothers can resist talking about their children. After you've found out about the children's activities, it will seem very natural for the wife to start talking about how she and her husband spend their leisure time.

Get them looking forward to meeting an intelligent, concerned, and knowledgeable friend. As you approach setting an appointment, you may want to leave the exact time open and have them call you when they arrive. If they're flying in for a quick house-hunting trip, they may not rent a car, and instead will rely on you for transportation. Don't fail to make this offer.

When you set out with them for the first time, give them an overview of your area. Have a route worked out in your mind for a quick tour of points of interest; and to introduce them to the various communities and neighborhoods they should be considering. As you drive, reel off your prepared scripts—the sales dialogues described in Chapter 23. Hand them both a simplified map of your area (a sketch you've had duplicated works great for this purpose) to help them get oriented quickly.

Remember, the quicker you can make them feel they know the area, the quicker they'll make a decision. As you cruise the various communities, keep verifying your assumptions—and change your plans if you realize you're off the mark in what you thought they'd want in a house.

First, zero in on the community they feel comfortable in; then start showing houses. If you have a large Quick-Speak Inventory, you'll have no problem switching directions quickly. Many times people coming to a new area change their requirements when they see, for the first time, what's available in their price range.

Remember, the transferee has many problems and sources of anxiety. Let's consider the typical two-income couple. One has been transferred, promoted, and given a fat raise. However, the spouse might be giving up a well-paying job to make the move. If the spouse hasn't—or can't—line up an equally good position in your area, it may be costing them many thousands a year to take the promotion. The Lender Qualifier form (at the end of this chapter and on the accompanying CD) must be introduced and explained to them.

Perhaps you'll be called on to help the spouse find a job in order to firm up the move and make the house sale on your end. Every case is different. Get a head start on the second income aspect of transfers by learning all you can in your initial phone conversation with them. Many times I've called hospitals for incoming nurses and schools for incoming teachers to find out about licensing and to help the spouse get started on finding a suitable job sooner. It's all part of the services a real estate practitioner provides.

"Should every agent in the office be allowed to handle the referrals your company receives through its relocation affiliation?"

My answer is a loud "No." Only the active agents—the ones who work the field, find prospects on their own, and bring business in—should be rewarded with agency referrals. The sit-around agents—the ones who get all their sales from floor time and ad calls—shouldn't be rewarded for being part of the problem instead of part of the solution. Only companies with a tremendous competitive advantage can survive with agents who depend entirely on company-generated business. The rest of the industry must have agents who knock on doors, work fizz-bos, and generate fees independently—or we go out of business.

The individual who gets the relocation agency referrals must have a patient personality. Some agents are not good with out-of-state referrals. Working with them means many trips to show property. Sometimes months go by before the sale is made—the first step might involve finding them a rental for six months. In other cases, pictures of property need to be taken and mailed, along with detailed information about schools and other interests. The person you choose to get the referral business not only must be a knowledgeable and well-prepared agent, but also must be detail-oriented and organized. Many pros have secretaries who can do much of the follow-up work, leaving the agent free to work with more people.

The agents selected to handle relocation agency business must be committed to the agency and to giving good service—this one agent can lose the whole account. Some people say, "Forget relocation business. The people are too picky, and for the commission you get, it isn't worth it."

In my experience, relocation agencies prefer to work with one person in each office who will then funnel the referrals to a few outstanding agents. The manager is the ideal middle person to do this. If too many people get involved, confusion reigns—and the agency account is in jeopardy. Most relocation groups have certain forms they want filled out and sent back. Also be sure to use a communications log for every relocation prospect. (A suitable form for this purpose is illustrated in Chapter 24 and available on the accompanying CD.)

Keep the relocation firm informed every step of the way. Keeping up with the follow-up and detail work is a critical part of ensuring an ongoing flow of business to your company.

On listings you take through relo agencies, be sure to find out what to do when the homeowners move out. Some companies want you to have the utilities billed to your office, and then be reimbursed by them. When the employer intends to buy a transferred employee's house and move them out, the relocation agency will ask you to give a "market evaluation." Your market evaluation will then be put together with one or two appraisals they pay a fee for. Be honest and conservative with the relocation people—they need *realistic* prices.

At various times in some parts of the country, even owner-occupied personal residences have been bought and sold primarily as investments with the hope of rapid appreciation. This doesn't work in difficult markets when faith in the inevitability of appreciation has disappeared. Real estate is a commodity—its true value rests on the uses to which it can be put in the present, not on what its price may be in the future. Like the current price of any other useful thing, the price of real estate is based on the relationship between supply and demand—but its value to any given person, couple, or family depends on their present needs.

Relocation is competitive. Many firms fight for this business. Big brother is always watching when you're involved in relocation. However, if you're professional, and if you treat the company's money as if it were your own, you won't go wrong.

Create a relocation packet—a collection of data about your area organized so incoming people can quickly find what they want. Include a table of contents, on your letterhead, to use as the first page. The relo packet should contain the following items:

- Simplified map of the area's communities
- School district information
- Lender Qualifier form
- Recreational opportunities available in your town
- List of churches (omit addresses. Show them where their church is when they're in your car.)
- List of shopping centers (Again, plan to show them when they arrive.)
- Brief discussion of climate
- Map showing access to airports, to where they'll be working, and to points of interest
- List of several places they can reach on a weekend for recreation
- Financing information
- Your company brochure
- Several house flyers

Having a relocation packet stamps you as a professional. When you start working on yours, check with your local Chamber of Commerce and library. They may have brochures or other information you can use. Make up several relo packets before you need them. This will allow you to express one to prospects the same day you get the referral, or to hand it to a prospect coming in with no prior notice other than the phone call from the relocation center.

# New People

Active real estate agents constantly meet new people. Successful real estate agents not only meet *more* new people, they meet them *better*. In the vital meeting situations, where either the gain or loss of a new client (listing) or customer (buyer) will occur, the successful agent has a high success ratio.

A high success ratio is often determined in the critical first 15 seconds of a meeting with new people. What can happen in just 15 seconds?

Time yourself with your watch. Get up, walk to a window, look out, walk back to your chair, and sit down again. The chances are, you can easily do all these things in 15 seconds. A fourth of a minute is long enough for an enormous amount of nonverbal communication, plus a considerable amount of talk. It's time enough to say 40 words without hurry. It's time enough to get preoccupied, to show irritation if the new people interrupt you, or to stare at them as though you suspect they'll be a waste of effort. It's also time enough to demonstrate your friendliness and eagerness to work with someone new, and to indicate you're pleasant to be with, too.

Some agents don't warm up to new people quickly. Sometimes this stems from an unwillingness to accept the salesperson's role of being the first-mover, first-smiler, and first-greeter. Sometimes the slow warm-up mirrors an agent's behavior in purely social meetings, or is a defense against feelings of inferiority in the customer-agent relationship. Social equality or inequality between agent and prospect isn't involved; the relationship is professional, not social. It's vital to believe and feel this correct orientation. Agents who greet newcomers with hesitancy and suspicion are unaware of how badly they're wounding themselves.

When customers first walk in, do you run up to them and put your hand out, or do you watch for their signals? Does their arm go up a little bit?

If it does, catch on. Reach out and shake hands.

Some people don't like to touch right away. They seem to be saying, "Don't invade my personal space." Then don't. Build up slowly.

Some people walk in and hug you. This is fine too—it's their way. But, be careful not to crowd people who can't handle it.

# The Essence of Client-Capture

Bait your hook with knowledge. Depend on knowledge for the power, and on your winning personality and charming smile only for the assistance.

During your first face-to-face encounter, what you can tell them about your area and what you can learn about their needs without offending them by seeming to pry, are all-important.

## Flow with Their Stroke

Fit your attitude to your client's moods and personalities, and your schedule to their time limitations. You can't build strong rapport trying to make them dance to your tunes.

## Product Knowledge Is Serious Business

You'll wither unless you know the inventory of available housing thoroughly; you'll flourish if you do. Only top-flight real estate people take product knowledge as seriously as it should be taken. (Chapter 3 discusses how you can rapidly gain a large and detailed knowledge of your inventory.)

## Listen, Really Listen

Top producers invariably are intent listeners (at least to prospects); low producers tend to be sloppy listeners. When you listen, listen actively with your ears *and* your eyes. Keep asking yourself, "Exactly what does she mean by this? Why didn't he finish his sentence? Do they really mean it?"

Listen and watch for hints to follow up and keep them talking about their feelings. Treat what they say as important, and prove you think it's important by remembering what they tell you.

## Be an Expert

Be an expert on financing, and on all phases of residential real estate practice. Prospects know they'll be spending large dollars with you; they also know they're worth large service.

# Buyers' Tango

*Put your left foot forward, and your right foot out, and head in the direction where the buyers hang out!*

All we need is a great melody and we've got a sensational new dance—for three. You and a pair of buyers. Even without the beat, some agents get the steps down pat, and others end up doing the hokey-pokey all the time. But the buyers' tango, like all dances, can be learned if you've got rhythm in your head and desire in your soul. When done well, the dance is smooth, graceful, and flowing. It takes practice, practice, practice. Once you get the steps down, watchers can hardly tell who is leading and who is following. But you and I know who's controlling the movements—the real estate agent.

You can learn the steps anywhere and any time, but the complete performance must be polished with real buyers. With a strong but subtle lead and quick responses, you can have your clumsiest partners thinking they're dancing *Swan Lake*—all the way to homeownership.

# The Proof-of-Competence Phase

All the demanding work of promotion, phone and mail prospecting, door-knocking, holding open houses, and putting in floor time has but one objective: contact with a buyer or seller. Once you have contact, the search phase is over, and you are thrust abruptly into the proof-of-competence phase.

"Wait a minute," you say, "What about building rapport? Don't I have to demonstrate a genuine interest in solving their housing problem, should I regard them as unique and important individuals, and convince them they'll like doing business with me? Don't I have to create trust, confidence, and friendly feelings before I can take the next step?"

Not with action-imminent buyers or sellers, you don't. They're not looking for Smiley Jokester or Sally Sincere. They're searching for a capable expert who is socially acceptable. In actual practice, you'll blend competence-demonstration with rapport building as the situation dictates. When you've made your Breakaway you'll demonstrate your competence with relaxed alertness and win prospects by:

- **Responding to comments made by prospects with references to specific properties whenever possible.** These responses reveal your depth of knowledge while you develop useful information, "You'd prefer a larger dining room? I know of a lovely home with an impressive dining room. The carpet is powder blue. Do you like powder blue?"
- **Asking the right questions at the right time with the right words.** To a quiet couple who say nothing of consequence after your initial greetings, "Is this your first visit here?"
- **Speaking in an informed way about any phase of real estate the customers show interest in.**
- **Sliding your prepared sales dialogues smoothly into the conversation, tailoring them to fit the prospects' needs and tastes.** Once you gain the prospects' full attention, even if only momentarily, you have a golden opportunity. Seize it. Without

brag or bluster, and without knocking other agents or misrepresenting what you can do, demonstrate your real estate expertise. Show how you can help them get the house they want for the least amount of money possible, or sell their house advantageously.

- **Bringing out your cutting-edge technology.** Turn on your laptop and bring up a few houses they may be interested in. The computer age doesn't eliminate the need for having a large Quick-Speak Inventory—it simply gives you additional ways to cash in on the knowledge you've stored in the best computer you'll ever own—your brain.

Avoid saying, "I'm a hotshot agent." Don't overwhelm them with real estater's jargon; simply respond with casual competence to whatever questions they have with the confidence born of knowledge. Then guide the interview in the channels you want it to go, remaining always alert to the direction they want to go.

The challenge is to let them know you're hot stuff without directly saying so. You do this by drilling yourself on Quick-Speak.

## Capture Both Partners

Lots of pretty women work in real estate. If the salesperson is a woman and she only looks at the male half of the buyer pair—and the afternoon wears on with just those two looking at each other—there's trouble in Sales City. The saleswoman is operating as though the man will make the decision, which is always a risky assumption to place all your bets on.

While all this he-and-she looking is going on, the wife is thinking, "We're going to buy a house from *her*? *No way.* I've got an *ugly* girlfriend in real estate; we're buying from her."

Or the salesperson is a man who, making the same assumption, only looks at the husband. All day long they're talking man-to-man, while the wife is saying to herself, "This twit thinks I'm too stupid to be involved in a big decision like the choice of my own home. I'll show him. Tomorrow, we'll find an agent who'll involve me too, and then we'll get serious about buying."

**Look at them both equally and speak to them both equally.** Try to include them both in the minor decisions and discussions leading up to the one big decision. Even if you can't treat them equally because one spouse is so dominant, the less-aggressive half will appreciate what you're trying to do. Very often it's the quiet one who, though refusing to say much in public, casts the decisive vote in private.

**Operate on this theory: to capture either one as a customer, you have to capture both of them.** Two birds in the hand are worth more than one on your shoulder and another in flight.

# Tune in Emotionally

Ask yourself, "Who am I dealing with?"

In handling buyers, you must listen, and watch, and *think* if you want to understand human nature. Always keep in mind how many kinds of people there are, and how many different motives and moods they may be feeling at the moment. Be sensitive to the emotional level of your prospect. Meet it and build from there.

Maybe you're naturally outgoing and flamboyant. Tone this down when working with an engineer type who is analytical and calculating. You must become a numbers nut for this person. You must convince the client of one vital issue: His or her concerns are your concerns. Do this by demonstrating competence, not by making unsupported claims which often come across as bare-faced lies.

When you are working with an extrovert who is warm and understanding like yourself, but his wife keeps the books and is suspicious, you have to appeal to her more conservative ways and still be warm.

# Shoot Your Best Shot and Don't Worry About Competition

One of Kitty Jamison's experiences illustrates this point. An out-of-state referral, a single woman, gave explicit requirements and said she was seeing houses with another agent on Tuesday, but would be available to look with Kitty on Wednesday. Kitty knew there were only about half a dozen properties in Mission Viejo meeting the lady's requirements. After a thorough review of the MLS book, she found seven possibilities. Certain the other agent would show all seven of those houses to the buyer on Tuesday, Kitty called every active agent she could, trying to find some new or pocket listings to add to the seven. No luck. Time ran out.

Exuding a confidence she didn't feel, Kitty met the buyer on Wednesday and drove her to the first stop. The lady looked glum when she saw the house. After prowling through it silently, she said, "Now this is more like it."

"You haven't already seen this home?" Kitty gasped.

"Nothing I saw yesterday came anywhere near this close to what I want."

"The other six I've lined up are just as close," Kitty said.

"If they are, I'll buy one from you."

And she did. The other agent hadn't shown a single one of the seven houses meeting the buyer's requirements, even though all seven were in the book. Why not? The answer to this question explains why no more than 20 percent of the agents do 80 percent of the business in most real estate offices.

The top 20 percent doesn't work harder than the average agent; they work smarter. They make productive use of the time and energy others spend complaining and discouraging themselves. And the top producers in any sales organization have made the initial all-out effort success demands of us all.

# Recognize Lonely Charlie

It happens a lot. The husband reports for work at his new job and in his spare time starts looking for their next house while the wife stays back home with the kids to sell the home they're leaving. Not all husbands in this situation are Lonely Charlies. Men with heavy travel schedules, outside salesmen and regional executives, for example, are used to being away from home. Most of them have learned how to handle it.

But Lonely Charlie hasn't. Before his transfer he worked every day at the same desk with the same people. Every day he bantered at the same coffee urn with the same office friends. Every day he drove to work at the same time, parked in the same space, and drove home by the same route. Evenings and weekends he spent with his family in even more familiar surroundings.

Then the transfer jerks Charlie out of his comfortable rut. His wife must stay behind until their old house sells, or until the kids finish school. Suddenly Charlie's world is gone: no wife, no family, no home to care for, no personal friends, an unfamiliar work routine—no grass to mow, no albums to paste stamps in, no kids to yell at. The streets are strange and the climate is off-key. He has to learn which light switches do what all over again. His new job helps during the day. But his evenings are grim: the four motel walls are closing in on him. And his weekends are endless.

No wonder Lonely Charlie looks at houses—and looks, and looks. And with whom? A friendly, attractive saleswoman. He's in no hurry. His house hasn't sold yet. And, as soon as he makes his choice, there's no reason for her to spend time with him anymore. So—even if Lonely Charlie doesn't have trouble on his mind—he does need a socially acceptable, and cheap, way to fill all those lonely hours. Maybe

Lonely Charlie doesn't even admit to himself what he's doing—but consciously or not, he'll waste as much of your time as he can.

Charlie is a needy person during this lost interlude between the secure home-office situation he's left behind, and the secure home-office situation he'll create as soon as he possibly can. Meanwhile, he's hurting. A saleswoman needs to be very professional when working with Lonely Charlie, and she must set limits on how much time she'll spend with him. The longer she works with Charlie, the more the wife back home hears about her, and the less likely it is that the wife will permit the purchase to be made through the long-suffering agent.

Even without this complication, there's rough air to fly through here. Lonely Charlie is the easiest customer-capture around for the saleswoman—and the hardest to close. It's nearly impossible to close with the true Lonely Charlie. Before you invest a huge amount of time, pretty lady, investigate. Ask to call his wife, no matter where she is. A long distance call will cost a fraction of what the time you can put into him is worth. Tell him you want to talk colors, and such. If he squirms at the idea of you calling his wife (no matter how plausible his reasons sound) he's a full-blown Lonely Charlie. Or, if you do get the chance to phone his wife and she's suspicious and unfriendly, you're not going to get the business anyway, so forget it.

## Smile Mysteriously

Sometimes buyers have told me, "We came to you because we hear you've got properties no one else knows are for sale."

I smile mysteriously and say, "I have a little luck now and then."

Of course I have. Every active agent knows a half-dozen fizzbos or expireds who'll go for a one-party show, or people who've said, "I'm going to list with you in a couple of months, but if you get some hot buyers for a house like this in the meantime, bring them around."

And an active lister usually knows, at any given moment, one or two people who can't make up their minds whom to list with, or when. But this information isn't what made my reputation for knowing more properties than anyone else. What did? Knowing the inventory in the Multiple Listing Service's book better than anyone else. How did I do it? By working hard, smart, and alone; by keyviewing and reviewing the inventory until I had everything in my area of specialization on Quick-Speak (see Chapter 2 for more on learning Quick-Speak).

You can do it too by spending every spare hour during the entire week studying houses. This means you cut off the fun-time caravaning.

When your crowd from the office piles into one car and laughs their way through a few houses, firing zingers at each other and telling funny stories all the way, it's great fun. You see half as many houses as you would traveling alone, and you remember none of them.

I liked fun-time caravaning as much as anyone. If I was losing touch with the people in the office, or getting punchy from the pace and needed the camaraderie, I'd go with the crowd and have some fun too. But if you make it a habit rather than an exceptional treat, ha-ha caravaning will cost you more than a new Mercedes.

## Lunching with Buyers

You can't save a lost sale by taking the buyers to lunch, although you often can use a lunch to make amends for an inconvenience you've inadvertently inflicted. Except for special circumstances, save your lunch money for buyers you have great rapport with, or for the times when you're on the verge of getting an offer and need to review with the buyers what you've seen together. But make very sure they really want to have lunch with you.

Tell them, "I'd be pleased (flattered, honored, happy) to join you for lunch now, but I hope you'll be candid with me. You're about to make an important decision, and if you need the time to talk privately, I certainly think your private talk is more important than my pleasure at this moment. The vital thing is to solve your housing problem."

If I had been showing property from 9:30 A.M. or so, when about 11:30, I'd say something like, "Let's take a break now. Maybe you all would like to get a bite to eat. I'll give you two a chance to be alone, and talk about the houses we saw this morning. Would you like to meet at 1:00?"

Be selective. If you're a new salesperson, you should conserve your funds. There are people around who'll not only waste your time, they'll happily waste your money too.

Should a saleswoman, showing houses to a married man, looking without his wife, ask him to lunch? Not, unless he's an old friend, she knows the wife well, and is on a solid footing with her. Say to him, "Have a nice lunch. Let's get back together at 1:00 and resume our tour."

Should she accept lunch from him? For the same reasons, no. She should tell him, "I want to devote as much time as possible to you because I know you need to find a home for you and your wife. You need to have me available to assist you, so I'd like to use the lunch hour to catch up on phone messages at the office."

Obviously, if you've already told him he's your first customer, and you don't have *anything* else to do, you've put yourself squarely in line for Lonesome Charlie's full trip.

If you've been out with them two or three times and they're very close to making a decision, say, "Would you two like the opportunity to be alone during lunch so you can discuss what we've seen this morning—because I know you've seen a couple of houses you really like. Or may. I have the pleasure of taking you to lunch?"

A sales*man*, working with a wife looking alone, should show the same degree of professionalism. Even with couples, unless they're friends of the family or repeat customers, going to lunch with prospective buyers usually hurts rather than helps. Use lunchtime to plan your next move with them, to scout out new houses to show them, to think over what they've said and not said, and to reflect on whether you've missed something. The lunch hour away from them will often give you the unpressured time to step back, look at the situation, and figure out how to keep their interest up. Use the time well. Don't fritter it away in chit chat. Then you can charge back after lunch and guide them to purchasing the home they need.

In light of what you've learned about them in the morning, the chances are you'll be able to locate some additional houses they should see. Perhaps they asked questions you weren't prepared to answer. Use this time to get the answers.

# Expanded Folk Wisdom

It's not what you say but how you say it. Let's expand this compressed bit of folklore into four specifics for real estate.

### 1. Never present negative information with:

- an enthusiastic, "Isn't this just peachy keen?" manner. This always rings false because it is false. With most prospects, once your credibility is cracked it can never be mended.
- an arrogant, "Take it or drop dead," attitude,
- an inflexible, "This is how it's got to be," stance unless you've tried all the softer approaches first, or
- a hand-wringing, "You're going to kick the furniture apart about this" posture. This tells them they're expected to throw a tantrum. Many people can't resist the invitation.

### 2. State negative information clearly and directly, with few words and no excuses. Sympathetic half-smiles and small gestures are often better hard-fact softeners than words.

Watch your customers closely while you're talking. Allow them just long enough to understand the negative (a split second may do it) and then say something upbeat, or ask a positive question.

3. **When you've handled a situation poorly.** Summarize the situation in a brief written paragraph at your first opportunity and decide how you could handle the same circumstances better the next time. Write down the smooth phrases you think up after the event, and practice saying them so you'll be ready the next time.

4. **Acknowledge every statement by a customer.** "I understand," is a good phrase for this. Allow a second to pass before you change the subject. And take time to understand what your customer is telling you. If you keep on saying, "I understand," while you're thinking about something else, the customer will soon realize your mouth is on automatic pilot. Most of us learned in childhood to hate this.

# Another Window of Understanding

Another window to an understanding of your customers' emotions is to consider how large the sum of money involved in the house purchase looks when it's compared to the sums of money they deal with in their daily work. The wheeler-dealers who make decisions involving millions are at one extreme; the hourly workers who make no money decisions in their regular work are at the other.

These people will have vastly different attitudes. The hourly worker may be humble or antagonistic; he's sensitive to being condescended to. Be careful not to big-deal the hourly worker. He's vulnerable, especially in front of his wife. You can wound him by highlighting his lack of knowledge—he's almost certain to be tender in this area. Guard his ego.

If he snaps, "I know that," respond with a cheerful,

"Great! I see you're much better informed than most of my customers are."

# Don't Tell Them You're New

When I was new, people would ask, "How long have you been in the business?"

If it was someone referred to me by a personal friend, I'd say, "I'm green but I'm growing." Everyone else I'd tell, "I entered the profession this past year." The last 12 months are the past year, right?

If you started in December and it's January, you can honestly say, "I'm working my second year in real estate."

But don't let it drop there. What they're really saying is, "Are you competent to handle our business? This is an important matter to us. We don't mind helping you get started, but we don't want to pay for a beginner's mistakes."

They need reassurance. Give it to them. "I've been very fortunate so far." Say this firmly, your tone indicating you've made lots of money because you know what you're doing. Then continue with, "I don't expect to ever stop learning; the need to keep learning makes this business exciting. But if I don't have an answer, I know where to get it fast." Then ask them a question about their requirements and get on with finding them a house.

Some new agents are so defensive about being new they overcompensate by trying to prove they know it all. This turns people off because, most of the time, they've heard or they can tell you're fairly new. Do your homework, know your job, and you won't have trouble with people worrying about you being new.

## Use Your Buyers' File Constantly

Do you call your buyer prospects without first reviewing everything you know about them—everything you've carefully noted in your buyers' file? You won't need to do this if you're calling them every day, but if much time has gone by, you run a great risk of forgetting something they've told you (something they'll remember telling you).

When you forget how many children they have, or something they want in their next home, your act of forgetting is taken as if you'd said, "I don't care enough about your housing needs to remember."

Capture customers by caring enough to recall their uniqueness.

## The Hungry Breath

Long time, no commission! I'm beginning to doubt, and it's beginning to show. It's no longer the comfortable, "Would you like to buy?" look. Now it's the hungry, "You gotta buy" look. It's the old, "Don't waste my time unless your suitcase is ready" pitch. The hungry breath of a salesman casts an odor. No one comes near. Somebody give me a breath freshener. I smell terrible! Avoid this problem by working my circle formula at the end of Chapter 1.

# Winning Scripts

"We're large enough to serve you, and small enough to care."

"We are members of the Multiple Listing Service. Although we are very active listers in this area (buyers want to know whether you and your office control a lot of listings), we also keep current on all the other brokers' properties on the Multiple Listing Service. Have you highlighted some ads you'd like me to inquire about for you?"

During the first few minutes of talking to prospects, build on the common denominators. If it's a referral situation, mention the people who referred you right up front in the conversation. This is important because they may have been referred to three other agents by various friends, and now they can't remember who you are.

So you say, "Mr. and Mrs. Palmer, it's so nice to talk to you. I've heard a lot of nice things about you from Mary and Bill."

They think, "This is the gal who helped Mary and Bill get their neat place on North Drive—Okay." Their defenses come down a bit.

"Are you presently working with another broker?"

I always ask this. If prospects are already working with someone they feel loyalty to, I want to honor their loyalty whether it's to an agent in my company or not. I also want to conserve my time for prospects where my chances of earning a fee are better.

During my first meeting with buyers I always say, "When I look for a house for my own family, nothing bothers me more than the possibility of missing something. It's maddening to house-hunt with an agent you know isn't on top of everything available. The one house he doesn't know about might be the perfect home for you, and a good buy too. Believe me, I've been there. I know the feeling. It keeps me constantly hustling all over this town making sure I'm familiar with everything on the market. I know my prospects don't want to miss anything. So I know all these properties like I know my children's birthdays.

# Lender Qualifier Form

The next chapter tells you how to integrate effective qualifying technique into your sales system. Use the following Lender Qualifier form with the customer early in the interview. Have them fill it out. Determine your house selections from this information. Download this form into your computer from the accompanying CD.

---

## LENDER QUALIFIER - A FORM BUYER FILLS OUT AT FIRST INTERVIEW

EXAMPLE:

For a family with gross income of $42,000 and monthly long-term obligations of $400 (installment debt, auto loans, credit cards, child support, etc.)

A. Gross Annual Income     $42,000
(Before Taxes)

B. Gross Monthly Income     $3,500
$42,000 divided by 12

C. Monthly Allowable Housing Expense     $1,260
and Long-Term Obligations
$3,500 multiplied by .36 (36% of gross monthly income is usually allocated for principal, interest, taxes, insurance and monthly long-term obligations)

D. Monthly Allowable Housing Expense     $860
$1,260 minus $400 (subtract monthly long-term obligations from line C. Remainder is allowable principal, interest, taxes, and insurance payment.)

> NOTE: Monthly Allowable Housing Expense on line D should not exceed 28% of Gross Monthly income on line B. If it does, enter the lesser amount on line D and continue.

E. Monthly Principal and Interest     $774
Payment
$860 multiplied by .90 (90% is the amount of the monthly allowable housing expense usually allocated to principal and interest payment only, excluding taxes and insurance.)

F. Estimated Mortgage Amount*     $96,149
$774 divided by 8.05 m multiplied by $1,000 (8.05 is the factor for a 9% loan amortized over a 30-yearterm. Factors for other interest rates and terms-consult a lender.)

G. Estimated Affordable Price Range     $120,186
$96,100 divided by .80 (80% is the mortgage loan amount, assuming a 20% down payment. Use .90 for a 10% down payment.)

\* Rounded to the nearest $100

© 1989 Danielle Kennedy Productions, P.O. Box 1395, Sun Valley, Idaho, 83353

ACTUAL:

    Monthly Long Term Obligations:     $ 400.00

A. Gross Annual Income     $ 42,000.00
(Before Taxes)

B. Gross Monthly Income     $ 3,500.00
Line A divided by 12

C. Monthly Allowable Housing Expense     $ 1,260.00
and Long-Term Obligations
Line B multiplied by 36%

D. Monthly Allowable Housing Expense     $ 860.00
Line C minus long-term obligations OR Line B multiplied by 28%, whichever is less.

E. Monthly Principal and Interest     $ 774.00
Line D multiplied by .90

F. Estimated Mortgage Amount     $ 96,149
Line E divided by the appropriate factor from the interest rate chart multiplied by 1,000

G. Estimated Affordable Price Range     $ 120,186
Line F divided by .80 or .90 depending on down payment

> Should you select an adjustable rate loan, your Sales Associate can also show you how to use this worksheet and Interest Rate Factor Chart to determine your affordable price range and monthly payments.

This material is intended for example purposes only and is not a commitment for financing.

This worksheet is intended for use on primary residences. Your mortgage amount and price range will vary depending on the size of your down payment, the specific terms of your loan, other monthly obligations and the amount of association fees, if applicable.

# CHAPTER 15

# Cut-to-the-Chase Qualifying

**Why Do It? ● How to Dodge the Qualifying Problem ● Backstroke with Style ● Help Rosebuds to Open Up ● Maintain Privacy ● Set Up the Close When You Qualify ● Silence Is Golden ● Maintain the Office ● Winning Tactics in the Qualifying Interview ● Winning Scripts**

## Why Do It?

Agents often skip the qualifying interview when working with buyers for the first time. Some agents mistakenly believe it's easier to delay qualifying, and many fear they'll offend the buyers. Other agents, in their eagerness to show property, charge out of the office with whomever comes in, and hope it'll all pay off, somehow, somewhere down the road.

By omitting the up-front qualifying session, however, agents raise more barriers between themselves and a collected fee. Showing people houses they can't afford can drive away prospects who would be able to buy a lower priced property. Working with people who can't buy makes you unavailable for people who can. Getting an offer accepted for someone who can't obtain a loan won't feed a parakeet. Curb your hunger: You'll get to the feast quicker if you know where it is.

There's a lot more to effective qualification than simply finding out how much prospects make. After a properly conducted qualifying interview you also have a clear idea of what your buyers want in their next home; you've learned much about working smoothly with them;

you know where the power lies between wife and husband; and you understand where they're coming from, and why, and when.

It's just as important to understand your client's motivation when they're buyers as it is when they're sellers. *Why do they want to move?* Do they both want to move, or are they split: The wife wants to stay, the husband wants to move (or vice versa). If so, the move may be months or years away.

If buyers have a house to sell, discuss interim financing with them. Tell them about the problems involved in making offers contingent on the sale of their house. Whether it's stated in the offer or not, they can only make an offer contingent on their own house selling if this has to happen before they'll have the money to complete the purchase of their next home. Most people don't understand these financial issues; it's one of the reasons they need you.

You won't be able to start the process of moving the people you hope are buyers into a house until they're willing to reveal their reasons for wanting to move, and their capability of doing so. Unless they will reveal this information, the odds are they are not ready to move yet. If so, they are lookielews (just looking around) and, while such people often become active customers in the future, you can't afford to work with them now when doing so prevents you from working with present-time buyers. The active agent must constantly make these decisions. You'll rarely go wrong by giving priority to people who have trusted you with information about themselves over those who won't.

When I began selling real estate, I hated to qualify prospects. Perhaps I was so afraid to qualify people because, when I was little, my mother always told me, "Never discuss your father's income, or anybody's income, with anybody. It's nobody's business; money is personal." Then, suddenly, I'm in real estate; suddenly it's critical that I say to these people sitting in front of me, "Can you give me an idea of the income you're earning per month, so I can better serve your needs?"

I couldn't do it.

If you can't do it either, your fall-out rate will be fierce, because you'll be dancing around mansions with people who can't buy a shanty unless they stretch their budget. Three weeks later you sell them Default Villa and a lender connects you with reality. Bang. Pow. Ouch.

You've got to get this fear of qualifying behind you. You've got to develop the hard-headedness to back away from hopeless situations. I was a strong lister who couldn't sell except by accident until I learned to qualify. Don't make the same mistake—it'll save you so much heartache. Use the Lender Qualifier form in Chapter 14 early in your relationship.

Show me a salesperson who continually faces cancellations and I will show you a salesperson who is a poor qualifier. In Chapter 24 (and on the accompanying CD), we have included a Buyer's Analysis form. Use it with your prospects and you'll see great results in keeping everything together all the way to the closing. This form gives you the exact sequence of questions to ask on the qualifying interview; it's an efficient tool for new salespersons who fear being direct with their people. The Lender Qualifier form can be filled out after you use the Buyer's Analysis.

## How to Dodge the Qualifying Problem

You can avoid the whole qualifying situation by choosing among the lenders pounding on your office's door looking for business. Any of them will be glad to do the qualifying for you, and call to say, "Your buyers, Mr. and Mrs. Nguyen, qualify for X$. Go get 'em buddy." Pick a reliable lender's agent who will be able to fund the loan when the time comes, and show this person all the loyalty you can.

However, as with most conveniences, there's a price to pay—you'll never see many of the buyers again when you send them away to get qualified before you show property. Some will find another agent who'll take them right out to tramp through houses. Others weren't really present-time buyers at all. On the up-side, you will save time and frustration.

There are other popular ways to lose buyers, such as showing houses people love but can't afford. When you're new, you probably won't want to risk losing buyers by sending them off to get qualified. That's when you need to be a financing expert and know what mortgage products are available and at what cost. In other words, you need to learn how to "backstroke."

## Backstroke with Style

The more qualifying interviews you conduct, the more aspirations you'll shave with the sharp razor of reality. Always treat prospects with courtesy and style. It costs no more, and it'll bring them back to you in the future. You'll find scenes like the following.

The couple found their dream house on their own, and then came to see you about making an offer on it. In the qualifying interview you find out they don't qualify. Of course you won't wilt them with a contemptuous smile and say, "Guys, let's face it, this house is too rich for your blood."

You'll take an extra moment and be empathetic. "We all want to buy as much house as we can. I know what you're thinking: 'It'll be tight for a while, but our income will be higher before long, and then we can handle this house easily.' I understand. I sympathize with that. Believe me, I've been there . . ."

Pause. Make helpless gestures. ". . . But we have to put this through a lender's loan committee. They only look at today's numbers . . ."

Fix a firm, sympathetic look on them. ". . . And our problem is, today's numbers just don't work out right for us."

If the people can't afford to buy anything at all, go into a pleasant farewell speech and tell them, "I hope to see you again soon."

With people qualified to buy a less-expensive house, get right into solving their housing problem, "Today's numbers don't work on that particular house, but we have a lot of terrific properties where your numbers will absolutely *fly* through a loan committee. Let me tell you about this really neat place over on. . . ."

Make an obvious effort to be especially cordial to these people you've had to bump from first-class to tourist accommodations. Refuse to be embarrassed—for them or for yourself—and demonstrate by your courtesy how highly you value them as customers. You're dealing with prickly pride and bruised egos now, so be up, be enthusiastic, and don't refer to the bump-down again if you can possibly avoid it. Also, be equally careful not to treat them as though they've done something socially unacceptable in trying to buy beyond their means.

What about the people who can't afford anything in your sales area? Why bother with involved diplomacy with such folk? Why not get rid of these time wasters fast with a few blunt words?

Because today's can't-buys become tomorrow's buyers. People get promotions, inheritances, substantial aid from parents, or they join with another couple to buy a house. They also get calls to advise friends who are buying now. In real estate, as in life, courteous concern for others returns good things, and arrogant action paves the road ahead with troubles.

# Help Rosebuds to Open Up

I love big, full, long-stemmed yellow roses. But they aren't big or full when they're delivered. They come in a box as tiny, tightly folded buds. Some people are like this when we first meet them in real estate—they hold onto themselves, their arms folded tight, their eyes fixed on the floor or on your throat. You can almost hear an inner voice saying, "This agent's just out to sell me any old house, whether I want it or not. But I'm not going for it! I won't smile, move, or talk. I'm not giving this salesperson any opening to get at me."

We put the rosebuds in a water-filled vase, and then we put the vase in a sunny window. Soon we see the miracle of roses unfolding into full bloom. Think of those tight-lipped customers of yours in the same way. Like the rosebuds, they're protecting themselves until conditions are right for them to open up.

If they weren't softies deep down inside, they wouldn't be so fearful. If you try to open a rosebud by pulling at its petals, you'll destroy it. Provide the warmth and light, and it will open itself.

Create that right environment for your tense prospects so they can smile pretty too. They've been hurt, cheated, and hassled in the past until they can't relax. They really want to open up and become your customers, but they don't know it yet. They won't know until it happens—and it'll happen just as soon as you beam the warmth and the light on them they're seeking.

## Maintain Privacy

New salespeople are ill at ease when qualifying a prospect in front of their associates. They're concerned about having their performance critiqued. Managers should be careful *not* to listen. They should be especially careful *not* to go in and take over the qualifying interview because they think they'll do a better job than the new agent can. Unless their aid is called for, they must keep out of it, or they'll find themselves unable to build a capable staff.

And, often, the buyer hates being interviewed about very personal business where several strange people may or may not be listening. If at all possible, conduct the qualifying interview in private. If you have to talk at your desk, speak very softly—unless your buyers act like they want to tell the world their business.

## Set Up the Close When You Qualify

The point of qualifying is to find out what (if anything) you can close them on. Use the qualifying interview to get them used to being in the closing room. And always call it the *conference room*, never the *closing room*. Even in the natural close I teach, there's the tension of large decision making to contend with. So it helps to take them back to a room they've been in before. We're all more comfortable in familiar surroundings. And, on their second trip into the conference room, your prospects understand a vital point: business is conducted there.

However, if the jet stream of desire for a home is driving the people you're talking to at an open house, qualify them there; or at a coffee shop booth in the hotel where you meet out-of-state referrals. Be prepared to qualify prospects anywhere reasonably private and free of interruptions. But avoid unseemly haste to get at business. Offer them coffee or other refreshments, invite them to sit down and make themselves comfortable, and exchange a brief bit of small talk first.

## Silence Is Golden

Silence is never more golden than in the qualifying interview—except when you're showing property, closing customers, and negotiating offers for them. Silence, beautiful silence, is golden because it's the least offensive way known of saying, *"No, this is the way it has to be." "This is our best offer." "We really mean it; if you want this agreement, you'll have to improve your offer." "I'm willing to wait you out, but you'll never get a better offer from us."*

Yes, silence is amazingly communicative. We should really say, *silence talks.* How else can you say, "I'm firm, I'm strong, I'm confident. You need me more than I need you. If you don't do something to save it, this transaction won't happen." Given the right situation, silence will say any or all of that for you, without committing you, without giving offense.

Silence is such a powerful tool—why are we so afraid of it when we're with people? When silence settles in, we don't think, we panic.

"It's so quiet in here, I could hear an ant sing. I'm going crazy. I gotta think of something to say. Anything! This tension is killing me."

Whenever you feel silence-cramps coming on, quietly take a deep breath, hold it, and see how high you can count before your customer starts talking or you have to breathe again. Recite the alphabet *backwards* in your thoughts. Relive your first date, or any other first that will relax you while you remain confidently alert. Do any sort of mental gymnastics, but don't talk, and don't bang the tangibles around just to make some sound waves hit your eardrums.

Remember all the things the prospects have to think about during this high-pressure time. Remember the difference in pressure: you're in for about 2 percent and they're in for about 100 percent. You've asked them penetrating questions, or you've pushed them hard against a huge decision; they need time to consider the implications of it all. So let there be little quiet times along the way. Be generous with silences, not afraid of them.

As you become more relaxed in the qualifying interview, you'll notice the customers becoming more relaxed. They're thinking, "I'm okay! I'm with someone who's capable and confident; I'm in good hands."

However, if the salesperson is nervous, the customers are thinking, "I wonder if this agent can really do the job. And why is he so uptight? I wonder if someone's trying to pull a fast one on me—and is afraid I'll catch on."

When buyers start to doubt, all the negative stuff starts creeping in, and your difficulties escalate.

# Maintain the Office

When people walk into an office, no matter whose customer they are, they look at the overall picture of the environment: coffee cups all over the place, overflowing trash cans, filled ash trays. Don't be one of those salespeople who says, "Well, it's not my mess. Why should I have to clean it up?" Work together with team spirit; tomorrow somebody may have to clean up *your* mess. The overall office environment goes a long way toward promoting competence, both in the closing room and outside of it.

# Winning Tactics in the Qualifying Interview

Watch to see who is the leader between the husband and the wife, or whether it's an equal opportunity situation. The loudest, or the quickest to speak, isn't necessarily the leader. You can miss this if you're not watching closely.

Gear your remarks to the level of each individual, but be careful not to talk down to anyone. Pay a lot of respect to the man where he has the full responsibility for providing income to the family but, especially if you're a saleswoman, be careful not to make the wife defensive about not having a job outside the home. Where the wife provides the greater part—or all—of the couple's income, be sure not to show any surprise. Househusbands may be even more defensive than housewives about their status.

When working with a couple where the husband is submissive, try to draw him out without irritating his dominant wife. If you're a saleswoman, be feminine and warm, and find out what the husband, as well as the wife, likes. Pulling people up and making them feel good about themselves will always make your sales go more easily. Convince people, on the gut level, that you really care about their welfare. Call it "heart power." When you can express and demonstrate heart power sincerely—and have it accepted without embarrassment—your success will be unlimited.

Your job is to help people achieve what they want in housing. If achieving what they want isn't practical at this time, it's also your job to tell them so with gracious honesty.

When buyers tell you they want a four-bedroom view home, find out their price range during the qualifying interview. With your inventory knowledge, you'll then be able to give them a quick overview of what they can expect to find in the way of square footage, lot size, and amenities in four-bedroom view homes within their price range. Tell them right away. Why show them ten houses that will just disappoint them? They may translate their disappointment in housing prices into dissatisfaction with you—and rightly so. By giving them an overview before you leave the office, you can save them, and yourself, a day of dismay.

If they're serious about a house in your sales area, but want more house than they can afford (the buyers' usual dilemma), the sooner you start guiding them toward practical compromises, the better are your chances of closing them on an offer before heart and foot aches close their minds. Of course, don't refuse to show them specific houses they want to see, even if you know those houses will disappoint them. Just don't show them such houses exclusively, or even primarily. Be sensitive. Probe for the weak items in their list of requirements. If they want a pool, and it's out of their price range in the smallest house they'll accept, then point out recreation facilities nearby.

Your job is to give the buyers alternatives in housing if they can't find everything they want. This calls for creative thinking on your part. It's important to constantly ask problem-solving questions to the buyers like a true counselor. Encourage them to look into all alternatives. You have to see things objectively, and guide them, because they can't be objective and find their way without your help.

Sometimes it takes two or three meetings for buyers to open up. I never showed a lot of homes until buyers opened up to me with their needs and their capabilities so I could know their price range.

# Winning Scripts

Here's how to introduce the Buyer's Analysis for Better Service form and the Lender Qualifier form after your preliminary remarks are made, some chit chat is exchanged (be careful not to prolong it), and the coffee is on the table.

*Agent:* It's very important to me to serve you courteously *and* productively, Mr. and Mrs. Bailey. I know you are busy people. (Make lots of statements that emphasize their importance.) So many times, people will randomly look at houses with an agent, not really knowing what they want. The agent just does some guesswork and, when their time together is over, everyone is frustrated. I pride myself on my ability to make every minute count with people. But, before I can do this, I need your permission for something.

*Customers:* What's that?

*Agent:* Our company has compiled a questionnaire called the Buyer's Analysis for Better Service and the Lender Qualifier. With the aid of these forms, we interview our clients before we look at property so that our time together today will be more meaningful. Would you be offended if I ask you some of the questions on this form? (When you've acquired the confidence to work without the form, omit all reference to it by saying instead, "Would you be offended if I asked you some questions so I'll know how to make our time together meaningful?")

*Customers:* Sure.

*Agent:* Thank you both. I assure you that this is done in your best interests. We really do want to serve you well.

Make lots of affirmative statements in an enthusiastic tone throughout your entire time with your customers. This can be overdone, of course, but more often it's underdone—or left entirely undone. Reinforce the rapport you've already instilled into your agent-customer relationship by affirming your determination to serve them well whenever you have a natural opportunity to do so.

## Flashdeck These Questions

Create a flashdeck of the questions from the Buyer's Analysis for Better Service form and become a qualifying pro in a hurry. Make runs through this flashdeck twice daily until you can roll off these questions perfectly anytime you're with people. When you can do this, you will have stepped into the top 5 percent of salespeople with respect to this vital skill. Make no mistake about it, if you can't qualify effectively you can't be a strong producer. Here are some questions:

"Is this your first visit to our community?"

"Where are you folks from?"

"How long have you been looking for a home?"

"How many are in your family?"

"Then you have _____ children?"

"May I ask their names and ages?"

"Where do you live now?"

"How long have you lived there?"

"Are you investing in your present home, or do you rent?"

"How is the resale market in your area?"

"May I ask, Mr. and Mrs. _____, where are you employed?"

"How long have you been there?"

"Have you seen any homes you really like?"

"What prevented you from owning that home?"

## Urgency Questions

"How soon are you thinking of making a move after you find the right home?"

"How much time will you have to see homes today?"

"How many bedrooms will suit you best?"

## Current Owner Questions

"How much do you feel you will realize from the sale of your home?"

"Will it be necessary to sell your present home to purchase the new one?"

"Will you be converting any of your other investments to cash in order to complete the purchase of your next home?"

"If we are fortunate enough to find the right home today, will you be in a position to make a decision to proceed?"

"Not to be personal, but to do a better job for you, may I ask, how much of your savings do you wish to invest in your home?"

"What price range have you been considering? Better yet, since most people are concerned with their monthly outgo, how much do you feel you could comfortably invest each month in your new home, including everything?"

"Please take a few minutes to fill out this Lender Qualifier form. It's a perfect guide."

## Lower-Price-Range Property Questions

"The monthly housing expense and long-term obligations should be less than 36 percent of gross monthly income, according to the rule of thumb most lenders use. (This would include principal, interest, taxes, insurance, and monthly long-term obligations.) Are we in line here?"

"Please take a moment, Mrs. _____, to describe your present home to me, including all your likes and dislikes."

"What are your special requirements for your next home?"

"Are there any other special requirements I haven't noted yet, such as _____ (suggest some of the popular amenities available in your inventory) things you'd like to have in your next home?"

## Follow-Up Statement

(Memorize this one.)

"You might like several properties I have in mind. I'll set up appointments so we can view these homes. But please do me a favor—if my first houses aren't in line with what *you* have pictured in *your* mind, promise me you'll tell me. I won't be hurt. I know the inventory so well, I can adjust the homes to view on a minute's notice to what you *are* picturing and hoping to see. Will you tell me if I'm off the mark? (if I'm not hitting the nail on the head? if I'm playing rock when you want to hear Bach?)"

Use whatever metaphor suits you and the situation, but get them to commit to telling you if you're not showing them what they want to see. Otherwise, they'll grumble behind your back, and you'll never know why you couldn't solve their housing problem.

Place the inventory sheet next to the qualifying form, and glance at the housing listings as you qualify them. Keep trying to mentally place them in some of the houses that fit into their price range. Arrange your inventory sheet by price, lowest to highest, so you can instantly locate the price range where they belong and avoid scanning the entire inventory.

Keep in mind how much tension your customers are under, and how tension makes many people impatient. During this interview they watch to see how quickly and brightly you respond. Short words and quick movements are vital now; keep the pace fast so your people won't start wishing and planning to be someplace else. And keep a sharp eye on their reactions; don't frighten them by going too fast, either. When you smoothly and confidently ask the right questions, you get the needed answers.

Take a show list form and fill in the properties you intend to visit with them. While you make the appointments, ask them if they'd like to use the rest room or have another cup of coffee.

By knowing the inventory and the qualifying questions, you're in control. Sure, they can scan through the inventory on the monitor, but bowling them over with your firm's technology doesn't impress them with your personal competence. Know the inventory so well you set a standard that few agents can match, should those prospects work with someone else for an afternoon. Any agent can crank up the computer, but what will bring buyers back to you is having the inventory on Quick-Speak.

## Commands for Customers

Success here isn't as difficult as you might think, if you know the limits and how to do it. A command to a customer must always tell them to do something they want to do, something that clearly furthers their interests.

The command must be softened with a polite preface:

"What we should do now is. . . ."

"Would you mind. . . ."

"May I ask you to. . . ."

"After you."

"May I urge that we. . . ."

"May I suggest that we. . . ."

"The most important thing for us to do now is. . . ."

"The next step is for us to. . . ."

"To accomplish *your* purpose, what we must do now is. . . ."

"I know it's an annoyance, but the lenders insist on. . . ."

Such "commands" get things done.

## Speed, the Internet, and Preventing Cancellations

If you enlist the help of a reputable lender early in the qualifying process you will save yourself lots of headaches. The beauty of the Internet is the speed in which you can find out the truth about any prospect that crosses your path. You and your loan rep can e-mail back and forth in a matter of minutes all the information you need. There is no reason to go out and show anyone property until you have nailed down the truth about their situation. If you know the truth from the start, your cancellations will be next to nothing, because you will not be putting people and houses together who do not belong together. That is the true value of the Internet. The truth travels twice as fast as before.

# CHAPTER 16

# Virtual Touring, In-Person Showings— And Finalizing the Sale

## The Secret of Successful Showing

*Eenie, meanie, mynie, moe,*
*I've got twenty homes to show.*
*Why show this one, why show that,*
*When I know not bird from bat?*

The secret of successful showing is effective preparation. The secret of effective preparation is doing it intensely, on a daily basis, for all buyers you may encounter. You do it for all buyers because you can't know in advance what precise opportunities may be yours before any day ends. So you must prepare for a range of opportunities. Intense, daily preparation means that you:

- Use the Quick-Speak concept and keyview regularly.
- Develop sales speeches and a property catalog.
- Train yourself on your area's streets until getting disoriented there is impossible.
- Watch the local and national financial situation.
- Keep current on general real estate and business trends.

- Know your board's sales and listings for last week, month, and year.
- Know your area's appreciation rate, average days on the market, and average prices paid.
- Know your community's events, opportunities, schools, and shopping.

Yes, it takes all this knowledge, plus fine showing and selling techniques, to attain the high success ratio top producers enjoy. You don't start on top, of course. You climb there rung by rung. As you acquire the product knowledge, practice the following techniques on as many live buyers as possible.

# Virtual Touring

Yes, there are buyers today who purchase homes online. They virtual tour a home and they buy it. Usually they are affluent buyers. A middle class buyer is not going to risk his only hard-earned savings or equity and buy sight unseen online. But *yes* it is being done. It can be done because the technology is constantly improving.

I go online all the time and tour properties. You have to understand I have always been a passionate, house fanatic. I watch the Home and Garden channel the way some people tune into Oprah or the soaps. I *love* homes. And virtual tours really feed my real estate addiction. In the privacy of my home I can preview homes I might want to buy when I retire. Or if I am speaking in a seminar or doing consulting work, I can tour the neighborhood before I get there. I can become intimate with your market from my own home. Then I am so much more prepared for our work together.

For you, generally consider the virtual tour as a great screening device. While buyers who are investing their lifetime savings in a home, will eventually want to see what they are getting in person, virtual tours and open houses are a great way to eliminate homes that are of no interest. It is a great way to eliminate showing people too many homes. It is also a wonderful aid for agents who want to do some caravaning from their home offices.

As you read this chapter, think of ways to use the Internet to assist you with some of your preliminary research for both listing and selling appointments. You still must have an extensive knowledge of the inventory. Especially now since buyers can access all listings, make sure your prospect is not more on top of the market than you are.

# Danny K's 23 Ways to More Paydays

## 1. Show your people houses they can afford.

Chapter 15 told you how to qualify your buyers. Thorough qualifying is the key to successful showing, closing, and fee collecting. You can't win a thing by trying to sell houses people can't buy.

## 2. Respect your buyers' stated top limit.

Follow their limit even when they name a figure well below what they can qualify for. Let them make this decision. Make every effort to satisfy their needs within their comfort zone as to price.

Suppose you qualify the Rufus Klings to purchase a $300,000 house. Mr. Kling tells you, "I don't want to go over $200,000." Don't show them any house that costs more than $200,000. It's astonishing how many agents take a stated top limit as a challenge and would show the Klings houses in the $275,000 to $350,000 range.

Work for your buyers, not against them. Show them the best properties available within their stated top limit. Let them decide how much of their income they'll put into housing. If you find something the Klings like at $190,000—great. Four times out of five, the Klings will only live in that $190,000 house for a year. Then they'll come back to you, if you've handled them right, wanting to move up. At that time you'll list their present $190,000 home, and also sell them their next home for $299,000. Three transactions for you—none for the agents who made the Klings mad by showing them over-limit houses in the beginning. Referral business doesn't just happen—it's built by service tuned to the customers' wavelengths.

## 3. Ask house-eliminating questions (HEQs).

As you gain skill in qualifying, learn how to probe deeper into your buyers' likes and dislikes in the qualifying interview, and as your Quick-Speak Inventory increases, you'll find yourself narrowing down your show list to fewer and fewer houses. Your ability to match buyers to houses will grow rapidly; and the time it takes you to sell each set of buyers will drop dramatically. The key is (1) a thorough knowledge of the inventory; and (2) developing an effective list of house-eliminating questions and an easy manner of asking them so your buyers are comfortable answering.

Be alert for the house-eliminating questions arising naturally as you show property to buyers. When you ask one, make a mental note of it, and add it to your list.

You are showing property to the Cosbys. You've asked them a number of questions, but haven't checked about backyards. At one house, you find a small backyard—all concrete and pool. You don't know if they want a big yard or a small yard, so you say, "George, I don't know whether yard work really thrills you, but this is definitely low maintenance."

He may say, "I travel a lot. I don't have time to work on a yard. This is perfect."

Another buyer will say, "I pound concrete all day long. What I want in a backyard is some nice soft grass."

"Aha," you think, "another house-eliminating question. I'll just add that gem to my list of HEQs. Next time, I'll ask something about backyards in the qualifying session."

Showing houses is an ongoing discovery process between you, your customers, and the available housing. With many buyers, you'll be able to gain a very clear picture of what they want and take them right to it when you know two things very well: what's available and what to ask.

With buyers whose aspirations far outrun their pocketbooks, your primary task is reconciling them to what they can afford. But even with such people, having a good set of house-eliminating questions will enable you to cut through the confusion and focus on their achievable needs in the shortest possible time. Develop a list of questions to reveal what buyers like and don't like. Phrase your questions to elicit a broader reply than a *yes*, a *no*, or a grunt.

## 4. Analyze their expressed likes and dislikes.

A person's likes and dislikes sometimes conflict. A man wants a large, lush backyard, but doesn't want to do the maintenance work or pay a gardener. When you hear such conflicts, don't take them too seriously at first. Point out the conflict sympathetically, and ask for direction. If they seem stuck on dead center, tell them the question will resolve itself, and ask for permission to show property on both sides of the conflict. Usually, careful analysis of what they're saying will guide you straight to what they want—if you're willing to listen closely and carefully weigh their words.

*Huffing, bluffing, till day is done,*
*I'll swear is hardly that much fun.*
*I wish I'd previewed every one,*
*'Stead of taken looks at none.*

## 5. Listen, really listen, when your buyers talk about what they want.

Ask about their likes and dislikes. Listen to the answers. Remember the answers. Make notes and refer to your notes.

Some agents remember to ask, but don't bother to tune in for the replies, much less memorize the information as it's given to them. Agents who don't remember what the customers say are easy to spot: they're the ones standing around the office complaining about buyers having no loyalty.

## 6. Don't show houses you haven't previewed online or in person.

You can't fake this. People will tell you, "I hate blue carpet and I can't stand dark-paneled rooms. I want a large dining room, and we need a huge backyard."

How are you going to avoid showing them houses that are packed with their negatives but have none of their positives, unless you have a large Quick-Speak Inventory?

*Now they're angry, grumpy, sore—*
*'Spected me to know the score.*
*Realty is such a great big bore*
*'Less you know the in-ven-tore.*

## 7. Show buyers what they want to see.

No, we're not insulting your intelligence. We're hammering away at a point some agents find difficult to act on. If your buyers tell you they like simple, clean lines and can't stand gingerbread, don't show them a provincial for *any* reason, especially not any of these eight: (1) you know of one in their price range; (2) it has a $1,000 bonus to the selling office; (3) you promised the listing agent you'd show the house; (4) it's your listing; (5) you think it's cute; (6) it's on the way; (7) showing it will kill some time; (8) the provincial is one of the few listings you can drive to without getting lost.

If you can only show three houses meeting their general specifications, do it, and try for a later appointment when you'll be better prepared. Explain that you have other pressing business. This won't anger them, but wasting their time showing them the wrong kind of houses surely will if they've stated their preferences clearly.

*Tell me, have I nipped my greatest chance*
*On the easy closing to advance?*
*Oh, when all I want is just the fee,*
*Why so unreasonable must they be?*

## 8. Plan your parking technique.

Whenever you keyview a property, decide where you'll park when you bring customers to see it. When showing houses with good curb appeal, don't park right in front, or pull into the driveway. An important part of such a property's emotional impact is the prestige its street view conveys. Usually, the best vantage point to absorb that impact is from across the street. Approach the house from a direction that makes it natural to park across the street. Then sit in the car for a moment, looking at the house. Ask your buyers to pause, if they're about to scramble out, and look too. If the front view isn't inspiring, park right out front. If it's really bad, pull into the driveway. The Winning Scripts section has effective phrases for these situations.

## 9. Learn when to use (and not to use) the demonstration technique.

The demonstration of unique features must be a key element in your sales presentation, whether you're selling can openers or computers. But, when you're solving housing problems for customers, don't insist on demonstrating a house's details to buyers who aren't excited about its floor plan or location.

Beyond the basics of shelter and indoor plumbing, a house's most sales-worthy functions are in the emotional sphere, where they relate to prestige, comfort, and security. You can show the view from every window, and push a hound through every pet door; but unless the house taps the buyers' feelings, there's little chance it'll become their home.

If buyers are cool, don't delay the house-finding process by demonstrating the cute little goodies found there and risk turning the buyers into bye-sayers. Fees are not won by such methods. But if the basic house ignites their interest, then the skillful demonstration of neat details can fan the flame of interest into a red-hot offer.

Some buyers, however, are slow browsers. For them, crank every gimcrack in every house you show. Never mind your own impatience.

If your buyers browse like cows, help them chew all the grass. Try that with the fast-moving folk, though, and you'll soon find yourself back at the office wondering whether her headache was the real thing as they drive off.

Then there are the buyers who expect to be led like sheep. For the sheep and the cows, you must know the demonstration technique. Just don't try it on the fidgeters, and the scamperers, or you'll have a conflict you can't gain from. Flow with the buyers, and dance to their rhythm instead of trying to make them polka to your tune. Customers who want you to take a strong lead will say so, or will indicate this desire by sticking close to you instead of trotting off in every direction.

Here's how to assume the control necessary to demonstrate features. When entering a house, suddenly take a few quick steps ahead, turn to face your customers, spread your hands a little, and start talking confidently about a feature they can see from where they are standing. The feature may be an amenity you can physically demonstrate by turning a dial, opening a panel, or throwing a lever, or it may be a feature requiring an explanation before its full value can be understood. It will become easier to claim their attention each time you use this technique on a given couple—when you handle it right.

If you're telling them things they want to hear, if you're not pounding their ears when they want to quietly absorb a house's ambience, they'll listen because they know you're saying something interesting. But, if their attention is getting harder to seize each time, you're not being selective enough in choosing amenities for demonstration, or you're going into too much detail—for them—at that particular stage of their progress toward a house choice.

Speak briefly and to the point. In cases of doubt, don't demonstrate a feature or explain an additional point. They'll ask about whatever is important to them at their current level of interest in a given house. Avoid mentioning the obvious, and never chat about the obvious for the sole purpose of killing the quiet. If silence with a buyer troubles you, reread *Silence Is Golden* in the previous chapter.

Choosing a good position when you take your demonstration stance helps. Any break in the interior will do: a step between levels, a doorway, an open space between rooms. If they continue talking to each other (why should they instantly shut up?) wait, silently and without moving, until they conclude their exchange. Then say your piece, and move on. Your control will be intermittent, and will grow throughout the showing session if you don't try to maintain it in rooms and houses without anything worth demonstrating. If you feel compelled to dominate the entire showing session, consider joining the Marines; they still need a few good people for drill sergeants.

There's one time you'll want to demonstrate features even if you expect your buyers to have little interest in them. This is where you show your own listing and the sellers are at home. Prepare your buyers for this before they get out of your car.

"At this point, I know you're mainly interested in the overall picture, but the lady of this house will probably be home now, because she's expecting her children home from school. If she's there, and I don't tell you about a few of the improvements they've made here themselves, she'll be quite upset. Please bear with me this one time."

How can they refuse?

## 10. Go back to year one.

Buyers are interested in the area they're moving to, and giving them a little history subtly establishes you as an old-timer and an expert.

"Do you know that in 1900, the Iversons bought 50,000 acres here for a dollar an acre?" I ask my buyers.

There's history all over North America. I could go into any town, talk to some alert and knowledgeable agents about their area's early landowners, and then be able to tell an interesting tale in the car while I'm driving buyers from one house to another. And my buyers—anywhere—will be impressed. Mix a touch of history in with your discussion of recreational facilities, schools, shops, and churches. Knowledge of all these features is vital. Sell the area while you're touring it.

## 11. Don't show too many houses.

If you show buyers more than five or six houses the first time out, you're going to confuse them. They're not going to remember.

"Now was that the one with the blue tile roof or the red?" It all gets muddled in their minds.

## 12. Give the house a chance to speak.

Don't be afraid of silence. If your buyers aren't talking, it's a good sign. It means they're reacting on an emotional level with the house, and they have to do this to fall in love with the place. So be sure that your mouth isn't in motion purely to eliminate a silence because it frightens you. Don't be a talk-pest when people are making the intimate selection of their new home. This doesn't mean you don't say anything, it means you don't talk unless what you say will advance the sale.

## 13. Sell possibilities.

It was a plain little house; a box; no style. But its price was as high as the neat young couple I was showing it to could go. They wanted more but couldn't stretch their dollars. The place had no dining room. The dining area looked out on a grubby but fully fenced side yard where dogs had been kept. The house was vacant and the side yard was filled with junk. I told my buyers how easy it would be to replace the window with French doors, pave that sideyard, and create a romantic outdoor dining court.

"You've even got room for a fountain," I said.

They loved it. When we got back to the office, they immediately spoke of the house, "where we could have a dining court with a fountain." They bought the house. A few months later, they called up to rave about their dining court and invite me over to see it. They bought an idea—something that wasn't there—and then proceeded to install and enjoy it.

Train yourself to spot salable possibilities. You'll miss many opportunities if you only talk about what's there now. Possibilities no one else has seen are free. Sell them. It's a beautiful way to create genuine value to bridge the gap between what the sellers will take and what your buyers will give.

*Next time, next time, I'll surely know*
*All For Sales, and in the warm glow*
*Of great knowledge, hard won, will earn*
*So much silver I'll have to learn*
*New ways to spend, new sights to see*
*New joys to sing of with such deserv'd fee.*

## 14. Play the ace last?

Here's some practical psychology that often seems to work. Many agents swear by this system, but I use it selectively.

Play-the-ace-last calls for you to route customers first through the houses you think they'll like *least*. Then, after they've rejected a few properties, you take them to the house you've decided they'll like *best*.

This theory stands on two legs: (1) people feel better about making a *yes* decision after they've demonstrated control by saying *no* a time or two, and (2) your ace, the house you've picked to sell them, looks better by contrast to the others than it would have, had you shown it to them first.

In the beginning, I always placed the ace last—sometimes by accident—because I had to show people several houses to find out what they wanted. Then, when the right house for them popped into my head, I'd get excited and say, "Wait'll you see the next house I'm going to show you. I promise you it'll be the very best you'll see all day. It really fits your needs." This approach always worked fine because I built up enough rapport to carry it off before using it. When you have this rapport, people react with delight to your spontaneity, enthusiasm, and involvement. They appreciate your injection of excitement and fun into their big decision. If they're positive people, they'll react this way; if they're negative, go slow with the high excitement until you're sure it won't just make them more negative. Even now, I would show markedly negative people the homes I thought they'd find least attractive first, and save the best till last, so they could run their grouch-string out before getting down to business.

However, with normally pleasant to highly positive people, when you've reached the stage of knowledge, credibility, and confidence, where you immediately know the house they'll buy, why waste time? Show them the house they'll love first and tell them that's what you're doing. Then everything else they see just can't compare and, when they get tired of looking at can't-compares, you close them. But this stage of confidence takes a while to reach.

Later on, when you've perfected deep-dish qualifying, you can find out what buyers want in a hurry. When you have a Quick-Speak Inventory large enough to enable you to match them one-to-one with the right house, lead with your ace—if you have rapport and they're positive-thinkers. But always game-plan your people based on their personalities.

Play your hunches. It's how you develop reliable intuition about people. And in the beginning, unless you have a hunch to the contrary, show your buyers at least two other houses before you play your ace. You can show the ace in the middle of two or more can't-compares.

## 15. Steer clear of razzle dazzle.

It's always safer to give people information at a deliberate, friendly pace than to rattle off intricate details too fast for them to understand. Let them hurry you along—and feel superior and smart—rather than make them slow you down and feel inferior and stupid. When you spew out information faster than they can comprehend it, people think about—and resent—*you* instead of thinking about what you're telling them. They know you've drilled yourself on the data, and now you're showing off. Your methods are showing. You don't sound like someone who really cares about them. Slow down, relax, and smile. Make sure your listeners are listening. Make sure your words are turning prospects into customers, not turning customers into walk-aways.

## 16. Read their signals.

Buyers send messages to you constantly with body language even when they're not talking. You can't necessarily understand, or rely on, the words more than the unspoken signals. Both often conflict with other parts of their total message. Don't try to read their minds; don't evaluate them; but do ask courteous questions to clarify how they feel. And, when your questions reveal important contradictions, ask further questions to clarify their meaning, purpose, or preference. Be careful not to sound argumentative or superior. Soften your questions with phrases such as: "So I'll understand exactly what you mean, could you. . . ."

Hearing the meanings between their words—and reading their body language signals—will tell you more than some people will deliberately say to you at this stage. You are a professional devoted to putting the customers' welfare first. Keep thinking this as you watch their body language and listen to their words. It will help to foster the feeling in their minds that you are someone they can trust.

Folded arms indicate tension unless the person is feeling chilly. You may have moved too fast too soon, or invaded their comfort zone. The distance people want you to stand varies. Be sensitive to the bubble of private space most people need. Don't bear-hug everyone, but don't keep a ten-foot-pole distance from everyone either. Take your cue from their feelings. Time your approach to their comfort zone, rather than rigidly applying your own get-close, or stand-off, feelings to everyone.

When you detect signs your buyers' emotions are churning, proceed with caution to find out what's happening inside their heads. You may need to close them, pull back, or make some other move.

Smile a lot when you're with buyers. Cultivate a relaxed manner. Otherwise your tension infects them. After they've opened up, a little pat on the shoulder, and saying, "I'm going to take care of you," can work wonders at reassuring them.

Watching your buyers' facial expressions is vital. When you see a lot of confusion or a frown on the buyer's face, gently find out why. Watch for restlessness or you'll lose them. Restimulate them if possible. Be alert for boredom and move along if you detect it. When the customer interrupts, or becomes hostile, in many cases they're feeling the onset of buying fear.

Yawning can be a sign of fear too. Some people will yawn when they see the house they know they should buy, because now they're up against the big decision—and the pressure scares them.

Others will smile to conceal irritation. Excessive throat clearing or coughing can indicate fear, annoyance, hunger, boredom, or other causes. And, of course, the yawners can be tired, the smilers happy, and the coughers sick. The signals of body language, like words, are often spoken with a forked a tongue.

Be alert for signs of fatigue in buyers. Some buyers tire quickly from the emotional strain, and fatigue stops all positive thought. Be careful not to exhaust your buyers with an overload of information and hustle before you show them the house you think they'll love. Don't take them there so tired they can't react to it.

## 17. Create involvement.

The wife mentions a favorite grandfather clock, or the husband tells you his hobby is woodworking. Be alert for opportunities to ask the wife how her grandfather clock would look in this hall, or how well that garage would serve the husband's hobby needs.

## 18. Build from their emotional tone.

As you proceed with your showing presentation, buyers will either get excited about what you're showing them, or become discouraged. If you suspect discouragement, draw them out; don't allow them to suffer in silence. In my area, out-of-staters often say, "We didn't realize prices were so high out here. For this much money you get a mansion where we come from."

Turn their discouragement into enthusiasm by talking about lifestyle advantages. Winning Scripts (under *Lifestyle*) gives you some ideas.

## 19. Show bright.

Show buyers five properties initially, but be prepared to show more. Especially with the ready-to-buy-today prospects, mix other brokers' listings in with your showing of in-house listings. Unless you do, the buyers will realize you're only showing them one company's share of the market. Such actions tell them, loud and clear, "You better find another agent or you'll probably miss the best buy on the market." Don't be disloyal to your buyers' interests.

Take the most attractive routes to the various properties with your prospects. Relax with them, and enjoy their company. Talk about the community and the reason why it's a nice place to live. This is a tension-filled task at best (for your buyers too), so be as relaxed as you can.

If you're showing many properties, take breaks. If your buyers see more than five houses, all those properties start swimming together. Then it's time to suggest lunch or coffee.

Don't show more than five properties to buyers getting a "feel" for the area, but who are not in a financial position to buy today. Say this, "I would like to familiarize you with the area. I have selected a cross section of properties best suited to your range and needs. This will give you an opportunity to evaluate what you see today and make some decisions at home."

## 20. Be excited.

Be excited about your showing presentation. Say, "If you enjoyed the last property, I know I'm on the right track. So I'm really excited for you to see this next one." Be sincerely involved in the drama of fitting the clues together (like in a mystery story) between the proper home and your buyer.

Your initial goal should be to develop the ability to pick three to five homes that zero in on your buyers' needs during the qualifying interview. You need to be able to pick those homes and drive to them without searching through the Multiple Listing book or switching on the computer. You can soon reach this point by putting forth the necessary effort. Then your goal should be to raise your professional skills to the level where you can pick out and show *the* house, their future home, to buyers *first*. You'll never be able to choose *the* house every time, of course, but doing it at all takes a high degree of sensitivity and expertise. To hit it occasionally is an admirable, and highly profitable, talent—and the source of much satisfaction.

> *Now they're here, I have no choice.*
> *Could I claim I've lost my voice?*
> *Off we go till sun does set.*
> *You must know how far I'll get.*

## 21. Prepare your car.

Before your buyers arrive, wash your car and clean the inside. Also clean all your other problems out of your head. Nothing will help you more than having a fresh mind and a large Quick-Speak Inventory of houses, winning scripts, and streets.

Be prepared for people. Give each person one of your imprinted memo pads, and suggest that they keep notes for later evaluation. Have an extra amortization book in the car. CPAs, bankers, and engineers especially like to poke around among the tables of figures while you're driving around. Keep a few inexpensive games and toys in the trunk in case your buyers bring along children; keeping them happy and occupied will enhance your chances of selling to their parents.

## 22. Transform an argument.

Never get caught between a husband and wife having a disagreement. Of course that's easier said than done when they're disagreeing about what house to buy. Hearing from a third party often helps resolve the problem. To help, the agent takes the disagreement and rephrases it in a positive light.

Let's consider an argument that flares between Joe and Clare after you've shown them some houses.

*Clare:* I like the two-story, three-bedroom that needs work. The location is better, and we could easily repaper and paint some rooms.
*Joe:* I'm sick and tired of spending my weekends painting, papering, and fixing up when I could be relaxing. I like the little one-story four-bedroom with everything done. And it's cheaper than the pit you like.
*Clare:* You're plain crazy if you think I'll move into that stupid little phone booth.

(At this point you must become creative and, in an unbiased way, start getting through the problem. The way to solve any problem is to go through it. So you must start sorting. Check out the way to get through this murk.)
*Agent:* Now, as I understand this, Clare, you like to go in and put your own stamp on a home. You and Joe usually work together to renovate a property, is that correct? Good. Well, you must both have talent for that sort of thing. I'm all thumbs when it comes to taking something apart and putting it back together again.
*Clare:* Oh, we've done some marvelous work on the houses we've lived in, haven't we Joe?
*Joe:* Yeah.
*Agent:* Sounds like you're really talented, Joe.
*Joe:* Well, I'm probably the best darn wallpaper hanger in town—and the least willing.

*Clare:* Joe's really done some very nice work.

(Notice that we are trying to restore some affinity and admiration between them. That's step one. Step two is finding the path to the solution.)

*Agent:* Now, you have two choices here. First of all, you could renovate the two-story, something you're both good at, or you could move into the house that doesn't need quite as much work. Is there some special reason, Joe, why you don't want to tackle another project right now?

*Joe:* Yeah, there sure is. I'm sick of fix-up work. I'm good at it—but it just takes too much time, and I want to start playing a little golf and enjoying life. Heck, I'm 45.

*Agent:* Have you ever considered doing this for people who aren't as talented? You and Clare could start a business.

*Clare:* Well, that's a thought. But Joe, are you really getting tired of it?

*Joe:* Yeah, Clare, I am. Maybe you'd like to start playing golf with me.

*Clare:* I hate golf.

*Joe:* Well, I know you like to play tennis, and so do I. With the money we'd save on that smaller home, we could travel more. Remember, you said you wanted to go to Tahiti.

*Clare:* Oh, Joe, could we?

Now the solution is in sight. By remaining neutral and maintaining a professional attitude, the agent changed an argument into a discussion. Then the agent could act as the discussion's moderator. By staying cool and by looking for ways to renew their good feelings about each other, the agent toned their anger down and got them back to the business at hand.

If you can't do this, you're almost certain to lose bickering couples as prospects. Stepping in, finely and calmly, at least gives you a chance to save the situation and your opportunity for a fee. Whenever I'm working with a couple who aren't getting along, I always try to get them talking about something good that exists between them. Even if there's no argument, two good openers are: "Tell me how you met" and "How long have you been married?" Once they're talking about the good old days you can cut right through the core of their problem and drum up a solution that pleases everyone.

## 23. When they're too agreeable.

Your buyers love everything. It's driving you frantic. How can you deal with it?

First, recognize that their excess of good feeling is because (1) they can't afford what you're showing them; or (2) they desperately want everyone, including their agent, to love them. So they just can't bring themselves to tell you what they dislike about the properties you're showing them.

It's almost always one or the other. If love-need seems unlikely, probe deeper into their finances. If you continue to work with them, they're going to be taking up lots of time—so find out if you're drilling a dry hole. Of course you found out what they claim their financial situation is during the qualifying interview. Go back and examine your notes intensely. Call people where they come from. Run a credit check on them. It's cheaper, and less frustrating, than continuing to work under a cloud. Set up a confidential lender interview.

With people who seem to need everyone's love, you'll need to show a touch of displeasure when they avoid making decisions. If this doesn't work, have increasingly blunt discussions with them—over a period of a few days—and either bring them to a decision or send them on their way.

# More Good Ideas

Choose competent agents to associate with, and exchange information about houses of special interest. Working with buyers will cause you to miss caravan days occasionally, so develop contacts who can quickly fill you in on the newly listed houses you should check out on your own.

When your buyers live nearby, if they're comfortable with the idea, see their present home. Ask them what they like and dislike about the dwelling. Notice their favorite colors and the furniture they'll take with them to the home they're going to buy through you. Sometimes you'll want to measure some of their furniture. Take notes on your clipboard.

Possessing this information about their lifestyle (but only if they welcome your interest) will give you a strong hold on their loyalty, and enable you to quickly steer them to the best house available for their needs. Be very professional as you gather this information so you never seem nosy.

# L.A. to Seattle, and the Loyalty of Buyers

Whenever I think about loyalty, or the lack of it, that buyers display toward us worthy, hard-working agents, I'm reminded of a scene I witnessed. I was catching a plane for Seattle at Los Angeles International

Airport right after Thanksgiving. I was flying north to present a training seminar. In the LAX terminal that afternoon there were a lot of college kids going back to school. I noticed one young couple embracing and carrying on with all of young parting's sorrow. He was going to Seattle; she was staying in Los Angeles. I felt sad for them. It reminded me of my college days, and of all the tears shed when I used to say goodbye to my sweetheart as he went one way and I went another. I felt like walking up to them and saying, "Don't worry. Before you know it, all the pain will be over. You'll be married, you'll have kids and house payments—and everything will be peachy."

I got on the plane and watched the young man I'd felt sorry for. When we landed at Seattle, he walked ahead of me toward the terminal. I figured he'd crawl out, weighted down with sadness because his girlfriend was still in Los Angeles. All of a sudden, I noticed he had this little spring in his step. I decided to follow the guy into the Seattle terminal.

And there, waiting for Mr. Sad-Down-South, stood a beautiful blonde. They hugged and kissed, and were so happy to see each other. I wanted to yell, "Hey, wait a minute, his girlfriend's back in Los Angeles!"

Buyers are the same way, and they can't help it either. So just take it as a fact of life when they're motivated and it's hurting, you better be working, because if you don't handle their needs somebody else will.

# Selling the Navarros: A Role Play in One Act

Cast:    Manager
         Danny, the agent
         Mary Navarro
         Jack Navarro

This role play is to be read by four people at an office meeting for training purposes. If all four members of the cast have copies of this book, no rehearsal is required. The manager or broker conducting the meeting obtains volunteers to play the other three parts, and reads the manager's role himself or herself. The agent may be a man or a woman.

Props required: three chairs, arranged to represent the front and back seats of an agent's car. Comments to be made directly to the audience are enclosed in parentheses (like this). Stage directions [enclosed in brackets like this] are not to be spoken.

*Manager:* (The time is 11 A.M. Our agent, Danny, has just finished a fine qualifying interview with Jack and Mary Navarro, played for us today by _____ and _____. As the action starts, Danny and the Navarros are ready to go out and see property. Five houses are on Danny's show list. Appointments have been made to show four of the houses. At the fifth house, no one answered.)

[Danny and the Navarros enter from the side and walk toward the three chairs set up to represent the car.]

*Danny:*  Here are copies of the show list, and memo pads. [Hands a set to Mary, and then a set to Jack.] You can make notes on the houses if you care to.

I'm certainly happy that you've given me the opportunity to show you our town today and hopefully, to serve you in the manner that you're accustomed to. I'd like to ask both of you a favor before we begin. [Pauses.]

*Jack:*  What is it, Danny?

*Danny:*  Well, I'm a real estate agent, but I'm also a human being with the same needs you have. I own a home, and I had to look for property when I first moved to this area, just like you're doing. I wasn't in real estate then. Anyway, I remember how disheartening it was to look at homes that were too much money, or too far from my taste—and then go back to the motel discouraged. I hated to say anything to the agent for fear I'd hurt his feelings because I knew he was excited about the properties he was showing, and he thought they were special. [Pauses.]

*Jack:*  So what are you saying?

*Danny:*  I just want you to know, although I took a lot of information from you at the office, and sense what you need in a home, I'm never really sure until I get some "audience reaction," as I like to call it. It's sort of like the opening of a play—you never know how it will turn out until you read the reviews. So, if I am on the right track and you like what I am showing you, great. But, if I'm off track, please do me a favor and tell me—when the seller isn't present—or in the car. I can change my game plan fast. And I'm not the owner of any of these properties, so there's no way you can hurt my feelings. I'm interested in what you feel, think, and want. Please promise me you'll confide in me.

*Mary:*  Of course we will, Danny. You seem anxious to please.

*Danny:*  I am. [Makes car-starting motions and noises.]

*Manager:*  (Danny, of course, has carefully thought out the best route to each property.)

*Mary:*  How are the schools here, Danny?

*Danny:*  We'll be looking at homes in two school districts. My children have been in one district for the last eight years, and I'm very pleased.

The other district has also established an excellent reputation. I've visited both district offices, and they seem very similar. I have clients and close friends with children in the other district, and I get good reports about those schools. And I followed the reports of the college board exams of kids out of both districts. They've scored high on college preparation.

*Jack:* Sounds like you keep informed.

*Danny:* I have to, or I wouldn't be doing my job. Real estate agents have a deeper responsibility to their people than just showing homes. I can tell you about good doctors, lawyers, gardeners—almost any service you might need later. Just ask me, or call—anytime.

*Mary:* Oh, I'm glad to hear that. I hate like heck to give up my pediatrician. I just love him—and my two-year-old does too.

*Danny:* Well, our kids love Dr. Zwillig. I'll give you his number when we get back to the office.

*Manager:* (Danny parks across the street from the property because it has curb appeal.)

*Danny:* [Raises arm as though to open car door and pauses, staring across the street. Jack and Mary follow their agent's gaze.] Well, this is our first showing. I pick out homes with pride of ownership whenever possible. This one is clean and neat and a delight to show. It may not be right for you though, so please let me know. Don't forget our agreement. [Gets up, making motions of opening car door. Mary and Jack follow, as Danny walks ahead of couple to the front door.]

*Manager:* (Have your lock-box key handy, and a card ready to leave at the property. Keep cards in a side pocket of your blazer or suit, or in an easy access area of your purse, ladies.)

*Danny:* The owner said she was leaving. [Makes knocking motions.] We'll just give it a moment to make sure we're not disturbing her.

[Danny turns toward lawn area and looks through Jack and Mary. This causes them to turn around also.]

*Danny:* Lovely front yard, isn't it?

*Jack:* Someone here has a green thumb.

*Danny:* Everyone has a green thumb in this county. Nothing to it. Automatic sprinklers. The sun's free. Just throw ten bucks worth of fertilizer on the lawn now and then. Well, I guess she's not here. [Uses lock-box key to open door.]

[The Navarros walk slowly into the house as Danny holds the door open, closes it, and then walks quickly—but smoothly, around them to get in front. Danny pauses, and looks in all four directions. The Navarros stop and imitate her four-corner glance.]

*Jack:* [Tentatively.] Nice place.

*Mary:* It's not bad.

*Danny:* Follow me. I'll take you through the living areas first.

*Manager:* (Danny leads the buyers through the house, walking with a confident stride that's not too fast, not too slow. The stage has been beautifully set at this house. The lights are on, and music is playing softly.)

*Danny:* As we go. I'll point out a few things you might not otherwise notice. The owner tells us this carpeting was installed just six months ago; it has over 9/16-inch rubber padding. It's in perfect condition, don't you think?

*Mary:* It's beautiful.

*Manager:* (Now our agent takes the buyers down the hall and steps aside to let the Navarros go into the bedrooms. So no one feels crowded, our agent remains in the hall.)

[Danny stands back as though holding a door knob; Jack and Mary take a few steps and then stand, looking about.]

*Danny:* Though you'd never know it, due to the excellent craftsmanship, this master suite has a new bathroom. The large Jacuzzi tub is an addition, and so is the matched pair of basins. Aren't they neat features?

*Mary:* Yes, they are.

*Jack:* It drives me up the wall to share a single basin with Mary. Double basins are an absolute must for us.

*Danny:* Okay, I'll make a mental note of it—and I'm going to scratch the next house on the list because it has a very small bath in the master suite—no chance to add the second basin as these people have done.

*Jack:* Yeah, scratch it—let's not waste time.

*Danny:* Did you notice the large walk-in closet?

*Mary:* [She looks.] Yes, it's sure big.

*Manager:* (Throughout the showing our agent has been alert for any sign of impatience, or for any sign of desire to linger. The pace of the showing has been matched to the couple's natural rhythm of absorbing and reacting. Our agent has maintained a good balance of silence between brief comments on the less-obvious amenities this particular house contains. Then, after they've seen the whole interior, our agent pops the question.)

*Danny:* I'm eager to hear your feelings about the basic floor plan and the color scheme here.

*Jack:* It's a very nice home, Danny, but it's too small for us. I can't stand a family room off the kitchen, because it means I have to listen to the dishwasher every time I catch a game on TV.

*Mary:* Jack, I like having the family room right off the kitchen because I can watch Tim and Cindy play in there while I'm getting dinner.

*Jack:* But I hate the noise.

*Danny:* How about taking a quick peek at the yard now? We can discuss family rooms in the car. I have some thoughts about them.

*Manager:* (Why take them back to see the yard now? Because Mary likes the house, and Jack may decide later to let Mary have her way on the family room since she's there all week, but he's only home on the weekends. Then our agent can say, "Remember? It had a very nice yard, too.")

[Danny leaves a business card, and they quickly go through the motions of leaving the house. At the door, they pause while Danny makes exaggerated—but fast—lock box gestures. Then the three of them get back in the car.]

*Danny:* [Making car-starting motions.] Now, let's think about this. Mary, you like the family room off the kitchen, and Jack likes some privacy. How about using a fourth bedroom for a combination den and guest room? Jack could put a TV in there and have a place to call his own. And Mary, we'll find you a floor plan with at least a small family area off the kitchen.

*Mary:* Great. But is there such a beast in our price range?

*Danny:* There sure is. I was going to show you one just before lunch, but now I'm excited about that house because I see you have a specific need for it. What do you say we go over there right now? Jack—is it okay?

*Jack:* Sure. But, listen—I like the idea of the den, but I'm less than happy about the idea of also using it as a guest room.

*Mary:* Jack, how often do we have anyone stay over? About twice a year?

*Jack:* But the double bed and your sewing machine and the stuff in our fourth bedroom takes up all the space.

*Danny:* Instead of having a double bed taking up space all year, how about selling it and using the money to buy a convertible sofa? They have reasonably priced ones now that fold down fast to very comfortable beds.

*Mary:* I'd put my sewing stuff in the family room so you could have a nice, private den, Jack.

*Danny:* It's astonishing how cheap portable TV sets are these days.

*Jack:* I'm not too big on small screens.

*Mary:* At least you could always see what you want. Old softie here always lets the kids watch their programs except for football.

*Jack:* Well, getting a small TV is a thought. How much would you guess a fairly good convertible sofa would cost, Danny?

*Danny:* I don't have to guess. They start at _____ [ad-libs a current sofa price]. I have a couple of brochures in the trunk about the convertible sofas our local furniture shops carry.

*Jack:* You're a traveling encyclopedia. Danny.

*Danny:* Just part of my complete service. [Danny makes parking motions, then looks intently to the left.] There it is, folks. Take a careful look, because I really feel it's your next home.

[All three stare to the left with great interest.]

*Manager:* (Our agent has made this house-hunting expedition exciting by reacting quickly to clues about what will make these buyers buy. The vital element is knowing the inventory well enough to make quick choices.)

*Jack:* [Doubtfully.] Does it have double wash basins?

*Danny:* Sure does.

*Jack:* How much are they asking for it?

*Danny:* [Ad-libs a current price for a four-bedroom-with-family-room home in your locality.]

*Jack:* Will they take less?

*Danny:* I know they'll take the price I mentioned. Anything less I'm perfectly willing to present to the sellers, and work with them to negotiate an agreement both parties will feel good about.

*Jack:* But what's your feel for it? Do you think they're soft?

*Danny:* I wouldn't think so. This house just came on the market, and it's priced right—

*Jack:* [Interrupts] It's priced right, huh?

*Danny:* Definitely. So we really shouldn't look at it with the idea of buying it for less. It's a very sound value as priced.

*Jack:* Can you back that statement up?

*Danny:* Absolutely.

*Mary:* Guys, I'm dying to see the inside. Let's not sit here all day.

[Mary gets out of the car. Danny and Jack follow her, still talking.]

*Jack:* I don't mean back the price up with a list of numbers on a printout. I want to see some of the houses you feel justify this price.

*Danny:* No problem. I can drive you right to several that will.

*Jack:* Yes, I'll bet you can. I get the impression you know what you're doing.

*Danny:* Jack, I have to—for my own self-respect. Real estate is heavy stuff. The decisions are very important to the people who make them. I treat this business as a very serious matter.

*Jack:* It shows.

[They arrive at the front door.]

*Danny:* I didn't get an answer when I called here, but the lady is very neat, so I'm sure she left it nice. Do you mind waiting here at the door just for a minute while I run in and turn on some lights and open the drapes? I'd love for you to get a good first impression.

[Danny hustles around, making light-switching and drape-opening motions.]

*Mary:* Okay—but hurry. Danny can't hear us right now. Jack, what do you think? Could this be it?

*Jack:* Could be. This neighborhood gives me a good feeling.

*Mary:* Can we swing it?

*Jack:* Listen, we wouldn't be here if we couldn't. We're with an agent who's loaded for bear.

*Mary:* I'm so excited.

*Danny:* Come in—come in.

[Spreads hands wide as Jack and Mary walk forward, and gestures in time to] Ta ta ta *ta*—BOOM.

[Mary and Jack take a few steps forward, stop, and look around.]

*Mary:* I love it. I love it.

*Jack:* Not bad. Not bad at all. Where's my den?

# Winning Scripts

## Lifestyle

Here's how to turn house hunters' discouragement into enthusiasm:

*New-to-the-sunbelt-buyer:* We never dreamed we'd have to pay so much for such a little house in this area.

*Agent:* I understand how you feel. I'm from a colder climate too, and I thought the same thing when I first came here. Then I discovered it doesn't matter as much as I thought it would. You see, you don't want so much space inside because the accent here is on the outside. No one else has a huge house either. Our warm sun just pulls you outdoors constantly. Before you know it, you'll find yourself sailing on the lake in January wearing a swimsuit, or playing tennis in shorts in February—without giving it a second thought. And your kids won't spend as much time indoors anymore, so they don't need large bedrooms.

Natives should say, "I understand how you feel because so many people say the same thing when they first come here. Then, before you know it, they're in the swing of things here and saying it doesn't matter anymore because—"

Reverse the reasoning if your buyers are coming the other way.

*New-to-cold-climate buyer:* I'm not used to these huge rooms. I don't know if I want the hassle of keeping this much space clean.

*Agent:* On our cold winter days, you'll be glad to have the extra room so the children can get out from under your feet and play games indoors to keep from getting bored. And, of course, they can always learn to keep their own space tidy. It's easier to do it when they aren't cramped.

## Park Across the Street

"Doesn't this home make a fine impression from the street?"

"Wouldn't it be fun to have your guests see this impressive front when they drive up?"

"Doesn't this home give you a good feeling of strength and stability, just looking at it from across the street?"

"This home seems to say to the world, 'Important and cultured people live here.' Do you get this feeling too?"

"They've taken great pride of ownership in this particular home, haven't they?"

"You have to get inside to appreciate the real charm (the secret, the fine quality, the emotional appeal, the many features, the outstanding value) of this one."

## Crossed Arms as a Buying Sign

Go gently. Pretend you are mentally removing one arm, and then the other, from the crossed position. Try a smile and say, "I see a little glimmer of hope in your eyes. Could it be that I've struck oil?" Humor is the best tension-breaker.

## When You Haven't Excited Your Buyers

People always respond to honesty, or to your admission of a mistake. When the houses you select don't excite the buyers, say, "I'd like another crack at this. My houses today weren't what you like, so please let me select a few more, because now I have a better understanding of your needs."

## New Home Competition

"Before I make a decision. I want to look at new homes."

This happens frequently in areas where new tract homes, or semi-custom (speculative) houses are available directly from the builders.

Here's the medicine.

"I certainly understand your desire to look at new property. Please feel free to do so, because I want you to have total peace of mind when you make your purchase, especially if it's with me. However, keep in mind the home you're considering with me has approximately _____ thousand dollars worth of landscaping improvements (the owner gave me these figures) and the work was done five years ago, so you can imagine what the cost to reproduce the outside of their home would be today.

Also, be sure to include in the price comparison the carpeting and drapes and, of course, the extra mirrors, paneling, wallpaper and so on you'll be getting here. In the resale all this work is in. It's part of the purchase price, and included in the new loan you'd be getting. But on the new home, all those improvements will be additional cash out of your pocket. And be prepared to live with dirt and dust for a while. I know some folks who didn't have carpeting laid until the initial landscape was in because they hated to get their new carpets and drapes full of dust and dirt. I tell you these things not to discourage you, but to give you some reality on what a new home involves, as opposed to a resale home.

Look at these issues carefully—not only at the cost of improvements but also the time and trouble involved in putting them all in."

If you are a resale salesperson selling new tract homes for a builder, as well as resales, turn it around, "I know you're considering a resale home, but keep in mind this new home has never been lived in. It will truly be yours to decorate and landscape in the colors and ways you feel fits your family, rather than being stuck with someone else's choices. Your new home will have the unique touch only you two can create. It will be an original because you are the original owners. It may take a little longer, but don't you always have to wait for quality? Your new home is worth waiting for because you can be assured it's what you want."

## Ask These Questions at the Right Time

"Are you presently working with another agent?"

"Is there anything I could do to better serve you; perhaps something that isn't being handled right now with any other agent you are working with?"

"I want to serve you so well you won't feel any need to go to another agent in this area. I can't help you in all areas of the county, but this area is my specialty. It really is easier if you have one person you can count on for everything in each area. Otherwise, you may feel confused and torn in your loyalties. That takes energy away from house hunting. I really want to fill all your needs. Is this possible, do you think?"

"Tell me about yourself. Do you spend a lot of time in your home? Are you goers on the weekends? Do you prefer just being home and having projects and hobbies around the house? I want to know as much as I can, so I can better serve you."

"Describe your color scheme inside your present home. Do you want to repeat those colors in your next home?"

"What's the outside of your present home like? colonial? contemporary? I don't know about you, but when people think of me they see country and oak and tiny windows. What do you think your friends see when they picture you and your home?"

"I wish I could see your home. It would help me get into your skin and be you for awhile. It would increase my awareness of how I can serve your important housing needs."

"How am I doing? Am I on the right track? Are you disappointed at what we have done together so far, or pretty satisfied?"

## Know Where Buyers Stand

Always confront the buyers along the way so you know where you stand. Don't ever be afraid to confront the truth.

"I'm really enjoying our time together. Please don't hesitate to point out anything you feel I've forgotten to inform you about."

"Let me tell you about our wonderful school system here." (Use the sales speech you prepared for this purpose.)

"Let me tell you about the convenient shopping we have here."

"Let me tell you about the terrific access to freeways (highways, the interstate) this area has."

"Do you like sports and athletics? Here's a schedule of what's going on at the local (YMCA recreation center, public park)."

"We have some great night life just minutes (miles, hours) away. Here's a list of some of our best nearby restaurants."

List all the amenities your area offers and write winning declarations similar to the ones just given, to be used when qualifying and working with buyers. This is all great glue to laminate buyers to you.

"I'm going to take real good care of you two."

"I know everything on the market around here, so you can be absolutely sure I'll show you every house you'd be interested in owning."

## Overly Talkative and Reactive

Your buyers may be nervous about their coming change. This occurs frequently with the first-time buyer.

"Do you think we'll qualify? I've only been on this job a year, and my wife just got her degree."

Try to make them feel safe about their decision. "Now listen here, guys, I wouldn't do a thing to harm you and every step of the way I'll make sure that this is right for you. Remember we've already figured what you can afford on the Lender Qualifier form. We have respected loan people to assist you, too."

# CHAPTER 17

# Closing Those Golden Nuggets Before They Turn into Lead

The Natural Close Is the Greatest Close ● Closing Craft ● There Are Limits to Closing ● When to Shut Off Your Yak ● What Is the Seller's Motivation? ● When You Sell One Spouse or Partner First ● Three New Things You Said ● Add a New Facet to Your Powers of Persuasion ● Do You Take This House in Rain and in Sleet? ● Ten Tips on Obtaining Salable Offers That Stick ● Winning Closing Scripts

Unless we can close—unless we can bring about a situation where the customer will make, and carry out, a buying decision—success in real estate will elude us. Effective closing isn't a clutch of verbal traps to force people into decisions they don't want to make. Salespeople create this unprofitable situation for themselves by failing to qualify buyers thoroughly, and by failing to fully understand their customers' needs, desires, and capabilities.

I've already talked about closing in many chapters in this book, in fizzbo, listing, and prospecting. In this chapter, we're going to work on the classic closing situation: getting the buyers' name on the line, and separating them from their earnest money.

The agents I see creating the most trouble for themselves are the ones who regard buyers and sellers as adversaries to be defeated. Certainly, some customers are disloyal, eager to take unfair advantage, careless of our time, and unaware of our rights as persons. But we must remember the situation most people are in when they make real estate decisions: suddenly they are dealing with sums of enormous size compared to their usual decisions. They are frightened. Be charitable. Learn to be genuinely warm-hearted and kindly toward your clients. Cherish the concept of serving their needs first in order to serve yourself well, but second. Never think of sellers and buyers as enemies. Your life becomes a war if you decide to make war. You can also decide to make peace. You can act on a firm resolve to serve your buyers to the best of your abilities in spite of whatever quirks their natures have.

This attitude is never more helpful than in closing. Unless you are in tune with your buyers, and working for them, you won't be able to take advantage of the natural close.

# The Natural Close Is the Greatest Close

A natural close is just part of the big picture. First you build rapport with your buyers, then you talk money and quality before you show the property with light-hearted skill. Next you balance the good points against the bad points as you fill out a buyer's net sheet. You call the listing agent to get the feel for the sellers' motivation, and end with, "I don't know about you guys, but I think this must be the place."

*This* is the natural close. It's as natural as going to sleep when you're tired, eating when you're hungry, and buying a home when you need shelter. This close occurs by itself when you follow all the natural steps leading to it. You don't wait to build rapport until after you write up an offer; you don't write up a purchase agreement before you show the property.

The natural close is a powerful performer because it respects the buyers' needs and concerns. The only reason agents have trouble with it is they get impatient—they try to put the roof on before they're through pouring the foundation. The natural close is the greatest close when you take it step by step. You simply do all the things you're supposed to do; and you do them thoroughly, skillfully, and at the right moments. The natural close is *you* being *you*, loving what you do, and knowing what to do. It's combining your knowledge with the needs and wants of people who are just like you and me.

# Closing Craft

The agents who can bring people to a decision about a home are the agents who believe in what they're doing. They feel certain their buyers will benefit, personally and financially, by taking their help and advice on real estate matters. These agents believe in their own worth, and believe their job is important to the continuing prosperity and security of their country. If you don't believe this, convince yourself. If you can't convince yourself, find another line of work. Your disbelief—by robbing you of all pride and joy in your work—will ring through to the buyers, where it will multiply your problems twenty times.

When I first began in the business, I wasn't really proud to be selling real estate. It was the only way I could think of to make more money than I'd spend on babysitters, and still have time to mother my four small children and the fifth who was on the way. I didn't know about the outstanding people who had dedicated their lives to selling real estate, and to creating a better work environment in the industry. I wasn't aware such people existed. I didn't know they were giving generously of their time in political action committees, and at state and local levels of real estate jurisdictions. I thought most agents were too pushy. I was simply selling real estate as a stepping stone to something else I hadn't even thought of yet. You have a conflict when you feel this way about a job, whether or not you're aware of it. You subconsciously feel guilty because you're doing something you don't believe in. Unconsciously, you rationalize ways to be less effective and to be less than totally committed. Perhaps you even question whether you're leading people astray by selling them property, instead of knowing that their purchase, on your recommendation, will ultimately increase their net worth and immediately increase their well-being.

The sharp edge of doubt cuts deepest on what should be the closing stroke. This is when all our guilt comes crashing down, blocking our path to a smooth close.

Agents who fall into this category frequently make the following mistakes:

- Doubting agents fail to see opportunities to close. This means they never sell anything, although they will allow people to buy from them if the buyers are sufficiently anxious to do so.
- Doubting agents may get this sort of reply from a feeble attempt to close:
    **Buyer:** I'll have to think about this. And I want to talk to my sister—she knows quite a lot about real estate.
    **Doubting Agent:** (with relief, because now he can go home) Can't say I blame you. Go ahead. Think on it. I'll call you in the morning.
  At best, Doubting Agent may say: Well, what is it you want to sleep on? Can't we bring your sister down here, and discuss this together?

- Doubting agents can't close even though they have all the proper closing statements memorized. But, these fine words are delivered without heart, conviction, or drive. Doubting agents won't close in a closing situation simply because they're saying one thing while all their nonverbal language shouts the opposite. If the buyers like the house well enough, they will go to another broker because they need to be told they're doing a wise thing with sincere, unfaked conviction. The agent who convinces the buyers that *he* believes they should buy will sell them.

Every active agent will frequently encounter situations where people want to buy a house they should not buy, where the agent must advise against the purchase in question, or even against any purchase at all. But apply doubt selectively, and don't project your own internal uncertainties into other people's lives.

Belief in what you're doing must come from within yourself, but it is the product of what you choose to put into your mind. Retailing bad news is a giant industry. If you're hooked on it, if you insist on your daily fix of worldwide disaster, don't be surprised if your lack of optimism costs you a bundle. You can also choose to look for the brighter side of the news. It's a little harder to find, because it doesn't sell as well as bad news, but it's there. Being an optimistic realist is as valid as being a pessimistic realist because prediction is always very chancy.

The buyers' ability to carry the investment in question is established in the qualifying interview. This leaves only one doubt to be resolved: Have you shown them every valid solution to their housing problem? Any valid solution must be a reasonable compromise of their preferences and dislikes, and be available within their price range. Once you've convinced yourself they've seen every valid solution to their housing problem, you'll feel good about heartily recommending the purchase of their choice.

When buyers see in your eyes and actions:

- well-meaning intentions,
- the conviction you have their best interests at heart,
- confidence in your own expertise,
- and confidence in your own worth as a person,

your closing scripts will carry tons of persuasion—and they'll work! The same words, spoken with no genuinely felt conviction, won't even carry ounces of persuasion—and they'll fail every time.

# There Are Limits to Closing

There are limits to closing beyond which it's not wise to go. Here are some cases:

- When your buyers have listed their present home for sale and must sell it to buy, and you know the house-sale contingency isn't acceptable in your community on offers.
- When the husband and wife are deeply upset with each other, and you must pit one against the other in order to close them. Wait it out. It's far better to remain friends with them both, and let them straighten out their marital situation at home.
- Overly excited people who are easy to close. "Everything is wonderful!" they gush and "money is no problem."

They're ready to sign after one session in the car with you. Always suspect the easy ones. One time I did have a miracle occur, as they do now and then with the easy-come, easy-fallouts. On a Sunday morning, one of my sellers called. A couple driving by, completely new to our area, saw the sign in front, went up to the door, and were shown the house by the sellers. They loved it.

"Call your agent, and tell her to bring a purchase agreement over here; we want to buy it."

I was deeply suspicious. Believe me, when you're one of the walking wounded, you're suspicious. So I went over there rather reluctantly, purchase agreement in hand. (I was a three-year veteran salesperson when this happened. Had I been new, I would've expected this one to be easy. Then, when it went "thunk," I would've been crushed. But, thank goodness, experience teaches us not to celebrate until the check is in hand, and the closing statement is delivered.) As I went through the qualifying interview in the presence of the sellers, alarm bells were ringing in my head.

After the buyers approved the purchase agreement and left, I told the sellers it was highly unusual to sell so easily. "Don't pop the bubbly yet, because our buyers have to meet strict loan qualifying rules." The sellers, of course, just felt I was being overly cautious (like new salespeople feel when their broker tries to convince them to use the Buyer's Analysis for Better Service form *before* they show property). In this case, the buyer's credit had been very bad, and there were a lot of job change problems. I never worked so hard for a transaction, but we did finally close this one.

However, more times than not, overly excited buyers who drop out of nowhere and instantly fall in love with a home need to be checked out the closest. Of course, you can always run into a dream situation, but please regard them strictly as icing on the cake.

- When they need to borrow money from relatives—who aren't with them—in order to purchase the property. Such buyers always say, "No problem. Our relatives will love it."

  Tell your buyers, "I'm positive your Uncle Arnold and Aunt Matilda will adore this place, and want you to have it, but let's get them in on this now, before we involve the sellers in our excitement." Keep the pressure on your buyers to do what they must do before they can buy.

- When only one partner is present. This often happens when half of the couple comes out to start a new job, and the other remains behind in their old home. Put a contingency in the purchase agreement: the offer is subject to the missing partner's approval within a stated period, perhaps five or ten days. Make the sellers and their agent aware they have nothing firm until Big Mama sees the house and says *yes*. It doesn't matter how often Pop tells you she'll be crazy about it.

- When they have an appointment with another broker or two after you. They love one of the houses you've shown them, but they have a hang-up. In the past, they've always bought a house in each new area they've been transferred to from the first agent they've worked with. Then they never stop worrying that they might've missed a better buy. This time they've vowed to keep their other appointments.

"But we're really excited about this house, and we don't want to run the risk of losing it while we're looking around."

Tell them to submit an offer through you calling for their final decision within 48 hours. This will put them under some obligation to you, and also allow them to ease their curiosity about other properties.

In this situation, many agents try to talk the buyers out of keeping their other appointments by saying something like, "Do you really feel it's necessary to see the other agents? I'm a Multiple Listing agent. I can show you any property another agent can show you. May I ask if you feel I'm doing a good job for you?"

If you know the inventory well, and did a professional job of matching their needs to it, how much chance is there another agent can show them a better house? You destroy your credibility by applying too much pressure now, especially if they say they won't buy any house you showed them through anyone else. Insisting they don't need to check with another agent will convince many buyers that they'd be stupid not to.

Also, some people can't handle much pressure in a straightforward way. Push them hard and they'll sign an offer and give you an earnest money check. Then they'll hustle out to look at houses with other agents. If they find something they like better, you'll get a message canceling the offer they placed through you, an offer the sellers have accepted in the meantime. The only certainty in the resulting havoc is a lot of trouble for you in coping with it. Closing is much more than merely getting an offer and earnest money. Closing is building enough conviction in your buyers' minds to carry them through to the settlement of the transaction.

The limits you must consider when you close are the following:

- Is the buyers' situation financially sound?
- Will your close merely create a temporary sale that's certain to fall out? Show me a salesperson who pushes too hard, and I'll show you someone with a phenomenal cancellation rate who is getting more bitter and pushy every week.
- Do the buyers really like the home, or are they the type of people who'll say anything to get out from under the pressure of decision making?
- Do they like you?
- Do you like them?
- Have you done a thorough job, or are you simply hungry for a sale?
- Are you handling too many customers at once? For example, do you need to move on to your next appointment, so you try to speed up people who think slower than you do?
- Do they really want it, but you know it will be detrimental to them at this time?

With hard work and creative financing, I was able to get Max and Tina into their first home. During the following year, the appreciation rate was sensational, and they got the move-up itch. Max and Tina called me over to determine what their net would be if they decided to sell. We were all impressed with the figure, but they were a one-income family, and his take-home pay hadn't increased enough to carry the larger house they liked. They were eager to move up in the community although Max was getting bored with his job, and a promotion to another area was a possibility. I knew I could list their home, and also sell them the move-up, but I also knew Max and Tina would be stretched too tight for safety in the larger house. I felt this situation was outside the limits, and refused to close them. I said what had to be said as nicely as I could, and left them feeling unhappy. Six months later I did list and sell their house when Max got a healthy raise and a transfer to an area with less expensive housing. I missed one transaction with Max and Tina, but I gained many more elsewhere because of the faith I gained in myself by doing what I knew was right for them. There's no better investment than in your own integrity.

# When to Shut Off Your Yak

Knowing when to stop talking is one of the most valuable sensitivities an agent can develop. Some agents are blabber-junkies with a $40,000-a-year habit. They're terrific closers. The problem is, they're also terrific reopeners. A cure for their loose lips would make more money for these agents than anything else could. Excessive talking can be caused by anything from simple high spirits to deep-seated anxieties. Cures range from validations (see Chapter 27) and in-depth review of one's goals and capabilities, to professional counseling and therapy.

Most of us don't have such a deep-seated chatter problem. We just talk too much part of the time. *Shut off your yak* means you don't say anything unless it has to be said. Watch and listen, analyze what you already know about the situation, and keep silent until you can say something with a good chance of advancing the cause.

Here are some good times to shut off your yak:

- When showing property. This, of course, is when you set up the close. You can't set yourself up for a smooth close by talking when there's no need for your input. Avoid expressing features too cutely, "Ooo, I just love this darling little kitchen, don't you?" The recital of obvious facts such as, "this room has a huge window," don't advance your cause. If you irritate your buyers by talking too much, they'll think you'll probably irritate the sellers when you present an offer. Guard your words well when you're with buyers.
- When the buyers are fighting with each other. Even if you know who is right, and a clarification of some point has to be made, wait until the steam blows off these people to speak. You can only fuel the flames by talking when the battle rages. Sit quietly, and let them fire their shots. "You guys work it out, and then I'll follow your lead. As my Dad used to say, I'm a lover, not a fighter."
- When a third party, a friend or relative of the buyers, drops in and disagrees with everything you've told your prospects. You're the professional; keep your cool until your buyers see the axe the third party is grinding.

- When buyers and sellers talk at the property. Otherwise, your buyers will wonder if you're trying to conceal drawbacks of the area. Let the seller be the expert on the community at this moment. You can talk about other advantages of living there when you're alone with the buyers again. However, if the conversation gets lopsided, rescue your buyers by saying, "I hate to break in, but we should be going now because the sellers are waiting to leave at the next house, and there's no lock-box key."
- **Be especially sure to shut off your yak at the hardest time to do so: when you return to a property with excited buyers who need to be by themselves and absorb the loveliness of the moment.**

# What Is the Seller's Motivation?

Keep your antennas extended to catch any hints of seller motivation as you keyview houses and talk with other agents. Understanding why sellers are selling sharpens your eye for the perfect fit of buyer and seller.

For example, Agent Footmouth has a very strong buyer who needs a house fast, and can make a clean offer. It's the slow season, there's an oversupply of properties on the market, and the ideal house for Footmouth's buyers is listed at $459,900. His buyers' top limit is $390,000. They are reluctant to look at the $459,900 house because they don't want to get excited about something they can't afford, Footmouth assures them he'll be able to talk the sellers into accepting their offer because of the season and the oversupply.

His buyers love the house and say go. Footmouth presents their $390,000 offer on the $459,900 property—and the sellers reject it contemptuously. Only then does Footmouth discover the sellers' new home won't be ready for six to eight months. They don't want a quick closing, like most sellers do, because they want to stay where they are until they can move directly into their new home. So Footmouth's most important selling point for his low offer—a quick close—counts as a negative with them. They are not willing present-time sellers.

Had Footmouth known this before exciting his buyers about the property, he would have avoided showing it and losing them altogether. Now, after reminding Footmouth they only looked at the property because he said it could be had for their price, they find themselves another agent.

Following are some clues to seller reactions.

| *Sellers' Situation* | *Sellers' Willingness to Compromise* |
| --- | --- |
| Quick transfer | Often willing to negotiate, especially if the employer will pay the brokerage. |
| Waiting for new home to be built | Depends on time span. Usually easier to negotiate with as completion date of new home approaches. |
| Purchased next home with swing loan and is now, or soon will be, making payments on two houses unless this listing sells | Often willing to negotiate. |
| Purchased next home with savings | Usually far less willing to negotiate than a swing-loaner. |
| Listed, but have nowhere to move yet | Difficult to negotiate with unless unusual circumstances exist. |

Chapter 18 has Winning Scripts for these seller motivations.

# When You Sell One Spouse or Partner First

When either half of a pair of home-hunters finds the house they want before the other half comes looking, don't try to sell the second person. Let the one you've already worked with do this for you. Be ready to answer questions, but stay far enough away so they can talk privately. If the one you saw first can't sell the house to the other, you can't either.

# Three New Things You Said

Be aware of what you're saying to clients, and ever on the lookout for effective sayings. After each meeting with a buyer, take a few moments to think about the conversation. Write down the three new things you said that went over best on $3 \times 5$ cards, and review these cards frequently. This habit of writing down your best words will remarkably increase your memory for what you've said. It will also provide you with your own rapidly growing arsenal of Winning Scripts. These will be especially effective for you because they are your original words.

# Add a New Facet to
# Your Powers of Persuasion

"At this point in time, I'm not sure what you're thinking or feeling."

You could say the same thing with fewer words, as in, "I don't know your mind now," but the shorter version is much too abrupt for many people when they're skipping about on the hot skillet of decision.

Buyers have a lot to think about in the closing room, and abrupt speech can crowd them. Unless they're snapping back their replies quickly, use comfortably slow, roundabout phrases to stretch out your meaning, and allow their preoccupied minds time to cope. School yourself in this technique, and its opposite, staccato speech stripped down to bare essentials. When you need to keep the ball in their court, you can do it with a quick zip of short words. The effect is heightened if you've been speaking in long-winded phrases and then switch to abrupt language. Compare:

| Forceful Phrases | Long-Winded Phrases |
| --- | --- |
| now | at the present time |
| today | during the current year |
| think about | give careful consideration to |

There are hundreds of these odd pairs. Collect them and practice switching back and forth from the quick and forceful to the slow and long winded. Learn to alter your speaking style at will, and add a new dimension to your powers of persuasion.

# Do You Take This
# House in Rain and in Sleet?

Do you take this house in rain and in sleet, to have and to hold, in dark of night and shine of day, when payments fall due, and when flowers bloom at your door? Do you take this place to be exclusively yours, to be your refuge from the world's cares, to be the shelter where your children grow and your friends gather?

Say *yes*.

The agent is searching for the right words, the right timing, and the right price to draw four people's okay to an agreement for the benefit of all of them. You're just the go-between; only they can perform the act of buying and selling, of replacing the tired old wishes under this roof with fresh new dreams. Don't push too much, and don't lie, but somehow provide the reassuring phrases and setting required to be the conductor of this transfer-of-hopes symphony, the minister for this union, the successful bearer of expertise in your community's housing.

# Ten Tips on Obtaining Salable Offers That Stick

1. **Qualify with finesse.** Draw intelligent conclusions from the qualifying interview and avoid showing people homes they can't afford. Don't whet their appetite for what they can't buy. It's cruel to their feelings—and brutal to your pocketbook.

2. **Plan your pacing.** Wait for the moment to ripen before you try to close. Your buyers must really want the house. Wanters will be eager to hear your full explanation of the buyer's net sheet. They will listen intently as you describe how an offer works. When they've reached this point, it's time to say, "Are you ready to proceed? I'd like to make this home part of your future."

3. **Clue into the sellers' motivation first.** Always call the listing agent to get a feel for the sellers' motivation before settling on how high the offer should be, and discuss what you learned with the potential buyers before writing the offer.

4. **Be careful on a low offer.** If your buyers insist on low-balling the offer, push hard for:
   - no contingencies,
   - timing the close to suit the sellers' convenience,
   - allowing the sellers to cash out if they so desire,
   - no unusual or nit-picking clauses,
   - no grabs for the sellers' furnishings,
   - and an extra large deposit.

   Meeting all six of these requirements gives a low-ball offer its best chance of being accepted. Take the following paragraph as a rough guide—the best possible because every case is so different.

   The first complication introduced into a low-price offer cuts its chances of being accepted to 50 percent, the second complication halves your chances again to 25 percent, the third to 12½ percent, and so on. **Low price offers must be clean!**

   You may question whether a low-price offer is damaged as much by a trifling provision (a request for the patio furniture, for example) as it is by a major item. Perhaps you've never seen, as I often have, a seller grow pale when the price is stated, and then flush with rage when the trifle is mentioned. Never forget the part emotion plays in all aspects of real estate. When you have to go with a low price, fight hard to eliminate every other negative.

5. **Get a sufficient deposit.** Even on full-price offers, low deposits are a red flag to sellers.

6. **Type it.** If possible, type the offer. If this isn't practical, take the time to print carefully. (If both your cursive writing and block printing look like the work of a five-year-old with a sore hand, it can start hurting you in the wallet now. Libraries and bookstores have books on printing legibly. Get one, practice ten minutes a day for three weeks, and you'll be able to print beautifully for the rest of your life.)

   Difficult-to-read offers, or those with clumsily worded clauses, turn sellers off. They haven't even deciphered the whole offer yet, and already it sounds like a troublesome transaction. You may not be able to type it, but you can always print it. And you must insist, for their benefit, on your customers giving you enough time to word their offer clearly and concisely.

7. **Reinforce the commitment.** At the time you write and they approve the offer say to the buyers, "I'll be presenting this offer to the sellers in good faith. In other words, I'm going in there with the understanding that if your offer is accepted, you are committed to purchasing this property. You do understand this, don't you?"

8. **Don't socialize after you write up the offer.** Get down to business and present it as soon as possible. Have the buyers go for a cup of coffee or whatever until you can get back to them.

9. **Be sure the buyers are given a signed copy of the offer before you leave them.**

10. **Leave on an upbeat note.** Be sure you close your meeting with your buyers on an up tone. "I will do everything in my power to secure this property for you. If I get a counteroffer, it won't be because I didn't give all I've got—and that's plenty. But wish me luck."

# Winning Closing Scripts

To be effective, closing scripts must be spoken with sincere empathy. Your buyers have to know you're interested in them, you're concerned about their welfare, and you want them to have a trouble-free transaction. To instill confidence in them, emphasize those points repeatedly.

## Closing Scripts to Be Used in the Car on Your Way to See Property

"Let me tell you a few things about this great community. The school system here is the finest. I happen to live just two blocks from this home, and I can tell you personally—this grade school has as dedicated a staff as you'll find anywhere. And my friends tell me this applies to our entire school system. Our recreation and parks system is _____. The public library is within walking distance and it's _____. The stores here are _____."

"One of the things I like best about living here is _____." (By now you've learned what appeals to their interests. Use this information to paint a picture of how the change they're making will help them enjoy their interests.)

## Closing Scripts to Be Used at the Property

Find an area with the features, such as proximity to work or highways, of special importance to them. Then emphasize those features whenever possible. "I know how important freeway proximity is to you, Jim. Guess what, this house is only two blocks from the main artery to the freeway. Also, the hospital is only four miles away, Isabella. Perhaps we can go by there right now and see if there are any nursing positions open at this time."

"Can you picture your furniture in this room?—How's it fit?"

**When You Get the First Objection.** *Ignore it.*

There are a lot of things the buyers like about this house, but they say, "The color of the carpeting is bad. No way could I live with it." Ignore the statement. Pretend you didn't hear it. And then say something like, "Oh, I forgot to tell you! This house has air conditioning."

Ignore the objection and bring out something you know they want. The second time the objection comes up, *go for it.* "But I told you, Danny, this carpeting—the color's atrocious. There's a lot of good things here, but I don't want to put new carpeting in. Any time I spend $1.4 million for a house, I want the carpet to be the color I want and in good shape."

"Okay."

*Be happy* they're telling you what the objection is, because it means they feel safe with you now. *Rephrase the objection* when they say, "I don't want to spend $1 million four on this place and have to re-place the carpet too."

*Pause.* Think a moment. Then say something like this (and make it sound as sarcastic as possible when you rephrase it), "Oh, this carpet clashes with your furniture, does it? Then we've eliminated this house from consideration."

Now you've given them perspective, and brought what they're doing into focus. If there's any possibility they might buy this house, they'll say something like, "Oh, it's not *that* bad, but—."

**After You've Rephrased the Objection, Get All the Problems Out in the Open.** "Is there anything besides the car-peting you don't like about this house?" Ask this after you know they like the home. They're serious about it. Your cancellation rate will be much lower if you'll take the time to explore all your customers' ob-jections this early in the game. Some people are reluctant to reveal ob-jections. Gently urge them to do so. Show empathy. Give your buyers time to find words for their feelings.

Here's how to overcome objections after they've given you all of them. It depends on what they don't like. If it's the carpet, say, "You know, you can't change the location of a house. We can't physically move the acreage; we can't change the floor plan without great ex-pense. But the carpeting we can always change. And, quite frankly, this is one of the finest locations in the area. So let's think in terms of a car-pet allowance the seller might accept. I'm not sure (because you're not), but it could be an option."

(However, it's unwise to mention things like a carpet allowance to buyers you suspect will be low-ballers. See *Ten Tips on Obtaining Salable Offers That Stick* (Number 4).

As salespeople, we provide *options* by opening the customers' eyes to them, by negotiating with them, but primarily, by seeing them. An important part of our job is to be alert for options the customers aren't aware of. Very often, what buyers object to is something they can live with temporarily. In the case just mentioned, they can manage with the carpet's unwanted color—if they choose to—until they are ready to recarpet.

"In view of all the other advantages this home has, is the carpet color something you can live with for a while?"

"Tell me what you're thinking about the possibility of purchasing this property. It's really important for us to keep in good communication so I'll know if I'm truly serving your needs. Am I on the right track?"

I often interject something like this into conversations with my buyers, "If you decide to make a proposal to the owner, do you feel you'd want to include the furnishings in your offer?"

"I think this place pleases you both. You're indicating to me that you'd possibly like to make an offer on it. Let's talk about this now."

## Closing Scripts to Be Used in the Car on the Way Back to the Office

If they've found the house they like, and you're on your way back to the office, take the pressure off in the car.

The primary earner is thinking, "Oh oh, he or she's going to want to buy it."

You just know these thoughts are happening and there's the give-away buildup of tension in the car. You should relieve the pressure a bit, because it is not only painful to them, it raises the possibility that the key person will find a way to escape. Say, "Now, Mr. and Mrs. Chen, I don't want you to do anything you might regret later. I want all the facts out in the open. So, as soon as we get back to the office, I'm going to prepare a buyer's net sheet for you, and tell you exactly what it's going to cost to purchase this property, what the monthly investment will be, the loan origination fee—everything. Then we'll look at the whole picture and see whether you feel comfortable with it."

They think, "Oh, boy. She's not going to write up a purchase agreement. She's not going to try and close us."

They're sitting back like the rosebuds were when we first met them, all tight and tucked in again. Relieve some more pressure by saying, "I want you to see the facts and figures before you make a decision. It's gotta be right, guys. If it's not right, I'm not going to live with it either." They feel safe again. You've created a safe environment, and they'll love you for doing it.

"Won't it be nice to have this decision out of the way?"

"It'll be great when you're all settled in and living in our community. I know you'll love it. I sure do."

## Closing Scripts to Be Used at the Office When You've Returned with Interested Buyers

**"I Want to Think It Over."** This is the house for them; they really love it; they want to move in. But the husband says, "I want to think it over."

Is their present home sold? Maybe it's the contingency problem again, or perhaps swing financing. Think about all these things again. If their present house is sold and all systems are go, but they're saying they want to think it over, try one of the following two tactics.

## 1. Property not available

"It's funny how many people have said, 'I want to think it over,' and I can understand why—I don't like to feel pressured either. But then, when I call to be sure the property is still available the next day, a lot of times it's gone. The market is excellent in March, April, and May. So I feel an obligation to tell you this, Mr. Buyer, the property might not be here tomorrow. Are you willing to risk it?"

## 2. 24-hour first right of refusal

Suggest a 24-hour first right of refusal. If they've pretty much settled into the house you've shown them, but they've got an appointment with another broker, and there's no way they're going to make a decision tonight, try to get an offer with a 24-hour contingency requiring their final approval tomorrow evening at 5:00. The listing agent and the seller have to go along with it, of course. I've used this device and saved sales I would otherwise have lost.

**"The Interest Rate Is Too High."** One person wants the house; the spouse is hesitating. The interest rate is the peg he's hanging his fears on. He expresses concern about having their fun money consumed by high interest.

"As far as not being able to do things with your family—(What these buyers really need now is outflow. If they can talk out their anxieties and frustrations, these things will reduce themselves.)—what type of activities do you engage in with your family?"

"Well, we like to ski."

"Oh, so do I. But, you know, you can't ski all year round. Perhaps you could have everyone save money throughout the year for your ski fun in winter time. But your property and your real estate investment isn't a seasonal, sometime item. It's a permanent security-building investment for you and your family over the years. When you consider the tax advantages, and the ongoing effect of inflation, it's really vital to get started on owning your own home.

"I know the interest rates are higher than you expected, but it's not the whole picture. Consider what this home will cost in another year. Our rate of appreciation last year was ____ percent. Over the last three years it's averaged ____ percent. Okay, let's take the lower figure of 3 ½ percent. You're considering a $600,000 home, a property which will be worth $621,000 in 12 months' time if present inflation and price trends continue, and I don't see any indications they won't.

"I think interest rates are going to hold steady, or go up, but what do you think is the most they can go down in the next year? a point?

two points? Okay, let's figure what you'd save if rates dropped *three* full percentage points, because I just happen to know it means a savings to you of about $2.20 per thousand of the loan, per month, on the term we'd be using, 30 years. Okay, on the $480,000 loan you'd need to buy now, this works out to $12,672 in annual interest savings—*if* interest rates drop *three full percentage points*. It's a lot of savings, but to get it, you'd have to pass up $21,000 in annual appreciation. Depending on what happens to interest rates, you'll lose between $8,328 and $21,000 a year by waiting.

**When It's a Seller's Market.** "Property in this area is on the market for an average of only _____ days right now. Homes priced right for today's market, as this one is, are being snapped up even faster than the average. Based on this reality, it's simply not to your advantage to delay executing the decision I think you've made. There just isn't much property available here now, and the property you like on _____ Street won't wait long for a buyer. If you want to live there, the time to act is now—right now."

"I just talked with the listing agent on this property, and there is presently another offer pending. So, I suggest writing up a full-price offer if we expect to acquire it."

Of course, you never say this unless it's true.

**Your Own Stamp of Approval Is Required.** "This is absolutely and positively the best way for you to go."

You can never use this strong of a statement successfully unless you've worked closely enough with the buyers to have strong rapport as a person, and strong credibility as a real estate expert. However, if you've achieved this great rapport and credibility, but fail to use it at the right moment by decisively placing your own stamp of approval on the purchase they're considering, your strength will be a loss. Credibility and rapport are self-defeating unless employed positively. Your buyers' faith in your integrity and knowledge makes an imperative demand: You believe they are doing the right thing—and you tell them so with no ifs, ands, or buts about it. If you don't, they'll believe you—and not buy. If you force them to pull reluctant approval from you, their faith in you will make them back away from buying.

**When It's a Buyer's Market.** "I live and work in this town, so it benefits me to not just make a sale but to make a friend for life. I'm going to run in to you at the grocery store, the bank, almost anywhere. Lots of people in town will ask you about your house and how you found it. My reputation is at stake here. Someday you'll thank me for bringing you to see this house—I have to be sure of this."

**Buying Low in a High-Interest-Rate Market.** In a high-interest-rate market, tell your buyers, "Now is the time to buy in order to ensure you'll have the best selection and the best terms."

"People think buying property when interest rates are high is a poor decision. Most people don't understand what's going through the sellers' minds today. When someone puts a house up for sale in this market, they're motivated. They need to sell. So they'll carry paper, and they'll take a lower price than they would in a more favorable market. What a great way to buy on the lower end of the appreciation scale—before the next upward cycle of prices."

"Buy low—when interest rates are high!"

Here's another effective sales dialogue for a hard market with high interest rates.

"Most people follow the crowd, but the crowd is almost always a step behind. When purchasing real estate, don't follow the crowd—lead them. The best buys in anything are made according to the contrarian theory of going against what everyone else is doing.

"When percentage rates are high like they are now, most people won't buy. This is foolish because there are far more houses to choose from now, and the percentage of highly motivated sellers is also high. And, don't forget, when interest rates drop you can refinance."

Then go back to discussing with your buyers how their negotiating power is far greater today than it would be in a lower-interest-rate market where the selection of available housing is poor, the prices are escalating, and the sellers are greedy.

**Approaching the Offer Write-Up.** "I'll do everything in my power to make this transaction run smoothly. This is what is necessary if you decide to make a proposal to the seller: First, we fill out this purchase agreement. (Bring it out of the drawer, and have them touch and read it.) Then I'll need a check from you for an earnest money deposit of about $_____. Your check will be deposited upon the acceptance of this offer, or returned to you if the offer is declined. Then I will proceed to do all these things. (Present them with a checklist of the steps involved in the processing of their transaction from beginning to closing.)

Start telling your "Here's what happens when I present your offer" speech to every buyer. If they say, "Oh, we've been through this many times," say, "Oh, you know how this works? Good. Then we won't go through all these details."

However, most of the time, buyers will listen while you explain how offers work. Tell them how you will make an appointment with the listing agent.

"I'll go over there and present this offer. If the offer isn't accepted, you get your check back. It's invalidated. If the sellers change anything on this agreement, you have another chance to make another decision." Explain the whole process.

"If you decide on this property, I intend to make it as easy for you to buy it as possible. I'd like to introduce you at the bank carrying the present loan. We can all go to the bank together and fill out the necessary paperwork, and perhaps get a new account started for you in this state. It'll be my pleasure to help you through this busy period."

"If you both decide to buy this property . . . I should say, if you both want to *try* to buy it by making an offer to the owners—then what happens next is I'll call the listing agent and get the latest facts regarding possession and general motivation from him about his sellers. Would you like me to call the listing agent and see what the scoop is?"

This only calls for a minor *yes.* Many of the people who will give you this minor *yes* would freeze up and say *no* to "Shall we proceed?" because they aren't there yet. Then, while you talk to the listing agent, they have time to get used to the idea. And, by allowing you to call the listing agent, they've put their foot in the air to take the next natural step: approval of your suggestion to write an offer.

**For the Still-Not-Sure.** "Let's go back there again and look at the property as if it's already your own home. Let's just go in there and relax—and enjoy the place. I'll sit on the living room couch, and let you people walk through and look, and measure, and picture your own furniture in there. Really get in there and pick it apart in your minds."

Say this, get up, and start moving toward the door. Keep in control.

# Negotiating for a Lifetime Customer

Never Go Directly to Sellers ● Seal Your Lips ● Don't Talk Outside the House ● Prepare for the Offer Presentation ● Warm Up the Buyers' Image ● Accent Minor Positives Before Price ● Don't Wait Too Long to State the Price Offered ● Presenting a Realistic Offer to Unrealistic Sellers ● Counteroffers and Your Obligation to the Sellers ● The Talk-Alone Ploy ● Selling the Counteroffer ● The Eight-Dollar Persuader ● The Penny Persuader ● Take the House Away from Them ● If the Buyer Says "Yes" ● Try the Three-Day Option When All Else Fails ● Winning Scripts

In Chapter 17 we discussed methods of obtaining the most salable offer possible. Let's assume you've done this. Now you're ready for the next step—negotiating the sale.

## Never Go Directly to Sellers

Make an appointment to present the offer to the sellers through the listing agent. If the listing agent isn't available promptly, ask for the manager or broker, explain your problem cordially, and ask someone in the office to make arrangements with the sellers to be there when you present the offer.

Ordinarily you'll be able to reach the listing office immediately, but if you can't reach someone within a reasonable time, call the homes of everyone who works there. Burn up the wires to everyone *except the sellers.*

Never go directly to the sellers with an offer. Doing this is the same as criticizing their agent for not being on hand no matter how you phrase it. Not only is such conduct unethical, it damages your offer's chances of being accepted. Unprofessional conduct on the part of agents frightens sellers, and there's no worse time to frighten sellers than when they're about to hear an offer.

If the listing office consists of just one person, and if diligent effort fails to locate someone in the listing office to represent the sellers, call an officer of your Local Board of REALTORS® for help. Your Board of REALTORS® has very specific rules for this problem.

# Seal Your Lips

News travels fast. Don't discuss the offer with the listing agent, the sellers, or with anyone else before you present it to the sellers and their agent in person. Don't telephone the sellers during the time you have an unpresented offer. If it's absolutely necessary for you to communicate with them, have a third party (their listing agent, if possible) relay the message. Don't give the sellers an opportunity to question you about the offer before you're eyeball to eyeball with them.

If you know the sellers personally, they may call you and try to discuss the offer over the phone. It's quite easy to avoid doing so.

"Oh, Mary, I understand how eager you are to know what's happening, but you see, I'm required to honor my agreement with your listing agent. I know you wouldn't want to put me in a difficult position. I'll see you at 7:00. Thanks, Mary. Goodbye."

When you have an offer on your own listing, it's just as vital not to discuss the offer with your sellers on the phone. If you allow phone negotiations to start, your seller may say, "Call them back and tell them to bump up their offer $2,000. And don't come over until you've got their okay on it."

If you don't take the offer seriously, why should your sellers?

With some sellers you can simply say, "I don't want to get into the terms until I see you. Is 7:00 okay?"

With other sellers, you may have to explain further, "If this was an offer on someone else's listing, I'd never discuss it on the phone. I'm representing you in this transaction, and this particular set of buyers too, and I don't think it's fair to you or to them to make a phone offer. Will 7:00 be a good time for you, or should I come right over?"

When another broker in the office has an offer on one of your listings, you don't want to know what the offer is. Tell the buyers' agent *not* to tell you what the terms and the price are if she sounds like she's going to. This way you can truthfully say to the seller, "I'm sorry, but I don't know what the offer is."

They'll often reply, "Oh, come on—you must know."

"No, I don't. When I'm working an offer, I never tell the listing agent what it is. After we all get together and hear the offer, I'll help you analyze it and decide what to do."

"You really don't know what the offer is?"

"Absolutely not. And it's better this way because I'm your representative, not the buyers'. It's my job to get you the best price and terms I can within your time schedule. There's no advantage to my knowing what the offer is before you do because I can't accept or reject it. But there are several reasons for me not to know. For one, some sellers would think I've teamed up with the buyers' agent to try and get their offer accepted. One of the ways to avoid suspicion is to avoid acting suspiciously. It's one reason why I don't want to hear the offer before you do."

Sellers feel exposed when an offer is coming. Keep everything open and above board. This discussion assumes the custom in your area is to have both agents present when the offer is presented to the sellers. If the custom where you work is for only one agent to be present, of course be guided by the custom. Your broker will explain precisely how this crucial step is to be handled in this case.

# Don't Talk Outside the House

Agents from each side, talking on the doorstep is one of my pet peeves. Buyers' agents chattering on sellers' doorsteps have strained many fragile client relationships for me, and I believe several transactions were blown apart by this bit of carelessness. Here's how it should work.

An agent calls from another office and tells me, "I've got an offer on one of your listings."

"Terrific. Thanks for showing it. Thanks for taking the time. I really appreciate it."

"When can we present, Danny?"

"Let me call the sellers. I'll get right back to you."

I call the sellers, make the appointment, then call the offering agent back.

"We're all set. I'll meet you at the property at 7:00." End of conversation.

I didn't stay on the phone chatting with the buyers' agent, nor did I ask any questions about the offer. Had I done so, I could very quickly find myself knowing more about the offer than I'd want to admit to my client.

I also said, "I'll meet you at the property." Not in front of it, or around the corner from it, but *at* the property.

Here's a recipe for disaster: Two cars pull up in front of the seller's house a few minutes early. The seller is watching from the window and sees one of the agents climb in the car with the other agent. While the two agents chat—probably about other matters, or even sports—the seller is thinking, "I'll bet they're figuring out how they'll try to beat my price down. Those turkeys! I'll show them. I'm not budging a dime off my price."

Don't start chatting with anyone. Just get out of your car, walk right up to the seller's door, and ring the bell. If the other agent is standing there, don't talk to her. Get inside the house with the sellers and then talk.

# Prepare for the Offer Presentation

If you represent the buyers, prepare a Guidelines to Market Value form and a seller's net sheet. Maybe the listing agent will have the Guidelines form, but don't count on it. Have two forms rather than lose the transaction because you have none. As the buyers' agent, you're the only one who can have a net sheet filled out because you haven't told the listing agent what the offer is in advance.

Have all this vital data in hand. You're on the one-yard line now, which is no place to take a loss after all your hard work to get there. Go prepared. Psych yourself up and take the tools you need to give your offer its best possible launch.

# Warm Up the Buyers' Image

When the sellers open the door, I introduce myself to them and to the listing agent. Then we all sit down and have a brief bit of small talk before getting down to business. But I don't present my offer just yet. First I say something like, "Let me tell you a little about Joseph and Yolanda Chang. They have three children. They love your house. Their five-year-old boy is just about the size of your Mary over there, and your kitchen facing the backyard fits their needs perfectly. The swimming pool is great—they're a very sports-minded family. She's expecting, so it'll be just great for her. She won't have to drag all the stuff into the car to go down to the rec center—she can stay home and exercise by the pool."

I give the sellers a profile of the buyers. Many houses are sold because the sellers liked the buyers better than the price. People often have put a lot of themselves into this house they can't live in anymore, and they want it to go to someone they feel good about. So talk up your buyers early in the game; it's usually the only chance you'll get. After the price hits, what the buyers are like has less impact.

## Accent Minor Positives Before Price

First I talk about the buyers and then I get in to the purchase agreement. I've worked out my game plan well before the meeting. Every game plan is different too, to fit the particular offer. Here's one example.

Before writing the offer, I find out (from the listing agent) when the sellers want to finalize the sale. Since my buyers' offer meets this important seller requirement, the favorable settlement date is the second item I talk about after the buyers' profile.

The sellers want to carry back a second mortgage and earn some interest on the equity they don't need for their next home. Since a second mortgage is part of my offer, this is the third item I tell them about.

The sellers asked for a large deposit. Any money item gives them a good opening to say, "Okay, now we're talking dollars. What price are they offering?" For this reason, I discuss the deposit as the final item before stating the price offered.

By speaking firmly and getting to the point, I have no trouble remaining in control. I'm able to guide the conversation the way I want it to go, without being loud or pushy, because I keep it moving.

## Don't Wait Too Long to State the Price Offered

What you say about the buyers should be well thought out and right to the point. Don't drone on and on; the sellers have a lot hanging on the amount of the offer. Especially if you have a low offer, don't play all 18 holes first. I've seen agents lay on a fabulous presentation and build up to a dramatic crescendo: ". . . and they're offering $420,000!" The seller almost throws a punch across the table at the buyers' agent because he's been listening to this build-up for 59 minutes and his asking price is $559,950.

Sellers aren't stupid. They'll react well to a little concise drama, but not to a wearisome ramble down Yaketty Yak Lane. Talk briskly, clearly, intently, and don't waste words before the price comes out.

You should also come on early with the price when the offer is weak in other ways, such as the specified possession date isn't convenient for the sellers, the buyers may not qualify, there are contingencies, the terms offered do not meet those set forth in the listing, and so on.

# Presenting a Realistic
# Offer to Unrealistic Sellers

We discussed working with your own overpriced listing in Chapters 11 and 12; now we're concerned with negotiating the sale of someone else's overpriced listing.

How you should proceed depends on how long the property has been for sale, and on how active the market is. There's no point in pressing owners to sell a new listing at a figure well below their asking price in a rising market. At the opposite extreme is a long-time listing in a falling market. Here your realistic price is probably a genuine shocker to the sellers and whether they will accept it may depend on their acceptance emotionally, rather than financially. Come on softly in this situation even though you're in control and the sellers are not.

Tell the sellers you're here to help all parties reach a solution helpful to everyone concerned. Emphasize your buyers' concern about coming into an inactive market at any price and justify their need to make an intelligent decision for themselves. Defuse the situation with sympathy and understanding.

Most transactions take place between these extremes, on listings that have been available a few weeks in a moderately active market. If you're at the beginning of the normal selling season, emphasize the uncertainty of it all, the number of houses on the market, and the possibility of interest rates rising and knocking sales in the head. If the selling season is over, work this fact hard. Ask the sellers to give careful consideration to the likelihood that they'll have to carry the house through to the next selling season.

You're playing match point, so fight for it. Remember you fight best when you remain courteous, calm, and considerate, but you can do this and speak forcefully too.

# Counteroffers and Your
# Obligation to the Sellers

If your offer is not accepted, and the sellers and their agent start talking about a counteroffer, say, "There's something I'm obligated to tell you. If anything is changed on my offer, it's invalidated. I no longer have an offer. I have the responsibility to tell you this."

If there's not a large spread between the offer and the asking price and terms, go a step further. Tell the sellers, "My offer is firm, and you can sell your house right now by accepting it. You can put all this uncertainty behind you so you can devote your energies to moving forward. But a counteroffer puts us back to square one. I don't know what my buyers will do with it. Is it worth the risk of waiting for the next buyer? Who knows what the market's going to do in the coming weeks and months. But here we have this fine couple ready to sign on your property now."

## The Talk-Alone Ploy

When you really feel the sellers should take your offer because of market conditions, press on with this script.

"Before you are committed to making a counteroffer, Mr. and Mrs. Sellhigh, wouldn't it be wise for you to talk about this privately? Maybe we (indicate the other agent) should leave you alone for 15 minutes. Don't you think it would be worthwhile to discuss this? This is an important decision, and I feel you're rushing into a bad one."

Get up and start moving toward the door. Unless they stop you, you've probably saved the transaction. The way this usually works is that the more fearful of the sellers talks the other one into accepting the offer as written, without risking a counteroffer. But it only happens in private.

## Selling the Counteroffer

Prepare the buyers for a counteroffer when you write their original offer. There's no guarantee any offer will go through. To improve your chances, talk to the listing agent and learn everything you can before you write up the offer.

Then, after finishing the offer, tell the buyers, "I'm going to try just as hard as I can to get this offer accepted. I'm really going to work for you. But there's always the chance it won't fly. As you know, they have five months to sell this house, so they don't want to move out soon. We're asking for possession at settlement in 90 days. This makes it tough, especially since we're not meeting their price."

At this time, very nicely review all the weak points of their offer. "So be prepared. This may not get off the ground."

Many buyers will then say something like, "That's as high as I'll go. If you come back with anything changed on our offer, I'm not going for it."

Tell them, "That's understandable. Let's play one domino at a time. I'll sure do everything I can to put this through for you. By golly, I'll go in there and give 'em both barrels."

## Your Negotiating Posture

Your negotiating posture should always be calm, pleasant, and patient. Whenever another party speaks, listen attentively and hear them out fully. But don't expect the same courtesy in return from the principals in the negotiation. Make allowances for the emotional strain of both buyers and sellers, and retain your professional cool. Steer the conversation toward problem-solving decisions and away from personality conflicts. If emotional demands or arguments are made, restate them in concrete and impersonal terms and ask the person who spoke emotionally if your restatement is correct. Stress benefits and work on problems; avoid attacking others.

*Never try to make anyone admit* they've been unethical, unreasonable, unsmart, unkind, or un-anything. Don't get sidetracked from real issues involving money. Not only is it difficult to get people to admit they've done something wrong, you can't put such admissions in the bank—unless you're the one who makes them.

"I agree with you; on this point the sellers are being unreasonable. Unfortunately, they feel very strongly about it. You're absolutely right, but is it worth passing up this terrific buy because of a trifle?"

Sympathetic gestures, facial expressions, and empathic phrases, work wonders at smoothing the way over the rough spots. There are 12 empathic phrases in the Winning Scripts at the end of this chapter. Memorize each one for frequent use.

## Influence the Counteroffer

First, get the lowest price the sellers will accept at this stage nailed down. Then go for the other items of importance to your buyers. You know what they are. Make sure the sellers understand the value to them of giving the buyers selling points to help get the counteroffer approved.

## Take It to the Buyers in Person

When you get a counteroffer take it to the buyers in person. Unless it's a long-distance transaction, don't call them on the phone if at all possible. Don't overlook the dramatic impact of a long trip by car or air which can often swing the decision your way.

Phone the buyers and tell them, "I need to talk to you and I'm on the way. I'll be there in ____ minutes."

## Start with the Positive When You Present the Counteroffer

To continue the example, the buyers told you they must be settled in about 90 days. It's a rock-solid requirement. To present the counteroffer, lead off with, "Hey, you know what? They didn't fight the 90 days. Even though they don't have a place to go, they said they'll find a place and pay rent."

You could also start out with something like, "I want to give you the good news first. The bad news isn't so bad we can't work it out."

## Sell the Difference

Sell the difference, not the price. Some agents sound like they're announcing the world's heavyweight championship fight when they tell their buyers, "The sellers countered for **SIX HUNDRED AND FIFTY-EIGHT THOUSAND DOLLARS.**" This leaves no doubt in the buyer's minds: it's a very frightening amount of money. No wonder so few of these agent counteroffers are accepted.

It's just as accurate to calmly say, "They countered for $3,000 more."

Your buyers know what was offered. They can add 3 to 655 and come up with 658 every time. Never mention $658,000 until you have the counter signed. Here's how it sounds using both strategies.

"The sellers countered for $658,000," says agent Bongwords.

"Wow," says the buyer. "That's a lot of money—almost two-thirds of a million dollars. Unreal! I can't believe I offered $655,000 and got turned down. They're nuts! You could buy a great house for $155,000 not so long ago—never mind the extra half-million. They can keep their stupid house—let's forget the whole thing."

"The counter is for $3,000 more," says Agent Smartwords.

"They want $658,000, huh?"

"Yes, $3,000 more."

Repeat the difference, not the price. Then get right on with some perspective.

# The Eight-Dollar Persuader

If you're working with 30-year loans, each additional thousand-dollars of the loan amount will increase your customers' monthly investment by the following.

| INTEREST RATE (%) | MONTHLY COST (PER THOUSAND DOLLARS) |
|---|---|
| 4 | $ 5.14 |
| 5 | $ 5.37 |
| 6 | $ 6.00 |
| 7 | $ 6.65 |
| 8 | $ 7.34 |
| 9 | $ 8.05 |
| 10 | $ 8.78 |
| 11 | $ 9.53 |
| 12 | $10.29 |
| 13 | $11.06 |
| 14 | $11.85 |
| 15 | $12.64 |
| 16 | $13.45 |
| 17 | $14.26 |
| 18 | $15.07 |
| 19 | $15.89 |
| 20 | $16.71 |

As we continue the example, let's assume a 9 percent interest rate and a counteroffer difference of $3,000.

Tell your buyers "You're already going in with enough of an initial investment, so we can put all the difference on the loan. The spread amounts to $24.15 more a month. As you consider this counteroffer, the effective figure to keep in mind is $24.15."

Why talk about $658,000 when you can realistically talk about $24? The $8.00-a-month persuader is not a gimmick; it really is the effective, important figure to a person buying a home. It's vital for you to keep putting costs back into proper perspective for your buyers. In the counteroffer situation, both buyers and sellers tend to lose perspective. If you and the other agent aren't careful, your negotiations will degenerate into a power struggle. The principals will take and hold to positions regardless of what's best for them. Don't let them lose sight of the benefits to flow from agreement. Steer them away from power plays. Get your buyers back to why you're working for them, to what the real problem is, and to how you are all going to solve it.

Sometimes they'll say, "I'm just not going to pay this price."

They can afford the house. They want the house. But an ego item is interfering with their thinking. Buyers and sellers can irritate and frustrate each other without ever meeting. Be the peacemaker. Think of nonaggressive words to express what has to be said. You're there to soothe everybody and clear the rabbits off the runway. So always sell the amenities.

## Sell Amenities

Never argue over money. Steer the conversation away from money and toward the features. Sell the amenities.

"Don't forget, this house is close to the schools. The kids can walk from here. And there's a beautiful park just down the street. From the other house the kids would have to take the bus to school. And you'd have to take them to the park, Yolanda."

"Yeah, but it's $3,000 more," Joseph says.

Now is the time to hit them with even more perspective.

# The Penny Persuader

With 30-year loans, each extra thousand dollars added to the loan will increase the buyers' daily investment as shown in the table on the following page.

Pick out an amenity and sell the savings value of the amenity against the difference. We're still working on the $3,000 difference with Joseph and Yolanda Chang. The interest rate is 9 percent, so the $3,000 will cost them 81 cents a day.

You look at Yolanda and say, "We've covered the whole area and we know what's available. We know you can buy the house you like best for a price you're happy with, plus 81 cents a day. This is really what we're talking about—81 cents. I know it all adds up, but so do the other costs, like driving the kids around. I don't think gas will get cheaper, and I know you'd rather have your kids walk to school than go on the bus three miles each way. But it's hard to reduce a benefit of this kind to dollars and cents, isn't it?"

"I have a feeling you're about to," Joseph says.

"I wouldn't try. Quality-of-life values just don't translate into dollars. Anyway, the money has to work out for you, or it's not a good

| INTEREST RATE (%) | DAILY COST (PER THOUSAND DOLLARS) |
|:---:|:---:|
| 4 | $.16 |
| 5 | $.18 |
| 6 | $.20 |
| 7 | $.22 |
| 8 | $.25 |
| 9 | $.27 |
| 10 | $.29 |
| 11 | $.32 |
| 12 | $.34 |
| 13 | $.37 |
| 14 | $.40 |
| 15 | $.42 |
| 16 | $.45 |
| 17 | $.48 |
| 18 | $.50 |
| 19 | $.53 |
| 20 | $.56 |

situation—and I wouldn't want you to go on it. I really mean it. Okay, zero for the kids walking to school, but how often would you say you'll drive to school yourself, Yolanda? Once a month? Or once a week, counting the different activities for three kids."

"At least once a week."

"Okay, six miles round trip at 10 cents a mile—60 cents. That only pays for about one day a week. I don't know how often the kids will want to go to the park. . . ."

At this point Yolanda says, "Joseph, I can't believe we're sitting here talking about 80 lousy cents. I want that house."

Give the counteroffer to Joseph and say, "I know you folks are going to love the place. I'm really happy for you." Put your finger where he should sign and say, "This is where you approve it, Mr. Chang." Then hand it to his wife for her signature. And away you go.

It isn't always this easy, of course. But, if they can qualify for the loan and want the house, you're dealing with personality hang-ups. These problems yield to the right approach. Here's another one with a high success rate.

# Take the House Away from Them

Run through their other house choices again in your mind and then say, "Joseph and Yolanda, I think we should forget this house we've made an offer on."

Address the person who wants the house most, and address him or her, "Yolanda, what do you think? Shouldn't we take another look at your second and third choices? Maybe, in view of this counteroffer, you'll see them in a different and better light now. We could see them both in 30 minutes. What do you say? Shall we take off right now and go look at them?"

You have just snatched the house she wants away from Yolanda's eager grasp. Sit still, close your mouth, and wait. Your silence will eventually force one of them to say something. Give it time because Yolanda is working on Joseph with her eyes. Don't watch. If you'll just sit there counting the nails in the paneling, the chances are the buyer will say, "Yes."

# If the Buyer Says "Yes"

Notify the sellers as soon as you have a signed offer. Do it right away because another offer may be in the wind, and somebody on either end may have an attack of remorse.

## Give Everyone a Copy of the Documents

Many transactions have been lost because everybody didn't have a copy. The listing agent, the sellers, the buyers, and the buyers' agent must all have a signed copy of the offer and counteroffer, if any. Get those copies signed and delivered before you go to bed so you don't have to worry.

## Now Pat Yourself on the Back

Go back to the office, jump up and down, and hug everybody. Then go home, tell everybody there that you're great, pat yourself on the back again, and *take time to celebrate.* Really do this! Take the time to feel good about what you did. What you just did was no easy job. Some days it goes on and on for hours and far into the night.

There are solid reasons why you should make a big deal of patting yourself on the back immediately following a success. Unless you do, you'll cheat yourself out of a vital, sustaining part of the reward, and weaken your future drive.

# Try the Three-Day Option When All Else Fails

One very effective strategy is to wait three days and resell the original offer. Waiting is dangerous. But let's assume you haven't been waiting. You've kept on working with Joseph and Yolanda Chang, and after three days they're still in the market. They still want the Sellhigh's house but they won't—or can't—pay $658,000 for it.

When you go back to the sellers with the same offer, don't schedule the full offer presentation meeting. That would be an irritating formality at this point. Anyway, you tried it face-to-face, it didn't work, and now the only thing you can change is the presentation method.

Call the listing agent at home about 8:00 or 9:00 on the third night. Ask him to participate in a conference call about the original offer right then with the seller. You'll pay for the call.

Never go around the listing agent and call the sellers directly. They'll turn you down cold and complain to their agent, who'll then file a complaint against you at your Board of REALTORS®. Stay clean with the listing agent, get her or his permission to make the conference call, or don't do it. The listing agent will tell you whether other sales activity on the Sellhigh's house makes your rehash of the old offer pointless.

The third night after the original offer was turned down seems to be the right moment for this option. Maybe your buyers will sweeten their offer, moneywise or otherwise. But, sweetened or not, make the call.

After three days, the sellers are very likely having third thoughts, "My house hasn't been shown since the Changs were here; the selling season is almost over for this year; how much longer can I wait?"

This option can work in any market when you're not very far apart, as in this example, and it can work in quiet markets when you're much further apart.

Few agents come back after three days and present the same offer. It takes very little time or trouble—you've already done all the work. You only need to get 1 success from 100 tries to justify the effort, and your success ratio with this move will be far higher.

# Winning Scripts

## Use a Dozen Forms of Empathy

Trade rhetorical concessions for substantive concessions, verbiage for concrete, and points of discussion for points of value. It costs nothing to say, "I know you're right. If this were a just world, it would work as you say. Unfortunately, there isn't much justice, so we won't be able to do it."

But it can cost you a great deal not to say those blow-softening words when the occasion arises for them. If you can't give them the value, at least give them, whenever possible, the satisfaction of hearing you justify their position. Here are some soft phrases you should be quick to drop into negotiations to smooth the way:

- "I understand." Very simple, yet very powerful. Practice saying it with varying tones and emphasis.
- "I know what you mean."
- "I've been there."
- "I know what you're saying."
- "I sympathize with that."
- "I know the problem well."
- "You're right."
- "I agree."
- "I see your point."
- "That's only right and reasonable."
- "I'm with you 100 percent."

## Scripts to Help Close These Seller Motivations

**Quick Transfer.** "I would have been delighted to bring you a full-price offer, but this is the very best I could do, based on my buyer's thinking and the other properties on the market now.

"May I emphasize again how financially sound my buyers are, and their ability to complete this purchase quickly. Within _____ days, you'll be cashed out of this house, free of the monthly payments here, and off and running in your new life. Won't it be great when this problem is solved?

"I'm happy to say, I've got the solution. All you have to do is approve it right here."

**Waiting for a New Home.** "Because you have time, you have a cushioned price on this property reflecting a future evaluation, rather than today's price. My buyers obviously prefer your home to all others, or I wouldn't be here with an offer from them. But they've become experts on today's values in our area in the last few days.

"They want your home, but they want to buy it at today's price. This is a very cyclical business, and there's no guarantee prices will actually rise (continue to rise, turn around) over the next six months.

"In half a year, the scene might look very different, so I believe we're justified in asking for our offer to be considered in light of today's market conditions only."

"Is it possible for you to consider interim housing? Perhaps my buyers would be interested in a rent-back situation for you. Would you consider it?"

**Purchased Another Home.** "Obviously, it's no fun paying out all that interest. I am offering you a well-qualified buyer who can eliminate this problem for you within _____ days from today. We'll make this as free of worry as possible for you."

**Nowhere to Go Yet.** "You wanted to wait for a well-qualified buyer before you went ahead with purchasing another property. My people want to give you 60 days to close this one out, and to find your next home."

**Distress Sale.** In cases of pending foreclosure, divorce, bankruptcy, or financial disaster brought on by the loss of a breadwinner's income, it's important to help people save face. Even if they're hurting and you know it, play this aspect down.

"I wish I could have brought you a full-price offer, but this is my buyer's best shot. Due to the number of homes available now, he's taking a rather hard line. If you have the holding power, then this offer may not be for you. Holding power is mostly an emotional issue rather than a financial question. Most folks would rather sell it and go on to something new."

# CHAPTER 19

# Fallout Avoidance

Do It Now ● Look Ahead with a Checklist ● Sleeping Dogs Wake Up and Bite ● Avoid the Meatball Mortgage Company ● Acceptance Is Only Half the Battle ● Get It Moving! ● Keep Your Clients and Customers Informed ● Work with the Appraiser ● Choose Hard-and-Now over Later-and-Easier ● Assume Nothing ● How to Push Details with Minimum Effort ● Be There at the Settlement

Some transactions collide with immovable obstacles and can't be saved no matter what you do. Don't grieve over what might have been. Think about the lost transaction only long enough to understand what really happened. You've paid a high price for knowledge, so make sure you know the lesson. Instead of blinding yourself to the truth by seeking someone to blame, look at the circumstances with impartial eyes—and learn from the mistakes.

Was your performance faultless? Probably not—at least not in the rear view mirror. By hindsight you can almost always find things you'll wish you had handled differently. Learn from the fallout and avoid beating yourself up over it. More importantly, be careful that the experience doesn't cause you to be resentful, suspicious, and quick to jump to negative conclusions about people. Your next prospects aren't responsible for your last fallout. And don't talk on and on about the dead transaction. Bury it. Go on to newer and better things.

Sales that shouldn't have been made because the buyers can't qualify are covered in Chapter 15, and are not considered fallout. A fallout is when a transaction fails to close due to circumstances arising or changing after the purchase agreement is signed. And circumstances can change radically at any time.

# Do It Now

The first principle of fallout avoidance is that small problems not promptly solved will kill transactions. Minor paperwork details left uncompleted kill transactions. So do unsigned documents, loan applications not pursued with vigor, and inspections not made. The list is long; it includes every detail necessary for the close. Today's easily handled small problem becomes the day-of-closing's unmanageable monster.

Transactions fall out for reasons as countless as snowflakes in a blizzard. New reasons occur every day. Fortunately, the best method of saving your transactions and collecting the fees you've earned is to rely on simple common sense. Basic to avoiding fallout is checking frequently with the lender and the escrow officer (or whomever is processing the paperwork) to make sure everything required is started, and then is completed, in good time.

After a fallout disaster, surprisingly enough, an agent may say, "Nobody ever told me the darn thing had to be done."

As an agent you need to understand something basic. When you hang your license on the wall, and tell the world you're in the real estate business, it's *your responsibility to know* what's required. Study your office's file of closed transactions; ask your escrow officer, lender's representative, or manager what's required; and then bulldog those requirements through.

# Look Ahead with a Checklist

It's also surprising that agents often fail to make a list of all the items to be done before a transaction can close. The night the sale is made, it's easy to get carried away in the excitement, and to be certain that no item will be forgotten. The sellers are enthusiastic and happy, and you know how badly they need to get their money out of the house. You believe them when they assure you they'll get right on with replacing the water heater and finding the permit for the greenhouse, as they agreed. Then they simply don't get around to it; something it never occurred to you could happen. Another idea that might not occur to you—you could just plain forget about these items. Every day of the settlement period generates its own pressures. You're working on new sales and listing opportunities with the intensity that real estate demands. These pressures blow those water heater and permit problems right out of your mind—until you get a phone call, a few hours before the scheduled close of the transaction, telling you there'll be no close unless the permit is on file and the water heater is replaced *today*.

Now it's tear-hair-and-tires-time. Maybe you have an appointment to show property, and no time to handle these details. But you must handle them, and postpone your appointment to show property, whether you lose those buyers or not.

So, sit down, the morning after each sale, and think through everything it will take to get the transaction closed, and your share of the fee safely tamped down in your bank account. Go over the purchase agreement's special provisions word-by-word; review the negotiations step-by-step. Think about each room in the house, the appliances, and the grounds. Don't overlook the counteroffer. Compile a special check-list of tasks that must be completed for the closing as you do this. Then check your list regularly. Keep everything moving. You're the one who gets paid or doesn't get paid—for doing all this.

# Sleeping Dogs Wake Up and Bite

If you're working on a government-financed transaction and there's a patio cover attached to the house, don't assume there's also a building permit for a patio cover. Any additions or remodeling work done since the original construction are a time bomb ticking away unless you have copies of the building permits for the work in your files, especially if you're working on a VA-financed transaction.

Instead of worrying about it, find out. Call or visit your city or county building and safety department, and make sure building permits have been issued, and the work was properly signed off. Get copies of the documents.

Sometimes you'll find yourself working with buyers who are ready to make an offer on the weekend. If so, protect your buyers by inserting this clause into their offer:

"Sellers to furnish copy of building permit for patio cover within five days of acceptance of this offer."

Then make sure you get the permit copy.

If you've ever made a last-minute, tire-screeching run to the building department with a transaction hanging in the balance, you'll swear there's nothing worse than not avoiding this avoidable problem.

# Avoid the Meatball Mortgage Company

Above all, select with great care the lender you recommend to your buyers. Then closely follow the path through approval to funding that their loan application must take.

When approval of a customer's loan application takes longer than promised, you better worry even though the loan representative says, "Don't worry." In fact, you'd better cancel the application and take the loan to a more reliable lender. If you don't wait too long, maybe there's still time to save the transaction. Losing a deal at the last minute because Meatball Mortgage Company ran out of money and couldn't fund the loan, ranks very high on real estate's list of greatest frustrations. (I found this out the hard way.)

# Acceptance Is Only Half the Battle

Foresight and prompt action can save most of the transactions threatening to fall out between offer acceptance and the settlement and collect-your-fee time. I say "most" with confidence, because *most* of my transactions have squeezed through tight places. Many experienced agents swear *every* transaction hangs by a thread at some point during its perilous journey from acceptance to settlement. Only half the battle is getting an offer accepted and the transaction opened. The second—and often the toughest—half of the battle is getting your open transaction closed. Heed this warning: Your work is only half done when an offer is accepted.

# Get It Moving!

Start processing your transaction the first available business hour. Create a schedule with your closing checklist, showing when each item required for the close must be completed. If the transaction hangs on a contingency, consider whether you should incur any processing cost until the contingency is removed. Unless you plan to pay for those costs yourself if the transaction falls out, make sure it is clearly understood who will pay for the processing charges (for example, an appraisal fee to a lender) if the transaction doesn't go through.

# Keep Your Clients and Customers Informed

"I've got the termite report in my hand. No problems."
"The appraisal came through okay. Isn't it great?"
"Good news: We have loan approval."
Whether you're working with the buyers or the sellers, they've made a big decision, and they'll have moments of doubt about the

wisdom of it. Perhaps they'll have moments of panic. You are the flight attendant during the transaction's bumpy flight from opening to settlement, and part of your job is to reassure the anxious passengers—your customers. You are also the navigator and pilot, so use all the outside help you can get. Your problems will multiply if you try to do everything yourself.

What if the news is bad? Tell your people. Keeping them informed includes the bad news. Everything concrete affecting their interests—except items obviously too trivial to mention—must be promptly divulged to all interested parties. Bad news (something actually happened) must be immediately passed on to your customers; bad mouthings (nothing actually happened) need not be passed on. Remember, when something necessary to the settlement of the transaction does not happen on time, this nonhappening is bad news; both buyer and seller must be promptly informed. Use a communication log for all good and bad news connected with the transaction. Record all conversations you have with your clients on this log. Record every conversation with all parties involved during the open transaction period. See Chapter 24 for forms to keep track of conversations. Forms are also found on the accompanying CD.

## Work with the Appraiser

Meet the appraiser at the property, and give him or her a list of comparable sales. A copy of the Guidelines to Market Value you used to make the sale will work fine. Never make appraisers dig up the list of comparables for themselves.

Why bother? You need to bother because appraisers don't have much time. Compare their fee to yours and you'll see why they don't. They can't dig and dig. They have to furnish your appraisal fast and go on to their next assignment. So they'll very likely miss the best comparable sales you used to justify the sales price to the buyer. If this happens the appraiser won't appraise the property high enough to carry the loan. By the time you go through the whole process with another lender, something else can change and kill the transaction. It happens all the time.

## Choose Hard-and-Now over Later-and-Easier

Drive over to your customers and get those documents signed. Go see for yourself whether the missing screens were replaced, as agreed. Between the time the Sold sign goes up and the close of escrow or settlement, you must supervise the details. When things don't happen on schedule find out why not by going to the source of the problem.

Let's assume you represent the buyer. Your accepted offer called for a preliminary title report within ten days, but on the eleventh day you still don't have it. Call the title company first and ask them what's holding up the report. Then call the listing agent and ask why they aren't abiding by the contract.

# Assume Nothing

Certain things have to happen if your transaction is to finalize. Make sure everything does. Don't wait until the transaction is in serious trouble to start rescue operations. At the first hint of danger, move fast, with courteous but relentless persistence to cure the problem.

# How to Push Details with Minimum Effort

Select dependable people and companies to perform the services called for on your checklist. Make inquiries before using anyone. Then meet the people involved. Tell them you're going to do a lot of business with them. Tell them that you expect prompt and efficient service, and you'll be loyal to them if they will perform for you.

## Be a Good Customer

Always order the work as soon as you can. The service companies you use have other real estate agents they must please also if they're going to stay in business; never forget this. Always strive to cooperate. Don't waste the time of your service people. Limit your demands for special attention to those occasions when you really need it, and you'll find they'll come through for you.

## Be Forceful, But Always Be Courteous

As you're pushing the details along, remember that many of the people you're dealing with are salaried. They'll get paid whether your treasured transaction falls out or closes, so don't expect them to feel as intensely about the deal as you do.

## Bug People Briefly, Respectfully, and Frequently

Repetition is more effective than rage. Firm persistence pays. Make people want to help you, not determined to foil you.

# Be There at the Settlement

In some states, you must sit in on a settlement ceremony at which papers are signed and a deed is exchanged for a check. There's no such settlement meeting in California, but the principle remains the same—both agents must be available to react to any sudden emergency. If you can't be in town the day your transaction closes, designate another competent agent in your office to cover for you, and make sure everyone concerned knows who is covering.

After hundreds of transactions, I still worked with checklists. Although the sixth sense for trouble I developed usually served me well, sometimes my sixth sense was out to lunch. A checklist never is out to lunch.

Tailor the basic checklist given in Chapter 24 (and on the accompanying CD) to your state laws, climate, local conditions, and customs.

# CHAPTER 20

# A 100 Percent Referral Business

Develop a Farm First ● The Referral ● But What Will They Take? ● Doing Volume Business ● Put Warmth in Your Fast Professional Job ● Return Messages ● When They Move In ● How to Get Letters of Recommendation ● Getting Referrals ● "We've Moved" Cards ● Stay in Touch ● Remembrance Programs ● Inhale New Information, Exhale New Business ● Drop One, Pick Up Seven ● Winning Scripts

You can make big money in real estate by farming—but not the top dollar. So why bother with a farm in the first place? You should bother because farming is one of the fastest and surest ways to build referral business.

## Develop a Farm First

First develop a farm until it's producing a steady crop of fine listings. While you're doing this, the phone will start ringing with the following kind of call.

"I hear you really know what you're doing, so I want you to come over and list my house."

Then it'll ring again.

"I'm Joe Justgotin. I'd like to see some houses. Herbert Kelly said you were the best agent to call."

All of a sudden you've got referral business—but you can't slack off in your farm yet. You still need to promote. You still need to send thank-you notes, advertise, work open houses, and put in floor time. The business will keep on coming to you because you've earned it—by effective promotion and then by effective performance for your clients.

At first, you'll spend all your nonlearning time searching for buyers and sellers. When you're working with a good amount of customers, you'll perhaps cut your search-for-clients time in half, but you'll still have to farm or you'll soon have no clients and no income. It will come home to you very forcefully how much more you could accomplish if you started each day with a client or customer who has a need, rather than with your need to find a client or customer.

This whole book is about how to maximize your time so you can create a loyal clientele who will keep on feeding you the first shot at listings and sales. Then, by knowing how to hit the target with lots of those first shots, you will earn a large income.

By stick and piece, just as a house is built, you will build your loyal clientele. First, you acquire the site—your real estate listing farm. Guided by plans, as a contractor is, you will work effectively at preparing your site. You will lay the strong, straight foundation for a loyal clientele by performing the basic services of real estate with competence, friendliness, and integrity.

Always make sure people are glad you are their agent. In house construction, as in clientele construction, a crooked or weak foundation results in a ramshackle structure of little value and no permanence. Erect the walls of your clientele structure by following through, by using your expertise to foresee problems, and by doing the extra things we'll talk about in this chapter.

Roof your clientele structure by asking for referrals. Furnish it by keeping in touch with former clients so they will remember to recommend you when real estate comes up in conversation. Your clientele structure can be a shack or a mansion; it depends on how much effort and material you're willing to put into its construction.

One of my closest clients was a husband and wife who had been married 60 years. They were the closest couple I ever knew. I'd sold the family several houses: to the grandparents, the parents, and the newlywed children. Every time they had a real estate problem during the last five years, they'd call me up.

"What should I do about a home improvement loan?"

"Who should I call for a swimming pool bid?"

I was the real estate member of their family.

On Christmas Eve, the patriarch of the clan called me. "My wife died today. I wanted you to be the first to know." He was sobbing on the phone. Because his single son lived with them and there were three names in joint tenancy on the title, and he was very concerned about what he had to do legally. He said, "I can't think of anyone I'd rather call, because you're part of our family."

When you're building a clientele, remember what an intimate family you want to become. Approach every listing presentation, and work with every buyer, with this in mind.

Before I ever made a listing presentation, I instinctively looked on everyone in my farm as someone who could decide to move tomorrow. I did this because I couldn't tell the move-sooners from the stay-put-forevers back in those days. Truthfully, I still don't know how. People have told me, "I'm never moving; my roots here are driven all the way to the center of the earth," and four months later they're calling the moving van. You never know. Everyone on your farm is a possible client, and a source of vital information and referrals.

The first place I went when I started in this business was out to greet people. All the housewives vacuuming on Saturday morning, and all the husbands shining their cars in driveways, turned and looked when the big mama made her first appearance in the local neighborhood. I came equipped with giveaways: free litter bags for the husband's car, rain hats for the wives. Information began leaping (along with baby in the tummy) my way.

"Hey, the guy next door is being transferred." The leads kept coming at me because I kept going back after them.

"My brother may want to move out here. Do you have any information about Mission Viejo you could mail him?" I sure did.

"Brad Johnson just decided to take the job in Pennsylvania. Told us so last night."

This is how it went. Looking back, I can remember dozens of leads of this kind. Not all of them worked out, but I followed up on every one. Those early leads to a fee still stand out in my memory, but the hundreds of doors I knocked on, and the thousands of phone calls I made which led nowhere, have long been forgotten.

I did things differently later in my career. In the early days I was looking for a break, couldn't find one, and then I realized I had to make my own breaks. I worked a farm and the for-sale-by-owners, and checked birth announcements for leads to people who might need to move up, held open houses, and so on. Later my major real estate sales work consisted of handling three areas: (1) come-list-me requests; (2) show-me-homes requests; and (3) servicing listings and open transactions.

# The Referral

The phone rings. They want me! Me; lil' ol' me.

"We heard you're good."

They are giving me their Academy Award. I love it.

"We heard you really know the score."

Hot diggety! A firecracker goes bang! I've arrived in someone's mind. Whoop-dee-doo! Wow! Wham! It's the Fourth of July to me!

I kept a Rolodex file of all my closed transactions, and worked the file at least twice yearly. Sometimes I sent out crazy notes, or dropped over and said "Hi" to clients. Every Christmas I had special tree ornaments made up and delivered to my clients and customers. I sent out a lot of flowers all through the year.

The 100 percent referral business doesn't mean you go up on a mountain, squat in front of a cave, and wait for people to climb up to you. You're still working; you're still farming; only now you're exclusively watering and fertilizing and reseeding your Everybody-I-Know Farm. You may spend more money on giveaways now than you ever did on the ordinary 300-house farm, but the returns are far greater because you average more payoff work each day. Your gifts now go to people who've already worked with you, are likely to do so again when they have a need and, in many cases, have already given you fee-winning referrals. Instead of trudging door-to-door recruiting strangers, much of your time is spent on the phone gathering information and pushing transactions toward their closings.

The Rolodex file is your stock in trade. It's your umbrella of protection against the rapid changes of climate hitting the real estate business every now and then. Start filling your Everybody-I-Know Farm Rolodex today.

## But What Will They Take?

When the buyer says, "They're asking $169,000, but what will they take?" *please* don't answer, "Oh, I know it's just an asking price. They'll take less."

Remember, today's buyer is tomorrow's seller. When they ask this question (and every buyer does), look at them and say, "I know they'll take $169,000." Pause an instant, and then say, "I'm perfectly willing to present anything less to the sellers, and work with them to negotiate a good result for all parties."

A significant part of today's buyers will remember how you handled their question when tomorrow comes and they find themselves selling. Three years after buying a house from me, I've had people call up and say, "C'mon over; we're moving." I take the listing and, as we're talking afterwards, one of them says, "You know why we listed with you? Your Christmas tree ornament was nice, and we liked getting your notes, but the real reason is that when you were showing us a million houses before we bought this one, we remember how you represented all those properties. You never said, 'I know they'll take less.' We thought then, that someday, if we ever sell again, we don't want an agent who'll tell every buyer, 'I know I can chisel them down,' like the first guy we worked with said. On about half the houses we'd go in, he'd say, 'Here's what they're asking, but you can get it for a lot less.'"

Whether it's your own listing or not, don't knock the price. Some agents on an open house will announce to everyone who walks in, "They're asking $249,900, but this is my listing and I know the price is soft. Believe me, it's *soft*. They're really motivated." This agent believes he can tell a genuine buyer from a self-appointed spy—if he's ever even thought about sellers' spies. Before long, he's telling the seller's uncle or bridge partner how soft the price is, and a short time later he's groaning around the office, "I just can't believe this. I've always been solid as granite on my $249,900 listing, and they were all set to extend it for another 90 days. So just now I call up and he's an iceberg—says he's listing with Sell Fast Realty tomorrow. Wouldn't give me a reason; wouldn't hardly talk to me. And after all the open houses I've held for them! People sure are ungrateful."

# Doing Volume Business

Doing volume business means working efficiently. You don't have time to patch avoidable mess ups because there are so many *un*avoidable mess ups coming at you.

Working efficiently means that you do the following:

- **Stay on top of phone numbers and names.** If you have only one transaction a month, you can spend 30 minutes looking for the phone number and name you wrote with eyeliner on the back of a candy wrapper. The top producer can't do this.
- **Caravan alone.** You don't have time for jolly chit chat in a car full of wise-cracking agents. You can't afford their distraction while you're emotionalizing a home into your Quick-Speak Inventory.
- **Work to a plan.** Certain things have to be done each day or your problems multiply. List what you have to do and make people wait, if it's unavoidable, while you do those tasks.
- **Schedule time off and take it.** Without time off you burn out, mentally and physically. Sustained high production must be supported by quality recreation.

## Put Warmth in Your Fast Professional Job

Many otherwise strong agents fail to build a large and loyal clientele because they are too coldly efficient, too much the big operator, and too surface slick. Their clients know they were well served, but feel vaguely taken advantage of; machine-processed instead of treated by a warm and caring person. Let a wart or two show and prove you're down to earth, friendly, and real. Make clients glad they've contributed to your success. It's better not to be absolutely perfect. You're in a highly emotional business and, while you can easily get too involved in your customers' problems, you can also easily be too aloof, too uncaring, and too determined to preserve a strict professional relationship.

Functioning on a large scale in residential resales requires more than efficiency. It requires an efficiency coated by friendliness and warmth. Work on achieving the happy medium between concerned, unforced friendliness and overinvolvement in your clients' problems. Sometimes only a fine line divides the two, and the fine line runs in different places for different people at different times. There are no simple rules, but you should be thinking about whether you're operating at the right distance from each set of clients every time you meet with them.

## Return Messages

Return messages from customers just as fast after the sale as you did when you were showing them property. This can be difficult sometimes, but you've got to give them consistently good service if you're going to build a loyal clientele. If you don't, people will think, "She sold us a house and got what she wanted from us—so now we're nobody. When she was showing us property, she always got back to us the same day. Three days ago I called her, and she still hasn't called back. All she cares about is quick money."

When these people decide to move again, in two months or two years, they'll remember how you slighted them after they bought, not how you catered to them before the sale.

Agents who unconsciously—or deliberately—slow down services after the sale are sometimes heard to say, "I'm the unluckiest person in the world when it comes to finding loyal clients."

# When They Move In

## Help Them Move In

While the sale is in process, hand them your flyer with information on utilities, cleaning services, schools, and so on. Some utilities require the owner to sign or make a deposit, others don't. Arrange to have utilities connected on whatever date your buyers specify if possible. Tell your buyers to consider your office as being their message center while they're en route.

## Dinner on You the Night They Move

This is remembered with special gratitude by wives too tired from unpacking to shop and cook, by husbands who're a bit edgy about unexpected moving expenses, and especially by single parents. You'll save time and money and make a better impression by not inviting yourself to this dinner. Let them go by themselves and relax.

The free dinner is easily arranged by talking to the manager of a good restaurant, and perhaps making a cash deposit. One highly successful agent runs a tab for this purpose at a country club, and needs only to call and say, "Mr. and Mrs. Kimito Katayama and their two children will be in for dinner tonight. Put the charges on my bill."

Don't worry if your clients have the extra thick filet mignon just because you're paying; they will feed you referrals—a far richer diet for you than any restaurant will serve them.

## Bring a House-Warming Gift

Give your buyers a home-furnishings gift certificate or a card to a local health exercise class if they are fitness-oriented people. How about a lush green house plant or maybe a pen-and-ink sketch of the home framed? Brainstorm gift ideas with fellow salespeople.

# How to Get Letters of Recommendation

Ask for recommendations. Do it softly, and wait until they're settled. Ask enthusiastic people, not those who see everything in two shades of gray. When you make your second follow-up call to see how they're getting along three weeks after they're in, if they say something like, "I knew I liked this home before, but now I love it. My kids are on the swim team, and everything is really clicking."

This is the time for, "Can I ask you a favor? Would you mind writing a letter of recommendation, saying I did a good job for you? I want to put it in my Listing Presentation Manual. And I'll keep a copy in my desk, so when I have a down day, I can read it, and remember I helped somebody, and feel good about myself again."

*Ask* for letters of recommendation; you'll get a hundred times as many as you would if you never asked.

# Getting Referrals

You have to ask for referrals too. You have to tell people you're eager and able to handle more business. You might think it's always obvious to everyone, but you can so easily slip into appearing hassled, over-worked, and in desperate need of time off—when you're really in desperate need of a hot buyer more than anything else. Never let a client think for an instant you're anything but thrilled with the real estate business. For clients and customers you should always be up.

Referred customers are quicker to refer their friends to you than picked-up customers are, partly because referred clients often are the sort of people who habitually seek recommendations when faced with important decisions. Refer to the Winning Scripts at the end of this chapter for referral-breeding phrases to use with them.

With pick-up clients and customers, there's even less reason to leave the referral idea to chance. Do it delicately, but plant this thought firmly in their brains: recommending you to their friends is something you need and want. Unless you take the initiative, it may never occur to them to refer you to their friends.

They may even like you so well they won't refer you. Here's an example of how this happens. Art and Cheryl Hermosillo are a charming young couple you pulled in from an ad call. They buy their first house from you, they love it, and you too. A few weeks later, their friends, Joe and Scrappy Loudslap, come over to see their new house.

After a few more visits, the Loudslaps are very enthusiastic about your area. When Art and Cheryl talk it over, however, they decide not to mention you to Joe and Scrappy. They feel their friends are too crude for you, they probably won't buy a house anyway, and you're so busy you'll be annoyed with them for bothering you with the Loudslaps.

Fortunately, you run into Art and Cheryl and, as you're talking to them, you realize they have something on their minds. You draw them out and then assure them you'll be happy to take your chances with Joe and Scrappy. So Art and Cheryl put their crude friends in touch with you.

An experience like this convinced me I had to be more direct about asking for referrals. (I sold a house to the couple like the Loudslaps in three days. They were fun to work with.) I'd been Shy Sheila when it came to telling people that I wanted and dreamed about, referral business. So I started making a more concentrated effort of asking for referrals in a nice way, and I began getting a lot more of them.

## "We've Moved" Cards

My friend Marleen has ten of the notice below typed up for each of her buyers after they've moved in. She drops them off a day or two after they arrive, before the newcomers have time to send their new address to their friends. These cards are complete with the customers' name and new return address typed on the envelope. They get used because they're so convenient, which means Marleen's personally endorsed advertisement goes all over the country. She tells me it's a real business-builder for her.

---

*We are proud to announce we have recently moved to Huntington Beach. Our new address is:*

*98281 WORTHPORT DRIVE*

*HUNTINGTON BEACH, CA 92646*

*We would also like to mention our Realtor, Marleen Litzel, who helped make our move a pleasant one. If you're looking for a home in this area or thinking of selling your present home, give Marleen a call at (800) 555-9999. We're enclosing her card for your convenience, so be sure to mention us!*

*Our schedule is a little hectic right now since we're in the midst of boxes, but we're looking forward to seeing you soon.*

---

## Stay in Touch

Stay in touch with your sellers who move away. You never know when they might move back. And, wherever they go, people around them will know where they came from, people will tell them when someone is moving to their old hometown, and they'll have a chance to send you a referral.

With your buyers who stay in town, keep in touch. You can't bury yourself in your office and your daily routine of working with new clients and expect your old clients to remember you when they move three years later. If your old clients haven't heard from you, you won't even be fourth on their list.

Staying in touch means an annual gift plus a phone call, a visit, or a note every six months. Magnify your impact by varying your touch: phone sometimes, visit sometimes, send a note sometimes.

Don't direct all your keep-in-touch efforts toward just the wife, or to just the husband, or to just one member of a less traditional household. You can learn this the hard way, or you can take this tip from me, and save the fees you'll lose otherwise. I kept in touch with only the wife in several couples who'd bought from me because it was easier— and I first learned they were moving when their houses appeared on the hot sheet as new listings.

I had slipped up on keeping in touch with the husbands because I thought I was solid with the wives. But when it got down to the "Honey, I'm sorry but we're moving again" stage, the locker-room referral won out. Never put all your eggs in one basket. A couple is two people (count 'em two) and they are both important in the listing decision.

# Remembrance Programs

Schedule time to remember your entire clientele during each of two off seasons during the year. Stick to your schedule, or your referral business will dwindle, not grow. Decide what your annual gift system will be: birthday, anniversary, Christmas, Mother's and Father's Day. You can also create your own gift day: Jive up January Day, September Surprise, or another creative idea. A note saying you're striking a blow against dull February, when enclosed with a gift, will have more impact than the same amount of money spent two months earlier at Christmas. Do what turns you on, suits your personality, and fits your schedule. Stay within your budget—but think big. Careful planning will maximize your impact, which will maximize your income.

Don't overlook stopping by, and leaving the good old memo pad extolled in Chapters 6 and 7. If no one answers your knock, write a note like, "Sure hope you like your home now as well as you did the day you moved in. Just thinking about you, Maria Jian."

The important part of your program is to make those twice-yearly contacts every spring and fall, and deliver a unique special remembrance sometime during the year. Instead of a gift, some agents follow a birthday and anniversary card program. I've never done this, but other agents have, with good results in building up clientele. If you feel comfortable with this approach, do it.

## Keep Clients and Customers Informed of Your Success

Clients love to hear about your success! They really do. If you have done all the things suggested here, all the detail work, and all the follow-up, then you're not an agent to your clients, you're a friend! They'll love you! You're part of the team they're rooting for. When your picture is in the paper, or they hear you're doing this or that, write them and say, "Thanks. I couldn't have done this without you. I get by with a little help from my friends."

# Inhale New Information, Exhale New Business

It pays off well to keep current with happenings by reading the local papers, but it pays off fabulously well to stay ahead of what's printed as news. You'll reap more benefits from getting out and seeing the people and the places, and then doing something about what you learn.

For example, going to your office from an early morning meeting with a seller, you follow your usual practice of keeping your eyes open while you take a route through an area you haven't been in for a few days. In a shopping center you see a merchant putting a "Going Out of Business Sale" banner in the window of his paint store. You have no intention of diluting your concentration on the home resale market, so you call a business opportunities broker you know, and tell him about the banner.

Your friend says, "So Charlie Pealing has finally had enough. He just isn't the type to be in retail sales. I'll hustle right over and see him. Charlie should sell the business, not close it. The right owner could make a bundle. Do you have an in with Charlie?"

"Not at all. See if you can find out whether they're planning to sell their home and move out of town, will you?"

Two days later, Biz Op Agent calls you back.

"I listed the paint store. And the Pealings are leaving town. Charlie's wife's name is Mabel. I'd go over and see her this afternoon, if I were you."

# Drop One, Pick Up Seven

When I met Steve and Tina for our second appointment to look at property, Steve said, "I guess we wasted yesterday morning for you, Danny.

We've decided a view isn't so important after all. Everything else is still the same. Sorry to spring this on you without warning."

"No problem at all, Steve. Okay, I can think of . . ."

"You'll need some time to research a new bunch of houses, won't you?"

I shook my head reviewing my inventory in my head. "Just give me a few minutes to phone our new group of sellers. And yesterday wasn't wasted, because now I know exactly the right house for you."

Steve and Tina looked at each other a little oddly, so I explained quickly, "But there are three other really sharp homes I want you to look at also. While you finish your coffee, I'll let the owners know we're coming."

A few minutes later, we were on our way. "Do you want to see the house I think you'll like first, or shall I save it for last?"

"Save the best for last," Tina said.

They went through my three comparison houses carefully. Today the emphasis of their search was on finding reasons to eliminate each house; yesterday they had talked about how they could repaint the walls and change the carpet. I realized they'd already found a house they really wanted.

Driving toward the last house, the one I thought they'd really like, the tension felt like it would pop open the doors of my car. At last we turned into a small cul-de-sac where only one house was for sale.

"I knew it," Steve said. "Did I tell you, or didn't I tell you, Tina?"

Both of them jumped out of the car and hurried up the sidewalk toward the house I'd brought them to see. But not for the first time, obviously. Here I'd thought I was smart to hit on just what they wanted in two days—but somebody else had done it in one afternoon!

I forced a smile, let them inside, and watched while they dashed off in different directions. I stood there, knowing there wasn't anything I could do to sell them; somebody already had done it. I qualify all my customers before showing houses, so I knew they could afford the place or I wouldn't have brought them there. I also knew the house was priced right.

Steve and Tina finally put their heads together for a moment of quiet talk. Then they walked up to me, eyes shining.

"This is it, Danny. Let's go back to the office and write it up."

The listing agent on the property was a well-known agent who closed a lot of buyers she picked up on open houses. She hadn't been able to close Steve and Tina though. Neither had I; they'd closed themselves—but, I thought, we all need some gravy now and then.

Driving back to the office, I named the listing agent.

"I'm surprised she held that house open—it's tough to find. She likes to work the ones right off the busy streets."

"It wasn't open yesterday," Steve said. "We floundered in there with a brand new agent. Look."

I glanced at the card he held out, and saw "Julie Spice" written neatly on a local realty firm's cards.

"She was working her very first open house somewhere around here."

"Julie might be brand new, but she was really sharp to take you to that house right off," I said.

"Pure dumb luck," Steve said. "She thought it had a view until we got there. We only went in to be nice, and then—whammo. Who wants an agent who doesn't know what she's doing to represent them? If I lived out here and could stay on top of it—maybe."

"Except for her being new, did you like her okay?"

"Sure," Tina said. "But we've got to fly back home as soon as possible, and Steve doesn't think she can look out for our interests the way you will. After all, we'll be 2,000 miles away."

"Let her get some seasoning first," Steve said. "She doesn't even know her way around town."

"Oh, you just rattled the poor girl," Tina said. "When we walked into her open house, it was really sweet how excited she got. She hadn't seen anyone for three hours, and she was just closing up. So we just had to let her show us some other houses."

I remembered the feeling. You're so new it hurts, and you know it shows. You're scared of all the things you don't understand about the business, and you wait, and wait, and wait on those endless open houses before you learn how to use your time. You're praying people will come because you need a transaction bad—and at the same time you're afraid to have anyone come because there's so much you don't know. I remembered—in an eye-moistening flash.

Tina kept on talking, "We stayed at our house—Steve, I'm already calling it our house—until it got dark on us. So it took her a few minutes to find her way back to where we'd left our car, and old grump here . . ."

"I just told her she needed to learn the streets," Steve said.

"But by this time, Julie was quivering from head to toe," Tina said. "She figured she had made her first sale."

"Because she'd had some dumb luck," Steve said, "I don't see how we owe her anything. In fact, we gave her some badly needed experience—free."

We were back at my office by this time. Thinking about the new agent, I led the way inside. It's no fun to be quivering hungry for a sale.

I've been there and I know. But those days were past for me; by this time I had three very good years behind me.

"Steve, Tina—it'll break Julie's heart if you buy the house she found for you through me. We can work this out so you're protected. I know her broker and he's good. I'll call him right now and get his word that he'll stay on top of this transaction all the way through, so there's no way you'll have problems with her inexperience."

"Danny, you took us there today. What did she really do for us?"

"Steve, she took you there first. Now she's pacing the floor, wondering what happened, sweating out the phone, jumping every time it rings thinking it's you or Tina wanting to make an offer. Please go through her. Let's all feel good about the great house you've found."

That's the one I dropped. I'm no Pollyanna. Had I been struggling, I never would've done it. But I had money in the bank and a success pattern established. I didn't need to step on heads. So I called her broker, explained the situation, and of course he agreed to watch the transaction. Steve and Tina were pleased with how it went.

The seven sales I picked up came about because Julie's office sold nine of my listings the following year, compared with only two the year before.

# Winning Scripts

Let's say you've wrapped up a sale to Martin and Georgia, who were referred by Jack and Helen. After the wrap up, it's quite easy and natural for you to say, "Martin and Georgia, can I tell Jack and Helen you're satisfied with my service?"

"You certainly can," Martin says. "In fact, I'll call Jack myself and tell him what a great job you did for us."

(If Martin calls Jack, that's great, but don't depend on it. Call Jack and Helen later and thank them for the referral yourself.)

Tell Martin, "I'd appreciate it so much if you would call Jack. You know, people feel responsible when they recommend someone, and that's just one reason why I go all out to justify the confidence referrals have in me. I depend completely on referrals from satisfied clients—from *very pleased* clients, I hope—and I really like it this way. It's so much nicer to work with clients who've been referred. I can do a much better job for people when there's a feeling of mutual confidence from the start. Martin and Georgia, don't you think we had mutual confidence right from the beginning?"

"We did. We certainly did," Martin says. "We saw everything we needed to see, we didn't waste time, and we bought right. I feel good about the whole thing."

"Wonderful. I can't tell you how pleased I am to hear you say so. Would it be asking too much if I'd say I hope you'll recommend me to your family and friends if the opportunity arises?"

"Oh, we certainly will," Georgia says.

"You wouldn't happen to know of anyone who's thinking of a real estate move now, would you?"

Martin shakes his head. "No, 'fraid not. You know, we hate to rush off, but . . ."

"Martin," Georgia says, "What about the Hensons?"

"Oh, right," Martin says. "Funny I'd forgotten about them—must be all the excitement. Now, with us living here, I think the Hensons might move in too. They've talked about it for a couple of years, but they didn't want to go where they didn't know anybody. I'll give you Bill's phone number—you should call him."

Even if you don't sell the Hensons, you can ask for referrals. Sometimes you'll show property to people for three or four days, and they think you're great, but they buy in an area outside your working range.

When a client calls to drop the bad news that they've bought elsewhere, why not say, "I'm really glad you found what you wanted. I really am."

"Well, we just wish we could've bought it through you."

"Do you feel I did a good job showing you this area?"

"I sure do."

"Can I drop you a couple of my business cards in the mail? Would you mind referring people to me who might be moving down to this area?"

If you're this close to them, they'll always tell you they'll be happy to refer you. And this works—I've sold several people who were referred to me by people who had bought elsewhere.

# CHAPTER 21

# Time Planning with or without Paper

Time—Do You Have Enough? ● Use a Personal Digital Assistant ● How to Plan Your Day ● Setting Priorities ● Use a Pencil ● Use a Checklist ● Use a PDA or a Laptop ● How to Close Rings ● Controlling the Phone Monster ● Interruptions ● Time-Log Yourself ● Schedule Your Days, Weeks, and Seasons ● Juggling Personal and Professional Time ● Communicating Right the First Time ● Watch for Danger Signs in Communication ● The $8 Million Listener ● Set Aside Some Alone Time ● When Depression Starts Eating Up the Clock

Life offers us only two things: time and each other. The 86,400 seconds in every day are all we'll ever have. Time is like no other concept—it is life itself. Because its importance to us all cannot be exaggerated, we want to devote an entire chapter to the effective use of time, both personal and professional.

## Time—Do You Have Enough?

"Do the most productive thing possible at every given moment."

This is a great concept. There are other ideas, and we will suggest a few effective systems here. But the biggest problem people face with time isn't *time* management—it's *self*-management. You and I can try to control everything happening in our immediate universe, but we can't be effective if we're nonselective. Getting control of your life means letting go in the areas where you are ineffective, and taking more control in the areas where your time is well spent. It means you make, and carry out, basic decisions about how you'll invest your most precious, irreplaceable, and nonrenewable asset: time.

The trend that's been running ever stronger for decades will get even more intense in the twenty-first century. Fewer agents—superstars—will control more of the business than ever. For a long time there have been areas with more agents than transactions—and yet a few agents are making huge incomes there. How can the superstars do it? They do it by using all their working time to do what pays the most: farming, listing, prospecting, negotiating, and selling.

As soon as possible, a superstar agent will hire a personal assistant—perhaps a licensed person—to do routine things the agent doesn't have to do personally. But you have to do it all at first, until you have acquired the necessary funds, knowledge, and skills to hire help. Until then, your focus has to be on controlling your time effectively—never an easy task in a business as filled with unexpected opportunities and challenges as real estate.

We lose control (and lose the ability to further our growth) in areas of our life where we have closed our minds to positive change. All too often, we do this by giving control of our lives to the small emergencies of the moment instead of to our own carefully thought-out plans. Closing off areas of our life from positive change means we have ceased to grow in those areas. Since we cannot remain constant, when we stop growing in an area, we start decaying there. Life is a series of growth or decay rings, each one connected to the others. We open a new growth ring by choice, compulsion, or chance. Then we either nurture it with care, action, and energy—or we allow it to wither. And finally, either right away or later, we close the ring. Call it change, call it growth, or call it getting older, life is a series of rings. Each ring has an opening, an effective period, and a close. Each ring of your life is either a growth ring—or a decay ring.

Learn to think in terms of change. Be aware of how everything is growing or decaying: your love, your skills, your friendships, your spirit, your fortune, your health, and your surroundings. But don't hate or fear decay; it's the natural process providing us with nutrients for future growth rings.

When you think in terms of change, you can see more clearly how you are making choices—or are letting circumstances make them for you. Make choices after weighing your conflicting opportunities instead of just letting things happen to you. Before you can be effective, you must plug your mind into now—this day, this hour, this minute, this second. *Plug into now.*

Some people should carry around a tape player to endlessly repeat "Plug into now, plug into now, plug into now." Living in yesterday or yesteryear, regretting what was or wasn't said or done five minutes or five years ago, is living in a decay ring. Living in the now, while preparing wisely for the future, is a growth ring. Living in the future is a decay ring. How great can the future be unless you take great care of *now*? The future hits with a shattering blow of reality to the people who try to live in it.

How can you plan your time in a business which requires you to be at the beck and call of buyers and sellers? Recognize that it isn't easy. Then go on from there. Of course any time plan you set up will be interrupted—frequently, you hope—by the urgent demands from your clients and customers. Clients clamoring for your attention means business, and business means fees. If people interrupt your schedule, make them pay for the privilege—don't begrudge them.

Recognize also that you'll frequently have to decide whether to abandon a planned day because something just came up, or refuse to change your game plan. Rehearse how to say *no* politely. Always be ready to say, "I can't make it today, but do you have any free time to-morrow?" Make your nonbusiness, nonfamily appointments tentative so you can jump on a fast-breaking opportunity. And regard most family appointments as sacred and unbreakable, regardless of the opportunity's glitter. You only have one family, but hundreds of business opportunities will come your way.

"I'll do it later when I have the time," is an illusion you can't afford. You'll never have more time. Unless you retire to Mars, you're never going to have more than 24 hours between now and this same minute tomorrow.

Using time productively is the most valuable skill you can have; recognizing this fact is the largest step you can take toward packing your hours with action, success, and fun. With this skill, anything physically possible can be achieved. Without it, very little of your potential will be used, and you'll achieve only a fraction of the success you're capable of.

# Use a Personal Digital Assistant

Using a personal digital assistant (PDA) futhers your time management abilities. Try to prioritize and then keep your eye on each targeted task all day. But plan it without paper. Purchase your personal digital assistant and follow all the instructions of this chapter. Just do it electronically. Some of you won't go for the no paper idea. You love your scraps of paper. I am not going to argue with you. Just make sure that you complete what you want to complete each day.

# How to Plan Your Day

Plan your day the night before, and do it every night.

In the beginning, allow 15 minutes each night for this vital element of your personal growth, income, and time control system. You'll soon learn to do a thorough job of planning your day in 5 minutes or less.

## Three Actual Time Plans

On the following three pages are daily time plans prepared by three successful real estate agents. Note how much easier the veteran's time plan is. He's paid the price for a 100 percent referral business, and now he's enjoying a high degree of control over his time along with a high income.

Make planning tomorrow an integral part of your bedtime routine. Follow the same steps each night and you'll find your planning going faster, and nothing will slip past you. Here's my step-by-step system for daily planning:

**1.** I review my monthly and weekly pages for all the items I've accumulated over the past few weeks that must be done tomorrow.
**2.** I list these items on the daily work plan, along with the new tasks popping into my mind at this time.
**3.** I give my short- and long-term goals a fast mental run-through, and set activity targets (how many doors I need to knock on, or how many fizzbos I should see, for example) to enable me to reach my goals.
**4.** I highlight the *must-be-done* details; the ones that may turn into monsters if they're not handled when they should be handled.

This is all there is to it! When I first stated doing this, it was a hard quarter-hour's work, but the results on those first tomorrows were so great I've never stopped planning my days this way. After a week or two, I was getting my planning done in two or three minutes a night, and I often felt I'd saved two or three hours a day because I was organized. It adds up fast—as extra listings taken, and more houses sold increase the time pressure.

Planning tomorrow every night lets you sleep better. When I first got into real estate, I didn't do this planning for months. I'd toss and turn in the middle of the night, wondering what time I had to be where the next day, and how I'd get the loan documents delivered before 10:00 so the loan would fund on time. I was doing my planning the

| FEBRUARY | MARCH | APRIL |
|---|---|---|
| S  M  T  W  T  F  S | S  M  T  W  T  F  S | S  M  T  W  T  F  S |
|            1  2  3  4 |            1  2  3  4 |                        1 |
| 5  6  7  8  9  10  11 | 5  6  7  8  9  10  11 | 2  3  4  5  6  7  8 |
| 12  13  14  15  16  17  18 | 12  13  14  15  16  17  18 | 9  10  11  12  13  14  15 |
| 19  20  21  22  23  24  25 | 19  20  21  22  23  24  25 | 16  17  18  19  20  21  22 |
| 26  27  28 | 26  27  28  29  30  31 | 23  24  25  26  27  28  29 |
|  |  | 30 |

### Monday March 13

| Time | | Task | Time |
|---|---|---|---|
| **8** | | Pick up kids at Jr. High | **3** |
| | Floor time | Basketball game (Jeff, Sue, Jamie) | |
| **9** | Return messages | | **4** |
| **10** | Organize what to show, check if available, set appointments to preview | Prepare dinner | **5** |
| **11** | Organize newsletter, ad or flyer | | **6** |
| **12** | Preview properties | Go over listing presentation, comps, etc. | **7** |
| | Printer—newspaper appt. | | |
| **1** | Calls to customers, escrow prospects | Listing presentation | **8** |
| **2** | Children home—call | | **9** |

### NOTES:

| | |
|---|---|
| Married woman | 3 million volume |
| 4 children | |
| 2 years in real estate | |

hardest way possible—with my conscious mind in gear instead of asleep. Then I discovered the subconscious mind works on your problems in the middle of the night if you'll commit them to writing. Then your conscious mind rests, and the subconscious takes over and does its job. You wake up and the solution to many of your problems is as plain as the new day's sun.

But, and this is important, the next morning when you wake up, do present-time exercises—DON'T READ THE TIME PLAN YET.

| FEBRUARY | MARCH | APRIL |
|---|---|---|
| S M T W T F S | S M T W T F S | S M T W T F S |
|       1 2 3 4 |       1 2 3 4 |            1 |
| 5 6 7 8 9 10 11 | 5 6 7 8 9 10 11 | 2 3 4 5 6 7 8 |
| 12 13 14 15 16 17 18 | 12 13 14 15 16 17 18 | 9 10 11 12 13 14 15 |
| 19 20 21 22 23 24 25 | 19 20 21 22 23 24 25 | 16 17 18 19 20 21 22 |
| 26 27 28 | 26 27 28 29 30 31 | 23 24 25 26 27 28 29 |
| | | 30 |

### Thursday March 16

| | |
|---|---|
| **8** | Door knocking (15)     **3** |
| **9** Check Multiple Listing book, hot sheets, expired in office | FSBO appt.     **4** |
| **10** Printing pick up | Expired appt.     **5** |
| **11** | Cold calls     **6** |
| Floor duty | |
| **12** No lunch today—Do mail-outs | **7** |
| | Appt. expired listing |
| **1** Preview property | **8** |
| **2** Post office run | **9** |

NOTES:

| |
|---|
| Single guy          2 million volume |
| 31 years old |
| 3 weeks—no days off |
| 3 days—goes & hides |
| 2nd year in real estate |

Wait until your morning routine is out of the way and you've reached your work area. Then open the planner, and tear into your first growth ring of the day with all your first-task eagerness. Check off each item you complete; each one is a win you should feel good about. It's so nice to see lots of boxes checked off at the end of the day, and to know you've done all you could do to achieve your goals in those hours.

| FEBRUARY | MARCH | APRIL |
|---|---|---|
| S M T W T F S | S M T W T F S | S M T W T F S |
| 1 2 3 4 | 1 2 3 4 | 1 |
| 5 6 7 8 9 10 11 | 5 6 7 8 9 10 11 | 2 3 4 5 6 7 8 |
| 12 13 14 15 16 17 18 | 12 13 14 15 16 17 18 | 9 10 11 12 13 14 15 |
| 19 20 21 22 23 24 25 | 19 20 21 22 23 24 25 | 16 17 18 19 20 21 22 |
| 26 27 28 | 26 27 28 29 30 31 | 23 24 25 26 27 28 29 |
| | | 30 |

### Monday March 20

| | | | |
|---|---|---|---|
| **8** | Exercise program & tennis | Constant follow-up on leads | **3** |
| **9** | | | **4** |
| **10** | Office to service transactions | | **5** |
| **11** | | Dinner | **6** |
| **12** | Lunch with old client | Phone canvassing | **7** |
| **1** | Showings | Listing presentation | **8** |
| **2** | | | **9** |

NOTES:

Single guy
4 million dollar volume last 3 years
6 years in business

## Make Tasks to Do Pop into Your Mind at Daily Planning Time

As you run across tasks through the day to go on tomorrow's time plan, enter them in your PDA, jot them down on your calendar, or record them on your micro recorder.

Fill out your tomorrow's plan in a quiet place where you can be alone—go in the bathroom and lock the door if necessary. Take a moment to relax and free your mind of hassles. Then jot down your things to do as fast as your memory pours them at you. Don't slow down the process by assigning priorities. Do this tomorrow morning.

What a thrill it is—what a tremendous feeling of power it gives you—when this system is working reliably for you.

## Check the New Day's Growth Rings

Every night, before planning a new day, check today's plan for any growth rings you haven't closed today. Make a decision on each one. Carry the project forward to tomorrow, plug it into a later date, or abandon it.

I always plan both my personal and professional time together each day. Keeping your promise to a child about attending a 3:00 P.M. basketball game is just as important as keeping a 6:30 P.M. listing appointment. Any type of agreement should be honored, both at home and in business. Of course, you can't make more agreements than you have time to honor. The solution is simple. Set priorities, and learn how to say *no*.

## Getting into Present Time

Get into present time when you wake up in the morning. Maybe you had a bad dream. Maybe your fears about a sale falling out made you sleep fitfully. Maybe you just have a sick feeling of impending disaster. If so, first concentrate on the now, on what action you can take right away. Work out your own routine for getting into present time and putting yesterday away. These exercises put me into present time in the morning:

Sitting on the edge of the bed, let your feet rub the rug. Feel its texture. Look out the window at something outside that you like. Look at something in your room that you like. Turn on music and stretch. Reach for the ceiling. Touch your body, your shoulders, and your nose. Touch three walls in your room fast. Pick up a perfume bottle or a vase. Feel its shape.

Do sit ups to music. Touch your toes repeatedly. Make up a creative dance. Sing in the shower. Buy a water massage and enjoy it in your early morning shower. Go out and jog or if you're not in shape, start walking.

Pick up a book and read a familiar happy passage. Do all this fast. The goal is to get into present time quickly, to feel good about yourself, to feel aware of now.

Now commit your day to a force greater than yourself, to God if you're a believer. Pray something like, "Please help me be all that I can be today. Help me play my part in the creation of a better world. Help me concentrate on just today, so at the end of this day, I'll know I did all I could do, as fairly, wisely, and effectively as I could."

## Setting Priorities

List everything to be accomplished the following day, both personal and professional, but don't assign a priority until the next morning. Then, when you arrive in the work area the following morning, use ABCs to set priorities.

A showing appointment and a child's dental appointment are both *A* priorities. Put an "A" beside all these appointments on the time plan. As you go over your list, also mark *B* priorities, task like making a bank deposit, shopping, and auto maintenance. In the middle of October, a *C* priority might be "start Christmas list." You could do it a week or two later, but if time permits, today is the day.

Apply priority setting to clients and open houses also. For example, you've listed a vacant house. It's Tuesday. You get a note from a couple in New Jersey you've been corresponding with. They are arriving in California this weekend, but they don't say when you'll hear from them. Plan an open house at your vacant listing as a *B* priority, and make showing property to the people from New Jersey an *A* priority if they show up. What's nice about priorities is they give you options. And in this business the more options you have, the better your career will go.

You also need to set priorities at home. If you plan on setting your farm on fire this month to build up a big listing bank, then everything on your time plan for this month should reflect this goal. Don't create conflict by telling the family you intend to see a lot of them this month when the farm is foremost in your mind. If you set career priorities this month, set some personal priorities with your spouse and the kids for next month. Balance is the key to an effective juggling act between personal and business demands.

## Use a Pencil

Use a pencil when time planning. Let's face it, you must be flexible in real estate. The best laid plans frequently get flushed down the drain in real estate. You start on expired listings, intending to work on them all day, but a hot buyer pops in off the street. Naturally, you go for the buyer. With no trouble, you erase your original time plan, and plug the expired listing routine into another day. If your schedule is in ink, you'll feel guilty.

# Use a Checklist

Checklists are the greatest way to keep control of the changing patterns in real estate. People often ask me how I kept on top of 20 to 30 transactions a month as a salesperson. I had checklists inside every folder, and I used a communication log for each transaction to record every conversation, phone or in person, relating to the transaction. When you call the lender, and the loan officer tells you the loan on one of your transactions has been approved, record this information in writing, along with the date, time, and name of whomever told you. Also write down when you called the customers to inform them of the good news. When you and another agent are arguing about who was supposed to order the termite reports two hours before the closing, you can refer to the entry in your communication log dated two weeks ago where she promised to order it right away. These communication logs are powerful allies in court, should this ever be necessary.

Since the form has the names at the top, you will need at least one form for each transaction you're working on. In order to keep the forms organized, you might want to keep them in a loose leaf binder, alphabetized by client name, and keep the binder handy to the phone. When the sheet is filled, it can go into the client folder and a blank one with the client's name can be added to the binder.

Checklists for servicing listings, holding houses open, and pulling up-time are all gathered together in Chapter 24 and are available on the accompanying CD-Rom. You'll find step-by-step checklists there to help you keep on top of things in a variety of real estate situations. A sample of the communication log also appears in this chapter.

Imagine yourself with a just-sold listing, another sale made two weeks ago on which the VA appraiser is due out any day, and a third transaction about to close in need of loan documents signed and a cashier's check. How do you manage all these transactions without feeling overwhelmed? It's easy—if you've been working systematically. By reviewing the checklists, you know the exact status of each one. But, don't forget, all this servicing must not take up the major portion of your time. To maintain volume, your main effort must still be directed at contacting new business. You have open houses to set up, and fizzbos to call on. How do you know what invitations you have sent out, which owners you are working with, and a few hundred other details? You have checklists on each of these programs, and cards filed on each of these people. By pulling the card from your file, you can tell the status and progress of each situation.

## Use a PDA or a Laptop

As we mentioned earlier, if you want to eliminate all the paper scraps, do it all on your PDA or your laplap. Microsoft® Office or another software program can shape you up fast. It's your call. Folks think that all this electronic time planning has eliminated time waste and procrastination. You wish! It's just getting more expensive now to realize what a procrastinator you are. So do what works for you.

## How to Close Rings

One of the biggest problems real estate people have is not being able to finish phone conversations, meetings, and projects. Many things get started, but nothing gets finished. So what happens? Confusion, guilt, and problems multiply, as they always do when people fail to complete what they've started. Agents get nervous and ineffective.

Notice how it works in a real estate office. First thing in the morning, the salesperson comes in with the best of intentions. She's started her growth rings for the day properly. The night before she wrote her plan, and she walked into the office ready to go. She's going to write 20 open house invitations to start this morning off strong. After her floor time, she's going to brown bag it for lunch, and then rap knuckles on three blocks' worth of doors. But what happens? She never closes any of these rings. She starts. But visitors, phones, and donuts get in the way. The routine paperwork she should have done six weeks ago now is *A* priority urgent, and must be done *now*. And suddenly the day is done but the work is not.

The following sections describe how to handle interruptions in your day, from people and from paperwork.

## Controlling the Phone Monster

The phone is strictly a message machine. It's not a living, breathing organism able to attack our day and make us its slave. At one time the phone controlled me. I would be eating dinner, talking with my family, and giving them some badly needed time, when the phone would ring. My goodness, it might be the big deal of the year! It might be Ford! It might be Sony! It might be Rockefeller! So, like Pavlov's dog salivating on signal, when the phone rang I'd pick up the receiver ready to do anything it told me to do. Now, the phone is a big item in the life of a real estate agent, especially the real estate agent who needs to connect with any possible house buying or selling creature. However, there are times when this instrument must be excluded from your life. Let your answering machine handle it.

## Don't Prolong Conversations

Someone says, "I'll see you Saturday night," and you immediately introduce a new matter into the conversation. "Oh, did I tell you, my brother bought a new house?" We do this subconsciously. We do it because we hate endings—even phone conversation endings. It's our fear of finality. Train yourself not to introduce new topics into old phone conversations. If the other party tries it on you, say something like, "I want to hear all about it when I see you on Saturday, but I've got to run now."

## Don't Always Have to End Up on Top

Some agents are so competitive they fight to win even when nothing worth winning is involved. For example, you call in to report a sale, and you're just as excited as can be. You've been with these customers for two days straight, so you haven't had a lot of time to service your other transactions. Last night you were at it until almost midnight catching up. You call in to ask the up-person to write your sale on the board. Whoopee!

Instead of sharing congratulations, the up-person lectures you for not returning Mrs. Brown's calls about a termite inspection you know isn't needed for 30 days.

"She called back twice, and boy, is she mad," the up-person says.

You spend the next 10 minutes trying to make the up-person admit you're right about your priorities so you can come out on top. But the up-person packs a big ego too and won't give an inch. It's all so useless. Be alert for no-win conversations, and chop them off with a quick, "I'm real sorry about it, bye." Quit playing games with the precious minutes of your life. Don't hang on to petty squabbles, hang up.

## Open Your Phone Conversations Closer to Their End

You'll save chunks of time by getting right to it on a call. Let's take this situation. You need some information about a listing from an agent you know.

The slow-and-open phone start goes, "Hi, Ed. This is Danny. How's it going?"

Isn't this friendly and polite? Unfortunately, Ed believes it's not nice to tell people you're anything but "fine." He says, "Not too good, Danny. I was talking to a fellow in the parking lot yesterday and a beer truck swung wide and ran over my big toe."

"How terrible." The appraiser, who is standing at your elbow waiting for Ed's information, shifts his weight impatiently.

"Listen, Ed, I'm terribly sorry but . . ."

"Thanks, I appreciate your sympathy. I really do. You know what else happened to me this week? You won't believe this, but . . ."

Let's try the quick and close-to-the-end phone system on Ed's big toe. Say all in one breath, "Hi Ed. Has the sale of your listing on Poplar settled yet?"

"It settled yesterday, Danny. Say, did you hear what happened to me?"

"The appraiser is standing here waiting, Ed. I'll talk to you at the Board of REALTORS® breakfast. Thanks, bye."

When you have calls by the score to make, as every agent handling several transactions at one time does, you have to press on to keep those calls from eating up your get-new business time. Start practicing this vital art now.

## Other Phrases to End a Phone Conversation

"I sure look forward to seeing you on Tuesday, bye." (The call was to arrange Tuesday's meeting.)

"I sure appreciate all your information. It's all I want today, but I'll call you again when I need further help."

"My doorbell's ringing."

"I have a commitment—sorry, gotta run." (You do have a commitment—to yourself to use your time wisely. Be careful. Don't allow yourself to be the most neglected friend you have.) Commitment covers a multitude of sins. Use it freely.

## Use a Time-Efficient Call-Back System

Return messages right before quitting time or lunch. People thinking about going to lunch or leaving for the day don't want to keep on jabbering.

# Interruptions

## Controlling Drop-ins

See your friends on a regular basis, and really work on the friendships. Then fewer people will drop in on you quite as easily and say, "Where have you been?"

If you're busy in a back office, set up a fellow salesperson to help you out when a visitor drops-in to eat up your time. Prime her to say to the visitor (usually the other salespeople know who the pest is), "Would you like me to interrupt him?"

With the garden-variety pest, this usually wakes them up to reality: yes, you are busy right now.

If you are interrupted, stay on your feet—and fidget. Keep looking back at your desk. Or put a limit on the visit by saying, "I am right in the middle of preparing a Guidelines to Market Value for a seller, so I only have a minute right now" or "I have a commitment so we've got to make this quick."

## Limit Coffee

In terms of income lost by wasting time, many agents have a $500-a-day coffee habit.

"I gotta have a cup of java. I just can't get started without a cup of coffee."

Then, of course, you must have donuts with the coffee—which leaves you with sticky fingers you have to wash.

If you worked all the time you spent drinking coffee and snarfing down donuts, you'd close one or two more transactions a month. How about rewarding yourself with one coffee break a day—if you're on target with all your goals. But put a time limit on it.

## Lovely Long Lunches

Lovely long lunches slay time. Oh, they're fun, but what violence they do to your production and energy level for the entire afternoon. The time and money you'd spend on daily long lunches could finance a terrific referral-business builder of the sort staged each month by a broker friend of mine in El Paso, Texas. She hosts lunch and welcome get-togethers for her recent buyers and past clients. Everyone meets one another, and this gives her a priceless opportunity to follow up with clients and customers in a social situation. It's a profitable idea and lots of fun.

## Paper Interruptions

Does your desk look like a paper trap? Do you regularly spend a few calm seconds filing papers where you can go right to them, or do you regularly spend frantic minutes searching through the rubble for papers you must have? If you're a paper junkie, take the clutter cures in the next chapter.

# Time-Log Yourself

Unrealistic time plans are worse than useless. Instead of efficiency, they deliver frustration. Connect yourself with reality on time planning by logging a 48-hour stretch of your life. First, time-plan the 48 hours you're going to log. Then record the hours and minutes you spend on all your activities. Include sleeping, eating, dressing, lunching, shopping, taking care of the car, the yard, and your home. Also record time spent on commuting and recreation, and of course, the time you spend working.

After you've logged the real time spent on your cycles of action for two days, compare how much time you estimated for each activity and how much time you actually spent doing it.

The data you gather this way will guide you to creating realistic time plans able to vastly expand your efficiency.

# Schedule Your Days, Weeks, and Seasons

There's a optimal time to do everything. When your timing's right, your efforts go further. Good timing multiplies your effectiveness by a factor of ten.

Below are the best times of the day, week, and year for working your opportunities.

## For-Sale-by-Owners

Stop in or call fizzbos at 5:30 P.M. on Sunday night. From September through December the resale market usually slows up for everyone—but check the pattern in your locale. Fizzbos need extra help. Take an especially long listing—through March, if possible.

Send fizzbos a note of encouragement timed to arrive on Saturday, "Hope the weekend is going well for you. I might stop by Sunday after my last showing to give you an update on the area's general market activity."

## Your Farm

Work your farm from 3:00 P.M. to 6:00 P.M. on Friday afternoons, and from 10:00 A.M. and 12:00 noon on Saturday mornings.

Double your prospecting schedule between September and December. You'll get few signatures on listings, but you'll create follow-up opportunities you can convert into listing agreements from January through March.

## Cold Calls

Make calls any day between 7 P.M. and 8:30 P.M. (Don't worry about calling on Saturdays or Sundays. Most people will think you're hard working.) Again, work September to December doing lots of phoning and prospecting so you'll have many opportunities to solidify after the first of the year.

## Listing Presentations

Intensify your efforts in this area from September through December. Many of these presentations will be for later follow-up. "We want to wait until after the holidays," is a common refrain. Be sure to send these new prospects Christmas cards, and January letters with predictions about next year's market. A good time for appointments with prospective sellers is 7 P.M. to 8:30 P.M., nightly or on weekends. January through June are big months for new listings. Make sure of your share of those listings by laying heavy groundwork to get them during the final third of the preceding year.

## Showings

Showing is activity intense from March through August. It starts building, depending on climate conditions, between January and March. Plan to keep your days free to show quite a bit. Many companies transfer people right after the first of the year. Do errands and follow-up listings at night and in the early mornings. Leave 10 A.M. to 6 P.M. free to show property.

## Expired Listings

Work expireds the same day your Multiple Listing book is published. Try early morning phone calls. Your comment might be something like, "I noticed your home was removed from the Multiple Listing. Are congratulations in order?" (no pause) "Has it sold?" *Wait* for their reply.

"Oh, what a shame—I remember thinking how lovely your paneled den is with all your seascape paintings."

They're delighted when you remember things like this. It certainly helps you get your foot in the door. But you'll need to have your Quick-Speak down pat.

## To Heal Wounds

Schedule the next day after a disappointment for office catch-up. Time-plan a heavy day of specific goals. Then hit the office early and tear into those projects. Double-check your transaction files. Catch up on all your reports. Organize some new sales and listing aids. Clean out your desk. Answer any correspondence. Send notes to people you think about on a hunch. Sit at your desk for the time-planned number of hours and pound out all the dirty work. All day long, cross off items like crazy on the detailed list of Things to Do you prepared the night before. At the end of the day, you'll have a great sense of accomplishment because you've done a lot of tasks you dislike. A day like this relieves guilt and releases energy. The following day, you'll want to get out amongst them again.

## Schedule One Service Day a Week to Tie Loose Ends Together

Spend one full morning each week (preferably a Monday or Friday) working on open transactions. Call lenders and check on the status of all outstanding loans and funding. Make sure the client and customer has delivered or sent everything necessary. Prepare comparables for appraisers. Check on inspection reports, patio permits, and the like. If the buyer needs to secure a projection of future earnings from his or her company in order to qualify, is it ready to be picked up? Check on your present listings that are still unsold. Call the owners and give them a pep talk. Call agents who have shown your listings and communicate the feedback to the seller.

# Juggling Personal and Professional Time

## Get Help If You Need It

This section is written especially to the ladies (but show it to your husbands).

How can you possibly clean the house, wash the clothes, cook everyone's meals, care for the children (a full-time job in itself) and knock on doors, show property, have listing appointments, and still sleep at night? You are not Houdini! For a long time, I thought I was, and tried to prove it to my family and neighbors.

"I'll show them," I thought. "I can do it all without help. If anyone sees a cleaning crew coming to my house, they'll think I can't handle the pressure. I sure don't want them thinking I'm neglecting my children."

After three years of doing laundry at 2 A.M., and generally not enjoying life or the money I'd had the good fortune to make, I decided to employ a full-time helper.

At first the family didn't think they'd like having someone "hanging around all the time." But, after much discussion, we all reached the same conclusion: having clean socks in the morning and a Mom who could sit down five minutes out of the day would far surpass any loss of privacy we might experience.

Finding the right person wasn't easy. We ran through a few people until the right lady came along. I don't need help now. I just have a once-a-week cleaning service. But things change as kids grow up. It takes time, patience, good recommendations, and perseverance, but good help is out there if you need it.

If you live near a retirement community, there are a lot of able-bodied and capable people there who are lovely, and need other people to care about. Run an ad in the retirement community's local paper and say something like, "We have an active, happy home with two children and two working parents who need domestic assistance. We like people, and will enjoy the company and aid of another member of our team."

Another idea is to run an ad in the local junior college or university's paper. Get to know some of the counselors (try the high schools, too) and tell them about yourself. Maybe they can match you up with a student who will blend well with you and with your family's personality. Also try the employment agencies, or run an ad in several newspapers. A dear friend of mine, who is raising his children on his own, did this. He got the cream of the crop!—a couple in their fifties who love kids and do cleaning, cooking, grocery shopping—the works.

But never forget your status: you are the parent. Outside help should provide you with more quality time for your family. In the summer, go to the office at the crack of dawn, after telling the children, "At 1:00 I'll toot the horn out front. Everybody be ready to run out and jump in the car, 'cause we're heading for the beach."

Then you have the rest of the day to enjoy your family without having to worry about dishes, clothes, and food because you have capable people doing the chores. Having reliable help should be one of your first goals as you progress up the real estate ladder.

## Establish Family Goals

Goals are great. Cut out a picture of the luxury car of your choice, put it on your desk, and tell yourself, "If I make X amount of dollars next month, I'll buy this one for me." It's a neat goal you'll soon achieve. Then ask a travel agent for posters from some top ski and snowboard resorts. Tack them up on your 9-year-old's bedroom wall and say, "If I achieve X number of listings, we're all going skiing next month." Watch how those kids will keep you posted on happenings to help your career. Including them in the family's goals makes the youngsters accept your being away much better.

## Spouses

You must make up your lost time to your spouse frequently by saying, "Okay, tonight is our night," and then don't let the phone, clients, or kids interrupt. Workaholics beware! When you finally feel ready to be with the husband, wife, or other soul mate you've been neglecting, this person might not still be there for you.

## Sometimes the Family Has to Wait

Keep in mind that sometimes the work will come first. If you have out-of-state customers and they need to find a house in three days, you and I know you'll be with them early, all day long, and until well into the night. This is when I would say to the gang, "Okay, for the next couple of days, you'll need to make your lunches the night before, get up in time for school, and generally help keep the place straightened up, because Mom is helping some people find a home in our area."

## WorkingMoms.Calm

Buy this book: *WorkingMoms.Calm: How Smart Women Balance Family & Career.* I wrote this to lighten your load. I pass on all my secrets of juggling and so do 30 other trailblazing working mothers. Go online or to your local bookstore to buy the book today.

## Sometimes the Business Has to Wait

At other times business has to wait—for a school play, a Little League game, a parent-teacher conference, a graduation, or maybe just a lost child who needs your attention. Often a misbehaving child is simply a discouraged child who needs some good communication with Mom or

Dad. The rule of growth applies here just as it does to business details; small problems can become huge if neglected at home, too.

## Do the Things You Hate Most Earliest in the Morning

Do the things you hate first. It might be making a casserole for dinner, answering phone messages, writing follow-up notes, picking up keys and lock boxes—or dropping bad news on someone. Then you have a free mind for the rest of the day; you can concentrate on the really important things like facing clients and giving them 100 percent of your attention.

# Communicating Right the First Time

Communicating right the first time saves a huge amount of time. Good communication means taking an idea and putting it into clear and concise words; delivering it to a receiving point (hopefully, a listening ear); and then receiving acknowledgment from the mouth of the receiver saying she or he understood it. Breakdowns in communication occur when people don't listen properly, and can't duplicate exactly what the message was. That's when misinformation spreads.

Consider this case of trouble in Unsettled City. Manny, the listing agent, is telling others how Mary, who represents the buyer, said the escrow officer would order the termite report. What she actually said was, "You're the listing agent, so please order the bug report, and be sure to tell the escrow officer when you've done so." But Mary didn't enter what she told Manny on a communication log form, so now no one believes she told him to get the report.

The message didn't get through because during their conversation (1) Mary yelled at another agent to take a message from someone holding on the other line for her, (2) Mary had a donut in her mouth, and (3) the listing agent wasn't listening. At first Manny's attention had been riveted on a pretty redhead walking by his office. Then Mary's donut-muffled voice annoyed him so much he put down the phone while she was talking and went over to the candy jar for a chocolate drop.

This is communication? Sadly, it goes on every day in real estate offices across the country with the funds of our buyers and sellers at stake. Please follow these simple rules during communication, and no one will be able to believe the way you handle 20 transactions at once without getting rattled.

## Use a Communication Log

There's a sample communication log form in Chapter 24 and on the accompanying CD. Record all phone conversations pertaining to a transaction on this log. Make a new entry in the communication log for every phone conversation with the client, lender, escrow officer, attorney, mother-in-law, or whomever. You don't have to quote verbatim, but give the sense of the conversation. Write something like, "12-14: Talked to Sunny Westbrook of American Savings. Appraisal ordered, bank verifications returned, buyer loan application filled out and back, expect to go to loan committee on the 6th of next month." Record the length of the conversation in minutes.

## Be Single Minded

Concentrate on the person you're with, the project you're doing, and the day and hour you're living. Push everything else out of your mind. Tell anyone pushing a distraction at you, "I'll handle it later."

Do this especially when you're with clients or customers. Make them feel there isn't another living soul on earth, and you have nothing but *time* for them. I used to say to my hot prospects, "You are my most important concern right now, so don't worry about me being busy with anyone else." They loved that! It sure beats the salesperson who thinks he can catch every fish in the sea.

"Well, I have until 3:00 and then I have to pick someone at a hotel." How would you feel?

## Acknowledge the Message

When someone calls you, sends you something, writes you a note, or just says hello, acknowledge it. Say *thank you*, say *yes*, say anything, but let the person know you received their message. We all want to know where we stand, whether the beautiful pass we threw 30 yards downfield was received and carried for a touchdown—or fumbled. And, when you send or speak important messages, follow up until you get acknowledgment, and know you've completed your communication.

## Communicate Right with Loved Ones

Quality communication is just as vital with your loved ones. Have you ever heard, "Home is where you go when you're tired of being nice to people."? It's a sad thought and a recipe for personal disaster, and it can come true for any of us. Often the phone is ringing when you walk in.

The house is a mess. "Get this place cleaned up," you yell as you walk to the phone. Then you pick up the phone and say in your *wonderful-me* voice, "Hello there, can I help you?" And when you hang up, it's scream time again. If this describes you, take note and fix it.

# Watch for Danger Signs in Communication

## Blame Sentences

It's easy to fall into the blame game. Do you use sentences like these?

- "They are to blame."
- "She made me feel bad."
- "It's his fault."
- "He made me late for the appointment."
- "She didn't do what she was supposed to do."

Fixing the blame on others is a waste of time better spent on fixing the problem.

## Fatigue Stops Positive Communication

If you're tired, shut up and go to bed before you make a fool of yourself. Who cares about anything when they're tired? You'll definitely get messages mixed up, so put a blanket over the phone and let it sleep too.

# The $8 Million Listener

Listen, listen, listen! Listen more than you speak, and you'll save lots of time. Listen especially with clients and customers on listing appointments and property showings. A friend of mine did almost $5 million in volume in one year. Barbara is basically a quiet, reserved person. But does she listen! Her follow-through is legendary. From her files, Barbara can duplicate every significant conversation she was party to concerning each one of her transactions.

# Set Aside Some Alone Time

Everybody needs time for themselves occasionally. You just can't keep pouring from the pitcher forever without stopping to fill it up. I escape for a few minutes almost every day to be by myself. Maybe to walk along the beach—I love the sea. Or I throw myself into music. My new alone-time favorite is skiing down a mountain listening to music with earphones. After I've had a lot of transactions to keep up with, or a week away from home giving seminars, I really need to heal myself. We all do when we've run our battery down. Then you have a choice to make: you can sink into relaxation for a couple of days and regain emotional energy, or you can get sick.

## When Depression Starts Eating Up the Clock

When I feel depressed, I find a close friend to be with. Then we stay clear of the serious issues, and how heavy life can be. Just laughing, dancing, and enjoying their company snaps me back fast. Everyone needs three or four people they can be perfectly themselves with, and know that their genuine self is accepted and appreciated. We have to learn how to protect our spirit above everything else. Life is for growth rings, not decay rings.

Certain people or events will have a destructive effect on you; if you identify with them your future and the attainment of all your goals are at risk. Either you change your thoughts and disconnect from the destructive person or influence, or you will go into a downward spin. Associate with people who make you feel good about being you. Remember, all we have is time—and each other.

# CHAPTER 22

# Self-Organization

## SOLD

**Winning the Paper War ● Clutter Cures ● Your Real Estate Car
● Profit Stations ● Work Methods ● Think Ahead with Kits**

Using your low-pressure time to organize is vital, because it allows you to be cool and competent when the pressure shoots up. Then you can use the high pressure time to drive your career forward instead of blowing it apart. The money is where the high pressure is. Organize yourself and your workspace to handle it. Organize for specific purposes that include the following:

- To take a listing without prior notice
- To show property without prior notice
- To qualify new customers anytime
- To close old customers anytime
- To use large blocks of time effectively
- To use odd moments effectively
- To prospect efficiently
- To learn efficiently
- To succeed with open house and up-time
- To follow through successfully
- To have time for your loved ones
- To enjoy life

Self-organization has a specific objective: to free you from as much frustration as possible so you can concentrate your time and energy on fee-earning tasks.

Organize now. Organize so you stay organized. You'll need to organize yourself, because no one else can. And do it fast. That's the secret—speed. Make the minutes count as you organize yourself. Act boldly and act with speed. Then you'll have the time to organize, and the benefits you receive will encourage you to keep on spending a few minutes a day organizing and remaining well organized.

Once accomplished, maintaining a high level of organization requires little effort. Although you can never neglect it entirely, most of the necessary action becomes automatic. It's merely a matter of forming the right habits.

# Winning the Paper War

"What paper?" you ask. You say you have gone paperless and I see you figuring things out on your PDA (personal digital assistant). But then I go back to your office and the place is still full of paper. You are still not paperless! You still have paperwork. Until you *really* can go paperless, let's organize what is in front of you.

Have you ever noticed the way many agents go through the pile of paper in their office slot? First, they look through it quickly for something important, such as a check made out to them. Not finding one, they leaf through the material dispiritedly, reading nothing, throwing nothing away, and then they set it *all* aside in one pile to be gone over later. This stack of papers is all important—too important to be thrown away, not important enough to be acted on now. But action waits until later, "Until I have more time," you think.

Don't fool yourself. The first step toward uncluttering your desk is to unclutter your mind of the idea that there'll be more time later. It will never happen. You're working hard to *increase* your clientele—to *increase* the demands on your time. You'll have less time to waste tomorrow, less time on every tomorrow. The real estate business, our legal system, technology, and life in general are all becoming more complicated every day. Convince yourself of this: "Since I won't have time tomorrow to catch up with what I should've done today; I'll do today's work today. And I'll organize today for my busier tomorrows."

# Clutter Cures

To get organized you'll need to go through the pile of paper in your office slot and be done with it when you reach the last item. To do this, grasp the pile by a corner, shake out all the same items—phone messages and letters—and act on them first. Dispose of each item as you touch it. Do one of the following:

- Throw it in the wastepaper basket
- File in it an easy-clean file (see next section)
- Act on it. Pick up the phone and call someone, e-mail or snail-mail somebody about it, note what has to be done on tomorrow's action list, refer it to somebody else for handling, or file it in a specific file—do whatever is required.

The secret to organization is to touch paper once, and only once, whenever possible. Easy-clean files let you do this without losing control of anything you need. If you're suffering the pangs of paper-choke because you can't separate what you may need later from what you'll never need, here are some specific remedies guaranteed (provided you actually put them to use) to heal the most virulent case of keep-it-all-itis.

## Easy-Clean Files

**This/Last Files.** To be sure of being able to find any item you might need quickly, set up a this/last file for each type of document you receive 20 or more of each month. If you get a daily hot sheet from your Board of REALTORS®, and you've been letting them pile up on your desk and in your attaché case because you hate to throw them away, label a file folder, *Hot Sheets/This Month*. Keep this folder in the ready position and you'll never have to worry about whether you'll want to look at last week's hot sheet again or not. Look at each hot sheet when you first see it. Concentrate an instant to remember any detail you might need, jot down in your appointment book any action you'll take on this hot sheet in the future, and then pop it in the *Hot Sheets/This Month* file.

On another file folder put the label, *Hot Sheets/Last Month*. On the first day of each month, dump the contents of the *Hot Sheets/Last Month* in the garbage, transfer the contents of *Hot Sheets/This Month* to the last-month folder, and you've easy-cleaned your hot sheet file.

It's a matter of moments, once a month, to clear several this/last files. Here are some other this/lasts you might want to set up:

- Caravan sheets
- Other broker's flyers on their listings
- Loan company flyers
- Other service flyers

You might ask, "Why not just have a this-month file and dump it once a month?"

Then you'll be dumping out yesterday's material, along with 30-day-old items. This/last folders guarantee you'll keep every item at least 30 days, so there's no worry about throwing away items you'll need. It's a system you can set up quickly, put on habit control, and forget about.

## Rotating Monthly Files

**Keep for One Year Folders.** Label one dozen folders, one for each month. If you start the system in March, the first folder in the group is March, then April, May, and so on through December, followed by January and ending with February. During March, drop everything into the *March* folder that you might want to keep for an extended period of time. These folders are great places to drop various bits of paper you might—but probably won't—need again such as raffle tickets, claim checks, free lunch coupons, receipts, and miscellaneous notes.

The advantage is, you don't have to think whether to keep a doubtful item; you just drop it in the current month's *Keep For One Year* rotating folder. At the end of March, put the *March* folder behind February's, and start dropping incoming items into the *April* folder. Repeat this process through the 12 folders. On the first of March of the following year, dump the one-year-old material from the *March* folder in the garbage without looking at it and start the process all over again. Unless you rescue an item within the year, out it goes.

Finding a needed item will be easy. Think about when it came in, and then skim through the items in one or two of the monthly folders until you see it. The rotating monthly file allows you to keep items readily accessible for a full year, and to clean the file in less than one minute per year.

These two filing systems will prevent the paper blizzard from stalling your movement forward. You can set up the necessary file folders in only a few minutes and start efficiently disposing of all the papers you're not sure you'll need again, but still be able to find if you do. This takes care of the most numerous and least important papers. With them out of the way, you can concentrate on handling vital papers effectively. To do this, set up fast-working tickler files.

**Monthly Rotating Tickler File.** Label 12 folders, *ACTION January 1*, *ACTION February 1*, and so on through December. These are great for reminders to pay bills, order farming tools, send anniversary cards to clients, and numerous other needs. Put everything you need to handle each item in these files so you can work through them quickly. On the first of each month, pull the folder, do the work, and put your repeating reminders back in the folder. (The Smith's anniversary will be in April next year too, so it should stay in *ACTION April 1*.) Then put this folder at the back of your *ACTION* folders and let it start working its way to the front again.

**Tickler 1/31 System.** Electronic organizers are great for their intended purposes. However, there's no convenient way to put miscellaneous papers in them. Any office supply store will have a set of folders numbered 1 through 29, and 30-31. To set up a tickler 1/31 filing system just put these folders in your desk and start using them. Here's how they work.

Suppose today is the 20th of the month. Take the folders numbered 1 through 20 and put them behind 30-31. You'll then have a set of folders arranged as the dates will come up for the next 30 days. File all your action notes in the folder for the day you should take action, and the tickler 1/31 system will automatically place the right papers in your hands at the right time. All you need do is clear the file once a day. Three effective uses are:

- To trigger follow-up on your transactions. ("Loan documents due back from Smiths.")
- To remind you of events. File the complete invitation or announcement. When the date comes, just pull the papers and avoid hunting for the ticket.
- To kick off follow-up on your leads. Choose the date you want to call a party back, and drop the paper with the information in the right day's folder. The Fast Fact Grabber form in Chapter 24 (and on the accompanying CD) is set up for this kind of operation.

Less obvious, but more powerful in its effect on your income, is the heightened sense of timing you'll develop with this system. Use tickler 1/31 to spread your workload to the lighter days, to trigger phone calls at the best moments, to put yourself in the right place at the right time. The advantage of tickler 1/31 over the calendar pad or PDA is that you can drop original documents or complete files into it—no copying is necessary.

Every night, as you're working up tomorrow's action list, go through the next day's tickler 1/31 folder. If it's the night of the 19th, pull the folder marked "20," take all the papers out of it, and file the folder behind "19." Don't carry the tickler folders around with you or, when you need them to file new tickler material, they'll be gone.

Put tomorrow's material in a folder labeled *Action Now*, a folder you carry with you as a ready-made plan of action for the day. Tickler 1/31 works best when kept at the desk you visit and work at every day, where you make most of your fee-winning calls.

**Daily Action Folders.** This set of seven folders is easy to carry in your attaché case. It lets you constantly rearrange your schedule for the next few days, as developments demand. Label them *Action Monday*, *Action Tuesday*, and so on through the week.

Use these rotating tickler systems to control your organization and to refine your tomorrow's action list.

## Tomorrow's-Action-List Yourself to Big Money Fast

Success is certain if you do these two things: (1) Each night, prepare a list of the things you must do tomorrow to achieve your goals and, (2) *do* those things tomorrow.

On your TAL, your tomorrow's action list, rank the opportunities you've set out for yourself in their order of importance. Jump on those items you like least the very first thing in the morning and get them out of the way. Keep them from hanging over you all day. This habit of making sure you *clear all disagreeable tasks first every day,* will do wonders for your morale and double your efficiency. You no longer will carry guilt around all day, and go in fear of the unpleasant duty. By doing what you don't want to do early, you save hours of excuse-making and exhausting internal debate. And while you're procrastinating, the nasty problem is getting worse, and your fear of dealing with it is getting stronger.

After the disagreeable tasks are out of the way, tackle the tasks on your TAL in order of their importance. Push item 1 as far forward as you can before moving on to item 2. The TAL form is shown in Chapter 24 and is available on the CD.

## Name and Phone Naildown

Every real estate office periodically sees one of its agents tearing her desk apart searching for a client's phone number because, unless the number can be found, the opportunity for a transaction with the party is gone. A common surname, when the city they live in isn't known, or an unlisted number, can cut off all chances of getting back to a prospect.

Curiously, even after hearing about a few of these fiascoes, agents will continue to jot phone numbers on any scrap of paper and let it go—until they need the number.

**Always write the number in a second place. At once.** An excellent second place is your calendar or organizer—paper or electronic. The quick scribble, "Jones, 234-0987," can save you a frantic hour— or a large fee. But do it as soon as the prospects give you their number. Write it in a second place while you're talking to them. They won't mind you taking them seriously.

# Your Real Estate Car

Although it's great for casting an aura of excitement and glamour, you don't have to drive a luxurious four-door sedan to sell real estate. I won top volume awards in our Board of REALTORS® showing property in a little red squareback Volkswagen. Keep the car you're using clean. Don't let trash accumulate in it. Store the stuff bouncing around in the car's trunk in your garage, and use that space to carry the following:

- *Kid Controller Kit.* Gather some games, puzzles, and books (they don't have to be new or expensive) for the occasions when your customers bring their children. Avoid gooey eatables that kids can smear on the fabric of your car seats.
- *Last Week's Multiple Listing book.* Carry this week's MLS book with you, but if you mislay it, last week's copy in the trunk will see you through.
- *"Just Sold" doorhangers* you can spread in the neighborhood the same day you close a sale. News is the most perishable commodity in the world. Get it out fast.
- *Giveaway Kit.* Always carry a supply of your personalized memo pads. Give them, and other farming items, out at every opportunity. People remember gifts someone they know personally hands them far better than gimmicks hung on their doorknob by a phantom.
- *Keep a few of your customer-catcher maps* made up and ready to go in your trunk, too. Chapter 9 describes this useful sales tool in detail.
- *Forms Kit.* Keep a few extra copies of listing forms, purchase-agreement forms, counteroffer forms, buyers net sheets, sellers net sheets, and any other forms you might need handy in your

car's trunk. You can't close without these vital forms, and by the time you get back from a run to the office, Cousin Charlie may have called and said he's getting into real estate.

- *Coping Kit.* Pack it with items able to keep the small, unexpected problems small. Include a small pair of pliers, a screwdriver, a few extra ballpoint pens, a handful of bolts and nuts for your signs, a Sold sign, a For Lease sign, paper clips, and various kinds of tape. Also include a few boxes of raisins for when there's no time for a regular meal, a spare battery for your laptop, and an extra calculator.

Protect all paper items carried in your trunk from dust and moisture or they'll probably be unusable when you need them. Plastic bags closed with rubber hands are great for this because you can see what's inside. Cardboard boxes with lids taped on with masking tape work well too. Label them so you won't tear everything apart when you need something in a hurry.

All these kits will easily go in one 10" × 12" × 14" cardboard *Bankers Box* with lid, available at office supply stores.

# Profit Stations

Doesn't *profit station* sound more inspiring than *work station*? If you can't immediately have a large, well lighted desk in a separate room, with computer, telephone, and files handy, don't let this stop you. A profit station can be very profitable even if it's only a shelf in the pantry within reach of a wall phone, as my home profit station was. Don't knock the shelf in the pantry. In those primitive days before cell phones, a 25-foot cord allowed me to range far and wide, stirring soup and quieting restless babies, while prospecting, following up, or negotiating on the phone. Now cordless phones and cell phones can make any shelf or nook an effective profit station if you have a place to write, and a shelf to keep your files. The less space you have, the more pressure there is to get down to essentials.

An open house is an effective profit station if you are organized to work effectively while you're there, in addition to holding the house open. Chapter 9 discusses this in detail.

## The Traveling Profit Station

Get a second attaché case and gather everything you need to prospect effectively to follow up on expireds, to court fizzbos, to handle your current clients, and service your transactions. Your first attaché case contains your laptop computer or your Listing Presentation Manual and all the forms and tools you need to list and sell. By grabbing these two cases, you're ready for anything.

As a real estate agent you're an outside person. The money is out in the field. You do your business where it can be done, in your clients' homes, in vacant houses, in coffee shops, or on the hood of your car. Make it a firm habit to keep the book or electronic planner you use to control your activities with you at all times.

# Work Methods

## Mood Governed or Scheduled Batch

Be aware of how you work now. You may want to change your fundamental method to a more productive system. One of the most popular work methods is to allow your mood to govern your pace and direction. You work continuously at whatever seems like a good idea at the time until your mood changes. Then you do something else as dictated by your new mood.

The new mood may be created by a phone call or another outside stimulus. If this is your work method, your output is controlled by external forces, not by your internal determination. People who swing rapidly from periods of enthusiastic action to glum apathy are not organized well enough to take full control of their careers. Discipline and the sense of purpose success demands require a keen sense of your own worth; a warm regard for yourself as your own best friend; and a set of goals you want to achieve, believe you can achieve, and are excited about achieving. Success requires the habit of encouraging (positively validating) yourself.

This is the essence of self-organization. Take control of your career. Instead of letting those you come in contact with govern your mood, and then letting your mood govern your output, take control of your life. Set goals, work to schedules, control your mood and yourself. A better work method is scheduled batch:

## Scheduled Batch

No matter how efficient you are, there will always be more work available in your real estate practice than you can perform. You can work until you're exhausted, and you'll always feel defeated. Or you can schedule a batch of work, finish it, and feel good. By organizing a constant flow of wins in this way, you reinforce your good feelings about yourself and build your confidence. You begin a cycle of working happier, of having more success, and of achieving your goals. As your abilities grow, and negative thinking grabs you less and less, you'll find yourself setting higher and higher goals—and continuing to achieve them.

Plan your work in batches. Schedule yourself to do preparatory work during the hours when you can't door-knock or phone. Set up batches of ten expireds or ten fizzbos to visit or phone at the right time of day and week. Research these opportunities by driving past each of the houses, and having the files all set up so you can start promptly when the good time rolls around. Plan ahead so you can get through your batch with smooth self-confidence. Let your constant mood of confidence inspire people to place their trust in you. Govern them with your positive mood instead of allowing their fear, anger, guilt, and failure to govern you.

## Think Ahead with Kits

You get a come-list-me call.

"José just came in, and he got the terrific promotion I told you about."

"How wonderful, Felicia."

"The only thing is, they want him there in two weeks, so we want to put our house on the market right away. Can you come over now?"

"I can be there in ten minutes."

From your files, you pull the Guidelines to Market Value you prepared when Lisa first told you her friends would probably be moving soon.

Grabbing your attaché case and your listing kit, you hustle out to your car. Everything you need to take a listing is in your two hands because you think in terms of kits, not long lists of miscellaneous items. And you won't forget anything in the hurry and excitement because you've carefully organized those kits during your quiet time.

Note: If you *really* would commit to the PDA and the laptop listing presentations you could finally once and for all free yourself from the clutter. Go ahead. I dare you. Go completely electronic!

# CHAPTER 23

# Prepare and Perform— Or Pass Out

Preparation Is the Vital Concept ● Preparation Prevents Poor Performance ● Be Mentally Prepared ● How to Create Sales Dialogues Fast ● Make Money on Your Area's Yearly Buying Pattern ● Your II (Important Information) Notebook ● Services ● Put the Numbers Book Away ● Buy Software That Does the Work for You ● Fast Numbers Are Fee Earners ● The Figure to Remember Is $44.25

Imagine that you're lying in a dentist's chair, staring goggle-eyed at the ceiling, hoping it won't hurt. A man you don't know walks in wearing a white coat. He leans over you, starts the drill, gives you a cheery smile, and says, "I hope you don't mind me practicing on you. You see, I'm kind of new at this—I've still got a few things to learn. But trust me—I'll take good care of you."

Have you ever sat nervously in a doctor's office, and noticed all the diplomas and certificates hanging in neat frames on the walls? Reassuring, aren't they? Since the competence of a real estate agent can have a heavy impact on their financial health, clients and customers expect you to be prepared. When you first contact them, they're looking for some reassuring signs of knowledge and experience. They're seriously thinking of relying on your competence in making a major decision that may involve nine times their annual income (including interest). That's important money to anyone.

## Preparation Is the Vital Concept

Preparation is the key to closing a sale. Preparation is the key to closing a listing.

Learn the inventory. Know your area intimately. Understand thoroughly all the different financing methods available, all the costs of borrowing, and all the closing costs involved. Understand, and be able to explain concisely, the tax and investment advantages of owning a home.

# Preparation Prevents Poor Performance

In real estate, the same situations repeat over and over again in endless variations on a few basic themes. Prepare in depth to meet these situations with smooth confidence. Learn the closes, the qualifying methods, and the techniques. Watch the hot sheets. See new listings constantly—I did it every single week, for years.

People say *prior* preparation prevents poor performance, but *all* preparation *has* to come before need, doesn't it? You can't buy fire insurance after your house has burned down; you can't pull on a life vest after you've drowned; and you can't put the caller on hold while you learn the inventory.

When the ad or sign call comes in, you've got to know more about what's in the house than the ad tells—more than can be seen from the street. If you don't, why should the caller talk to you? And you've got to know more of what's on the Multiple Listing than just the one property he or she called about. Prospective buyers immediately spot the salesperson who knows the inventory. She just stands out as knowledgeable.

Know the area. Know about schools, parks, churches, doctors, baby sitters, bowling alleys, tennis clubs, soccer teams—know it all. And, especially, know the unique, outstanding, or unusual features of your area. Know its history, special parades, and customs. You're not just selling homes, you're selling a way of life.

Know the comparables. This means you've got a terrific comparable file you're constantly updating. Save time and do it on a computer. A buyer should be able to come up to you and ask any question about the area's housing when you're actively listing and selling, and you have the answer on the tip of your tongue.

Don't cheat yourself. When opportunity walks in, it takes preparation to be able to grab it before it walks right out again. The difference between an outstanding salesperson and an average salesperson is preparation. One is armed, the other isn't. One has the weapons to win; the other has only a silly grin and a naive trust in luck.

# Be Mentally Prepared

Being mentally prepared means that when I close the door to my house and get in my car, no matter what's happening there, all my home problems click off. Before I'm moving toward a meeting with clients, all of my attention is directed toward them.

Sometimes it's not easy to do. But often it's the best possible way to handle your personal problems—to put them out of your mind for a while and let one of the world's greatest healing systems—good honest hard work—do its magic.

"I'll think about it later—right now the best thing I can possibly do is to concentrate on solving Mr. and Mrs. Kimura's housing problem."

Turning off your inner conflicts is an excellent habit and skill to develop. Find the tricks that work for you: squeeze your toes, whistle "Dixie." or take three deep breaths.

# How to Create Sales Dialogues Fast

You'll need a tape recorder to practice your sales dialogues. Why are they *dialogues* when you're obviously going to do most of the talking—why not *monologues*? They're dialogues because these sales talks should be two-way communications between you and the client or customer. Don't set them up for you to go on and on. Constantly insert questions like the following:

- "This makes sense, doesn't it?"
- "Do you agree?"
- "Are you with me?"
- "This is my profession; I work with real estate concepts every day. So it's easy for me to forget how my clients are experts in other fields, professions I know nothing about. So please interrupt if I get carried away. I haven't been throwing too much realty jargon at you, have I?"

Keep your customers involved. You're not selling them or listing them if they're staring at you with blank faces, wondering how they can get away from your relentless speech and all the information they don't understand or need.

Define exactly what each dialogue is to cover. Rambling sales speeches result when your purposes are vague. Effective sales speeches result when you have specific objectives. For example, "Objective: To persuade someone to list with you."

Pick someone you've met (a client, a friend, anybody) to address your speech to. Let's say you choose Roger Lane, a 40-year-old bachelor who's an engineer. Imagine talking to him when you tape your sales dialogues. The second time you tape each sales speech, imagine that you're addressing someone other than Roger, a young married couple, for example. The third time, address a retired couple.

Before you start taping, outline your speech. Do this quickly by taking five minutes or less to jot down two or three words to remind you of each of your main ideas—the six or seven reasons why Roger Lane should list with you. Take another minute to recopy your notes into logical order. Put your strongest point last, and your second-strongest point first.

Now tape your speech. Talk to the imaginary person or couple. If you can think of real people, that's even better. Don't talk for more than three minutes.

Listen to the recording once for content. Stop the tape to make notes on parts you want to add or cut. Listen to the tape again. This time be alert for avoidable repetition of the same word, for "ahs," "ohs," and slurred words, and for talk that's too fast or too slow, too loud or too soft. Make sure your speaking style is easy and natural. You don't want to sound stiff, superior, or condescending, nor do you want to come across as a hard-selling phony. Make sure you're not throwing in real estate jargon. Use plain English. Cut unnecessary words; they obscure your meaning, but do repeat your basic ideas in other words.

As in any good speech, tell them what you're going to tell them, *tell them,* and then tell them what you've told them. This applies only to your main ideas. Go over your main points in plain but varied language when you express them the second and third times.

Listen to the tape and think about how to improve, and then immediately make a second tape of your speech. Repeat your double analysis. Then tape the day's final version. This third version will be your starting point when you review your short speech tomorrow.

Use this method to tape all nine sales dialogues called for in the Breakaway Schedule of special achievements given after Chapter 28. On the following page is a list of dialogues and the day they're scheduled.

As you listen to these tapes, and learn your nine dialogues thoroughly, you'll need to guard against repeating them like a mynah bird. Practice constantly at speaking with conviction and clarity. Pause occasionally for effect. Ask your imaginary listeners questions. Use a bright and pleasing tone. Vary the speed and force with which you speak. But be careful you aren't going for a Shakespearean perform-

| Day | Dialogue |
|-----|----------|
| 12 | "Why you should list with me." |
| 13 | "What's happening now in our local resale housing market?" |
| 14 | "The community of Green Pretty Valley (your area)." |
| 15 | "Why Green Pretty Valley is a great place, Mr. and Mrs. Homebuyer, for you and your family to grow and prosper in." |
| 16 | "What happens in today's market when you limit your offer with contingencies." |
| 17 | "The outlook is optimistic." |
| 18 | "The tax advantages of home ownership." |
| 19 | "Why you should buy a home now." |
| 21 | "The various ways you can finance a home purchase, and the advantages and costs of each method." |

ance; talk naturally or you'll sound insincere—and you'll talk yourself right out of business.

When you've made the best tape you can, put it aside for a few days. Then listen to it again. Make a new tape whenever you think you can improve on your old version. Keep your first tape or two. When you listen to them a month from now, you'll be impressed with how much you've improved.

Listening to your own tapes frequently will raise your critical abilities to new heights. You'll find yourself making minor but important improvements in facets of your speech you didn't even notice the first few times you listened to your voice. Listening to your perfectly delivered lines, you'll discover, is a very effective learning device for the content of the sales dialogues.

When you're actually face-to-face with a buyer or seller, you'll want to break your speeches up into small segments. What the clients want to say is more important than what you want to say to them. Your chance will come. Be prepared to make your chances count with effective, expressive speech that compels attention because it's informative and direct.

Rehearse spontaneity, verve, and facts *in*; rehearse drone, hesitation, and ramble *out*. Tips on four of the dialogues follow. You'll find ideas for the others in the chapters on listing and selling. Remember, the real power of planned and practiced sales speeches comes from the accurate and up-to-date information in them. Only you can supply this vital element.

## Day 14: "The Communities of Green Pretty Valley"

Tape your remarks and listen to them carefully. Make sure you're not speaking condescendingly about any part of your sales area. The locality you knock will be the only one some of your buyers will feel comfortable in. Make sure you don't talk yourself out of the chance to sell in any area.

## Day 16: "Here's What Happens in Today's Market When You Limit Your Offer with Contingencies"

Tailor this speech to your prospects' degree of sophistication in real estate. If you haven't had experience with this issue yet, talk to several other agents. Call someone in the Multiple Listing book who has several listings. Ask that agent, "If I had a customer interested in your listing at 12345 First Street, how would your sellers feel about an offer contingent on my buyers selling their home?"

When market conditions change, update this dialogue accordingly.

## Day 17: "The Outlook Is Optimistic"

You'll need this dialogue when buyers ask you questions like, "Where do you think the general economy is going? Are we headed for another recession? Aren't we about due for another downturn? Aren't interest rates too high?"

They're really saying, "I'm afraid. Tell me something to ease my worries about taking on the risk of buying a house. I need reassurance."

Give them reassurance.

Those buyers need a crutch. Unless you shove strong support under them fast, they'll fall victim to their fears and back off from investing in their future as they should. Prepare your optimistic outlook speech before it's needed. Stiffen it with facts. Make it a strong argument; practice it until you can deliver it with convincing power.

Organize a steady flow of useful facts. The Internet is a terrific source of up-to-the-minute information. Check out news magazines, newspapers, bank newsletters, and various subscription newsletters. Be on the lookout for good news constantly. But don't wait. From what you know now, or can quickly find, perfect the first version of your "Optimistic Outlook" sales dialogue. Improve it in the future whenever you can.

## Day 19: "Why You Should Buy a Home Now"

Talk with understanding about the real reasons why people buy homes instead of renting apartments. Include buyers' desires to satisfy their yearning to belong; their urge to call some territory their own; and their aspirations for prestige, security, and comfort. Work in some words about the indestructible nature of a land investment, the accumulation of equity, and the appreciation of value. Simply mention the tax advantages, which another dialogue covers in detail.

Don't let dollars dominate this discussion, as so many agents do. Money reasons are rationalizations people use to justify their emotional decisions. If you outline the money advantages adequately, while treating the emotional factors with dignity and completeness, you will create a powerful selling tool in this sales dialogue.

When higher housing prices and interest costs seem imminent, include these items in the sales talk, but your basic speech should be built around the unchanging emotional factors. Don't be discouraged if your first attempts don't sound convincing or detailed enough. You're dealing with deep emotions here. It's worth working hard on this talk over a period of time. Do the best you can now. Continue to develop and refine this sales dialogue in the coming months until your clients and customers listen carefully, and nod their heads in agreement, as you talk.

# Make Money on Your Area's Yearly Buying Pattern

The demand for housing in your marketing area may have a pronounced seasonal pattern, or perhaps a calendar-events such as school summer vacation pattern. This pattern of change in month-to-month demand repeats itself annually. Other factors influence the demand for housing in your area, of course. Changes in the economy make it more difficult to see the yearly pattern but it's still there. Knowing the pattern intimately makes you a local real estate expert.

Being able to discuss this pattern in detail and with confidence not only will impress prospects, and help you convert them into clients and customers, it will frequently provide you with powerful arguments to induce your clients to make realistic price decisions.

Suppose your sellers are considering an offer well below their asking price. It's late in the year and the beginning of the slow season. You know they should take the offer because, first, they can't afford to carry the house through the winter. Secondly, your chances of remaining as their listing agent until spring are doubtful. So accepting the offer is vital for them and important to you. In this situation, most real estate agents can't fire any ammunition except vague but vehement assertions such as, "The market around here is really dead in the winter."

"How dead is it?" the seller says.

"Well, all I do in the winter is public relations. I might as well be ice fishing."

It doesn't sound very professional or convincing, does it? Even when delivered by the grayest of heads, such arguments won't bend bull-headed sellers intent on being their own worst enemies (such sellers are a breed you'll encounter often). A better tactic is based strictly on facts of record, such as,

"Based on the record, only about 13 percent of our annual sales are made in the winter months. Of course, if house sales were evenly distributed throughout the whole year, 25 percent of the sales would be made in the winter fourth of the year. So winter sales are roughly half of the average for the entire year. But the 12 percent not sold in the winter get added onto the rest of the year, so the difference between winter and summer is more like three to one. Are you with me? The actual average for the last three years is 13.2 percent in the winter and 38.4 percent in the summer—just about exactly three to one."

Let your words sink in for a moment. "I've got my sales charts right here. Would you like to look at them?"

You show them the figures. "Excuse me for throwing all these numbers at you so fast, but they're important for you to know. If you're going to make the best decision on this offer, the seasonal buying pattern has to be a key element in your decision."

After you get this point across, follow up with this clincher you've dredged up from your statistics, "There's another vital aspect to this seasonal pattern you should also give careful consideration to. Winter prices are lower than summer prices by an average of 9 percent. My data cover the last three years, and they're adjusted to eliminate the effect of inflation. In other words, I've isolated the price effect of the season.

"Now, what does that 9 percent price differential actually mean? Well, it tells us that for the most part, only the most willing sellers sell their houses in the winter. Putting it another way, nobody sells in the winter unless they sell for less. Since you're working on the high side of the market price, what this boils down to is, in all probability you'll carry your house through the winter if you turn this offer down. Maybe all the way to summer—unless you decide to take considerably *less* than this offer in the meantime.

"Of course, what I'm attempting to do now is predict the future, and no one can be sure of what the future will bring, but the recent history of this area bears out what I'm saying. The choice is between taking a long gamble against the future's odds, or taking the sure thing now."

Now let's consider a conversation with a fizzbo. It's January 14, and your fizzbo wants to move out of state, so you tell him,

"In each of the last three years, resale home sales in this area have peaked in March. Before then, the best month was always August. But every year—the largest number of new listings—and the largest number of total listings—still hits in August.

"What does this mean to you? If you want to delay listing your house until summer, like you're talking about doing, the odds are you'll have to accept less than you could get for your house in March, simply because they'll be so many more houses on the market.

"We're talking about a supply-and-demand situation here. You have a very unique house, one that people will fall in love with. But why put *the buyers* in the strongest possible bargaining position, and *yourself* in the weakest possible bargaining position? If your house is on the market well before the peak—and not too many people know our market has been peaking in March—buyers are thinking, 'he's got the whole summer to sell; he won't go for a low offer now.' But if you're trying to sell in August, then the buyers are saying to themselves, 'If he doesn't sell in the next couple of weeks he's stuck with the place until spring.' This is an enormous difference in buyer attitude.

"My graphs detailing sales patterns are in my car. I'd like you to think about the advantages of having the entire Multiple Listing Service on your team—all _____ (give number of agents on your Board of REALTORS®) of us—plus a strong, professional agent—me—directing the marketing effort. And, as an extra bonus, your house will automatically be listed in hundreds of real estate offices across the country, and the listing will be available worldwide on the Internet. If you're like most people, your plans hinge on selling your house. Wouldn't it be wiser to put this gigantic team to work for you at the *best* season rather than at the poorest season? Is it worth taking the chance to wait?

"Would you think about all this, please, for the moment it'll take me to run out to my car and get my graphs? I think you'll be impressed with the market information. You know, I've spent a lot of time on research. I'm a professional. I devote much energy to searching out ways to help my clients sell faster and for more money. There are so many aspects to marketing real estate; it takes a dedicated professional to think about and have access to all of them."

You must have your facts documented in case you're challenged. To gather the data that will support your statements, check with your Board of REALTORS® for the following information summarized by month for several recent years:

- Total number of housing units sold, per month
- Average price

Let's say that for Green Pretty Valley in one year the sales were as follows:

| Month | Units | Percentage of Year's Sales |
|---|---|---|
| January | 195 | 3.9 |
| February | 250 | 4.7 |
| March | 320 | 6.2 |
| April | 410 | 8.0 |
| May | 520 | 10.1 |
| June | 601 | 11.7 |
| July | 690 | 13.4 |
| August | 640 | 12.4 |
| September | 599 | 11.6 |
| October | 415 | 8.1 |
| November | 395 | 7.7 |
| December | 110 | 2.2 |
| Total | 5,145 | |

Plot the data on graphs. Show each year in a different color. You will make two curves on one graph.

- Price curve. See the sample graph on the following page.
- Monthly sales as percentage of the year's sales. Set it up similar to the Price curve.

This is powerful information. It just takes a little preparation—perhaps four hours' worth. What is the average commission you expect to earn? Divide it by four to get your hourly rate for preparing this data if it only sells one transaction for you, or wins one salable listing, during the several years you'll use it. You will, of course, need to spend an

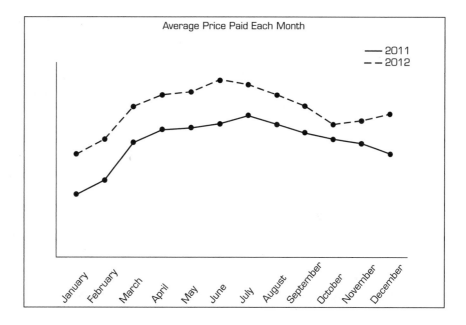

hour each year updating the data. If your average net commission is $9000, you will have made $150 a *minute* for updating this data after it's saved one transaction for you.

# Your II (Important Information) Notebook

In whatever device you use to keep track of numbers and other details, enter all the vital information you might need at any moment:

- Advertising phone numbers, deadlines, and rates
- Deadlines for caravans, ads, and the Multiple Listing book
- School district boundaries and phone numbers
- Local tax rates
- Utility office locations and hook-up information

Do more than just work on this valuable data on floor time or at open houses. Make up flash cards and memorize everything in it.

# Services

You should always be ready to recommend someone to perform every conceivable household repair and type of construction work. Suppose a client calls and you don't know about the service she needs. In your file, you've got electricians, plumbers, roofers, chimney sweeps, and tree sprayers, but Dr. Sasanka Mukerji, who bought a house from you, needs a tile-setter.

You can say, "Sorry, Doctor, I've never had a call for a tile-setter. Can't help you on this one." Translation: "I'm not as much of an expert as you thought I was."

**Instead, you say,** "Tile-setter, yeah—who is the fellow who does this? Doctor, you'll have to give me a minute on this one—I just can't think of the man's name. I'll check my file at home (at the office if you're at home) and call you back."

Then get on the phone, locate a tile-setter, and get back to Dr. Mukerji the same day. Be sure everyone you recommend has a proven track record with someone you know—preferably you. A bad recommendation can hurt you more than none at all.

# Put the Numbers Book Away

You look like a beginner when you pull out the little book of numbers and drop your nose in it to figure loan amounts. Usually, at any given time all you need is one number, which you memorize or write on a strip of tape and stick to the back of your calculator. When interest rates are moving, perhaps you'll need three numbers at your fingertips, ready to punch into your pocket calculator. On the following page are some numbers giving the monthly cost of 30-year loans.

Suppose you're figuring a buyer's net sheet for a loan of $367,310 on a 30-year loan at 10.5 percent.

A glance at the information you've written on the back of your calculator tells you that $9.1474 is the payment for each thousand dollars of such a loan. Enter 9.1474 in your calculator and hit the multiply button.

Now enter the loan amount: 367.31. (Since one thousand dollars is your unit, the comma after the thousands in your loan amount becomes your decimal point: $367,310 = 367.31. The final zero in the loan amount means nothing in this calculation.)

9.1474 × 367.31 = $3359.93 monthly investment for 30 years to pay off a loan of $367,310 at 10.5 percent.

This answer is accurate to the penny.

Where do you find $9.1474[*] in your real estate numbers book?

In the monthly payment schedules, on the 10.5 percent page for 30-year loans, find $100,000 at the bottom of the page. That figure, the

---

[*] Some amortization books give this value as $9.1475, which adds 4 cents to the monthly payment, or $14.40 to the total paid over the life of the loan.

| Interest Rate (%) | Monthly Cost Per Thousand |
| --- | --- |
| 6 | $ 5.9956 |
| 7 | 6.6531 |
| 8 | 7.3377 |
| 9 | 8.0463 |
| 9.5 | 8.4086 |
| 9.75 | 8.5916 |
| 10 | 8.7758 |
| 10.25 | 8.9611 |
| 10.5 | 9.1474 |
| 13 | 11.0621 |
| 14 | 11.8488 |
| 15 | 12.6445 |
| 16 | 13.4476 |
| 17 | 14.2568 |
| 18 | 15.0709 |
| 19 | 15.8889 |
| 20 | 16.7102 |

monthly investment to retire a $100,000 loan, is $914.74. Moving the decimal point two places to the left divides by 100, giving the answer carried out to 4 decimal places for a $1,000 loan. Note that the figure given in the table for a loan amount of $1,000 is $9.15. Applied to the loan in this example, the rounded figure of $9.15 gives an answer that's about 96 cents higher per month from the actual payment.

Why worry about less than one dollar a month? Because some people, when they're making a major commitment, are put off by rounded figures about their monthly investment. They prefer rounded figures on house values, closing costs, and the like, but the monthly outgo figure, if given approximately and without conviction as to its accuracy, is a wonderful excuse to put off the decision. Close this loophole by giving them the exact figure. It's easy when you know how.

# Buy Software That Does the Work for You

The next time you go to the National Association of REALTORS® convention, shop for some great software at the trade show. Buy the lender qualifying packages that does all the number crunching for you. Then you won't have to worry about the figures—let your computer do the figuring.

## Fast Numbers Are Fee Earners

Whipping out the numbers fast allows you to concentrate on your clients and customers. Learning the number shortcuts frees you of fluster and distraction at the crucial moments when people make their big decisions. Why inflict the serious handicap on yourself of being slow at, and afraid of, the arithmetic you know is required to earn a fee? While you're fumbling, buyer's remorse is whispering in your customer's ear, "Wait. Don't commit yourself. Think it over."

## The Figure to Remember Is $44.25

That's how much the principal of a $100,000 loan is reduced by the first monthly payment of $877.58, when the rate is 10 percent and the term is 30 years. The other $833.33 is the first month's interest cost.

Sellers often overestimate how much they've reduced the balance of new loans. Many of them reason somewhat like this, "Okay, my payment is $877.58, so I'll figure $300 for interest. Let's say, $377.58 for quick figures, and to be on the safe side. So I must be paying the loan off at about $500 a month. Let's see. I took the loan out last December, so I've made six payments. We can't owe more than $97,000 now." The man thinks he's paid off more than $3000; actually, he's paid off *less* than $300.

By remembering $44.25, you can quickly estimate rough payoff figures for any size loan if it's fairly new, carries an interest rate in the 10 percent range, and has a term of 30 years or more. This rough estimate will warn you when your prospects are indulging in wildly wishful thinking. Here's an example of how this can help you.

George and Mary Silverstein, walked into your open house and said they want a larger home than they now have. Your first goal is to capture them as clients. Even though George has recently been promoted, you suspect it's going to be a tight squeeze to qualify them for the loan they'll need. You need to know how much equity the Silversteins have in their present home, but they're hazy about their loan's exact terms. Most people are. When they bought two years ago, they're certain they took out an $85,000 loan. They guess their interest rate at 9 or 9 1/4 percent, and the loan's term at 35 years.

George says, "We must've paid it down to about $81,000 after all this time, wouldn't you think?"

"Instead of taking a wild stab at it," you say, "let me make a quick calculation. I take it you haven't made any extra payments."

"No, we just made the regular payments."

It's obvious to you, of course, that in only two years the Silversteins paid off far less than $4,000 on a long-term 9 percent loan. But rather than slap George down by instantly saying *no*, you dignify his wishful statement by calculating an answer.

You have a number in your head, $44.25, which you know is the first month's payoff on $100,000 at 10 percent for 30 years, and that 35-year loans pay off even more slowly. But you don't think they've got a 35-year loan, though you don't say so yet.

- Enter $44.25 in your calculator.
- Multiply it by 85 percent (Use .85 if your calculator doesn't have the % button. $85,000, of course, is 85 percent of $100,000.)
- The result, $37.61, is the first month's payoff for an $85,000 loan for 30 years at 10 percent simple interest. This is close enough for ballpark figures. Multiplying the payoff by 24, the approximate number of monthly investments the Silversteins have made to date, gives $902.64 as the answer.

The Silversteins have paid off about $1000, give or take $100 or so, not the $4000 they think they've paid. Of course they get statements regularly giving them their exact balance, but many people never bother to read them. Now you need to let them down easy, without making them feel stupid or poor.

"Well, you know, George and Mary, these long-term loans pay off very slowly at first. I work with them every day, and I'm still surprised every time I figure one. If you happen to remember the exact amount of your payment, I could figure the whole thing for you in a minute."

"That's easy," George says. "I write the check every month. It's $699.28."

"Does that include property tax and fire insurance?"

"No. I pay those separately."

"Okay, this is great, George. You've given me everything I need."

Divide $699.28 by 85 on your calculator. The answer you get is $8.2269. A flick of your wrist allows you to consult the numbers you've written on a piece of tape stuck to your calculator's back. You see that $8.2268 is the payment per thousand dollars of original loan amount for a 30-year loan at 9 1/4 percent.

"You've got a 30-year loan at 9¼ percent interest," you announce.

"That's right," George says. "I remember now. You really came up with those numbers fast."

They're impressed. They no longer have any doubt about you being competent to handle their real estate needs. Now you can get on with solving their housing problems and earning a fee.

"Knowing the numbers is just part of my service, George. My clients and customers have more important things to think about than the details when they're making a big decision like buying or selling a house. Okay, if I can just have another second."

On your laptop, you bring up the loan progress chart—it has a different name in some books—or pull out the little book of real estate numbers and flip to the page for 9.25 percent loans, which you know is the interest rate the Silversteins have been paying.

- The heading reads "Original term in years." Their loan term is 30 years, so you look at this column.
- Their loan is two years old. In the "Age of Loan" column you find 2. On the 2 line in the 30 column is "986." This number means that for every $1000 the Silversteins borrowed originally, they now owe $986.
- The original amount of their loan was $85,000. Multiply $986 by 85 to get the current amount they owe: $83,810.

"Your loan has a balance of $83,810. But, of course, you've gained two full year's appreciation on your house. You put down 20 percent when you bought?"

"Yeah," George says. He's blinking from the shock of being told he owes $2,810 more than he thought he did.

You then multiply $85,000 by 125 percent (1.25) and get $106,250. The Silversteins took out an 80 percent loan on their present house when they bought it; 80 percent of $106,250 is $85,000.

"I take it you paid about $106,250 for your house?"

George gives you a surprised look. "That's exactly what we paid."

You know the appreciation rate was 8 percent two years ago and 12 percent last year. You multiply $106,250 by 1.08, leave the result in the machine, and multiply that number by 1.12. Your answer is $128,520.

"George and Mary, let me ask you something, and we're just talking. What do you think your house will sell for on today's market?"

"I wouldn't take a dime less than $120,000," George says with a touch of belligerency. "I've really put a lot of work and money into it.

I've added sprinklers, a concrete patio, lots of things. And I just painted the place."

They were able to get a full 80 percent loan going in, so there's a good chance they bought at a fair market price. If so, their home has probably appreciated at about the average rate, and should now be worth about what you figured: $128,500.

Multiply $128,500 by 92 percent or .92 to get $118,220. They will gross about $118,220 if their house sells for $128,500. Subtract what they owe, $83,810, to get their net walkaway of $34,410. However, you don't drop this number on the Silversteins yet because they would lock onto it. Then, if it turns out they've got strange decorating or house-keeping taste, or have otherwise downgraded their home's salability, you're in trouble. Their house won't bring an average price, and you've needlessly thrown away a pad able to put you into two transactions.

"Let me work out a sellers' net sheet for you based on $123,000," you say.

"Will our home sell for *that* much?" Mary asks.

"Well, Mary, we've been talking for a few minutes, and you know by now that I'm a conscientious professional, so it goes without saying that I'd want to do my usual thorough market study of your house be-fore giving you a definite answer to this vital question, but . . ." pause just an instant " . . . I'd never mention the figure I did unless I felt pretty sure it's a distinct possibility, based on what you've told me. If your house could be sold for $123,000, would you folks definitely be inter-ested in the home you said you liked over on Terry Street?"

Now zip your lip and let the big question hang in the air. Enjoy the silence, as only a pro can. One of the most important parts of sales-manship is knowing when to keep silent—and having the emotional control to remain silent for as long as necessary. While communicating nonverbally, wait. Don't straighten things up, fidget, make notes, or run figures on your calculator. Sit still and count spots on the opposite wall. Let the pressure build.

Your fast methods have kept you right up with them anyway. Their net walkaway figure is $29,350 from a sales price of $123,000. (.92 times $123,000, less $83,810, equals $29,350.) Call it $30,000 for round numbers. That's about what they'll have for a down payment without drawing on their savings. Since 5 times 20 is 100, 4 times the down payment available gives you the 80 percent loan that's necessary. The Silversteins can pay about $150,000 for a house, if they can qual-ify for a $120,000 loan—you figure this in your head in a flash.

The interest rate is 10 percent, and 30-year 80 percent loans are available. That works out to $8.7758 per thousand dollars borrowed, a figure you have memorized because it's the going rate on the most common type of loan at the moment.

No calculation is necessary to get a tight figure on an easy number like $120,000. Jot down rounded figures from $8.7758.

| $878 | for the hundred thousand |
| 88 | for ten thousand |
| 88 | for another ten thousand |
| $1,054 | is the payment on the house you plan to sell them |

Multiplying $8.7758 by 120 with the calculator gives the payment as $1,053.10. The rounded figure at $1,054 is close enough at this stage.

Don't wait until you're with people to learn the real estate numbers. Professionals practice prior to performing. Amateurs don't. Anyone can tell the difference—professionals earn fees; amateurs work for nothing.

# CHAPTER 24

# Money-Making Forms and Checklists

**MONEY-MAKING FORMS:** Quick-Speak Inventory Slot Sheet ● Fizzbo Cross-File Cards ● Communication Log ● Buyer's Progress Chart ● Fast Fact Grabber ● Results Record ● Show List ● Tomorrow's Action List ● Farm File ● Lender Qualifier Form ● Buyer's Analysis for Better Service ● Guidelines to Market Value ● **MONEY-MAKING CHECKLISTS:** Prospecting ● Checklist for Farming ● Checklist for Up-Time ● Checklist for Listing Appointments ● Listing Presentation Manual (LPM) ● After-Listing Checklist ● Open House Checklist ● Checklist for Property-Showing Appointment with Buyers ● Checklist for Your Real Estate Car ● Coping Kit ● Fallout Avoidance Checklist—After-Sale Checklist for Both Buyers' and Sellers' Agents ● Marketing Plan of Action

I get many requests every year regarding the forms in this chapter. They are available on the accompanying CD. They can also be ordered from Danielle Kennedy Productions (P.O. Box 1395, Sun Valley ID 83353; 208-726-8375; daniellekennedy@svidaho.net). These packets cost $16.95 and are camera ready for copying or scanning.

There are two kinds of forms: those you fill out for someone else's convenience, and those you can *choose* to fill out for your own benefit. For many of us, the mere sight of the word *forms* brings up sour memories of drudgery, test-taking, and income taxes. But forms play an organizing, time-saving, money-making role if you'll let them. The trick is to choose forms designed to help you achieve your goals, and to use forms in a systematic way. These will allow you to get more work done in less time. They will free your mind of detail, and allow you to concentrate on the clients and customers, and on fee-earning points. Used wisely, effective forms put the right facts in front of you when you need them, and these facts will often make the difference between capturing or losing a client, between closing people or opening them up for another agent.

Good forms and checklists are priceless. They'll prevent errors which at best are time consuming to correct, and at worst destroy opportunities. If you think of forms as barriers to progress, and checklists as crutches for the incompetent, you're cutting yourself off from tools of great value. If the following forms and checklists don't fit your area and work methods, adapt them or design and compile your own.

# Money-Making Forms

Forms will help you organize your work for maximum efficiency. Using effective forms and checklists will make an enormous difference in your production.

## Quick-Speak Inventory Slot Sheet

The walk-in customers looking for an elegant view home in Exclusive Heights won't be impressed by your knowledge of the fixer-uppers in the valley. A buyer interested in smoked glass and wood won't be charmed if you show them brick. A wide variety of property is available in your sales area, and most of it falls into the broad categories people ask for. Your inventory knowledge will be bunched into a few of these categories—leaving you unprepared to cope with buyers in the other categories—unless you work effectively to prevent this natural bunching. We'll call these categories "slots" for short. The Quick-Speak Inventory Slot Sheet (QSISS) provides you with a fast and dependable way to categorize. It allows you to design your Quick-Speak Inventory to meet the widest possible range of buyer needs. It guides your keyviewing and QSI flashdecking along the lines you've selected as being the most efficient for you. As your Quick-Speak Inventory grows, you may want to use additional slot sheets to cover more localities. On the following page is the form to put this idea to work.

Select your first zone of specialization for your first slot sheet. This should be an area of at least 1000 houses or condominiums. Write five headings at the top of a blank form to be used for a specific zone. (Write in pencil at first.) The headings should classify the housing in your zone in ways beyond the number of bedrooms each unit has. Classify them by price, number of stories, style, lot size, and specific amenities. Choose headings reflecting what buyers want and how they think in your area. Price, of course, is where the heaviest cut almost always comes, so you'll probably want to head some of the vertical

QSISS  Quick-Speak Inv

V=Vacant   O=Occupied

| UNDER 200K | UNDER 150K | | CONDOS | ELM DIST | CLUB ESTATES |
|---|---|---|---|---|---|
| 140 W "E" ST | | V | 66 S NET | 5502 W. ACE | |
| 1020 Bluff | | O | 2131 4th E | 4901 DANTE | 65 PRESS WAY |
| | | V | | | |
| 2 Bedrooms | 2 Bedrooms | O | 2 Bedrooms | 2 Bedrooms | 2 Bedrooms |
| | | V | | | |
| 3 Bedrooms | 3 Bedrooms | O | 3 Bedrooms | 3 Bedrooms | 3 Bedrooms |
| | | V | | | 49 S. 60TH |
| 4 Bedrooms | 4 Bedrooms | O | 4 Bedrooms | 4 Bedrooms | 4 Bedrooms |
| | | V | | | |
| 5 Bedrooms | 5 Bedrooms | O | 5 Bedrooms | 5 Bedrooms | 5 Bedrooms |

| Fixer-Uppers | Great Terms | VIEW | POOLS | |
|---|---|---|---|---|
| | | | | |
| | | | | |
| | | | | |
| | | | | |

© Copyright 1989 Danielle Kennedy Productions, P.O. Box 1395, Sun Valley, Idaho 83353.

columns, *Under* $250,000 (250K), or whatever figure now marks the top of an active demand slot in that zone.

Now, get busy finding houses to fill those slots. When completed, the QSISS tells you what sort of houses your Quick-Speak Inventory needs to give you a complete sample of what's available. You will know exactly what to look for so you'll be prepared to work with every serious buyer for which your zone can provide housing.

The slot sheet aims at developing an inventory you can show on the shortest possible notice—preferably with no notice at all. For this reason, the form gives special attention to vacant houses. In each row of slots, the top line is marked *V*. Property on this line must be vacant, available for showing without having to notify anyone, and its house key should be in a lockbox on the premises, or in your office.

The lower lines are marked *O* for occupied homes which require a phone call before you take buyers to see them. For each slot, select the property representing the best available-now value. As your inventory knowledge increases, and as new properties come on the market, update your QSISS; make sure it lists the best buys in every slot.

For example, you might decide to call your first zone of specialization *Green Pretty West.* Use the first two headings to focus attention on hot price categories. Three areas of special interest to you, a condominium development, an average neighborhood, and a prestige section, should have their own columns. Since houses with a fine view, a pool, or solar-assisted heating are in special demand in Green Pretty Valley, use the spaces for special categories at the bottom of the form to spotlight best-buy properties with those amenities. To speed the updating of the slot sheet, prices are not given because they should be flashdecked and memorized.

Additional tips for fast building of your Quick-Speak Inventory are given in Chapters 2 and 3.

## FSBO Cross-File Cards

When filed by phone number (which can be written in large numbers in the corner) the FSBO X-File gives you a quick and effective way to work fizzbos. Chapter 5 shows a partly filled-in form, and tells you how to pack loads of money-making follow-up information onto this 3 × 5 card.

FSBO X-File

| MB 9/7 | DC 9/14 | | | 123-9876 |
|---|---|---|---|---|

WHERE/WHEN ADS WERE RUN BY THIS FSBO — PHONE NUMBER

*Stone*

MAN'S *Jerry* **M**

WOMAN'S *Rita* **W**

LAST NAME — FIRST NAMES

*4126 Barmie Dr      Westport*

ADDRESS — CALL RECORD

| DATE: | TIME: | DATE: | TIME: | DATE: | TIME: | DATE: | TIME: |
|---|---|---|---|---|---|---|---|
| 9/7 | 11 AM | 9/14 | 8 AM | 9/16 | 9 AM | | AM |
| PERSON REACHED M | | PERSON REACHED M | | PERSON REACHED M | | | M |
| *Call 9/14* | | *Call 9/16* | | *Appt for 9/17!* | | | |

© Copyright 1989 Danielle Kennedy Productions, P.O. Box 1395 Sun Valley, Idaho 83353.

## Communication Log

In the sample communication log shown on the following page, the transaction is Stuart selling to Meigs. Your client is Stuart and you are the listing agent. It's important to show who your client is on this particular document because you might be representing Meigs in a few weeks. The first conversation started at 11:10 A.M. on June 9, and lasted two minutes. This data about time, date, and length of call makes all the difference if your word is questioned later. You'll find it's a solid

# COMMUNICATION LOG

| CLIENT/SUBJECT | | | | TRANSACTION | | YEAR: | PAGE: |
|---|---|---|---|---|---|---|---|
| John Smith Incorporated | | | | | TO | 1999 | 25 |

| START TIME | D A T E | STOP TIME | C O D E | CODE KEY: | L Letter |
|---|---|---|---|---|---|
| | | | | Name of person contacted and summary of communication | |
| 11:10 AM | 6/9 | 11:12 | OC | | |
| | | | | | |
| | | | | | |
| | | | | | |
| | | | | | |
| | | | | | |
| | | | | | |
| | | | | | |
| | | | | | |
| | | | | | |
| | | | | | |
| | | | | | |
| | | | | | |
| | | | | | |
| | | | | | |
| | | | | | |
| | | | | | |
| | | | | | |
| | | | | | |
| | | | | | |
| | | | | | |
| | | | | | |
| | | | | | |
| | | | | | |
| | | | | | |
| | | | | | |
| | | | | | |
| | | | | | |
| | | | | | |
| | | | | | |
| | | | | | |
| | | | | | |
| | | | | | |
| | | | | | |
| | | | | | |

© Copyright 1989 Danielle Kennedy Productions, P.O. Box 1395, Sun Valley, Idaho 83353.

foundation to say, "According to my communication log, I gave you the information on September 12 at 2:05 in the afternoon. I'm sure you remember now. My log shows that we talked for six minutes."

If gripe come to growl, your communication logs will carry great weight in court—provided you've made a consistent practice of keeping them.

The first call noted on the sample log was made by you, as indicated by the code *OC* (as explained on the form). The subject of the call is given next. You'll often use several lines for a single communication.

Don't clutter up the page with pointless detail, but take sufficient space to record the basis of the conversation. In the last column, note the other party to the communication. With a little practice, you'll find yourself entering this information without difficulty or delay as you talk.

## Buyer's Progress Chart

Whether you represent the sellers or the buyers, you'll want to keep close tabs on what *isn't* happening. Staple a buyer's progress chart to

| BUYER'S PROGRESS CHART | | FINAL ITEM COMPLETION | | | |
|---|---|---|---|---|---|
| **DATE of SALE:** | **TARGET CLOSING DATE:** | | CHECKLIST | | |
| **STEPS REQUIRED TO CLOSE** | **PHONE** | DATE ORDERED OR SENT | DATE COMPLETION EXPECTED | DATE ACTUALLY COMPLETED | DATE CLIENT INFORMED |
| APPLICATION FOR LOAN | ( ) | | | | |
| | ( ) | | | | |
| | ( ) | | | | |
| APPRAISAL | ( ) | | | | |
| | ( ) | | | | |
| | ( ) | | | | |
| BANK VERIFICATIONS | ( ) | | | | |
| | ( ) | | | | |
| | ( ) | | | | |
| CREDIT REPORT | ( ) | | | | |
| | ( ) | | | | |
| | ( ) | | | | |
| EMPLOYMENT VERIFICATIONS | ( ) | | | | |
| | ( ) | | | | |
| | ( ) | | | | |
| INSURANCE, FIRE OR HOMEOWNERS | ( ) | | | | |
| | ( ) | | | | |
| | ( ) | | | | |
| LENDER FUNDS AVAILABLE | ( ) | | | | |
| | ( ) | | | | |
| | ( ) | | | | |
| | ( ) | | | | |
| PRELIMINARY TITLE REPORT | ( ) | | | | |
| | ( ) | | | | |
| | ( ) | | | | |
| REPAIRS | ( ) | | | | |
| | ( ) | | | | |
| | ( ) | | | | |
| TERMITE INSPECTION | ( ) | | | | |
| | ( ) | | | | |
| | ( ) | | | | |
| INITIAL INVESTMENT DEPOSITED | ( ) | | | | |
| | ( ) | | | | |
| | ( ) | | | | |
| | ( ) | | | | |

© Copyright 1989 Danielle Kennedy Productions, P.O. Box 1395, Sun Valley, Idaho 83353.

the inside of your transaction folder, review it at least once a week, and keep the fees flying to you. Chapter 19 talks about fallout avoidance in detail, but the heart of the matter is using this form. You'll have far fewer fallouts if you'll diligently do the detail work on time.

## Fast Fact Grabber

This form lets you catch information quickly while you're prospecting and find the information rapidly when you follow up. On the back of this form are spaces for scheduling and recording ten calls. Just as important are the three boxes at the bottom designed to direct your attention toward figuring out how to turn each contact into a transaction.

## Results Record

Most of us tend to remember the negatives, and dwell on our failures more than our wins. It's easy to overlook the steady progress you're making. Results records keep the good stuff up front. Complete one of these forms (an example is found on page 456) for all your prospecting sessions even if you make only one call.

Study the results records you've completed occasionally. The more results records you accumulate, the more you'll learn from them. Unless you keep track of where you're going, you can't correct your route.

## Show List

The show list will impress buyers by showing houses in a professional, hassle-free way. It's highly effective in Boards of REALTORS® issuing a weekly Multiple Listing book. Where a weekly Multiple book is not provided, make the appropriate changes to the form.

After completing this for a particular set of buyers, run it through the office copier and make a copy for each individual.

On the form, *page number* is the page number of the current Multiple Listing book where the listing appears. This is handy when a customer starts asking questions about several houses.

Under *status, o/o* and *t/o* for owner-occupied and tenant-occupied. This distinction is important when you're showing property. Tenants may be less cooperative and less careful than owners about setting the stage. The *OK* means you've reached whoever lives there and received their permission to show the property. An example of a show list is found on page 457.

## FAST FACT GRABBER

| DATE OF FIRST CONTACT | | PRIORITY | BEST TIMES TO CALL |
|---|---|---|---|

LAST NAME

| FIRST NAME | H U S B A N D | SEE OVER | DON'T CALL TIMES |
|---|---|---|---|

WORKS AT

JOB OR TITLE

| FIRST NAME | W I F E | | A C T I O N |
|---|---|---|---|

WORKS AT

JOB OR TITLE

| **NOW** | OWNS | LEASES | RENTS | BEDROOMS | BATHS | STORIES |
|---|---|---|---|---|---|---|

STYLE

CONDITION

AMENITIES

| **WANTS** | TO SELL | TO LEASE-OPTION | BEDROOMS | BATHS | STORIES |
|---|---|---|---|---|---|
| | TO RENT | TO BUY | FINANCING DESIRED | FHA | |

STYLE & LOCATION WANTED

SPECIAL REQUIREMENTS

| HIS | HERS | OTHER | TOTAL INCOME $0 |
|---|---|---|---|

| PRICE RANGE OF HOUSE THE WANT TO BUY | TO SELL | PER | MO |
|---|---|---|---|

| CASH AVAILABLE FOR INITIAL INVESTMENT | SOURCE | SALE OF PRESENT HOME |
|---|---|---|

WHAT'S ON THEIR MINDS NOW?

SPORTS, HOBBIES, SPECIAL INTERESTS

| PETS | RELATIVES LIVING WITH THEM | CHILDREN |
|---|---|---|
| CATS | | LIVING WITH THEM |
| DOGS | FAST FACT GRABBER | |

© Copyright 1989 Danielle Kennedy Productions, P.O. Box 1395, Sun Valley, Idaho 83353.

FAST FACT GRABBER *(continued)*

| Name | | | | | | | Phone Number | | |
|---|---|---|---|---|---|---|---|---|---|
| **FOLLOW UP CALL NUMBER** | 1 | 2 | 3 | 4 | 5 | 6 | 8 | 9 | 10 |
| **PLANNED DATE TO CALL** | | | | | | | | | |
| **ACTUAL DATE CALLED** | | | | | | | | | |

**RESULTS OF CALL NUMBER**

1
2
3
4
5
6
7
8
9
10

**FAVORABLE ASPECTS**

**UNFAVORABLE ASPECTS**

**HERE'S HOW I'LL CONVERT THIS CONTACT INTO A TRANSACTION:**

© Copyright 1989 Danielle Kennedy Productions, P.O. Box 1395, Sun Valley, Idaho 83353.

## RESULTS RECORD

| START TIME: Enter: 1:30 for 1:30AM, 13:30 for 1:30PM | DATE CALLS MADE: Enter mm/dd/yy |
|---|---|
| **1:30 PM** | |
| STOP TIME: Enter: 1:30 for 1:30AM, 13:30 for 1:30PM | TYPE OF CALLS MADE: |
| **4:30 PM** | |

| TALLY OF CALLS MADE: | TOTAL TIME SPENT: | |
|---|---|---|
| | TOTAL NUMBER OF CALLS MADE: | AVERAGE TIME PER CALL: |
| SOURCE OF PHONE NUMBERS: | | |
| **FSBO ADS** ▼ | | |

THE THREE BEST THINGS I SAID DURING THIS PROSPECTING SESSION WERE:

1 _____

_____

_____

2 _____

_____

3 _____

_____

_____

_____

_____

_____

_____

_____

REMARKS:

_____

_____

| I MADE 123 CONTACTS DURING THIS PROSPECTING SESSION THAT I WILL FOLLOW-UP WITH IN THE FUTURE | **123** |
|---|---|

© Copyright 1989 Danielle Kennedy Productions, P.O. Box 1395, Sun Valley, Idaho 83353.

## Tomorrow's Action List

Use an appointment book planner, a TAL, or a plain piece of paper, but every night take the time to plan your tomorrow. Unless you do, every breeze will push you off your route. You won't get where you want to go until you take charge of your life. An example of a TAL is found on page 458.

| SHOW LIST | | | | | | | | B E D R O O M S | B A T H S | S T O R A G E | A G E O F H O U S E | S T Y L E |
|---|---|---|---|---|---|---|---|---|---|---|---|---|
| PREPARED ESPECIALLY FOR | | | | | | | | | | | | |
| DATE: December 12, 2002 | SALES COUNSELOR: | | | | | | | | | | | |
| ↑PROPERTY PERSON TO CONTACT ↓ | | ↑PRICE　　PHONE ↓ | | PAGE #. | STATUS ↓ OK ↓ | | | | | | | |
| 1 | ADDRESS | $132,000 | | 23 | G O O D | | | | | | | |
| | CALL BEFORE | ( __ ) __ 8888 | | | | | | | | | | |
| 2 | ADDRESS | $132,000 | | 34 | F A I R | | | | | | | |
| | CALL BEFORE | ( __ ) __ 8888 | | | | | | | | | | |
| 3 | ADDRESS | $132,000 | | 45 | P O O R | | | | | | | |
| | CALL BEFORE | ( __ ) __ 8888 | | | | | | | | | | |
| 4 | ADDRESS | $132,000 | | 56 | V G E O R O Y D | | | | | | | |
| | CALL BEFORE | ( __ ) __ 8888 | | | | | | | | | | |
| 5 | ADDRESS | $132,000 | | 67 | V P E O R O Y R | | | | | | | |
| | CALL BEFORE | ( __ ) __ 8888 | | | | | | | | | | |
| 6 | ADDRESS | $132,000 | | 78 | G O O D | | | | | | | |
| | CALL BEFORE | ( __ ) __ 8888 | | | | | | | | | | |
| 7 | ADDRESS | $132,000 | | 89 | G O O D | | | | | | | |
| | CALL BEFORE | ( __ ) __ 8888 | | | | | | | | | | |
| 8 | ADDRESS | $132,000 | | 100 | G O O D | | | | | | | |
| | CALL BEFORE | ( __ ) __ 8888 | | | | | | | | | | |

© Copyright 1989 Danielle Kennedy Productions, P.O. Box 1395, Sun Valley, Idaho 83353.

## Farm File

The farm file form (found on pages 459 and 460) provides a space to record all the good things you'll learn about the people in your farm. Knowing these details helps you talk to them and earn their friendship and trust.

The farm file has space for entering information about the house they live in. Transfer the permanent part of this data to your property catalog.

Each time you work your way through your farm, try to record at least one additional fact about every family you visit. Do this immediately after you talk with them in order to capture small details; they are vital to winning control of your farm. You must walk a fine line here. You must show pleasant interest in your people, but not come on as a nosy busybody. Back off whenever you encounter a secretive and suspicious person; you can gain nothing by pressing such people.

Before you hit any house again, quickly review the form for the details you've already learned through your past casual conversations. This will allow you to start off the new conversation about where the last one ended. People are flattered by what you remember about them if you're not too obvious about it.

A word of caution: Never write anything offensive in your farm file. Let this thought be your guide before making any entry: Would I be willing to show this item to the family involved?

# T.A.L.
## TOMORROW'S ACTION LIST

DO DATE: _____

| MUST DO | DONE |
|---|---|
|  |  |
|  |  |
|  |  |

PRIORITY

| | |
|---|---|
| ☐ | |
| ☐ | |
| ☐ | |
| ☐ | |
| ☐ | |
| ☐ | |
| ☐ | |
| ☐ | |
| ☐ | |
| ☐ | |
| ☐ | |
| ☐ | |
| ☐ | |
| ☐ | |

© Copyright 1989 Danielle Kennedy Productions, P.O. Box 1395, Sun Valley, Idaho 83353.

## Lender Qualifier Form

This is a form the buyer fills out at the first interview. See Chapter 14.

It is a form real estate agents use when they interview a buyer prior to previewing homes.

All forms in this chapter are included on the CD or can be purchased on hard copy from Danielle Kennedy Productions (P.O. Box 1395, Sun Valley, ID 83353; 208-726-8375; daniellekennedy@svidaho.net).

# FARM FILE

| ADDRESS: | | | | LAST NAME: | |
|---|---|---|---|---|---|
| | | | | | |
| | ⟵ HIS | FIRST NAMES | HER ⟹ | | |
| CHILDREN | | | | | |
| | | | | | |

**HOUSE INFORMATION** | | | | | BEDROOMS |

**CAREER INFORMATION** ⟵ HIS   HER ⟹

**LEISURE INTERESTS** ⟵ HIS   HER ⟹

| VISITS | LAST NAME | DATE MOVED |
|---|---|---|

© Copyright 1989 Danielle Kennedy Productions, P.O. Box 1395, Sun Valley, Idaho 83353.

# FARM FILE

| DATES | FACTS LEARNED |
|-------|---------------|
|       |               |

**FRIENDS AND RELATIVES**

**REFERRAL POSSIBILITIES**

© Copyright 1989 Danielle Kennedy Productions, P.O. Box 1395, Sun Valley, Idaho 83353.

# SELLER'S NET SHEET

PREPARED FOR: _____        DATE: _____
REGARDING: _____
SALES COUNSELOR: _____

MANAGER'S APPROVAL:

SELLING PRICE        _____

## ESTIMATED SELLING COSTS

TITLE INSURANCE                                    _____
TAX STAMPS                                         _____
ESCROW FEES                                        _____
TERMITE INSPECTION AND REPORT                      _____
OTHER INSPECTIONS                                  _____
PREPAYMENT PRIVILEGE, IF ANY                       _____
RECONVEYANCE FEE                                   _____
BENEFICIARY STATEMENT                              _____
PRORATION OF INTEREST                              _____
FHA or VA LOAN DISCOUNT FEE                        _____
DISCOUNT to CASH OUT BUYER'S SECOND TRUST DEED     _____
_____                 _____
_____                 _____
_____                 _____
_____                 _____

*APPROXIMATE TOTAL OF SELLING COSTS         | $0.00 |    | $0.00 |

## LOANS

(Indicate where the information was obtained by circling one of the sources for each loan)

FIRST TRUST DEED        Seller    Lender    Document    _____
SECOND TRUST DEED       Seller    Lender    Document    _____
OTHER ENCUMBRANCES      Seller    Lender    Document    _____

TOTAL ENCUMBRANCES                                   | $0.00 |    | $0.00 |
TOTAL of ESTIMATED SELLING COSTS and ENCUMBRANCES          | $0.00 |    | $0.00 |

### *APPROXIMATE NET CASH TO SELLERS              | $0.00 |

*This estimate has been prepared to assist you in computing
your costs. And net walk-away cash. Whenever possible, we        ABOVE:
have used the MAXIMUM charges that are expected.

However, unusual circumstances may arise, and lenders,
inspectors, and others may vary their charges. Therefore,
these figures cannot be guaranteed.

© Copyright 1989 Danielle Kennedy Productions, P.O. Box 1395, Sun Valley, Idaho 83353.

# Money-Making Checklists

## Prospecting

For every prospecting session, gather the phone numbers you plan to call *before* the best time to prospect. Have the following items handy when you begin calling:

- *Pad of fast fact grabber forms*, or plain paper.
- *Results record form.* Fill in the date, time you'll start calling, type of call, and source of the phone numbers before you start. Keep track of what you're doing so you can evaluate what

# BUYER'S NET SHEET

PREPARED FOR: _____

PROPERTY ADDRESS: _____  SELLING PRICE: _____

SALES COUNSELOR: _____      DATE: _____

● 
FINANCING METHOD                    ┌──────┐ ┌──────┐ ┌──────┐
                                    └──────┘ └──────┘ └──────┘

_____ LOAN FEE:                          _____  _____  _____

INTEREST ON NEW LOAN:                         _____  _____  _____

  at an interest rate of:                      _____    _____    _____

SETTLEMENT ESCROW FEE:                        _____  _____  _____

DRAWING LOAN DOCUMENTS:                       _____  _____  _____

TITLE POLICY:                                 _____  _____  _____

TAX SERVICE:                                  _____  _____  _____

RECORDING FEES:                               _____  _____  _____

FIRE INSURANCE:            PREMIUM: _____

(or HOMEOWNERS')           or IMPOUND: _____   _____  _____  _____

PROPERTY TAXES:            PORATION: _____

                           or IMPOUND: _____   _____  _____  _____

CREDIT REPORT:                                _____  _____  _____

APPRAISAL:                                    _____  _____  _____

INSPECTIONS:                                  _____  _____  _____

ASSOCIATION DUES AND TRANSFER FEE, IF ANY:    _____  _____  _____

_____             _____  _____  _____

_____             _____  _____  _____

MISCELLANEOUS:                                _____  _____  _____

        TOTAL CLOSING COSTS:                  _____  _____  _____

        INITIAL INVESTMENT:                   _____  _____  _____

        TOTAL CASH REQUIRED TO CLOSE:         _____  _____  _____

MONTHLY INVESTMENT (See other side for Breakdown):   _____  _____  _____

**MANAGER'S APPROVAL:**

© Copyright 1989 Danielle Kennedy Productions, P.O. Box 1395, Sun Valley, Idaho 83353.

you've accomplished, and make any necessary changes to improve results during future prospecting sessions.

- *Mirror.* Keep it in front of you as you call so you can constantly check your expression. The stress showing in your face will travel over the phone to the other person.
- *Pen and pencils.* Make sure you have plenty.
- *Timer.* A stopwatch works best, but any clock will do.
- *Cassette recorder* if you want to tape yourself.

## BACK—BUYER'S NET SHEET

### BREAKDOWN OF MONTHLY INVESTMENT

●    ☐    ☐    ☐

Principal and Interest
      On First Mortgage      _____   _____   _____
      On Second Mortgage     _____   _____   _____

Association Dues, if any                _____   _____   _____

Monthly Cost of Fire or Homowners' Insurance     _____   _____   _____

Monthly Cost of Property Taxes          _____   _____   _____

TOTAL MONTHLY INVESTMENT                _____   _____   _____

*AMOUNT DEDUCTIBLE on your federal
              Income Tax return      _____   _____   _____

**\*NOTE: YOU MUST VERIFY THIS AMOUNT WITH YOUR TAX ADVISER BEFORE RELYING ON IT TO MAKE A DECISION ABOUT REAL ESTATE. THESE DEDUCTIONS MAY NOT BE AVAILABLE TO YOU.**

**All figures given on both sides of this form are based on present information. Actual figures at the settlement may vary.**

© Copyright 1989 Danielle Kennedy Productions, P.O. Box 1395, Sun Valley, Idaho 83353.

- *Paper or electronic planner* to record all appointments you acquire during this session. Be ready to set up meetings not in conflict with your present commitments.
- *Your office's current sheet of listings and the Multiple Listing book or your computer showing the best web site for listings* in case some of the conversations turn into property inquiries.
- *Your comparables file.* Some agents prefer to give very little information over the phone with the intention of doing this in person with a Guidelines to Market Value form. Other agents give all

---

Date: _____

## BUYER'S ANALYSIS FOR BETTER SERVICE

Names of Clients: _____

Is this your first visit to our community? _____

Where are you folks from? _____

How long have you been looking for a home? _____

How many are in your family? _____

Then you have _____ children? _____

May I ask their names and ages? _____

Where do you live now? _____

How long have you lived there? _____

Are you investing in your home or do you rent? _____

How is the resale market in your area? _____

May I ask Mr/Mrs. _____ where are you employed? _____

_____

How long have you been there? _____

Have you seen any homes you really like? _____

What has prevented you from owning that home? _____

_____

_____

_____

How soon had you thought of making a move after you've found the right home? _____

How much time will you have to see home today? _____

How many bedrooms would suit you best? _____

*If they own now:*

How much do you feel you will realize from the sale of your home? _____

Will it be necessary to sell your present home to purchase the new one? _____

---

© Copyright 1989 Danielle Kennedy Productions, P.O. Box 1395, Sun Valley, Idaho 83353.

the information asked for on the phone with the aim of building trust and making people feel comfortable. Choose which way you'll operate beforehand, and check results over a period of time.

- *Winning scripts.* Have handy a list of statements to make and questions to ask.
- *Goal.* Always set a goal for each prospecting session; make it no more than a reasonable stretch beyond your comfort level. Build on your wins.

---

# BACK—BUYER'S ANALYSIS FOR BETTER SERVICE

Will you be converting any of your other investments to cash in order to complete the purchase of your next home?

_____

If we were fortumate to find the right home today, will you be in a position to make a decision to proceed?

_____

Not to be too personal, but to do a better job for you, may I ask, how much of your savings do you wish to invest

in your home? _____

What price range have you been considering? Better yet, since most people are concerned with their monthly outgo

how much do you feel you could comfortably invest each month in your new home, including everything?

_____

_Use on lower price range properties:_

A rule of thumb most lenders use is that the monthly investment should be approximately one-fourth of a person's

gross monthly income, after payments on long term bills are deducted.  Are we in line here?

_____

Please take a moment, Mrs. _____ to describe your present home to me, including

all your likes and dislikes.  _____

_____

_____

_____

_____

What are your special requirements for your next home?

_____

_____

_____

Are there any other special requirements that I haven't noted yet, such as (Suggest some of the popular amenities

available in your inventory) that you'd like to see in your next home?

_____

_____

_____

© Copyright 1989 Danielle Kennedy Productions, P.O. Box 1395, Sun Valley, Idaho 83353.

# Checklist for Farming

## In your car:
- Bottle of ice water
- Multiple Listing book
- Farm file
- Property catalog
- Backup supply of giveaways

GUIDELINES TO MARKET VALUE

Prepared For:
Regarding:
Prepared By:
Date:

*Range* $ _____ *to* $ _____

| RECENT SALES | SALES PRICE | DATE LISTED | DATE SOLD | LIST PRICE | AMENITIES | FINANCING | LOCATION | | |
|---|---|---|---|---|---|---|---|---|---|
| | | | | | | | | | |
| | | | | | | | | | |
| | | | | | | | | | |
| | | | | | | | | | |

| HOMES AVAILABLE NOW | LIST PRICE | DATE LISTED | DAYS ON MARKET | AMENTIES | | FINANCING | LOCATION | | |
|---|---|---|---|---|---|---|---|---|---|
| | | | | | | | | | |
| | | | | | | | | | |
| | | | | | | | | | |
| | | | | | | | | | |

| EXPIRED LISTINGS | LIST PRICE | DATE LISTED | DAYS ON MARKET | AMENTIES | | FINANCING | LOCATION | | |
|---|---|---|---|---|---|---|---|---|---|
| | | | | | | | | | |
| | | | | | | | | | |
| | | | | | | | | | |
| | | | | | | | | | |
| | | | | | | | | | |

© Copyright 1989 Danielle Kennedy Productions, P.O. Box 1395, Sun Valley, Idaho 83353.

**In your purse or pocket:**
- A supply of your business cards

**In your hand:**
- A few of your current giveaways
- A few of your imprinted memo pads

**In your heart:**
- Firm resolve to meet your farming goal for the day
- Firm belief that a single soft *yes* is worth 100 hard *no's*

**In your brain:**
- Your goal for how many contacts you want to make today
- A number of opening remarks
- Alertness

**On your face:**
- A confident smile

## Checklist for Up-Time

The tea cart checklist is given in Chapter 10.

## Checklist for Listing Appointments

- Clipboard for taking notes during the tour
- Calculator
- Multiple Listing book
- Title insurance rate card
- Amortization book
- Your Listing Presentation Manual. As soon as you can, put your LPM on a laptop computer you're confident with and expert at operating.
- Listing folder containing:
  - Guidelines to Market Value form filled out for the property you're there to list
  - A seller's net sheet form to be filled out during the appointment
  - A blank listing form
  - Your marketing plan of action flyer
  - An imprinted memo pad
  - Copy of your latest newsletter
  - Flyer-packet of your other listings, or of a sample of your office's listings. Place them on top of a copy of your profile of a pro (you).
  - A copy of your personalized flyer, "A Dozen Tips to Bring My Sellers More Money." (See Chapter 12.)

## Listing Presentation Manual (LPM)

If you're using a paper LPM, the most convenient page size is 8 1/2 × 11 inches. Choose a stand-up variety that is easy for your prospects to review, and leaves both your hands free. You have two choices of format in this size sheet:

- *Laptop.* Download all your important papers on the laptop. Endorsements, photos, lender qualifiers, and so on. Everything you do on paper can be done on the computer. Go paperless and cutting edge.
- *Flip Chart.* The horizontal page size is 11 inches, like a school notebook turned on its side. Use plastic sheet protectors.
- *Easel Binder.* The horizontal page size is 8 1/2 inches. Get top-loading sheet protectors to make updating your LPM fast and easy. If your office supply store doesn't have these items in stock, they can order them.

I preferred the flip chart to the easel binder because most of the certificates and $8 \times 10$ photos I used in my LPM were horizontal in orientation and were right side up in the flip chart format. The flip chart also looks less like a high-school notebook and more like professional working equipment.

Select the format you prefer and use lots of color to produce great-looking pages displaying your most powerful LPM points. Highlight important items. Strive for a smooth presentation, but keep it very personal to yourself. Remember, the most important element in your presentation is *you*, so sell yourself with subtle and persistent strength.

Your LPM should have three sections. Set it up to flow smoothly from one section to the next as you use it.

## Section One: Sell the Real Estate Industry
### Explain the Multiple Listing Service

- Show a sample page from the MLS book.
- Highlight the number of agents involved.
- Emphasize the referrals from other areas that all these agents get.
- Give the volume done by the entire Board of REALTORS® last year in graph form. As you talk, tell your prospects what the volume was last month and last week.
- Show a printed copy of the code of ethics, published by the National Association of REALTORS® (if you are a member).

### Show the Diagram of Buyers

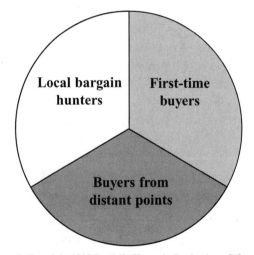

© Copyright 1989 Danielle Kennedy Productions, P.O. Box 1395, Sun Valley, Idaho 83353.

If your prospects are considering selling on their own, show this diagram and explain how first-time buyers are afraid of fizzbos, and buyers coming in from distant points don't have time to work with fizzbos. Both kinds of buyers want a professional they trust to represent them. Without professional help, fizzbos are left with the local bargain hunters and the lookielews. Don't bring this up unless the sellers intend to try to sell themselves. Don't plant the idea in their minds.

## Section Two: Sell Your Company

- Show $8 \times 10$ color pictures of your entire staff, and the interior, and exterior of your office. If you have a good location, talk about it now.
- If your company rates favorably in your community on sales volume, include a page showing how strongly they rate, and then tell your prospects.
- Show them samples of your company's advertising.
- Explain how advertising works in the local real estate resale market. A diagram showing how much business comes from signs, classified ads, and other sources will back up your information on advertising.
- Show the special awards your company has won or a photo of your staff holding trophies. Show your pride in your office and tell how your staff works together.
- Talk about deadlines for getting the listing into the Board of RE-ALTORS® office, for advertising, for getting their listing on the Internet, and for having their house caravanned. If your office has its own preview of new listings, tell them about it now.
- Show your company's relocation affiliation, and talk about it.

## Section Three: Sell Yourself

- Talk about the cutting edge technology you're using to stay on top of the real estate market. Show them your sophisticated methods of showing property to buyers via computer.
- Include training certificates that show the sellers how you keep up with new trends in marketing homes.
- Show sample flyers from some of your listings.
- Include your profile of a pro flyer.
- Discuss briefly your "Dozen Tips to Bring My Sellers More Money" flyer.
- Talk about your track record, if you've been in the business long enough to have an impressive one.

- Show them photos of your office awards.
- Include newspaper clippings of your awards or other personal publicity.
- Include some samples of ads you've placed yourself.
- Include letters of recommendation from satisfied clients and customers. These are powerful convincers.
- Discuss and illustrate your marketing plan for selling their home, should you be selected to represent them. A sample marketing plan is given at the end of this chapter.
- Use several photos of you and happy clients putting up Sold signs. These have great emotional impact.
- Include a blank Guidelines to Market Value form, and a blank seller's net sheet. This makes for a smooth transition to the money phase of your presentation.

At this point set the LPM aside, put your listing folder on the table, take out the guidelines form, and go for it.

## After-Listing Checklist

- Put your temporary For Sale sign in the front lawn.
- Obtain a key from the sellers and place it in the lockbox.
- Have your broker approve the listing form.
- Submit a copy of the listing to the Multiple Listing Service.
- Order the permanent For Sale sign installed.
- Distribute Just Listed doorhangers in the neighborhood.
- Check with the present lender about the existing loan or loans. Can they be assumed? Is there a prepayment privilege? What costs are involved?
- Explore what other lenders will do for a buyer now, so you'll be able to answer when asked.
- Have an extra key made if the sellers will allow it.
- Put your marketing plan into high gear.

## Open House Checklist

- Open house signs, arrow signs, and flags
- Refreshments, if desired. (Bring paper cups, napkins, sugar and creamers, if needed, paper plates, trash bag, and everything you'll need to clean up.)
- Your plan for making effective use of your time at the open house
- Display on the most visible table, or on an easel:
  - Purchase agreement
  - Guest log

- Information flyer about the property
- Stack of customer-catcher maps
- Stack of flyer-packets
- Giveaway package promoting your area
- Stack of your imprinted memo pads
- Business cards
- Net sheet made out for asking price of the property
- Have available, but not necessarily in sight:
  - Listing forms
  - Amortization book
  - Title insurance rate card
  - Calculator
  - Multiple Listing book
  - Your appointment book
  - Pad of fast fact grabbers or plain paper
  - Something to eat
- Display in the front room:
  - Easels with storyboards about your area and you

## Bring If the House You're Holding Is Vacant

- Card table and three folding chairs
- Roll of hand towels, box of tissues, and soap
- Drinking cup
- High-intensity lamp with extension cord

## Checklist for Property-Showing Appointment with Buyers

- Show list prepared for these buyers
- Deposit receipts (purchase agreements)
- Title insurance rate card
- Calculator
- Amortization book
- Multiple Listing book
- Counteroffer forms
- Buyer's net sheets
- List of schools and churches in the area

## Checklist for Your Real Estate Car

- Open house signs, arrow signs, and flags
- Temporary For Sale sign
- *For Lease* rider

- *Sold* rider for your office's sign
- Kid kit with games to occupy children
- Coping kit (see next section)
- Backup kit containing a supply of your:
  - Business cards
  - Personalized memo pads
  - Latest farming giveaway
  - Latest newsletter
  - Buyer and seller net sheets
  - Listing forms
  - Purchase agreements
  - Counteroffers
  - Lockboxes
  - Extra batteries for your calculator
  - Supply of pens and pencils
  - Extra amortization book and title rate card
  - Stationery, letterheads, notes, and envelopes
  - Stamps
  - Customer-catcher maps
  - Flyer-packets

## Coping Kit

- Masking and transparent tape
- Some push pins, paper clips, and rubber bands
- Stapler, scissors, screwdriver, and pliers
- Handful of bolts, nuts, and washers for your signs
- Work gloves
- Box of tissues
- Band aids
- Large flashlight
- Measuring tape (cloth, not metal, so as not to scratch furniture)

Put the above items in a small cardboard box and keep them in your real estate car's trunk. You'll be pleased at how often they'll ease your way, and keep you looking cool and competent.

## Fallout Avoidance Checklist— After-Sale Checklist for Both Buyers' and Sellers' Agents

Be alert for developments possibly able to blow your *current* transaction apart. Every real estate transaction is unique. The most important item on your fallout avoidance checklist is alertness and a quick reaction to whatever occurs in a cool, professional manner laced with plenty of sound common sense. Chapter 19 has more details on fallout avoidance.

The following items will help avoid fallout:

- All copies of the accepted offer (and counteroffers, if any) signed by all parties. Copies of each of these documents delivered to all parties.
- Buyer's loan application delivered to lender
- Complete legal description of property to lender and to the person processing the paperwork
- Inspections ordered promptly. Termite, roof, mechanical—whatever is required in your area and by the special provisions of this purchase agreement.
- All other special provisions of the purchase agreement cleared
- All contingencies, if any, cleared
- All repairs required by the agreement ordered in good time, and completed
  - Who has responsibility for each item?
  - Are they doing what has to be done?
- Are the sellers making timely arrangements to move out?
- Loan approval
- Keep a communication log on all conversations involving this transaction
- Use a buyer's progress chart to keep track of the vital steps necessary to close
- Will the lender have the money to fund the loan?
- New fire insurance obtained by buyer
- Preliminary report of title, if required by this purchase agreement
  - Ordered?
  - Received?
  - Any problems?
- Have escrow instructions (or whatever document is used in your state to tell the person handling the paperwork exactly what to do) been signed and returned?
- Have the buyers done whatever must be done before they can get the necessary initial investment money?
- Have the buyers deposited the money in escrow or the proper account?
- If the buyers are to move in before settlement or close of escrow, has a rental agreement been signed and a substantial amount of

money released to the sellers before they take possession? (Allowing the buyers to move in before the property is legally theirs should be avoided whenever possible. This removes all incentive to complete the purchase from some people and others find little things around the house to bicker about. However, sometimes it's the only way to save the transaction when things the buyers can't control delay the close.)

It's your responsibility to protect your clients' interests, and also to help them give friendly and honorable cooperation to the other party. Transactions have been lost because one of the agents felt that loyalty to his or her client or customer permitted rude or unreasonable conduct to the other party. Your job is to solve problems, not create them—never forget this.

## Add These to the After-Sale Checklist If You're the Buyers' Agent

- Introduce your buyers, by telephone or in person, to the processor (or whoever will be handling the paperwork involved).
- Think through the paperwork problems involved in this particular transaction, and work out a schedule to get everything done on time.
- Whenever possible, allow yourself a pad of time to cover slip-ups in the paper flow. If necessary, hand-carry documents or fly to get them signed. Send them by express overnight service if necessary.
- Review with your buyers all the details to be cleared before they can get title to their new house. Do this as soon as possible after their offer is accepted.
- Order fire insurance.
- Make sure a copy of the fire insurance policy is delivered to processor or lender.
- Work through the listing agent to make sure the sellers have arranged to move out on time.
- Make sure your buyers understand what type of check is required. If they show up at the closing with a personal check drawn on an out-of-state bank for the amount of the initial investment, your transaction won't close—unless they can have the funds wired from their bank to a nearby correspondent bank *today*.
- Know about the keys to the house (and garage door openers). When, where, and from whom will you get them? Don't wait until the last minute to get these answers. The listing agent may

be out of town when the sellers move out with the keys in their pockets.

- Purchase a housewarming gift to give the buyers. (Buy them dinner on you the day they move in?) Cement your relationship with them and ensure future referral business.
- Ask for referrals.
- Call two weeks after they move in.
- Add these customers to your twice-yearly contact file.

### Add These to the After-Sale Checklist If You're the Listing Agent

- Notify your office, and your local Board of REALTORS®, of the sale.
- Obtain your broker's approval of the purchase agreement.
- Make copies of any permits for alterations and additions in the file if required.
- Put a *Sold* rider on your For Sale sign.
- Remove the lockbox. Tell the sellers, "With your permission I'll keep the key in the safety of our office so I can let the appraiser and the inspectors in and not have to bother you. Will this be okay?"
- Distribute *Just Sold* doorhangers in your area.
- Prepare a list of comparables for the appraiser.
- Meet the appraiser at the property with a list of comparables, and the key.

## Marketing Plan of Action

Adapt this plan to your area and methods, and add one to your Listing Presentation Manual. Put a copy in the listing folder you make up for each listing appointment.

I.  **Sales Promotion and Advertising**
    A. List property. Place lockbox, if agreeable.
    B. Distribute listing to all members of the staff.
    C. Submit listing to Multiple Listing Service, and check book weekly to make sure the listing is accurately recorded.
    D. Caravan for our staff on Tuesdays, and acquaint them with the amenities and strong sales features prior to entering client's home.
    E. Caravan for Saddleback Valley Board of REALTORS® members on Thursdays, with refreshments served to encourage

their lingering to enjoy the home. Phone offices for a personal invitation prior to caravan.

F. Write no less than three ads about the property for advertising in some or all of the following media: *The Register, The Pennysaver, The Saddleback News,* and the *Los Angeles Times.*

G. Print and distribute a marketing sheet. Sheets are given to offices of the Saddleback Valley Board of REALTORS®, distributed at Board of REALTORS® breakfasts, and also left in client's home for those viewing it.

H. Hold open house, when convenient for client.

## II.   Monitoring

A. Ask sellers to save all business cards of agents for you to follow up.

B. Follow up with people met during open house.

C. Send personal notes notifying neighbors and others of listing and open houses.

D. Telephone top salespeople in Board of REALTORS®.

E. Make continual effort to keep client's property in front of Board of REALTORS® members, and to sell to each agency calling in about the client's home.

GOAL—To continually, and always in good taste, keep client's home in front of MOTIVATED salespeople and MOTIVATED BUYERS until SOLD!

## III.   Financing the Sale of the Home

A. Contact the current lender, inquiring about their lending policies.

B. Conduct a lender survey of interest rates, loan fees, and other data to compare with current lender.

C. Report and discuss findings with client.

## IV.   Contact with Owners

A. Present samples of all sales promotions and advertising.

B. Call and/or visit client frequently about the progress of the sale of the home, response of showings, and general market activity.

C. Re-evaluate marketing program often for possible changes.

## V.   The Processing Period

A. Suggest and implement, if possible, hand-carrying of documents.

B. Follow up to make sure all necessary documents are signed and delivered to the proper parties as soon as possible.

C. Keep in constant contact with processor, lender, title company, and buyer's agent during the entire processing period.

# CHAPTER 25

# Dead Cats, Weeds, and Holes in the Wall

The Diamond ● The Water's Cold, All Right ● All-Out Effort Makes Success Certain ● A Load of Independence ● Fallbehind, Movingup, and Hyflier ● Danny's Dozen for Success at Listing and Selling ● Watch Your Jargon ● A Good-Stuff Notebook (Inner Trainer Journal) ● Stay Away from Jolly J. Floppe ● Weeds ● Even Out the Peaks and Valleys ● Make Habits Work for You; Don't Fight Them ● Check Your MOO Every Month ● The Pigeon-Toed Undersold Real Estate Agent ● The Rules ● Excuses Accuse ● Develop Your Powers of Decision Making ● Old Hand to New-comer ● Holes in the Wall

About noon on a hot September day, I got a call from an agent who said she would show one of my listings in an hour to a very ready buyer if I would get rid of the dead cat in the backyard. It smelled pretty bad, she said. When she previewed the house, one of the neighbors had complained to her about the cat. As I walked out of the office I told Melinda on the up-desk, "I'll be back in 20 minutes. I've got to run over and bury a dead cat."

I picked up a shovel at my house and drove over to the listing. It was a vacant house the owners had left in immaculate condition, but as soon as I stepped out of my car, I realized the neighbor had good reason to complain.

I dug a deep hole in the backyard with the shovel, placed the poor little creature in his grave, and refilled the hole. Then I drove back to the office and called the showing agent.

"You're all set."

"When's it going to be taken care of? I can't show that property to my people unless I know for sure . . ."

"It's done. I took care of it myself. And I turned the sprinklers on for a bit. It's April in Paris around there now."

When I checked with Melinda for messages, she said, "Danny, did you really go out just now and bury a dead cat?"

"I took care of it, Melinda. I'm sure it had been somebody's darling pet, but I couldn't leave it in the back yard. What a total turn off for buyers."

"Of course. Only—why you?"

"Because I'm the *listing* agent, Melinda. The owners are a 1000 miles away."

"But couldn't you have called someone?"

"Like who? I figured I could take care of it myself quicker than I could locate someone to do it for me. How would you have handled it?"

Melinda shook her head. "I don't know—except I wouldn't do it myself. I'm a real estate agent, not a yucky-thing-doer."

I thought about this incident two months later when Melinda dropped out of real estate. She just couldn't bury the dead cats.

# The Diamond

The hardest and, at the same time, the most beautiful fact about this fascinating business of ours is this simple truth: You get paid exactly what you're worth. This will seem very hard when you've just had two transactions fall out, four offers turned down, and eight bills you owe go delinquent. It will seem beautiful when you bank more in one month than the average wage earner takes home in a year.

"There's a lot of pure, dumb luck in this business and all of mine is bad," we often say—and even believe—when things go wrong. Whenever you're tempted to lay your problems on some nebulous force outside yourself, it's time for you to have a little talk with yourself.

"Friend, I tell this to you for your own good, you make your own luck 99.99 percent of the time. In listing you make your own luck. In selling you make your own luck. In every aspect of life you make your own luck. So get out there and make yourself some good luck. Sitting around complaining pays just what it's worth: nothing. The longer you talk negative, the longer you'll earn nothing—and friend, you can't afford it."

Are you throwing yourself into real estate with all your energy or are you just testing the water, dipping a toe in to see if it's too cold?

# The Water's Cold, All Right

Pull on a wet suit and dive into that water or get in your car, drive away, and forget about it. There are determined, knowledgeable agents already in the water—and they think it's just fine. One thing you haven't done is join a monopoly; there is no protective tariff holding off the competition.

However, there is space for everyone who's willing to work effectively. The world in general, and the real estate business in particular, will always have room for another effective worker. So learn to be effective.

Being effective means, quite simply, doing what has to be done to open and close transactions. This doesn't mean using trickery, misrepresentation, or unethical conduct. All unfair tactics are degrading and self-destroying. Learn how to win people's trust and confidence. There's no better way to begin than by convincing yourself of your own trustworthiness and competence.

Many people unconsciously hold back from all-out effort in real estate because then they'll have no excuse if their all-out effort fails to bring them success. They can't face the risk of defeat without a prepared excuse. These people do not grasp a pair of simple facts: half-hearted effort always fails and all-out effort ensures success.

# All-Out Effort Makes Success Certain

If you've chosen realistic, achievable goals, all-out effort makes success certain. Success in real estate is an achievable goal for anyone capable of obtaining a real estate license. But, you must make a full commitment of your energy and resources and not hold back. You must make this decision and only one other, "I must change and adapt and grow; the world won't change to suit me, and it won't adapt itself to me."

Do what has to be done to merit your clients' and customers' faith in you. Tell them the truth, the whole truth, and nothing but the truth. As far as you know the facts, tell them everything legitimately affecting their interests and everything important to the decisions they must make. Be honest and up-front even when you talk yourself directly out of a fee. It will come back to you. Believe in your own integrity, and others will believe in you too. *Nothing can happen in real estate until people like and trust you.*

Do what has to be done to prepare a property for sale. Tell the sellers the doggie do-do in the backyard must be shoveled up and the bathroom fixtures must be cleaned and shined. Do it diplomatically— but do it.

Sometimes serious problems with the property have to be corrected before it will sell. If the sellers are merely slow to accept reality, work with them. But you have to make a decision in this situation. Will the sellers fix the problems before they decide it's your fault the property hasn't sold? Look ahead and make this decision early. The most effective use of your time may be to work on listing other properties to replace the problem house. A large part of being effective is successfully avoiding unpromising situations.

Agents who have only one listing or one buyer will often put up with a lot of flakiness in the client or customer. As you pick up a good group of people to service, also pick up wisdom about when to let a client go. This will give you a load of independence.

# A Load of Independence

Keep your balance, but remember that people can keep you working so furiously you never realize how much money they're preventing you from making.

A few sellers and some buyers are too demanding, too unreasonable, too destructive of your time, energy, and positive feelings. You can't make money even if you succeed in closing a transaction with them. By the time you've collected your fee, you've spent more time working with them, and more time healing yourself afterwards, than you would've spent earning two or three fees with normal people.

If you're starting to wince every time the phone rings, if you're beginning to suspect you secretly hate people, stop and consider your clients. Are you selecting the worst people to work with by allowing such people to monopolize your action? If so, they're blocking you from having sufficient time and energy to find prospects who are more of a pleasure, and less of a pain, to work with. Remember, lots of nice people are out there, mixed in with lots of not-so-nice people. For the sake of your health—and for the benefit of your bank account—start sloughing off the worst of the grumps and growlers as soon as you can. Start jumping for the prospects who say *please.*

Remember, the *please*-sayers are the kind who'll go away quietly if they're neglected. Let the howlers howl when you give priority on your time to the *please*-sayers. This is the way you select a reasonable clientele instead of allowing an unreasonable clientele to select you. Relax and keep your mind refreshed. Put yourself in the way of pleasant people to work with. You'll make more money and like your days better if you do.

# Fallbehind, Movingup, and Hyflier

You'll encounter more properties with minor problems than with major problems such as landscaping that needs attention, doors that squeak, and a broken window that lets in rain.

Agent Hyflier calls a dependable handyman.

"Fix it. I'll pay you," Hyflier says. Hyflier may or may not get repaid by the seller at the close.

"My time is valuable," Hyflier says, having done the things necessary to make it so. "No handyman can do what I get paid the most for, but he can take what I'd get paid the least for off my back."

Agent Movingup feels the same, but can't afford the handyman yet, so she makes the repairs personally—and gets the house sold.

Agent Fallbehind is too busy squeaking his office chair to do what must be done. Things slide until, three days before the listing expires, Fallbehind has a sudden burst of energy. He makes lots of phone calls. He puts intense pressure on people to move fast. Money is spent. Things get done. But, it's too late. The sellers list with someone else.

Fallbehind sinks back into a dazed funk, rousing occasionally to refill a coffee cup and badmouth Hyflier.

"He just knows an awful lot of people." Something underhanded is going on there somewhere, Fallbehind intimates darkly, pounding back to his desk. "And this new kid, Movingup—let me tell you, nobody goes that fast in this business without cutting too many corners. She's just a flash in the pan—no real depth there. Wait'll things get really tough. Wait'll the chips are down. Then we'll see if that prima donna can sing."

When the market turns and the chips *are* down, Hyflier is flying too high to notice, Movingup is solidly entrenched with a 100 percent referral business, and ex-agent Fallbehind goes to work as a security guard "until the market straightens itself out."

The following dozen ideas, if followed, will turn Fallbehind into Movingup, and Movingup into Hyflier.

# Danny's Dozen for Success at Listing and Selling

1. Honor your time and your integrity.
2. Keep specific, written, achievable, and exciting dreams always fresh and alive in your thoughts.
3. Positively validate yourself every morning and night.
4. Build your pride on your achievements won fairly; never forget or apologize for a humble beginning.
5. Know your inventory.
6. Know your area.
7. Make promises you can keep and then keep them.
8. Learn the golden phrases people need to hear in order to make decisions favorable to them and to you.

9. Find your winning shots and construct a strong game plan. Play it hard.
10. See the world through your clients' eyes; feel their hopes and fears; be part of their ups and downs. Develop referral business by putting your peoples' needs ahead of your own.
11. No matter how busy you become, take time to be kind to your body, and to learn and to live and to love.
12. Be responsible to and for yourself, to and for your family, to and for your company, your community, and your country.

## Watch Your Jargon

Think about your words. Clients don't know the real estate language.

*Caller:* I've decided to sell, Tillie. Come over and list my house.
*Tillie:* I can't. I'm on the floor.

## A Good-Stuff Notebook (Inner Trainer Journal)

Keep a notebook to record what you've done well. *Good-strokes* go in the front section. These are all the clever dialogues, zingers, and convincing arguments you thought of *after* the people walked out the door and it was too late to use them. Also record here the effective lines you *did* think of in time to use.

Briefly jot down the circumstances that set the stage for your good stroke after you record the good stroke itself. Make a habit of capturing your effective words in your notebook as soon as you're alone. Read them over and role play them occasionally so they'll be on the tip of your tongue the next chance you get to use them. You'll get many chances; the situations of real estate constantly repeat themselves.

*Feel-goods* go in the back section. These are your victories. Read them to pep yourself up when things go wrong. Read them when things go right to accelerate your enthusiasm. We tend to remember and dwell on our defeats and rejections, large and small, and to forget our good shots. Turn this around: Reject your rejections and dwell on your sharp shots. Take note of the quick one-liner you saved a shaky negotiation with. Remember the time you listened carefully to a grumpy garbage-can kicker and came away with his listing. Recall the fee-winning hunch you acted on. Jot down your smaller victories too. If you're held back by fear of someone reading your feel-goods, abbreviate them in code. Keep a list of the scores you've made. Read and relive them when you're tempted to dwell on defeat. If you prefer hashing over faults and failures to remembering strengths and successes, it's proof that you're self-destructing your enthusiasm, forcing a defeatist attitude on yourself, and driving fees from your pocket.

Take delight in your victories. Remember what you did right. Record your right moves, your strengths, your effective phrases. Review them constantly. Build confidence to match your rapidly growing competence. Low achievers have neither; mediocre performers have one without the other; high achievers have both. Success flies on two wings.

## Stay Away from Jolly J. Floppe

Every office has a few jolly junkhead flops—people who have loads of failure fables on Quick-Speak.

"That's me, the fall-out king of the South."

"I've screwed up so many deals, I've learned to look good doing it."

"When it's your turn to get a good break, it'll find you wherever you are. No sense knocking yourself out looking for it."

"Take it easy. Rome wasn't built in a day."

"You don't have to do this stuff."

"Nobody does *that* anymore." (J. J. Floppe will tell you this about any effective technique—such as working fizzbos or expireds—that the Floppe is too negative, fearful, or lazy to do.)

The Floppes think they know exactly how much business they have to do to hold their desks—which is sometimes next to nothing. Occasionally they have to find a new wall to hang their license on. By doing well—especially if you're newer in the business than they are—you become a serious emotional problem for them: *You're prospering, why aren't they doing as well?*

If you're a comer, the J. J. Floppes may not admit, even to themselves, that they aren't really for you. Don't let them pull you down to their level.

## Weeds

Weeds in the lawn or landscaping are easily removed. Find a neighborhood kid to take care of them for you for a little cash. Hardware stores have some terrific weed-eater gadgets for the price of a good dinner for two. Get one if you have a weed problem on vacant houses. It might be worthwhile having a weed-eater to lend your sellers who still occupy their houses. Shape-up that landscaping somehow and sell their well-tended house faster and for more money.

## Even Out the Peaks and Valleys

Consider investment income to even out the peaks and valleys of the real estate cycle. Buy a fixer-upper at the year's low point, fix it up during the slow season, and put it back on the market when demand quickens. Or build up a rental portfolio. Invest in the field you know. You'll gain insights and make career-boosting contacts you wouldn't otherwise acquire.

## Make Habits Work for You; Don't Fight Them

"I'm set in my ways. They're winning ways. I change my ways whenever I learn something better. Habits are my friends, not my masters, not my enemies. They help me do more, and get it done better and faster. My habits don't control me; I control them."

If you don't believe all of the above paragraph, congratulations! You've just located a serious barrier to your success and happiness—and one you can easily beat down. After all, you put the barrier up, so get busy and knock it down.

If you find the idea of changing your personality unsettling, explore your fears. Why don't you want to change? When you can answer this question, you'll be ready and able to take charge of yourself.

## Check Your MOO Every Month

The real estate market is changing constantly. The *methods of operation* (MOO) that worked well last month may not work as well next month. Long distance races aren't won on dying horses, and your real estate career is definitely a long distance race.

**Consider every month whether you should adopt new methods to deal with changes in:**

- The resale market as it is today and as it is likely to be in the immediate future
- Your growing referral business
- Your increasing professional stature

### Every month, consider these questions:

- Should you find more creative financing methods to maintain volume in the face of a tightening money market?
- Should you concentrate on finding buyers or on acquiring new listings?
- Should you farm more or stop farming altogether?
- Should you work on fizzbos more or not at all?
- Should you concentrate on expired listings?
- Should you look for an assistant?
- Should you advertise more? in newspapers? by mail?
- Should you spend more time with clients, and less time elsewhere?
- Should you review fundamentals?
- Should you take some time off and heal yourself so that you'll be more effective?

# The Pigeon-Toed Undersold Real Estate Agent

It's 6:00 P.M. He's been pounding the pavement all afternoon.

"Hi, I'm Paul Roberts, your local real estate expert. Can I be of service?"

This morning he sat on floor duty at the office. Not one decent prospect came his way.

"Sell Fast Realty, this is Paul . . . I'm sorry, Mr. Jones isn't in right now. Can I take a message?"

After four hours of taking messages and an afternoon on the street, now he's home.

"Hi, Paul. How's my honey? How'd you do today? Any listings? Did you show anyone property, or sell a house?"

It sounds easy. But it isn't. I'd like for those who think it's easy to swap skin for a week with the real estate professional—no salary, no steady flow of income—only yourself to rely on. Let others experience our days of desperation and loneliness. Let them earn our days of self-fulfillment, cocksure power, and creative drive.

# The Rules

Always, always, play it strictly by the rules. Take this from me as the absolute truth, and save yourself a lot of hard knocks. The rules give you your best chance. Ethics aren't entanglements to hinder you; they are defenses that protect you. Follow them and be wise.

During my ten-year career as a salesperson I was never called to court—not once. I'm more proud of this than of my track record.

# Excuses Accuse

Whenever you're tempted to marshal lengthy arguments rather than admit an obvious failure on your part, remember this: The more you excuse yourself, the more you accuse yourself. Confess the mistake. Don't ramble. Accept full responsibility for the error and move on fast. When blame hangs in the air, it clouds the client's view of you.

"It's my fault. I was very busy then, although being busy is no excuse. I should've handled it but I didn't. It won't happen again, I guarantee you. What's done is done. Now let's focus on the future . . ."

# Develop Your Powers of Decision Making

Quick decision making is a skill you can turn into a habit; and both the skill and the habit can be developed. Indecision is also habit; it can be curbed with your new habit of decisive action. Here's how to do it:

- Make important decisions when you're fresh. A tired mind makes weak decisions, if it makes any at all.
- Don't postpone decisions and do nothing. If you need more information, decide how much new information you need and when and how you'll get it. Then make a decision about when you'll make the important decision.
- Always make small decisions fast. Always make big decisions deliberately. Always make the distinction. The common practice is to make large decisions fast, perhaps because analyzing their pros and cons seems overwhelming, and to reserve the longest periods of indecision for the smallest matters. Turn these issues around. Make the right decisions about decisions. Quickly snap off the little decisions, where mistakes hurt little, or not at all. Put your long thoughts and detailed reasoning into the large decisions.

When you've paid your dues in this business, and the volume you're doing starts attracting attention, eager beginners will ask you for more help with their problems than you have time to give. Tell them to read the following poem.

# Old Hand to Newcomer

*How's it going?—See you later;*
*We'll talk when you're much, much greater.*
*Don't bother me kid; go do as I did.*

*Though it wouldn't be a strain to,*
*I hardly get paid to train you.*
*I have eager people to see*
*Who are waiting for me;*
*I have lots of doorbells to ring*
*And some very hot deals to swing.*
*Don't bother me kid; go do as I did.*

*Let me make you this blunt declaration:*
*I'm no part of your indoctrination.*
*All this time of mine you'd like for free,*
*is time able to earn me a great big fee.*
*Don't bother me kid; go do as I did.*

*You see, my time is all I've got,*
*And if it seems I'm such a sot,*
*As not to give a jig or jot,*
*Not a worry about your lot,*
*Say, don't be so very dense*
*I mean no great big old offense.*

*Sure, I was a slow starter once,*
*Now I'm busy 'cause I'm no dunce.*
*Let me wish you the best of luck*
*And hope you make the great big buck.*
*But bother me not, just do as I did.*

*Learn wide, learn deep, and on your own,*
*Knowledge so learned is never on loan.*
*I wouldn't say: this you should do,*
*Unless I know it's true, true, true,*
*Because, deep inside this cold shell, you see,*
*Lives the warm memory of how it was for me.*

# Holes in the Wall

People often move out leaving the interior of their house looking like the O.K. Corral after its worst day. Those holes in the wall then become the main topic of conversation whenever the house is shown. It's a disaster, pure and simple.

Root around in the garage for the rusty, skinned-over cans of wall-matching enamel such people usually leave. Buy a small can of spackle in a hardware store, and enough children's water color brushes to give you one for each color needed. Press dabs of spackle into the picture holes with your thumb or a putty knife and then touch up the spackle with the paint. Take the time to work carefully and you can do a beautiful job of hole repair your first time out. Even tired old paint dries out to match.

Effective real estate agents adjust to reality. There's no justice. Sometimes you must bury the cat, pull the weeds, and touch up the holes. Sometimes, the way this unjust world operates, you'll make $1000 an hour doing such simple jobs as these.

# CHAPTER 26

# Every Day Is a Birth Day

**Success Is Born of Purpose** ● **Pick Four Targets** ● **Do Your Targets Balance?** ● **Hazy Targets Are the Hardest to Hit** ● **Ask Yourself These Questions** ● **Give Yourself Wins** ● **Update Your Targets Frequently** ● **Break Up Your Work Cycles** ● **Everybody's Most Essential Goal**

Every morning as you open your eyes and see the new day, you get another chance. It really is a birth day. You get a chance to birth something new into your life each day. No matter what happened yesterday, it is over. Today is a new opportunity. You are alive! What a gift! It shouldn't take a crisis for you to appreciate your health and your circumstances. Even if your circumstances aren't what you want, start with where you are today.

What do you want to do with your life each day? Knowing that answer gives you your purpose. People with purpose find goal setting easy. Their purpose is more important to them than the difficulties they face in carrying it out. Their minds are too filled with purpose to allow space for difficulties to expand there. They are impatient with barriers, and think constantly of how to avoid or get through them, not on how formidable and distasteful those barriers are.

## Success Is Born of Purpose

Successful, purposeful people have no interest in difficulties except to solve them. For this reason they constantly achieve goals, and then set newer and higher goals for themselves.

**489**

The future looks far different to people without purpose. Forced to function without a driving purpose to crowd their minds, they find their problems expanding like hot air in a balloon. Purposeless people devote most of their time and energy to trivialities, and see their lives enclosed by walls. They never find a purpose outside their self-imposed walls because they think the walls can't be scaled. With purpose, one sees the handholds, scampers over the wall, and races away to the great world outside the walls.

It all comes down to purpose. Is your mind filled with expanded purpose—or expanded problems? Your mind must be dominated by one or the other; it cannot be dominated by both. Pump up your purpose, expand your positive side, and your negative side has to diminish.

You're here on this planet. Why not make an impression? Why not be an influence? Why not have a special effect on one person? Why plod when you can fly? The limitations you place on yourself are enormously greater than any imposed from the outside.

It all comes down to purpose. To me, purpose derives from having other human beings in your life who care about you, who love you—and yes, who are dependent on you. Nothing nourishes purpose from acorn to great oak like being special to your own special people.

Find your purpose. Find big and small reasons to want more from life. Then fulfill your potential. Everyone must develop on their own, at their own pace. But growth would be dull without people who care about us, who provide the spark, and who encourage our development.

# Pick Four Targets

Take your laptop or a notebook to a quiet place. Go there alone and get comfortable so you can think in clear and large terms about the four vital areas of your life. Consider each in turn. Begin by writing two words across the top of a page in your notebook: *Financial Targets.*

## Financial Targets

Below this heading, write a short paragraph to describe what you want to attain financially. Don't begin with specific sums of money, but focus on what you want the money for.

Your first paragraph might read something like this:

"My purpose is to be financially independent for the rest of my life, and to support myself and my family well. This means providing each of my children with a college education, and my spouse and I with two wonderful trips together each year."

Think about what this will cost, and then write a second paragraph:

"My purpose is to have a steady income of X$_____ for the rest of my lifetime. I can realistically achieve this in the field of real estate by attaining a volume of X$_____, and by investing in _____ on this program: _____."

On this first page, keep your thoughts on the overall picture. Then write out your financial purposes in greater detail on succeeding pages as you refine your thinking.

Work at recording your purposes with all the freedom you can develop from the intensity of your desire for success. You can always revise your purposes whenever you close one series of growth rings and open another. Set your purposes on what is vibrantly alive for you now.

The next target area to cover, with a fresh page in your notebook, is: *Social Targets.*

## Social Targets

On this page write your purpose reflecting your own emotional needs.

"My purpose is to have three significant people in my life who are outside my family. These three will be people I love, and people I can count on in times of joy and sorrow. I would like to share common interests with these three. I am not a club joiner, and prefer a small, select group of intimate friends. I recognize this will take time and patience to develop."

You may be a club joiner. That's beautiful! You may prefer having a wider circle of friends. Perhaps traveling abroad, and developing friendships with people of other cultures intrigues you. There's an enormous variety of social purposes. What's vital is to have social targets to strengthen your growth and purpose, not how many friends you have.

Head another page of your notebook: *Spiritual/Mental Targets.*

## Spiritual/Mental Targets

"I will read at least two books a month, and attend at least one seminar quarterly. I want to go back to college and _____. I will develop my spiritual awareness, and increase my understanding of the supreme forces in my life by _____."

Now explore the last of the four target areas: *Physical Targets.*

## Physical Targets

"My body is healthy and I intend to keep it this way through good diet and adequate exercise. To this end, I will _____ (jog, lose weight, play tennis, walk). I will reach this weight, _____ and remain there.

### Target Barriers

The most common barrier to strong purpose is the failure to throw off negative childhood training. Many of us are blinded to what we want by our compulsion to do what we think other people value. We're so busy worrying about what someone else thinks we don't tune in to what we think. We must hear our own inner voice to have strong purpose.

You may have to think about these four target areas over a long period of time before you can truly set targets in all four areas. However, unless you write out your purposes, they will remain as fleeting as the clouds. Write them out now. Your initial targets may stand for the rest of your life, or you may change them tomorrow. What's vital is to start the process of building powerful purpose through knowing exactly what you want from life.

## Do Your Targets Balance?

As soon as you finish writing your four targets, take a critical look at the way they balance. Some people are too work-oriented; others are too play-oriented. Too much work or too much play isn't what sends workaholics and high-life addicts to the mortuary too soon, it's the lack of balance. I know about the destructive force of an out-of-balance lifestyle—I've been there. In my case, addiction to work threw my life into turmoil. I'm not sure this problem is more easily cured than alcholism, but you have the energy to attack it. Balance your income and outgo, not only of money, but also in the social, spiritual, mental, and physical targets as well.

You can sell more real estate when you work smarter, not harder—a vital short-term benefit. Over the long term, you'll make more money by keeping your balance, enjoying life, acquiring new skills in other areas, and keeping your purposes strong.

## Hazy Targets Are the Hardest to Hit

Now let's get down to specific goal setting. Decide how many doors you will knock on today to pay for your trip to Europe—or the rental property you want to buy. In the other areas of your life, set goals just as specific. If your target is to be a better parent, decide how much time each day you are going to spend with your children.

# Ask Yourself These Questions

Are your targets realistic or unattainable? Determine this by asking yourself:

- How realistic are my goals considering my time schedule?

If you have floor time today and a dance to chaperone tonight, plus seven kids to drive around in between, your commitment to knock on 50 doors each day for the next two weeks is in trouble. At least it is today. Cut down your overall goal a bit, or modify it when your personal schedule is heavy. This decreases frustration and increases your energy for the hours when you can throw yourself fully into your work.

- How realistic are my goals, considering my natural talents?

This is a tricky area, because your natural talents are so much greater than you probably think they are. Push yourself beyond your comfort zone.

- How realistic are my goals considering the people close to me who frown on my every move?

Don't draw back just because people don't agree with what you're doing. But, if you have a spouse or loved one who gives you a lot of trouble, your communication skills with this person need work—by you, not by the other person. When loved ones feel compelled to hold you back, deep-seated problems need to be pulled into the light and solved. Such problems don't get better without loving attention bestowed in time. A neutral counselor may be required.

- How realistic are my goals considering my budget?

Suppose your target is a super-promotion in your farm every single month this year, but you haven't had a transaction close in six weeks—and you're about to miss your second house payment. I suggest you cut the super-promotions, order a good supply of memo pads, and go from there.

# Give Yourself Wins

Some people never pat themselves on the back. I have a tendency to be this way. After I give a speech to a group, and even before I tell myself, "Hey, I did good," I go for the critique cards. Sometimes, I catch myself hurrying through the wins looking for the listener who hates me. Then I have to get hold of myself, and take time to bask in the wins so when I hit the losses, I can keep my perspective.

When you make a goal and achieve it, stop and smell the roses. I don't care if your goal was only to close one transaction this month, and you sit next to Ms. Real-Estate who has 30 transactions in escrow. You made your goal, so go to the best dress shop, men's shop, hobby shop, or whatever you like—and go for it. Then grab your loved one and jump for joy. Record your wins on the calendar. Write the goals you have achieved in tall letters and add some fun drawings. Learn how to let yourself feel really good about winning—you'll win more often if you do.

# Update Your Targets Frequently

Decide if what you're doing is still what you want to do. You're changing into a more successful and better person, so keep your targets current. Schedule regular review of your goals and targets. Goals age faster than we do. Keep on studying, growing, and reaching for a more distant star.

# Break Up Your Work Cycles

You have a sharply defined purpose in life. You're attacking your goals with vigor, knocking down your barriers left and right, and hitting targets regularly. You need to intelligently deal with the possibility of burn-out. Do it **now,** *before* burn-out knocks you off the fast track. Burn-out may only wipe out a year or two of your life, but many people never recover from it.

## WorkingMoms.Calm: How Smart Women Balance Family & Career

Burnout victims are often working moms (and dads too). So get my book *WorkingMoms.Calm: How Smart Women Balance Family & Career* online or at your local bookstore. If you are married share it with your spouse and the children. It's filled with how to balance family and career from 30 of the smartest working moms I know. Of course I share all my juggling tricks too. Working families in real estate need a guide for balancing their lives as much as they do for listing and selling.

## Stop and Smell the Roses

Learn to take mini-breaks: two minutes of quiet meditation, five minutes to run up and down a flight of stairs to break up a long session at your desk, an hour three times a week, a long weekend now and then. On these mini-breaks use another capacity, preferably a physical one. Exercise is the best healer for the pressures of real estate. An hour's exercise (especially if it's doing something you enjoy) can repair a hard day's damage—and leave you fresh for an evening's work or play.

Break your big goals down into simple, small tasks. If your goal is to become the listing king or queen, and this means you have to double your production, break your ambition into small daily wins. Contact so many fizzbos, call so many expireds, write so many notes a day. And, as soon as you can afford it, hire an assistant to handle the things you don't have to do yourself.

# Everybody's Most Essential Goal

To be blunt about it—you're no good to yourself or anyone else if you're dead. Nor are you of much use if you're dragging yourself around half-dead. **So your most essential goal is to stay alive, healthy, and energetic.**

This seems too obvious to write and yet every year three wildly popular killer lifestyles claim the lives of many Americans long before their time, and sap the energy of even more. How many people do you know whose lives ended too soon because they put on too much weight, smoked, or avoided exercise?

## Permanent Weight Control

Being overweight is the first wildly popular killer lifestyle, and losing weight is a multi-billion-dollar industry. Fortunately, there's a permanent low-cost cure. It's called *The Anti-Diet Book.**

Warren Jamison helped to write this practical guide for training your metabolism to burn fat efficiently. This book is packed with tips for learning to love eating right to enhance your health, energy, and ability to perform better under stress so you can make more money and enjoy life more.

* Jack L. Groppel, Ph.D., *The Anti-Diet Book*. Orlando: LGE Sport Science, 2000.

## Banish Tobacco and Live!

The second wildly popular killer lifestyle is the smoking habit. *The Official Guide to Success,** another book Warren helped write, contains an effective way to stop smoking without pills or patches. Several life-long smokers who were never able to quit any other way told me this system worked for them, and they were amazed at how easy it was.

## Learn to Love Exercise

The third wildly popular killer lifestyle is failing to get generous amounts of exercise regularly. The key to exercising more is to learn how to make it enjoyable. If you look on exercise as being pure drudgery and a boring waste of time, you won't do it. But for people in high-stress professions such as real estate, exercise is a wonderful way to blow away the pressures of the day and build energy to handle even more stress. Pick a few physical activities you enjoy, and make time for them. Just do it!

* Tom Hopkins, *The Official Guide to Success*. New York: Warner Books, 2000.

# CHAPTER 27

# Leading Team Players to Success and Profitability

In making the transition from sales to management, I never realized how different the skill requirements were. My track record as a top producer really did not convert me into a successful manager and trainer. Usually my past experiences as a high flier were not helpful with management problems. It was my parenting skills and my background in sports (competitive ice-skating) that proved helpful as a leader and a manager. Excellent managers are good coaches.

## Coaching and Honesty

Coaches are the role models for their team. The best coaches walk the talk and the team knows it. The team can smell a phony a mile away. So whether you are recruiting, training, or retaining, remember that *you* must exemplify the truth. You cannot expect to make progress with your team if you are not honest. If you expect them to be on time, you have to be on time too. Otherwise you are living a lie. If you want them to invest in on-going education, then you too, must invest in your own education.

I am always amazed that most of my audiences are "agent only" audiences (unless it specifically states that my session will be for managers only). The basics of listing and selling are not just for agents. They

**497**

are meant to be absorbed by the entire team. Why would a coach send her team to a seminar without knowledge of the content? Shouldn't the coach be right there with the team? Management needs a refresher too. Otherwise the team comes back to the office all fired up and there is no follow-up from management. Lack of follow-up is a major problem in this industry. The bottom-line is if the coach is living a lie, he is getting no respect. He may think he has his team fooled because the team appears to be his friend, but there is an underlying tension because the coach is not walking the talk. There is a big lack of respect and without respect and there is no team.

# Market Share and On-Going Training

One of the biggest oversights I see in management is that managers do not recognize the relationship between on-going education and market share. Look around your locale. I'll wager that the offices dominating the market are very education-oriented. They are spending lots on growing a smart team. When I owned and managed three offices we consistently dominated 30 percent of the market share. Why did that happen? We were training fanatics. Following is the typical education plan we offered.

## In-House Educational Programs

**Sales Meetings.** A 12-month agenda was prepared with the topics of each sales meeting designated. We were flexible when appropriate but each specific meeting had a timely subject that involved some type of teaching. Agendas were always passed out and every minute of the meeting was accounted for on paper. We stuck to the agenda and our meetings were well attended. We promised the truth and then we delivered what we promised.

**War Story Morning.** From 10 A.M.–11A.M. once a week, agents would come into the meeting room and tell a war story of the week. The story could not take longer than 5 minutes to tell and it had to have a moral. The storyteller had to determine the lesson learned and how to best communicate that lesson to the rest of us. It didn't matter if it was a successful or a failing story, but what was the lesson learned? This lesson was then passed on to the others in order to enlighten them for future similar situations.

**Telethons and Online Chats and Seminars.** We often gathered together at the office on Wednesday or Thursday nights to make group calls to targeted lists. Maybe our telethon was promoting low interest rates to renters or prospective first-time homebuyers. Sometimes we were doing a group call on moving up in the neighborhood. Two, three, or more heads are better than one. There are always the agents who feel especially comfortable making the calls and those who are shy. A telethon is a good way to mix them up together. Role modeling really does encourage the weaker links.

Today when I consult with companies, I suggest online seminars for homebuyers and sellers. Agents can sit at their laptops or at their desk computers and participate in the discussion online. This can be done from each agent's home now too. So the team can be together online to conduct the workshop for the buying and selling public. Even the shy ones can't really complain.

**Territory Visits.** Friday and Saturday afternoons were my field days with the new agents. Going out to the respective farms and passing out memo pads, visiting fizzbos, or delivering holiday treats was often a team effort. This was an example of management walking the talk. My agents truly respected my role modeling in the territories. It wasn't all talk and no action.

I didn't ever want the following conversation in my company, "Yeah, you know that 'has-been' broker of ours—Danny Kennedy? She supposedly door-knocked pregnant and sold 40 homes a year in her farm alone. She never comes out from behind her big fat desk these days. What a big shot!"

**Outside Seminars.** There were always seminars coming into town. Depending on what we needed at the time, you could count on our team attending the best ones.

**Jumpstart Training.** Every month, new agents went through our jumpstart program for 12 days. I created a video training series (which is now commercially available) for the new agents. I also wrote a manual with field assignments and homework assignments to compliment the video and live lectures.

**Seasoned Agents On-Going Training.** Quarterly, we offered the 12-day program to agents at all levels. When a middle-of-the-road agent wanted to take that next step, I knew that she needed to add more prospecting to the equation. The on-going video series allows the experienced agent to take a look at some other niches she has not been prospecting. Most of the time someone who needs to increase production also needs to expand territories or niches. Introducing additional niches to his or her daily prospecting agenda, soon is reflected in an increased bottom line.

## Hot Issues and Fast Solutions

The beauty of the Internet is that we can all get together in a flash when a problem arises. Certain problems go along with the current real estate climate in your area. Is it a rising market or a falling market? For example, in a rising, active market, what steps can agents take to prevent their buyers from being in a multiple contract situation? You can solve these problems with an online chat or workshop.

Other online discussion topics include:

- Is it always a positive outcome for sellers to have multiple contracts? If not, why not?
- What can or should listing agents do to represent their clients' best interest in a multiple contract situation?
- What can buyers' agents do to represent their clients' best interest in a multiple contract situation?

# Selective Recruiting

If you are seeking team play and profitability (and are we having any fun otherwise?) then 90 percent of your chances of succeeding take place during the selection process. It works this way in theatre too. All first-rate directors know that if they end up with a runaway, hit show, they can attribute most of its success to casting. Pick the right actors from the beginning and you pretty much have it made. The problem in our industry is we do not grasp this truth. It shows in our hiring practices and in our turnover ratios. In my book, *Double Your Income in Real Estate Sales* (Career Press, 1998) I wrote a chapter entitled "Leadership Management." It gives managers a complete format for recruiting, training, and retaining a team. I hope you will read that book, too. In addition to what I wrote in that book, let me add some recruiting suggestions here:

- Never hire someone on the spot.

If you are running ads in the paper or online, insist that candidates fax or e-mail you a resume when they call in. They may want to drop a hard copy off to your secretary, too. A good first impression is reflected in a well-thought-out, first-class resume. It still frightens me to know how easy it is to get hired at a real estate company. Management gets desperate, especially if a group of heavy hitters just exited or opened their own company (boy will they be in for a shock!!!), and bingo, managers are pulling anyone in off the street. Don't panic. There is no shortage of talent. In this century more young people are coming to us earlier in their careers. Many can be recruited right out of college. Younger generations are free-thinking entrepreneur types who do not desire to work for a big company. Real estate is one of the few free enterprises left and the younger generation knows it; and they want to explore the possibilities.

- Don't rely on one method of screening.

I have watched hiring trends come and go. Personality tests, intelligence tests, style of dress, and interview ability all have their value, but there is never a guarantee. When I joined the industry I was very pregnant and considered undesirable recruiting material. Several companies turned me down due to my "part time" status. Managers assumed I was part time based on how I looked. But I had a full time attitude. There are many agents that may appear to be full time, but they are part time in their commitments. And, of course, the opposite is true too.

- Interview candidates at least twice before hiring.

After you receive the resume, consider setting up two interview times. If you use a two-step interview process be sure you know what is going to happen at both appointments. Remember you are in charge, not the candidates.

- Listen more than you talk in an interview.

I have been in recruiting interviews with very respected managers and it was embarrassing listening to the manager giving a sales job. The goal seemed to be to "sell" the candidate on coming to work with the company. The opposite attitude should prevail—the candidate (I like calling the recruiting prospect a *candidate* too) should be selling the manager. Ask why the candidate wants to work at this particular company. Ask how the candidate will contribute to the team. Ask why the candidate is changing offices. (Do you really want to hire someone who openly criticizes his last broker?)

- Prepare investigative questions.

All managers need a treasure trove of questions that reveal needed information. The best questions are derived from observation and awareness. When you think about those agents in your company over the years who really are top notch, do you notice that there are certain common denominators all of these people seem to possess? Create questions which help you discover if this candidate has the *potential* of going in that direction. For example: No one can motivate you but you. No one can motivate me but me. This is a truth you can rely on when it comes to human nature. So if you are talking to a candidate who is changing offices because she wants her company to do more advertising, or she feels she is not getting enough relocation leads, what does that tell you about this person? She is not self-motivated. She does not understand that this is a self-generated business and that the best do not wait around the office for deals to happen. They are out prospecting as many different niches as they can come up with in a given day.

•   Hire only upon recommendation.

I am a fanatic about recommendations. Why would you hire someone to play on your team without an endorsement? This is a big step in the growth of your organization. Even a new agent should be able to provide recommendation letters from past satisfied employers or customers, or teachers from a school or work history. So many brokers have the best of intentions but they wimp out and hire before they either speak to the reference or receive the recommendation letters. Do not rush; wait and see. It's so easy bringing someone into the office, but so difficult to take yourself and the team out of misery if you are trying to help that person leave. Know what you are getting as best you can before you start playing ball. With new agents, a referral from a teacher or a past employer can help you determine if they have good skill potential for selling real estate. Maybe the candidate has never sold a house, but her people skills as a caring and expressive nurse are certainly transferable. With seasoned agents coming over to you, ask for a list of their most recent customers. You can find out just how respected someone is by talking to the buyers or sellers *after* the transaction closes. If the servicing of the client was as aggressive as the prospecting and capturing of the client, that tells you a lot about the candidate's character.

•   Recruiting equals prospecting.

Managers must commit to daily recruiting the way salespeople must commit to daily prospecting. However, most of the time managers recruit the way agents prospect. The agent runs out of money and closings. He panics and hits the fizzbos, past customers, or open houses again. The manager looks at his monthly stats and sees that closings are down and the office looks empty. Well then, maybe it is time to look for more bodies. Do not run a panic ship. No matter how prosperous times are, never stop keeping your eyes open for good candidates. They are everywhere: waiters and waitresses, doctors, lawyers, teachers, corporate middle managers, students, empty-nester moms, and retired people. One of my best agents retired at age 60 from the hotel business. She joined my company and was my top producer for the next 10 years!! If you want your bottom line to stay upward mobile, make prospecting for recruits your first priority, right along with on-going training.

# Building 360 Leadership

If you put the time into finding strong individuals to recruit on your team, you will have a much better chance of leading the team from every angle. Yes, the new agent on the totem pole can be a leader in your company. The top producing agent can be a leader. The consistent middle of the road producer can too. Why? Because they all possess leadership qualities. Maybe the new agent has a strong advertising background, the top producer is strong on follow-up, and the middle-of-the-roader does a thorough job and is very detail-oriented. These are all qualities a good team needs. And those who possess these qualities are great role models and teachers.

When you give everyone on your team the opportunity to be a leader, you are taking the heat off of yourself. I think most organizations today lack joint leadership efforts. We don't invest in it because it takes time, patience, and on-going training. The manager has to spot the talent and then show this talented player how to share it with others. You have to be on the lookout for ways to replace yourself. And this means a good manager is not an egomaniac—it is all right if somebody else on the team shines besides you. Actually, a 360 leader welcomes this type of group behavior.

Relationships today often do not have the history they used to have in an organization. In Fortune 500 companies, employees tell me that in a 10-year period, some workers have had as many as 10 managers. Part of the problem is that nobody wants to invest time in a relationship anymore. We walk away too soon. These relationships never have a chance to develop. Agents leave companies for trivial reasons: a commission split or a difference of opinion with another agent. We have to start thinking about building relationships again if we hope to have stronger teams.

Managers or salespeople should not stay in unhealthy organizations but we need a deeper sense of commitment. When conflict or trouble arises, we need to learn how to work through it. On the other side of the conflict are great lessons and the experiences from the lesson create strong teams.

# Choosing a Company

Agents often ask, "Should I work for a big company or a small boutique company?"

To new agents or seasoned agents, my advice is always the same, "Work for a company that shares your values."

The size of the company is irrevelant. If you have a good set of ethics and lots of integrity, how comfortable are you going to be at a company that subscribes to the philosophy, "Do whatever it takes but make the deal."

Both managers and candidates must be sure everybody is on the same page of music.

Our company was service-oriented. We prided ourselves on the numbers of our repeat customers. If you are a relationship-building company, your ethics will be impeccable. So it is a good idea to set up questions in the interview process that put a candidate's values on the line.

# Parting Company

When is it time for an agent to leave your company? Guidelines for parting company need to be resolved at the time of hiring. Most real estate firms have an independent contractor status agreement with their agents. It is important to set up these guidelines at the beginning of the relationship. What type of production does the candidate expect of himself or herself? Is it aligned with the company standards? When should an agent and a manager sit down and make a decision about continuing the relationship? These questions must be established as part of your hiring policies.

# CHAPTER 28

# Break Loose and Fly!

Now let's take off, and soar to new heights. I did—and you can too. But first, here's a few final reminders as you finish reading this book and get set to take the second step on your journey to becoming a real estate superstar: accepting the challenge of the Breakaway Schedule.

Start today to concentrate on just the next customer. Don't try to do everything we have mapped out for you in one week. Sometimes we look at the long haul and it scares us to death. We don't want you to do this. Instead, think, "Just one more person," and follow these suggestions to help you:

- *Break loose* from the people, places, and things exerting a downward pull on your performance. Seek out growth-causing situations, not those leading to stagnation. Honor your responsibilities, but shuck your bad habits.
- *Break loose* from negative thoughts and feeling sorry for yourself. As soon as you start feeling down, take a walk around the block. The poet Robert Frost always took his dog. Frost said he didn't know if it did the dog much good, but it sure helped him.
- *Break loose* from fear and panic. When you try something for the first time (like knocking on a door, or qualifying a buyer) it'll go better if you pretend you've already done it dozens of times. Relax; put your challenge in perspective. It's not like weapons

of mass destruction will rain down on your city if the task you fear doesn't go well.

- *Break loose* from taking yourself too seriously. Chew a blade of grass. Grin. Hum a happy tune. It really helps. Emphasize to yourself how much you want to do what you're doing. *Have-to* bogs you down; *want-to* gives you wings.

- *Break loose* from the grumps of this world; never let them control how you feel for even an instant. A few grumps stumble across everyone's path—but you don't have to join them. In fact, you can't join the grumps unless you choose to join them.

- *Break loose* from down days. You can just as easily choose to enjoy every minute of every hour of every day. When things don't go as well as you'd like, make believe you only care a little bit and the trick will keep you opening up, finding new friends, and making more joy and more money.

- *Break loose* from bad health patterns like getting no exercise and living on junk food. A sound body and mind go hand-in-hand. Pay attention to what you eat, and get an exercise program. What are your strengths in sports: golf, handball, weight-lifting, hockey, or tennis? Decide, make time, and do it. Taking care of your body is just as important as meeting a customer, so schedule your fitness time and keep your fitness appointments as though your life depends on it—which, by the way, it does. However, don't try to be too competitive! Exercise is supposed to relieve anxiety and frustration, not cause it (which may rule out golf). Some people do everything with the "kill" instinct. Relearn how to play if you've forgotten.

- *Break loose* from jealousy. It causes more physical and mental mix-ups than any other disastrous emotion. Become your own best friend, and don't worry about who is better off than you. Jealousy is a negative emotion, both in and out of real estate. We all get the pangs. When they come on, do something exactly opposite of the feeling. If someone else in the office makes a sale, force yourself to congratulate him. Put a note on his desk with a pleasant thought. Pretty soon, jealousy won't win.

- *Break loose* from feeling like one of the herd. Remember, you're an original, and no one can replace you. If a customer goes elsewhere, he won't be getting you.

- *Break loose* from being on the defensive. Ask yourself, "Would I rather be right or happy?" You may not always have all the answers—so accept this possibility.

- *Break loose* from complaining about personal problems and health.

- ***Break loose*** from gloomy facial expressions. Exercise your cheek muscles and start broadening the smile. Grandpa Barrett often recited,

  *Smile and the world smiles with you*
  *Weep and you weep alone.*
  *For the cheerful grin will get you in,*
  *Where the kicker is never known.*

- ***Break loose*** and find the kid in you again. Remember what it's like at age 6 or age 16, when you wake up on a summer morning, when the air smells clean, and the breezes are warm? It can still be that way. Real estate is great—but living is even greater. Life is so fragile. Cherish every second. Begin now and

Break loose—

BREAK LOOSE—

BREAK LOOSE AND FLY!

# GLOSSARY

## A

**Adjustable Rate Mortgage (ARM):** A mortgage with an interest rate that changes over time in line with movements in the interest rate index. ARMs are also referred to as AMLs (adjustable mortgage loans) or VRMs (variable rate mortgages).

**Adjustment Period:** The length of time between interest rate changes on an ARM. For example, a loan with an adjustment period of one year is called a one-year ARM, which means that the interest rate can change once a year.

**Amortization:** Repayment of a loan in equal installments of principal and interest, rather than interest-only payments.

**Annual Percentage Rate (APR):** The total finance charge (interest, loan fees, points) expressed as a percentage of the loan amount.

**Assumption of Mortgage:** A buyer's agreement to assume the liability under an existing note that is secured by a mortgage or deed of trust. The lender must approve the buyer in order to release the original borrower (usually the seller) from liability.

## B

**Balloon Payment:** A lump-sum principal payment due at the end of some mortgages or other long-term loans.

**Binder:** Sometimes known as an offer to purchase or an earnest money receipt. A binder is the acknowledgment of a deposit along with a brief written agreement to enter into a contract for the sale of real property.

## C

**Cap:** The limit on how much an interest rate or monthly payment can change, either at each adjustment period or over the life of the mortgage.

**CC&R's:** Covenants, conditions, and restrictions. A document that controls the use, requirements, and restrictions of a property.

**Certificate of Reasonable Value (CRV):** A document that establishes the maximum value and loan amount for a VA-guaranteed mortgage.

**Closing Statement:** The financial disclosure statement that accounts for all of the funds received and expected at the closing, including deposits for taxes, hazard insurance, and mortgage insurance.

**Condominium:** A form of real estate ownership where the owner receives title to a particular unit and has proportionate interest in certain common areas. The unit itself is generally a separately owned space whose interior surfaces (walls, floors, and ceilings) serve as its boundaries.

**Contingency:** A condition that must be satisfied before a contract is binding. For example, a sales agreement may be contingent upon the buyer obtaining financing.

**Conversion Clause:** A provision in some ARMs that enables you to change an ARM to a fixed-rate loan, usually after the first adjustment period. The new fixed rate is generally set at the prevailing interest rate for fixed-rate mortgages. This conversion feature may cost extra.

**Cooperative:** A form of multiple ownership in which a corporation or business trust entity holds title to a property and grants occupancy rights to shareholders by means of proprietary leases or similar arrangements.

**Certified Residential Broker (CRB):** To be certified, a broker must be a member of the National Association of REALTORS®, have five years' experience as a licensed broker, and have completed a certain number of required residential division courses.

## D

**Due-on-Sale Clause:** An acceleration clause that requires full payment of a mortgage or deed of trust when the secured property changes ownership.

## E

**Earnest Money:** The portion of the down payment delivered to the seller or escrow agent by the purchaser with a written offer as evidence of good faith.

**Escrow:** A procedure in which a third party acts as a stakeholder for both the buyer and the seller, carrying out both parties' instructions and assumes responsibility for handling all of the paperwork and distribution of funds.

## F

**Federal National Mortgage Association (FNMA):** Known as Fannie Mae. A privately owned corporation created by Congress to support the secondary mortgage market. It purchases and sells residential mortgages insured by the FHA or guaranteed by the VA, as well as conventional home mortgages.

**Fee Simple:** An estate in which the owner has unrestricted power to dispose of the property as he wishes, including by will or inheritance. It is the greatest interest a person can have in real estate.

**FHA Loan:** A loan insured by the Insuring Office of the Department of Housing and Urban Development of the Federal Housing Administration.

**Finance Charge:** The total cost a borrower must pay, directly or indirectly, to obtain credit according to Regulation Z.

## G

**Graduated Payment Mortgage:** A residential mortgage with monthly payments that start at a low level and increase at a predetermined rate.

**GRI:** Graduate, Realtors Institute. A professional designation granted to a member of the National Association of REALTORS®, who has successfully completed courses covering law, finance, and principles of real estate.

## H

**Home Inspection Report:** A qualified inspector's report on a property's overall condition. The report usually includes an evaluation of both the structure and mechanical systems.

**Home Warranty Plan:** A protection plan against failure of mechanical systems within the property. It usually includes plumbing, electrical, heating, and installed appliances.

## I

**Index:** A measure of interest rate changes used to determine changes in an ARM's interest rate over the term of the loan.

## J

**Joint Tenancy:** An equal, undivided ownership of property by two or more persons. Upon the death of any owner, the survivors take the decedent's interest in the property.

## L

**Lien:** A legal hold or claim on property as security for a debt or charge.

**Loan Commitment:** A written promise to make a loan flier a specified amount on specified terms.

**Loan-to-Value Ratio:** The relationship between the amount of the mortgage and the appraised value of the property, expressed as a percentage of the appraised value.

## M

**Margin:** The number of percentage points the lender adds to the index rate to calculate the ARM interest rate at each adjustment period.

**Mortgage Life Insurance:** A type of life insurance often bought by mortgagors. The coverage decreases as the mortgage balance declines. If the borrower dies while the policy is in force, the debt is automatically covered by insurance proceeds.

# N

**Negative Amortization:** Negative amortization occurs when monthly payments fail to cover the interest cost. The interest that isn't covered is added to the unpaid principal balance, which means that even after several payments you could owe more than you did at the beginning of the loan. Negative amortization can occur when an ARM has a payment cap that results in monthly payments that aren't high enough to cover the interest.

# O

**Origination Fee:** A fee or charge for work involved in evaluating, preparing, and submitting a proposed mortgage loan. The fee is limited to 1 percent for FHA and VA loans.

# P

**PITI:** Principal, interest, taxes, and insurance.

**Planned Unit Development (PUD):** A zoning designation for property developed at the same or a slightly greater overall density than conventional development, sometimes with improvements clustered between open, common areas. Uses may be residential, commercial, or industrial.

**Point:** An amount equal to 1 percent of the principal amount of the investment or note. The lender assesses loan discount points at closing to increase the yield on the mortgage to a position competitive with other types of investments.

**Prepayment Penalty:** A fee charged to a mortgagor who pays a loan before it is due. It is not allowed for FHA or VA loans.

**Private Mortgage Insurance (PMI):** Insurance written by a private company protecting the lender against loss if the borrower defaults on the mortgage.

**Purchase Agreement:** A written document in which the purchaser agrees to buy certain real estate and the seller agrees to sell under stated terms and conditions. Also called a sales contract, earnest money contract, or agreement for sale.

# R

**REALTOR®:** A real estate broker or associate active in a local Board of REALTORS® affiliated with the National Association of REALTORS®.

**Regulation Z:** The set of rules governing consumer lending issued by the Federal Reserve Board of Governors in accordance with the Consumer Protection Act.

# T

**Tenancy in Common:** A type of joint ownership of property by two or more persons with no rights of survivorship.

**Title Insurance Policy:** A policy that protects the purchaser, mortgagee, or other party against losses.

# V

**VA Loan:** A loan that is partially guaranteed by the Veterans Administration and made by a private lender.

# THE BREAKAWAY SCHEDULE

A self-training course able to give you high earning capability in 21 days—if you can meet the challenge this quickly.

**Note A.** The index gives the page numbers where explanations will be found for each of the special terms we've coined for Breakaway.

**Note B.** You can complete all *Special* Achievements in the 21-day schedule before you receive your license. Many of the *Repeating* Achievements require a license.

## *Special* Achievements of Day 1

**1.** Take aim at what you want. Reread Chapter 26, and make a written commitment in each of the four basic targets suggested there. Choose your initial goals. Your initial goals may be major or minor goals, but one should be the sum of money you want to make in the next 12 months. Another goal should be something exciting you'll do or buy with part of the money you're going to make.

To ensure your success with the dynamic goal-setting technique, set your initial goals fast, review them frequently, and revise them whenever they stop pulling you forward.

**2.** Reread Chapter 5.

**3.** Select your winning move from the variety of fizzbo techniques given in Chapter 5. Your selection isn't chiseled in granite— make it fast, you can always change it later. Then prepare a flashdeck of the winning scripts for the fizzbo technique you've chosen. Chapter 3 details the flashdeck method of high-speed learning.

**4.** Use your new flashdeck to create a blank-interval cassette. Chapter 3 tells you how easily blank-interval (BI) cassettes are made on a tape recorder, and how you can use this system to rapidly develop a convincing delivery of the many fee-grabbing lines in this book.

**5.** Select your specialization zone. This can be a neighborhood, a community, a type of house, everything east of the tracks, or any definable area or class of housing units. Don't spend much time picking your first zone. You're merely selecting an area you'll give special attention to until another area looks better. You won't farm there, but plan to drive your zone frequently, and give special attention to its houses on caravan. Make use of frequent virtual tours online too.

**6.** Prepare your Quick-Speak Inventory slot sheet. Chapter 24 shows you how. Chapter 2 tells you why this is the golden key to success.

**7.** On a printed map of your sales area, define 30 neighborhoods of about 20 streets each. This is the first step in gaining complete street knowledge of your area with the fast and effective named-neighborhoods method. Remember, getting lost with a customer in your car destroys your image of competence. Knowing your streets so well you can't get lost impresses customers and saves crucial time during property showings, when delay is dangerous. Chapter 3 gives you full details. Buy neighborhood map software; it's inexpensive and it will help you learn the area faster.

**8.** Read about rapid image building in Chapter 13. Then make an appointment with a professional photographer to have your portrait taken. Use this portrait on your letterhead, newsletters, business cards, web site, e-mails, and display advertising. You also need this photo of yourself for the single most important farming tool I know of: imprinted memo pads. Chapter 13 gives tips on designing effective ones. Complete your memo pad design now, and order 1000 of them as soon as you have your photo.

# *Repeating* Achievements of Day 1

**Note C.** Repeat each achievement every day until you've wrung the fullest possible benefit from it.

**Note D.** Achieve the *special achievements* for each day first; they provide the tools you'll need for the *repeating achievements*.

**Note E.** You must have a valid real estate license before performing many of the *repeating* achievements.

**A.** Keyview properties until you've filled five slots on your Quick-Speak Inventory form. Review Chapter 3. It tells you how to use the keyview concept for total house recall. (See special achievement 6 on page 513.)

**B.** Using the high-speed learning method given in Chapter 3, put the first two named neighborhoods in your memory.

**C.** Make three runs through your flashdeck this evening.

**D.** Follow immediately with three runs through your BI cassette. Use the flashdeck to coach yourself when necessary. Don't stop. Keep the tape moving and concentrate on speaking the lines with sparkle and clarity.

**E.** Make up your tomorrow's action list. Chapter 22 has tips on this simple technique. If you make this a firm habit, it will earn more money for you in fewer minutes than anything else.

**F.** Just before retiring for the night, review the goals you selected today. Give each one a few seconds of deep concentration. Experience yourself doing, having, and being what you want to achieve.

# *Special* Achievements of Day 2

**1.** Reread Chapter 11, on listings.

**2.** Flashdeck Chapter 11's Winning Scripts.

**3.** Use your new flashdeck to create a BI cassette.

**4.** Hyperlearn your listing form. Chapter 3 has the techniques to enable you to conquer this form quickly.

**5.** If you don't have a farm yet, consult your manager and determine what areas are open. Then reread the sections in Chapter 6 on selecting a farm. Take your time making this important decision. On each of the next three days, an achievement is scheduled to help you select the best farm available by Day 6.

**6.** Reread Chapter 21, on time planning. Write a daily schedule for yourself. Then choose three time-saving systems from this chapter and put them into action. If you can afford a digital time planner, and you think you will use it, invest in one now.

**7.** Conquer the seller's net sheet (often called "seller's net proceeds"). Give this form one hour of concentrated attention. Study the closing statements in your office's file of completed transactions so you'll understand the end result of the seller's net sheet. If you discover anything on the form you wouldn't be able to explain to a client, find the answer. If you don't know the answer, you can be sure a prospective client or customer will ask the question. Direct your questions outside your office—to processor, title, and lender's loan production people. E-mail your favorite loan officer and ask for a download of a qualifying program you can master. Scan my forms and practice net sheets on your laptop, if you have one.

# *Repeating* Achievements of Day 2

**A.** Review your goals as soon as you wake up. Visualize each one. Emotionalize them—make them live in your mind.

**B.** Make three fast runs through your flashdeck in the morning.

**C.** Follow immediately with three runs through your BI cassette.

**D.** Go online and check the daily hot sheet of new listings. Have any changes occurred in the five houses you put into your Quick-Speak Inventory? If so, update your QSI flashdeck, your slot sheet, and your memory.

**E.** Keyview enough properties to fill five more slots on your QSI slot sheet and to replace any expired or sold properties (Chapter 3). You can do this online through virtual touring too. That counts!!!

**F.** This evening make three runs through your new and old flashdecks.

**G.** Make three runs through each of your BI cassettes.

# *Special* Achievements of Day 3

**1.** Reread Chapter 8, on prospecting.

**2.** Flashdeck this chapter's Winning Scripts.

**3.** You guessed it: Make a BI cassette for solo role working these Winning Scripts. Chapter 3 tells you the difference between role playing and role working.

**4.** Write your "I'm in the real estate business" letter for your Everybody-I-Know farm. Chapter 6 has sample letters, and Chapter 13 gives writing tips. Estimate how many copies you'll need (at least 300) and order what you need from a printer or make copies at a copy shop. Create documents of all these letters on your computer.

**5.** Start your Everybody-I-Know Farm. On file cards, list the names of 25 individuals or couples you know well. Chapter 6 tells you how to work the people-I-know farm. Install a client contact management system. Get these names in your computer now.

**6.** Define on a map the various farms available. Then drive all the streets of each possibility. You may immediately eliminate some from further consideration. When you return to the office, determine the turnover rate of each farm you're still considering with the method given in Chapter 6. Read the discussion there on applying past turnover rate to your decision about the future.

**7.** Reread Chapter 22, on self-organization. Then organize your automobile for maximum real estate efficiency.

*I never said this would be easy;*
*Becoming a professional never is.*

## Repeating Achievements of Day 3

Some fizzbo material may have passed the overlearned stage. If so, drop those cards to weekly review, as suggested in Chapter 3, and limit the fizzbo cassette to one or two runs of solo role playing every other evening. This overlearned stage is ideal for developing the relaxed, confident delivery most likely to convert prospects into clients.

Here's a new achievement to be repeated daily until thoroughly learned:

**A.** Go online and study inventory via virtual tours. Open your office's inventory of listings, and prepare seller's net sheets for the first three houses you find. Push yourself. Work hard and fast. Check your results. Then ask your broker to check and correct the forms. Never give a net sheet to a client until you have your broker's permission to do so. Your company is liable for your errors and, through them, you are too. Whenever you figure a net sheet, remember that some of the dollars you're writing down could come out of your pocket if you make a mistake. You can't get a professional's rewards without accepting a professional's responsibilities.

## Special Achievements of Day 4

**1.** Reread Chapter 15, on qualifying.

**2.** Flashdeck the Winning Scripts for the buyer qualifying session and make a BI cassette.

**3.** Spend two or three hours with a loan processor, attorney, title company officer, or whomever settles (closes) transactions in your state. Watch them and learn how they do their jobs. Make an appointment and they'll give you a pleasant reception. Later on, you'll find you're making money from what you learned watching these people.

**4.** Decide on the format for your farm file (see Chapter 6, and the form in Chapter 24). Obtain the materials you'll need for it so you can start developing this basic file as soon as you pick your farm on Day 6. Create the farm document in your computer.

**5.** Start your important information notebook (see Chapter 23) by copying into it all the frequently-used listing form remarks and special provisions you find by studying your office's file of closed transactions and current listings. Work with only two or three files at a time, and be careful to return them promptly to their proper file positions. Create your notebook on the computer or store it in your electronic organizer.

**Orphan Clients.** Ask your broker if you can have the orphans you find. Orphans are clients of agents who've left your company—unless they've already been given to someone currently active in your office. The orphans who bought a house three or four years ago are due to move up, and some people expect to be transferred to another area even sooner. Create a document to handle orphans.

**6.** Visit the farms you're considering. Walk around each one and get a feel for the different localities. Look at the way the people take care of their properties. Notice the cars they drive. Just by casually glancing from the sidewalk, you'll form an idea of the attitudes held, the lifestyles lived, and the recreational activities the people there enjoy. Which farm do you feel most comfortable in?

The better you relate to the people in your farm, the more affinity you have for them, and the better you'll do there. Talk to anyone you happen to meet who seems to live there. Tell them you're selecting a farm and ask for their advice. People love to give advice, so listen carefully to what they say. (If you haven't received your real estate license yet, be careful not to offer your services as an agent. Don't talk about the values of specific properties, or do anything else requiring a real estate license.) Don't be swayed by a grouch or booster; talk to several people in each farm. Ask them how they like their particular street. Is it convenient to shopping and highways? Are there any special problems in the area? If several of them tell you a certain agent has this neighborhood all tied up, you might want to look elsewhere. Investigate the farm fully before you commit yourself. You'll be making heavy and continuing investments of time and money in your farm for a long time, so pick it carefully.

**7.** Reread Chapter 23, Prepare and Perform—or Pass Out. Review your schedule, goals, and validations; consider whether you're preparing yourself adequately to achieve those goals. Add the achievements below to your daily schedule.

# *Repeating* Achievements of Day 4

**A.** Add 25 more names to your Everybody-I-Know farm file. Continue to input 25 people a day until you get through all your old and new school, club, and church rosters. Then work through your Christmas card list, shower party lists, and any other list you have of people you know.

When you've worked through all your rosters, add the people you do business with, friends, relatives, and acquaintances—anyone you know.

When you have input everyone you now know, don't stop. Every day you meet new people. Add at least one new name to your list every day. If you add these names to your client contact management system daily, inputting on the computer will not be such a gigantic chore later. Keep it constantly updated.

**B.** Send handwritten notes announcing your entry into real estate to three people in your Everybody-I-Know farm file. Handwritten notes are a must for people you know well. Yes, even in this electronic age!!!

# *Special* Achievements of Day 5

**1.** Reread Chapter 10, on up-time.
**2.** Flashdeck Chapter 10's Winning Scripts.
**3.** Use your new flashdeck to create a BI cassette for solo role working the ad call and sign call situations and responses in those Winning Scripts.
**4.** Develop your knowledge of all forms of conventional financing currently being offered by banks, savings and loans associations, and other private mortgage loan sources in your area. Enter the details in your important information notebook. Have your banker or loan representative forward you all these forms so you can scan them into your computer to study.
**5.** Consider your farm possibilities from the standpoint of providing a wide price range and selection of housing types. It may be necessary to select three mini-farms in three different locations

to achieve this purpose. Can you do this? Do you want to? Explore these questions today; find more details in Chapter 6.

**6.** Flashdeck or input (Microsoft Office is good) the deadlines you'll be working with:

- Your company's deadlines for cooperative advertising.
- Local newspaper advertising deadlines. (Call the newspapers for this information; don't ask around the office and get tagged as a pest.)
- Your local Board of REALTORS® deadline for getting new listings online or in the next issue of the Multiple Listing directory, if your association issues one. There may be different deadlines for extensions and other changes in existing listings. Know them all. Find the deadline for adding a house to the next caravan. If this information isn't printed in each issue of the book, call the office.

**7.** Conquer the buyer's net sheet form (sometimes called the "buyer's closing costs"). Learn how to quickly figure what the buyers' initial investment in their new home will be, and how much they'll be investing in it every month. Chapter 23 has helpful tips. Create a document for this on your computer. Ask a computer store about software for qualifying or attend the National Association of REALTORS® convention and browse the trade show for these types of products.

# *Repeating* Achievements of Day 5

Add this to your schedule and keep at it every day until you've acquired professional competence:

**A.** Browse online the office's listing inventory at random and prepare buyer's net sheets on three houses. Work as fast as you can; then carefully check your work. Research any areas of uncertainty in your office's file of completed transactions, with lenders' agents and title people, or with the person who processes open transactions for your firm. Leave the agents around you out of this; they have their own problems.

Add the following achievement to your schedule, and keep at it until you're operating smoothly at the level of success you've chosen for yourself:

**B.** Put your winning fizzbo system to work by contacting five for-sale-by-owners a day.

## *Special* Achievements of Day 6

**1.** Reread Chapter 6, on farming.

**2.** Flashdeck the Winning Scripts in Chapter 6.

**3.** Create a BI cassette of the verbal opportunities and barriers in those Winning Scripts and of the responses that enable you to take advantage of the opportunities and get around the barriers.

**4.** Weigh all the information you've gathered about the available farms, and select yours. Choose the farm scoring highest on diversity, promise, and affinity and inform your broker.

**5.** Decide how you'll compile your deed details folder on your new farm. Chapter 6 tells all about this folder. Work out a plan to get this information as soon as possible, and put your plan in motion now. One suggestion is a client contact management system.

**6.** Start a property catalog of your farm by registering one-tenth of your farm's properties today. Remember to record facts about properties, not about people, in your inventory catalog. Enter this on your laptop. Chapter 6 tells you how this listing and sales aid will make you money, and how to create it. On each of the next nine days, a repeating achievement will be to record another tenth of your farm in your property catalog. Do this, and by Day 15, you'll have every property in your farm computerized, if you are computer savvy, or organized on hard copy.

**7.** Organize your work station at home for maximum real estate efficiency.

## *Repeating* Achievements of Day 6

Continue your daily schedule of *Repeating* Achievements from Day 1 through Day 5. You now have six BI (blank-interval) cassettes:

| | |
|---|---|
| Fizzbo | Qualifying Buyers |
| Listing | Up-Time |
| Prospecting | Farming |

All the cards for your flashdecks of this material, plus the deadlines flashdeck you compiled yesterday, should now be in three groups:

- In your twice daily drill deck: material not overlearned.
- In your once or twice weekly review decks: learned material.
- In your monthly review deck: overlearned material.

Complete mastery is your learning goal for all these phrases, facts, and skills. When you're able—instantly, accurately, and sincerely—to respond to the situations these tools are designed for, you'll usually be able to turn them to your advantage. Half learning won't get it. Continue your daily drills until using each item becomes second nature. Some of these situations don't happen often. If you depend on prospect contact to keep these words and skills fresh in your mind, you'll be unprepared for the less frequent situations when they suddenly occur. Schedule regular review of the overlearned material.

Add the following new achievement to your schedule:

**A.** Study the filled-out listing forms in your office's file for 30 minutes a day. Continue this daily study for as long as it helps you. Put some of these documents in your computer. You can study them anywhere you go if you own a laptop.

# *Special* Achievements of Day 7

**1.** Reread Chapter 7, on Danny Kennedy's full-year farming almanac.
**2.** Make a tentative schedule for your next 12 months of farming activity.
**3.** Select this month's giveaway (one you can get quick delivery on), and order enough for your entire farm. (If you're on a tight budget as a new salesperson, order memo pads only until you can afford the monthly giveaway suggestions.) Don't order anything until you've checked with your broker, and made sure it's okay in your area.
**4.** Order next month's giveaway for your farm.
**5.** Order the following month's giveaway for your farm.
**6.** Pick your monthly farm decision day. Chapter 6 tells you why this is vital to an efficient farming program, and what to do. If you select the 10th day of each month, write "Farm Decision Day" in your yearly appointment book (or digital system) on the 10th of every month remaining in the year.
**7.** High-volume phoning plays tricks on you unless it's kept in control. Use the fast fact grabber and results record (in Chapter 24) to help you make phone prospecting pay off big. Order these forms today, or design your own and have a local print shop run off 100 copies of each.

**Before you start on a phone-prospecting campaign,** check with your broker and make sure you won't be violating any local ordinances or rules.

## *Repeating* Achievements of Day 7

Add this item to your daily schedule:

**A.** List another one-tenth of your farm's property catalog. (See *Special* Achievement 6, Day 6.)

Let's review some of the items on your daily schedule:

- As soon as you wake up, review your target commitments and goals. Take a moment to see yourself in full color enjoying each goal or living each achieved target. Emotion is what works the changes. Practice "seeing" your success clearly for a second or two on each target and goal. Don't linger. The twice daily repetition of these mental images will start working their wonders as soon as you learn how to make them vivid.
- Make three fast runs through your new and old flashdecks each morning and night. Concentrate—and never hesitate. Unless you know the response or answer instantly, turn over the card, read it intently, and go on to the next card.
- Make three runs through all your BI cassettes every evening and morning. Coach yourself with the flashdecks if necessary. Say your lines with confidence and sincerity.
- Check today's online hot sheet for changes in your QSI. Make any necessary corrections in your slot sheet, QSI flashdeck, and memory.

## *Special* Achievements of Day 8

**1.** Reread Chapter 14, on capturing customers.
**2.** Flashdeck the Winning Scripts in Chapter 14.
**3.** Use your new flashdeck to create a BI cassette for solo role working those customer-capture situations.
**4.** You'll soon be working with buyers—and writing offers and counteroffers. Before you do this on your own, get your broker's approval. Mistakes in offers could be costly to you both, so don't rush in before you're ready. Take the time to prepare. Don't terrorize your buyers into backing out by groping for words, and floundering through the form. Buyers making offers need reassurance, not reasons to run—they scare themselves enough without our help. Know the forms thoroughly; memorize the phrases covering common purchase situations; get ready for fast work at decision-making time. Do your job before their desire to

buy cools. Chapter 3 gives you a rapid learning technique and tells you how to learn—before the need—all the purchase offer situations frequently encountered in your locality, and what phrases best cope with those situations. Use them to make up a purchase offer flashdeck.

**5.** Spend one hour reviewing your income, personal, and family targets. Revise your written list of goals to include at least three achievable goals able to inspire you in each of those three categories.

You should now be able to drive without hesitation to about 160 streets in your sales area through your work with the named-neighborhoods program (*Special* Achievement 7, Day 1). In the coming months and years, this knowledge will win many extra fees for you. If you want to take virtual tours to save gas, go right ahead.

# *Repeating* Achievements of Day 8

**A.** Add to your daily schedule: Use the purchase offer flashdeck (today's *Special* Achievement 4) to drill yourself on making out this form fast. If it is already on your computer, great! Take 30 minutes to drill, then spend another 30 minutes researching your office's files. Add any new offer problems you find—and clauses designed to control them—to your purchase offer flashdeck.

**B.** Reread the tips in Chapter 6 on farming. Then knock on 15 doors in your farm. Learn at least one fact about each family or house.

# *Special* Achievements of Day 9

**1.** Reread Chapter 9 on how to make money holding *weekly* (on both weekends and weekdays) open house.

**2.** Flashdeck Chapter 9's Winning Scripts for open houses.

**3.** Prepare a BI cassette for solo role working the open house situations in those Winning Scripts.

**4.** Add to your important information notebook by copying into it the frequently-used purchase agreement (deposit receipt) clauses you find in your office's file of closed transactions. Scan these documents and store them in your laptop.

# *Repeating* Achievements of Day 9

Schedule yourself to hold open houses all week long. The big listers in your office will welcome your offer to give their listings this exposure to the public because you're demonstrating a high level of drive, enthusiasm, and competence.

# *Special* Achievements of Day 10

**1.** Reread Chapter 17, "Closing Those Golden Nuggets Before They Turn into Lead."

**2.** Flashdeck Chapter 17's Winning Scripts.

**3.** Use your new flashdeck to prepare a BI cassette for solo role working the closing situations in those Winning Scripts.

**4.** From memory, sketch your sales area's highways, major roads, and most important streets. Use as many sheets of paper as you need to show all the major traffic arteries in your area, and how they connect. Don't take more than one minute per sheet. When you're through, compare your work with the printed map. If your sketches are wrong or incomplete, you've discovered a weakness you can correct before you get lost with a customer. Chapter 3 tells you how to do so quickly. Check into buying local map software.

# *Repeating* Achievements of Day 10

Add this to your daily schedule:

**A.** Prospect for people interested in buying or selling real estate by making ten cold canvass calls in your sales area. Chapter 8 provides you with techniques for successful cold calling. Keep your results count for cold canvass calls separate from the other two types of calls you'll be making soon. You can use e-mail with this method too.

   You are, of course, trying for an appointment to view a house, with the intention of expanding the appointment into a listing presentation. Don't be discouraged if you don't get an appointment; your goal is to complete those ten calls in a courteous and professional manner. If you do succeed in making an appointment, build on your success—go for more appointments by finishing your ten calls. Then concentrate on preparing the strongest listing effort you can make today. Review Chapter 11 on listings—you'll find much there worth brief and intense study right now.

You have now filled all 50 slots in your basic Quick-Speak Inventory. You started this project on Day 1 with *Special* Achievement 6 and *Repeating* Achievement A. Will these 50 slots adequately cover your sales activity? If not, design another slot sheet and start filling it in with five houses per day. Continue replacing sold and expired houses on your original slot sheet. Virtual tours should allow you to increase the numbers.

## *Special* Achievements of Day 11

**1.** Reread Chapter 18, on negotiating.
**2.** Flashdeck Chapter 18's Winning Scripts.
**3.** Use your new flashdeck to create a BI cassette for solo role working the negotiating situations in those Winning Scripts.

## *Repeating* Achievements of Day 11

Continue your daily sessions with each of the incomplete achievements. Add this to your daily schedule:

**A.** Make ten image-building calls into your farm. Keep track of who you're calling in your farm. If you don't have a farm, make ten additional cold canvass calls or e-mails into your sales area. Note: Cell phones allow you to make more calls during down time, while waiting for appointments, etc.

## *Special* Achievements of Day 12

**1.** Effective farming will make you a lot of money. A 100 percent referral business will make you a lot more, because all your time will be spent working with clients who've called you. That happy situation is reached by doing a superlative job of farming, by working effectively with buyers, and by developing your contacts into a reliable referral network. Chapter 20, "A 100 Percent Referral Business," tells you how it's done. Reread it now. Let it inspire you to do such a superlative job of farming you'll soon be cashing in on referrals. Make referral business your goal. Start training yourself now to explore the referral possibilities of every person-to-person contact you make.

**2.** Assemble the best Listing Presentation Manual (LPM) you can from what's immediately available to you. Then list every item that will strengthen your LPM and plan how you'll obtain each item. Tips on preparing your LPM are given in Chapters 11 and 24. Consider putting your LPM on your laptop.

**3.** A method for creating effective sales dialogues fast is given in Chapter 23. Use this method to develop a "Why you should list with me" speech for use with your Listing Presentation Manual. Consider making a quick video clip of the speech and duplicating it on a CD business card to leave with prospects.

**4.** Start your farm people flashdeck by listing a family name on one side of a 3 × 5 card, and their address on the card's reverse side. Take this information from any directory you can. The crisscross is the most convenient directory to use. Do 30 cards today, or one-tenth of the households in your farm. This is the start of a project to be completed over the next nine days as a *Repeating* Achievement. Chapter 6 tells you some of the ways a farm people flashdeck will help you gain control of your farm quickly. Go paperless and do it on your laptop.

# *Repeating* Achievements of Day 12

Add this to your daily schedule:

**A.** Call the owners of ten expired listings. Chapter 8 has helpful tips for this. Keep a results record (see Chapter 24) on each call and hold onto it for future analysis. Do you have an expired list on your laptop? Delete any expired names that have been off the market or sold for over six months.

# *Special* Achievements of Day 13

**1.** Reread Chapter 13, on promotion, so you can sell your listings faster and sell yourself better.

**2.** Develop this sales dialogue: "What's happening now in our local resale housing market."

**3.** Develop your knowledge of government, home-purchase financing used in your area. Learn about any veteran or special financing your state may offer along with the federal FHA and VA programs. Call the loan production departments of mortgage companies for this information, or call the lender's agents who leave their cards in your office. Enter the details in your important information notebook and save it on your computer.

**4.** Make up a master for your buyer show list form. Make 100 copies at the local quick-print shop—you're going to need them. The sample in Chapter 24 works great; it saves time and impresses customers too. Use it as is, or modify it to suit the housing in your area. This is a valuable form to send as an attachment to prospects.

# *Repeating* Achievements of Day 13

You should now be:

- Talking with 15 people on your farm each day. This will take you around your farm once a month.
- Talking with at least 5 fizzbos a day.
- Making 10 cold canvass calls.
- Making 10 image-building calls a day into your farm.
- Calling 10 expired listings a day.
- Sending 10 e-mails a day.
- Leaving 10 voice mail messages or text messages with agent-friendly prospects.

# Special Achievements of Day 14

**1.** Make up the best "Our Beautiful Area" sales book you can from what's immediately available. Include common floor plans; lists of churches, clubs, schools, cultural, and recreational facilities; maps showing locations of malls, shopping centers, and scenic areas; driving distances to regional attractions and nearby cities; and local tax information and utility rates. Include all the things people moving in want to know. Save this to your computer so it can be sent online.

**2.** List what you need to improve your sales book and plan how to acquire each item. Create a document entitled *Sales Book*, so your customers 3000 miles away will be able to download it onto their computers.

**3.** Develop this sales dialogue: "Fine communities of Green Pretty (your sales area) Valley." Describe the areas as you would to prospective buyers making their first visit to your area. State the types of housing available in each community and give price ranges.

**4.** Flashdeck all the churches in your sales area. On one side of each 3 × 5 card write the denomination; on the other side write the name of the church and its location or cross streets. Not knowing where the churches of buyers' faith are in your area will hurt you badly with some people. Don't lose a fee before you act on this advice. Make a map if it'll help, but learn where the places of worship are. Save it to your computer.

# Repeating Achievements of Day 14

Your printed "I'm in real estate" letter will be ready by now. Save it to your computer. Add this to your daily schedule:

**A.** Hand-address envelopes and mail this printed letter to 20 people in your Everybody-I-Know farm. Continue your mailing at 20 letters a day until you've mailed to everyone you know. You could also send it online.

# Special Achievements of Day 15

**1.** Know your area's yearly buying pattern. Chapter 23 tells you why knowing this will make you money, and gives you a powerful self-selling speech. Put this knowledge into a scripted speech tailored to your area.

**2.** Review the tentative goals you set for yourself on Day 1 and Day 8. Do they still excite you? Did you aim too low at first? Do they now seem too high to reach? Take time today to reset your income goals for the immediate future at achievable levels able to inspire you to greater, but not impossible efforts. Write down income goals (revised if you so decide) for each of the next 12 months. As you set these monthly income goals, bear in mind the 60-day sale-to-payoff delay built into the average transaction. Always set believable, achievable goals. But first reread Chapter 26. You'll see the discussion of goals there in a new light.

**3.** Develop this sales dialogue: "Why Green Pretty Valley is a great place, Mr. and Mrs. Homebuyer, for you and your family to grow and prosper in."

## *Repeating* Achievements of Day 15

- Complete your farm property file. This project began as *Special* Achievement 6 on Day 6, and *Repeating* Achievement A on Day 7.
- Add the final pair of named neighborhoods and bring your stock-in-trade of well known streets to the top professional level of 600. This project started on Day 1 as *Special* Achievement 7.

## *Special* Achievements of Day 16

1. Develop your knowledge of the seller-financed sales methods available in your state such as land contracts, second trust deeds, and all-inclusive trust deeds (wraparounds). Enter the details you learn in your important information notebook. Save it to your computer.
2. Develop this sales dialogue: "Here's what happens in today's market when you limit your offer with contingencies."

## *Repeating* Achievements of Day 16

A. Schedule yourself for two open houses this week. Make a reputation for doing a superlative job representing property on open house and you'll soon find your office's top listers lining up to get you to hold their listings open whenever you have time. Being able to select the best open houses will give you the best possible shot at buyers.

## *Special* Achievements of Day 17

1. Reread Chapter 19, "Fallout Avoidance."
2. Make up your own checklist of items to watch out for, and take action on, between sale and settlement. Refer to Chapter 24. Save it to your computer.
3. Develop this sales dialogue: "The outlook is optimistic." You'll need this speech when buyers ask you such questions as; "Where's the country going? Are we headed for another recession? Aren't we due for another turndown?" Unless you're ready to deal with these fears, you'll lose some fees. Chapter 23 has more about this.

**4.** If you're part of the Multiple Listing system, flashdeck the coding and abbreviations used by your Multiple Listing Service. Include everything a buyer or seller might ask you about.

# Repeating Achievements of Day 17

**A.** Would a call-back to any of the people you've already contacted be worthwhile now? If so, do it. Are you entering your call-backs in your appointment system? Unless you do, you'll miss out on vital follow-up. Calling back *at the right time* where you sniff business is the difference between success and failure on the phone. Set up your call-back system (keep it simple) and call prospects back precisely when they say is the best day and hour. The back sides of the fact grabber forms (Chapter 24) and tickler 1/31 (Chapter 22) combine to make an effective call-back system. Build this information into your office software.

# Special Achievements of Day 18

**1.** Develop this sales dialogue: "The tax advantages of home ownership." Every time you give this talk, be sure you warn your clients and customers to get their tax advice from tax experts, not real estate experts. Tell them your remarks are only intended to alert them to possibilities of tax savings.

**2.** Analyze all the results record forms you've compiled so far. If you have 1 appointment and 3 opportunities for later follow-up to show for each 100 calls, rejoice—you're doing great. Anything more is sensational! Study every little part of your prospecting procedure. Look for the winning things you're doing—and do them more often. Also be on the lookout for any nonproductive habits you might have slipped into. Now would be a good time to tape your side of a few prospecting calls if you haven't been doing this regularly. Play the tapes back, try to put yourself in the other person's shoes, and ask, "What can I do better?" On your results record forms, if you've filled one out (completely) every time you've prospected, you'll find clear statements as to what wins and what loses. You've been talking, now listen to yourself. Be sure to take your own advice.

**3.** Your experiences have given you a changed viewpoint on the value of self-organization in the past two weeks. Read Chapter

22 again. You'll find some valuable tips there you may have missed before.

4. Read entirely through Chapter 3, on the hyperlearn system. Then select three of those methods and continue your breakaway from the pack.

# *Repeating* Achievements of Day 18

Fit this into your daily schedule:

A. Each day add one new goal, update an old one, or add an additional detail to your target commitments to your goal flashdeck. See Chapter 27 for a full discussion of targets and goals.

# *Special* Achievements of Day 19

1. Develop this sales dialogue: "Why you should buy a home now."
2. Note reminders in your appointment system for monthly review and improvement of "Why you should buy a home now."

# *Repeating* Achievements of Day 19

A. You've been making ten image-building calls per day into your farm. Continue at this rate until you've called your entire farm once. Then drop back to five image-buildings calls a day, and install the five calls as a permanent part of your daily work schedule. You always need a reason to call, so be continually on the alert for reasons. Chapter 6 talks about this in more detail. Use a specific cell phone for prospecting calls only. Program it for text messaging.

# *Special* Achievements of Day 20

1. Reread Chapter 21, on time planning.
2. It's been one week since you developed your "What's happening now in our local resale housing market" speech. Update this sales dialogue with the latest weekly data issued by your Board of REALTORS®. Add details and smooth out its flow. By now, you've probably given this talk to prospects on the phone many times. Tape yourself giving it, and then critique your delivery.

## *Repeating* Achievements of Day 20

Since Day 10, you've made a total of 100 cold canvass calls and 80 calls to expired listings, plus many other calls, e-mails, and voice messages.

Congratulations! You're now a communication pro. You've talked to some great people and you have business in sight. Keep after it!

Use your results record form to help you decide which of the two prospecting fields is most productive for you. Split your future 20 calls a day between cold canvass calls and expired listings so most of your calls go where you see the greatest return. But continue to make at least 10 calls a week to the least productive field. There may be a seasonal factor, competitive condition, or soft spot in your technique preventing you from striking pay dirt in the least-productive field now. By making calls to this area, you'll soon discover what the problem is and be able to correct it.

**A.** On your permanent daily work schedule system, block out time to make 20 prospecting calls a day, divided between cold canvass calls and expired listings.

## *Special* Achievements of Day 21

**1.** Write "A Profile of a Pro" about yourself. Chapter 13 tells you how to make money with this self-advertisement, gives writing tips, and has a sample profile to help you. Save it to your computer.

**2.** Develop this sales dialogue: "The various ways you can finance a home purchase, and the advantages and costs of each method." Save it to your computer.

**3.** You've worked hard during the past three weeks, and you've tentatively formed many effective new habits. Make those winning habits a permanent part of your personality: Read the rest of this section about consolidating your gains.

> *And now at last its finally over,*
> *Time's come to gather the sweet green clover.*

Congratulations, Awaybreakers! You've learned a great deal very quickly.

Now you're at a crossroads. Will you use this new input, review it, expand on it, and continue to grow—or will you slowly slide back to your previous level of performance? Here are some specific suggestions on how you can continue your growth habit.

# Consolidate Your Gains After Breakaway—Make a Smooth, Swift Takeoff into Rapidly Rising Income

Reward yourself. *Now.*

You'll sustain your drive longer and make more money if you'll alternate hard-driving work with high-quality play. Select whatever reward you think you should have, not what someone else thinks you should have. When you've done the job, collect the reward from yourself. Then continue the good habits you've learned through Breakaway:

- Prepare a tomorrow's action list every night. (Do this even on vacation—it maintains the habit: "(1) Get up late, (2) Go to beach, (3) Have fun.")
- Add five houses to your Quick-Speak Inventory every day your time isn't fully occupied with clients.
- Continue hyperlearning information about real estate in general and your area in particular until you have enough data on Quick-Speak to graduate from unpaid amateur to highly paid professional.
- You've learned how to prospect fast, and you've had success at it. Its terrors are behind you. Any day you don't have an appointment with a client or customer, get out in the field and prospect for two hours in the morning, and another two hours in the afternoon.
- While others stand around and gab before the weekly office meeting starts, sit down in a corner and make a few prospecting calls, or keep on top of your transactions, appointments, and action list. Carry your prospecting kit in your attaché case. If a customer calls in to say, "Sorry—I'll be 45 minutes late," pull out your prospecting kit and rap out a few more calls. Squeeze fees from those vagrant minutes by making them work for you.
- Leaf through the Breakaway schedule, and privately score how thoroughly you've put the material there to use. If you haven't squeezed all the benefits you can from Breakaway, then do it over.
- Repeat the course. Pass over the items you've thoroughly learned or completed. Look again at the achievements you were reluctant to try three weeks ago. The achievements you don't want to think about are the ones best able to dramatically improve your income.
- Are you charging ahead now? If your answer is *no*, do you lack drive? Have you chosen goals that really excite you? Do you really believe you can achieve them? You have? You do? Then are you reviewing your targets and goals twice daily to power your drive?

Or are you afraid to change? Are you afraid to be a winner? *No.* You're probably not. But if not, why aren't you charging ahead? Your problem probably stems from noninspiring goals, or from failing to use the target/goal system with emotional intensity. If you're not thrilled with your performance, restudy Chapters 26, 27, and 28. Remember, I'm rooting for you every second. Consider me your invisible partner. Between you, me, and someone greater than both of us, we can make your career spectacular!

# INDEX

# SEVEN FIGURE SELLING

## Proven Secrets to Success from Top Sales Professionals

DANIELLE KENNEDY

Sales professionals, entrepreneurs, and small business owners alike will learn sales strategies and gain the mindset that can truly lead to surpassing $1,000,000 sales and business goals! Tactical strategies and candid stories from legendary sales professionals— like Jenny Craig, Founder and President of Jenny Craig International; Helen Gurley Brown, Editor of Cosmopolitan; Judi Sheppard Missett, Founder of Jazzercise International; Fred Segal, Owner of Fred Segal Stores; and many more—offer new insight into the "out-of-the-box" thinking that set these businesses leaps and bounds ahead of the rest.

Danielle Kennedy, a sales legend in her own right, pulls the "*best of the best*" success strategies and the characteristics of a business winner into one dynamic resource providing the tools needed to launch a sales career or business to the next level of higher profits. Learn about:

0-324-18751-3 ©2003

- Using Imagination as a Powerful Business Force
- The Rewards of the Payback Philosophy
- Predicting Patterns of Buying Behavior
- Creating Excitement and Building Trust
- Renewing Your Energy for Unparalleled Performance
- How to Listen Like a Lover

*Order your copy today!*
http://www.thomsonlearning.com/catalogs/
1-800-354-9706, option 4

ISBN 0-324-18751-3

# WORKINGMOMS.CALM

## How Smart Women
## Balance Family & Career

### Danielle Kennedy

*A way of life, not a web site!* Calm living is an oxymoron for most working moms. But, this book provides the next best thing—balanced living. Every working mother strives for this "unobtainable" goal—the perfect balance between family and work. Now, this once unobtainable goal can be a reality!

*WorkingMoms.Calm* brings together the success and failures of successful women who have strived to achieve a balanced life. In her passionate and inspiring manner, Danielle Kennedy—herself a mother of eight and successful entrepreneur—shares the secrets of more than 30 successful women. Apply the wisdom and practical solutions of this book and gain the confidence to live a life that fully embraces family and career.

Solutions include how to:
- Avoid the common trap of guilt.
- Be alert of the dangers of perfectionism.
- Enlist the help of family members.
- Work with your company to meet your children's needs.
- Create energy both physically and emotionally.
- Be present for your children.

### *Order your copy today!*
http://www.thomsonlearning.com/catalogs/
1-800-354-9706, option 4

ISBN 0-324-18750-5